Management of Physical Education and Sport Eleventh Edition

Charles A. Bucher
(deceased)

Professor, School of Health, Physical Education,
Recreation, and Dance University of Nevada,
Las Vegas

Former President, National Fitness Leaders
Council

Consultant to the National Fitness Foundation

March L. Krotee

Faculty, School of Kinesiology and Leisure
Studies, University of Minnesota,
Minneapolis

Fellow, Research Consortium, American
Alliance for Health, Physical Education,
Recreation and Dance

Past Chair, International Relations Council,
American Association for Active Lifestyles
and Fitness

Past Chair, Sport Sociology Academy, National
Association for Sport and Physical
Education

Consultant to the President's Council on
Physical Fitness and Sports

Educational Mentor, Athlete Educational
Mentoring Network United States Olympic
Committee

Kellogg/Partners of the Americas Fellow

Sports Ethics Fellow, Institute for International
Sport

Fulbright Scholar

Boston   Burr Ridge, IL   Dubuque, IA   Madison, WI   New York   San Francisco   St. Louis
Bangkok   Bogotá   Caracas   Lisbon   London   Madrid
Mexico City   Milan   New Delhi   Seoul   Singapore   Sydney   Taipei   Toronto

WCB/McGraw-Hill

A Division of The **McGraw·Hill** *Companies*

MANAGEMENT OF PHYSICAL EDUCATION AND SPORT

Copyright © 1998 by The McGraw-Hill Companies, Inc. All rights reserved. Previous edition(s) 1955, 1963, 1967, 1971, 1975, 1979, 1983, 1987, 1993 by Mosby-Year Book, Inc. Printed in the United States of America. Except as permitted under the United States Copyright Act of 1976, no part of this publication may be reproduced or distributed in any form or by any means, or stored in a data base or retrieval system, without the prior written permission of the publisher.

This book is printed on acid-free paper.

1 2 3 4 5 6 7 8 9 0 DOCDOC 0 9 8 7

ISBN 0-8151-1302-1

Vice president and editorial director: *Kevin T. Kane*
Publisher: *Edward E. Bartell*
Sponsoring editor: *Vicki Malinee*
Developmental editor: *Sarah Reed*
Marketing manager: *Pamela S. Cooper*
Project manager: *Marilyn M. Sulzer*
Production supervisor: *Deborah Donner*
Designer: *Michael Warrell*
Compositor: *Carlisle Communications, Ltd.*
Typeface: *10/12 Times Roman*
Printer: *R. R. Donnelly*

Library of Congress Cataloging-in-Publication Data:

Bucher, Charles Augustus, 1912–
    Management of physical education and sport / Charles A. Bucher,
March L. Krotee—11th ed.
      p.   cm.
    Includes index.
    ISBN 0-8151-1302-1
    1. Physical education and training—Administration. 2. Sports
administration.   I. Krotee, March L. II. Title.
GV343.5.B787   1997
613.7   068—dc21
                                                     97-26467
                                                      CIP

www.mhhe.com

To my wife
Leslie,
my two sons
Chip and Rob, their wives Liz and Kim,
and their families,
without whose love and support such
an undertaking
would be impossible.

                              I love you.

preface

The eleventh edition of *Management of Physical Education and Sport* is designed to provide a comprehensive, contemporary text for administration and management courses dealing with physical education and sport in the educational setting. The text has been carefully revised based on developments and trends that have taken place within our dynamic profession and therefore reflects the most current thinking and research available. As in past editions, seminal works have been maintained and referenced to provide a solid foundation from which newer management concepts, skills, and techniques may be built.

NEW TO THIS EDITION

This eleventh edition has maintained the conceptual framework of the previous edition; however, the content has been revised and shaped to reflect the most current patterns concerning the organization and management of physical education and sport. Where appropriate, crucial issues such as race, ethnicity, gender, age, and disability have been addressed and contemporary educational initiatives concerning multiculturalism and internationalization have been included.

Changes in the text include the addition of leadership and total quality management (TQM) to the introductory chapter that focuses on the management process. Chapter 2, Management Organization to Achieve Objectives of Physical Education and Sport, has been revised and incorporates new physical fitness development objectives. It also now includes a section on the globalization and internationalization of physical education and sport.

Chapter 3, Physical Education Instructional Programs, includes the timely addition of period

and block scheduling, as well as updated information about teaching and coaching certifications and programs for individuals with disabilities. New participatory information is included in chapters 4 and 5 as is an expanded discussion of Title IX and its effect on physical education and sport programs.

The chapters covering public and private sector physical education and sport programs, human resource management and supervision, and program development (chapters 6, 7, and 8) have been extended in scope. Expanded coverage concerning professional growth and potential employment opportunities, mentoring, and program development assessment and evaluation systems are presented. Chapter 9, Facility Management, has also been expanded and now includes the total facility management package (TFMP) concept as well as the latest information on joint partnering ventures. Chapters 10 and 11 offer the most up-to-date information about fiscal management and purchase and care of equipment. Chapter 12, Management and the Athletic Training Program, expands its previous coverage concerning the important role that athletic training plays for the teacher, coach, and sport administrator. Chapter 13, Legal Liability, Risk, and Insurance Management, has been revised and includes additional court cases, risk management tips, and guidelines for safe and effective teaching, coaching, and supervision. The chapter on public relations has been enhanced to include marketing and its accompanying strategies used to generate support for physical education sport programs. The final chapter, covering office management, has also been refined to make the eleventh edition of *Management of Physical Education and Sport* the most up-to-date and authoritative text in the profession. More than 100 new photographs have been incorporated for the reader to be able to readily identify with the written content of the text.

PEDAGOGICAL FEATURES

To facilitate its use by instructors and students, several pedagogical aids have been incorporated into this edition. These include the following:

Instructional Objectives   Each chapter begins with instructional objectives that introduce the main points of the chapter. Attaining these objectives indicates fulfillment of the chapter's intent.

Introductory Paragraphs   A short introduction begins each chapter. This provides students with a transition when progressing from the previous chapter.

Summaries   Each chapter ends with a brief review of the critical material presented in the chapter. This summary assists students in focusing, understanding, and retaining the most important concepts covered in the chapter.

Self-Assessment Activities   Each chapter includes a set of activities that enables students to determine whether they understand the main points in the chapter. This activity serves as an evaluation for both the student and instructor.

References   Each chapter provides both foundational and contemporary references that may be used to acquire further information about the materials presented.

Suggested Readings   Additional readings have been selected and, where appropriate, annotated for students to further inquire into related material.

SUPPLEMENTS

An Instructor's Manual/Test Bank is available to qualified adopters and provides instructors with additional material to facilitate the conduct of the course. The Instructor's Manual contains the following features for each chapter:

Chapter Overview   This overview provides a brief review of the main points covered in the chapter.

Instructional Objectives   These objectives provide a framework for preparing lesson plans. They are designed to focus on the objectives and competencies to be achieved by the student.

Topical Teaching Outlines   These outlines provide a point of reference for organizing lectures, class projects, and presentations.

Multiple Choice and Discussion Test Questions

These questions are based on the objectives and competencies presented in each chapter. An answer key is also provided for use by the instructor.

ACKNOWLEDGMENTS

I would like to thank Paul F. Blair, Leslie L. Krotee, and Jonathan Sweet for their assistance in the preparation of the manuscript. Special thanks are also accorded to Vicki Malinee and Sarah Reed of McGraw-Hill for their confidence, patience, and diligence while bringing this project to completion. In addition, I would like to personally thank the reviewers of this and previous editions who have provided invaluable input in order to ensure the integrity of the text:

Frank Ashley
Texas A&M University

Charles Chase
West Texas A&M University

Maureen Fitzgerald
University of Missouri

Mark Fohl
University of Minnesota—Morris

Diana Gray
Indiana University

Graham Hatcher
University of North Carolina—Wilmington

Erica Knowles
Walsh University

Keith Lambrecht
Northern Illinois University

Kathleen McCann
University of North Dakota

Rick W. Nelson
Northland Community College

James Reynolds
Jacksonville State University

Ralph Sabock
Pennsylvania State University

Vernon Vradenburg
University of Wisconsin—Platteville

Victor Wallace
Lambuth University

Jim Wasem
Eastern Washington University

I would also like to acknowledge Gerry Vuchetich, Women's Intercollegiate Athletics, University of Minnesota; Wendell Vandersluis, Men's Intercollegiate Athletics, University of Minnesota; The School of Kinesiology and Leisure Studies, University of Minnesota; The Department of Recreational Sports, University of Minnesota; The Department of Dance, University of Minnesota; The University of Nevada at Las Vegas; Minnesota State High School League; AAPHERD; NASPE; PCPFS; The Cooper Institute for Aerobics Research, Dallas, Texas; Alan Blum and Eric Solberg, DOC, Baylor School of Medicine, Houston, Texas; Special Olympics International, Washington, D.C.; Donald Krotee Partnership, Planning, and Architecture, Santa Ana, Calif.; Joanne Lombardo, Comprehensive Planning Services, Newport Beach, Calif.; Hellmuth, Obata, and Kassabaum, Inc., Sports Facilities Group, Kansas City, Mo.; Grafton Adams, Photograf, Sports Photography; Mary Ann and Gerard Knight, Waymouth Farms; Mike Mularky, Pittsburgh Steelers, Wayzata, Minn.; P. A. Rull, Leisure Policy Division, Urban Services Division, Hong Kong; Trina Tinti, Department of Intercollegiate Athletics, University of California at Berkeley; Jerry Yeagley, Department of Intercollegiate Athletics, Indiana University; USA Basketball; Garth Weiss, United States Tennis Association; Tom Snicker and Heidi Martin, Wayzata School District, Wayzata, Minn.; and Dr. Thomas C. Slettehaugh, Commissioner, Minneapolis Arts Commission, for their assistance in securing photographs and materials for this eleventh edition.

I would also like to thank the many friends and professional colleagues who helped in many ways with the revision of the eleventh edition—from answering crucial questions to proofing to loaning reference books. Thus, the eleventh edition is truly a team effort by professionals who continue to pursue excellence and strive to provide a quality educational experience for both students and teachers.

Finally, as you know, this text will be the second edition that will go to press without a good friend and colleague, Charles Bucher. Charlie did much to shape the roots of the profession, specifically management and administration of physical education and sport, and through his dedicated career, touched the lives of many young aspiring professionals. For this, I dedicate the eleventh edition to him and hope that "our" text continues to reflect the spirit of this truly great man.

March L. Krotee, Ph.D.
Fulbright Professor
University of Minnesota

brief contents

vii

contents

ix

The Management
Process

The Management Process

Instructional Objectives and Competencies To Be Achieved

After reading this chapter the student should be able to

- Describe and contrast the traditional and modern views of management.
- Appreciate the advantages and problems associated with a democratic and participatory management.
- Discuss a modern philosophy of management.
- Identify the factors and qualifications essential for effective physical education and sport management.
- Enumerate the major duties of a manager in a physical education and sport setting.

- Outline the preparation necessary to be an effective manager.
- Explain why the study of management is important to the physical educator, athletic and activities director, or sport manager.
- Identify issues relevant to modern physical education and sport management.

This text is concerned with the study of management as it is applied to the domain of physical education and sport.* Although management skills and concepts are applicable over this

---

*For the purposes of this text, the terms *physical education* and *sport* include a comprehensive spectrum of movement as adapted from the Physical Activity and Sport Continuum developed by Krotee in 1980. The continuum, illustrated here, ranges from play to professional and performing sport and dance.

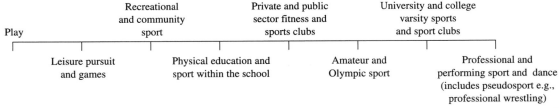

broad continuum of organizational and institutional settings, the primary focus of the text remains the management of the traditional delivery systems of school physical education, interscholastic, intercollegiate, and recreational sports. Management is a crucial ingredient in any physical education or sports program and must be soundly implemented if that program is to be conducted in an effective, efficient, and meaningful fashion. Management involves the interaction between those who administer and those who participate in the physical education and sporting processes. It involves, but is not limited to, such important matters as personnel, long-range planning, programming, facilities, budget, legal liability, marketing, and public relations. This text explores these managerial dimensions and examines ways in which they can be effectively and efficiently employed.

WHAT IS MANAGEMENT?

DuBrin, Ireland, and Williams (1989) define management as the coordinated and integrated process of utilizing an organization's resources (e.g., human, financial, physical, informational/technological, technical) to achieve specific objectives through the functions of planning, organizing, staffing, leading, and controlling (see figure 1-1).

Hersey and Blanchard (1982) note that management is "working with and through individuals and groups to accomplish organizational goals." The American Association of School Administrators (1955) describes management as "the total of the processes through which appropriate human and material resources are made available and made effective for accomplishing the purpose of an enterprise." The National Association of Sport and Physical Education (NASPE)–North American Society of Sport Management (NASSM) Joint Task Force on Sport Management Curriculum and Accreditation (1993) further identifies sport management as "the field of study offering the specialized training and education necessary for individuals seeking careers in any of the many segments of the industry.

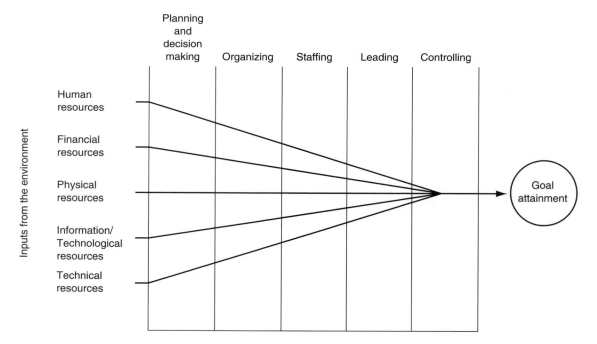

Figure 1-1. The management process

The antecedents of the theory and practice of management as we think of it today have their roots in the ancient civilizations of humankind. Leakey's diggings of the hand-axe man (predating 3000 B.C.) of Olorgesailie (Kenya) and Olduvai Gorge (Tanzania), the cuneiform tablets of the Sumerian society (circa 2500 B.C.), the physical evidence of Machu Picchu (Peru), the pyramids and the tombs of Beni Hasan (Egypt) and the Great Wall each serve as testimony to the management processes requisite to accomplish various societies' sociocultural objectives. Other often-cited examples of early management mastery include the Roman Empire (circa 753 B.C. to A.D. 476), the Chinese civil service system (circa 165 B.C.), and the Roman Catholic Church (circa A.D. 110). Thus management is recognized as a fundamental integrating process designed to achieve organized, purposeful, and meaningful results.

The term *management* was derived from the French word *menager,* meaning "to use carefully" and the Italian word *maneggiare,* meaning "to handle." The term was originally applied to the training of horses and later was extended to the operations of war and the reorganization of the military, referring to the general notion of taking charge or control. Contemporary management implies an ongoing process by which managers create, direct, maintain, and operate purposive organizations through coordinated, cooperative human effort.

WHAT IS A MANAGER?

A manager is someone whose primary activities are part of the management process. Specifically, a manager is someone who plans, makes decisions, organizes, staffs, leads, motivates, and controls organizational resources. Managers may be physical education teachers or department chairs; athletic coaches and directors; commissioners of leagues; general managers of professional teams; directors of health, golf, or racquet clubs, managers of country clubs, corporate or community fitness centers, Ys, or ski areas; managers may be involved in any number of positions of responsibility within a traditional education system or the multibillion dollar sporting industry.

More than six million individuals in the United States hold managerial positions, and as technology and information continue to expand and packaging, promoting, and marketing become more sophisticated, even more well-trained and prepared individuals will be called on to perform the myriad managerial duties required to effectively and efficiently manage successful physical education and sporting operations. The art of management is now becoming a science.

There are many different kinds of managers. Some possess warm, friendly personalities that foster a relaxed working environment and are popular with their staffs, whereas others are cold and unresponsive to human needs. Managers carry out their responsibilities in various ways. Some will shape members of their staffs; others are known for their inaction (seemingly waiting for problems to solve themselves); some are despots and authority figures; and others believe in providing democratic and situational leadership for their organization. Each manager is different, influenced by such characteristics as training and preparation, personality, experience, beliefs, and values. These managerial characteristics often play a significant role in determining how managers utilize the resources at their disposal (table 1-1).

In today's marketplace, some managers are not sufficiently trained to assume managerial roles. Although this trend seems to be reversing itself within the profession, it is still apparent that contemporary managers need to equip themselves with the necessary conceptual, human, and technical skills that are required for what Peter Drucker has noted as a most "crucial resource" for developed nations, as well as one of the most needed resources in countries that are struggling to develop.

WHY PURSUE A MANAGEMENT CAREER?

Many reasons motivate individuals to pursue a career in management. Some persons like the recognition and prestige that frequently accompany a person who is a chairperson, dean, athletic director, or corporate fitness manager. The fact that management positions usually carry a higher

Table 1-1. Examples of resources employed by sports organizations

Organization	Human	Financial	Physical	Informational	Technical
Minneapolis Public Schools	Athletic director Coaches Municipal employees	Tax revenue Gate receipts	Municipal building Parade stadium	Scheduling Transportation	Open enrollment PL 94-142
University of Minnesota Division of Kinesiology	Physical education students Sport and exercise science students Faculty and staff	State funding Grants Contributions Endowed chairs Shared positions	Aquatic center Golf course Fieldhouse Laboratory of sport sciences	Publications Public relations Development Funding opportunity	Web site Computer systems Equipment repair
University of Minnesota Athletic Departments	Student athletes Faculty representatives Academic counseling Sport psychology	Government grants Alumni contributions Fund-raising	Williams Arena Golf course Training complex	Sports information Public relations Publications Media guides	Lexicon system Drug testing protocol
Eden Prairie Community Center	Director Aquatics coordinator	Rental of ice time Bond issues	Ice arena Aquatic center Racquetball courts	Shared utilization Senior citizen programs	Energy cost Pool operation and maintenance
Clark Hatch Fitness Centers	Fitness director Business manager Staff	Corporate memberships Guest fees	Computers Weight training equipment	Promotional packages Nutritional programs	Computers Equipment repair
Minnesota Vikings	Players Corporate executives and board members Player personnel	Television profits Stockholder investments Skyboxes Parking and concessions	Metrodome Training complex Weight training and rehabilitation center	Sales forecasts Playoff revenue Television commercials	NFL Players Association Contracts Internet

salary than other positions in the organization can be a strong motivating factor for some. Authority and power may also be reasons for seeking a management position.

The manager usually controls functions such as recommending salary increases and promotions, making personnel decisions, and determining workloads and travel, all of which appeal to some indi-

viduals. Some persons prefer management duties to those of teaching and coaching. Others seek to create, build, and put into operation their own ideas for helping the organization grow and gain a better identity. Clearly, individuals enter management and become managers for many different reasons.

Whether individuals are successful in getting into the field of management (e.g., department

The modern management process utilizes cooperative effort and up-to-date technology.

chair, principal, head coach, athletic and activities director) depends on the particular situation and other factors. A physical education teacher who is experienced, respected by students and faculty, and a leader in the school or a coach who is experienced, popular with players and staff, and active in the community may be selected. People are selected for managerial positions based on such factors as academic preparation and certification for the position, maintaining a thorough knowledge of the position, experience in the field, management skills, and philosophy. Other valuable managerial commodities that may assist one in gaining a managerial position might include social and communication skills, problem-solving and decision-making skills, poise and self-discipline, self-confidence, a cooperative demeanor, motivational skills, in-house political savvy, and technical skills (e.g., computer, legal, or financial).

THE IMPORTANCE OF MANAGEMENT

How well an organization such as a school, community center, fitness or racquet club, or aquatic complex charts its course and achieves its objectives depends on how well managers outline and perform their jobs. Therefore it is imperative that all physical educators and sports personnel thoroughly understand the importance of effective and efficient management. Some of management's important contributions follow.

The way in which organizations are managed determines the course of human lives. Human beings are affected by management. It influences the type of program offered (e.g., consumer oriented, rehabilitative), the climate or environment in which the program takes place, the goals that are sought, and the health and happiness of members of the organization as well as those being served.

Management provides an understanding and appreciation of the underlying principles of the science of this field. Methods, techniques, strategies, and procedures employed by the manager can be evaluated more accurately and objectively by staff members if they possess managerial understanding. Also, sound management will be better appreciated and unsound practices more easily recognized.

Studying management will help a person decide whether to select this field as a career. Increased understanding and appreciation of the management process will help individuals evaluate their personal qualifications and potential within the field.

Most physical educators perform some type of management work; therefore an understanding of management will contribute to better performance. Management is not restricted to one group of individuals. Most staff members have reports to complete, equipment to order, evaluations to make, and other duties to perform that are managerial in nature. An understanding of management will help in efficiently carrying out these assignments.

Management is fundamental to associated effort. Goals are created, stated, and reached, ideas are implemented, and esprit de corps is developed with planning and cooperative action. A knowledge of management facilitates the achievement of such aims.

An understanding of management helps ensure continuity. A fundamental purpose of management is to carry on what has proved successful rather than destroy the old and attempt a new and untried path. An appreciation of this concept by all members of an organization will help to ensure the preservation of the best traditional practices that exist in the organization.

A knowledge of management helps further good human relations. An understanding of sound management principles will ensure the cooperation of the members of the organization and produce optimal efficiency and productivity.

Managers contribute to the realization of a better society. Because managers influence productivity and establish organizational policies and goals, they collectively influence a nation's standard of living and quality of life.

Management is rapidly becoming a science, and the study of this science is essential to everyone. It can result in a better-ordered society through more effectively and efficiently run organizations. Every individual belongs to formal organizations. Through a democratic and cooperative approach to management, the individual can aid in carrying on what has proved to be successful in the past.

MANAGEMENT IN TRANSITION

The role of management has changed markedly in recent years. The role of the manager has evolved from where "the manager" most often possessed the only voice in the governance of the organization (including such key decision making as hiring, salary, assignment, and advancement) to today's team-oriented management approach. The contemporary manager has become keenly aware of the importance of the individual within the organizational framework. This awareness has developed because of the complexity of the tasks involved in managing a classroom, gymnasium, sport club, or team or in successfully operating a

Teachers and coaches should be well skilled in managing group dynamics and team building.

ski area, aquatic complex, or community or fitness center. Physical education and sport have become a "shared" or team-related phenomenon, one that is gradually becoming multicultural in nature, requiring increased consciousness and appreciation concerning race, ethnicity, and gender. The manager is part of that team whose job might be to facilitate, implement, or remove constraints to help other team members within the organizational framework achieve their respective goals and develop to their full potential. In this respect, today's manager has become a coach. Today's manager must be thoroughly informed and an expert in group dynamics, role differentiation, motivation, goal setting, decision making, and positive reinforcement. These types of interpersonal processes must be masterfully exercised if the individual, the organization, and management are to be successful.

Despite the perpetual state of transition and adaptation that managerial roles are in, some work characteristics remain somewhat stable. Managers often work long hours at an unrelenting pace. Some seem to never catch up! Their day is broken up into a large number of brief, diverse, and fragmented managerial activities. Managers meet, interact, network, and maintain contact with a large number of people. They often have little time for reflective thinking or planning, and many seem to prefer oral to written communication. Much of the manager's work is initiated by others, and oftentimes managers do not control their own destiny.

If prospective managers of physical education and sport programs are thinking about being in a position to possess power over other individuals, force personal ideas on other members of the organization, or provide opportunities for making unilateral decisions, then they should not go into management because they are doomed to failure. The formula for success is to be creative, adapt ideas, set goals, motivate, promote social justice and equality, and make shared decisions with members of the organization. The power of the *organization* is crucial, not the power of the *individual*.

MANAGERIAL FRAMEWORK AND FUNCTIONS

The conceptual framework for the study of management has evolved since classical school management pioneers such as Frederick W. Taylor (1911) and Henri Fayol (1929) proposed various ingredients, possessions, duties, and responsibilities that served to shape the management process. Thus the modern manager's makeup, which may be characterized as dynamic, continuous, fluid, and controlling in nature, has grown into a complex interrelated spectrum of duties and responsibilities influenced and tempered by the manager's personality, capability, and experience as well as the environment in which the organization must function (table 1-2).

Table 1-2.   A framework for the shaping of the management process

Ingredients	Possessions	Duties and Responsibilities
People personality and needs (affiliation, aspiration, power, attitude, achievement, motivation)	Dynamic Continuous	Leadership, motivation, and communication Training programs and delegation of tasks
Environmental influences (social, cultural, political, economic, race, gender)	Fluid (continually changing and adapting)	Effectiveness and performance evaluation
Physical and mental ability and experience (education, knowledge, opportunity, training)	Directs and controls (the nature, extent, and pace of the organization)	Goal setting, decision making, and feedback

Dynamic leaders help shape the direction of interscholastic and intercollegiate sport.

Within this framework, some of the commonly identified functions of management follow.

Planning

Planning is the process of logically and purposefully outlining the work to be performed, together with the methods to be used and the time allotted for the performance of this work. The total plan will result in the accomplishment of the purposes for which the organization is established. Of course this planning requires a clear conception of the aims of the total organization. To accomplish this planning, the manager must have vision to look into the future and prepare a strategy for what is seen. He or she must forecast the influences that will affect the organization in order to arrive at prudent decisions concerning future organizational challenges.

Organizing

Organizing refers to the development of the formal structure of the organization whereby the various management coordinating centers and subdivisions of work are arranged in an integrated manner with clearly defined lines of authority. The purpose behind this structure is the effective accomplishment of established objectives through a coordinated marshalling of human and physical resources.

The structure should be set up to avoid red tape and provide for the clear assignment of every necessary duty to a responsible individual or cooperative work unit. Whenever possible, standards should be established for acceptable performance for each assigned duty.

The coordinating centers of authority are developed and organized primarily on the basis of the work to be done by the organization, the services performed, the individuals available in light of incentives offered, and the efficiency of operation. A single manager cannot perform all the functions necessary except in the smallest organizations. Hence responsibility must be logically assigned to others. These individuals occupy positions along the line, each position being broken down in terms of its own area of specialization. The higher up the line an individual goes, the more general the responsibility; the lower down the line the individual, the more specific or focused the responsibility.

Staffing

The management function of staffing refers to the entire personnel duty of selection, assignment, training, and staff development and of providing and maintaining favorable working conditions for all members of the organization. The manager must have thorough knowledge of staff members. He or she must select employees with care and ensure that each subdivision in the organization has a competent leader and that all employees are assigned to jobs in which they can be of greatest service. Personnel should possess talent, energy, initiative, and loyalty. The duties of each position must be clearly outlined. All members of the organization must be encouraged to use their own initiative. They should be praised and rewarded fairly for their services and informed (and perhaps reprimanded) if performance is not up to standards. Vested interests of individual employees must not be allowed to endanger the general interests of the majority. Work environment and conditions should be made as pleasant and as ideal as possible. Physical, social, and multicultural factors should be provided for. Personnel

Management functions of organizing, controlling, and communication are crucial to physical education and sport activities.

who feel good about themselves and their work environment produce significant results.

Leading

Leading is a responsibility that falls to the manager as head of the organization. The manager must lead, positively motivate, and influence the individuals who make up the organization and therefore will affect the operations and conduct of the program. This means implementing and carrying out approved plans through work of employees and staff to achieve or exceed the organization's objectives. A good leader is influenced by the nature of organizational plans and structures as he or she elicits behavior that will support the achievement of the organization's objectives. A good leader maintains sound interpersonal relationships while developing systems and structures that motivate employees and satisfy their needs.

The ability to motivate is an integral part of leadership in order for the employee, organization, and manager to develop to their fullest potential. Motivation is associated with the "why" of human endeavor. Motivation in physical education and sport involves effort, persistence, and purposeful and goal-directed behavior as they relate to governing choices that affect achievement and productivity. Factors such as discipline, satisfaction, achievement, recognition, and advancement may all contribute to the enhancement of human potential.

Managerial effectiveness is determined by the ability to guide, assist, and direct others successfully toward established goals. Managers who are good leaders receive high marks in determination, persistence, endurance, and courage. Good leaders affirm values, create options, explain and clarify, inspire, unify, and serve as role models. They clearly understand the organization's purposes and keep them in mind while guiding the way. Through leadership, managers maximize communication, cooperation, and shared decision making to ensure the integrity, success, and "culture of quality" of the management process.

Controlling

Controlling ensures the proper execution of plans and consists of several factors. Job standards or expectations should be set, and methods and procedures for measuring whether standards are met should be established. Controlling should be done in light of the goals of the organization. Corrective action should be taken when goals are not met or if they may not be met. Controlling also means interrelating all the various phases of work within an organization; therefore the organization's structure must clearly provide close relationships and competent leadership in the coordinating centers of activity. The manager should meet regularly with chief assistants to make arrangements for unity of effort to eliminate obstacles to coordinated work.

Coordination should also take place with management units outside the organization when such out sourcing responsibilities are necessary. Controlling means that subordinates must be kept informed through regular reports, research, monitoring, and evaluation concerning performance in relation to expected standards and outcomes. In this respect the manager is a point of intercommunication. In addition to accepting the responsibility for reporting to a higher authority, managers must continually know what is going on in the area under their jurisdiction. Members of the organization must be informed on many topics of general interest, such as goal achievement, progress, strong and weak points, and new areas proposed for development.

OTHER MANAGEMENT FUNCTIONS

There are myriad other interrelated and associated managerial functions found throughout the literature. Those functions most often mentioned include the following:

- *Decision making:* the sequence of steps completed to select a course of action from two or more alternatives. This may include various interpretive phases by the management team.
- *Problem solving:* approaching a problem in a systematic way in order to enhance the probability of arriving at the proper decision.
- *Budgeting:* strategic planning to allocate resources required to support institutional objectives. The budget is most frequently associated with the control function.
- *Evaluating:* the process of measuring progress, comparing it with objectives, and taking needed corrective action.
- *Communicating:* the ability to articulate a clear and concise viewpoint or message to others. Effective communication leads to respect, trust, and increased performance outcome.
- *Reporting:* the ability to provide meaningful feedback, including analysis of data, in a clear and concise fashion in order to determine if organizational goals are being met.
- *Delegating:* the process by which authority is distributed by the manager downward in the organization. Delegating should be a form of positive motivation if planned and properly conducted.
- *Innovating:* the ability to introduce a new idea, technique, method, or purpose into the management process.
- *Coordinating:* the ability to interconnect the aims of the organization with the aspirations and needs of the participants.
- *Representing:* serving as the spokesperson, figurehead, or liaison for the organization or team to various outside organizations, groups, or individuals.
- *Creating:* the ability to originate, envisage, fashion, devise, or design a new system or strategy concerning the management process.

■ *Motivating:* the process by which behavior is mobilized and sustained in the interest of achieving organizational objectives.

FUNCTIONAL, EFFECTIVE, AND EFFICIENT MANAGEMENT

Qualifications

The qualifications of physical education and sport managers are many and varied. Sound health and fitness for the job is requisite for any physical education or sport position. It is not uncommon, because of the stress of managerial positions, to find health (including burnout) to be a contributing factor to resignation. A thorough knowledge and understanding of the tasks and associated risks of the position are also keys to not only job qualification but also job satisfaction. Clearly, possession and command of the managerial skills associated with the position and the willingness to accept responsibility are crucial qualifications at

Qualifications such as experience, teaching and communication skills, and personal integrity are requisite to good leaders.

any managerial level, including teaching, coaching, or directing a sport or activities program.

Other associated qualifications include, but are not limited to, the following:

Experience

Teaching skill

Previous and continued involvement in physical education and sport

Coaching or sport administrative duties at various levels or other managerial, practicum, or internship experience

Community and public relations

Education

College or university preparation and degree

Communication skills, computer skills, and coursework related to the job position, including child development, legal issues, and human relations

Certification (e.g., first aid, CPR, WSI, NATA, NSCA, lifeguard training, pool operator's license, teaching and coaching license or certification, or adapted/developmental physical education certification)

Attendance and active participation at clinics, staff development workshops, and job-related conventions, seminars, and conferences

Personal traits

Honest, trustworthy, fair, cooperative, intelligent, creative, original, personable, dedicated, professional, ethical, and decisive, among others

Just as the qualifications and abilities of managers vary, so do the tasks and responsibilities. To complete managerial tasks successfully, certain skills are required, whether from a top, middle, or frontline manager. The three primary skill areas deemed crucial to effective and efficient management practice are technical, human (interpersonal), and conceptual (Katz 1974).

Skills and Levels

Technical Skills

Technical skills involve the ability to employ specialized knowledge and expertise with various equipment, procedures, methods, and techniques to perform the given task. The manager must understand the product (e.g., physical education, interscholastic ice hockey, or Special Olympics) or service that is being managed and the processes involved by which the product is created, packaged, marketed, and delivered. Frontline managers often rely heavily on operational and technical skills (e.g., website analysis, computer graphics) to make certain the organization provides its services as effectively and efficiently as possible.

Human Skill

Human skill deals with the ability and judgment to work with and through people. Communication, attitude shaping, cooperative effort (teamwork), and motivation are key ingredients that a manager must master to achieve the organization's goals and objectives. Knowledge and understanding, character, sound judgment (predicting, diagnosing, and attributing), common sense, social and intercultural sensitivity, and ability to influence behavior (behavior modification and stress management) are just some of the skills especially critical to middle managers as they attempt to integrate the work of first-level employees and staff with the desires of top management.

Conceptual Skill

Conceptual skill implies the ability to see the "whole picture" of the organization and the envi-

Conceptual skills are crucial to future leaders.

ronment or culture in which the organization must function. It entails the ability to think in the abstract and analyze and understand the cause-and-effect relationship of the various interrelated organizational interests and interdependent functions. Conceptual skills are used to formulate and implement an organization's strategic plans and are most often associated with top-level management.

Leadership

Another often-mentioned management skill or trait is leadership. Leadership is the skill of influencing the activities of an individual or group in an effort to have them willingly strive for goal attainment in a given situation.

Knezevich (1981) recognizes three kinds of leadership: (1) *symbolic leadership,* which is primarily a personality attribute; (2) *formal leadership,* which involves the use of a title, status, or position denoting a leadership role in a formal organization; and (3) *functional leadership,* or the role performed in an organized group. Leadership is a social process that involves activating and working with people. Personality traits and attributes such as charisma and optimism will not in themselves result in leadership. Furthermore, conferring a title does not necessarily induce leadership. Instead, the existing situation and the ability of the person to lead in that situation are critical. Leaders embed and transmit their message or culture through building trust and instilling values and standards, paying attention to and rewarding the people around them, allocating resources, performing role modeling, handling crises, and attending to recruitment, selection, promotion, and retention. Leaders are individuals who are inventive, who take risks, and who are entrepreneurial. They provide vision of potential and promise, and they possess the ability to attract and mobilize others. People usually function best under leadership that is creative, dynamic, and imaginative. Leadership cuts across all levels of management and is present in any situation in which someone is trying to influence the behavior of another. Leadership helps shape personal philosophies of management, management style and decision making, and is crucial in charting a successful course for any program or organization.

The management domain is structured in a number of ways and consists of various interrelated systems, stages, and levels. Figure 1-2 is a dual schematic that reflects various managerial levels (top, middle, and frontline), the amount of time (in percentage) that a manager at a particular level might engage in human, technical, and conceptual skill functioning, and the decrease in managerial opportunity as the management ladder is climbed.

Roles

The roles that managers play in physical education and sport organizations are varied and multidimensional in nature. Mintzberg (1973) offers ten distinct roles of an effective administrator, which have been adapted to the physical education and sporting process (table 1-3).

Other Considerations

Regardless of where physical education and sport is delivered (e.g., schools, private clubs, commu-

nity), the need for the development of a functional, effective, and efficient management scheme is required. This means developing an organizational structure that lends itself to delegating authority, resolving organizational conflict, making meaningful decisions, and forming sound policies and procedures for safe and efficient conduct of the programs set forth by the organization.

Delegating Authority

The effective manager delegates responsibilities and with them the authority to make the necessary decisions for carrying out such responsibilities.

Many managers are overwhelmed with their assigned duties. In many cases it is impossible for one person to discharge all of these duties. Therefore it is important to delegate responsibilities to qualified people who can perform effectively on behalf of the organization.

A clear understanding should exist between the manager and the people to whom the duties are being delegated. The latter must be willing to assume such responsibilities and must know exactly what their responsibilities are.

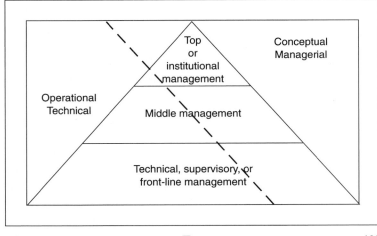

University presidents, corporate directors and vice presidents, superintendents of schools, owners of sports teams and fitness complexes

Deans of college faculties, general managers, principals, athletic and activities directors, head, regional, and national team coaches

Department chairs, area coordinators, curriculum supervisors, directors of elementary and secondary education, heads of special and adapted physical education, teachers, and coaches

Figure 1-2. Management skill schematic. A dual schematic reflecting managerial levels (top, middle, and frontline), the amount of time (in percentage) of managerial skill functioning (human skills held constant and crucial at each level), and the decrease in managerial positions as the educational, athletic, or corporate ladder is climbed

Table 1-3 Ten physical education and sport managerial roles

Role	Description	Management Activities of Teachers, Coaches, Athletic Directors, Officials, Sport Managers, and Administrators
Interpersonal Roles		
Figurehead	Symbolic head; obliged to perform a number of routine duties of a legal or social nature	Ceremonies and banquets, fund-raising solicitations, alumni outings
Leader	Responsible for the motivation and activation of subordinates; responsible for staffing, training, and associated duties	Virtually all managerial activities involving subordinates
Liaison	Maintains self-developed network of outside contacts and informers who provide resources and information	Acknowledgment of correspondence; internal and external work; other activities involving external sources such as conferences, media, and local, state, regional, and international visitations
Informational Roles		
Monitor	Seeks and receives wide variety of special information (much of it current) to develop a thorough understanding of other organizations and environments; emerges as nerve center of internal and external information of the organization	Handling all correspondence and contacts categorized as concerned primarily with receiving information (e.g., periodical news, conference newsletters, rule guidelines, legal matters)
Disseminator	Transmits information received from outsiders or from other subordinates to members of the organization; some information factual, some involving interpretation and integration of diverse value positions of organizational influencers and shapers	Forwarding correspondence into organization for informational purposes, verbal contacts involving information flow to subordinates (e.g., review sessions, instant communication, construction of web sites, flow of facts)
Spokesperson	Transmits information to outsiders on organization's plans, policies, actions, results, etc.; serves as expert on organization's industry, posture and culture	Staff meetings; handling correspondence and contacts involving transmission of information to external sources such as the community and involving printed and electronic media
Decisional Roles		
Entrepreneur	Searches organization and its environment for opportunities and initiates "improvement projects" to bring about change; supervises and designs certain projects	Strategy and review sessions involving initiation or design of improvement projects (e.g., facilities, media production)
Disturbance Handler	Responsible for corrective action when organization faces important, unexpected disturbances or problems	Strategy and review sessions involving disturbances and crises (e.g., eligibility lawsuits, harassment charges)
Resource Allocator	Responsible for the allocation of organizational resources of all kinds; makes or approves all significant organizational decisions	Scheduling; requests for authorization; any activity involving budgeting and the programming of subordinates' work
Negotiator	Responsible for representing the organization at major negotiations	Negotiation (e.g., facility rental, travel, media contracts)

In physical education programs, the director or chair of physical education often delegates to others the responsibilities for the physical activity program, recreational sports, and curriculum development. The director of athletics frequently delegates authority to coaches, trainers, and equipment supervisors. The manager should recognize that in delegating responsibilities, he or she is still responsible for the conceptual and overall functioning of the unit, whether it is a school division, department, or program.

Resolving Organizational Conflicts

Wherever human beings and the variant of social change or development are involved, conflicts may develop. Conflicts may arise around such human needs as security, status, esteem, or self-actualization. When certain needs are not satisfied, conflict may arise. People have physical needs, such as the need for physical comfort; psychological needs, such as a feeling of belonging and recognition; or social needs, such as the desire to work with a certain group of people. Organizational conflict might occur when employees perceive a lack of consistent supervisory practice or fail to see how they fit into their assigned roles. Reward, recognition, status, job assignment input, and job task equity are other trouble spots for managers. Conflict often results in poor performance, absence, frequent turnover, and organizational dissociation.

Organizational conflicts, as far as possible, should be solved swiftly and effectively by the manager. This means creating an environment in which employees want to work and can achieve self-esteem and self-actualization. It means providing opportunities for personal growth and opening channels of communication to improve both situational and employee relations. It means making work as interesting and challenging as possible to ensure positive and productive performance. It also means involving employees in decisions that affect their well-being, morale, pride, and job effectiveness.

Organizational conflicts are kept to a minimum if the management is aware of human needs and tries to satisfy these needs in the best interest of all concerned. It is mandatory that the manager be a master of conflict resolution.

DECISION MAKING

Decision making in the management process requires that certain steps be followed to bring about meaningful action. This problem-solving approach usually includes recognizing a problem, defining the problem, gathering relevant data, analyzing the data, identifying a set of alternative solutions, and finally arriving at a decision. Management, however, must not stop at the point of arriving at a decision. Figure 1-3 presents a model of sequential phases that extend the problem-solving and decision-making processes to ensure that effective and meaningful decisions are being implemented. The model includes the following phases:

Perceiving. The process of recognizing that a problem exists is the starting point of successful decision making.

Defining. Defining the problem is sometimes not an easy task. Conflicting facts requiring skillful interpretation, as well as personal reluctance to address a delicate problem, often arise. Managers need an understanding of norms, standards, and ethics that govern the selection and definition of problems. They need to know what the critical factor is.

Gathering relevant data. This may be accomplished by observation, interviewing, production of special reports by task forces or committees, and distributing questionnaires, personnel evaluations, or other appropriate sources. Information close to the source is desirable even though such sources may contain bias.

Analyzing data. After the significant and relevant information is gathered, the data is evaluated using either an objective or a qualitative approach. Decisions that are made for appearance or for the enhancement of the management record rather than for inherent validity or logic should be avoided.

Identifying alternative solutions. A set of solutions should be studied, if possible, before

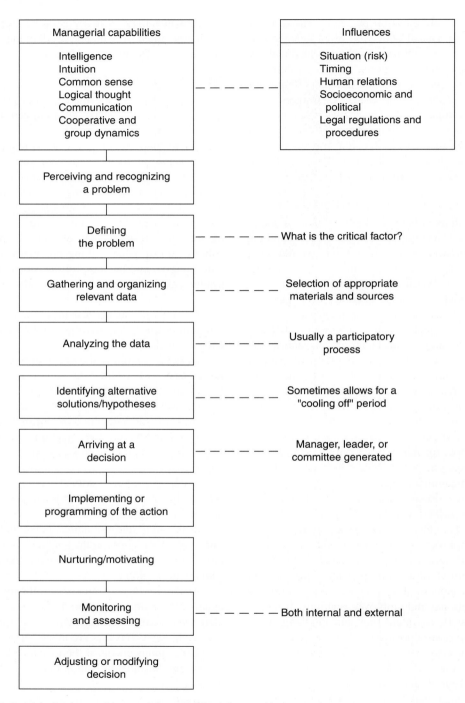

Figure 1-3. Model for problem solving and decision making

Decision making is a cooperative effort.

arriving at the final decision. This is necessary because of the ramifications that the decision itself may generate. This process should allow for creativity, brainstorming, and group participation, especially when developing new projects, programs, and proposals. This synergistic approach may yield a large number of creative solutions to complex decision situations.

Making the decision. Decisions are often affected by the environment, personalities of decision makers, timing, and communication as well as by those who will be affected by the decision. Decisions are sometimes made by the manager alone; however, ad hoc, advisory, or standing committees may play a significant role. Participation and due process should always be part of sound decision making. Oftentimes a manager selects a good but not optimal or perfect solution because of circumstances such as time constraints or inaccuracy of information. Such "satisficing" is related to the need for suboptimization, which occurs when organizational objectives cannot be pursued independently because they are interdependent and often in conflict.

Implementing the decision. After the decision is made, resources in the form of planning, budget, equipment, personnel, and so on should be mobilized to support the decision.

Motivating. As the program or position is set into operation, continued motivational support (i.e., funds, reward structures, increased commitment) should be visible. This nurturing and continued interest and support will assist in the development of proper organizational attitude and add to the productivity of the program or individual.

Monitoring and assessing. This dimension of the problem-solving process may be established over a prescribed time period (e.g., monthly or quarterly) and is an attempt to determine whether the decision was effective. This input in the form of monthly or quarterly reports will serve as a primary source of data to determine if the decision might be adjusted, modified, or allocated more resources to continue to be productive. Internal and external reviews might also be employed.

Managerial decisions are rarely as rational and calculated as managers like to believe. Most decisions are a result of bounded rationality because of the myriad influences that pervade the decision-making process (e.g., conflicting goals, ill-defined problems, missing facts, laws, regulations, contracts). Managers become effective decision makers through exercise (trial and error), and sometimes less than desirable results will occur. The manager must accept the reality and learn from past omissions or errors, yet not become too cautious because this might lead to lost opportunities for both the organization and the decision maker.

Tips for Decision Makers

1. Prudent planning should minimize the number of decisions with which the manager must contend.

2. Insist that subordinates (e.g., division heads of physical education, coaches, aquatics directors) assume responsibility for their programs and line staff.

3. Assess the impact of organizational politics, biases, and attitudes when others are invited into the decision-making process.

4. View problems as opportunities to demonstrate problem-solving and decision-making prowess.
5. Seek out the best alternatives rather than the most convenient. Be creative when generating alternative solutions and do not critically analyze while the generation process is underway.
6. Decision making involves risk, and a manager who never makes a wrong decision is often short-changing the organization as well as the decision maker.

Forming Sound Policies

The efficient management of a physical education or athletic department requires the establishment of sound policies if it is to achieve its goals. Policies are essential to the efficient and effective management of any department, school program, business, or other organization. Without policies, there is little to guide the activities and conduct of the organization in the pursuit of its goals. With well-reasoned policies the organization can function efficiently and effectively, and its members will better understand what is expected of them. Policy making is decision making that restricts managers' discretion and provides limits within which acceptable decisions and behavior must fall.

Policies are guides to action that reflect procedures that, when adhered to, fulfill the best interests of the organization and the purposes for which it exists. If properly selected and developed, policies enable each member of the organization to know what duties are to be performed, the type of behavior that will result in the greatest productivity for the establishment, the best way the departmental goals can be accomplished, and the procedure by which accountability can be established and evaluated.

Management policies are statements of procedures that represent the legalistic framework under which the organization operates. As such, they are not frequently changed; they possess some sense of permanence. Management policies are not developed on short notice or hastily drafted without the input of the management team and those charged with organizational compliance.

Although policies are considered and formulated carefully, they should be reviewed periodically in light of any new developments that occur. For example, at present some high schools are involved with open enrollment. This new freedom for students makes some existing policies concerning athlete participation outdated and obsolete. Therefore, policy review and change are needed.

How Policy Is Developed

Policy emanates as a result of many phenomena. For example, the Constitution of the United States sets forth various conditions that affect policy development in organizations throughout the country. Educators, for example, must comply with such conditions as equal rights for all in the public schools and separation of church and state. Other conditions educators must comply with are the various conditions inherent in the democratic process and those included in such legislation as Title IX and the Individuals with Disabilities Education Act (IDEA).

Because education is a state responsibility, the state government also issues policies that must be adhered to by local education authorities. These policies include such items as the number of days schools must be in session, certification qualifications, core subject requirements, and salary schedules for teachers and coaches. Within the framework of these policies or guidelines established by federal and state agencies, however, local education authorities, such as school boards, are permitted freedom to develop their own policies. Thus they establish policies pertaining to students' driving to school, attendance, chemical abuse, physical education requirements, student-athlete eligibility, and many other crucial factors. Sometimes local policies conflict with state policies, in which case the local policies are declared invalid. In other instances, local policy (e.g., core class content or status) might conflict with institutions such as the NCAA (NCAA Initial-Eligibility Clearinghouse). These conflicts may be negotiated.

Policy is developed in many ways in physical education and athletic departments. In some organizations it is done autocratically, with a manager establishing policy unilaterally. The process is devoid of deliberations and creative input from the members of the organization. The trend now, however, is toward greater involvement of staff members in developing policy.

As a general rule, the expression "many heads are better than one" is true of policy development. Policies must be carefully researched and thought through before they are drafted and presented to authorities. Therefore it is usually better to involve people who look at problems affecting policies from many different angles. Although staff members may participate in policy development, it should be recognized that the formulation and development of policy is different from the execution of the policy. Execution of policy is usually a management responsibility and should be recognized as such.

Writing Policies

Before a policy is written, much research must be done to determine what goes into the substance of that policy. This research can be accomplished in several ways. One method is for the director of physical education or athletics to appoint a committee to research or strategically plan and to recommend policy to the management. When the committee to recommend policy has been formed, the members will want to gather and investigate the facts thoroughly. They may decide to research the status of policies regarding this problem; what other similar organizations are doing; what policies already exist; the stand taken by selected national professional and athletic associations; views of other managers; the position of the American Civil Liberties Union, teachers' unions, and school board lawyers; and other specialized sources of information. After gathering the data, the committee will want to deliberate carefully and then make a recommendation. If the recommendation is approved, the director of physical education or athletics may then recommend it to his or her superior for approval, who in turn may recommend it to the school board, regents, or other responsible group for the final approval as the policy governing the organization.

The policy that finally emanates from the committee should be written clearly and concisely. There should be no ambiguities or possibilities for misinterpretation of what is intended by the policy statement. The statement of policy formulated by the committee should be reviewed carefully by the staff members, management, and compliance experts to further determine that the statement clearly says what the organization's position is on this particular issue.

When Policy Is Needed

Only the most important items facing the department or organization should have policy statements. Policies on trivial matters should not be carried on the books, because confusion and failure to adhere to many of the policies can result when policies are not known or understood. Furthermore, too many policies may cause the important ones to be obscured by the proliferation of those less important. It is usually better to have only a few carefully researched policies that cover major management functions. The other matters, if they need attention, can be covered by rules and regulations or in some other manner.

PHILOSOPHICAL AND THEORETICAL DIMENSIONS OF MANAGEMENT

One of the fundamental components of management, and one that is often neglected, is the establishment of a sound philosophy concerning physical education and sport. Philosophy is the process of critical examination, reasoning, and insight undertaken in an effort to arrive at truth and reality. It promotes the development and clarification of beliefs and values that serve as a foundation for the behavior and, ultimately, the performance outcome of the management team and organization.

Critical to the multidimensional management process are philosophical and theoretical questions that might be raised by a master manager. These might include the following:

- Does the present management process positively affect the manager and others involved?

- Does the process include meaningful integration and interaction between the individuals involved and the environment?
- Are management actions based on accomplishing the most good for the majority of those involved?
- Do management's actions positively contribute to the improvement of the quality of life of humankind and society?
- Does management strive for inclusion and fair and equitable opportunity, or for exclusion?

Of course these questions and the whole management process are strongly tempered by contemporary philosophical and theoretical constructs, values, politics, economics, nationalism, education, religion, ecology, and numerous other sociocultural forces that play a significant role in not only shaping the management process, but also in building a personal philosophy of management.

Management has traditionally been divided along a bipolar authoritarian-democratic continuum (figure 1-4). Managers, for the most part, acquired their management style or orientation from prior experience, former mentors, schooling or formal training, and/or environmental or situational circumstance. Traditional management evolved from its initial stages of classical and scientific management where the employee was technically trained and required to improve task and outcome performance to the behavioral or human relations phase. This behavioral approach focuses on staff feelings, attitudes, and needs and on a more integrative approach in which philosophical and theoretical constructs forge a new multileveled and eclectic approach.

Traditional theories of philosophical and theoretical managerial orientation include authoritarian, democratic, and laissez-faire. From these as well as from the more recent systems and eclectic approaches, future managers can adopt, develop, and refine their own personalized management orientation or style.

Authoritarian

The authoritarian orientation implies one-person leadership with decision making imposed on group members by the manager. An example of this orientation is the chairperson of a physical education department who seldom holds a staff meeting. Instead, directives are issued from the office dictating the policy and procedures that each staff member is expected to follow. This style is often associated with McGregor's Theory X, in which employees often dislike their assigned tasks or tend to shun responsibility. Authority seems to reside in the position as the head of the administrative unit. As a result, staff members frequently hesitate to disagree, and their creativity is often stifled.

Democratic

The democratic or egalitarian philosophy implies a manager who submits important matters to group discussion and involves group members in both the input and output (decision-making) process. This follows McGregor's Theory Y, in which employees are assumed to be committed to the task at hand and seeking responsibility and ownership.

An example of this orientation is the secondary school athletic director who holds regular staff meetings in which items that affect the sport programs and student-athletes are discussed. Each member of the staff is respected as a person as well as for his or her expertise, creative suggestions, and ideas. The staff helps in formulating goals and procedures that influence the operation of the sport program. The athletic director realizes that for the organization to achieve its goals, the staff must cooperate and feel like an integral part of the organization.

Laissez-faire

The laissez-faire orientation is an extension of the democratic approach in which little guidance is provided and decision making is frequently left to group members.

An example of this orientation is the physical education chairperson who does not provide active leadership. He or she believes that problems will solve themselves if given time. This individual frequently spends much time in activities that are personal in nature or that do not have

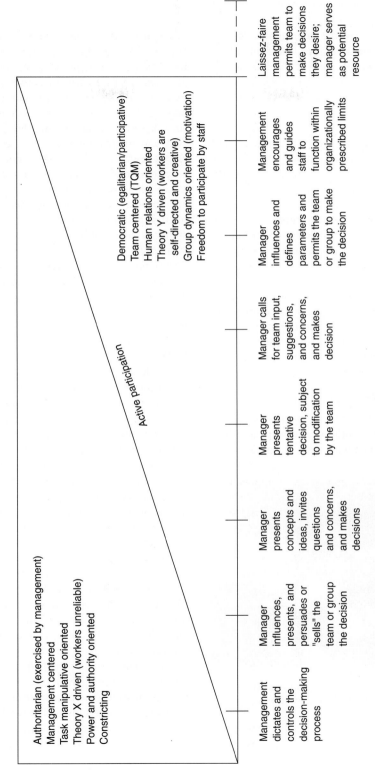

Figure 1-4. Management philosophical and theoretical orientation continuum

Authoritarian (exercised by management)
Management centered
Task manipulative oriented
Theory X driven (workers unreliable)
Power and authority oriented
Constricting

Democratic (egalitarian/participative)
Team centered (TQM)
Human relations oriented
Theory Y driven (workers are self-directed and creative)
Group dynamics oriented (motivation)
Freedom to participate by staff

Laissez-faire management permits team to make decisions they desire; manager serves as potential resource

Active participation

Management dictates and controls the decision-making process

Manager influences, presents, and persuades or "sells" the team or group the decision

Manager presents concepts and ideas, invites questions and concerns, and makes decisions

Manager presents tentative decision, subject to modification by the team

Manager calls for team input, suggestions, and concerns, and makes decision

Manager influences and defines parameters and permits the team or group to make the decision

Management encourages and guides staff to function within organizationally prescribed limits significant importance in the management of the organization. To a great degree, staff members function on their own because of the absence of leadership in the organization. This fragmentation often leads to low morale and ineffectiveness.

Systems

The systems theory of management has stemmed from the rapid growth of technology and management in recent years. By borrowing techniques from the business world, managers have constructed models that bring together in a unified fashion the many facets of an organization. The systems theory is a method designed to collect data on interrelated and interacting components that, when working in an integrated manner, help accomplish a predetermined goal or goals. The systems approach provides a conceptual framework for integrating the various components within an organization and for linking, for example, human resource management (recruitment, selection, development, assessment, adjustment) with larger organizational needs.

Total Quality Management

Total quality management (TQM) has its philosophical foundation in valuing and respecting the contributions of individuals and in meeting the

Total quality management leads to success, as evidenced by the USA basketball team. Courtesy of USA basketball.

needs of the people (e.g., user groups, consumers, children, student-athletes, fans) who use or benefit from the service or product provided. TQM managers assign or empower more responsibility and decision making to those who are carrying out the process (such as an aquatics director) and who should possess greater knowledge for both the conduct and improvement of the program. TQM includes teamwork, better communication between employees and management, more attention to customer relations, and statistical analysis of outcomes and problems as a measure of quality and improvement. It requires changing the system, letting go of authority, and instilling self-confidence in a well-trained and committed staff. These systems changes lead to open, team-centered behavior in which employees seek out and share new concepts and ideas. TQM encourages people to look outside traditional boundaries that formerly tended to shackle thinking and restrict vision.

Eclectic

The eclectic approach might be considered the offspring of management's traditional philosophical and theoretical constructs and systems theory. In this regard, the eclectic approach is adaptable, fluid, and situational in nature and might build on any number of the best and most appropriate management orientations (i.e., a mixture of democratic and laissez-faire). The manager must therefore be aware of the spectrum of contemporary management orientations in order to ensure that the eclectic approach functions at full effectiveness. This spectrum might range from Ouchi's Theory Z (in which the design of the organization serves to motivate and develop employees who are deemed as keys to productivity and quality) to Management Science (in which the quantitative orientation focuses on mathematical and network modeling as well as on computer and information systems). The full spectrum is implemented to support management's decisions. Knowledge, understanding, and appreciation of the systems approach, in which the organization is viewed as an interrelated set of subsystems working synergisti-

Effective management leads to positive outcomes.

cally, of the contingency theory, which suggests that organizational behavior cannot always be generalized or extrapolated from the apparent situation, and of TQM, in which teamwork is the cornerstone, should all be an integral part of the manager's philosophical and theoretical repertoire.

A PHILOSOPHY OF MANAGEMENT FOR PHYSICAL EDUCATION AND SPORT

Humankind and the environment in which we live represent the most important considerations in the world. The real worth of a field of endeavor, organization, or idea is found in what it does for people. The most important and worthwhile statement that can be made about a particular vocation, organization, or movement is that it contributes to the betterment of humankind.

Individuals possess goals that represent a variety of human objectives. Those goals include the need for health and security for oneself and one's family, the desire to obtain an education and to be employed in a worthwhile, meaningful, and gainful occupation, and the right to engage in a free society and to enjoy leisure pursuit.

People do not miraculously work together. They do not spontaneously band together and strive to accomplish common objectives. Because many groups and individuals possess common goals, however, through associated effort they help each other achieve goals that would be impossible for someone to accomplish alone. No one person, for example, can establish a comprehensive school for his or her children's education, but through cooperative effort and support many people join together to make quality education possible.

Organizations, to function effectively, need machinery to help them run efficiently, to organize and execute their affairs, and to keep them operating smoothly, so that the goals for which they have been created will be achieved. This machinery is management—the framework of organizations and the part that helps organizations implement the purposes for which they have been established.

Management, therefore, exists to help individuals achieve the goals they have set to live happy, productive, healthful, and meaningful lives. Management is not an end in itself; rather, it is a means to an end—the welfare of the people for whom the organization exists. Management exists for people, not people for management. Management can justify itself only while it serves the individuals who make up the organization, helping them achieve the goals they possess as human beings and as members of society.

SUMMARY

Management is the process by which key personnel provide leadership so that an organization functions efficiently and effectively in achieving the goals for which the organization exists. Management involves such functions as planning, organizing, staffing, leading and motivating, and controlling. Problem solving and decision making are also important facets of the management process. A philosophy of management for physical education and sport should recognize that the needs and welfare of the human beings who make up the organization are paramount to success. The contemporary manager also needs special qualifications, as well as skills (technical, human, and conceptual) that take into account various philosophical and theoretical underpinnings of management. These skills, combined with the appropriate measure of knowledge, sound judgment, experience, and training, will prepare the contemporary manager to effectively lead any program or organization as well as to achieve success and satisfaction.

SELF-ASSESSMENT ACTIVITIES

These activities will assist students in determining if material and competencies presented in this chapter have been mastered.

1. Take a sheet of paper and divide it into two halves as indicated here. On the left side, list the skills and functions of a manager, and on the right side, list specific preparation you would undertake to acquire these skills.

Skills and Functions of a Manager	Preparation for Skill Acquisition

2. Assume you are a manager who believes in participatory management. Describe how you would implement this orientation as the manager of a program of physical education.

3. Discuss your philosophy of management.

4. You are superintendent of schools of a large school system and are interviewing applicants for the position of director of athletics and activities. Construct a job description for the position.

5. List what you consider to be the major roles performed by a manager of a physical education and sport program.

6. You aspire to be the manager of a community fitness center. Briefly describe the steps in the decision-making process that you would employ to solve a major conflict.

7. Construct a policy concerning participation in physical education for all levels (K–12) of a public school.

REFERENCES

1. American Association of School Administrators. 1955. *Staff relations in school administration.* Washington, D.C.: American Association of School Administrators.
2. DuBrin, A.J., R.D. Ireland, and J.C. Williams. 1989. *Management and organization.* Cincinnati, Ohio: South-Western Publishing.
3. Hersey, P., and K.H. Blanchard. 1982. *Management of organizational behavior: Utilizing human resources.* Englewood Cliffs, N.J.: Prentice Hall.
4. Katz, R.L. 1974. Skills of an effective administrator. *Harvard Business Review,* September-October, 90–102.
5. Knezevich, S.J. 1981. *Administration of public education.* New York: Harper & Row.
6. Mintzberg, H. 1973. *The nature of managerial work.* New York: Harper & Row.
7. NASPE-NASSM Joint Task Force on Sport Management Curriculum and Accreditation. 1993. Standards for curriculum and voluntary accreditation of sport management education. *Journal of Sport Management* 7:159–170.

SUGGESTED READINGS

Blanchard, K., and S. Johnson. 1982. *The one minute manager.* New York: William Morrow.
  Presents a compilation of findings and management implications from medicine and behavioral science.

Brassie, P.S. 1989. Guidelines for programs preparing undergraduate and graduate students for careers in sport management. *Journal of Sport Management* 3(2):158–164.
Discusses programmatic training and experiences necessary to become an effective manager of human resources as they pertain to physical education and sport.

Conner, D. 1992. *Managing at the speed of change.* New York: Villard Books.
Focuses on organizational and human behavior issues and concerns in management.

De Sensi, J.T. 1994. Multiculturalism as an issue in sport management. *Journal of Sport Management* 8:63–74.

Douglas, J., S. Klein, and D. Hunt. 1985. *The strategic management of human resources.* New York: John Wiley and Sons.
Presents a thorough overview of the converging forces that play a significant role in the management process. Motivation and other psychological concerns are well represented.

Drucker, P.F. 1980. *Management in turbulent times.* New York: Harper and Row.

Kraus, R.G., and J.E. Curtis. 1990. 5th ed. *Creative management of recreation, Parks and Leisure Services.* St. Louis: Mosby Year Book.

Phi Theta Kappa. 1995. *Leadership development studies.* Jackson, Miss.: Phi Theta Kappa.

Roberts, K.H., and D.M. Hunt. 1991. *Organizational behavior.* Boston: PWS-KENT Publishing.
Discusses resources and views of such theorists as Peter Drucker, Abraham Maslow, and Max Weber as applied to leadership at the department level.

Scott, B. and S. Soderberg. 1985. *The art of managing.* Hampshire, England: Wildwood House.
Reviews the essentials of job management and suggests a balanced approach to the art of management. Offers interesting case examples.

chapter 2

Management Organization to Achieve Objectives of Physical Education and Sport

After reading this chapter the student should be able to

- Discuss how and why management organization is important to the effectiveness of physical education and sport programs.

- Identify the objectives of physical education and sport for which the organization and structure exist.

- Outline the principles that should be followed in establishing an effective organization for physical education and sport programs.

- Describe a formal and an informal type of organization and structure and provide rationale for each.

- Outline the factors that need to be considered to develop a functional organization.

- Describe the organization and structure of physical education and sport programs that exist in elementary and secondary schools, colleges and universities, and other representative organizations responsible for the delivery of physical education and sport.

- Prepare a management organizational chart for a physical education and sport program.

The first chapter covered the nature and scope of the management process. Such things as managerial functions, skills, roles, qualifications, and philosophy were presented. This chapter discusses the objectives of physical education and sport and the management organization and structure needed to accomplish these goals.

Schools, colleges, and other organizations do not function efficiently without some element that

holds them together and gives them direction so that they can achieve the goals for which they exist. This element is management. Management is the glue that bonds the various units and provides the control, communication, motivation, and leadership needed to achieve success. To accomplish these functions, a structure is needed that provides an efficient and effective way of operating and carrying out the various duties and responsibilities existing within the organization. The structure illustrates the roles various members of the organization play in achieving established goals. The structure indicates to whom each member reports and who is responsible for carrying out duties. It presents a blueprint or plan of action for getting the job done.

The primary purpose of structure in physical education and sport is to make it possible to achieve goals and objectives. Unless the organization and structure perform this function as efficiently and effectively as possible, it is headed for failure and should be abandoned. The structure is a means to an end, not an end in itself. Because this is true, it follows that the goals or objectives of physical education and sport must be clear in the mind of management before the establishment of the organizational structure takes place. Therefore the first task is to clarify the objectives that are being sought for physical education and sport.

PHYSICAL EDUCATION OBJECTIVES TO BE ACHIEVED

The objectives of physical education discussed here pertain, in general, to all educational levels—elementary, junior high or middle school, secondary, college, and university—although there could be further delineation of goals for each level. In addition, the objectives also relate to most other agency and institutional programs.

A study of humankind reveals four general directions, or phases, in which growth and development take place: physical fitness development, motor skill development, cognitive development, and social-emotional-affective development. Well-managed, safe, systematic, progressive, purposeful, and informative physical education can significantly contribute to each of these phases.

Physical Fitness Development Objective

The physical fitness development objective deals with the program of activities that builds and maintains power in an individual through the development of the various organic systems of the body. It results in the ability to sustain adaptive

Effective teachers and coaches guide students to ensure that objectives are being realized. Trina Tinti, head coach of gymnastics, University of California at Berkley.

effort, to recover, and to resist fatigue. The value of this objective is based on the fact that an individual will be more active, perform better, and be healthier if the organic systems of the body are adequately developed and functioning properly.

Muscular activity plays a major role in the development of the organic systems of the body, including the digestive, circulatory, excretory, heat regulatory, respiratory, and other body systems. Participating in activities such as hanging, climbing, running, throwing, leaping, striking, carrying, kicking, and lifting helps these systems function more efficiently. Health is also intimately related to muscular activity.

Vigorous muscular activity also produces several other beneficial results. Krotee and Hatfield (1979) point out that the various aspects of health-related fitness—cardiovascular and cardiorespiratory efficiency and endurance; appropriate body composition; muscular strength, endurance, and power; and flexibility and relaxation—represent basic elements essential to proper functioning. Research supports the fact that these components, when developed, can improve quality of life. The trained heart provides better nourishment to the entire body. It beats more slowly and pumps more blood per stroke, delivering more food to the cells and more efficiently removing waste products. During exercise, the trained heart's speed increases more slowly and has a longer rest period between beats, and after exercise, it returns to normal much more rapidly. The end result of this state is that the physically fit or trained individual can perform work for a longer period of time, expend less energy, and operate more efficiently than can the untrained or unfit individual. The physically fit individual also decreases his or her risk for cardiovascular heart disease as well as other illnesses related to a sedentary lifestyle. Whether participating in physical education class, performing routine tasks, or responding to emergencies, this trained or fit condition facilitates a vigorous and active quality of life. Therefore, physical education should aid in the development of the physically fit individual so that he or she will be able to live a healthful, happy, and productive life.

Motor Skill Development Objective

The motor skill development objective (Sage 1984) is concerned with developing body awareness, making purposeful physical movement with as little expenditure of energy as possible, and being proficient, graceful, and aesthetic in this movement. This objective has implications for work, play, and other activities that require physical movement.

Effective motor behavior results in aesthetic qualities of movement and in the development of a movement sense, which in essence is the development of motor skill together with appropriate knowledge and understanding about the skill and a positive attitude toward its development and use. In other words, proper control of movement during life's patterns and routines takes place in the movement-educated person.

Effective movement depends on a harmonious working relationship of the muscular and nervous systems. Effective movement results in greater distance between fatigue and peak performance; it is found in activities involving running, hanging, jumping, dodging, leaping, lifting, kicking, striking, bending, twisting, carrying, and throwing; and it will enable one to perform daily work efficiently without reaching the point of exhaustion too quickly.

Motor skill development is evident in many forms, such as dodging in a soccer game.

In physical education activities, the function of efficient body movement or motor skill is to provide the individual with the ability to perform with a degree of proficiency, which results in greater enjoyment of participation. Most individuals enjoy doing those particular things in which they have acquired some degree of mastery or skill. For example, if a person has mastered the ability to throw a ball consistently at a designated target and has developed batting and fielding prowess, he or she will be likely to choose to play baseball or softball. If the person can kick and trap a ball with some degree of effectiveness, then soccer might provide the challenge. Few individuals enjoy participating in activities in which they have little skill. Therefore, the objective of physical education is to develop in all individuals as many physical skills as possible so that the participants' interests will be wide and varied. This development will not only result in more enjoyment for the participant, but at the same time will allow for better adjustment to the group situation. Other values of motor skill are that it reduces expenditure of energy, contributes to confidence, promotes affiliation and recognition, enhances physical and mental health, makes participation safer, and contributes to the aesthetic sense.

The motor skill development objective also has implications for the health and recreational outcomes of the program. The skills that are acquired during physical education will help determine how leisure time will be spent. If a person excels in swimming, much leisure time may be spent in a pool or lake, or pursuing another aquatic endeavor. If the person is successful in racquet sports, he or she may be found frequently on the courts. Physical educators should develop in all individuals an understanding and appreciation of human movement as well as each individual's unique movement potential.

Young people who are in school should obtain fundamental skills that will afford them maximal satisfaction and happiness throughout life. To achieve these skills, a balance should exist in any physical education program between team, dual, individual, and lifetime sports. Team sports such as football, basketball, soccer, volleyball, and softball perform a great service by providing an opportunity for students to develop physical prowess and enjoy exhilarating competition. In many school physical education programs, however, team sports dominate the curriculum at the expense of individual and dual sports such as tennis, badminton, swimming, weight training, and golf, not to mention dance. In such cases, students are being deprived of the opportunity to develop skills in activities in which they can participate throughout their life span. It has been estimated that only 1 out of every 1,000 students who play organized football, for example, will ever play the game again after leaving school, whereas many will swim, jog, skate, ski, canoe, dance, and play tennis, racquetball, or golf well into their older years. Only through a well-balanced program of exercise and team, dual, individual, and lifetime sports will it be possible to develop a well-rounded individual.

Physical educators can and should be proud of the contribution they make to humankind. It is within their power to help many individuals learn physical skills and thus help them to lead healthier, happier, and more meaningful and productive lives. The world is a better place to live in as a result of the work of competent and committed physical educators, because the development of motor skill has significant value.

Golf instruction provides insight into motor skill development and neuromuscular control.

Cognitive Development Objective

The cognitive development objective (Barrow and Brown 1988) involves the accumulation of knowledge and the ability to think and interpret this knowledge.

Physical education is about human movement. Physical education's body of knowledge has its roots in the sciences, humanities, and other sources that interpret the nature of human movement and the impact of movement on the growth and development of the individual and on his or her culture. Scientific principles regarding movement—including those that relate to such factors as time, space, flow, and how humankind interfaces with machines—should be considered. The study of human movement should be part of the education of each individual who comes in contact with a physical education program.

Physical activities must be learned, hence, the necessity of thinking by the intellectual mechanism. The techniques and coordinations involved in various movements must be mastered and adapted to the environment in which the individual lives, whether it be walking, running, driving an automobile, in-line skating, playing arachnophobia, or stroking a crosscourt forehand with topspin in tennis. These movements require the participant to think, analyze, synthesize, and coordinate the muscular and nervous systems. Furthermore, this type of knowledge is acquired through trial and error, practice, cooperative effort, affordance, and opportunity and then, as a result of this experience, meaning and sophistication in the movement situation (for example, pattern or performance outcome) changes.

The individual should not only learn to move, but should also acquire a knowledge of rules, techniques, safety, and strategies involved in physical activities. In basketball, for example, the participant should know the rules; the strategies for offense and defense; the tactics involved in the transition game; the various types of passes; the difference between screening, blocking, and blocking out; and finally, the values that may be derived from participation. Techniques learned through experience result in knowledge that should also be acquired. A ball travels faster and more accurately if one steps while making the pass, for example, and time is saved when the pass or shot is made from the same position in which it was received. Furthermore, a knowledge of followership, leadership, courage, cooperation, self-reliance, assistance to others, interdependence, safety, etiquette, multiculturalism, and adaptation to group patterns should be transmitted or transferred in each class meeting.

Knowledge about health should also play an important part in the program. All individuals should know about their bodies, the importance of cleanliness, factors in disease prevention, the merits of exercise, the necessity of a well-balanced and nutritious diet, the importance of adequate rest, values of sound health attitudes and habits, facts concerning smoking, alcohol, and substance abuse, and which community and school agencies provide health service and counsel. With the accumulation of knowledge of these and other relevant facts, participation in physical education activities acquires a new meaning, and health practices are associated with definite purposes.

Leadership, courage, and cooperation are requisite to climbing the wall.

Physical educators can and should intellectualize their activities more. Physical activities are not performed in a vacuum. Physical educators should continually provide appropriate knowledge and information for participants and encourage them to ask "Why?" *Why* is it important to participate in this activity? *Why* should an hour be devoted to physical education each day? *Why* is exercise important? *Why* is it important to play by the rules? *Why* do I warm up? *Why* should I cooperate? Physical educators should also provide participants more opportunities to think, that is, allow participants to make choices, plan strategies, and select appropriate activities instead of usurping all this responsibility themselves. *The more thinking that takes place on the part of the participant, the more educating the activity becomes.*

Social-Emotional-Affective Development Objective

The social-emotional-affective development objective (Gensemer 1985) is concerned with assisting an individual in making personal and group adjustments as well as adjustments as a member of society. Physical education activities can offer valuable opportunities for making these adjustments if proper management is provided.

Physical educators should find as many ways as possible to positively influence human behavior. The rules of the game often reflect the standard of the democratic way of life. In games, one sees democracy in action and an individual is evaluated on the basis of ability and performance. Ethnicity, economic status, cultural background, race, gender, or other characteristics should not play a role, but differences should be recognized and appreciated. Performance and participation are the criteria of success.

Another aspect of the social objective of physical education is the need for each individual to develop an appropriate self-concept. Participants need to develop wholesome attitudes toward themselves as maturing persons. During the various stages of physical growth and development that young people experience, they are often accepted or rejected by classmates because of physical characteristics and/or physical prowess. It is therefore important for individuals to develop themselves physically not only for reasons of their own self-awareness but also because of the implications that their physique and physical skills have for their psychosocial image.

Each individual has certain basic social needs that must be met. These include a feeling of belonging (affiliation), recognition, self-respect, and love. When these needs are met, the individual becomes well adjusted socially. When they are not met, antisocial characteristics and negative behavior may develop. For example, the aggressive bully may be seeking self-respect, the gang member may be seeking affiliation, and the sub-

Physical education contributes to social-emotional-affective development. Crest View Elementary School, Brooklyn Park, Minn.

stance abuser may be seeking recognition. The needs theory has implications for the manner in which physical education programs are conducted. The desire to win, for example, should be subordinated to meeting the needs of the participants. Students today "need" more support, more success, and more positive experiences than at any time in history. Physical education *must* contribute its fair share.

All human beings should experience success. This factor can be realized through physical education. Through successful encounters in physical activities, people develop a positive self-concept and satisfaction in their achievements. Physical education can provide for this successful experience by offering a variety of challenges and invigorating activities as well as developing the skills necessary for successful participation in these activities.

In a democratic society all individuals must develop a sense of cooperative consciousness. This should be one of the most important objectives of the program. Therefore in various activities the following factors should be stressed: assistance for the less skilled participant, respect for the rights of others, subordination of one's desires to the will of the group, and realization of cooperative living as essential to the success of society. Individuals should be made to feel that they belong to the group and have the responsibility of directing and contributing their actions in the group's behalf. The rules of fair play, followership, and leadership should be developed and practiced in all activities offered in the program. Qualities such as courtesy, sympathy, fairness, ethical behavior, honesty, respect for authority, and abiding by the rules will help considerably in the promotion of social efficiency.

Another factor that should not be overlooked is the plus factor of affective development. Physical educators cannot be content once they have developed the physical body, mapped the skills in the nervous system, and developed the amenities of social behavior. Something else still remains— affective development—and this represents one of the greatest challenges to the field in which so many young people have a drive to engage.

Affective development is about attitudes, appreciations, values, and beliefs. Therefore physical education should be concerned with such things as helping individuals develop a healthy response to physical activity and recognize the contribution that physical education can make to health, to performance, and to the worthy pursuit of leisure. The individual should develop a positive attitude toward physical education, respect for others, self-discipline, and a wholesome attitude toward cooperative group work and play. In sum, the adoption of a healthy lifestyle for all is the ultimate goal of the profession.

Members of the physical education profession should help young people set goals and clarify and think through their value judgments, appreciations, and attitudes. Although physical educators should not indoctrinate students with

the educators' own value systems, they should recognize their position as role models and realize that much can be done to motivate and facilitate learners of all ages in formulating, analyzing, reevaluating, and renewing values and attitudes.

THE OBJECTIVES OF SPORT

Although the theoretical relationship between physical education and sport in the educational setting becomes increasingly complex as we move through the Physical Activity and Sport Continuum, each maintains many of the same general objectives already presented. At the same time, sport has additional goals that relate directly to the achievement of a high degree of skill and competitive success. Some physical educators believe that in certain situations the goals of sport programs are not compatible with the goals of physical education. Furthermore, the goals of highly competitive sport differ in various respects for each educational level and each institutionalized sport program.

Sport in the Elementary School

The sports program in the elementary school should stress what is good for the child and provide opportunities for a variety of positive experiences. All sports activities should be geared to the developmental level of each child and not just to his or her weight, grade level, or chronological age. Children at this stage vary greatly in physical and psychosocial development; therefore both an informal program and policies that recognize individual differences should be initiated.

The sports program should provide a wide variety of developmental (physical, motor, and psychosocial) experiences and should focus on lower organizational games and large muscle activity (e.g., running and jumping). Sports offerings that are selected should be broad based and diverse, and opportunity for all to participate should be encouraged. There should not be undue concentration on developing skill in just a few sports or sport-specific positions; nor should children be pressured into conforming to adult standards in a rigid, authoritarian, highly organized, and highly competitive sport program. Contact sports, particularly tackle football, are considered by many experts to be injurious for children of this age. Indeed, many football programs have been phased out of elementary school environs and picked up by myriad community-based organizations.

Sports activities—including playdays, clubs, and field trips—should be part of an overall well-organized and integrated school and community education program. Competent personnel, medical supervision, and safety procedures should be emphasized.

Sport in the Junior High or Middle School

The junior high or middle school sport program should be adapted to the needs of boys and girls in grades 6, 7, 8, and 9. This is a period of transition from elementary to senior high school and from childhood to adolescence. It is a time when students are trying to understand their bodies, gain independence, achieve social status, acquire self-confidence, and establish a system of values. It is a time when a sport program is needed to challenge the abilities and broadening interests of the student.

Interscholastic sport of a varsity type, if offered, should be provided only after the prerequisites of sound physical education (including adapted) and recreational sport programs have been developed and implemented. Selected varsity sports should be permitted only after the assurance of special controls in regard to such items as qualified management (coaches and officials), medical supervision, health status, safety, facilities, game adaptations, and appropriate classification of players. Some worthy goals at this level are to build team spirit, nurture the competitive drive, teach self-discipline and self-control, and develop pride in accomplishment and hard work. There should be room for everyone on the team, and playing time should be planned for maximal participation. The governance of the sport programs should also lie within the same educational structure as that of physical education.

High school soccer. Lexington High School, Lexington, Mass.

Sport in the Senior High School

Representative goals of sport at the senior high school level are usually articulated by each school district. Common goals often espoused by high school officials include promoting physical excellence; engendering an appreciation of competition and the will to win; instilling morale, honesty, fair play, and self-discipline; achieving goals such as self-assurance, group loyalty, and responsibility; providing a wholesome channel for expression of emotions; integrating various aspects of the self (social, emotional, physical, and intellectual) into action; and developing qualities of good citizenship and other valuable personal qualities such as leadership and empowerment. Other goals include providing an outlet for the release of personal energies in constructive ways, using sports as a unifying force for school, home and community, and providing activities that will help students live a balanced life.

Sport in College, University, and Associated Programs

The objectives of highly organized and competitive sport programs in many junior colleges and colleges, universities, and associated programs include developing excellence in sports competition;

providing a program that is financially self-sufficient; establishing a leadership position in sports among peer institutions; satisfying needs of the spectators, athletes, alumni, community, and coaches; and providing sports programs for the gifted student-athlete. In some colleges (Division III) and associated programs, sports may take on a low profile. Programs at this level often foster student participation and may not depend on spectators and gate receipts for their existence.

Overall Objectives of Physical Education and Sport

It is crucial to realize that the overall objectives of physical education and sport across the totality of the Physical Activity and Sport Continuum have traditionally been embodied in the goals of education as set forth in 1918 by the Commission on the Reorganization of Secondary Education. The commission's Seven Cardinal Principles include (1) health, (2) command of fundamental processes, (3) worthy home membership, (4) vocational competence, (5) effective citizenship, (6) worthy use of leisure, and (7) ethical character.

These principles, together with the 1938 *Purposes of Education in American Democracy* tenets of self-realization, human relationships, economic efficiency, and civic responsibility, have set the tone for physical education and sport in the United States. This tone has been more recently conceptualized and globalized by organizations such as UNESCO (International Charter of Physical Education and Sport, 1993), NASPE (The Physically Educated Person, 1990), and the North American Regional Forum (AAHPERD 1995). The latter, a joint statement by the American Alliance and Canadian Association for Health, Physical Education, Recreation, and Dance, summarized that physical education and sport has a vital role in the design of education for the future. It empowers individuals to learn about their world and be active participants within it. In doing so, human and social values are nurtured, and human rights and freedoms are encouraged; in these ways, our humanity can be most profoundly expressed. (See Appendix A for UNESCO's International Charter and the

AAHPERD/CAHPERD Global Vision for School Physical Education Statement, which also includes The Physically Educated Person).

The aim of organized physical education and sport programs is to create an environment that stimulates selected movement experiences resulting in desirable responses that contribute to the optimal development of the individual's potentialities in all phases of life. Sheppard and Willoughby (1975) further articulate what education should encompass:

> A growing commitment to the full realization of human potential will place permanent emphasis upon the development of competent, productive, responsible, inquiring, questioning, value-judging, sensitive, compassionate, loving, humane individuals and their individuality as expressed by the concept of self: self-esteem, self-direction, self-control, and self-actualization. Along with this will go the preparation to play many and varied societal roles—citizen, spouse, lover, parent, colleague, worker, player—and an emphasis on skills which are of life-long importance. Schools will actually attempt to prepare students to live a life, not merely to educate them.

Education should be available to, and meet the needs of, all citizens. It should furthermore be delivered in a dynamic, diverse, and professional fashion.

DEVELOPING A MANAGEMENT STRUCTURE THAT WILL ENABLE OBJECTIVES OF PHYSICAL EDUCATION AND SPORT TO BE ACCOMPLISHED

After the goals and objectives for physical education and sport programs have been identified, a management structure that will contribute to the achievement of these goals should be developed.

The structure refers to the framework whereby such things as titles of positions, role assignments, task allocations, functions, and relationships are graphically illustrated. The structure implies lines of communication, coordination, cooperation, and decision making.

Planning, developing, and organizing the structure for a physical education or sport program are important management responsibilities. Efficient organization and structure result in proper delegation of authority, effective assignment of responsibilities to staff members, adequate communication among the various units of the organization, clarification of the tasks assigned, and a high degree of morale among staff members. All these factors determine whether the organization's goals are achieved.

Loen (1971) suggests guidelines for developing a management blueprint that are organized around activities rather than around people. His suggestions include the following:

- Review the program and its objectives at least once a year because realignments in duties and responsibilities may be necessary.
- Design each position so that a short label describes its primary responsibilities. Each title should be descriptive yet short enough to use in normal conversation.
- Assign each person clear-cut duties, responsibility, and authority, so that each position holder will possess freedom to act. When people know exactly what they are responsible for and to whom to report, they can concentrate on getting things accomplished rather than wondering if they are infringing on someone else's prerogatives.
- Establish line and staff positions that will enable management to realize the advantages of both centralization and decentralization.
- Establish each position on the basis of the knowledge and skills likely to be found in an individual.
- Design each position so that the position holder can make maximal use of his or her knowledge, understanding, talents, and skills.
- Design positions so that decision-making authority is as close as possible to the scene of the action. Routine decisions should be made by the individuals "on the line."
- Give managerial staff responsibility for as many positions as possible. This is both economically and organizationally efficient and effective.

PRINCIPLES FOR MANAGEMENT ORGANIZATION AND STRUCTURE

Experts in many areas have developed principles to aid in effective management organization. Some of the most significant principles include the following:

The management structure of an organization should clarify the delegation of authority and responsibility. For the goals of the organization to be met efficiently and successfully, management must delegate some of its powers to responsible individuals. These powers and the associated tasks should be clearly defined to avoid overlapping authority.

Management work may be most effectively organized by function. The doctrine of unity maintains that all personnel engaged in a particular type of work should function under a single authority.

Span of control should be considered in organizational structure. The number of subordinates who can be supervised adequately by one individual determines the span of control.

Successful management depends on communication. Communication is essential to effective management because it helps avoid waste and

Organization and communication are necessary for every physical education staff.

duplication and promotes cooperation among departments and staff.

Coordination and cooperation among various departments in an organization are necessary for effective management. Coordination among departments keeps each subsystem well informed and working together in a complementary and synergistic manner.

The manager must be an effective leader. An effective leader appreciates both the goals of the organization and the personnel working for the organization. Both are essential for the success of the organization.

Staff specialization aids effective management. To achieve objectives, organizations must perform many different tasks that require the abilities of various area specialists.

Authority must be commensurate with responsibilities, and lines of authority must be clearly drawn. An organizational chart is useful to illustrate the lines of authority. These lines should be well defined and unambiguous.

Organization and social purpose cannot be separated. The structure of an organization is a means to an end, and not an end in itself.

There is no single correct form of organization. Such factors as size, personnel, and economic constraints often determine the most appropriate organizational structure for a particular situation.

TRANSLATING THE MANAGEMENT STRUCTURE INTO GRAPHIC FORM (ORGANIZATIONAL CHARTS)

Once the desired type of management structure has been determined, the next step is to prepare it in graphic form so that it can be easily understood by members of the organization and by other interested individuals.

Organizational charts are frequently used to illustrate and clarify the structure of an organization. These charts clearly depict the management setup of an organization and the key management positions and their functions. Management uses these organizational graphic representations to orient new staff members to their responsibilities and their place in the total structure of the organization. These charts also serve as a public

relations instrument to show the community how it is intimately linked to the physical education and sport process.

Petersen, Plowman, and Trickett (1962) outline a six-step procedure for the development of organizational charts.

1. *Identify the objectives of the organization.* These objectives are designed to meet the goals of the organization, which in turn determine the structure that must be developed.

2. *Arrange objectives into meaningful functional units.* This step requires assessing the organization with its differentiated parts and units and organizing it to bring about a harmonious and integrated whole. If this step is successfully accomplished, it reduces friction and fragmentation and brings about a closely coordinated, smoothly functioning organization.

3. *Arrange the identified functional units into appropriate management units, such as departments.* This step varies in each organization, but it should represent the most effective and meaningful relationships for achieving the goals of the organization.

4. *Prepare a model of the structure of the organization and perform a trial run.* To make sure that the model represents the best management structure for the organization, it should be used initially on a trial basis.

5. *Revise the model in light of input received.* Views from personnel within and outside the organization should be sought and the model revised where necessary to achieve the most satisfactory, efficient, and effective structure possible.

6. *Evaluate the final design and assign staff who work within the organization to appropriate functional units.* As a result of this final step, each member of the organization can see where and how he or she fits into the total organizational structure.

Line and Staff Organization

The most common type of organizational chart is a line and staff chart (figure 2-1). A person in a

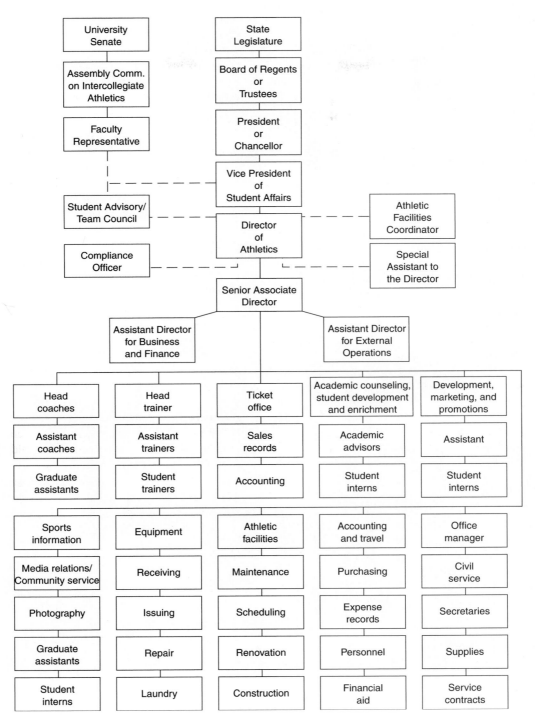

Figure 2-1. Organizational structure of an athletic department at a large college or university.

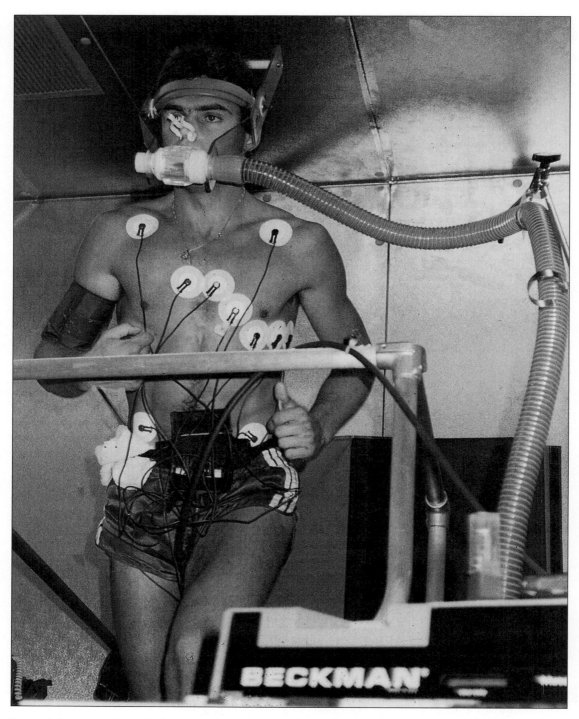

Research is vital to physical education and sport programs. Courtesy of the Division of Kinesiology, Laboratory of Physiological Hygiene and Exercise Science, University of Minnesota.

line position has direct responsibility and authority for a specific objective or objectives of the organization. For example, a senior associate director of athletics would be in a line position, with direct responsibility for duties assigned by the director, and in turn would report directly to the director. A person in a staff position has an indirect relationship to a specific objective or objectives of an organization. Staff personnel often have advisory positions or are in positions that are not responsible for carrying out the central mission of the organization. An example would be a facilities coordinator in the athletic department of a university or college program. Staff personnel do not have authority over line personnel. Line positions are related to, and derive authority from, the management head. In charts, staff positions are usually indicated by broken lines and line positions by solid lines. Line personnel are depicted in a vertical line in an organizational chart reflecting the hierarchy of power, whereas staff personnel are often depicted in a horizontal line.

Small management units with limited staff, such as interscholastic departments of physical education or athletics, frequently have little distinction between line and staff personnel because very few, if any, staff positions per se exist.

FORMAL AND INFORMAL ORGANIZATION AND STRUCTURE

Organizational theory and structure require that first, there must be a need for an organization to exist, and second, the organization must know the goals it is trying to achieve. To accomplish these objectives, a structure should be provided that enables the management to plan and make decisions, organize, staff, lead, motivate, control, and evaluate. These tasks can be performed through either a formal or an informal organization.

Formal Organization

A formal organization is based on a hierarchical job structure, with tasks assigned by managers to subordinates, concomitant with their job-task hierarchy and communications network. Figure 2-2 illustrates an interscholastic athletic and activities department and its formal relationship within a public school setting. Such an organizational structure is concerned first with the positions to be filled (coaches) and tasks to be accomplished (the conduct of sport programs), and then with the persons to be assigned to these positions and tasks. Clearly delineated lines of authority and formal rules and regulations are earmarks of formal organization, as are dependence, obedience, discipline, reward, and chain of command.

A formal organization is employed because it provides a clear picture of the positions that exist and the tasks to be performed. It represents a way to get things done by the use of authority and chain of command. It places subordinates in positions where they must perform as instructed; thus things get done. It assumes that control of behavior is accomplished through rational judgment and that the manager is the person most qualified to make decisions and solve problems. It assumes that people should be instruments of production and is authoritarian by nature and design.

Informal Organization

An informal organization realizes that many relationships exist that cannot be illustrated in an organizational chart. In other words, things get done outside the formal relationships that a chart reflects. It assumes that relationships occur in many informal settings where ideas are generated; productivity is enhanced; and cooperation, loyalty, and high morale are developed. Figure 2-3 represents such an informal structure concerning the articulation of physical education, recreational sports, and intercollegiate athletics at a large university.

Advocates of informal organization contend that this structure reflects how tasks are actually accomplished and thus oppose the formal, authoritarian type of organization. They also maintain that people who hold rank in an organization do not always behave rationally nor do they have complete access to reliable information at all times. Advocates of informal organization also

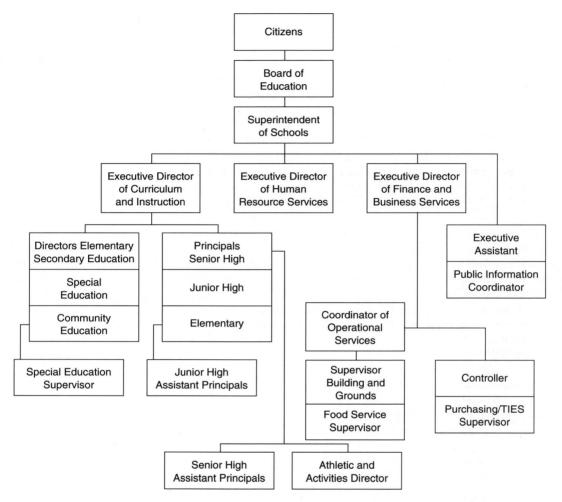

Figure 2-2. Formal organizational structure of a public school system athletic and activities department.

believe that members of an organization are not merely instruments of production, but instead have desires, values, needs, and aspirations that must be taken into consideration.

Modern theories of organization and structure indicate a shift away from the formal organizational structure toward an informal orientation recognizing the value of the human relations perspective. These modern theories and approaches (i.e., systems, behavioral management, contingency, etc.) are based on the fact that although most persons agree that some type of organizational framework is usually needed, most

individuals are capable of some self-direction and self-motivation to perform admirably on the job.

One aspect of informal organization is the formation of subgroups that do not appear on organizational charts. For example, employee unions represent an important group with whom managers must interact. In some organizations committees, commissions, councils, and task forces also represent influential subgroups. Therefore management must understand and appreciate what a staff member wants or desires and needs from his or her position, whether it is increased wages or benefits, job security, improved working

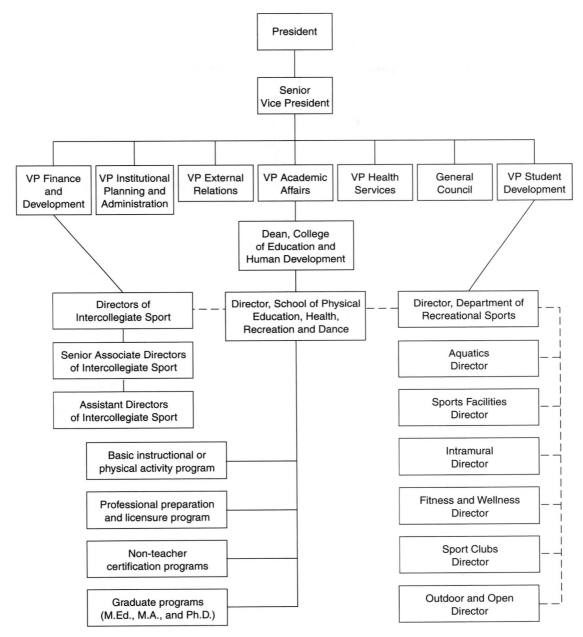

Figure 2-3. Informal organizational structure for physical education at a large college or university.

conditions, a share in the decision-making process, or some other condition.

Modern theories of management are moving more and more toward an eclectic and participa- tory philosophy in which staff members and managers both are involved in many organiza- tional decisions. Employees will better identify with an organization if they are involved in the decision-making process, and research suggests that performance outcome may also be significantly enhanced.

MANAGEMENT STRUCTURES FOR PHYSICAL EDUCATION AND SPORT PROGRAMS

The management structures currently employed for physical education and sport programs in elementary, junior high or middle school, secondary schools, colleges and universities, and community organizations are presented and discussed on the following pages. The examples offered are models and may be adapted and modified to fit each individual physical education and sport-specific circumstance.

The Organization and Structure of Physical Education and Sport in Elementary, Junior High or Middle Schools, and Secondary Schools

The school district is the basic management unit for the operation of elementary, junior high or middle schools, and secondary schools, and is a quasi-municipal corporation established by the state. In the United States, this basic educational unit ranges from a one-teacher rural system to a large metropolitan system serving thousands of students. A system may be an independent governmental unit or part of a state or county government or other local administrative unit. The governing body of the system is the school board.* The chief administrative officer is the superintendent of schools.

The school board is the legal management authority created by the state legislature for each school district and usually consists of a chair, vice chair, clerk of the board, and treasurer. The chair works intimately with the superintendent and is responsible for conducting school board meetings. The vice chair serves in this capacity in the

---

*The term *school board* is used throughout the text although *board of education, school committee, community-school board,* and *board of directors* are used in some regions of the United States.

absence of the chair. The clerk of the board is legally responsible for the board's records and documents, and the treasurer works closely with the executive director of finance and business. The responsibility of the elected board is to act on behalf of the residents of the district. It has the duty of appraising, planning, and initiating state-mandated educational programs (i.e., graduation standards, special education, birth-through-age-21, assurance-of-mastery, etc.). It selects executive personnel and performs duties essential to the successful operation of the schools within the district. The board develops policies that are legal and in the interest of the people it serves. It devises financial means within its legal framework to support the cost of education. It keeps its constituents informed about the effectiveness and needs of the total program, and it solicits citizen advice and counsel.

An example of a mission statement for a school board would be to prepare all students for the future by providing a challenging education that builds academic competence, encourages creativity, promotes lifelong learning, advances critical thinking skills, instills commitment to personal wellness, and fosters respect for self and others.

The key management personnel charged with carrying out the mission of the school district within each school system usually consist of the superintendent of schools, executive directors or assistant superintendents, principals, and directors (figure 2-4).

Superintendent of Schools

Within a large school system, a superintendent has management responsibility of the school program. Executive directors or assistant superintendents are in charge of academic services, resource management, and various other phases of the program, such as elementary and secondary education. There is also usually a superintendent's position associated with smaller schools. These managers are known as district superintendents; they are often responsible for many schools within a wide geographical area.

The superintendent's job is to carry out the educational policies of the state and the school board. The superintendent acts as the leader in educational matters in the community and provides the board of education with the professional advice it needs as a lay organization. The superintendent also supervises the executive assistant, who manages the daily functions of the superintendent's office. The executive assistant attends all meetings, functions, and retreats of the school board and serves to ensure that the operations of the school board are in compliance with the legal requirements, policies, and procedures set forth by the school board and the state.

Executive Director of Curriculum and Instruction

The executive director of curriculum and instruction supervises the divisions of elementary education, secondary education, special education, athletics, community education, and summer school education, and is responsible for the staff development of teachers and all district employees. The principals of elementary, junior high or middle schools, and secondary schools, as well as directors of physical education and directors of athletics and activities, fall within the curriculum and instruction director's domain. The executive director of curriculum and instruction is also involved in the development and evaluation of curriculum and the organization and supervision of instruction and preservice and in-service teacher training. The executive director of curriculum and instruction is first in line to perform the duties of the superintendent of schools in the event of the superintendent's absence.

Executive Director of Human Resource Services or Director of Personnel Services

The executive director of human resource services is the chief personnel officer of the district and, as such, manages the personnel functions for all licensed (teachers, coaches, administrators, etc.) and classified (secretaries, clerks, etc.) staff. The executive director also assists the superintendent in district management and represents the district in assigned school-community relations. In addition, aspects of employee relations such as negotiations of union contracts, fringe benefit packages, and insurance coverage for teachers and coaches also fall within the human resource manager's domain. In the absence of the executive director of curriculum and instruction, the human resource director represents the superintendent.

Executive Director for Finance and Business Services or School Business Manager

The finance and business manager serves as head of business affairs and supervises the controller, purchasing, operations, and the total information educational systems (district computer consortium for record keeping, grading, athletic eligibility, etc.) employed by the district. Buildings and grounds, food service, and the business office staff also usually fall under the domain of the finance and business manager. The executive director of finance and business is last in line to assume duties during the superintendent's absence.

Principal

The position of principal is similar to that of the superintendent; it differs mainly in the extent of responsibility. Whereas the superintendent is usually in charge of all the schools within a particular community, the principal is in charge of one particular school. The duties of the principal include executing educational policy as outlined by the superintendent, appraising educational offerings, making periodic reports on various aspects of the program, directing the instructional program, promoting positive relationships between the community and the school, and supervising the maintenance of the physical plant.

Supervisor

The supervisor is generally responsible for improving instruction in a specific subject area, although sometimes a supervisor is responsible for the entire elementary or secondary instructional program.

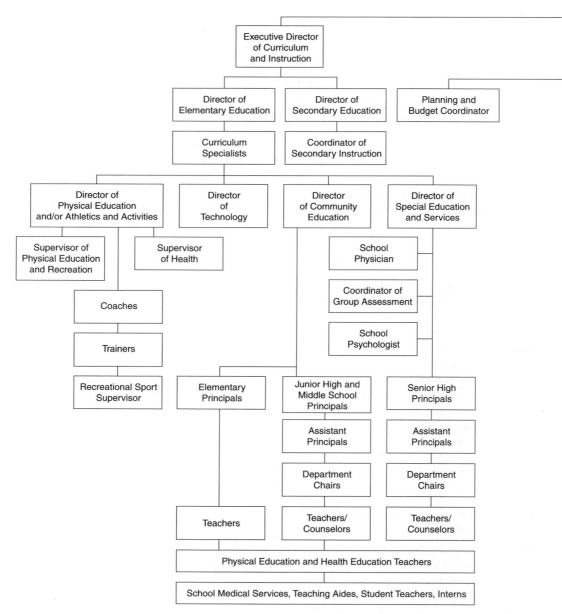

Figure 2-4. Organizational structure for a public school system.

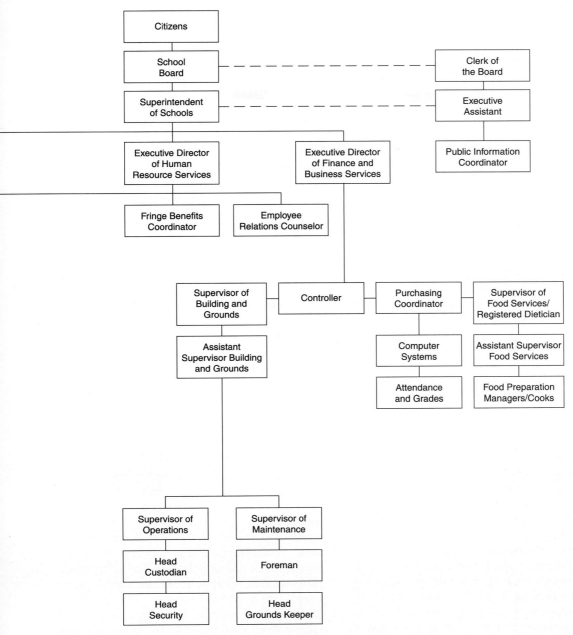

Figure 2-4. Organizational structure for a public school system—cont'd.

Director

The director is responsible for functions of a specific subject matter area, such as physical education or athletics and activities or a particular educational level (i.e., elementary or secondary). The responsibilities have administrative and supervisory implications.

At some secondary schools, the positions of *director of physical education* and *director of athletics and activities* are consolidated into one position. Other school districts, however, separate the two responsibilities into two positions.

The *director of physical education* provides leadership, programs, facilities, and other essentials concerning the conduct of the program, which includes grades K–12. Specific responsibilities include the following: providing coordination between physical education and athletics; supervising inside and outside physical education facilities; overseeing equipment and supplies for special areas (includes maintenance, safety, replacement, and accounting operations); maintaining liaison with community groups (includes holding educational meetings to interpret and improve the program and serving on various community committees); preparing periodic reports regarding areas of activity; and supervising the total physical education program (classroom, gymnasium, adapted, aquatic, intramural, and extramural programs). The director of physical education provides leadership for other staff members, evaluates personnel, and is responsible for long-range planning, including curriculum and program development.

A *director of athletics and activities* assumes many duties similar to those of the director of physical education. There is, however, little organized, competitive sport (e.g., Spring Track and Field Day) at the K–6 level. Many junior high or middle schools also maintain minimal competitive sport programs (sometimes limited to football, soccer, volleyball, and basketball). In many parts of the United States, community youth and recreation and park board sport programs have filled this competitive sport void.

The director of athletics serves to provide leadership, sport programs, and facilities in a coordinated and cooperative effort with the physical education department and community education or recreation department of the district as well as with other community youth sporting groups. The athletic director monitors and evaluates coaches and attends to the health status, eligibility, and behavior (e.g., awards or misconduct) of the student-athlete. The director must also budget, plan, purchase, allocate, and oversee maintenance of programs and equipment. It is necessary for the athletic director to keep up with the latest safety codes concerning equipment and facilities. Scheduling of games and officials, coordination of special game events (e.g., bands, dance lines, cheerleaders, etc.), insurance, and medical supervision also fall under the jurisdiction of the athletic director. Public relations (e.g., television, radio, and print media), marketing, production and sales, fund-raising, booster clubs, and accounting for finances provide the athletic director with a full-time position that has become an integral part of our educational system. In many communities, the term *activities* has been added to the athletic director title, thus enlarging the managerial scope to include most extracurricular school activities ranging from debate to dance line.

High School Sport Councils

In some high schools, sport councils are formed to serve in an advisory capacity to the school board and the administrative officers of the school. Membership might include principals, athletic and activities directors, physical education directors, students, physicians, athletic trainers, coaches, parents, and community leaders. The sport council performs such functions as recommending policy, awards, eligibility, and budgets and making sure that the athletic program is managed according to acceptable educational standards. Many state high school leagues/associations provide additional guidelines for these standards.

The Organization and Structure of Physical Education in Colleges and Universities

A college or university is characterized by a governing board, usually known as a board of regents or trustees, which is granted extensive powers of control by legislative enactment or by its charter. The governing board of a college usually delegates many of its powers of management to the administration and faculty of the institution. The chief management officers, usually headed by a president and several vice presidents, are commonly organized into such principal areas of management as academic affairs, student personnel services, business, and public relations. The members of the faculty are usually organized into colleges, schools, divisions, and departments of instruction and research. Large institutions frequently incorporate a university senate or assembly committee that is the voice of the faculty and serves as a liaison between faculty and administration.

Physical education (also referred to as kinesiology, exercise science, sport studies, etc.) is organized as one management unit for men and women in almost all colleges and universities in the United States. The management unit may be either a college, school, division, or department. The manager in charge of the physical education program may be called a director; chairperson; or division, department, or area head (see figure 2-3). In most institutions of higher education, these managers are responsible directly to a dean, but they may be responsible to the director of athletics. In some institutions, recreational sport is included as a part of the physical education program. However, in many institutions, recreational sport programs maintain a separate identity and often report to a vice president of student affairs, whereas physical education reports to an academic dean or vice president.

The duties of the head of a physical education department (depending on the size of the institution) may include coordinating the activities within the particular unit, requisitioning supplies and equipment, preparing schedules, making budgets, conducting meetings, teaching classes, coaching, hiring and dismissing personnel, developing community relations, supervising recreational sports and intercollegiate athletic programs, evaluating and appraising the required or basic physical activity program, representing the

department at meetings, facilitating the raising of external funds, and reporting to superiors.

Physical education in colleges and universities is commonly organized in four components: (1) the basic instructional or physical activity program, (2) the teacher preparation and licensure program, (3) the nonteacher certification programs such as exercise science, athletic training, sport studies, and sport management, and (4) graduate programs (figure 2-5). The basic instructional or physical activity program provides physical education instruction for all students, including people with varying disabilities. Basic skills, movement patterns, rules, strategies, and enjoyment of mastery are the prime focus. Surveys indicate that basic physical activity programs remain a high priority not only because of their cost effectiveness but also because of their popularity among students, staff, and faculty. Many institutions have discontinued their physical activity requirements and have infused their curriculum with attractive and creative "impact" courses, ranging from aerobic dance to kayaking.

The teacher preparation program is for students interested in pursuing a teaching career and includes basic skill courses, physical education major activity and pedagogy courses, and various physical education content courses, such as applied physiology, biomechanics, history and philosophy, school law, motor behavior, organization and management, sport psychology, and sport sociology. The experience usually culminates in a

Impact skills course offerings make physical education an attractive curriculum elective.

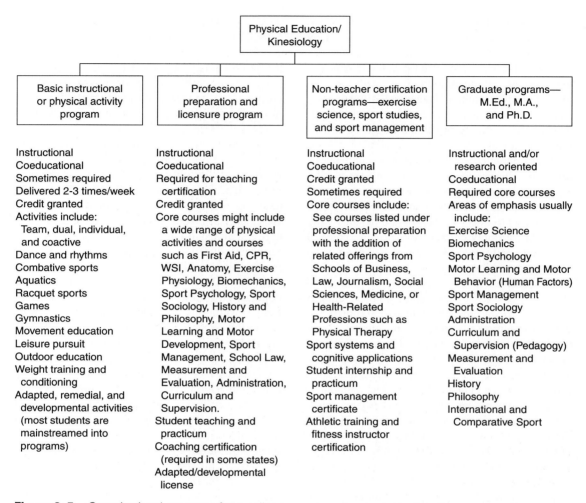

Figure 2-5. Organizational structure for a college or university physical education program.

student teaching and practicum setting. Also associated, and often integrated, with the professional preparation program are certification and licensure programs (e.g., adapted/developmental education or coaching). These programs usually reflect current state mandates and remain integral parts of most college programs. Some colleges are in fact moving to five-year professional training programs leading to a master's degree in teaching.

The nonteacher certification component of physical education is rapidly expanding in many colleges. These programs provide a basic core of traditional physical education/kinesiology content courses integrated with appropriate core courses from schools of business, law, journalism, management, medicine, and health-related professions such as physical and occupational therapy. An internship (e.g., cardiac rehabilitation center, corporate fitness center, YMCA/YWCA, professional sports organization) usually serves as the culminating experience in this nontraditional physical education delivery system. Certifications in athletic training, sport management, fitness instruction, strength and conditioning, and dance instruction are often awarded in conjunction with associations such as the National Athletic Trainers' Association (NATA), National Association for Sport and Physical Education (NASPE), American College of Sports Medicine (ACSM), National Strength and Conditioning Association (NSCA), and the International Dance Exercise Association (IDEA).

The fourth component of many college and university physical education departments is the graduate program. For the most part, advanced and concentrated work in physical education major content areas (e.g., sport psychology, sport sociology, sport history and philosophy, sport management, international and comparative sport, biomechanics, motor learning and development, exercise physiology) is prescribed with statistical methods and computer application techniques forming a research foundation or core. A minor or supporting area (e.g., law, business, marketing, international relations, counseling, special education, child development, school administration) is usually required, thus providing the potential graduate with an increased scope of the domain of human movement.

The Organization and Structure of Sport in Colleges and Universities

Because athletic programs are organized and administratively structured differently in colleges and universities than in high schools, the organization of sport in colleges and universities (see figure 2-1) requires further elaboration and discussion.

The Director of Athletics

The athletic director in colleges and universities is responsible for the management of the intercollegiate athletic program. In large institutions, this is a full-time position, whereas in smaller institutions, it may include other responsibilities involved with physical education, teaching, administration, and coaching.

Some of the key duties of many athletic directors include scheduling contests and preparing contracts, arranging for team travel, appointing, supervising, and evaluating the coaching staff, making arrangements for home sports contests, representing the institution at athletic association and league meetings, securing officials, checking and preparing player eligibility and insurance lists, preparing the budget, fund-raising, and overseeing facility supervision and maintenance.

Directors of athletic and activities programs should promote their programs and their student athletes.

Faculty Athletic Committee

Most colleges and universities with sport programs of significant size have a faculty athletic committee. This committee serves in an advisory capacity to the president of the institution or, in most instances, a vice president. The membership of such committees frequently includes faculty representatives, students, coaches, student-athletes, community leaders, and alumni. The athletic director and administrative representative are usually ex officio and nonvoting members. The faculty athletic committee is involved in functions such as approving budgets, developing eligibility standards, approving financial awards, authorizing schedules, acting on problems that arise, developing policies, investigating infractions, reviewing scholarship decisions, and deciding to what extent certain sports might be added or eliminated.

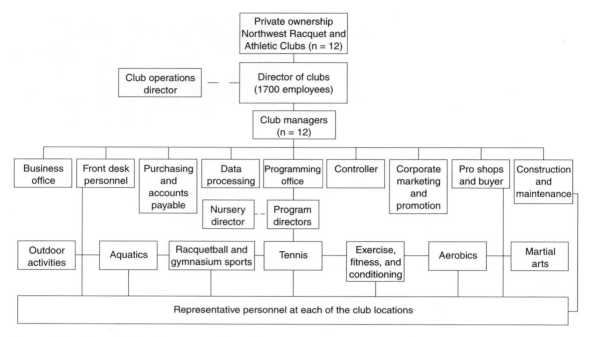

Figure 2-6.   Organizational structure of a private-sector, owner-operated enterprise.

Faculty Representative

Many colleges and universities have a faculty athletic representative. The athletic representative is a member of the faculty who represents the college or university at national association meetings such as the National Collegiate Athletic Association (NCAA) and the National Association of Intercollegiate Athletics (NAIA), as well as the conference to which the institution belongs (e.g., Big Ten, Pac-Ten, Big East, Big Twelve, S.E.C.). The faculty representative usually attends faculty athletic committee meetings as a nonvoting member and presents periodic reports to the faculty athletic committee. The faculty representative serves at the behest of the faculty committee and usually votes according to institutional policy.

Structure of the College or University Athletic Department

The structure of athletic departments on college and university campuses usually depends on institutional enrollment, tradition, budget, funding sources, and focus of each specific institution of higher education. Figure 2-1 reflects the structure necessary for the conduct of a Division I NCAA sport program that provides balanced offerings for both men and women. The roles, duties, responsibilities, and support service personnel, of course, would have to be modified, adapted, or collapsed somewhat for institutions offering fewer sports or less revenue driven sports programs. Regardless, sport participation opportunity and their associated support systems and services should be equitable across gender lines.

The Organization and Structure of Physical Education and Sport in the Private and Public Sector

Physical education and sport programs exist in settings other than school systems and institutions of higher education. Because of the current interest in health and physical fitness, a variety of delivery structures have evolved. From executive and corporate fitness programs to community-service-oriented programs such as community centers and Ys, not to mention the booming fitness club industry, the quest for enhanced physical activity and sport opportunities has developed into a multi-billion-dollar enterprise. The

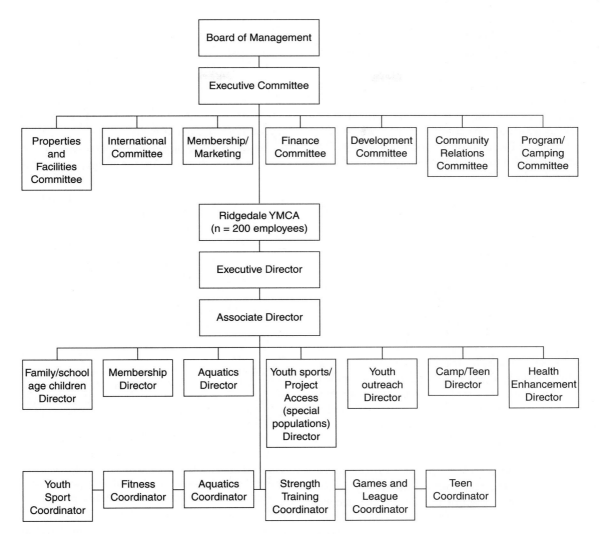

Figure 2-7. Organizational structure of a community YMCA.

organization and structure for such enterprises range from being operated by a private owner to being accountable to a community board of directors. Some structures are motivated by profit, whereas others might be community-service oriented, and still others might exist as part of a health-related employee fringe benefit package.

Regardless of the situational circumstances, the need to provide well-trained managers and personnel to meet the consumer demand is apparent and provides yet another attractive profes-sional marketplace for those who are well prepared, skilled, schooled, and certified in the delivery of physical education and sport-related services. The physical education personnel involved in these programs include people trained in physical education specialties such as exercise physiology, biomechanics, sport management, coaching, nutrition, fitness training, dance, sports writing, public relations, and marketing. Figures 2-6 and 2-7 represent organizational structuring of various private-sector enterprises.

WHAT DETERMINES AN EFFECTIVE ORGANIZATION

Whether in the public school environment or the private sector, an organization at any level must possess certain ingredients to be effective. The effective organization needs a well-trained, skilled, and dynamic leader who can formulate sound aims and objectives and set goals in order to achieve the mission of the organization. The organization must also possess a functional, integrated infrastructure, staffed by motivated team members who work cooperatively to meet the goals and challenges of the organization. The end result will be a job well done with a high degree of satisfaction achieved by all involved.

SUMMARY

One of the functions of management is to develop an organizational structure through which the goals of physical education and sport can be accomplished in an effective and efficient manner. The physical education and sport objectives to be achieved include physical fitness, motor skill, cognitive, and social-emotional-affective development. To meet the needs of all students, including those with varying disabilities, the objectives of physical education and sport will vary at each educational and institutional level. However, the adoption of a healthy lifestyle remains a constant at all levels.

Management structures for physical education and sport are organized differently for elementary, junior high or middle schools, secondary schools, and colleges and universities. Fitness centers, Ys, and organizations other than schools and colleges also maintain their own organizational schemata. Furthermore, it is important to recognize that an informal as well as a formal management organization and structure affects most programs. It is therefore crucial in developing organizational structures that management principles and guidelines be incorporated.

SELF-ASSESSMENT ACTIVITIES

These activities will assist students in determining if material and competencies presented in this chapter have been mastered.

1. You have been asked by the head of a governmental organization to identify the objectives that physical education will be able to achieve for the citizens of that country and to show what management structure you would recommend to help achieve these objectives. Prepare a written statement for presentation before the country's legislative body.

2. Write an essay on the topic "Developing and organizing the structure for a sport program is an important management responsibility."

3. Cite at least six principles that should be observed in developing an effective management organization.

4. You are a consultant with expertise in management organization and structure who has been hired by an organization with a physical education and sport program to give advice about whether it should implement a formal or informal structure. What advice would you give to this organization? Defend your decision.

5. Form a team from your class and attend a local school board meeting. Interview at least one board member concerning his or her perception of the role of physical education and sport in the school district. Report back to the class.

6. Draw a structural organizational chart for each of your college physical education, athletic, and recreational sports departments, showing the various management components; discuss their responsibilities and relationships.

7. Tell how the management organization and structure you recommended in item 4 would provide for each of the following: *delegating authority* to the heads of the instructional program, the program for individuals with varying disabilities, recreational sport, and varsity sport; *resolving a conflict* between the directors of athletics and physical education; *determining budget allocations* for athletics; and *formulating policies* regarding Title IX.

REFERENCES

1. American Alliance for Health, Physical Education, Recreation, and Dance (AAHPERD). 1995. A glo-

bal vision for school physical education. *Update,* September/October, 1, 6.

2. Barrow, H.M., and J.P. Brown. 1988. *Man and movement: Principles of physical education.* Philadelphia: Lea and Febiger.

3. Gensemer, R.E. 1985. *Physical education: Perspectives, inquiry, applications.* Philadelphia: Saunders.

4. Krotee, M.L., and F.C. Hatfield. 1979. *The theory and practice of physical activity.* Dubuque, Iowa: Kendall/Hunt.

5. Loen, R.D. 1971. *Manage more by doing less.* New York: McGraw-Hill.

6. Petersen, E., E.G. Plowman, and J.M. Trickett. 1962. *Business organization and management.* Homewood, Ill.: Richard D Irwin.

7. Sage, G.H. 1984. *Motor learning and control—A neuropsychological approach.* Dubuque, Iowa: Wm. C. Brown.

8. Sheppard, W.C., and R.H. Willoughby. 1975. *Child behaviors: Learning and development.* Chicago: Rand McNally.

SUGGESTED READINGS

American Alliance for Health, Physical Education, Recreation, and Dance (AAHPERD). 1987. *Basic stuff series I and II.* Reston, Va.: AAHPERD.
The views of the profession concerning application of physical education to the curriculum.

La Point, J.D. 1980. *Organization and management of sport.* Dubuque, Iowa: Kendall/Hunt.
Provides a significant overview of many dimensions involved in competitive sport. Discusses sport-related issues and problems encountered by student-athletes, parents, coaches, athletic directors, and school boards.

Midura, D.W., and D.R. Glover. 1995. *More team building challenges.* Champaign, Ill.: Human Kinetics.

National Association for Sport and Physical Education. 1988. *Directory of professional fitness certifications.* Reston, Va.: AAHPERD.
A guide to opportunities for certifications in the profession of physical education and sport.

Peters, T. 1987. *Thriving on chaos.* New York: Alfred A. Knopf.
A guide on goal setting, power, accelerated change, and leadership. The author also delves into creativity and innovation.

Thoma, J.E., and L. Chalip. 1996. *Sport governance in the global community.* Morgantown, W.Va.: Fitness Information Technology.
Delves into governance issues ranging from national sports policies and the Olympic Movement to politics in sport. The book also includes treatment of bidding and hosting large events.

United Nations Educational, Scientific, and Cultural Organization (UNESCO). 1993. *International charter of physical education and sport.* Paris: UNESCO.

Vroom, V.H. and E.L. Deci. 1981. *Management and motivation.* New York: Penguin.
Presents an overview of motivation including theoretical constructs concerning attitude formation, job satisfaction, and performance. Organizational change is also covered.

Wuest, D.A., and C.A. Bucher. 1995. *Foundations of physical education and sport.* St. Louis: Mosby–Year Book.
Provides an overview of physical education and sport including philosophy, history, and core content. Career patterning and issues in the profession are also explored.

Wuest, D.A., and B.J. Lombardo. 1996. *Curriculum and instruction.* St. Louis: Mosby–Year Book.
Contains theoretical and practical considerations for the implementation of secondary school physical education programs.

part II

Management of Physical Education and Sport Programs

Physical Education Instructional Programs

Instructional Objectives and Competencies To Be Achieved

After reading this chapter the student should be able to

- Provide a description of the nature, scope, purpose, and worth of instructional programs in physical education.

- Outline management guidelines for preschool, elementary school, secondary school, and college and university physical education instructional programs.

- Describe management instructional strategies for physical education programs resulting from Title IX legislation.

- Justify the need for certain management procedures, such as scheduling, time allotment for classes, size of classes, instructional loads, class and locker-room management, uniforms, taking roll, selecting physical education activities, grouping, and area of student involvement.

- Understand the professional nature of selected management problems in instructional programs such as required or elective physical education, substitutions, credit, class attendance, excuses, instruction by specialist or classroom teacher, dressing and showering, records, and evaluation.

- Discuss what is meant by an adapted/developmental program of physical education.

- Describe the various elements that make up an individualized education program (IEP).

- Describe administrative procedures to comply with and implement Public Laws 94-142; 99-457; 101-336 (ADA), and 101-476 (IDEA).

- Discuss various motives that individuals have for participating in physical education programs.

Thus far in this text we have concerned ourselves with the nature and scope of management as they relate to physical education and sport. We have also discussed the objectives these programs are designed to achieve and the organizational structure needed to efficiently and effectively pursue and accomplish these goals. This chapter delves into the instructional physical edu-cation program and identifies associated guidelines, issues, and concerns.

By tradition, the basic instructional physical education program was graphically represented at the base of an isosceles triangle. The part immediately above the instructional base was the recreational sports program, and at the apex of the triangle was the varsity athletic program. What the isosceles triangle symbolized in the past is still true to the effect that a sound physical education program should serve as a firm and solid base for all other school and community physical activity and sport programs (figure 3-1). The instructional program in physical education is the place to teach skills, strategies, concepts, and essential knowledge concerning the relationship of physical activity to physical fitness, motor skill, cognitive, and social-emotional-affective development. It is a place to challenge, build competence, encourage creativity, promote life-long activity, advance critical action skills, instill commitment to personal wellness, and foster re-spect for others. It is also a place to introduce an awareness of the development and maintenance of optimal levels of physical fitness.

Skills should be taught from a scientific, theoretical, and progressive approach so that the various mediators and human factors that affect human movement are clearly understood by the participant (figure 3-2). Demonstration, films, videotapes and videodisks, computers, posters, and other audiovisual aids and materials enhance instruction and are required for optimal learning.

The physical education program presented throughout the school years should be sequential

in development and progressive in application. A physical fitness program should also be develop-mental and progressive in nature, starting with the individual's present state of mental and physical fitness and gradually moving to higher levels.

Performance objectives should be established and targeted for individual student achievement. When boys and girls advance from one grade to another, they should have achieved certain objec-tives in various physical education activities, just as they achieve various levels of skills, knowl-edge, and competencies in other school subjects. A plan for assurance of mastery in physical education must be developed and implemented.

Physical education should involve more than physical activity. As the participant understands more fully the importance of human movement; what happens to the human body during exercise and stress; the relationship of physical activity to one's biological, psychological, and sociocultural development; the history of various activities; and the role of physical activity in the interdependent global community, physical education will take on a new meaning, grow in intellectual respect-ability, and contribute to building a more healthy and productive society.

Just as textbooks, handouts, and resource materials are employed within other courses in the educational system, so should they be used in the physical education program. Textbooks should not only contain material pertaining to physical skills, but should also explore the totality of the subject matter of physical education (e.g., fitness, nutrition, stress control, etc.).

Grading and developmental records that fol-low a student from grade to grade should be maintained throughout his or her school life. These records will indicate the degree to which the objectives of the program have been achieved by the student. The level and degree of physical skill and fitness achievement, involvement in outside activity, health status, and social conduct may all serve to interpret what role physical education has played for the students as they meet the challenges of an ever-growing and complex society.

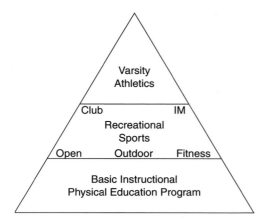

Figure 3-1. A traditional view of the relationship between the basic instructional or physical activity program, recreational sports, and varsity athletics.

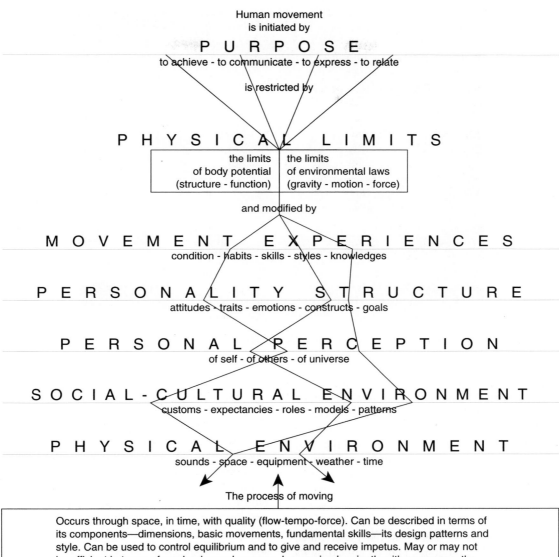

Human movement
is initiated by

P U R P O S E

to achieve - to communicate - to express - to relate

is restricted by

P H Y S I C A L   L I M I T S

| the limits of body potential (structure - function) | the limits of environmental laws (gravity - motion - force) |

and modified by

M O V E M E N T   E X P E R I E N C E S

condition - habits - skills - styles - knowledges

P E R S O N A L I T Y   S T R U C T U R E

attitudes - traits - emotions - constructs - goals

P E R S O N A L   P E R C E P T I O N

of self - of others - of universe

S O C I A L - C U L T U R A L   E N V I R O N M E N T

customs - expectancies - roles - models - patterns

P H Y S I C A L   E N V I R O N M E N T

sounds - space - equipment - weather - time

The process of moving

Occurs through space, in time, with quality (flow-tempo-force). Can be described in terms of its components—dimensions, basic movements, fundamental skills—its design patterns and style. Can be used to control equilibrium and to give and receive impetus. May or may not be efficient in terms of mechanics and purpose. Is perceived variantly with occurence, the mover, and observers.

and
IS A MODIFIER OF ITS OWN DETERMINANTS

Figure 3-2. Mediators of human movements serve to influence all physical education and sport instructional programs.

Karate class. University of Nevada at Las Vegas.

The basic instructional physical education program cannot be conducted in a hit-or-miss fashion. It must be planned in accordance with the needs and interests of the individuals it serves as well as the society in which they will become contributing members. Regardless of the individual's motives for participation (e.g., to pursue pleasure and satisfaction, to master skills, to attain or maintain fitness and health, to seek excellence), physical education class is where the process of a healthy lifestyle begins and where sound management is requisite. In this regard, physical education instructional programs may be guided by the AAHPERD/NASPE's Guidelines for the Physically Educated Person (see Appendix A).

MANAGEMENT GUIDELINES FOR SCHOOL AND COLLEGE PHYSICAL EDUCATION PROGRAMS

Physical education programs in schools and colleges have played a prominent role in educational systems since the turn of the century. Physical education programs exist at the preschool, el-

ementary, junior high, middle, and senior high school levels as well as at the college and university educational level.

Preschool Physical Education Programs

The concept of early schooling is no longer regarded as a custodial or compensatory undertaking. Instead it is viewed as a necessary provision for the normal growth and development of children. Research by psychologists, child development specialists, and sociologists has indicated that the early years are crucial for the child intellectually, physically, socially, and emotionally. In light of such findings, as well as the return of many mothers to the workforce, nursery schools and child day-care centers have gained wide popularity.

Preschool educational programs should involve indoor and outdoor play-learning activities. Physical education activities should include the development of fundamental movement skills, fitness, self-testing and team building activities,

Movement exploration is a key ingredient in elementary physical education.

music and rhythmic activities, and rhymes and story plays. A sound program of selected physical activities helps the child develop a positive self-concept; practice, develop, and test social skills; enhance physical fitness; and improve cognitive and sensorimotor skills. Research maintains that a relationship exists between perception and motor development and that perception is related to cognition; therefore physical movement experiences play a crucial role in cognitive development.

Preschool programs are becoming an integral part of educational systems in this country, and physical education is playing an important role in such programs.

Elementary School Physical Education Programs

Contemporary elementary physical education programs continue to focus on the foundation of the profession—human movement. Physical education takes on an important part of the schools' instructional program and is designed to foster development of fundamental motor skills, health-related fitness, and knowledge and attitude relative to physical activity through a carefully planned curriculum that includes, for example, movement, skills, fitness, ball skills, rhythms and dance, rope jumping, and tumbling. These learning experiences help students understand how to move and to become more aware of their body within the environmental framework of force, time, space, and flow. The experiences of, through, and about physicalness are managed in such a fashion that exploration, problem solving, cooperation, and challenge contribute to the development of positive feelings toward oneself and others as well as of physical activity as a valuable contribution to a wholesome and healthy quality of life.

Physical education at this level should promote the individual child's standard of performance and establish a physical activity comfort level so that each child may develop to his or her fullest potential.

Elementary schools also combine movement skills and perceptual motor development, and in some schools, an interdisciplinary approach is utilized, whereby the subject matter of physical education is integrated with certain other subjects such as health, music, science, history, and art.

Here are some management guidelines for elementary school physical education programs. The program should meet the needs of all children, including those with learning or physical disabilities, the culturally or environmentally deprived, and the gifted. The program should include a variety of developmental experiences that will help the child form a sound foundation on which to build more complex skills, techniques, strategies, and concepts. The program (ranging from basic motor skills to beginning related games) should provide developmental and progressive experiences in a safe and wholesome environment. It should foster creativity, challenge, self-expression, social development, team building, positive self-concepts, and appreciation for the importance of health and fitness.

Secondary School Physical Education Programs

The junior high, middle, and senior high schools of the nation should build on the physical education foundation provided at the elementary school level. Here are some management guidelines that represent important considerations in secondary school physical education programs. Most of the guidelines set for the elementary school also have merit in developing programs for secondary schools. The secondary program should be based on the developmental tasks of secondary school students. The program should consist of a variety of activities, including gymnastics, self-testing activities, rhythm and dance, movement skills, aquatics, physical fitness activities, outdoor education, and individual, dual, and team sports. The program should provide a thorough understanding of the human body and the impact of physical activity on its various organic systems. The *Basic Stuff Series I and II* developed by the National Association for Sport and Physical Education (NASPE) of the American Alliance for Health, Physical Education, Recreation, and Dance (AAHPERD) contains concepts, principles, and

developmental ideas extracted from physical education's body of knowledge and might serve as a valuable K–12 programmatic guide. The program should teach a variety of skills progressively, eliminate excessive repetition of activities, and ensure the inclusion of lifetime sports and health-related fitness concepts. The program should be open to all students, including those with varying disabilities, who should be provided an opportunity to function in the least restrictive environment. The program should encourage vigorous physical activity in and outside of class, including individual fitness and participation in community, recreational, and varsity sport.

In addition, to these management guidelines, the following points should be stressed:

The physical education class provides the student with a safe and wholesome environment in which to learn the skills, strategy, appreciation, understanding, knowledge, rules, regulations, and other material and information that are part of the program. It is not a place for free play, intramurals, or varsity practice. It is a place for proactive and dynamic instruction. Every minute of the class period should be devoted to teaching students the skills and subject matter of physical education.

Instruction should be fundamental and interesting. Skills should be broken down into basic components and presented so that each individual may understand clearly what is expected to be accomplished and how it is to be done. Use of demonstrations, computer simulations, videotapes and videodisks, and other audiovisual aids and materials can help make the instruction more meaningful and interesting.

Instruction should be progressive. There should be a definite progression from basic to complex skills. Just as a student progresses in mathematics from basic arithmetic to algebra, geometry, and calculus, so the physical education student should progress from basic skills and materials to more complex and involved skills, techniques, and strategies.

Instruction should involve definite standards. Students should be expected to reach individualized standards of achievement (assurance of mastery) in the class program. A reasonable amount of skill—whether it is in swimming, tennis, dance, or another activity—should be mastered, keeping in mind individual differences. Upon graduation from high school, students should have met definite assurance-of-mastery standards and goals that indicate that they are *physically educated.*

Instruction should involve more than physical activity. All physical education classes do not have to be conducted in the gymnasium, where physical activity predominates. A reasonable proportion of class time, perhaps as much as 10 percent to 20 percent, can be devoted to class interaction and discussion, guest lecturers, independent study, cooperative projects, field trips (e.g., skiing, bowling, sailing, or golf), *Basic Stuff Series I and II,* and working on individualized fitness and learning packages. Physical activity should not be conducted in a vacuum; if it is, it has no meaning and will not be applied when the student leaves the class and school setting. As the student understands more fully the importance of physical activity and sport, what happens to the body during exercise, how to cooperate to succeed, the roots of the various activities in which he or she engages, and the role of physical activity across cultures (such as the breaking of racial and gender barriers), physical education will take on a new meaning and perhaps play a significant role throughout the life span of each individual.

There should be records. The instructor should keep accurate records to provide tangible evidence concerning the degree to which student objectives are being met. This means that data concerning skill achievement, physical fitness level, critical knowledge, and other information, including social conduct—such as fair play, cooperative effort, and out-of-class participation—should be a part of the database.

There should be homework. It is just as reasonable to assign homework in physical education as in biology or math. Much subject matter is to be learned, many skills are to be mastered, and fitness levels must be improved or main-

Individual lifetime sport foundations are promoted in secondary schools.

tained. Teachers who require their students to work on various skills (physical and mental), endurance activities, and knowledge acquisition outside of class will find more time for meaningful and targeted instruction during class.

Each student should have a thorough medical examination before participating in the physical education program. An annual health examination should be regarded as a minimum, essential not only to ensure the student's safety but to effectively prescribe the frequency, duration, and intensity of the physical activity to best meet each student's needs.

The teaching load of physical educators should be determined not only by the number of instructional class periods assigned but also by the total number of activities handled by the teacher both in class and outside of class. For teachers to be effective, their normal daily workload should consist of not more than five hours of instruction, or five class periods. In addition, provisions should be made to ensure one hour of class-preparation time. Attached to the teaching load will be requests for active involvement in extracurricular activities (e.g., coaching, intramurals, clubs, etc.). Regardless of assignments, a teacher's time management skills will be put to good use.

Trends and Innovative Ideas in Secondary School Physical Education

Many innovative instructional programs are being employed in physical education at the secondary school level. These include programs that stress personalized, individualized, and cooperative learning; that emphasize performance objectives, competency packages, and goal setting; that concern career and leadership opportunities; that stress flexibility in scheduling; and that concentrate on specialized electives and group experiences such as camping, sailing, skiing, backpacking, and outdoor and wilderness leadership activities during which the student interacts with the environment as well as with other cultures.

College and University Physical Education Programs

Colleges and universities should provide instruction in physical education that meets the following management criteria:

- The program should be available to all students.
- The program should not be a repetition of the high school program, but should offer more advanced work in physical education. However, instruction in the development of basic skills should continue to be an integral part of the program.
- The program should include innovative features to meet the needs of students and at the same time be interesting and challenging.
- Management should not permit athletics, band, ROTC, recreational sports, or other activities to serve as a substitute for physical education.

- The program should provide a wide range of course selection including individual, dual, and team activities as well as aquatics, health-related fitness, dance, and outdoor pursuits.
- The program should stress knowledge and understanding of the value of physical activity and its relationship to the environment.
- The program should stress the study and practice of the science and art of human movement.
- The program should focus on lifetime activities.
- The program should be conducted by well-trained and fully certified faculty and staff members.

Since the 1970s, many (approximately 50 percent) colleges and universities in the United States have moved physical education from a mandatory to an elective status. Institutions still requiring physical education typically do so for a one- to two-year period. Classes usually meet two or three times per week, with some colleges still requiring standards of achievement (most often swimming and basic fitness). The trend in today's physical activity programs is toward more emphasis on lifetime sports, outdoor pursuits, and fitness activities, including aerobics, conditioning, and weight training.

The growth of community and junior colleges has been significant. In many respects, the activities for these institutions are the same as those for colleges and universities. Many community and junior colleges require students to take physical education at least one year. Most of the programs require two hours each week and stress the successful completion of physical education as a requirement for awarding of the associate degree.

The college and university physical education program is the end of formal physical education for many students. Student age range in colleges and universities is wide, incorporating participants from age sixteen to sixty and beyond. However, most college students are in their late teens or early twenties and have matured in many ways. Many hold part-time jobs. They are entering the period of greatest physical efficiency and possess many interests, including physical activity and sport. Many want to prepare themselves for successful vocations, an objective that requires the physical educator to show how physical education can contribute to success in their future profession. College students are also interested in developing socially, and coeducational activities help provide a training ground for gender-free experiences in a wide variety of settings. In addition, students are interested in developing skills that they can use and enjoy throughout life as well as in becoming physically fit and looking good.

In formulating a program at the college and university level, one needs to remember that many students enter with limited physical activity backgrounds. Therefore the program should be broadly based and varied at the start, with opportunities to elect more advanced activities later. Considerable opportunity should exist for instruction and practice in those activities in which a student desires to specialize. As much individual attention as possible should be given to ensure necessary safety as well as skill, fitness, and attitude development.

The program of activities should be based on the interests and needs of students as well as on the availability of facilities and staff. Some colleges have introduced foundation courses, which cover basic subject matter ranging from nutrition and weight control perspectives to the philosophical underpinnings of physical education (Prentice 1997).

In college physical education programs, physical skill and fitness achievement tests should be employed to assess student status, set reasonable goals, and ensure progress. Special assistance, systematic feedback, and individually prescribed programs should be offered to help all students develop to their fullest potential.

MANAGEMENT FACTORS RELATING TO ONE OR MORE EDUCATIONAL LEVELS

Certain management factors relate to one or more educational levels (elementary, secondary, college and university). Some of the more pertinent factors include interrelationships of elementary, secondary, and college and university programs; instructional aids and materials; class management; interpretation of Title IX regulations for instructional strategies; and implications of the Individuals with Disabilities Education Act (IDEA) for adapted/developmental physical education programs for persons with varying disabilities.

Interrelationships of Elementary, Secondary, and College and University Programs

The physical education programs from the K–12 levels through the college and university level should be interrelated. Continuity and progression should characterize the program from the time the student enters kindergarten until graduation. Overall planning is essential to ensure that each student becomes physically educated and to guarantee that duplication of effort, time management, curricular omissions, and shortages do not occur.

Continuity and progression do not exist today in many of the school systems in the United States. Instead, to a great degree, each institutional level is autonomous, setting up its own program with curriculum-writing teams and consultants responsible for course content and development. If the focus of attention is on the student—the consumer of the product—then curriculum planning will provide the student with a

Dance class. University of Minnesota.

continuous program, developed to meet the dynamic needs and interests from the beginning to the end of the formal educational process (kindergarten through college or university and beyond).

Consideration and cooperative planning should also exist for the entire community to ensure that each child's needs are met. Many communities have school and community physical education directors and recreation program managers who regularly meet to ensure an integrated, coordinated, and continuous program of physical activity for the entire community.

In some communities, shared partnerships involving both physical and human resources ranging from aquatics to ice hockey arenas are commonplace. Computer documentation, tracking, and information retrieval makes it easier to construct a physical education profile for each student to not only accommodate, for example, K–12 developmental fitness level status, but also track each student's use and preference of community fitness resources as well. In this way, school and community should develop even stronger interconnectedness.

Management Guidelines for Selecting Instructional Aids and Materials

When selecting audiovisual aids or other instructional resources and materials, physical educators should consider the following principles that make using these aids effective, meaningful, and valuable.

Materials should be carefully selected and screened. The teacher should preview the materials to determine if they are appropriate for the unit and age level of the students and to ensure that they present information in an interesting, progressive, and stimulating manner.

Proper preparation of materials should be made. The teacher or responsible school official should check all equipment that may be necessary for the presentation of materials to make sure that it is in operating condition. Computers, camcorders, videotape players, record players, and movie and overhead projectors, in particular, need to be carefully checked before each use. Maintenance schedules and records should also be maintained on equipment.

The presentation of materials should be planned and integrated into the lesson. Students should be properly introduced to the topic, and materials should be strategically placed so that they influence the learning process and the student understands their relationship to the unit of study.

Materials should be presented to the students in a proper learning environment. Students should be prepared and positioned so that all may hear, see, and learn from the material being offered. They should realize that they will be held responsible for the information being presented.

Materials should be varied. Different types of materials should be chosen for presentation to stimulate and motivate the students. A teacher using videotapes or slides exclusively does not take full advantage of other supplementary materials that may have widespread appeal.

Use of supplementary materials should be limited. The teacher should place a reasonable limit on the use of supplementary teaching materials in order to maintain a balance between time involved in physical activity and time engaged in, for example, viewing the serving technique of a professional tennis player via computer simulation.

Care should be taken to avoid excessive expenses. A reasonable part of the instructional budget should be set aside for supplementary materials. This amount should be in accordance with the emphasis placed on this phase of the teaching program, and items selected should possess long-term redeeming value.

Records and evaluations should be maintained. All supplementary materials should be carefully cataloged and kept on computer file for future reference. This should save the unnecessary time and expense involved in reordering or duplicating materials and in culling outdated materials.

By following these principles, the teacher is able to supplement learning with materials that are interesting, meaningful, and valuable to the students. Here are various types of materials, activities, and personnel that can be used in the instructional process.

- *Reading materials:* textbooks, trade books, magazines, rulebooks, pamphlets, journals, news clippings, handouts
- *Audiovisual aids:* motion pictures, slides, learning loops, television, videotapes, record players, audiotapes, disks
- *Special aids:* computers, charts, photographic materials, bulletin boards, magnetic boards
- *Professional personnel:* presenters from professional associations and organizations
- *Community activities:* recreational activities, PTA/PTO-sponsored events, Special Olympics, events sponsored by Red Cross, Partners of the Americas, and other private volunteer organizations (PVOs)
- *Clinics:* special games and programs conducted by visiting teams, professional teaching organizations, community organizations, foundations such as the Women's Sport Foundation, sports federations, state high school leagues/associations
- *Computers:* computer-assisted learning and feedback, web site and home page information

Class Management

Sound management does not just happen. It requires careful thought, good judgment, and planning before the class begins. Management prac-

tices help to ensure that the class functions as a coordinated group in order to effectively and efficiently accomplish the goals and tasks that have been established. Quality management leads to enjoyable, satisfying, and worthwhile experiences. The teacher who is in charge of a class where optimal learning conditions exist has spent considerable time planning the details of the class from start to finish (Jensen 1992).

The following reasons for good organization should be recognized by every teacher and administrator:

- It ensures the participant's health, safety, and maximal performance outcome.
- It helps eliminate discipline problems.
- It gives meaning and purpose to instruction and to the assigned activities.
- It results in efficiency, provides proper focus, and allows the best use of precious time.
- It more fully ensures that the needs and interests of the participants will be protected and satisfied.
- It ensures meaningful progression and continuity in the program.

Behavior modification through physical activity presentation to physical educators at the International Special Olympic Games Symposium, University of Minnesota.

Video- and computer-assisted learning help both students and teachers to manage more effectively.

- It provides for measurement and evaluation of objectives as well as timely feedback of results.
- It encourages program adaptations to meet each individual's needs and interests.
- It reduces errors and omissions.
- It helps conserve the teacher's time and energy and provides the teacher with a sense of accomplishment.

Management Guidelines

- The classroom environment should be one that is safe yet unrestricted, and creative movement should be encouraged. The equipment should be in proper condition and placed appropriately for safe activity. Field and gymnasium markings, equipment arrangements, logistics for activities, and other essential details should be attended to well before class.
- Strategic and long-term planning for the semester and the year should be prepared as well as daily, weekly, and seasonal planning.
- A definite time schedule should be planned for each period, considering learning objectives and the priorities concerning dressing for class, taking roll, safety, warm-up, class activity, cooldown, and other pedagogical essentials.
- The activity should be carefully planned so that class proceeds with precision and dispatch, with a minimal amount of standing around and a maximal amount of activity for each student.
- Procedures to be followed in the locker room should be clearly established to provide for traffic, valuables, clothes, and showering and dressing.
- The instructor should always be early for class.
- Participants should be encouraged and motivated to do their best at all times.
- A planned program of assessment and evaluation should be provided to determine progress being made by participants and the effectiveness of teaching strategies.
- The instructor should wear appropriate clothing.
- The instructor should possess a thorough command of the subject, recognizing the value of demonstrations, visual aids, cooperative goal structuring, and other techniques and strategies that promote learning.
- Desirable attitudes toward and understanding of physical fitness, learning skills, fair play, safety, vigorous participation, and other concepts inherent in physical education should be continually stressed.
- Procedures for emergencies should be established, disseminated to all involved in class (students, classroom teachers who sometimes deliver physical education classes, paraprofessionals, nurses, principals, etc.) and maintained on file. Students' health status should also be known to school personnel involved with the delivery of physical education and of all activity.

TITLE IX

On May 27, 1975, President Gerald Ford signed into law Title IX (Clement 1988) of the Education Amendments Act of 1972, which states that no person, on the basis of sex, be excluded from participation in, be denied the benefits of, or be subjected to discrimination under any educational program or activity receiving federal assistance. Title IX clearly established a mandate for educational institutions that received federal financial assistance to eliminate gender discrimination within their programs, including physical education and sport. The effective date of the regulation was July 21, 1975. Title IX affects nearly all the nation's 16,000 public school systems and nearly 2,700 postsecondary institutions. As a first step, the regulation provides that educators (including physical educators) should perform a searching self-examination of policies and practices in their schools and institutions and take whatever remedial action is needed to bring them into compliance with federal law.

Reason for Title IX

The primary reason for the enactment of Title IX was testimony before Congressional and other committees to the effect that females were frequently denied enrollment in traditionally male courses and activities and that girls and women were continually denied equal participatory opportunity. A national survey conducted by the National Education Association showed that although women constituted a majority of all public school teachers, they accounted for only 3.5 percent of the junior high school principals and 3 percent of the senior high school principals. It was believed that by instilling and perpetuating traditional gender roles and sexual differentiation, educational institutions have, over time, denied women equal educational and employment opportunity and therefore equal participation in the sociocultural process. Title IX was legislated to correct this fundamental problem.

Implications of Title IX for Physical Education Teachers and Their Instructional Strategies

Physical education classes must be organized on a coeducational basis. Teachers and staff should ensure that instructional offerings and opportunities are coeducational or gender-balanced. Most activities should be coeducational in nature, and equal opportunity for participation and equal time must be afforded to all students. This regulation does not mean that activities must be taught coeducationally. Within classes, students may be grouped by sex for such contact sports as wrestling, basketball, ice hockey, rugby, and football. Also, within physical education classes, students may be grouped on an ability basis even though such grouping may result in a single-sex grouping. However, sex must *not* be the criterion for grouping. Furthermore, if an evaluation standard has an adverse impact on one sex, such as a standard of accomplishment in a physical fitness test, different evaluation requirements must be utilized.

Schools and colleges must provide equal opportunities for both sexes. Equal opportunity in this respect means that the activities offered must reflect the interests and abilities of students of both sexes. Adequate course offerings, facilities, and equipment must be available for both sexes in physical education and sport programs. Furthermore, one sex cannot dominate the facilities or the new equip-

ment. In addition, adequate time for practice and instructional assistance must be provided for both sexes. Again, one sex cannot dominate.

Schools and colleges must spend funds in an equitable manner. Although equal aggregate expenditures are not required, an educational institution cannot discriminate on the basis of sex in providing proper equipment, supplies, and associated services.

Title IX takes precedence over all state and local laws and conference regulations that might be in conflict with this federal regulation.

If an institution receives federal aid, it must be in compliance with Title IX, even though its physical or athletic education program does not directly receive any of this aid.

There can be no discrimination in respect to personnel standards. No discrimination can exist in respect to personnel standards by sex, including marital or parental status, for employment, promotion, retention, salary, recruitment, job classification, or fringe benefits.

Financial aid must be awarded equitably. The regulations require an institution to select

Coeducational physical education. Birchview Elementary School, Wayzata, Minn.

students to be awarded financial aid on the basis of criteria other than a student's sex.

Interpretation of Title IX Regulations

Some interpretations of Title IX regulations that affect physical education instructional strategies are listed here. Interpretations such as the following have come from various sources. Sex designations associated with class schedules, activities, and budgets are not permitted. The term *girls' gymnasium* can be used; however, the scheduling of this facility must be nondiscriminatory in respect to each sex. Policies and procedures in regard to items such as uniforms and attendance must apply to both sexes. Sex-segregated administrative units, such as departments, do not necessarily have to be merged, although having faculty men and women in integrated offices in newly combined administrative units is encouraged. If a significantly greater number of one sex is enrolled in a particular physical education class, the administration, if called on, should be prepared to provide the rationale for such organization. Supervision of locker rooms may be assigned to teacher aides, paraprofessionals, or teachers in other departments. Marks or grades given in physical education classes should reflect individual growth and performance and not compare sexes with one another. Standards of performance that provide an unfair comparison for one sex should not be employed. In some cases, separate standards might be used for each sex; for example, on a physical fitness rating, such as number of push-ups or chin-ups in sixty seconds, separate standards may be used.

Coeducational Physical Education Classes

Because the provision for coeducational classes is one of the key implications of Title IX regulations, this topic is discussed further here.

Problems in physical education classes concerning Title IX have been cited in the professional literature. Weber (1980) indicates that problems such as the following have developed as a result of Title IX: the teacher is not profession-

Coeducational dance instruction. University of Minnesota.

ally prepared to teach various activities in a coeducational setting; male and female teachers who traditionally made decisions on their own are finding it difficult to function as a team and share the decision-making process; students are also finding problems such as being unable to perform some activities satisfactorily in front of members of the opposite sex; and those with poor skills are excluded from participation on highly skilled coeducational teams.

Weber also points out that many of these problems can be solved by such means as teachers eliminating their personal sex biases, employing new instructional strategies and techniques, and reexamining philosophies concerning the teaching of physical education. The main consideration in establishing coeducational programs is to respond to the interests and ability levels of the participants. When conducting activities on a coeducational basis, appropriate modifications may be made in the rules and conduct of the activities to equalize competition between the sexes.

Other problems that have arisen in physical education classes as a result of Title IX include assignment of office space, scheduling of gymnasiums for various activities, teaching of activities such as wrestling, potential for sexual impropriety, supervision of locker rooms, and dressing standards.

Compliance with Title IX   Title IX is being enforced by the Office for Civil Rights of the federal government. The first step seeks to have voluntary compliance. This process should be the job of the physical education teacher, physical education department, and school administration. If violations are found, federal financial support may be cut off and other legal measures taken, such as referring the violation to the Department of Justice for appropriate court action.

In 1992, the U.S. Supreme Court ruled that if schools intentionally violate Title IX, the plaintiff could sue for damages. Typically most complaints have been about athletics, not physical education. Further information about Title IX may be found in chapter 5.

THE ADAPTED/DEVELOPMENTAL PHYSICAL EDUCATION PROGRAM

The adapted/developmental program refers to the phase of physical education that meets the needs of the individual who, because of some physical inadequacy, functional defect capable of being improved through physical activity, or other deficiency, is temporarily or permanently unable to take part in the regular physical education program or the phase in which special provisions are made for students with disabilities in regular physical education classes. It also refers to students of a school or college population who do not fall into the "average" or "normal" classification for their age or grade. These students deviate from their peers in physical, mental, emotional, or social characteristics or in a combination of these traits.

The principle of individual differences that applies to education as a whole also applies to physical education. Most administrators believe that as long as a student can attend school or college, he or she should be required to participate in physical education. If this tenet is adhered to, it means that programs may have to be adapted to meet individual needs. Many children and young adults who are recuperating from long illnesses or surgery or who are suffering from other physical or emotional conditions require special consideration concerning their full and vigorous participation in physical activity programs.

It cannot be assumed that all individuals in physical education classes do not possess some type of disability. It is unfortunate that many programs are administered on this basis. An estimate has been made that one out of every eight students in our schools has a disability that requires special provision in the educational program.

Schools and colleges will always have students who, because of many factors such as heredity, environment, disease, accident, drugs, or some other circumstance, have physical or other major disabilities. Many of these students have difficulty adjusting to the demands that society places on them. The responsibility of the physical educator is to help each individual enrolled in the school to be engaged in appropriate physical education. Even though a person may possess various disabilities, this is not cause for neglect. In fact, by legal mandate and professional challenge, it is required that each child enjoy the benefits of participating in physical activities adapted to his or her needs. Provision for a sound adapted/developmental program has been a shortcoming of physical education throughout the nation because of a lack of properly trained teachers, because of the financial cost of remedial instruction, and because many administrators and teachers are not aware of their responsibility and the contribution they can make in this phase of physical education. These obstacles should be overcome as the public becomes aware of the mandate to educate *all* individuals in *all* phases of the total educational process.

Physical education teachers instructing students with severe disabilities.

People With Varying Disabilities

The nation's estimated fifty million people with disabilities have engaged in an aggressive civil rights movement. These actions were aimed at obtaining the equal protection promised under the Fourteenth Amendment to the Constitution of the United States.

As a result of the actions on the part of persons with disabilities, the nation is finally awakening to their needs as well as to their human potentialities. Until recently, persons with disabilities were viewed as nonproductive, functionally disruptive, and draining on society. As a result, persons with disabilities have often become discouraged. Today, however, the picture has changed. Persons with disabilities are achieving their rights under the Constitution, under public laws such as the 1975 Education for All Handicapped Children Act (P.L. 94-142), its upgrades the 1986 Education for All Handicapped

Children Act Amendments (P.L. 99-457) and the 1990 Individuals with Disabilities Education Act (IDEA) (P.L. 101-476), and under (P.L. 101-336) the Americans With Disabilities Act of January 26, 1992. Persons with disabilities are gaining accessibility, receiving educational opportunities, gaining meaningful employment in the public workforce, and taking their rightful place in an accessible society.

Definitions Relating to the Adapted/Developmental Program

Many terms have been used to define and classify persons with disabilities. These terms vary from publication to publication. Categories of children designated by the U.S. Congress in relation to legislation for persons with disabilities will be the primary classifications used in this text; however, these terms will be modified to reflect the changing view concerning persons with disabilities, such as those infected with HIV or Fetal Alcohol Syndrome (FAS). These categories include the mentally disabled, hearing impaired, speech impaired, visually impaired, emotionally and behaviorally disordered, learning disabled, physically disabled, and other health-impaired individuals who may require educational services out of the ordinary.

Special Education

Under federal law, special education means specially designed instruction, at no cost to parents or guardians, to meet the unique needs of persons with disabilities, including classroom and physical education instruction, home instruction, and instruction in hospitals and institutions.

Physical Education

Physical education as it relates to the persons with disabilities under federal law is the development of (1) physical and motor fitness, (2) fundamental motor skills and patterns, and (3) skills in aquatics, dance, and individual and group games and sports (including recreational and lifetime sports). Physical educators must serve as part of the adapted student's resource team and be prepared to design specific and appropriate programs of physical activity for each student.

Individualized Education Program

The individualized education program (IEP) is the program or prescription written for each child in relation to his or her specific disability. This IEP might range from full mainstreaming or inclusion in regular physical education classes (sometimes with a paraprofessional) to a specialized physical education setting under the direction of a licensed adapted physical educator. The IEP will be discussed in more detail later in this chapter (also see Appendix B).

Least Restrictive Environment

In essence, the *least restrictive environment* means persons with disabilities are placed in a class or setting that is as similar to a normal class as possible and in which the child can function

safely. This location ranges from a full-time regular physical education class (inclusion), to a regular physical education class with consultation from specialists in adapted physical education, to part-time regular physical education and part-time adapted physical education, to adapted physical education with regular physical education only for specific activities, to full-time adapted physical education in a regular school, to adapted physical education in a special school. The current trend is to include the special student, if possible, within the regular physical education instructional class, where appropriate and safe activities may be enjoyed.

Functional Physical Education Goals for People with Disabilities

Selected goals that provide direction to the physical education program for the student with disabilities and that translate into objectives for each participant, as outlined by AAHPERD (Stein 1971), are presented here in the following modified format:

- Inform each student of his or her capacities, limitations, and potentials.
- Provide each student within his or her capabilities the opportunities to develop organic vigor, muscular strength and endurance, joint function and flexibility, and cardiovascular endurance.
- Provide each student with opportunities for social development in recreational sports and games.
- Provide each student with opportunities to develop skills in recreational sports and games.
- Help students meet demands of day-to-day living.
- Help students with disabilities in their social development.
- Help students develop personal pride in overcoming disabilities or other forms of impairment.
- Help students develop an appreciation for individual differences and an ability to accept limitations and still be an integral part of the group.

The Adapted Physical Education Council of AAHPERD and the National Consortium for Physical Education and Recreation for Individuals with Disabilities (NCPERID) also provide specific recommendations concerning national standards and competencies as well as national certification for people working in this enriching and challenging field (NCPERID 1995).

Public Law 94-142/Public Law 101-476 (IDEA)

A milestone in legislative proposals providing for persons with disabilities was the passage of the Education of All Handicapped Children Act of 1975, which was signed into law by the President of the United States as P.L. 94-142 (Singer 1985). The act has now been upgraded via P.L. 101-476, the Individuals with Disabilities Education Act, and is now referred to as IDEA-Part B or Subchapter II. This legislation spells out the federal government's commitment to educating children with disabilities and provides for annual funding on a sliding scale for this purpose. It provides educational services to children with disabilities who are not receiving a free and appropriate public education as well as assistance for those children receiving inadequate help. IDEA mandates that physical education services, specially designed if necessary, must be made available to every child with a disability receiving a free and appropriate education.

These services have now been extended from birth through age twenty-one. Children with disabilities, as defined in IDEA-Part B, are those who require some type of special education and related services. Related services, under the act, are defined as "transportation and developmental, corrective, and other supportive services, including but not limited to, occupational, speech, and physical therapy, recreation, and social, medical, and counseling services." Although gifted children might need special education and related services, they are not covered under the law.

Other specific stipulations of IDEA require the following:

- That state and local educational agencies initiate policies to ensure all children the right to a free and appropriate education in the least restrictive environment.

- The planning of individualized educational programs, including health and physical status and motoric ability, and the scheduling of conferences that include parents, teachers (including physical education and special education teachers), case managers, administrators, representatives of local educational agencies, and where appropriate, the children themselves. These conferences must be held at least once a year.

- Due process for parents and children to ensure that their rights are not abrogated.

- A per-pupil expenditure that is at least equal to the amount spent on each nondisabled child in the state or local school district.

- That the state and local agency carry out the mandates of the law according to specific timetables provided therein.

- The development of a comprehensive system of personnel training, including preservice and in-service training for teachers.

- That students with disabilities will be educated in the least restrictive environment. This means that they will be placed in the regular class whenever possible.

Aspects of IDEA related to physical education. The following requirements are stipulated for physical education:
(a) *General.* Physical education services, specially designed if necessary, must be made available to every child with disabilities receiving a free appropriate public education. (b) *Regular physical education.* Each child must be afforded the opportunity to participate in the regular physical education program unless

1. The child is enrolled full-time in a separate facility, or
2. The child needs specially designed physical education, as prescribed in the child's IEP.

(c) *Special physical education.* If specially designed physical education is prescribed in a child's IEP, the public agency responsible for the education of that child shall provide the services directly or make arrangements for services to be provided through other public or private programs. (d) *Education in separate facilities.* The public agency responsible for the education of a child with disabilities who is enrolled in a separate facility shall ensure that the child receives appropriate physical education services in compliance with paragraphs (a) and (c) of this section.

Individualized Education Programs for People with Disabilities

After identification and eligibility have been determined for students with disabilities, an IEP must be developed for each individual. IDEA specifies the requirements and guidelines for the development of such programs (also see Appendix B):

> The term *individualized education program (IEP)* means a written statement for each child with disabilities developed in any meeting by a representative of the local educational agency or an intermediate educational unit who shall be qualified to provide or supervise the provision of specially designed instruction to meet the unique needs of children with disabilities. The design of an IEP shall include:

A. An assessment of the present levels of educational performance of the child;

B. A statement of annual goals, including short-term instructional objectives;

C. A statement of the specific educational services to be provided, and the extent to which the child will be able to participate in regular educational programs;

D. The projected date for initiation and anticipated duration of the services; and

E. An outline of appropriate objective criteria and evaluation procedures and schedules for determining, on at least an annual basis, whether instructional objectives are being achieved.

The comprehensive IEP should be developed using the team approach. The following persons should be represented on the team: parent, teacher (classroom, physical education, and special education), administrator, case manager, student, and —when appropriate—the people responsible for supervising special education, related services such as guidance and counseling, and other agency representatives (e.g., social worker, therapist, etc.).

Adapted/Developmental Physical Education Facilities

Appropriate and adequate facilities, equipment, and supplies are important to successful programs of physical education for persons with disabilities. However, these items must be modified for special or adapted physical education students because facilities and equipment are usually designed for students in the regular class. Adaptations are often necessary when students are mainstreamed into regular programs.

The passage of the Americans with Disabilities Act (ADA) and the results of various legal decisions have prompted school districts to make available and accessible the necessary facilities, equipment, and supplies to ensure a quality education for all students. There is some question, however, about whether students with disabilities are being provided with adequate facilities, equipment, and supplies. The types of facilities and equipment needed for adapted/developmental physical education will vary according to the nature of the program (adapted or unified sports; remedial or corrective exercises; or rest, rehabilitation, and relaxation), the student's disability, and the school level at which the program is conducted. For example, the elementary school program in adapted physical education may be taught in the regular gymnasium or, in less desirable circumstances, in the classroom. In secondary schools and colleges, however, a special facility or gymnasium for adapted physical education may be provided.

The Virginia State Department of Education, in its instructional booklet entitled *Physical Education for Handicapped Students,* outlines some of the factors that should be taken into consideration for students with disabilities. A few of these factors with other considerations are offered:

Within building

- Doors easy to open, at least forty-eight inches in width, and two-way in design.
- Nonslip ramps, properly sloped, with handrails on both sides.
- Elevators or chair lifts when necessary with properly placed operating mechanisms (closing door, starting, assistance button in braille, etc.).
- Floors with nonslip surfaces.
- Restrooms with toilets at proper height (twenty inches), with rails provided, and with properly designed doors.

Outside building

- Loading and parking areas convenient to accessible entrances. These areas should be properly lighted, barrier- and curb-free and, if possible, covered.
- Ramps suitable for wheelchairs and accessible to all building levels.
- Doorways and sidewalks wide enough for two passing wheelchairs.
- Emergency exits for wheelchairs.

Other considerations

Certainly many other considerations are crucial in order for persons with disabilities to be able to function within the operating codes. Other considerations are listed below:

- Telephone (height, length of cord, raised numerals for visually impaired).
- Aquatic facilities (accessible dressing and changing facilities and hair dryer at proper height).
- Safety doors at exits.
- Water fountains (height and accessibility).
- Restrooms (accessibility).

All physical education, athletic, and recreational sport programs must operate with sensitivity to provide every student with the opportunity to equal access. This is one area in which we must strive to do a better job.

Adapted/Developmental Physical Education Equipment and Supplies

For the most part, equipment and supplies that are used in the regular classroom can be modified to meet adaptive needs, and certainly equipment that already exists at regular playgrounds can and should be employed. Special care and safety measures must be taken, however, to prevent children from getting struck by such items as moving swings, teeter-totters, and ropes. Of course specialized equipment can be purchased or constructed by creative school personnel. Programmatic needs can be met now by myriad supplies, information, and organizations, ranging from the Braille Sports Foundation and the National Beep Baseball Association to the Minnesota Outward Bound School for the Handicapped and the International Sports Organization for the Disabled. The U.S. Consumer Product Safety Commission (CPSC) also is a valuable resource for safety guidelines for both facilities and equipment.

MANAGEMENT MATTERS RELATED TO PHYSICAL EDUCATION INSTRUCTIONAL PROGRAMS

Scheduling

The status and role that physical education plays in the educational curriculum reflect the physical education leadership and its relationship with central administration. Physical education is more meaningful for participants when the schedule reflects their interests rather than administrative convenience.

Physical education instruction is usually scheduled in a six- or seven-period structure, block, flexible, or modular fashion. Scheduling should be done according to a well-conceived plan. Physical education should not be inserted in the overall master scheduling plan whenever there is time left over after all the other subjects have been scheduled. This important responsibility cannot be handled on a hit-or-miss basis because that basis disregards the interests and needs of the students. Instead, physical education should be scheduled first on the master plan, along with other crucial subjects that are required of all students. This allows for progression and for grouping according to the interests and needs of the individual participants. The three important items to consider in scheduling classes are (1) the number of teachers available, (2) the number of teaching stations available, and (3) the number of students who must be scheduled. This formula should be applied to all subjects on an equitable basis.

When appropriate, all students should be scheduled. If the student is able to attend school or college, he or she should be encouraged to enroll in physical education. Special attention should be provided, however, to those with disabilities or to gifted individuals to ensure that they are included in a program suited to their individual needs. Also, attention should be accorded those students who need extra help developing physical skills, strength, and endurance and who are searching to find their way in the psychosocial realm.

Physical educators should make a point of presenting to central administration their plans for scheduling physical education classes. Facility availability, equipment, supplies, weather, and student interest and attention span should be taken into consideration when preparing a master scheduling plan. The need for equitable consideration should also be discussed with the principal and the scheduling committee. Through persistent action, progress will be made. The logic and reasoning behind the formula of scheduling classes according to the number of teachers and teaching stations available and the number of students who must be scheduled should not be denied. The program should be planned according to these guidelines to ensure progression and safe, meaningful instruction.

Period and Block Scheduling

Many physical education programs have schedules based on a six- or seven-period day. In this system, the teacher might teach five or six 45- or 50-minute classes with one preparation period. Some primary or elementary schools limit their scheduled class periods to 30 or 35 minutes, in which the teacher may teach from eight to ten class periods daily.

Many junior high, middle, and senior high schools have moved to block scheduling. Block scheduling divides the school year into terms (usually four nine-week terms per year); a student might enroll in four or five classes during each term that meet daily and are each 90 minutes in duration. Research indicates that block scheduling tends to maintain or increase academic performance, student retention, higher order thinking and problem solving, while reducing drop-out rates and suspension (Carroll, 1994). The block system is demanding on human resources, but more and more progressive school systems seem to be adopting this scheduling system.

Flexible and Modular Scheduling

The introduction of flexible scheduling into school programs has implications for the management of school physical education programs. Flexible scheduling assumes that the traditional system of having all subjects meet the same number of times each week for the same amount of time each period is not always possible. Flexible scheduling provides class periods of varying lengths, depending on the course content being covered by the students, methods of instruction, and other factors pertinent to such a system. Whereas the traditional master plan makes it difficult to promote flexible scheduling, the advent of the computer has made this innovation a potential.

Flexible scheduling also makes it possible to schedule activities for students of varying abilities at different times so that all students are not required to have a similar schedule based on a standard format of the school day. Under the traditional system, all students who were academically at risk, for example, took as many courses as the brightest. Under flexible scheduling, some students may take as few as four courses and some as many as eight. In either case, physical education should be a part of every student's schedule.

Modular scheduling breaks the school day into periods of time called modules. In a high school in Illinois, for example, the school day comprises 20-minute modules, and classes may vary from one to five modules depending on the purpose of the course. The school is on a six-day cycle and operates by day one, two, or three rather than the traditional days of the week. In physical education, each grade level meets for three modules per day, four days each week. Each grade level also has a two-module group meeting once every cycle. In this meeting, guest speakers and classroom lectures provide students with physical education concepts.

In other schools employing modular scheduling, students frequently have unscheduled modules that can be used for elective aquatics or gymnasium activities. Recreational sports, open lab facilities, sport clubs, and school demonstrations or exhibitions also provide opportunities for students to actively and regularly utilize the skills they have learned in physical education class.

Dress

Dress does not have to be elaborate, but it should be comfortable, safe, and appropriate. An important concern is that the clothing ensures safety when students are engaged in physical activity. For both males and females, simple washable shorts and T-shirts or sweatshirts are suitable and most comfortable. Many schools still require uniforms, especially where laundry service is provided. Of course, appropriate footwear should be worn. It is important to keep the uniform clean. The instructor or physical education department should establish a policy concerning safe, clean, and appropriate attire and work diligently to see that hygienic standards are met by all. Students who do not dress for class should not be permitted to participate in activities.

Time Allotment

Just as scheduling practices vary from school to school, district to district, college to college, and state to state, so does the time allotment for physical education. Some states have laws that require a certain amount of time each day or week be devoted to physical education, whereas in other states, permissive legislation exists. For the most part, however, school districts set their own K–12 schedules. Some require 20 minutes daily and others, 30 minutes daily. Some districts also specify the time by the week, ranging from 50 minutes to 300 minutes. Colleges and universities do not usually require as much time in physical education as do elementary, junior high, middle, or senior high schools. At the college level, requirements take the form of semesters or quarters of physical education that are usually delivered in one-hour blocks two to three times per week. The general consensus among physical education leaders is that for physical education to be of value, it must be offered with regularity. For most individuals, this means daily or at least three times per week.

Some individuals believe that, especially in elementary schools, a program cannot be adapted to a fixed time schedule. However, as a standard, there seems to be agreement that a daily experience in physical education is needed as well as laboratory periods during which students can exercise and practice the skills they have acquired.

On the secondary level, it is recommended that sufficient time be allotted for dressing and showering in addition to the time needed for participation in physical education activities. Some leaders in physical education have suggested a double period every other day rather than a single period each day. This arrangement would assist in encouraging students to shower, which has long been a problematic issue. However, the importance of daily periods should be recognized and achieved wherever possible. Administrators should work toward providing adequate staff members and facilities to allow for a daily period of physical education. This remains a challenge in times of fiscal constraint.

The amount of time suggested for adults to spend in physical activity programs is a minimum of three times a week (not on consecutive days). However, a daily physical education regimen is considered optimal and should be the goal of every professional physical educator.

Class Size

Some school and college administrators contend that physical education activity classes can accommodate more students than so-called academic content classes. This is a misconception that has developed over the years and needs to be corrected.

The problem of class size seems to be more pronounced at the secondary level than at other educational levels. At the elementary level, for example, the classroom situation represents a unit for activity assignment, and the number of students in this teaching unit is usually reasonable (15–25). However, some schools combine various units or classrooms for physical education, resulting in large classes that are not safe and provide a less than desirable teaching and learning environment.

Classes in physical education should be approximately the same size as classes in other subjects offered in the school. Such a class size is just as essential for effective teaching, individualized instruction, and optimal performance in physical education as it is in other content subjects. Physical education contributes to educational objectives on an equal basis with other subjects in the curriculum. Therefore, the class size should be comparable so that its educational objectives can be attained.

After much research, many committees established a standard for an acceptable size of physical education classes. They recommend that thirty students make up a class, with enrollment never exceeding thirty-five for one instructor. A lecture or other activity adaptable to greater numbers may make it possible to have more persons in the class, especially if an assistant or paraprofessional is on hand. For remedial work, a suitable class size is from one-on-one to twenty to twenty-five and should never exceed thirty. Aquatics, gymnastics, and other high-risk activities also call for reduced student-to-teacher ratio with 20:1 being the upper limit. With flexible scheduling, the size of classes can be varied to meet the needs of the teacher, facilities, and type of activity being offered. Creative managers should employ this technique when units such as beginning swimming are introduced.

Instructional Loads and Staffing

The instructional load of the physical educator should be of prime concern to management. To maintain a high level of enthusiasm, vigor, and morale, it is important that the load be fair and equitable so that physical educators can perform to their fullest potential.

Some professional guidelines recommended that one full-time physical education teacher should be provided for every 240 elementary or 190 secondary students enrolled. Such a requirement would provide adequate professional staffing and avoid an overload for many of the teachers. This arrangement might also keep more physical education teachers involved in after-school extracurricular activities, especially coaching and intramurals.

Professional recommendations regarding teaching loads at K–12 educational levels have been made that would limit class instruction per teacher to five hours or the equivalent in class periods per day, or 1,500 minutes per week. The maximum would be six hours per day or 1,800 minutes a week, including after-school responsibilities. A daily load of 200 students per teacher is recommended, and this number should never exceed 250. Finally, each teacher should have at least one preparation period daily and other scheduled time for consultation and conferences with students.

It is generally agreed that the normal teaching load in colleges and universities should not exceed twelve to sixteen contact hours per week. At research universities, however, the load of the physical education (kinesiology, sports studies, etc.) professor is accommodated to take into account research, publishing, and service requirements. In many institutions, including K–12 levels, professional organizations, teachers' associations, and unions prescribe the length of the workday, including the instructional workload and number of contact hours.

The workload in a physical fitness center, which typically might open at 5:30 A.M. and close at 11 P.M. seven days per week, is often forty to fifty hours per week. Corporate fitness centers usually maintain an eight-hour working day.

Some, however, stay open at night, so the staff may have to work "off-hour" shifts. Regardless of position, the profession of physical education is a full-time labor of love.

Differentiated Staffing

Many innovations, such as differentiated staffing, are directed toward aiding teachers in the performance of their duties. Paraprofessionals, qualified undergraduate interns, teaching assistants, and student teachers provide many schools with valuable support staff.

Differentiated staffing relates to increased responsibilities or differentiation of functions among staff members. For example, in team teaching, higher salaries are given to team leaders or head teachers. Staff members who assume such roles as heads of departments or staff supervisors or assistants are usually compensated accordingly. In some school systems, highly competent staff members with expertise in certain areas are often assigned to special projects such as curriculum-writing teams and may also receive extra compensation for these duties.

The benefits derived from differentiated staffing are obvious from the responsibilities assigned to various staff members. In schools, for example, teachers are able to devote more time to helping individual students and to working with small groups to assist students in mastering learning tasks. Differentiated staffing allows the teacher to focus on teaching and not be directly involved in time-consuming clerical and physical responsibilities.

Paraprofessionals

Responsibilities include (1) supervised instructional assistance, (2) assisting with the swimming pool, (3) clerical duties, (4) student conduct supervision, and (5) preparation of learning materials.

Qualified Undergraduate Interns

Responsibilities include (1) clerical assistance, (2) record keeping, (3) preparation of learning materials, (4) conduct supervision in noninstructional areas, (5) individual assistance, and (6) observation.

Student Teachers

Responsibilities include (1) observation, (2) supervised clinical teaching experience, (3) assistance to supervising teachers, (4) preparation of learning materials, (5) individual assistance, and (6) extracurricular guidance.

Teaching Assistants

Responsibilities may be the same as those of an instructor at the college or university level. Physical activity programs at many larger universities are staffed primarily by teaching assistants.

Taking Roll

There are many methods of taking roll. If a method satisfies the following three criteria, it is usually satisfactory. (1) It is efficient—roll taking should not consume too much time. (2) It is accurate—after class, it is important to know who was present and who was not as well as who came late or left early. (3) It is uncomplicated—any system that is used should be easy to manage. The following provides some methods for roll taking:

1. *Having numbers on the floor.* Each member of the class is assigned a number that he or she must stand on when the signal for "fall in" is given. The person taking attendance records the numbers not covered.

2. *Reciting numbers orally.* Each member of the class is assigned a number that he or she must say out loud at the time the "fall in" signal is given. The person taking attendance then records the numbers omitted.

3. *Using a tag board.* Each member of the class has a number recorded on a cardboard or metal tag that hangs on a peg on a board in a central place. Each member of the class who is present removes his or her tag from the board and places it in a box. The person taking attendance records the absentees from the tags remaining on the board.

4. *Using the Delaney system.* This system uses a folder with cards that are turned over when a person is absent. It is a cumulative system that records the attendance of pupils over time.

5. *Using the squad system.* The class is divided into squads and the squad leader takes the roll for his or her squad and in turn reports to the instructor.

6. *Issuing towels and equipment.* The roll is taken when a towel is issued to each student or when it is turned in, or when a basket with a uniform is issued or returned.

7. *Signing a book or register.* Students are required to write their names in a book or register at the beginning of the class. Some systems require the writing of a name at the beginning of a period and crossing it out at the end. The person taking attendance records the names not entered from the master roll.

8. *Calling the roll.* This is the most frequently observed method; it is tedious yet effective.

Selecting Physical Education Activities

Physical education activities represent the core of the program. They are the means for accomplishing objectives and achieving educational goals. Because activities are so important to the physical education program, they must be selected with considerable care.

Criteria for Selection

Activities should be selected in terms of the values they have in achieving the objectives of physical education. This means that activities should serve to promote and develop not only body awareness, movement fundamentals, and physical fitness but also the cognitive, affective, and socioemotional makeup of the individual.

Activities should be interesting and challenging. Activities should appeal to the participants and present them with problem-solving activities and situations that challenge their skill, ability, and creativity. Activities should be adaptable to the growth and developmental needs and interests of children, youth, and adults. The needs of individuals vary from age to age. As a consequence, movement activities, the pattern of organization, and instructional delivery strategies must also change. The activity must be suited to the person, not the

person to the activity. Wherever possible, participants should be allowed some choice and input into their physical education program and class.

Activities should be modifications of fundamental movements such as running, jumping, throwing, walking, striking, kicking, and climbing.

Activities must be selected in light of the facilities, supplies, equipment, and other human and physical resources available in the school, college, or community. An extensive tennis program cannot be carried out if only one court is available.

Activities should be selected not only with a view to their present value while the child is in school, but also with a view to postschool and adult living. Skills learned during school and college can be used throughout life, thus contributing to enriched living. Patterns for many skills used in adult leisure hours are developed while the individual is in the formative years of childhood.

Health and safety factors must be considered when selecting activities. High-risk activities should be kept to a minimum.

The local education philosophy, policies, codes of conduct, and school or college organization must be considered.

Physical education class incorporating fundamental movement. Crest View Elementary School, Brooklyn Park, Minn.

School activities should provide situations similar to those that children experience in natural play and competitive situations outside school.

Activities should provide the participant with opportunities for creative self-expression.

Activities selected should elicit appropriate social and moral responses through high-quality leadership and role modeling.

Activities should reflect the democratic way of life.

Physical education activities are frequently classified into various categories. The following activities do not necessarily meet criteria that have been previously listed. They merely indicate some current offerings in physical education programs throughout the United States:

Team games

Baseball
Basketball
Codeball
Field hockey
Flag football
Football
Ice hockey
Soccer
Softball
Speedball
Team handball
Touch football
Volleyball

Outdoor winter sports

Ice hockey
Ringette
Roller-skating
Skating
Skiing (Alpine and Nordic)
Snow-boarding
Snow games
Snowshoeing
Tobogganing

Other activities

Camping and outdoor activities

Combatives (judo, karate)
Correctives (posture control)
Fly-fishing
Fly-tying
Games of low organization
In-line skating
Jogging
Mountaineering
Movement education
Orienteering
Progressive relaxation
Relays
Rock climbing
Self-testing activities
Yoga

Rhythms and dancing

Aerobic dancing
Ballroom dancing
Folk dancing
Gymnastic dancing
Modern dancing
Movement fundamentals

Rhythms
Square dancing
Social dancing
Tap dancing

Formal activities

Calisthenics
Marching

Water activities

Canoeing
Diving
Kayaking
Lifeguarding
Rowing
Sailing
Scuba diving
Swimming
Water games
Water polo
Water safety instructor
Windsurfing

Gymnastics

Acrobatics
Apparatus
Obstacle course
Pyramid building
Rope climbing
Stunts
Tumbling

Dual and individual sports

Archery

Badminton
Beach volleyball
Bowling
Broomball
Checkers
Cycling
Darts
Deck tennis
Fencing
Fishing
Golf
Handball
Horseback riding
Horseshoes
Paddleball
Paddle tennis
Platform tennis
Racquetball
Rifle
Rope skipping
Shuffleboard
Skeet shooting
Skish
Squash
Table tennis
Tennis
Tetherball
Track and field
Trapshooting
Volleyball
Wallyball
Weight training
Wrestling

Grouping Participants

Proper grouping of students in physical education classes is crucial to both obtaining desired results and complying with guidelines such as Title IX and IDEA. Because of considerations such as these, the physical educator needs to develop a broad spectrum of organizational strategies, ranging from homogeneous to heterogeneous groups.

By tradition, physical educators have tended to favor homogeneous grouping. The theory behind this strategy is that placing individuals with

Scuba diving class. University of Nevada at Las Vegas.

similar capacities and characteristics in the same class makes it possible to better meet the needs of each student. Grouping individuals with similar skill, ability, and other factors (e.g., height, weight, maturity) also aids in equalizing competition.

Current trends toward grouping students, however, take more of a heterogeneous approach. Research indicates that heterogeneous grouping promotes positive social interaction between students of differing ability, skill level, and other characteristics (e.g., race, gender, socioeconomic level, physical or mental disability) and enhances overall performance (Johnson, Bjorkland, and Krotee 1984). Moreover, heterogeneous grouping means that compliance with governmental mandates is easily accomplished.

Because of scheduling considerations, many schools group students by grade, which has inherent advantages as well as disadvantages. Grouping by grade provides many students with a sense of security since they are comfortable with their cohorts. On the other hand, height, weight and other developmental variations must be taken into account.

Perhaps the preferable class organizational structure is a combination of homogeneous and heterogeneous grouping. Grouping boys and girls into physical education classes by grade meets Title IX regulations and presents the physical educator with limitless possibilities for grouping strategies within the class. This, in turn, allows a variety of goal structures ranging from competitive to cooperative, with combinations thereof, to be utilized. In competitive situations in which height and weight are factors or in which it is inappropriate for boys to compete against girls (and vice versa), homogeneous groups can compete against others within their group. In other circumstances, teams formed homogeneously can be pitted against other teams from within the same skill division; on still other occasions, teams that are developed heterogeneously can compete against like teams.

Heterogeneous grouping provides unique opportunities for students to develop physically as well as cognitively and socially. For example, within a heterogeneous tennis class of thirty students, the instructor, after assessing skill level, can form six heterogeneous teams of five students. Each group practices as a team, teaching and coaching teammates, and when the competition round begins, the team plays against other teams so that number 1 players compete against other number 1s, number 2s play number 2s, and so on. This approach allows all players in the class to compete at their own level and to work toward a common goal (team victory) with students who are at different levels. It also enables the less skilled students in the class to make a meaningful contribution toward their team's success.

Many schools offer elective courses in physical education, which often is a very effective way of grouping students. Electives permit students to self-select and usually group students with similar interests and abilities in the class. Elective course-

Heterogeneous grouping promotes positive social interaction. Crest View Elementary School, Brooklyn Park, Minn.

work gives the innovative physical educator many opportunities for structuring task and goal interdependence in order to stimulate students physically, cognitively, and psychosocially.

Student Leadership and Involvement

In recent years students have been demanding greater involvement in the educational process, and in most cases, this increased involvement has been satisfactory to students, teachers, and administrators. Some of these areas of involvement are discussed briefly here.

General Planning

Students should be involved in planning meetings that discuss scheduling, curriculum innovations, and recent changes in educational methods and instructional strategies. Students might be invited to join community task forces, attend school board and parent association meetings, and also accompany teachers and administrators to other schools at which certain innovations may be directly observed. Some schools and colleges have instituted student advisory boards that meet with staff members to discuss problems, recommend changes, and participate in future strategic planning.

Curriculum Planning

Student surveys sometimes reveal the extent of curriculum changes desired by the student body. Administrators, teachers, and students should carefully weigh this information in light of current literature, research, and curriculum innovations in similar schools and colleges. Student participation and feedback are essential; however, students do have limited experience in educational matters, and this must also be considered. Frequently the limited use of experimental programs can help evaluate the change before it is implemented on a larger scale.

In a high school in Massachusetts, students take an active role in curriculum planning. Students, for example, plan what and how they are going to learn in a gymnastics unit. Several days are set aside for students to set goals, plan the steps needed to reach a specific goal, outline the evaluation requirements, and make a commitment to learning and improvement. The students put their goals in writing and then strive to achieve them. Instruction is provided, and grading is a cooperative venture between students and teacher.

Using the Student Leader

Student leaders may be used in the physical education program in several capacities.

Class Leaders

Opportunities abound in the physical education instructional class period for student leaders to be of great assistance. These duties include acting as squad leader; being a leader for warmup exercises; demonstrating skills, games, and tactics to be performed; taking attendance; assisting with locker-room supervision; and providing safety measures for class participation such as serving as a spotter and checking equipment and play areas.

Officials, Captains, and Other Positions

Student leaders can gain valuable experience by serving as officials within the class and recreational sports program; being captains of all-star or other teams; coaching recreational sport or club teams; and acting as scorers, timekeepers, referees, and equipment supervisors.

Committee Members

Many committee assignments should be filled by student leaders so that they gain valuable experience. These positions include being a member of a *rules committee,* by which rules are established and interpreted for games and sports; serving on an *equipment and grounds committee,* at which standards are established for the storage, maintenance, and use of these facilities and equipment; participating on a *committee for planning special events* in the physical education program, such as play, sports, or field days; and joining a task force on long-range strategic planning for the building of new facilities.

Supply and Equipment Manager

Supplies and special equipment ranging from basketballs and hockey equipment to audiovisual aids are among the items continually required for the conduct of the physical education program. The equipment must be removed from the storage areas, transported to where the activity will be conducted, safely set up, and then returned. The student leader can help immeasurably in this process and profit from such an experience.

Program Planner

Various aspects of the physical education program need to be planned, and students should be involved. Student leaders, because of their special qualifications and interest, are logical choices to participate in such planning and curriculum development. Their knowledge and input can ensure that the program more fully meets the needs and interests of all students who participate in the program.

Record Keeper and Office Manager

Attendance records, test scores, and inventories must be taken, recorded, and filed; bulletin boards kept up to date; visitors greeted; and other responsibilities effectively met. These necessary functions provide worthwhile experiences for the student leader to develop human and technical skills as well as to assist the teacher.

Student leaders assist the teacher in taking roll. Birchview Elementary School, Wayzata, Minn.

Special Events Coordinator

A multitude of details are always involved in play days, sports days, demonstrations, and exhibitions. Student leaders should help plan and conduct these events. This participation is a great way to experience sport management up close.

It is important to keep in mind that student leaders are to be accorded respect and rewarded for their work. They are invaluable volunteers whom the teacher wants to encourage, involve, and offer responsibility. Student leader experiences, however, should not detract from nor substitute for their physical education classroom learning experience. Student leaders or any staff members are not substitute teachers; safety and legal responsibility must always remain with the teacher.

SELECTED MANAGEMENT PROBLEMS IN INSTRUCTIONAL PROGRAMS

The manager of any physical education program is continually confronted with questions such as the following: Should physical education be required or elective? Should other activities be substituted for physical education? How much credit should be awarded? What is the policy on class attendance? How should an instructor deal with excuses? What grading system should the physical educator utilize? Who should deliver physical education at the elementary school level? These questions and other issues, including dressing and showering, record keeping, and safety considerations, are addressed in this section.

Should Physical Education Be Required or Elective?

General agreement is that physical education should be required at the elementary, junior high, and middle school levels. However, there are many advocates on both sides of the question of whether it should be required or elective at the secondary and college levels. Most professionals believe physical education should be required, whereas some school administrators and parents believe elective offerings are the order of the day.

Following are some of the arguments presented by each side.

Required

Physical education is a basic need of every student. Students need regular and vigorous physical activity to develop to their fullest potential and to release tension from the rigors of not only the academic setting but daily life as well.

The student considers required subjects most important, and if physical education is not required, many individuals who could benefit from active participation may choose not to do so.

Various subjects in the curriculum would not be provided unless they were required. This is probably true of physical education. Until mandated by state legislatures and school districts, physical education was ignored by many school administrators. This noncommittal administrative philosophy might cause physical education to suffer curtailment or possible elimination.

Even when required, physical education is not meeting all the physical, cognitive, psychomotor, and socioemotional needs of students. Therefore, an elective program may further inhibit student growth and development.

Elective

Physical education "carries its own drive." If a good basic instructional physical education program is developed in the elementary school, with students acquiring the necessary skills and attitudes, the drive for such activity will carry through to the secondary school and college. There should be no need to require physical education because students will want to take it voluntarily.

The objectives of physical education are focused on acquiring skills and learning activities that have carryover value, on assisting in the establishment of a healthful lifestyle, and on recognizing the importance of developing and maintaining one's body in its best possible condition. These goals cannot be legislated. They must become a part of each individual's attitudes and desires if they are to be realized.

Some children and young adults do not like physical education. This dislike is indicated in their manner, attitude, and desire to get excused from the program and to substitute something else for the course. Under such circumstances, the values that accrue to these individuals are not great. Therefore it would be best to place physical education on an elective basis so that those students who choose to participate actually desire to do so. In the day and age of freedom of expression and individual choice, it seems antithetical that requirements are a part of the educational curriculum.

Should Substitutions Be Permitted for Physical Education?

A practice exists in some school and college systems that permits students to substitute some other activity for their physical education requirement. This practice should be scrutinized and resisted aggressively by every educator.

Some of the activities often used as substitutions for physical education are athletic participation, Reserve Officers' Training Corps, and band. There is no substitute for a sound program of physical education. In addition to the healthful physical activity, physical education also develops an individual socially, emotionally, and mentally. Furthermore, the individual learns many skills that can be applied throughout life. These essentials are lost if a student is permitted to substitute some other activity for physical education.

Should Credit Be Awarded for Physical Education?

Whether credit should be awarded for physical education is another controversy with which the profession is continually confronted. Here again advocates can be found on both sides. Some think the joy of the activity and the values derived from participation are sufficient in themselves without giving credit. On the other hand, some believe that physical education is no different than any other subject in the curriculum, and therefore credit should be granted.

The general consensus among physical education leaders is that if physical education is required for graduation and if it enriches a person's education, credit should be awarded.

What Policy Should Be Established on Class Attendance?

It is important for every department of physical education to have a clear-cut policy concerning class attendance that covers absenteeism and tardiness. These regulations should be concise and clearly stated in writing so that they are recognized and understood. They should allow for a reasonable number of absences and tardies. Perfect attendance at school or college should not be stressed. Many harmful results can develop if students feel obligated to attend classes when they are ill and should be at home. There should be some provision for independent study and out-of-class activity as well as makeup work when important experiences are missed. Makeup work should be planned and conducted so that the student derives essential values from such participation rather than perceiving it as a disciplinary measure. There should also be written provisions for the readmission of students who have been ill or injured.

A final point to remember is the importance of keeping accurate, up-to-date attendance records to minimize administrative problems and maximize student accountability and safety.

What About Excuses?

The principal, nurse, or physical educator frequently receives a note from a parent or family physician requesting that a student be excused from participating in physical education. Many times, for various reasons, the student does not want to participate and obtains the parent's or family physician's support.

Most schools permit a student to be excused from daily physical education on the basis of a parental note, a memorandum from the family physician, or at the discretion of the physical education teacher. Although some schools accept the recommendation of any of these three persons, other schools might accept only an excuse from the school physician. At the college level, most programs accept the college physician's excuse or permit the instructors to use their own discretion in granting excuses to students.

Some prevalent reasons for granting daily excuses in physical education have prevailed over time. Secondary schools grant most of their excuses for participation in sports, school band, choir, debate, or some other school-sponsored activity. Some schools excuse athletes from physical education on game days, whereas others grant a blanket exemption from physical education for the entire sport season. Other reasons for excuses include makeup examinations, driver training, counseling, and medical considerations. Students who are excused usually are required to attend study halls or to score, officiate, or assist with the conduct of physical education class or assist the department in some meaningful task. Failure in the class usually results when too many absences accumulate.

Some school systems have attempted to control the indiscriminate granting of requests for excuses from physical education. Policies have been established, with the support of the board of education, requiring that all excuses be reviewed and approved by the school physician or nurse before they are granted. Furthermore, family physicians have been asked to state specific reasons for requesting excuses from physical education. This procedure has worked satisfactorily in some communities. In other places, physical educators have taken particular pains to work closely with physicians. They have established a physical education program in collaboration with the school physician so that the needs of each individual are met regardless of his or her physical condition. They have met with the local medical society in an attempt to clear up misunderstandings about the purpose and conduct of the program. Family physicians have been brought into the planning process. As a result of such planning, problems with excessive excuses have been reduced. In such communities, the values derived from participation in the program are clearly recognized, and because most parents and physicians want children to have worthwhile experiences, they encourage rather than limit such participation.

Cooperative effort between physical educators and physicians has resulted in the formulation of a list of statements with respect to this problem:

- Orient the student, parent, and physician at an early date in regard to the objectives of the physical education program.
- Route all excuse requests through the school physician or nurse.
- Discard permanent and blanket excuses. Instead of being categorically excused, students can be assigned an appropriate physical activity in keeping with their special needs.
- Students involved in excuse requests should be periodically monitored as to their school performance. Parents, students, and appropriate school officials should be involved.
- Cooperation between the school physician, nurse, counselor, and the head of the physical education department needs to be emphasized, especially in the case of continuous and excessive excuse requests.

Grading and Assessment of Students

To determine whether students are meeting the objectives of the physical education instructional program, it is requisite that each instructor develop meaningful, effective, and efficient methods for assessment. This assessment will assist in determining a grade or mark for each student that may be reported by semester, term, trimester, or quarter, and usually becomes a part of the student's permanent record. Grades are a serious matter and not only serve to inform students about their class progress but also may be used to gain admission to college, for employment, to qualify for a scholarship, or to receive preferred automobile insurance rates. Students are proud of their grades!

For grades or marks to be meaningful, they should be based on established criteria (e.g., school or national norms), which are clearly

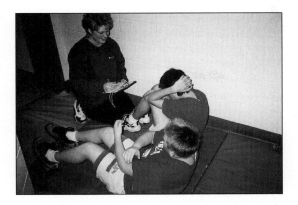

Assessment is crucial to the evaluation process.

presented to the student and class. A grade should reflect the student's progress toward these prescribed criteria as well as others designed by the student and the instructor. Grading is both a science and an art and should possess the following characteristics: (1) grades should be valid—they should reflect that which is intended (e.g., improvement in muscular strength or endurance, cardiovascular endurance, the defensive clear in badminton), (2) grades should be reliable—they should be a true reflection of the student's prowess and capability to perform, (3) grades should be objective—they should be based on well-defined criteria (e.g., making six out of ten foul shots reflects free throw proficiency), and (4) grades should be fair, equitable, and consistent—students performing at similar levels should receive similar grades.

Many different philosophies and methods are employed when it comes to the grading and assessment of students in a physical education class. Skill acquisition, performance, fitness level, effort, knowledge of the subject and an understanding of the rules are typical criteria. The teacher usually assigns a pass or fail, satisfactory or unsatisfactory, a grade from A through F, or sometimes a percentage. Regardless of the grading system employed, it is important to meet with each student in order to personalize grading. Finally, it is crucial to keep each student's yearly objectives and the teacher's and student's written assessments on file.

Who Should Conduct the Elementary School Physical Education Class?

The question of who should conduct elementary school physical education class has been discussed and debated for many years. Some educators suggest that the elementary classroom teacher instruct physical education classes, whereas physical education advocates prefer that a physical education specialist assume this responsibility. The regular classroom teacher usually possesses limited professional training in physical education. Most classroom teachers are not interested in teaching physical education. Furthermore, the renewed interest in physical education and the return to mainstreaming children with disabilities into the gym implies that qualified and certified teaching specialists should conduct these classes. The trend is toward more emphasis on movement education, perceptual motor development, physical fitness, lifetime skill acquisition, and other aspects of education with which the profession is concerned. There is an increased emphasis on looking to the physical education specialist for help and advice in planning and conducting the elementary school program, including both the regular and self-contained classroom. These developments have implications for sound in-service programs to assist the classroom teacher in doing a better job of delivering physical education.

In light of the present status of physical education in the elementary schools of this country, such recommendations as the following should be very carefully considered. Each elementary school should be staffed with a specialist in physical education. Although the classroom teacher may significantly contribute to the physical education program in primary school, factors such as the growth and developmental changes and interests taking place in boys and girls and the more complex specialized program that exists at this level make it imperative to seek the help of a specialist who possesses the ability, experience, and training required to meet the needs of the students. The physical education specialist and the classroom teacher should pool their experience to provide the student with an optimal learning environment. Each professional has much to contribute and should be encouraged to do so to reach the fullest potential of each student.

Dressing and Showering

The problem of dressing and showering is not so pertinent at the elementary level where the age of the participants and type of activities usually do not require special dress and showering. Some junior high, middle, and senior high schools require physical education uniforms. Reasons for this include safety, uniformity, and name identification. Those programs that do not require physical education uniforms request that students wear comfortable, safe clothing without zippers and buttons.

In the interests of comfort and good hygiene practices, ample time and provisions should be made for showering, drying off, and dressing. At the junior and senior high levels where no towel service is provided, many students choose not to shower. At this age, choices are important, and although showering may not be mandatory, it should be encouraged and its healthy benefits reinforced. Therefore schools should make special provisions for secure, clean, attractive places to dress and shower. Such places should be convenient to the physical education areas, be comfortable, and afford privacy. Although boys and girls are becoming increasingly accustomed to using group showers, many still prefer private showers. In the interests of these individuals as well as those students with disabilities, such facilities should be provided. When possible, there should also be a towel laundering service and hair drying facilities for the convenience of the students. Attractive and convenient showering facilities will lead more students to take advantage of this healthful practice.

Records

Records are essential in keeping valuable information regarding the participants' welfare. Records also are essential to efficient program planning and management. They should, however, be kept to a minimum and should be practical and functional. They should not be maintained merely as busy work and for the sake of filling files.

Some of the records should be concerned directly with the welfare of the participant and others with certain programmatic and administrative variables.

- Records that concern the health status, the cumulative physical education record, attendance reports, grades, and accident reports are of prime value.
- Health records are essential. They contain information on the most current medical examination, health appraisal, health counseling, and any other data pertaining to the person's health and medical status.
- The cumulative physical education record should contain information about activity participation, physical fitness appraisals, growth and development status, and other pertinent information concerning the student's participation in the physical education program. If a student has a disability, the student's IEPs should be on record.
- There should be special records for attendance, grades, and any other unique occurrences bearing on the participant that are not a part of other records.
- A year-end assessment for each student should be maintained.
- If a student is involved in a physical education class accident, a full account of the circumstances surrounding the accident should be recorded. Usually special forms are provided for such purposes.
- Management records should provide general information and equipment records, including a list of the year's events, activities, records of teams, play days, sports days, recreational sports, events of special interest, techniques that have been helpful, budget information, and any other data that would be helpful in planning for succeeding years. Memory often fails

Physical educators must be aware of safety and liability considerations.

over time, with the result that many good ideas are lost and many activities and techniques of special value are not used because they are forgotten. The computer is extremely valuable for this function.

■ There should be records of equipment, facilities, and supplies that show the current status, repair dates, inventory, new materials needed, and the location of various materials, so that they can be easily found. Records of such items as locker or basket assignments, lock combinations, and equipment checkout are essential to the efficient and effective running of a physical education program.

Computers in the Gymnasium

The use of computers and on-line information retrieval and delivery in the physical education and sport setting can serve to greatly enhance the programs. Software continues to develop for data management, ranging from Physical Best personalized fitness reports to individualized exercise and nutrition prescriptions to filmed simulation. Attendance reports, schedules, equipment status and inventory, facility usage, normative comparisons of fitness levels, and most record keeping and administrative functions can be facilitated with the computer. Computer-assisted instruction can also enhance student learning, from rules and safety to performance constructs. Educational technology is a tool and its use in the classroom and gymnasium must be prudently employed and managed (e.g., size and makeup of groups, type of feedback, task persistence) to ensure its effectiveness (Becker 1988).

Safety Considerations

The teacher of the instructional physical education program is responsible for the basic conduct of the program. This responsibility ensures that each class is operated in a safe, progressive, and prudent fashion. Teachers must provide a safe environment in terms of facilities, equipment, supervision, selection of age- and ability-appropriate activities, and an outline of proper procedures if an emergency should arise.

The teacher is also responsible for thoroughly explaining and demonstrating each activity, warning students of potential risks and hazards, employing proper and progressive skill techniques, requiring appropriate and safe dress, and providing prudent supervision to ensure optimal student learning and safety.

The teacher should be licensed and should maintain current certification (e.g., first aid, CPR, lifeguard training, coaching, adapted physical education) to ensure safety and provide the optimal learning environment for the students.

Each student should have a thorough medical examination by a qualified physician on file with the school or institution, and the physical education teacher should be aware of this health status (e.g., activity restrictions, medications, allergies).

Safety policies and procedures should be posted in several accessible and appropriate areas, and all students and their parents should be informed of these procedures and what is expected under emergency circumstances. Activity release and modified program forms, accident forms, and return-to-activity clearance forms should all be standardized and maintained in departmental records.

The teacher should also be encouraged to join the professional organization of his or her choice. Such organizations provide not only up-to-date professional information and ideas, but also insurance that covers potential professional injury and disability as well as legal liability.

CRITERIA FOR EVALUATING PHYSICAL EDUCATION INSTRUCTIONAL PROGRAMS

The following checklist (pp. 95-97) has been adapted for evaluating physical education instructional programs (Piscopo 1964). This checklist can serve to assess the instructional units or modules as well as the people who use (student) and deliver (teacher) the learning package. The checklist results can also guide both curriculum service and development of new instructional strategies.

SUMMARY

The instructional program in physical education is the place to teach such vital elements as skills, strategies, and understanding concerning the contribution of physical activity to total well-being.

Physical education instructional programs exist at all educational levels and in various community agencies and private volunteer organizations. Management guidelines exist for teaching physical education in all these settings as well as for selecting instructional aids, guides, materials, and appropriate educational technology.

Effective class operation facilitates successful management of a physical education organization.

Title IX affects the implementation of physical education instructional programs in all

Criteria for Evaluating Physical Education Instructional Programs

	Poor (1)	Fair (2)	Good (3)	Very Good (4)	Excellent (5)
Meeting Physical Education Objectives					
1. Does the class activity contribute to the development of physical fitness?	☐	☐	☐	☐	☐
2. Does the class activity foster the growth of ethical character and desirable emotional and psychosocial characteristics?	☐	☐	☐	☐	☐
3. Does the class activity contain recreational value?	☐	☐	☐	☐	☐
4. Does the class activity contain carryover value for later life?	☐	☐	☐	☐	☐
5. Is the class activity accepted as a regular part of the curriculum?	☐	☐	☐	☐	☐
6. Does the class activity meet the needs of *all* participants in the group?	☐	☐	☐	☐	☐
7. Does the class activity encourage the development of leadership?	☐	☐	☐	☐	☐
8. Does the class activity fulfill the safety objective in physical education?	☐	☐	☐	☐	☐
9. Do the class activity and conduct foster a better understanding of democratic living?	☐	☐	☐	☐	☐
10. Do the class activity and conduct cultivate a better understanding of and appreciation for exercise and sport?	☐	☐	☐	☐	☐

PERFECT SCORE: 50   ACTUAL SCORE: _____

	Poor (1)	Fair (2)	Good (3)	Very Good (4)	Excellent (5)
Leadership (Teaching Conduct)					
1. Is the teacher appropriately dressed for the class activity?	☐	☐	☐	☐	☐
2. Does the teacher know the activity thoroughly?	☐	☐	☐	☐	☐
3. Does the teacher possess adequate communication skills?	☐	☐	☐	☐	☐
4. Does the teacher project an enthusiastic and dynamic attitude in class presentation?	☐	☐	☐	☐	☐
5. Does the teacher maintain discipline?	☐	☐	☐	☐	☐
6. Does the teacher identify, analyze, and correct faulty performance in guiding students?	☐	☐	☐	☐	☐
7. Does the teacher present a sound, logical method of teaching motor skills, for example, explanation, demonstration, participation, and assessment?	☐	☐	☐	☐	☐
8. Does the teacher avoid the use of destructive criticism, sarcasm, and ridicule with students?	☐	☐	☐	☐	☐
9. Does the teacher maintain emotional stability and poise?	☐	☐	☐	☐	☐
10. Does the teacher possess high standards and ideals concerning his or her work?	☐	☐	☐	☐	☐

PERFECT SCORE: 50   ACTUAL SCORE: _____

Criteria for Evaluating Physical Education Instructional Programs—cont'd

	Poor (1)	Fair (2)	Good (3)	Very Good (4)	Excellent (5)
General Class Procedures, Methods, and Techniques					
1. Does class conduct yield evidence of preplanning?	☐	☐	☐	☐	☐
2. Does the organization of the class allow for individual differences?	☐	☐	☐	☐	☐
3. Does the class exhibit maximal activity and minimal teacher participation (e.g., proper emphasis on explanation and/or demonstration)?	☐	☐	☐	☐	☐
4. Are adequate motivational devices such as teaching and audiovisual aids effectively utilized?	☐	☐	☐	☐	☐
5. Are student leaders effectively employed when appropriate?	☐	☐	☐	☐	☐
6. Does the class start promptly at the scheduled time?	☐	☐	☐	☐	☐
7. Are students with medical excuses from regular class supervised and channeled into appropriate activities?	☐	☐	☐	☐	☐
8. Is the class roll taken quickly and accurately?	☐	☐	☐	☐	☐
9. Are accurate records of progress and achievements maintained?	☐	☐	☐	☐	☐
10. Are supplies and equipment quickly issued and stored?	☐	☐	☐	☐	☐

PERFECT SCORE: 50   ACTUAL SCORE: _____

	Poor (1)	Fair (2)	Good (3)	Very Good (4)	Excellent (5)
Student Conduct					
1. Are the objectives of the activity or sport clearly known to the learner?	☐	☐	☐	☐	☐
2. Are the students interested in the class activities?	☐	☐	☐	☐	☐
3. Do the students enjoy their physical education class?	☐	☐	☐	☐	☐
4. Are the students familiar with organizational procedures such as those for taking roll and obtaining excuses?	☐	☐	☐	☐	☐
5. Are the students appropriately dressed for the class activity?	☐	☐	☐	☐	☐
6. Does the class exhibit a spirit of cooperation in learning new skills?	☐	☐	☐	☐	☐
7. Do students avoid mischief or horseplay?	☐	☐	☐	☐	☐
8. Do students shower when the nature of the activity requires?	☐	☐	☐	☐	☐
9. Do lesser skilled students receive as much opportunity to participate as higher skilled classmates?	☐	☐	☐	☐	☐
10. Do students show respect for the teacher?	☐	☐	☐	☐	☐

PERFECT SCORE: 50   ACTUAL SCORE: _____

Criteria for Evaluating Physical Education Instructional Programs—cont'd

	Poor (1)	Fair (2)	Good (3)	Very Good (4)	Excellent (5)
Safe and Healthful Environment					
1. Is the area large enough for the activity and number of participants in the class?	☐	☐	☐	☐	☐
2. Does the class possess adequate equipment and/or supplies?	☐	☐	☐	☐	☐
3. Are adequate shower and locker facilities available and readily accessible?	☐	☐	☐	☐	☐
4. Is the equipment and/or apparatus clean and in good working order?	☐	☐	☐	☐	☐
5. Does the activity area contain good lighting and ventilation?	☐	☐	☐	☐	☐
6. Are all safety hazards eliminated or reduced where possible?	☐	☐	☐	☐	☐
7. Is first aid and safety equipment readily accessible?	☐	☐	☐	☐	☐
8. Is the storage area adequate for supplies and equipment?	☐	☐	☐	☐	☐
9. Does the activity area contain a properly equipped room for use in injury or illness or for rest periods?	☐	☐	☐	☐	☐
10. Does the activity area contain accessible toilet facilities?	☐	☐	☐	☐	☐

PERFECT SCORE: 50   ACTUAL SCORE: _____

Criteria	Perfect Score	Actual Score
Meeting physical education objectives	50	_____
Leadership (teacher conduct)	50	_____
General class procedures, methods, and techniques	50	_____
Student conduct	50	_____
Safe and healthful environment	50	_____
TOTAL	250	_____

educational institutions receiving federal assistance. To ensure compliance, all physical educators should be familiar with Title IX guidelines.

The adapted/developmental physical education program is designed to meet the needs of all individuals with disabilities. Public Law 101-476 (IDEA) mandates educational services for all students, usually in either the adapted physical education setting or in the regular physical education program and P.L. 101-336 (ADA) assures accessibility to appropriate facilities.

Management matters that relate to physical education instructional programs include scheduling, grading and assessment, class size, differentiated staffing, selection of appropriate activities, grouping of and instructional strategies for participants, and student involvement.

Selected management problems related to the instructional programs involve whether physical education should be required, who should deliver physical education at the elementary level, whether to permit the substitution of other activities for physical education, and the awarding of credit. Other issues to be addressed include the development of policies concerning class attendance, excuses, grading and assessment, dressing and showering, record keeping and emergency and safety considerations.

SELF-ASSESSMENT ACTIVITIES

These activities will assist students in determining if material and competencies presented in this chapter have been mastered:

1. You are a member of a physical education staff in a high school in which the instructional program is under attack by the faculty. It has been suggested that the program be abolished. Prepare a brief defense of the instructional physical education program that describes its nature, scope, and worth in the educational process.

2. You have been invited to speak to the PTO in your community on the topic, "The role of physical education in the community." Prepare a speech that describes the role of physical education and present it to your class.

3. Develop a model for a high school instructional physical education program and discuss how Title IX legislation has influenced your model.

4. Compare how traditional physical education instructional programs have been conducted with respect to students with disabilities and how they should be conducted as a result of inclusion or mainstreaming and IDEA.

5. Develop a list of principles for physical education instructional programs that would serve as guides for each of the following: scheduling, time allotment for classes, class size, instructional loads, uniforms, taking roll, activity offerings, grouping, and student involvement.

6. You are a director of a school physical education program and have been assigned by the superintendent of schools to plan an adapted physical education program for the entire school system. Prepare the plan you will submit to the superintendent, including the objec-

tives you will strive to achieve, the guidelines you will follow, and the activities to be offered.

7. You are a physical education faculty member and have been selected by your college to see that IDEA and ADA is fully implemented in your department. Prepare a plan that will ensure that your school physical education program complies.

8. Develop an emergency policy for the conduct of a junior high physical education program.

9. Form a team of four students and together list the pros and cons of showering at the high school level. Have the team develop a plan for implementing showering procedures at the high school level.

REFERENCES

1. Becker, H. 1988. *The impact of computer use on children's learning: What research has shown and what it has not.* Baltimore, Md.: Center on Elementary Schools, Johns Hopkins University.
2. Carroll, J.M. 1994. *The Copernican plan evaluated; The Evolution of a revolution.* Phi Delta Kappen. 76 (20), 105–113.
3. Clement, A. 1988. *Law in sport and physical activity.* Indianapolis: Benchmark Press.
4. Jensen, C.R. 1992. *Administrative management of physical education and athletic programs.* Philadelphia: Lea and Febiger.
5. Johnson, R.T., R. Bjorkland, and M.L. Krotee. 1984. The effects of cooperative, competitive, and individualistic student interaction patterns on achievement and attitudes of the golf skill of putting. *Research Quarterly for Sport and Exercise* 55:129–134.
6. National Consortium for Physical Education and Recreation for Individuals with Disabilities (NCPERID). 1995. *Adapted physical education standards, 1995.* Champaign, Ill.: Human Kinetics.
7. Piscopo, J. 1964. Quality of life: first priority. *The Physical Educator* 21:162.
8. Prentice, W.E. 1997. *Fitness for college and life.* 5th ed. St. Louis: Mosby–Year Book.
9. Singer, J.D. 1985. 10th anniversary of P.L. 94-142: A visionary law that has worked. *Education Week,* February 27.
10. Stein, J.U. 1971. A clarification of terms. *Journal of Health, Physical Education, and Recreation* 42:63.
11. Weber, M. 1980. Title IX in action. *Journal of Physical Education and Recreation* 51:20.

SUGGESTED READINGS

Allen, R.R. and T. Reuter. 1990. *Teaching assistant strategies: An introduction to college teaching.* Dubuque, Iowa: Kendall/Hunt.

Provides coverage concerning teaching roles, responsibilities, interpersonal relationships, creating learning environments, and assessment. Also included are tips on lecturing, leading class discussion, and facilitating student learning.

Dunn, J.M. 1997. *Special physical education.* 7th ed. Dubuque, Iowa: Brown & Benchmark.

Presents valuable information about managing the learning environment, learning developmental patterns, and understanding the myriad disabilities that physical educators will be involved with. It also includes lists, guidelines, and organizations and associations for physical education and recreational and competitive sports.

Glover, D.R., and D.W. Midura. 1992. *Team building through physical challenge.* Champaign, Ill.: Human Kinetics.

IMPACT II/The Teachers Network. 1996. *Teachers' guide to cyberspace.* New York: IMPACT II/The Teachers Network.

Provides information concerning innovative classroom projects as well as using the Internet and creating home pages.

Pangrazi, R.P., and V.P. Dauer. 1995. *Dynamic physical education for elementary school children.* Needham Heights, Mass.: Allyn and Bacon.

Provides a thorough view of elementary skills and activities for both physical education and recreational sports. Also offers curriculum and management concepts.

Payne, G.V., and L.D. Isaacs. 1991. *Human motor development: A lifespan approach.* Mountain View, Calif.: Mayfield.

Presents a conceptual view of motor development throughout the life span. Provides various assessment suggestions as well as managerial considerations regarding curriculum, computer utilization, and instructional strategies.

Rink, J.E. 1998. *Teaching physical education for learning.* 4th ed. St. Louis: WCB/McGraw-Hill.

Promotes teaching practices that make a difference in the learning of students. Guidelines and suggestions offered will help preservice and experienced teachers in their instructional roles. Task complexity and difficulty, learner readiness, and relatedness of sequential learning experiences are considered. Helps students become competent teachers by improving their skills and effectiveness in achieving desirable goals. Identifies the major components of the instructional process and describes, analyzes, and interprets the instructional process in light of the teacher's role.

Sherrill, C. 1993. *Adapted physical education, recreation, and sport: A multidisciplinary approach.* Dubuque, Iowa: Brown & Benchmark.

Provides valuable information for the professional physical educator working in adapted or developmental physical education. Practical strategies and desirable activities for specific populations are provided. Covers areas such as teacher qualifications, competitive sports, and physical education for persons with disabilities. Sets forth guidelines for areas such as program development and financial support.

Smith, T.K., and N. Cestaro. 1992. Saving future generations—The role of physical education. *Journal of Physical Education, Recreation and Dance,* 63(8): 75–79.

Provides a view of lifetime physical education for secondary school curriculum.

U.S. Consumer Product Safety Commission. 1992. *Handbook for public playground safety.* Washington, D.C.: U.S. Consumer Product Safety Commission.

Provides a resource guide for playground areas, facilities, equipment, and maintenance. Includes a section concerning parks and recreation for persons with disabilities.

U.S. Department of Education. 1994. *The goals 2000: Educate America Act—Launching a new era in education.* Washington, D.C.: U.S. Government Printing Office.

Willgoose, C.E. 1984. *The curriculum in physical education.* Englewood Cliffs, N.J.: Prentice Hall.

Discusses the curriculum of physical education in various educational levels against a background of societal needs, educational foundations, student characteristics, and research findings. Also discusses curriculum planning, program organization, the curriculum guide, individualizing physical education, and curriculum evaluation.

chapter 4

Recreational Sports: Intramural, Fitness, Open, and Sport Club Programs

---

Instructional Objectives and Competencies To Be Achieved

After reading this chapter the student should be able to

- Define *intramural, fitness, open,* and *sport club programs* and name the objectives each is designed to achieve.

- Prepare a list of policies that, if followed, will enable a person to organize and manage intramural, fitness, open, and sport club programs.

- Understand the roles played by various managerial personnel in conducting intramural, fitness, open, and sport club programs.

- Discuss how intramural, fitness, open, and sport club programs are administered in elementary schools, junior

high or middle schools, secondary schools, colleges and universities, and other representative organizations.

- Organize various types of competition for intramural and extramural activities.

- Show the importance of and the procedures for managing sport clubs, corecreation, and programs for faculty and for persons with varying disabilities.

- Discuss the importance of open or self-directed recreational activities.

---

hapter 3 discussed basic instructional physical education programs, one of the components of a well-rounded offering for students in schools and for members of other representative organizations. This chapter discusses the second component, the intramural, fitness, open, and sport club programs, which are often referred to collectively as recreational sports. By tradition, the term *intramural* denotes programming and competition "within" the institution, whereas the

term *extramural* depicts competition with "outside" schools. Sport clubs fall in between the two definitions. Recreational sports offer competition and other types of physical activities for individuals of all levels of skill and ability. A 1996 recreational sports student interest survey at a Big Ten institution revealed that 50 percent of the students participated in fitness activities. The survey indicated heavy interest in intramurals and open play (28 percent each), while sport clubs attracted about 10 percent of the students polled. In universities and colleges, as discussed in chapter 2, intramural, fitness, open, and sport club activities are usually organized into a department separate from physical education. This separation is also the case in some secondary and elementary schools, whereas in other schools, recreational sports programs are considered an extension of the physical education program.

Recreational sports make up that phase of a physical education program in a school, college, industry, or other representative organization that is geared to the abilities and skills of the entire student body or all the members of the organization. Recreational sports consist of voluntary participation in games, sports, fitness, open, outdoor, self-directed, and other activities. Recreational sports offer intramural activities within a single school or institution as well as extramural activities such as play days, festivals, and sports days that bring together participants from several institutions.

A sport club program is usually devoted to one activity, such as tennis, skiing, volleyball, or mountain climbing, and it encourages students and other individuals to participate at all levels of skill. Clubs compete within their own ranks as well as with other outside clubs. Sport clubs may be managed by members of the organization, such as students in schools and colleges, or by the central management of the organization. Members, advisors, or community volunteers usually provide instruction and coaching. Clubs are popular in schools and colleges as well as in other organizations. Many communities have tennis, swimming, running, hiking, racquetball, riding, and other types of clubs.

Intramurals were started many years ago as a result of student initiative in schools and colleges. At first they received little central administrative notice or support and were poorly organized. However, as student interest grew, the demand for departmental control kept pace. In 1913, intramural sports came under faculty control at the University of Michigan and Ohio State University. Since that time, intramurals, extramurals, and sport club programs have continued to grow and develop and in most educational institutions today are under the management and direction of fully trained professional personnel. The National Intramural-Recreational Sports Association (NIRSA) (formerly the National Intramural Association founded by Dr. William Wesson at Dillard University in New Orleans) was formed in 1950 and is considered the major professional organization concerning the conduct of recreational sports. Its *NIRSA Journal* is published three times per year.

RECREATIONAL SPORTS PROGRAMS

Objectives

The objectives of recreational sports programs are an indication of why such programs have expanded greatly throughout the country. These objectives are compatible with the overall objectives of physical education and also with those of education in general.

The objectives of the programs may be classified under four headings: (1) health and fitness, (2) skill, (3) psychosocial development, and (4) recreation.

Recreational sport is an integral part of the university community.

Health and Fitness

Recreational sports activities contribute to the physical, social, and emotional health of the individual. They contribute to physical health through participation in activities offering healthful exercise. Such fitness components as muscular strength, agility, flexibility, cardiovascular endurance, speed, and body control are developed and enhanced. Recreational sports contribute to psychosocial health through group participation and working toward achievement of group goals. Participation also contributes to emotional health by helping a person achieve self-confidence and improve his or her self-concept. It is estimated that nearly half the students at colleges and universities are involved with health- and fitness-related recreational sports activities that range from aerobics to weight training.

Skill

Recreational sports activities allow every individual to display and develop his or her skills in various physical education activities. Through specialization and voluntary participation, recreational sports offer individuals the opportunity to excel and to experience the thrill of competition and the satisfaction of open or self-directed activity. Most individuals enjoy activities in which they have developed skill. Recreational sports help participants develop proficiency in group activities in which each person is grouped according to skill, thus providing for equality of competition, which helps guarantee greater success and enjoyment. These programs also enable many persons to spend leisure time profitably and happily.

Psychosocial Development

Opportunities for psychosocial development are numerous in recreational sport activities. Through many social contacts, coeducational experiences, and playing on and against other teams, desirable qualities are developed. Individuals learn to subordinate their desires to the will of the group; they also learn fair play, courage, cooperation, group loyalty, social poise, discipline, and other desir-

Participation in recreational sports activities offers many opportunities for psychosocial development.

able traits. Participation in such a program is voluntary, and people who desire to participate under such conditions will do so by group codes of conduct. These experiences offer training for citizenship, adult living, and human relations.

Recreation

Recreational sports programs help participants develop an interest in many sports and physical education activities; this interest carries over into adult living and provides the basis for many happy leisure hours. These programs also provide excellent recreational activities and support groups during school days, when idle moments have the potential to foster less than desirable behavior. It is crucial that recreation opportunities be accessible not only to user groups but also to individual consumers, who have their own personalized agendas.

RELATION TO BASIC INSTRUCTIONAL AND HIGHLY ORGANIZED ATHLETIC PROGRAMS

Recreational sports activities and interscholastic and intercollegiate sports are integral phases of the total sport program in a school or college. This total sporting package includes the intramural and extramural programs, sport clubs, and varsity sport as well as the basic instructional physical education program. Each makes an important contribution to the achievement of educational and physical education objectives. It is crucial to maintain a proper balance so that each program phase enhances and does not restrict the others.

The basic instructional program in physical education is viewed by many physical educators as the foundation for recreational and competitive sports programs. The instructional program includes teaching such fundamentals as skills, concepts, rules, and strategies. Recreational sports programs provide opportunities for all students and others to employ these concepts, skills, and strategies in games and contests that are usually competitive. This part of the total Physical Activity and Sport Continuum is sometimes referred to as the laboratory, where the individual has an opportunity to experiment and test what has been learned in the physical education program.

Whereas recreational sports are for everyone, varsity sports are usually for those individuals who are highly skilled in sport-specific activities. The intramural phase of the recreational sports program is conducted on an intrainstitutional basis, whereas extramurals and varsity sports are conducted on an interinstitutional basis.

Very little conflict should exist between these two phases of the sports program if the facilities, time, personnel, finance, and other factors are apportioned according to the degree to which each phase achieves the desired outcome rather than the degree of public appeal and interest stimulated. One phase should not be designed as a training ground for the other. It should be possible for a person to move from one phase to the other, but this should be incidental rather than planned.

If conducted properly, each phase of the program can contribute to the other, and through an overall, well-balanced sports program, the entire student body or all members of an organization will gain appreciation for physical activity and sport and the great potential it has for improving physical, mental, psychosocial, and emotional growth (Espinosa 1994).

The philosophical model that was shown in figure 3-1 illustrated the placement of recreational sports within the province of physical activity. This triangular shaped model depicted an interdependence and a building of skills from the basic instructional physical education level to the recreational sports level and, finally, to the level of varsity and elite competition. This model conveyed the philosophy that instruction and opportunity in school and community recreation programs are basic to the other programs and that recreational sports skills are essential to producing the high-level skills found in varsity and elite play.

The diamond shaped model in figure 4-1 is presented because of its implications for viewing

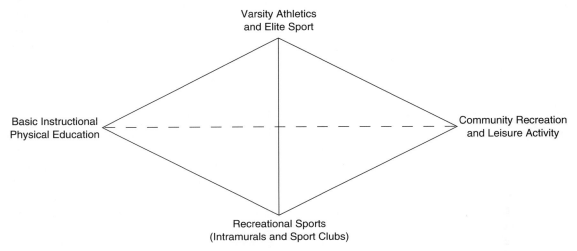

Figure 4-1. A modern conceptualization of the interaction of school and community physical education and sport.

the phases of the physical education program as both interdependent and equal. It establishes each phase as independent of the others. Recreational and varsity sports are placed close to each other because each is related to the other more closely than are leisure activity and basic physical education instruction. Community recreation is included in the model because of its contribution to recreational and varsity sport activities, both of which have as a primary objective the satisfaction derived from participation.

Although the basic physical education and recreational sports programs in a school or college are designed for every student, in practice they generally attract beginning students or those with moderate levels of skill. The highly skilled person usually finds a niche in the club sport or varsity program. This system has its benefits in that it is an equalizer for competitive structuring. In some cases further recreational sport skill divisions (e.g., "Jag" leagues, co-rec, first division, Division I) may be instituted.

MANAGEMENT PERSONNEL

Many management personnel are needed if a recreational sports program is to be a success. Some key persons involved are the director, student leaders, student directors and unit managers, recreational sports council members, and officials.

The Director

Many larger schools, colleges, corporations, and other organizations have established the position of director of recreational sports. In some cases other titles are used. The director is responsible for establishing programs, securing adequate funding, involving the community, and evaluating the success of the program. Some of the more specific duties of the director include planning programs; organizing tournaments and other forms of competition; supervising the maintenance of facilities, equipment, and supplies; attending and planning sports council meetings; interpreting the program to the membership, the management, and the public in general; supervis-

ing the program in action; preparing budgets; and evaluating the worth of the program.

Place in Management Structure

The director or person in charge of recreational sports in an elementary, junior high, middle, or secondary school is usually responsible to the director of physical education or athletics and activities. In some schools, these various components are not all under the same department.

At small colleges, the recreational sports department might also fall under the control of a director of physical education or athletics and in some instances, a student activities director. These program administrators usually appoint one person to manage the entire campus recreational sports program of which intramurals, fitness, open, and sports club activities are integral parts. In many schools, partial responsibility for recreational sports activities is delegated to students themselves.

In most larger colleges and universities, recreational sports departments maintain separate divisions, equal to the physical education or athletic divisions, and receive the same considerations concerning staff members, finances, facilities, equipment, supplies, and other departmental essentials. The department is usually headed by a director well schooled in physical education and sport or recreation management. Working with the director (when conditions warrant) should be associate and assistant directors, supervisors, student managers and assistants, and other staff members as needed, depending on the size of the organization. There should also be an adequate number of trained officials and support staff.

Student Leaders

Student involvement in all phases of education has been steadily increasing. Involvement in the management of recreational sports has been happening in high schools and on college campuses since the 1850s. Student leader roles may range from serving as board members to being managers, office assistants, coaches, and officials. For example, many colleges have drop-in centers where student supervisors are available to establish programs, reserve equipment, and arrange additional hours for the gymnasium or swimming pool. Some schools have student assistants who also supervise recreational sports activities.

Student Directors and Unit Managers

In some school programs, the director of recreational sports appoints an upper-level student who has been involved with the program to be student director. This student director may have such responsibilities as contacting officials, working with managers, issuing supplies, and scheduling.

Student unit managers have an important responsibility because they are in charge of a particular sport or activity. They usually work closely with the team captains and manage supplies and equipment, team rosters, and entry sheets; notify teams of the time and date of contests; and clarify eligibility rules.

Recreational Sports Council Members

An important feature of the overall management of a recreational sports program is a recreational sports council, which is usually an elected body with representatives from the participants, central administration, and recreational sports staff. The council is influential in establishing policy and practices for a broad recreational sports program. The council assists and advises the person in charge as well as the staff members. In some

Recreational sport provides students opportunities to participate and promote fair play through officiating.

cases, the council plays an important role in the decision-making process. Councils usually consist of representatives from the various participating units who disseminate information to the participating teams or individual membership. The council also helps make decisions about program operation and potential fee structures and serves as a sounding board for ways in which the program may be improved.

Officials

Excellent officials are necessary for a quality recreational sports program. They should have special qualifications, including a knowledge of the activity, the participants, the goals of the program, and the organization's philosophy of competition. Some of the responsibilities of the managers of the recreational sports program are to find sources for competent officials and then to recruit, select, and train them so that they enhance the program. Some of the duties performed by officials are to have game equipment ready before the contest, see that accurate score sheets are prepared, check for any safety hazards, prepare accident reports if needed, and officiate the game or activity objectively and impartially. Some institutions put officials through training sessions, supervise them during the playing season, and evaluate their performance after the season is over. Whereas most colleges pay their officials, elementary and secondary schools usually do not have the budget to provide compensation. Many schools seek voluntary help from students, staff, parents, and community workers; these volunteers need close supervision and should be offered some in-service training.

POLICIES AND PROCEDURES FOR ORGANIZATION AND MANAGEMENT

A list of policies and procedures governing the various features of the program should be in writing and well publicized, perhaps in handbook form. NIRSA possesses a large database and serves as an excellent resource for this undertaking (NIRSA 1996).

Policies and procedures for recreational sports should be developed in at least the following areas: student involvement in program organization and management, health and welfare of all participants, activities that meet the interests and needs of the participants, officiating, coaching, protests, eligibility standards, fees, forfeits, postponements, point systems, and awards. Policies and procedures concerning user groups, guest fees, rental structure, noise, food consumption, key control, equipment control, travel, and facility use should also be on record. The health and safety of the participants must be a top priority, and policies concerning emergency procedures should be well publicized.

MANAGEMENT CONCERNS IN K–12 SCHOOLS

The management of recreational sports at the elementary, junior high, middle, and secondary school levels presents some problems that are peculiar to these programs. In many colleges and universities, students live in dormitories and on campus, but students in K–12 systems do not have such living arrangements. Some students in K–12 systems have after-school jobs or have to catch a bus to take them home and cannot stay after school to participate in recreational sports. College students are more often able to participate because they are not faced with such problems, at least in institutions with dormitory living. Also, many times the parents of elementary, junior high, middle, and secondary school students do not see the value of recreational sports and so do not encourage their children to participate after school. College students, on the other hand, usually make their own decisions. Another problem faced by managers of K–12 recreational programs is the lack of facilities. Most schools have limited gymnasium and outdoor space. Varsity sports are often given priority in the use of these facilities, which causes a hardship on the recreational sports program. The question of financial and human resource support also exists in many schools, but recreational sports, especially at the junior high, middle, and high school levels, are clearly on the "hot zone" list for many school districts.

In light of these problems, managers of school recreational sport programs need to be creative when trying to initiate such programs. Some schools, for example, form partnerships with other schools, community parks and centers, YWCA, YMCA swimming pools, and Boys' and Girls' Clubs to provide facilities that meet the programmatic needs of their students (Jaundris 1980).

MANAGEMENT CONCERNS FOR COLLEGES AND UNIVERSITIES

Recreational sports have grown so large on the college campus that they present a different pattern of concerns and challenges than recreational sports in the K–12 school setting. It is estimated that 40 percent to 80 percent of college students participate in recreational sports. Despite this increase in participation, finances remain a prime concern. Most programs' primary sources of revenue are institutional funds and student fees. A trend toward decreasing institutional funding has challenged many programs to create alternative sources of funding (e.g., opening facilities to the public, providing instructional classes, operating sport camps).

Facility development, however, remains alive and well—one just has to visit Georgia Tech, Miami University (Ohio), University of Georgia, Tulane University, Texas A&M University, or the universities of Minnesota, Illinois, or Arizona, to mention a few that have invested in architectural showcase facilities. Furthermore, with the development of new and refurbished facilities, myriad opportunities exist for qualified and well-trained professionals to provide leadership in recreational sport management.

ORGANIZATIONAL CONSIDERATIONS

The organization of a recreational sports program involves selecting activities, scheduling, determining eligibility, establishing awards and point systems, maintaining records, planning health and fitness assessments, financing, and directing publicity and promotion.

Activities

The activities constituting the recreational sports program determine the amount of resulting par-

ticipation. It is therefore important to select the most appropriate activities. The following are recommended management guidelines that will help in selecting activities:

- Activities should reflect the needs and interests of the students or the members of the organization. These may include faculty and staff. Annual institutional needs assessments should be initiated each year.

- Activities should be selected in accordance with the season of the year and local conditions and influences.

- Coeducational recreational activities and recreational activities for students with varying disabilities should be provided.

- The activities included in the school physical education program should be coordinated with the activities included in the recreational sports program, which could serve as a laboratory experience for physical education.

- Many desirable activities require little special equipment and do not require long periods of training to prepare the participant for appropriate playing condition.

- Consideration should be given to such recreational activities as field trips, rock climbing, canoeing, backpacking, hiking, camping, bicycling, orienteering, and other outdoor pursuit activities.

- Activities should be selected with special attention to the ability and safety of the participant.

Open, self-directed, or informal recreational sports activities should play a primary role when organizing a program. Indeed, this phase of recreational sports programming is the most popular and rapidly growing phase. Opportunities should be provided for students to come to a facility and work out without having to enter a competitive environment, particularly in light of the physical fitness and health movement and of today's stressful lifestyle. The Recreational Sports Composite Activities box illustrates some offerings that have been used successfully in various recreational sports programs throughout the nation.

Recreational Sports Composite Activities

Selected Individual Activities

Archery	Orienteering	Squash
Badminton	Paddle tennis	Swimming
Billiards	Physical fitness	Table tennis
Bowling	Racquetball	Tennis
Curling	Rock climbing	Track and
Cycling	Rodeo	field
Deck tennis	Rope climbing	Tumbling
Golf	Scuba diving	Weight
Gymnastics	Shooting	training
Handball	Shuffleboard	Wrestling
Horseshoes	Skiing (Nordic	
Karate	and Alpine)	

Selected Recreational Activities

Camping and	Hiking	Kayaking
cookouts	Horseback	Mountain
Canoeing	riding	biking
Cycling	Hosteling	Rifle
Dance	Ice skating	Roller skating
Figure skating	In-line	Rowing
Fishing	skating	Sailing

Selected Team Sport Activities

Baseball	Lacrosse	Swimming
Basketball	Roller	Team handball
Broomball	hockey	Touch (or flag)
Field hockey	Rugby	football
Touch football	Soccer	Track and field
Gymnastics	Softball	Volleyball
Ice hockey	Speedball	Water polo

Scheduling

Recreational sports activities schedules will depend on student needs, student and faculty availability, facilities, season of year, community support, and budget constraints.

One of the most popular and convenient scheduling times for schools is late afternoon, especially in the fall and spring. This time has proved best for many elementary, junior high, middle, and senior high schools. It is an economical time because lighting is not required, outdoor space is available, and faculty supervision is readily available.

Evenings have been used quite extensively at colleges, and this trend has followed in many high schools. This time is not recommended for elementary, junior high, or middle schools. Some schools that have flexible or block scheduling use these hours during the school day. The physical education class, however, should have priority and use of this period for intramurals or extramurals does not conform to the standards set by the profession. Some schools have satisfactorily used free periods, activity periods, club periods, and even before-school hours for recreational sports programs when facilities were available.

The noon hour has also been utilized in some schools, especially in elementary, junior high, middle, and secondary schools and particularly in rural schools in which students do not go home or off campus for lunch. Because students will be active anyway, the lunch period offers possibilities in selected situations if overly strenuous activities are not offered.

Saturdays have also been used for recreational sports programs. Although the weekend is a problem in some localities because many individuals have to work or have planned this time to be with their families, weekend programs have worked successfully in many communities. On occasion, special days are set aside in many schools for field days, May Day for example, when all the students participate in a day or a half-day devoted entirely to the program's activities. These traditional sports days remain quite popular, especially at the K–6 level.

Recreational sports activities in the corporate setting, youth-serving agencies, and other organizations are scheduled at various times to meet the convenience of the members. Activities might be scheduled at any time during the day or night. With more single parents and more dual working-parent households, after-school activities have become standard rather than an experiment (Vannoy 1988).

Eligibility

A few simple eligibility rules are needed. These should be kept to a minimum, because the recre-

Recreational sports activities range from beach volleyball to broomball and from aerobic dance to outdoor pursuit.

ational sports programs should offer something for all students.

It is generally agreed that in schools and colleges players should not be allowed to participate in like activities when they are on the varsity team or squad. A student should be allowed to participate on only one team in a given activity during the season. Students, of course, are eligible to participate in more than one activity during a season (e.g., flag football, coeducational soccer) and should be enrolled in or affiliated with the school and conform to the institutional rules for participation.

Unbecoming conduct should be handled in a manner that is in the best interests of the individual concerned, the program, and the established code of conduct procedures. On occasion a student's eligibility may be forfeited for serious or repeated rules infractions.

Certain activities by their very nature are not appropriate for individuals with certain health problems. Therefore such individuals should be cleared by their personal physician or the school health department before being allowed to participate.

Several states have instituted policies linking academic achievement and attendance of students with their eligibility to participate in extracurricular activities (Bridgman 1985). However, some controversy has developed about whether a student should be denied the right to participate in such activities because of poor grades. In some cases, state officials have threatened to challenge such action in the courts.

Trophies and awards play an integral part in many programs.

Awards

There are arguments for and against granting awards for recreational sports involvement. Some recreational sport administrators argue that awards stimulate interest, serve as extrinsic incentive for participation, and recognize achievement. Some argue that awards make the program more expensive and that typically a few individuals capture most of the awards. Leaders who oppose awards also stress that there should be no expectation of awards for voluntary, leisure-time participation and that it is difficult to present awards on the basis of all factors that should be considered. Their belief is that the intrinsic joy and satisfaction received through participation are reward enough.

Research indicates that approximately four out of five recreational sports programs give awards. Awards, if presented, should be inexpensive, such as medals, ribbons, certificates, plaques, cups, or letters. Letters, pins, cups, medals, and similar awards have been used most frequently in K–12 schools, whereas trophies and plaques are given more extensively at colleges, universities, and in other organizations. A popular and relatively recent trend is the practice of giving T-shirts as awards. T-shirts can be imprinted with a school or recreational sports logo and provide excellent publicity for the program.

Point Systems

Many recreational sports programs have a cumulative point system figured on an all-year basis, which maintains interest and enthusiasm over the course of the school year and encourages greater participation.

An optimal point system should stimulate wholesome competition, sustain interest, and conform with the objectives of the total program. The point system should be readily understood by all and easy to manage. Under such conditions, points should be awarded on the basis of contests won, championships gained, standing in a league or order of finishing, participation, fair play, and contribution to the objectives of the program.

A point system might be based on the following items:

Each entry, 10 points

Each win, 2 points

Each loss, 1 point

Forfeit, –5 points

Each team championship, 10 points

Second-place team championship, 6 points

Third-place team championship, 3 points

Each individual championship, 6 points

Second-place individual championship, 4 points

Third-place individual championship, 3 points

Being homeroom or team representative, 10 points

Each meeting attended by homeroom or team representative, 2 points

Protests and Forfeitures

Procedures should be established in advance so that all persons involved know what the rules are when a protest is made and when forfeitures of contests take place. The circumstances under which protests and forfeitures will be acted upon, the decision-making process, and the penalties that will be assessed should be clearly set forth. An attempt should be made to have established policies that help prevent and discourage protests and forfeitures, because a great deal of time and effort are involved in such actions, and they also frequently result in bad feelings and negative public relations (Mueller and Reznik 1979).

Records

Efficient management of the program will necessitate keeping records. These records should not be extensive but should contain the information needed to determine the worth of the program and the progress being made.

Such records allow for comparison with other similar organizations. They show the degree to which the program is providing for the needs of the entire membership, the extent of participation, and retention and adherence rates. They track the activities that are popular as well as those that are struggling. They focus attention on the best units of competition, needs of the program, effective management procedures, and leadership strengths and weaknesses. Record keeping is an important phase of the program that should not be overlooked.

Use of Computers in Recreational Sports

Recreational sports can be managed much more efficiently using some of the versatile software now available for the computer. Virtually all information pertaining to the recreational sports program can be managed through computer programming. Names, addresses, telephone numbers, health status, entry fee information, eligibility, dropout rates, wins, losses, facility and team scheduling, and yearly point accumulation can all be recorded on computer. Computer literacy is requisite for all future managers in order to ensure maximal efficiency, accuracy, and effective use of time, thereby rendering better service to students and other clientele (Ross 1995).

Medical Examinations

Medical examinations should be required of all participants as a safeguard to their health as well as legal protection for the program. In some schools, this requirement is handled through annual school medical examinations and at other schools, through personal medical examinations given before a seasonal activity starts. The health status of all participants must be of the utmost importance for all managers of recreational sports programs.

Finances

The monies involved in recreational sports programs are raised in various ways. Because these programs often make more contributions to educational objectives than other parts of the educational program, they should be financed out of board of education and central administration funds just as other phases of the institution are financed.

Another method of financing programs that has proved satisfactory in some high schools and colleges incorporates offsetting the cost of running the programs by using a portion of the regular student activity fee that may also include the school newspaper, dramatics, the interscholastic or intercollegiate athletic program, and various student organizations. This method provides funds in proportion to the student enrollment and can be anticipated for future budget forecasting.

Other methods of financing used by some organizations include the use of varsity sport gate receipts, equipment rental, required participant or user entry fee, and special fund-raising projects such as sports nights, carnivals, and corporate sponsorship drives. Some argue that such practices discourage persons from participating and that requiring special projects to raise money should not be necessary for such a valuable phase of the institution. As mentioned previously, revenue generation and self-sufficiency have become vital in the conduct of recreational sport programs.

Publicity and Promotion

Members of an organization and the general public must understand the role of recreational sport programs, the individuals they service, the activities offered, and their objectives. Such information should be disseminated to the appropriate individuals through a well-planned and properly timed publicity and promotion campaign.

Newspapers and other print and electronic media should be used to provide appropriate space and publicity for the program and its activities. Brochures, bulletin boards, posters, and the school or organization's newspaper or newsletter can help focus attention on the program. Notices can be prepared and sent home to K–12 parents. A handbook can be prepared that explains the various aspects of the total program and can be distributed to all who are interested. Record boards and display cases can be constructed and placed in conspicuous settings. Clinics and workshops can be conducted on the various sports. Orientation talks and discussions can be held in school and college assemblies and at other gatherings. Special days can be slated with considerable publicity, and catchy slogans such as "It Pays to Play" can be adopted. Good publicity and promotion will result in greater student participation and better public understanding and support.

At Downers Grove (Illinois) North High School, where forty activities are offered each year, the managers utilize various promotional ingredients to publicize their program. These include a *Weekly Trojans Intramural Report,* T-shirts for champions, team uniforms paid for by local merchants, pictures of winners on the Recreational Sport Bulletin Board, community-oriented events such as the Trojan mile, and an annual Intramural Champions Pizza Party.

PATTERNS OF ORGANIZATION

Recreational Sports Programs in the Elementary School

The recreational sports programs in the elementary school should be outgrowths of the physical education program. They should consist of a broad variety of activities including stunts, rhythmic activities, relays, and tumbling. They should be suited to the developmental ages and interests of children at this level and should be carefully supervised (Humphrey 1994). The younger children in the primary grades probably will benefit most from simple games, lead-up activities, and low-organizational and cooperative games. In the upper elementary grades, more advanced activities can take place on both intragrade and intergrade bases (see the Suggested Program of Activities for Elementary Schools box). These programs should also be broadly based, varied, and progressive. Special field days and theme days, such as the Olympics

Suggested Program of Activities for Elementary Schools

Fall and spring

Beat the runner	Longball
Bicycle distance race	Playdays
Bocce	Prisoner out
Cosom hockey	Relays
Cooperative games	Rope jumping
Capture-the-flag	Soccer
Dodgeball	Softball
Endball	Speedball
Fitness day	Stealing sticks
Flag football	Tetherball
Foursquare	Track and field
Hopscotch	Wiffleball
Kickball	

Winter

Badminton	Ice skating
Basket shooting	Martial arts
Basketball	Newcomb
Battleball	Parachute
Bowling	Relays
Cageball	Rhythms
Cooperative games	Rope climbing
Cosom bowling	Shuffleboard
Cosom hockey	Tug-of-war
Dodgeball	Tumbling
Frisbee	Volleyball
Gym scooters	Wiffleball
Gymnastics	Wrestling

Elementary school recreational sports should be fun and well supervised. Crest View Elementary School, Brooklyn Park, Minn.

and the Pan-American Games, can add an international educational component to the program.

Guidelines for recreational sports programs in the elementary school follow.

- A basic instructional offering geared to the needs, interests, and growth and developmental levels of primary school children is prerequisite to and foundational for recreational sport programs.
- Qualified leadership should be provided, characterized by competencies involving understanding the physical, mental, emotional, and social needs of the child.
- Competition should involve only those children who are developmentally compatible (e.g., maturity, size, and ability).

- Cooperative and team-building games and large-muscle activities should be integral parts of the program.
- In the elementary school, recreational sports competitions should be limited to grades 4 through 6. Grades kindergarten through 3 should focus on the basic instructional physical education program, which should provide sufficient organized activity.
- Desirable health, physical, social, and emotional outcomes for students should be the goal of recreational sport programs.
- Tackle football and other dangerous contact activities should not be permitted.
- Program planning should involve students, parents, administrators, and the community.

Recreational Sports Programs in the Junior High or Middle School

The junior high and middle schools provide a setting in which many students develop a keen interest in sport. This is a time of limitless energy, physiological change, and immense psychosocial challenge. A full concentration of challenging recreational sports activities should be made available for all students who are not involved in seasonal interscholastic competition. In fact, many professional groups favor recreational sports programs at this level and are opposed to high degrees of competition. Activities conducted after school

(see the Suggested Activities for Junior or Middle and High Schools box) should provide the student with the opportunity to develop skills, gain self-confidence, have fun, socialize, gain recognition, develop self-worth, and break down cliques as well as racial and gender stereotypes.

Suggested Activities for Junior or Middle and High Schools

Team sports

A	Basketball	W	Gymnastics	A	Speedball
S	Baseball	W	Ice hockey	FS	Team handball
W	Broomball	FS	Kickball	F	Touch (or flag) football
A	Dodgeball	W	Ringette	S	Track and field
S	Fieldball	A	Soccer	F	Tug-of-war
FS	Field hockey	S	Softball	W	Volleyball

Individual and dual sports

A	Aerobic dance (varying levels of impact)	W	Gymnastics	A	Rope climbing
		A	Handball (1-wall)	F	Rowing
FS	Archery	FS	Horseshoes	A	Shuffleboard
A	Badminton	A	Jogging	A	Table tennis
A	Basketball free throw and field goal shooting	FS	Paddle tennis	FS	Tennis
		A	Paddleball	A	Tetherball
A	Bounce ball	FS	Paddle tetherball	FS	Track and field
A	Bowling	A	Quoits	AW	Tumbling
FS	Cross country	A	Racquetball	W	Wrestling
W	Deck tennis				

Corecreational activities

A	Badminton	F	Flag football	W	Skiing (Alpine, Nordic)
A	Bicycling	FS	Golf	W	Snow-boarding
A	Bowling	FS	Horseshoes	W	Swimming
FS	Canoeing	W	Ice skating	A	Table tennis
A	Dance (social and folk)	FS	Kayaking	FS	Tennis
W	Deck tennis	FS	Roller skating	FS	Track and field
		A	Shuffleboard	AW	Volleyball

Club activities

A	Bicycling	FS	Fishing	FS	Rock climbing
S	Canoeing	FS	Golf	FS	Roller skating
A	Dance (social, folk, square, modern)	A	Hiking	FS	Sailing
		W	Ice Skating	A	Tumbling
		A	Karate		

Special events

S	Baseball	FS	Field day	WS	Relay carnival
FS	Softball	A	Fitness day	FS	5K Fun Run
WA	Basketball skills contest	FS	Track and field meet		

F, fall; W, winter; S, spring; A, all seasons.

Skiing is a popular seasonal recreational pursuit at the middle school level.

The program should be well structured, properly supervised and managed by the school's physical education teachers, and student-run. Challenges by homeroom, grade, neighborhood, academic interest area, or school club are often used as motivators for maximal student participation. Weekends, lunch hours, and special event days featuring faculty challenges should not be overlooked as a means of building school pride as well as healthful, wholesome, physically active lifestyles that, it is hoped, will carry over into adulthood. The program should also be open to all students with any type of special need regardless of disability or physical limitation, and provision should be made for inclusion versus exclusion.

Recreational Sports Programs in the High School

At the senior high level, recreational sports should continue the pattern that has been laid down at the junior high or middle school level (Hammitt and Hammitt 1985; Jaundris 1980). Recreational sport activities should be varied and should focus on skill development, fun, building positive self-images, cooperation, and friendly challenges and competition as well as setting a positive tone for lifetime participation. At this

Intramural inner tube water polo. Lyons Township High School, La Grange, Ill.

level, activities can be conducted not only at noon, during prescribed activity hours during the day, and in the afternoon, but also in the evenings. The activities should cut across age, grade, and gender barriers, although wholesome rivalries by grade still seem to permeate the high school environs.

Personnel for the conduct of recreational sports programs should be well-trained professionals. Sound, creative leadership is needed if the programs are to prosper. Each school should be concerned with developing a plan in which proper supervision and guidance are available for after-school hours. Recreational sport clubs may be initiated to help train students to take an active role in the planning and conduct of the high school program. Qualified officials are also a necessity to ensure safe, equal, and wholesome competition. Facilities, equipment, and supplies should be apportioned equitably for the entire recreational sports program. No part of any group or any program should monopolize facilities and equipment, and a cooperative effort of the school and community is crucial to having a first-class high school recreational sports program.

Recreational Sports Programs in Colleges and Universities

College and university recreational sports programs offer an ideal setting for both men and women to participate in a wide range of physical activity (Henderson and Bialeschki 1991). These programs range from individualized activity such as weight training to a full complement of team and individual sports, from corecreational endeavors to carnival or special event days, and from aerobic dance to outdoor pursuit. The recreational sports center on a college or university campus is a place to gather, work out, and socialize and should offer a wide range of physical activity for the entire university community. It is a place that can and should bring a sense of community to the institution.

An example of one recreational sports department's mission statement reflects its commitment to the total educational process. They serve universities and colleges by

- Providing facilities for academic units and intercollegiate athletics

- Offering abundant opportunities for student employment and student development
- Cultivating interest and teaching skills in active leisure pursuits
- Increasing knowledge of wellness and physical fitness
- Promoting healthy lifestyle behaviors
- Providing facilities and programs that encourage interaction among members of the university community
- Introducing members of the public to university facilities and programs
- Hosting state, national, and international sports competitions and special events
- Making the university more attractive to both prospective and current students, faculty, and staff

One rapidly developing area of growth in recreational sports programming is sports clubs. These organizations provide participants with opportunities for high-level competition in many different activities. The University of Minnesota offers a wide range of opportunities that may be available for the college sport club participant (table 4-1). Many club sports, ranging from flag football to soccer and volleyball, sponsor national championship competitions. Championships and sponsorships seem to be the wave of the future.

Sport clubs, however, are only one component of the college and university recreational sport program. Intramurals (e.g., competitive A, B, and C leagues; recreational and corecreational leagues), extramurals, fitness (e.g., aerobics, lap swimming, weight training, running), faculty and staff leagues, and even summer sport camps are integral parts of the contemporary college recreational sports scene.

Open or self-directed recreation, in which individuals choose to play tennis, racquetball, squash, pick-up basketball, cycle, and so on, on their own is also growing in popularity and deserves the attention of recreational sport managers. Activities for men, women, graduate students, staff, faculty, family, and guests as well as corecreational sports, fitness assessments, coun-

seling, and outdoor and instructional activities are all delicately woven into the collegiate recreational sports endeavor (table 4-2). Safety, health status, eligibility, responsibility for the conduct of the program, and funding and facilities continue to be the salient issues to be addressed by sound management.

At many colleges and universities, student involvement in the management process is integral and ranges from the formulation of recreational sport constitutions to officiating. Many colleges still structure much of their recreational sport programming around units such as residence halls and dormitories, the Greek system (fraternities and sororities), or academic departments, although the traditional practice of competitions between teams that are arbitrarily formed at registration under labels ranging from the Nerds to M*A*S*H still seems to permeate recreational sports programs.

Recreational Sports Programs in Other Organizations

Recreational sports programs play a major role in many organizations outside the educational domain. For example, the corporate setting offers many recreational sport leagues for employees in a variety of sports as well as other physical activities. In many instances, softball diamonds, basketball and volleyball courts, jogging areas, platform and lawn tennis courts, swimming pools, fitness centers, and even golf courses are provided. Some companies compensate employees for joining nearby public-sector fitness clubs, and in other situations, businesses subcontract their recreational sports commitment to a private-sector enterprise. Employees usually take an active role in these programs, which contributes much to their morale, health, and physical and mental well-being; research attests to the increased work productivity and reduction of absenteeism.

Recreational sports programs may also be found in YWCAs/YMCAs, Boys' Clubs, Boy Scouts, Girl Scouts, Girls Inc., community centers, park and recreation districts, church organizations, military installations, and other youth- and adult-serving agencies. In addition to the

Table 4-1. University of Minnesota Sport Clubs

Team	Men's	Women's	Coed	Club Intercollegiate	Recreational Instructional
Aikido			✓		✓
Aikido, Yoshinaki			✓		✓
Archery			✓	✓	✓
Badminton			✓	✓	✓
Ballroom dance			✓		✓
Bowling	✓	✓		✓	✓
Boxing	✓			✓	✓
Crew	✓	✓		✓	
Cycling			✓	✓	✓
Fencing	✓	✓		✓	✓
Gymnastics			✓		✓
Ice hockey	✓	✓		✓	✓
Judo	✓	✓		✓	✓
Juggling					✓
Karate, int'l league			✓		✓
Karate, Japanese			✓		✓
Karate			✓	✓	✓
Kung Fu, Chinese			✓	✓	✓
Kung Fu, Vo Lam			✓		✓
Lacrosse	✓	✓		✓	✓
Marlinettes (synchro)		✓		✓	✓
Rodeo	✓	✓		✓	✓
Rugby	✓	✓		✓	
Sailing	✓	✓		✓	✓
Scuba			✓		✓
Ski, Alpine	✓	✓		✓	
Ski, Nordic	✓	✓		✓	
Skydiving	✓	✓		✓	✓
Soccer	✓	✓	✓	✓	
Squash	✓	✓		✓	✓
Swim Club			✓		✓
Tai Chi			✓		✓
Tai Kwon Do			✓		✓
Team handball	✓	✓		✓	
Tennis	✓	✓		✓	✓
Ultimate Frisbee			✓	✓	✓
Volleyball	✓	✓		✓	
Water polo	✓	✓		✓	
Water ski			✓		✓
White-water Kayak/Canoe	✓	✓		✓	✓

Table 4-2. University of Tennessee Recreational Sports			
Men	**Women**	**Faculty/staff**	**Corecreation**
Fall			
Team			
Flag football	Flag football	Flag football	
Bowling	Bowling	Bowling	
Volleyball	Volleyball	Volleyball	Volleyball
Golf		Golf	Softball
Indoor soccer	Indoor soccer	Racquetball	
Outdoor soccer	Outdoor Soccer	Tennis	
3-on-3 basketball	3-on-3 basketball	Turkey trot	
Wally ball	Wally ball	Free throw shooting	
3-on-3 football	3-on-3 football	Sand volleyball	
Individual and dual			
Racquetball	Racquetball		
Tennis	Tennis		
Golf	Golf		
Pass, punt, and kick	Pass, punt, and kick		
Turkey trot	Turkey trot		
Free throw shooting	Free throw shooting		
Table tennis	Table tennis		
Tennis classic	Tennis classic		
Spring			
Team			
Softball	Softball	Softball	Softball (5 male/5 female)
Tennis	Tennis		Tennis (2 male/2 female)
Track and field			
Racquetball	Racquetball		
3-point shoot-out	3-point shoot-out		
Basketball	Basketball		
Floor hockey	Floor hockey		
3-on-3 basketball	3-on-3 basketball	3-on-3 basketball	
Tug-of-war	Tug-of-war		
Sand volleyball	Sand volleyball	Sand volleyball	Volleyball (3 male/3 female)
Mud volleyball	Mud volleyball		
Individual and dual			
Golf	Golf	Golf	Golf
Racquetball	Racquetball		
Bowling	Bowling		
Summer			
Team			
Softball	Softball	Softball	Softball (5 male/5 female)
3-on-3 basketball	3-on-3 basketball	3-on-3 basketball	
Sand volleyball	Sand volleyball	Sand volleyball	Sand volleyball (3 male/3 female)
		Golf (2 players)	Tennis (2 male/2 female)
Individual and dual			
Tennis	Tennis		
Golf (2 players)	Golf (2 players)		

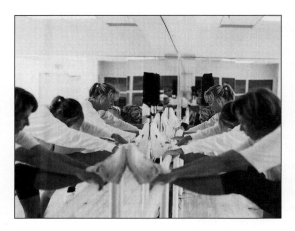

Open fitness is an important ingredient for many fitness centers, including hotels and convention centers.

organizations mentioned here, the NCAA and many sports federations and associations, such as those of golf and tennis, are also beginning to sponsor inter-city youth programs. Recreational sports represent an important part of many organizations' curricular and educational offerings.

The same types of formats for structuring multidimensional and creative physical activity and sport competition employed in schools and colleges are used by these nonschool organizations.

COMPETITIVE STRUCTURING

There are several different ways of structuring competition within most recreational sports programs. Three of the most common are leagues, tournaments, and meets. These modes of structuring take many forms, with league play popular in the domain of team sports, elimination tournaments used to a great extent after culmination of league play, and meets held to recognize the closure of a season or year of sports activity.

Various types of tournament competition have been employed extensively in recreational sports; descriptions of some competitive tournament structures will be included here.

The round robin tournament is probably one of the most widely used and one of the best types of competitive structures, because it allows for maximal play. It is frequently used in leagues, where it works best with no more than eight teams. Each team plays every other team at least once during the tournament. Each team continues to play to the completion of the tournament, and the winner is the one who has the highest percentage, based on wins and losses, at the end of scheduled play (figure 4-2, *A*).

The single, or straight, elimination tournament is set up so that one defeat eliminates a player or team (figure 4-2, *B* and *C*). This structure does not allow for maximal play; the winners continue to play, but the losers drop out. A team or individual is automatically out when it or he or she loses. However, this form of organization is the most economical from the standpoint of time in determining the winning player or team. Usually a drawing for positions takes place, with provisions for seeding the better players or teams on the basis of past performance. Such seeding provides more intense competition as the tournament moves toward the finals. Under such a structure, byes are awarded in the first round of play whenever the number of entrants does not fall into units to the power of two (i.e., 2, 4, 8, 16, 32, 64, etc.). The number of byes is determined by subtracting the number of entrants from the next higher power of two. Figure 4-2, *B* has 13 entrants (16 − 13 = 3 byes). Although such a tournament is a timesaver, it possesses a flaw because it does not adequately select the second- and third-place winners. The second or third best player may meet the best player, and eventual winner, in the first round of play, which often dampens the enthusiasm for the remaining games or matches in the tournament. Another weakness is that the majority of participants play only once or twice in the tournament.

The double elimination tournament (figure 4-3a, *A*) avoids some of the weaknesses of the single elimination because it is necessary for a team or individual to lose twice before being eliminated. This is also characteristic of various types of consolation elimination tournaments that permit the player or team to play more than once (figure 4-3a, *B*).

In some consolation tournaments, all players or teams who lose in the first round and those

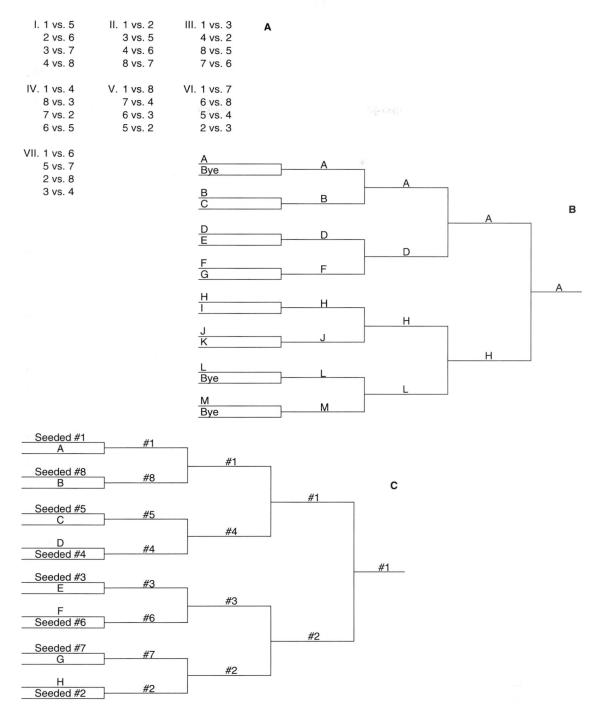

I. 1 vs. 5   II. 1 vs. 2   III. 1 vs. 3   **A**
   2 vs. 6   3 vs. 5   4 vs. 2
   3 vs. 7   4 vs. 6   8 vs. 5
   4 vs. 8   8 vs. 7   7 vs. 6

IV. 1 vs. 4   V. 1 vs. 8   VI. 1 vs. 7
   8 vs. 3   7 vs. 4   6 vs. 8
   7 vs. 2   6 vs. 3   5 vs. 4
   6 vs. 5   5 vs. 2   2 vs. 3

VII. 1 vs. 6
   5 vs. 7
   2 vs. 8
   3 vs. 4

Figure 4-2. A, Round robin tournament for eight teams. Team 1 remains fixed while the remaining teams rotate clockwise. B, Single elimination tournament with 13 entrants. C, Single elimination tournament with seedings.

121

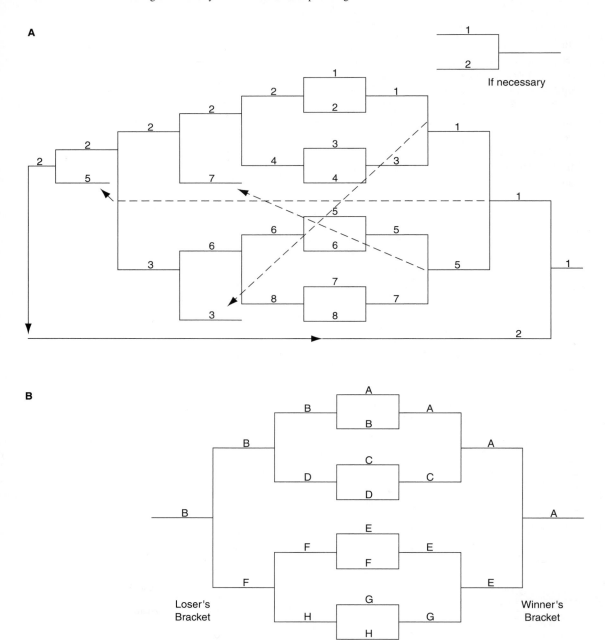

Figure 4-3a,b. A, Double elimination tournament. B, Single elimination tournament with consolation bracket.

who, because they received a bye, did not lose until the second round get to play again to determine a consolation winner. In other similar tournaments, any player or team who loses once, regardless of the round in which the loss occurs, is allowed to play again. Other tournaments include the Mueller-Anderson playback, in which the competitors continue to play until all places of finish have been determined in the tournament (figure 4-3b, *C*), and the Bagnall-Wild elimination tournament (figure 4-3b, *D*), which is a form of single elimination tournament that focuses on more accurately selecting the second- and third-place finishers. As was mentioned, the single elimination tournament sets up the possibility that the second or third best player is eliminated in an early round by the eventual winner. In the Bagnall-Wild, the players eliminated by each finalist participate in separate consolation tournaments.

The ladder tournament (figure 4-3b, *E*) adapts well to individual competition. Here the contestants are arranged in a ladder, or vertical,

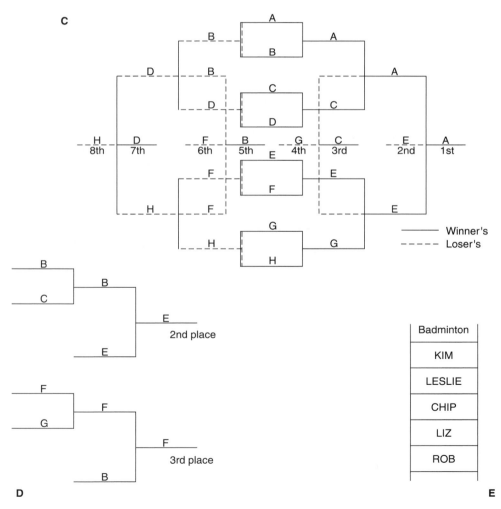

Figure 4-3c-e.   C, Mueller-Anderson playback. D, Bagnall-Wild brackets of a single elimination tournament. E, Ladder tournament.

formation, with rankings established arbitrarily or on the basis of previous performance. Each contestant may challenge the one directly above or in some cases two above, and if he or she wins, the names change place on the ladder. When a contestant loses to a challenger from below, he or she may not immediately rechallenge the winner, but must accept another challenge from below. This is a continuous type of tournament that does not eliminate any participants. However, it is not ideal because it may drag and interest may wane.

The pyramid tournament (figure 4-4) is similar to the ladder variation. Instead of having one name on a rung or step, several names are on the lower steps, gradually pyramiding to the top-ranking individual. A player may challenge anyone in the same horizontal row, and then the winner may challenge anyone in the row above.

The spider web tournament takes its name from the bracket design, which is the shape of a spider's web (figure 4-5). The championship position is at the center of the web. The bracket consists of five (or any other selected number) lines drawn radially from the center, and the participants' names are placed on concentric lines crossing these radial lines. Challenges may be made by persons on any concentric line to any person on the next line closer to the center. A player must defeat someone on his or her own level after losing a challenge in the immediate

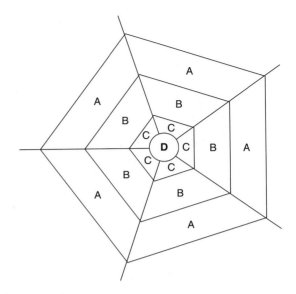

Figure 4-5. Spider web tournament.

inner tier of the web. This tournament provides more opportunity for competitive activity.

The type of tournament structure adopted should be the one deemed best for the unit, group, activity, or local interests. The goal should be maximal participation within facility and time constraints. Tournaments encourage participant interest and enthusiasm and are an important part of the recreational sports experience.

RECREATIONAL SPORTS CONSIDERATIONS

Recreational sport has the potential to make significant contributions to all levels of education (K–12 and college and university) as well as to the private and public sectors. In light of recent legislation, such as Title IX, IDEA, and ADA, special sensitivity is warranted and effort mandated to include opportunities for women and persons with varying disabilities as well as for other diverse populations. Recreational sports has led the way in opportunity for corecreational activities, and now recreational sports' overall objectives must be further extended. Objectives should include provisions for: (1) opportunities for both sexes as well as minorities and persons with disabilities (in the least restrictive environment) to

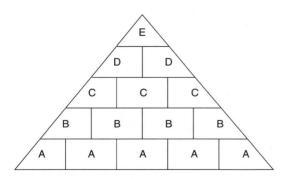

Any A may challenge any B.
Any B may challenge any C.
Any C may challenge either D.
Either D may challenge E.

Figure 4-4. Pyramid tournament.

Chess as a recreational activity. Division of Municipal Recreation and Adult Education, Milwaukee, Wis.

participate in wholesome play experiences, (2) cooperative experience through physical activity for all in order to enhance self-esteem and develop interdependence, (3) participants to enjoy themselves, develop friendships, improve personal skills, and gain mutual respect through both traditional and new activities, and (4) participants to gain the skills, information, and the support network needed for spending leisure hours constructively in wholesome physical pursuits.

The goal of having persons with disabilities participate in the least restrictive environment and to join the regular recreational sports program is challenging, to say the least. Programs such as "Special Friends" and "Unified Sports" (a program instituted by Special Olympics International) should be included. Special populations' participation in sports days, playdays, and invitational days—which have long been traditional intramural and extramural recreational sports ac-

tivities endorsed by AAHPERD and the National Association of Girls and Women in Sport—should also be encouraged.

At the college and university level, recreational sports managers should not forget graduate students (many older students are now returning to school), faculty and staff, and those individuals' families and significant others. The immediate community should also be included. Research suggests that an attractive recreational sport program assists in recruiting and retaining both faculty and students. Inclusion of significant others will contribute to sustained participation in physical activity throughout the life span. Certainly all managers of both physical education and recreational sport should not only address but actively promote such worthy inclusions (see the Checklist for Recreational Sports Programs box and the Recreational Sports Program Evaluation Checklist box on pages 126–128).

Checklist for Recreational Sports Programs

	Yes	No
1. Is the recreational sports program a normal outgrowth of the regular school program?		
2. Does the program have clearly stated objectives?	___	___
3. Does the program supplement the formal curriculum by increasing knowledge and skills?	___	___
4. Are recreational sports activities, including clubs, organized in terms of educational value rather than administrative convenience?	___	___
5. Does the administration set adequate policies to guide the program?	___	___
6. Have the aims and objectives of the program been determined?	___	___
7. Can any student participate?	___	___
8. Is a student limited to the number of recreational sports activities he or she may join?	___	___
9. Does each club have a constitution and bylaws that can guide students in the conduct of the organization?	___	___
10. Does recreational sports participation prepare the student for democratic living?	___	___
11. Do the activities help to develop school or organizational spirit?	___	___
12. Does the school schedule recreational sports activities so that they do not conflict with regularly scheduled school activities?	___	___
13. Does the school administrator support the program with adequate space, staff, and funds to carry on a worthwhile program?	___	___
14. Can a student discover and develop special attitudes and abilities through the recreational sports program?	___	___
15. Does the program offer opportunities for vocational exploration?	___	___
16. Is the individual student able to develop socially acceptable attitudes and ideals through the program?	___	___
17. Does the recreational sports experience provide situations that will contribute to the formation of improved behavior patterns in the student?	___	___
18. Do participants actively participate in program planning?	___	___
19. Are the projects and activities of the program initiated primarily by the students?	___	___
20. Do all the activities performed pertain to the program objectives?	___	___
21. Are the students allowed to select recreational sport activities according to interests?	___	___
22. Are students issued a calendar of events?	___	___
23. Does the school library make available books and periodicals needed by the program's participants?	___	___
24. Does the faculty advisor enlist the confidence of both boys and girls?	___	___
25. Is a faculty advisor willing to give time and thought to make the recreational sport, fitness, open, or club program a success?	___	___
26. Is a faculty advisor able to find his or her chief satisfaction in student growth and not in appreciation of personal efforts?	___	___
27. Does the administration of the school evaluate the program periodically?	___	___
28. Does the recreational sport program allow time for the evaluation of activities?	___	___

Recreational Sports Program Evaluation Checklist

A program can be evaluated in terms of the stated principles and objectives or according to prevalent acceptable standards.

How does the recreational sports program measure up to the acceptable minimum standards? By taking a few minutes to check off the items listed below, a quick evaluation can be made of the present status of the excellence of the program.

	Yes	No
Philosophy and objectives		
1. Is a written philosophy, mission statement, or a set of objectives available to the participants?		
Organization and management		
1. Is the director professionally qualified to manage the program?		
2. Does the director devote sufficient time per week to managing the program?		
3. Are participants included in the management of the program?		
4. Is there an advisory committee?		
Units of competition		
1. Are participants classified according to ability, age, height, or weight within the competitive unit?		
2. Within the basic unit, are participants permitted to choose the members of their teams?		
Program activities		
1. Does the director consult with the participants to make sure that their interests are of prime consideration in the selection of activities for the program?		
2. Are there both fitness and open or self-directed activities in the program?		
3. Are there both team and individual sports in the program?		
4. Are there at least five different sports making up the program?		
5. Do corecreational activities make up part of the program?		
6. Are there programs for persons with disabilities?		
Time periods		
1. Do the hours that participants are free receive top priority for scheduling?		
2. Is the noon hour used for programming?		
Methods of organizing competition		
1. Is the round robin tournament used whenever possible in preference to others?		
Point system of awards		
1. Is recognition of any kind given to the participants for their achievements?		
2. Is the award primarily for achievement instead of incentive for participants?		
Rules and regulations		
1. Are the rules defining such things as eligibility, health, safety, forfeits, postponements, and team membership distributed to all participants?		
2. Is the lack of fair play regarded as a rule violation?		
3. Is equipment provided for all activities offered?		
4. Is proper supervision required for all activities offered?		

Continued

Recreational Sports Program Evaluation Checklist—cont'd

	Yes	No
Publicity		
1. Is there a special bulletin board for recreational sports news and information?	____	____
2. Does a newsletter exist that carries recreational sports news and information?	____	____
Finances		
1. Does the organization provide funds for the operation of the program?	____	____

Rating scale

A yes answer must be given in each category if a program is to be considered good or excellent. Each Yes counts as 1 point.

Excellent	17 to 25
Good	14 to 16
Fair	11 to 13
Poor	10 or fewer

RECREATIONAL SPORTS PROGRAM PLANNING

One of the most important functions of the recreational sports manager is the continuous planning and evaluation of the program to see if its goals are being met. The program must also be evaluated in terms of budget and numbers of persons participating. In today's competitive climate, a program must be cost-effective or it faces the probability of being phased out.

Evaluation is a crucial component of the planning process of any well-managed organization. The planning process involves a number of steps or phases that can be modified for most management circumstances. The following planning process phases are offered for consideration.

A Mission or Vision of Accomplishment

This statement explains what the program should accomplish and how it fits into the conceptual and philosophical view of the organization.

Overview of the Situation

A managerial analysis of the conditions and complexities of the task serves as a guide to set realistic goals.

Specification of Goals

Goals must be realistic, reasonable, challenging, achievable, and quantifiable when possible (e.g., to increase the number of students with disabilities in the program from 16 to 50 participants). Goals may be long-range, intermediate, or short-term in nature. Growth, profitability, client satisfaction, retention, and social awareness are examples of areas in which organizational goals might be established.

Identification of Constraints

A description of the conditions and barriers that may hinder goal attainment, including alternative pathways toward goal attainment, should be outlined. Constraints may be human, technical, environmental, economic, informational, or sociopolitical.

Identification of Resources

Closely linked to the development of any plan of action is the establishment of information-gathering criteria to assist in the generation of sound ideas. Vital to this phase is research and input from consultants, students, staff, and community.

The Plan

For any plan to be effective, the manager needs to involve all the individuals (human resources) who

Recreational sport programs are attracting sponsors such as Schick, AT&T, Butterfingers, Cosmopolitan Magazine, and Nike.

are necessary for its implementation. Clearly defined tasks and roles, job descriptions and expectations, how the parts relate to the whole, timetables, cost, individual feelings, and direct input are vital to the plan.

Evaluation

Evaluation techniques will differ but generally should include (1) definition of the program goals; (2) data collection (e.g., number of participants, number of teams, games played); (3) an appraisal of players, coaches, officials, game scores, facility utilization, and so on; (4) recommendations from internal and external review groups; (5) consultant visitation; and (6) participant opinion and rating forms concerning the overall program.

On completion of the evaluation phase of the planning process, the recreational sports director and the program staff may want to revise, modify, or institute new programs to further meet the cognitive, psychomotor, sociocultural, and affective demands of the user group being served. The realization of the need for careful and prudent planning, as well as the total involvement of all recreational sports program participants, leads to sustained and successful programs.

SUMMARY

Recreational sports programs represent a very important component of the total educational process. They contribute to important qualities such as health, fitness, feelings of self-worth, skill, and social development. In addition, these programs provide an opportunity for all students to participate and interact on a voluntary basis. Activities should be selected that reflect and extend the basic physical education instructional program as well as student interests. The activities should be in consort with the laws of the land. The management of recreational sports programs at lower education levels is sometimes difficult because of a lack of transportation for students during after-school hours as well as a lack of facilities, finances, staffing, and parental support. To have a well-run program and to have the best interests of the students be served, the management of recreational sports should be concerned with items such as safety, supervision, health of participants, scheduling, awards, point systems, eligibility requirements, and officials. Many different types of tournaments can be employed in the recreational sports setting to increase the flavor of the competition. Programs should be carefully planned and evaluated periodically to determine if they meet the goals of the system in which they are housed and how they can be improved to better serve the clientele for which they have been established.

SELF-ASSESSMENT ACTIVITIES

These activities will assist students in determining if material and competencies presented in this chapter have been mastered.

1. Justify the role of intramural, fitness, open, and sport club programs, in terms of their objectives and activities, in the total educational plan of a school, college, or other organization.

2. You are the director of physical education in a high school, college, or other organization. You have been requested by your superior to develop a list of topics for a new recreational sports handbook for your organization. Prepare the topics in a table of contents format and submit them to your class for their critical evaluation.

3. Conduct a job analysis of the roles played by various management personnel involved with the recreational sports program of the college you are attending. Compare it with the personnel roles discussed in this chapter.

4. Develop what you consider to be a model sports club for an elementary school, high school, college, or large corporation.

5. Identify each of the following: round robin tournament, straight elimination tournament, ladder tournament, pyramid tournament, and double elimination tournament. Using one of these tournaments, prepare a hypothetical competitive league for 16 volleyball teams.

6. Describe the planning process you would employ for organizing a sailing club in your school.

7. Set up mock tournaments using single elimination, double elimination, and round robin formats. Determine a timeline or schedule for each tournament, the obstacles that may be faced with each structure, and the benefits offered by each format.

REFERENCES

1. Bridgman, A. 1985. Backlash: Its efforts to tie achievement with extracurriculars. *Education News,* 13 March.

2. Espinosa, C. 1994. Recrafting Programs: IM-Rec Sports and TQM (Total Quality Management). *NIRSA Journal* 18 (Winter): 18–20.

3. Hammitt, S.A. and W.E. Hammitt. 1985. Campus recreation activities—Planning for better use. *Journal of Physical Education, Recreation and Dance* 56:23.

4. Henderson, K.A. and M.D. Bialeschki. 1991. Girls' and women's recreation programming— constraints and opportunities. *Journal of Physical Education, Recreation and Dance* 62(1):55–58.

5. Humphrey, J.H. 1994. *Physical Education for the Elementary School.* Springfield, Ill.: Charles C. Thomas.

6. Jaundris, T. 1980. Possibilities and potentials— High school intramurals. *Journal of Physical Education, Recreation and Dance* 51(3):49.

7. Jones, T.R. 1971. Needed, a new philosophical model for intramurals. *Journal of Health, Physical Education, and Recreation* 43:34.

8. Mueller, C.E. and J.W. Reznik. 1979. *Intramural-recreational sports: Programming and administration.* New York: John Wiley and Sons.

9. NIRSA. 1996. *General and specialty standards for collegiate recreational sports.* Corvallis, Ore.: NIRSA.

10. Ross, C.M. 1995. Computers as a research tool: From on-line searches to statistical analysis. In *Valuing the Vision of Recreational Sports.* Corvallis, Ore.: NIRSA.

11. Vannoy, W. 1988. Latchkey intramurals. *Journal of Physical Education, Recreation and Dance* 59:82–84.

SUGGESTED READINGS

Davis, K.L. 1996. *The art of sports officiating.* Needham Heights, Mass.: Allyn and Bacon.
    Offers views on how to select, train, and maintain quality officials for your interscholastic, intercollegiate, and recreational sports programs.

Gibbs, R. 1995. The NIRSA natural high: An alcohol and other drug prevention program with promise. *NIRSA Journal* 20 (fall): 6–7.

Matthews, D.O. 1984. *Managing intramurals and recreational sports.* Champaign, Ill.: Stipes Publishing.

McLellan, R.W. 1984. Intramural-recreational programs—Selecting qualified coordinators. *Journal of Physical Education, Recreation and Dance* 55:57.
    Traces the roots of organized intramural sports programs and how they have become the recreational sports programs of today. Points out the many educational values of such programs.

NIRSA. 1993. *Instructional programming: A resource manual.* Corvallis, Ore.: NIRSA.
    Describes the general standards and procedures for certification, contracts, safety, liability, scheduling, and fee assessment as they pertain to recreational sports instructional programs. Goals, expectations, and evaluations as well as potential intradepartmental and interdepartmental conflict are discussed.

NIRSA. 1994. *Navigating the tides of change: Strategies for success.* Corvallis, Ore.: NIRSA.
    Presents a collection of papers ranging from assessment of recreational sports programs to leadership and building successful programs.

Rokosz, F.M. 1993. *Procedures for structuring and scheduling sports tournaments.* Springfield, Ill.: Charles C. Thomas.

Ross, J.G., C.O. Dotson, G.G. Gilbert, and S.J. Katz, 1985. Physical activity outside of school physical education. *Journal of Physical Education, Recreation and Dance* 56:35–39.
Provides the results and cites national trends and patterns of physical activity participation for students outside the school physical education program. Discusses the amount of time spent in such places as community or youth sports organizations and the types and trends of activity available outside the school setting.

Roth, D., and S. Hudson. 1994. The Impact of the Americans with Disabilities Act on campus recreation. *NIRSA Journal* 18 (spring): 22–25.

Special Olympics International. 1989. *Special Olympics Unified Sports.* Washington, D.C.: Special Olympics International.
Presents an overview of Special Olympics International's integrated sports offerings and strategies.

Interscholastic, Intercollegiate, and Other Competitive Sport Programs

- -

Instructional Objectives and Competencies To Be Achieved

After reading this chapter the student should be able to

- Discuss the purpose of and the values derived from participating in competitive sport programs.

- Specify the duties performed by such key management personnel in competitive sport programs as the athletic director, coach, athletic trainer, and members of the sport council.

- Explain some of the management considerations involved in sport programs relating to scheduling, providing for the health and safety of participants, contracts, officials, transportation, game management, crowd control, protests and forfeitures, awards, and records.

- Understand some of the central issues involved in such management problems concerned with competitive sport

- as recruitment, eligibility, proselytizing, scouting, finances, and extra compensation for coaching.

- Describe the nature and scope of competitive sport programs in elementary, middle, junior high, and senior high schools, colleges and universities, and other organizations.

- Identify some of the key sports associations and the role they play in influencing organized sport competition in schools, colleges, and other organizations.

- Outline key provisions and issues of Title IX and gender equity concerning the conduct of interscholastic and intercollegiate sport.

- ▬

T wo primary components of the Physical Activity and Sport Continuum have been presented: the basic instructional physical education program and the recreational sports program, which included intramural, fitness, open, and sport club offerings. This chapter focuses on

competitive sport in schools, colleges, and other organizations.

Interscholastic, intercollegiate, and other organized sport programs represent an integral part of the total spectrum of human movement experience. In some cases involvement in competitive

132

sport programs evolves from active participation in school physical education and recreational sports as well as the myriad sport programs that are housed elsewhere in the community.

Competitive sports, with their appeal to all age-groups, should play an integral role in the movement experience and help achieve the goals that have been discussed in previous chapters. They should also aid individual growth and development, and help all participants realize their full potential.

The competitive sport program is usually designed for those individuals most competent in sport-specific endeavors. It is the domain of the most talented and highly skilled, and it receives more attention and publicity than most other phases of the Physical Activity and Sport Continuum. The reason for this attention is not that the competitive sport program is more important or renders a greater contribution; instead, the attention is largely the result of popular appeal. Print and electronic media, alumni, parents, and others discuss competitive sport in glowing terms, and it involves competition of one school or college against another. This competition increases public awareness and creates enthusiasm and often a spirit of rivalry, which seems to be pervasive as sport plays out its role in society. The competitive spirit is not only a local phenomenon, but is nationwide and indeed has worked its way to the international sporting scene.

Interscholastic and intercollegiate sport programs concomitantly have had more attendant difficulties than most other phases of the sport continuum. The desire to win and to generate revenue has resulted in some unfortunate practices, such as unethical recruitment procedures, altering transcripts to make players eligible, admitting students to colleges and universities who may be academically unqualified, and the relaxing of academic and behavioral standards for varsity athletes, not to mention substance abuse, violence, and player exploitation issues and concerns. Large stadiums and sports complexes that require huge capital outlay and substantial revenue for their upkeep have been constructed. Indeed, many collegiate and some school programs have been enticed off campus in hope for the big payday.

The challenge of providing sound educational programs in competitive or varsity interscholastic and intercollegiate sports is one that all physical education professionals recognize. The challenge can be met and resolved if physical educators and other professionals bring to the attention of administrators, the community, and the general public the true purposes of sports in their respective schools and institutions of higher education. A need exists for maintaining competitive sport programs within the school that meet the needs of everyone; that are professionally organized and managed with the welfare of the individual in mind; and that are conducted in a manner by which educational objectives are not compromised even when exposed to pressures from parents, alumni, community members, and the media.

THE ROLE OF SPORT IN SOCIETY

It is no secret that millions of Americans engage in competitive sport (more than six million young girls and boys participate in interscholastic sport)

The Hubert H. Humphrey Metrodome, home of the University of Minnesota football team.

NCAA champion Marty Morgan, University of Minnesota.

on a yearly basis. Serving as testimony to the status of sport in contemporary society are the facts that sport is a multibillion-dollar industry, that more than one tenth of the *World Almanac* is devoted to sport, and that more people watched the World Cup than watched Neil Armstrong take the first step on the moon. Indeed, 217 million Americans report some type of participation in sport.

Sport's magnetism has been chronicled and debated by many who concentrate their effort on sport-specific exploration of our limits and inner selves; however, most researchers contend that sport possesses the following societal functions:

Emotional release. Sport serves to release emotions and relieve stress, acts as a safety valve, and provides a catharsis to relieve aggressive tendencies.

Affirmation of identity. Sport offers opportunities to be recognized and to express one's individual qualities.

Social control. Sport provides a means of control over and containment of people.

Socialization. Sport serves as a means of socializing those individuals who identify with it.

Change agent. Sport results in social change and new behavior patterns and is a factor that may contribute to changes in the course of history (e.g., interaction of classes, upward socioeconomic mobility based on ability, Ping-Pong diplomacy, gender equity, the demise of apartheid).

Collective conscience. Sport creates a communal spirit that brings people together in search of common goals, such as building community.

Success. Sport provides a feeling of success both for the participant and for the spectator when a player or team with whom one identifies achieves. To win in sport is also to win in life, and winning seems to be glorified by all.

BENEFITS OF COMPETITIVE SPORT

The values of participation in competitive sports are discussed under the headings of physical fitness, sport skill and knowledge, individual development, social development, and sport in the global village.

Physical Fitness

Competitive sports contribute to physical fitness by developing organic vigor, cardiovascular and cardiorespiratory endurance, neuromuscular skill, muscular strength and endurance, flexibility, and agility as well as desirable psychosocial attitudes toward play, fitness, and exercise. To develop and sustain a high degree of physical fitness, the individual must voluntarily submit to a vigorous program of exercise. Perhaps the most powerful force capable of motivating a person to engage in strenuous training regimens is the desire to excel in the arena of competitive sport.

Sport Skill and Knowledge

To achieve success in sport, individuals must develop neuromuscular skills that will enable them to respond instantly and effectively in a competitive sport situation. The resulting skill development will enable individuals to successfully respond to situations requiring strength, endurance, speed, and coordination, and to fit their skills within the framework of the sport decision-making process.

Acquiring skill through sport also leads to a high level of proficiency and a further desire to engage in physical activity. Some research indicates that persons who participate in sports when they are young are more likely to lead physically active lives as they age. The development and mastery of physical skill holds many other benefits, such as feelings of accomplishment, recognition, and affiliation as well as contributing to a more positive self-image.

Individual Development

Self-realization, self-sufficiency, self-control, and self-discipline are individual qualities frequently developed through competitive sport experience. Self-image and self-confidence are also enhanced through comparison of one's competitive interaction with others.

Participation in competitive sports facilitates the development of leadership, cooperation, fair play, and loyalty. Furthermore, commitment, decision making, and self-worth seem to be enhanced through the rigors of the competitive sport process.

Varsity student-athletes gain valuable social skills.

Social Development

Competitive sport provides opportunities for competition, cooperation, and individualistic participation. Although competition is a part of life, at the same time life demands cooperation, self-sacrifice, and respect for other people (e.g., race, ethnicity, gender, age, disability). Competition, cooperation, and individualistic sport behaviors, therefore, must be interdependent. Sport provides a natural opportunity to achieve this multifaceted objective, because individuals must be both competitive and cooperative in some situations, whereas under other circumstances, the sport environment may require individualistic behaviors. Fairness, adherence to the rules of the game, the ability to accept defeat, gaining respect for others, and the love of the game continue to shape the player as the player shapes the game.

Sport in the Global Village

Since circa 776 B.C., sport has served to bring the world together, stop war, and open barriers often closed by geopolitics. Sport, if managed properly,

NCAA All-American Todd Yeagley, Indiana University. (Courtesy of Indiana University Instructional Support Services, Nick Judy, Photographer.)

Table 5-1. Arguments For and Against Interscholastic Sport Programs

Arguments For	Arguments Against
1. Involves students in school activities and increases interest in academic activities.	1. Distracts the attention of students away from academic activities.
2. Builds the responsibility, achievement orientation, and physical vigor required for adult participation in society.	2. Perpetuates dependence and immaturity and focuses the attention of students on a set of values no longer appropriate in industrial society.
3. Stimulates interest in physical activities among students in the school.	3. Relegates most students to the role of spectator rather than active participant.
4. Generates the spirit and unity necessary to maintain the school as a viable organization.	4. Creates a superficial transitory spirit subverting the educational goals of the school.
5. Promotes parental, alumni, and community support for all school programs.	5. Deprives educational programs of resources, facilities, staff, and community support.
6. Gives students opportunities to develop and display skills valued in society.	6. Applies excessive pressure on student-athletes.

From Coakley JJ: *Sport in society: Issues and Controversies,* ed 5, St. Louis, 1994, Mosby–Year Book.

can facilitate peace and understanding, create lifelong friendships, and bring nations together. The 1996 Atlanta Olympic Games brought more nations (197) together on the field of competition than the United Nations roll call. Educational institutions and other organizations such as Athletes in Action (AIA) are taking advantage of the international competitive experience. The hosting via home stays of international teams at local tournaments such as the USA Cup in Blaine, Minnesota; an enlarged competitive format such as the *PAC 10* men's and women's all-star basketball tour to Asia; intercollegiate ice hockey that will soon compete against university all-stars from Canada, Europe, and Japan; these examples all serve as further evidence that sport can bring together the "global village."

There are, however, critics of the competitive sporting process, and Table 5-1 offers some popular arguments for and against it.

MANAGEMENT PERSONNEL INVOLVED IN SPORTS PROGRAMS

Key management personnel involved in sports programs include the director of athletics, the coach, the athletic trainer, and members of the sport council. In addition, the following personnel

are also involved in sport programs, particularly at the college level: assistant or senior associate athletic director, academic counselor, sports information director, athletic business manager, facility director, travel coordinator, administrative assistant, fund raiser, physician, sport psychologist or educator, equipment manager, game manager, ticket manager, and coordinator of special events. For the purposes of this chapter, however, only the major sport management positions applicable to both high school and college competitive sport programs will be presented.

The Director of Athletics

The director of athletics implements the athletic policies as established by the state, school board, or institution. Responsibilities and duties of the athletic director include preparing the budget; employing and evaluating coaches (figure 5-1); purchasing equipment and supplies; marketing and promoting the program; scheduling; arranging for officials; supervising eligibility and health status requirements; arranging transportation; seeing that medical examinations, insurance coverage, and medical treatment are available and adequate; and generally supervising the total conduct of the program.

```
                        DEPARTMENT OF ATHLETICS
Name_____    SCHOOL DISTRICT NO. 48      Evaluator _____
                           Beaverton, Oregon
Assignment _____                               Date _____
                         COACH'S EVALUATION
```

COACH'S SELF-EVALUATION (To be completed prior to the start of coaching assignment.)

1. Statement of personal goals and/or program goals as they relate to your coaching
    assignment.

    _____

2. Statement of self-evaluation on applicable criteria relative to completion of goals
    statement. (To be completed at the conclusion of your coaching assignment.)

    _____

3. ATHLETIC COORDINATORS EVALUATION (To be completed subsequent to the coaching assign-
    ment then reviewed with the coach.)
    CODE: Scale of 1 to 5, with 5 highest competency. If blank, not applicable.

    A. Management   Circle one
        1. Care of equipment (issue, inventory, cleaning, etc.)   1 2 3 4 5
        2. Organization of staff   1 2 3 4 5
        3. Organization of practices   1 2 3 4 5
        4. Communication with coaches   1 2 3 4 5
        5. Adherence to district and school philosophy and policies
            (eligibility reports, inventories, budgets, rosters,
            insurance forms, and follow-up, scores reported)
        6. Public relations   1 2 3 4 5
        7. Supervision   1 2 3 4 5
    B. Skills
        1. Knowledge of fundamentals   1 2 3 4 5
        2. Presentation of fundamentals   1 2 3 4 5
        3. Conditioning   1 2 3 4 5
        4. Game preparation   1 2 3 4 5
        5. Prevention and care of injuries (follow-up with parents) 1 2 3 4 5
    C. Relationships
        1. Enthusiasm   1 2 3 4 5
            a. For working with students   1 2 3 4 5
            b. For working with staff (support of other programs) 1 2 3 4 5
            c. For working with academic staff   1 2 3 4 5
            d. For the sport itself   1 2 3 4 5
        2. Discipline   1 2 3 4 5
            a. Firm but fair   1 2 3 4 5
            b. Consistent   1 2 3 4 5
        3. Communication with players
            a. Individual   1 2 3 4 5
            b. As a team   1 2 3 4 5
    D. Performance
        1. Appearance of team on the field or floor   1 2 3 4 5
        2. Execution of the team on the field or floor   1 2 3 4 5
        3. Attitude of the team   1 2 3 4 5
        4. Conduct of coach during game   1 2 3 4 5
    E. Self-improvement
        1. Attends in-district meetings and clinics   1 2 3 4 5
        2. Attends out-of-district clinics   1 2 3 4 5
        3. Keeps updated by reading current literature   1 2 3 4 5
4. Review by Building Athletic Coordinator with Coach
    (District Athletic Coordinator will review all evaluations before
    forwarding to principal.)

    _____

5. To be placed on file with principal and forwarded to the Human Resources office
    with yearly teaching evaluation.

Original-Building Principal
  Canary-District Athletic Coordinator   _____
    Pink-Building Athletic Coordinator   Signed by Coach
    Gold-Coach
                                           _____
                                           Signed by Evaluator
```

**Figure 5-1.**  An example of a form for evaluating coaches.
```

The athletic director should be professionally trained and possess a background in physical education and sport. Qualifications might include a major in physical education with additional preparation in sport management and business. Experiences as a player, coach, or manager should also remain experiential requisites. Although the scope of duties and responsibilities might vary from school to university level and from Division III to Division I, the human, technical, conceptual, and leadership skills remain constant.

In a well-organized school, college, or other organization with a large sports program, the athletic director might work closely with a business manager whose responsibilities might include hiring and scheduling of officials, office personnel, travel, and security as well as keeping financial records, paying guarantees, and other contractual arrangements (e.g., insurance and media contracts, gate receipts, and guarantees).

The director of athletics in some complex Division I programs usually has an associate and assistants to help with such responsibilities as scheduling, staff supervision, eligibility, fundraising, marketing, budgets, insurance, purchasing, travel, Title IX compliance, and academic counseling. There typically is a sports information director (SID) who prepares media releases, develops brochures, and manages such areas as photography, media, and public relations.

Coaching offers a challenging and rewarding career for many individuals.

The Coach

One of the most challenging management positions within the Physical Activity and Sport Continuum is that of coaching. Indeed, there are more than 350,000 high school coaches, many of whom have no sport-related education. Many students who show exceptional skill in an interscholastic sport feel they would make good candidates for various coaching positions. They believe that because they have proved themselves outstanding athletes in high school, their skills will carry over into the coaching domain. This carryover, however, is not necessarily true. There is insufficient evidence to indicate that exceptional skill in sport will necessarily guarantee success in the teaching and coaching profession. Many qualities and properties—such as a thorough knowledge of the sport, educational degree, coaching license, professional attitude, and teaching prowess, combined with such personal characteristics as personality, intelligence, fairness, flexibility, integrity, honesty, leadership, and a sincere interest in working closely with youth and young men and women—must provide the foundation for coaching success.

Coaching should be recognized as a form of teaching. Because of the nature of the profession, a coach is in a more powerful position to affect participants than are most other members of a school faculty. Youths, in their inherent drive for activity and action and the quest for the excitement of sports competition, often look up to the coach and, in many cases, believe that the coach is a person to emulate. Coaches should recognize this role modeling concept and strive to instill such values as character, honesty, self-discipline, and integrity. Although a coach must be a student and an expert of the game, these other characteristics are equally important.

Coaching is regarded by many as a position of insecurity, political or parental jockeying, and a hot seat of psychosocial turmoil. On the other hand, coaching offers an interesting and satisfying career for many individuals who seem to become permanent fixtures on the sidelines. However, the coach should recognize the possibility of finding himself or herself in a situation in which the pressure to produce winning teams may be so great as to cause unhappiness, insecurity, job discomfort, and sometimes ill health. One need not look at a school like Notre Dame or into the professional ranks to examine these coaching concerns because they exist within every local community. Lopiano (1986) suggests that if the competent, ethical, and well-trained coach is the key to elimination of undesirable behavior for which sport is now being criticized, it seems obvious that the better organized we are in training this individual and the more reflective we are in employing a coach, the better our programs will be.

Brian Ivie, captain of the U.S. Olympic volleyball team, conducts a coaching education seminar.

Of the qualifications needed to function as a credible coach, four are paramount. First, the coach must be a good teacher who is able to teach the fundamentals and strategies of the sport. Second, the coach needs to understand the player, that is, how the person functions at a particular level of development, with a full appreciation of human growth and development, including psychosocial parameters. Third, the coach must understand the game; a thorough knowledge of techniques, rules, strategies, and tactics is basic. Fourth, the coach must possess a desirable personality and character. Patience, understanding, kindness, honesty, sense of right and wrong, courage, common sense, solid communication skills, cheerfulness, affection, humor, enthusiasm, and unending energy are imperative.

Many times the coach is working part-time at the school, and in many cases, men are coaching girls and young women. These situations present certain logistical problems and are further reasons why the contemporary coach must be a thorough professional in all regards.

Coaching Certification and Licensure

In some situations, the only qualification coaches possess is that they have played the game or sport in high school, college, or sometimes, as a professional. It is generally recognized, however, that the best preparation for a coach is training in physical education (Sage 1989). In light of this fact, many states as well as state athletics and activity associations are requiring, or at least strongly recommending that coaches, particularly at the precollege level, have some training in physical education or exposure to various educational coaching programs offered through a variety of delivery systems.

Standards for coaching certification have been identified by the NASPE (National Association for Sport and Physical Education), an association of AAHPERD, through their National Standards for Athletic Coaches. NASPE identified 37 standards that are grouped in the following domains:

- Injuries: prevention, care, and management.
- Risk management.

- Growth, development, and learning.
- Training, conditioning, and nutrition.
- Social/psychological aspects of coaching.
- Skills, tactics, and strategies.
- Teaching and administration.
- Professional preparation and development.

Coaches should be encouraged to seek training, even if certification or licensure standards have not yet been required by their particular state or institution. Many coaching federations, such as the United States Soccer Federation, the United States Volleyball Association, and The Athletic Congress, provide outstanding coaching licensure programs. Private concerns such as the American Sport Education Program (ASEP), the North American Youth Sport Institute (NAYSI), the National Youth Sport Coaches Association (NYSCA), the Program for Athletic Coaches Education (PACE), the National Federation Interscholastic Coaches Education Program (NFICEP), and Special Olympics International also provide excellent coaching preparation opportunities. Although the trend toward certification is increasing, the thorough training of all coaches remains essential for the health, safety, and enhanced performance of each athlete.

A recent survey of the 50 states and District of Columbia provides the following information regarding coaching certification and education:

- 9 states require all coaches to hold a valid teaching certificate.
- 5 states require only the head coaches to hold a teaching certificate.
- 8 states require only selected sport head coaches to hold a teaching certificate.
- 12 states reported that coaches must be exposed to minimal education course content.
- 6 states leave the decision up to the individual local school district.
- 11 states require neither a teaching certificate, coaching licensure, or educational course work.
- Some states, such as Nevada, require personal background checks.

Table 5-2 illustrates some of the various states' teaching and coaching certification and licensure requirements.

The University of Minnesota has instituted one of the most comprehensive coaching certification programs, details of which are included in Table 5-3.

The now defunct Association of Intercollegiate Athletics for Women (AIAW) recommended a code of ethics for coaches from which any coach may benefit (AIAW 1979). Ethical considerations for the coach include the following:

1. Respect each player as a special individual with unique needs, experience, and characteristics, and develop this understanding and respect among players.
2. Have pride in being a good example of a coach in appearance, conduct, language, and fair play and teach the players the importance of these standards.
3. Demonstrate and instill in players a respect for courtesy toward opposing players, coaches, and officials.
4. Express appreciation to the officials for their contribution and appropriately address officials regarding rule interpretations. Respect their integrity and judgment.
5. Exhibit and develop in one's players the ability to accept defeat or victory gracefully without undue emotionalism.
6. Teach players to play within the spirit of the game and the letter of the rules.
7. Develop understanding among players, stressing a spirit of team play. Encourage qualities of self-discipline, cooperation, self-confidence, leadership, courtesy, honesty, initiative, and fair play.
8. Provide for the welfare of the players by:
   a. Scheduling appropriate practice periods
   b. Providing safe transportation
   c. Scheduling appropriate number of practice and league games
   d. Providing safe playing areas

Table 5-2.   State Requirements Concerning Coaching Certification, Qualification, and Education, 1997.

Professional/Teacher Certification

All coaches	*All head coaches*	*Selected head coaches*
Kansas	Alabama	Arkansas
Maryland	Arizona	Florida
Missouri	Georgia	Indiana
Nebraska	Iowa	Kentucky
New Jersey	Mississippi	Louisiana
New York		South Carolina
Texas		Tennessee
Hawaii		Oklahoma
Alaska		

Coaching Education Only	**State/District Decision**	**No Requirement**
District of Columbia	California	Delaware
Idaho	Colorado	Michigan
Illinois	Connecticut	Montana
Maine	Ohio	New Hampshire
Minnesota	Rhode Island	North Carolina
New Mexico	Massachusetts	Oregon
South Dakota		Pennsylvania
Utah		Vermont
Washington		Virginia
West Virginia		North Dakota
Wisconsin		Nevada
Wyoming		

Table 5-3.   Course Requirements for the University of Minnesota Coaching Certificate Program

Course Number	Course Name
KIN 3112	First Responder for Athletic Coaches and Athletic Trainers (3) or current American Red Cross Standard First Aid and CPR card (2)
KIN 3169 coaching	Volleyball Coaching (2), *3170* Baseball Coaching (2), *3171* Basketball Coaching (2), *3172* Football Coaching (2), *3173* Golf Coaching (2), *3174* Gymnastics Coaching (2), *3175* Ice Hockey Coaching (2), *3176* Swimming and Diving Coaching (2), *3177* Tennis Coaching (2), *3178* Track and Field Coaching (2), *3179* Wrestling Coaching (2), *3371* Soccer Coaching (2); Select one or more coaching courses
KIN 3111	Mechanics of Movement (3) or *KIN 3115* Physiological Application of Sports (3) or *KIN 3386* Exercise Physiology (4) or SpST 3620 Applied Sport Psychology (3)
KIN 3114	Prevention and Care of Injuries (3) or *KIN 5620* Practicum: Prevention and Care of Athletic Injuries (3)
KIN 3143	Organization and Management of Sport (3)
KIN 3624	Student Teaching: Coaching (3)

e. Using good judgment before allowing injured, fatigued, or emotionally upset players to play

f. Providing proper medical care and treatment

9. Use consistent and fair criteria in judging players and establishing standards for them.

10. Treat players with respect, equality, and courtesy.

11. Direct constructive criticism toward players in a positive, objective manner.

12. Compliment players honestly and avoid exploiting them for self-glory.

13. Emphasize the ideals of fair play in all competitive situations.

14. Maintain an uncompromising adherence to standards, rules, eligibility, conduct, etiquette, and attendance requirements. Teach players to understand and adhere to these principles.

15. Be knowledgeable in aspects of the sport to provide an appropriate level of player achievement. Have a goal of quality play and excellence. Know proper fundamentals, strategy, safety factors, and training and conditioning principles, and understand rules and officiating.

16. Attend workshops, clinics, classes, and institutes to keep abreast with and informed of current trends and techniques of the sport.

17. Obtain membership and be of service in organizations and agencies that promote the sport and conduct competitive opportunities.

18. Use common sense and composure in meeting stressful situations and in establishing practice and game schedules that are appropriate and realistic in terms of demands on players' time and physical condition.

19. Conduct practice opportunities that provide appropriate preparation to allow the players to meet the competitive situation with confidence.

20. Require medical examinations for all players before the sports season and follow the medical recommendations for those players who have a history of medical problems or who have sustained injury during the season.

21. Cooperate with administrative personnel in establishing and conducting a quality athletic program.

22. Accept opportunities to host events and conduct quality competition.

23. Contribute constructive suggestions to the governing association for promoting and organizing competitive experiences.

24. Show respect and appreciation for tournament personnel and offer assistance when appropriate.

25. Be present at all practices and competitions. Avoid letting other appointments interfere with the scheduled team time. Provide time to meet the needs of the individual players.

26. Encourage spectators to display respect and hospitality toward opponents and officials and to recognize good play and fair play. When inappropriate crowd action occurs, the coach should assist in curtailing the crowd reaction.

Athletic Trainer/Sports Medicine Specialists

The profession of athletic training has taken on greater significance in recent years because of the guidance of the National Athletic Trainers Association (NATA) and the concomitant increase in sports programs and the recognition that the health and safety of the student-athlete is a top priority. The role of the athletic trainer is the prevention, recognition, assessment, and management of injuries at all levels of competitive sport.

The contemporary athletic trainer needs special preparation to carry out training duties, which include prevention of injuries, first aid, post-injury treatment, and rehabilitation, as well as educational counseling. Such preparation, if possible, should include a major in physical education, NATA certification, or being a registered physical therapist. Also needed are such personal qualifications as emotional stability under stress, ability to act rationally when injuries occur, and a standard of ethics that places the welfare of the participant above the pressures for approval to play.

Many schools and colleges whose financial situation does not permit hiring a full-time certified athletic trainer are strongly encouraged to

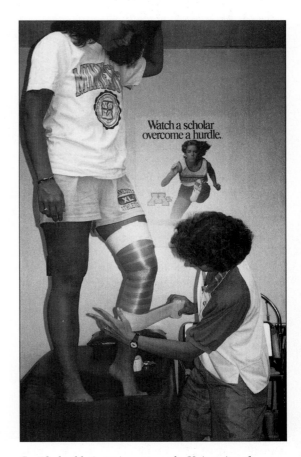

Certified athletic trainer at work; University of Minnesota, Minneapolis.

provide at the very minimum a part-time certified athletic trainer.

Qualifications for Athletic Trainers

Athletic trainers should complete a four-year college curriculum that emphasizes the biological and physical sciences. The courses required in professional preparation programs for athletic trainers also indicate some of the competencies needed. These courses include anatomy, physiology, exercise physiology, applied anatomy, biomechanics, sport psychology, sport sociology, organization and management of sport, first aid and safety, nutrition, remedial exercise, health, techniques of athletic training, counseling, and internship/practicum in the techniques of athletic training.

The certified athletic trainer is part of the sports management team and must work closely with administrators, coaches, physicians, school medical personnel, athletes, and parents in a cooperative effort to provide the best possible safety and health care. In some community situations, the athletic trainer is also responsible for staff development, in-service training, and supervision of a student athletic training staff.

Arnheim and Prentice (1997) list the following as the personal qualifications requisite for athletic trainers: good health, sense of fair play, maturity and emotional stability, good appearance, leadership, compassion, intellectual capacity, sense of humor, kindness and understanding, competence and responsibility, and a sound philosophy of life.

Additional information about the management of athletic training programs is provided in Chapter 12.

The Sport Council

Most colleges and many schools have some type of sport council, board, or committee that establishes and is responsible for the conduct of sport policies and procedures for the institution. Such councils, boards, or committees are responsible for providing proper direction as sport operates in the educational context of the organization.

The composition of such committees or councils varies widely from school to school and college to college. In a school, the superintendent or principal may serve as chairperson, or the director of physical education and/or athletics or other faculty member may hold this position. The committee may include coaches, members of the board of education, faculty, students, parents, and members of the community at large. In a college or university, the committee may consist of administrators, faculty, students, athletic directors, coaches, alumni, community leaders, and others.

Some of the functions of sport councils at the high school and college levels include making and reviewing policy, approving awards and eligibility, advising the athletic department on issues or concerns, endorsing and approving schedules and budgets, evaluating the athletic program, investigating complaints, interviewing and recommending to athletic directors potential athletic personnel for hiring, approving codes of ethics, reviewing scholarship programs, approving postseason play and international educational competitions, and deciding if various sport programs should be added or discontinued.

Academic Counseling

In the last decade, many colleges and universities have made a concerted effort to improve their academic image and the graduation rates of student-athletes. These program support services have as their mission to enable each student-athlete to become an educated, self-reliant, and self-confident member of the campus community. With the time demands, the stress of sport, and the pursuit of sporting excellence permeating all education levels, focused academic counseling for athletes has become an integral part of university sport and is now becoming part of high school programs as well, especially in regard to class load and content and NCAA eligibility.

Academic counseling services are an important support service for student-athletes; University of Minnesota, Minneapolis.

SELECTED MANAGEMENT FUNCTIONS IN COMPETITIVE SPORT PROGRAMS

Many management functions are pertinent to the directing of a competitive sport program, including the following concerns: event, game, and practice scheduling; contracts; health and safety of student athletes; injuries and insurance; officials; transportation; game management; crowd control; protests, forfeitures, and called games; awards and honors; and record keeping.

Event, Game, Facility, and Practice Scheduling

Scheduling involves maintaining a proper balance between home and away contests, seeking contests with organizations and institutions of approximately the same size and caliber of play, and trying to restrict the scope of the geographical area in which contests are conducted to minimize transportation costs.

Where leagues and conferences are in place, schedules are usually made many months or years in advance, leaving the athletic director or coach few windows of opportunity for nonconference matches. In most instances, the high school league or association, NCAA, NAIA, NJCAA, or other appropriate governing body limits the number of matches as well as the length of the season. All contests, games, and competitive sport events should have the sanction and approval of school, college, or other organizational authorities. Season lengths should be arranged so that they interfere as little as possible with institutional academic priorities. Practice schedules before the first contest should be adequate and appropriate so that the players are in match or game condition.

Some factors that may affect scheduling include environmental conditions, maximizing gate receipts, number of participants, state playoffs and invitational tournaments, transportation and logistics, availability of facilities, different sports that appeal to the same students, limitations concerning number of games or contests permitted, religious considerations, paid guarantees to travel and play, and potential educational impact on the student-athlete, ranging from tournament participation in Hawaii to number of class days missed.

Event, game, and practice scheduling should be fairly and equitably managed (following Title IX guidelines) permitting equal time, opportunity, and accessibility for all sport participants. All coaches and other personnel involved in facilities utilization, travel scheduling, and support services should be involved in management's decision-making process.

Contracts

Written contracts are usually essential in the management of interscholastic and intercollegiate sports programs (figure 5-2). On the college level in particular, games are scheduled many months and sometimes years in advance. Memories and facts tend to fade and become obscure with time. To avoid misunderstanding and confusion, it is best to have a written contract between the schools or colleges and all those concerned (e.g., athletic directors, coaches, business offices, officials, hotels, food service, transportation companies).

Contracts should be properly executed and signed by official representatives of all schools or colleges involved. Many sport associations, federations, and conferences provide specially prepared forms for use by member schools or colleges. Such forms usually contain the names of the schools, dates, times, and circumstances and conditions under which the contests will be held. In addition, they usually provide for penalties if contracts are breached by either party.

Health and Safety of the Student Athlete

Competitive sport should contribute to the health and well-being of the student athlete. Through wholesome physical activity, the participant should not only become more aware of the benefits of fitness and exercise, but also become more physically, cognitively, emotionally, and psychosocially healthy.

One of the first requirements for every participant involved in a sport program should be a

ATHLETIC EVENTS AGREEMENT
Department of Intercollegiate Athletics
University of Nevada, Las Vegas

ATHLETIC ACTIVITY _____

_____ VS UNIVERSITY OF NEVADA, LAS VEGAS

I. THE PARTIES HERETO HEREBY AGREE AS FOLLOWS:

(1) _____
         (Location)   (Date)   (Time)

(2) _____
         (Location)   (Date)   (Time)

(3) _____
         (Location)   (Date)   (Time)

(4) _____
         (Location)   (Date)   (Time)

II. THE FINANCIAL AGREEMENT SHALL BE SPECIFIED SUBSEQUENTLY:

(1) _____
    (Financial Sum)

(2) _____
    (Complimentary Tickets)

(3) _____
    (Other)

FOR: UNIVERSITY OF NEVADA, LAS VEGAS   **FOR: VISITING TEAM**

Signature: _____   Signature: _____

Title: _____   Title: _____

Date: _____   Date: _____

DISTRIBUTION:
    WHITE: University of Nevada, Las Vegas
    PINK: Visiting Team

Figure 5-2. Athletic events agreement.

Strength training and conditioning play important roles in contemporary sport; Kevin Yoxall, Strength Coach, University of California at Los Angeles.

thorough, vigorous, preparticipation medical examination by a trained physician to determine physical health status before engaging in strenuous activities. The nature of competitive sport and the sometimes stressful demands (both physical and psychological) placed on the participant make this examination imperative.

Everything possible should be done to protect the health and safety of the participant. A coach should always conduct the program with these objectives in mind. The coach should possess current certification in first aid and CPR and strictly adhere to progressive and prudent measures of training and conditioning.

Proper training and conditioning should take place before any player is subjected to competition. Such training and conditioning should always be progressive and gradual: The squad should contain ample players to allow for substitutions in the event a person is not physically fit or is otherwise unable to compete.

Proper facilities and equipment should be available to ensure the safety and health of the players. This means that facilities are constructed according to recommended standards concerning size, lighting, surfacing, and various safety features. Protective equipment meeting all current safety specifications (e.g., for football, lacrosse, and ice hockey) should be provided as required in the various sports. If appropriate facilities and equipment are not available, competition should be immediately suspended.

Games should be scheduled that result in equal and safe competition. The desire of small schools to compete against larger schools, in which case the competition is not equal, often brings potentially disastrous results to the health, safety, and welfare of the players (primarily in the case of collision sports). Under such circumstances, one often hears the remark, "They really took a beating." Competition should be as equal and fair as possible.

Proper sanitary measures should be taken. Individual towels and drinking cups or bottles should be provided. The day of the team towel, team water bottle, and uncared for mat has passed. Equipment should be approved and well maintained, and uniforms should be laundered as often as necessary. Facilities (e.g., weight training stations and mats) should be kept clean and up to code. Locker, dressing, shower, toilet, and other facilities used by participants should also be kept clean and sanitary.

Playing areas should be well maintained, clean, and safe. Gymnasiums, pools, and other facilities should be maintained at the proper temperature, and every measure must be taken to ensure safe, healthful, and optimal learning and performance conditions.

Injuries and Insurance

Prompt attention should be given to all injuries. Injured players should be examined by a physician and administered proper treatment. There should be complete medical supervision of the entire sports program. A physician should be present at all games and be on call for practice sessions, especially those involving contact and heavy exertion. The certified athletic trainer is not a substitute for a physician. The physician should determine the extent of injury. After being ill or hurt, a player should not be permitted to participate again until the coach receives an approved statement from the family, school, or college physician. The coach should make sure that, even though such permission is granted, the athlete is psychosocially and physically prepared for practice, match, or game conditions.

In many states, the state high school association sponsors an athletic insurance plan. Some insurance companies have plans that allow a sports participation rider to be added to the student's basic student insurance policy. Such plans pay various medical, X-ray and MRI examinations, dental, hospitalization, and other expenses according to the terms of the plan. The amount of any payment for an injury is usually only the amount of the actual expenses incurred, but not in excess of the amounts listed in the schedule of allowance for such injury. To collect benefits, plan requirements must be met.

The insurance provided by various state and independent plans usually includes benefits for accidental death or dismemberment, hospital expenses, X-ray and MRI examination fees, physicians' fees, and surgical and dental expenses as well as emergency transportation. Dental benefits may or may not be included in the schedule of surgical benefits. In some plans, catastrophe benefits are also available for injuries requiring extensive medical care and long-term hospitalization. Coverage is normally provided on a deductible basis, with the insurance company paying 75 percent to 80 percent of the total cost over the deductible amount up to a maximum amount.

Every school, college, or organization involved in the delivery of competitive sport should have a written policy concerning health, safety, injury, insurance, and other concerns relating to the competitive sport process. Furthermore, the administrator, coach, athletic trainer, team physician, parents, and players should be thoroughly familiar with the legal responsibilities, rights, and due process concerning all phases of the competitive sport program.

Officials

Officials play an integral role in any competitive sport program; therefore they should be well qualified, certified, and hold membership in their respective officiating association. They should know the rules and be able to interpret them accurately, recognize their responsibility to the players, be good sportspersons, and be courteous, honest, friendly, cooperative, impartial, and able to control the game at all times.

To ensure that only the best officials are employed, procedures should be established to register officials and determine which are qualified. Officials should be medically fit and required to pass examinations on rules and to demonstrate their competence. Rating scales have been developed to help make such assessments. Most sports associations have some method of registering and certifying acceptable officials. The National Association of Girls and Women in Sport, an association of AAHPERD, has a rating committee that certifies officials, as do state high school associations or leagues. In some states, the officials who are assigned then rate the schools or colleges regarding facilities, environment, and circumstances surrounding the game. Officials' ratings can provide important feedback on coaching behavior and site management, and in turn, coaches should rate every official.

Subject to contract differences, officials are frequently chosen by the home team with approval of opponents or the conference. The practice of the home team selecting officials without any consideration toward the wishes of other organizations has on occasion resulted in relations that have not been in the best interests of sport. The growing practice of having the conference or association select officials has nullified many of these situations.

Officials should be duly notified of the date, time, and location of the contests to which they have been assigned and contracts awarded. Officials' fees vary from school to school and sport to sport, although some associations have assigned standard rates. It is usually considered best to pay a flat fee that includes both salary and expenses rather than to budget them separately.

Umpires and officials play major roles in sports competition.

Transportation

Transporting athletes to and from sporting contests presents many management problems: Who should be transported? In what kinds of vehicles should athletes be transported? Who should drive? Is sport part of a regular day-school program? Should private vehicles or school- and college-owned vehicles be used? What are the legal implications involved in transporting athletes to and from school- and college-sponsored events?

The present trend is to view competitive sport as an integral part of the educational program so that public funds may be used for transportation. At the same time, however, statutes vary from state to state, and persons managing sport programs should carefully examine the statutes and policies concerning their own circumstance.

Many managers believe that athletes and representatives of the school or college, such as band members and cheerleaders, should travel only in transportation provided by the school. When private cars belonging to coaches, students, or other persons are used, the manager should be sure to determine whether the procedures are in conformity with the state statutes regarding liability. Under no circumstances should students or other representatives be permitted to drive unless they are licensed drivers, and under most circumstances students should not be used as drivers.

The business manager is generally responsible for transportation. This responsibility usually involves a great deal of advance planning,

One Day in a Monthly Schedule of Sporting Events

April 8

Depart:	3:00 P.M.
From:	Senior High School Parking Lot, West Exit
Team:	Junior Varsity Baseball
To:	Jones High School, 3 Oak St., Plymouth, MN 55447
Phone:	612-555-0123
Students:	25
Pickup:	5:30 P.M. at Jones High School Baseball Field
Remarks:	Construction on Route 12 may require travel on Route 55. Please check before trip.

and the coach, athletic director, and department representative assigned to handle transportation must work in consort both to provide for the safety of the participants and to minimize the costs associated with travel. The director of athletics should submit a monthly calendar of athletic events, listing the date, time, and place of departure; event; destination; number of participants; time of pickup; mode of transport; and remarks (see the One Day in a Monthly Schedule box). These calendars should be posted and sent to all coaches and athletes involved.

After the transportation has been scheduled with the appropriate school department or transportation company, a copy of the transportation contract is distributed to the athletic director, the coach, the principal, and the business manager. The procedure for submitting transportation requests varies in different schools and colleges, but written records should always be confirmed and scrutinized by the athletic director and coach.

Event and Game Management

Because so many details are associated with event or game management, it is possible to include only a brief statement of some of the more important items. To have an effectively and efficiently conducted event, good organization is important. Someone must be responsible. Advance planning must be done. Many details must be attended to, including (1) pregame responsibilities, (2) game responsibilities, (3) post-game responsibilities, and (4) preparation for away games. Before an event or game, details such as contracts (e.g., officials, transportation, security, and facilities), eligibility records, equipment, facility availability, tickets, public relations, medical supervision, and medical examinations must be thoroughly checked. Responsibilities for home games might include checking such items as supplies and equipment, pregame and halftime entertainment, tickets, security and volunteer ushers, scoreboards, public-address system, emergency care procedures, availability of physician and athletic trainers, and locker room facilities for visiting teams and officials. The responsibilities after a home game consist of checking such items as payments to officials and visiting school, evaluation of officials, attendance and participation records, and financial records and deposits. Preparations for an away game include such important details as parents' permissions, missed classes, transportation, funding, contracts, travel team, and records. In addition, after an away game, forms must be completed in order to accurately account for all travel related expenses (figure 5-3).

Crowd Control

Crowd control at sports contests is becoming increasingly important in light of potential security problems and incidents (as few as they may be when compared with recent international sporting events) that have occurred at high school and college campuses as well as at neutral sports venues. The elimination of evening sports events at the high school level has been on the increase, particularly in metropolitan areas. School districts and college authorities are taking increased precautions to avoid crowd problems at sporting contests. Good sports assemblies are being conducted, townspeople are being informed, and administrators are discussing the matter. Fair play assemblies are now presented at most state high school association competitions as well as at

UNIVERSITY OF NEVADA, LAS VEGAS

Controller's Office
Accounts Payable Department
CLAIM FOR GROUP TRAVEL EXPENSES

Note: Do not use this form for submitting Travel expenses for individual faculty/staff of UNLV.

Department to Travel:_____

Destination: _____

Dates of Travel: _____

Number of Students and Staff Members: _____

SUMMARY OF EXPENDITURES

Transportation:

    Method:_____

    Cost (Do not enter cost of any agency vehicle.) _____

Meals, lodging, and miscellaneous:

Dates						Total
Breakfasts						
Lunches						
Dinners						
Lodging						
Other						
Student Allowance						

Total Meals, Lodging, and Miscellaneous:...............................

Total All Expenditures and/or Student Allowances.......................
  (Must be substantiated by receipts)

Advance Received: ....

Balance Due or to be reimbursed......................................
  (If balance is to be reimbursed to the traveler submit a request
  for check in the amount of reimbursement.)

Account to be Charged:_____

Signed by: _____

Approved by:_____
               Department Head

UNLV AP 270 4-96

(1) Controller's Office
(2) Controller's Office
(3) Department

Figure 5-3.   Claim for group travel expenses.

college level tournaments. Organizations—including the AAHPERD, the National Association of State High Schools, and most conferences and high school leagues—have suggested numerous guidelines for crowd control, including fair play. A summary of these recommendations may be found in Appendix C. These approaches to crowd control should also be extended to include crowd emergencies such as lightning storms, earthquakes, tornadoes, and other environmental disasters in which crowd communication and safety are paramount.

Protests, Forfeitures, and Called Games

Procedures for handling protests and forfeitures in connection with sports contests should be a matter of written policy. Of course, careful preventive action should be taken beforehand to avoid a situation in which such protests and forfeitures occur. Proper interpretation of the rules, good officiating, elimination of undue pressures, and proper education of coaches about the philosophy and objectives of competitive sport will help prevent such action. However, the procedure for filing protests and forfeitures should be established. This procedure should be clearly stated in writing and should contain all the details, such as the person or responsible organization to whom the protest should be addressed. Time limits and time frame involved, person or group responsible for action, legal counsel, and any other necessary information should be readily available for the parties involved. One of the most frequent reasons for a protest is the use of ineligible players, which usually results in the forfeiture of any game in which ineligible players participated.

Calling games because of environmental (e.g., rain, snow, cold, lightning, tornado, earthquake) or other unforeseen conditions (e.g., sickness or tragic circumstance) also requires following the policies and procedures set down by management. Oftentimes, short notice is the great concern, which is why communication via phone, fax, electronic mail, and walkie-talkie must be readily available.

Awards and Honors

The basis for awards in interscholastic and intercollegiate sport is similar to that in recreational sport, except for some high school or NCAA limitations. There are arguments for and against granting awards. Some individuals believe that the intrinsic values derived from playing a sport—joy and satisfaction, physical and psychosocial benefits, among others—are sufficient and that no materialistic awards should be given. Others argue that awards have been a symbolic recognition of achievement since the time of ancient Greece, and they should be an integral part of the competitive sport program.

The awards policy should be determined by the sport council at each sporting level. The practice of granting awards in the form of letters, insignia, plaques, medals, or some other symbol is almost universal. Along with traditional sporting honors, many organizations are

Extrinsic awards are commonplace in competitive sport programs.

beginning to recognize the academic achievement of student-athletes (e.g., banquets for academic excellence). This practice is strongly encouraged.

When awards are given, they should be modest and meaningful. Some state athletic associations and other governing bodies have placed financial limits on awards to student-athletes. Furthermore, it seems wise not to distinguish between so-called major, or revenue-producing, sports and minor, or non-revenue-producing, sports when granting awards. Award criteria should call for equal treatment among potential recipients. Awards and honors (e.g., all-state, MVP, all-academic, captain) are personally meaningful for those student-athletes who receive them. College admissions officials or prospective employers often request such information, and sometimes admission and financial aid are directly related to such achievements.

Record Keeping

Management of any competitive sporting endeavor requires accurate records of all the details concerned with the sport-specific situation. The following records should be considered for inclusion in the computer or database file: medical status; parents' contact addresses, phone numbers, and insurance information and permission to participate; academic eligibility; budget and travel records; conference schedules; and transportation. Also on-line should be records on the conduct of various sports from year to year, season to season, and game to game, so that they can be compared over time or with other organizations or teams; statistical summaries of player participation and game performance tendencies that may assist the coach in determining weaknesses in game strategy or in quantifying players' or teams' performances vs. stated objectives; and other pertinent information essential to well-organized game preparation and management. Moreover, sound management practices demand accurate records of equipment and supplies, officials, financial reports, injuries, and other accountability items requisite for conducting a top-notch program.

SELECTED MANAGEMENT PROBLEMS ASSOCIATED WITH COMPETITIVE SPORT

Contemporary competitive sport at both the school and college levels has become a quagmire of seemingly ever-changing rules and regulations. Needless to say, the sport management team (athletic director, coaches, student-athletes, sport council, sports medicine staff, school and college personnel, etc.) is responsible for the conduct of a program of integrity. The management team is bound to encounter problems related to recruitment, eligibility, scholarships, proselytizing, scouting, finances, substance abuse, and compensation for coaching.

Recruitment

Recruiting student athletes is a controversial issue. Some educational institutions indicate that they do not condone recruiting for the primary purpose of developing winning teams. These institutions feel the admission process should be the same for all students, regardless of whether they are athletes, merit scholars, minority students, or others gifted in music, art, or architecture. No special consideration should be shown to any particular individual or group. The same standards, academic and otherwise, should prevail. This idealistic view, however, seems to be in constant conflict with most pragmatic practices at both the high school and college levels.

Some educational institutions, however, actively recruit athletes for their varsity teams. One has only to identify the country's leading football, basketball, or ice hockey high school teams to gain a realistic view of big-time high school recruiting. The main consideration here is to live up to rules of the state high school association or league, the conference, the NCAA, or other organizations in which the institution participates. To do otherwise should not be condoned.

In high school and college sports, teams should be made up of matriculated students attracted to the school or college because of its educational offerings, not its sports reputation. In some states, high school open enrollment continually causes problems that have not truly been addressed. At the college and university level, there is a population of student-athletes on whom millions of dollars are spent during the recruitment process. Management can do much to see that acceptable academic standards are observed in the recruitment process and that the cost of attracting qualified student-athletes is reduced. It should be made clear in writing that established rules will be observed and that any violation by the coaching staff will be dealt with severely. Also, at many universities, sport departments are hiring consultants to conduct seminars for the management team, including coaching staffs, about effective and legal recruiting practices.

Eligibility

Standards regarding the eligibility of participants are essential. These standards should be in writing, disseminated widely, and clearly understood by all concerned so that players, coaches, and other involved people will not become emotional when they "suddenly" realize they cannot use a star player who is ineligible to compete.

Standards of eligibility in interscholastic circles usually include an age limit of not more than 19 or 20 years; a requirement that an athlete be a bona fide student; rules concerning transfer students that frequently require them to be residents in the community served by the school; rules concerning international and exchange students; satisfactory attendance, academic standing, and grades in school; a limit of three or four seasons of competition permitted per sport (playing in one game might constitute a season); permission to play on only one team during a season; playing on an outside all-star or select team during or after the season; and a requirement that the participant have a medical examination, amateur status, and parent's consent. These eligibility regulations vary from school to school, conference to conference, and state to state.

The National Federation of State High School Associations considers a student ineligible for amateur standing if the student (1) has accepted money or compensation for playing in an athletic contest, (2) has played under an assumed name, (3) has competed with a team whose players were paid, or (4) has signed a contract to play with a professional team.

Eligibility requirements at the college and university level include rules concerning core courses, academic test scores, residence, undergraduate status, academic grade point average and progress, limits of game participation, transfer, substance abuse, and amateur status, including hiring of agents and professional tryouts. These rules have become quite complex, and athletic directors, coaches, counselors, and compliance officers must remain current.

Scholarships

Should athletes receive scholarships or special financial assistance from schools and colleges? Those in favor of scholarships and financial assistance claim that a student who excels in sport deserves to receive aid just as much as one who

Scholarships help student-athletes obtain a sound education while competing. University of California at Los Angeles.

excels in various other academic pursuits. Those opposed point out that scholarships should be awarded on the basis of the need and academic qualifications, rather than physical prowess in some sport.

The NCAA has recently reduced the number of allowable scholarships, which has caused a controversy concerning further limitations on students who without athletic scholarships would be unable to afford a Duke, Georgetown, or Stanford education. The complex web of sport scholarships is not confined to the college campus. The situation even extends into the private high schools and preparatory schools, which seem to be in steady supply of high-powered athletes, whether in football, basketball, soccer, or ice hockey.

The controversy is a difficult one; however, with competitive sport being an integral part of the educational process, it seems that if sport can enable young people to further their education or can assist them in gaining admission to highly selective institutions, the student-athletes should have those opportunities.

Proselytizing

Proselytizing is a term applied to a high school or college that has so strongly overemphasized sport that it has stooped to unethical behavior to secure outstanding talent or winning teams. High schools are not immune to this problem, and colleges seem to receive a lot of attention as well as visits from the staff of the NCAA office. Open enrollment, sports sponsorship, international exchange students, and gracious financial incentives offered by private high schools lead to legitimate concerns about the management of competitive sport at the high school level. For the most part, state high school athletic associations and leagues have attempted to legislate and control these problems and have realized a fair amount of success. The NCAA, however, seems to be continuously investigating unscrupulous proselytizing practices.

Scouting

Scouting has become an integral part of competitive sport at both the high school and college levels. Scouting might range from personally

Intercollegiate basketball provides opportunities for student athletes to gain an education both on and off the court.

attending games to watching game films. By watching another team perform, one can learn the formations and plays used as well as discover certain team or individual player tendencies or weaknesses. These discoveries might range from watching players to determine mannerisms they possess that might give away a certain play to evaluating the personality of the opponent under stress.

Many schools and colleges are spending considerable money and time on scouting. Some schools scout a rival team every game during the season, using three or four persons on the same scouting assignment, and some study endless footage of exchanged videos. It is believed by many athletic administrators that money could be spent more wisely if used to enhance other aspects of the game for the participants.

Scouting is considered an important part of the game, and if scouting does occur, the head coach at the institution has direct responsibility for the action. Prior arrangements should be made about the game to be scouted or videos to be exchanged with the opposing team's sports department. Although one hears stories of coaches falling out of trees while observing closed practices, scouting for the most part has been ethical and remains an important facet of game preparation.

Finances

Interscholastic and intercollegiate sport programs throughout the country are financed through many different sources. These sources include gate receipts, board of education and central university funds, donations and gifts, endowments, special projects, students' activity fees, pay-for-play assessment, physical education department funds, magazine subscriptions, parking, and concessions. In major college and professional sport, preferred seating, luxury boxes, and corporate sponsor signage, are also crucial strategies for producing new and enhanced revenue streams.

It has long been argued by leaders in physical education that competitive sport programs have great educational potential. They are curricular in

Interscholastic evening soccer match; Wayzata High School, Wayzata, Minn.

nature rather than extracurricular. This means they contribute to the welfare of students like any other subject in the curriculum. On this basis, therefore, the finances necessary to support such a program should come from board of education or central university funding sources. Sport programs should not be self-supporting or used as a means to support part or all of the other so-called extracurricular activities of a school or college. Sport programs represent an integral part of the educational program and as such deserve to be treated like other aspects of the educational program. This procedure is followed in some schools and colleges with benefits as well as limitations to all concerned.

Gate receipts are a primary source of funding for many competitive sport programs. Too often gate receipts become the point of emphasis rather than the vehicle that provides valuable educational opportunities and experiences to the participant. When this shift occurs, sport cannot justify its existence in the educational process.

Recent trends indicate that one out of every five U.S. schools has cut back sport programs, or may soon do so, as a result of fiscal difficulty. Gate receipts alone can no longer support the number of men's and women's sport programs that are being offered at many institutions.

In some school districts, a student fee, which is collected from the interscholastic sport participant, as well as the formation of booster clubs has managed to keep competitive sport programs intact. And yes sports sponsorship is beginning to make its way into the high school sports' programs. Schools, colleges, and universities will have to creatively address this fiscal issue as the decade of the 1990s comes to closure.

Substance Abuse

Substance abuse among junior high, middle, high school, and college students is a reality that must be recognized, treated, and combated with preventive measures. The student-athlete has no immunity to the use of drugs among students. Indeed, athletes and anabolic steroid abuse are often mentioned in the same breath, which tarnishes the traditional belief that the athlete was somehow above substance abuse.

The substance abuse problem in the world of professional and college sports is of great concern to all. The news media, public, parents, student-athletes, and particularly educators and coaches, should be equally concerned about the young athlete. Substance use and addiction are not limited to the adult world; they endanger the entire younger generation.

The Drug Education Committee of the NCAA has indicated that most athletes bring their substance use habits with them when they come to the college campus.

Therefore the committee concluded that "it may be more effective to deal with the problem at the secondary school level."

Alcohol is the most commonly abused drug, with 93 out of every 100 young athletes eleven to fourteen years of age coming in contact with this element. Marijuana is the next most popular drug on the list. The U.S. Department of Health and Human Services has pointed out that approximately one out of every three high school seniors has tried marijuana before entering high school.

Young athletes who hope to give themselves more energy use agents such as cocaine, including its derivatives crack and ice, and uppers such as amphetamines, caffeine, and ephedrine. Anabolic steroids are also being used by these sport neophytes who hope to make themselves bigger, quicker, and stronger for sport competition.

These drugs are taking their toll on our young athletes as well as on the community as a whole. Growth potential and maturity are being hampered, and side effects are causing poor health not to mention impairment of motor function, slower reaction times, improper coordination with poor execution of movement, altered perception of speed, and withdrawal and loss of friends. In sum, users are experiencing academic, psychosocial, and vocational failure.

Some school districts and high school leagues are coming to grips with drug abuse. Programs designed to identify those students who come to school under the influence of alcohol or other drugs are being implemented throughout the nation. Those students who exhibit overt behavior

of drug abuse are usually referred to the school principal. Students who voluntarily admit use of drugs are then referred to the student assistance and counseling program. Voluntary self-referral to the student assistance program for drug abuse in some school districts is not a violation of the athletic code and student-athletes can remain active participants. In many high schools, however, substance abuse is forbidden, and immediate suspension from the team for various time lengths is prescribed.

Bruce Durbin, executive director of the National Federation of State High School Associations (which represents 20,000 schools and 93,000 individual members), believes that a drug program should stress education rather than enforcement. Such programs should reach and be actively supported by coaches, officials, parents, students, and educators in general.

The Minnesota High School League (MSHSL) has been proactively involved in providing student-focused chemical health awareness programs since the early 1980s. The league's programs (see "TARGET Minnesota" in Appendix D) served as models for the National Federation of State High School Association programs which were designed to assist other states in addressing chemical abuse. In 1985, the MSHSL, the state of Minnesota, the Hazelden Foundation, and the KROC Foundation (founded by Joan Kroc, widow of McDonald's founder and San Diego Padre owner Ray Kroc) cooperatively founded Operation CORK and have constructed a $7 million training and treatment facility at Hazelden in Center City, Minnesota devoted to drug prevention and education. The MSHSL in cooperation with its region committees also select drug-free student athlete/activities leaders to serve on their 16 regional TARGET teams that provide chemical health awareness training and information to region schools.

Many universities and high schools have also taken a proactive stance toward substance abuse; some of those relevant ideas are offered in Appendix D.

Coaching Compensation

A frequent topic of discussion at school meetings is whether teachers should receive extra pay for

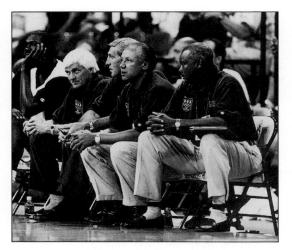

Coaching at the elite level can be a lucrative profession; U.S. Olympic basketball coaches. Courtesy of USA Basketball.

extra services. Parents, taxpayers, school boards, and administrators have been trying to decide whether sport coaches, adapted coaches, dance line coaches, cheerleading advisors, band leaders, dramatics supervisors, yearbook advisors, and others who perform services in addition to their teaching load should receive additional compensation.

A sensible solution to this problem is essential to the morale of a school staff. Most school systems are demanding more and more services and have formulated pay scales to cover the extra duties. These scales often have compensation formulas including hours spent, length of season, number of participants, and experience, which may culminate in as much as $4,000 to $5,500 for a head coach of football or basketball and $1,500 to $3,500 for an assistant coach in a typical suburban senior high school.

Coaching loads should be equalized as much as possible. If inequalities exist that cannot be corrected through extra pay, then extra staff and, sometimes, release time may be considered.

The compensation involved in competitive sport at the college or university level is not as clear-cut as in high school. At the NCAA Division III level, coaching might be part of the teaching or administrative responsibilities, whereas at the Division I level, coaching and its associated duties may be the only assignment. Within sport, differences range from six-figure salaries, radio and television shows, cars, shoe and apparel contracts, and country club privileges to the "no perks club" of many non-revenue-producing sports. There seems to be a distinction between revenue-producing and non-revenue producing sport coaches' compensation not to mention gender-based salary equity concerns.

For the majority of coaches, however, at both the high school and college level, compensation for coaching is similar to pay for teaching. It needs to improve and should be a top priority.

MANAGEMENT GUIDELINES FOR COMPETITIVE SPORT PROGRAMS

Competitive sport programs have existed in schools, colleges, and universities since 1852 when the Harvard and Yale crews dueled on the calm water of the Winnipesaukee River in New Hampshire.

Elementary, Junior High, and Middle Schools

Since competitive sport was first introduced to college campuses throughout the United States, high schools have embraced sport as part of their educational offerings. As a result, most high schools in America today have some form of interscholastic sport. It did not take long for our junior high and elementary schools to feel the impact of interscholastic sport programs. A survey by the National Association of Secondary School Principals (which included 2,296 junior high schools) revealed that 85.2 percent had some program of interscholastic sport.

For the most part, interscholastic sport has been phased out of the elementary school level, where educators agree that physical activities should focus on the development of basic motor skills and positive attitudes toward physical activity. An informal recreational sport program should be a part of all elementary programs, as should traditional May Days and Field Days at which competitive intramural and extramural sport may be introduced.

The special nature of grades 7 through 9, representing a transition period between the elementary school and the senior high school and between childhood and adolescence, has raised a question in the minds of many educators about whether an interscholastic sport program is in the best interests of the students. Many junior high and middle schools do, however, have football, soccer, basketball, volleyball, and track and field for young boys and girls.

Management Guidelines for Elementary School Sport

Many of the guidelines of the American Academy of Pediatrics may be applied at the elementary school level and to the type of sport competition that should be offered:

- All children should have opportunities to develop skill in a variety of activities.
- All such activities should take into account the age and developmental level of the child.
- Sport activities of elementary school children should be part of an overall school program.
- Competent medical supervision of each child should be ensured.
- Health observation by teachers and others should be encouraged and help given by the physician.
- Sport activities outside the school program should be entirely voluntary without undue emphasis on any special program or sport and without undue emphasis on winning. These programs should also include competent medical supervision.
- Competition is an inherent characteristic of growing, developing children; therefore, competitive programs organized at the school, neighborhood, and community levels that meet the needs of children should be provided. State, regional, and national tournaments, bowl games, and charity and exhibition games are not recommended for this age-group. Commer-

Low organized sport focusing on skill development; Brooklyn Park, Minn.

cial exploitation in any form should be avoided.

- Body-contact and collision sports, particularly tackle football and boxing, are considered a physical risk and have no place in programs for children of this age.
- All competitive sport programs at this level should be organized with the cooperation of interested medical groups, who will ensure adequate medical care before and during such programs. This care should include thorough physical examinations at specified intervals and advising parents and coaches about such factors as injury, response to fatigue, individual emotional needs, and the risks of undue physical and emotional strains.

With a proper blend of common sense and sound management and leadership, competitive sport activities at the elementary school level can lay the foundation for a lifetime of wholesome physical activity. The primary consideration

should be toward a diversity of wholesome childhood experiences that will aid in the proper
physical and emotional development of the child
rather than toward highly organized competition.

Management Guidelines for Junior High and Middle School Sport

The research regarding a highly organized sport
program at the junior high or middle school level
indicates the following points of substantial
agreement:

- This age range is a period of transition from
  elementary school to senior high school and
  from childhood to adolescence. It is a time
  when students are trying to understand their
  bodies, gain independence, achieve adult social
  status, acquire self-confidence, and establish a
  system of values. It is a time when a challenging and enjoyable program of education unique
  to this age-group is needed to meet the abilities
  and broadening interests of students.
- The best educational program at the junior high
  school level provides for enrichment that meets
  the needs of students in grades 7 through 9. A
  distinct and separate educational climate for
  these grades is needed to ensure that the program will not be influenced unduly by either
  the elementary or the senior high school.
- Coaches are needed whose full responsibilities
  lie in the junior high or middle school and
  whose training is appropriate to the needs of
  these students.
- The junior high school should provide for
  exploratory experiences with specialization de-
  layed through the completion of senior high
  school.
- The junior high school competitive sport environment should provide for the physical, social,
  mental, and emotional development of students
  as well as for the development of a sound
  standard of values.
- The principal and other members of management have the responsibility for providing
  sound educational leadership in all school matters. The type of physical education, recre-

ational, and competitive sport programs offered
will reflect the type of leadership provided.

The interscholastic sport program, if offered
at this level, should be provided only after fulfilling the prerequisites of physical education programs, adapted/developmental programs, and recreational sport or intramural programs and only if
special controls regarding health and safety, facilities, game adaptation and supervision, classification of players, leadership, and qualified, certified coaches and officials have been provided.

The competitive sport program should offer a
favorable social and emotional climate for the
student. The program should provide freedom
from anxiety and fear, absence of tensions and
stress, a feeling of belonging for each student, a
social awareness that contributes to the development of such important traits as respect for the
rights of others, and an atmosphere conducive to
growing into social and emotional maturity.

All sport activities should be professionally
supervised and a physician or certified athletic
trainer should be intimately involved to ensure
optimal health and safety conditions.

Competition itself is not the factor that makes
sport dangerous to the student. Instead, the crucial
factors are items such as the manner in which the
program is conducted, type of activity, facilities,
leadership, and physical condition of students.

Competitive sport, if properly conducted, has
the potential for satisfying such basic psychological
needs as recognition, belonging, self-respect, and
the feeling of achievement as well as providing a
wholesome outlet for the physical activity drive.
However, if conducted in light of adult interests,
community pressure, and other questionable influences, it can prove psychosocially harmful.

Interscholastic sports, when conducted in accordance with desirable standards of leadership,
educational philosophy, activities, and other pertinent factors, have the potential for providing
beneficial social effects for the student; but when
not conducted in accordance with desirable standards, interscholastic sports can be socially detri-
mental to all involved.

Management Guidelines for Interscholastic and Intercollegiate Sport Programs

Selected recommended standards for high school and college sport programs follow.

Organization

The wholesome conduct of the sport programs should be the ultimate responsibility of the school administration along with the school board or board of regents.

Sport policy should be developed, evaluated, and supervised by a faculty committee.

Sport policy should be implemented by the director of athletics and activities.

Sport should be organized as an integral part of the department of physical education at the high school level and should maintain strong positive relationships with associated departments (e.g., physical education, kinesiology, sport and leisure studies, public health, physical therapy) at the collegiate level.

Staff

All members of the coaching staff should be members of the faculty.

Coaches should be hired based on their qualifications to assume educational responsibilities and not on their ability to produce winning teams.

Coaches should enjoy the same privileges of tenure, rank, and salary accorded other similarly qualified faculty members. This remains a major point of contention at many large universities.

Public school coaches should be certified educators and hold a coaching minor or coaching certification including first aid and CPR training.

Finances

The financing of interscholastic and intercollegiate sport should be governed by the same policies that control the financing of all other educational activities within an institution.

Gate receipts should be considered a supplemental source of revenue, as should the myriad fund-raising enterprises undertaken by both schools and colleges.

Health and Safety

An annual, thorough, preparticipation medical examination should be required of all participants; a physical examination on a seasonal basis would be preferable.

Each school should have a written policy spelling out the responsibility for sport-related injuries and should provide or make available athletic accident insurance.

Each school should have a written policy for the implementation of an injury-care program.

A physician and certified athletic trainer should be present at all sport contests.

Only equipment that is fully certified as offering the best protection for the student-athlete should be purchased and utilized.

All protective equipment should fit players properly.

Competition should be scheduled between teams of comparable ability.

Games should not be played until players have had a minimum of two to three weeks of physical training and conditioning.

Good officiating is requisite for the protection and safety of the participant; Minnesota State High School League soccer play-off.

Playing fields and surfaces should meet standards for size and safety for the participants.

Eligibility

All schools should join, and fully participate, honor, and respect the eligibility rules and regulations of, respective local, state, and national sport associations.

Recruiting

The sport teams of each school should be composed of bona fide student-athletes who live in the school district or who were attracted to the institution by its educational program.

All candidates for admission to a school should be evaluated according to similar standards.

All financial aid should be administered with regard to need and according to the same standards for all students. The recipient of financial aid should be provided a statement of the amount, duration, and conditions of the award.

Sport scholarships, when possible, should be allocated on a full rather than partial basis to avoid inequitable distribution among team members.

Awards and Honors

The value of sport awards and honors is sometimes questioned. However, when the program is properly managed and kept in perspective, awards are a meaningful part of high school and college sport programs and are a positive recognition of hard work, dedication, skill, and school commitment. Many institutions have developed comprehensive award programs in which scholar-athlete honors and all-academic honors share the spotlight with traditional sport awards such as all-state, all-district, all-conference, and most valuable player.

Evaluation

Just as evaluation and assessment of physical education instructional programs, recreational sport programs, coaches, and officials should be practiced on an on-going basis, so should evaluation and assessment of interscholastic and intercollegiate sports programs. This scrutiny helps

Awards can play a meaningful role in recognizing hard work and significant sport and academic achievement; All-American and Olympian Marie Roethlisberger, University of Minnesota.

ensure, maintain, and enhance quality competitive sport programs.

Management Guidelines for Competitive Sport Programs in Other Organizations

Competitive sport programs also exist in forms other than the formal educational setting. Community organizations and businesses, recreation and park districts, Ys, and the traditional golf and tennis clubs offer tremendous opportunities for all age-groups to compete. State games, local sports festivals, police athletic leagues, church leagues, aquatic clubs, Athletes in Action, and the military are just some of the many sports delivery systems available to the competitive sport consumer.

These sport programs need to be geared to the age and needs of the participants. Youth-serving agencies, for example, should observe the established standards for interscholastic programs, whereas adults and seniors might follow the standards applicable at the college and university level. Many advantages accrue from belong-

Evaluation of a High School Sport Program

	Yes	No
1. Sport program as an integral part of total curriculum		
a. The sports are an outgrowth of the physical education program	___	___
b. A variety of sports is available for all students	___	___
c. The educational values of sport are foremost in the philosophy	___	___
d. All students have an opportunity to participate in a sport	___	___
e. Sports are used appropriately as a school's unifying force	___	___
f. Athletes are not excused from courses, including physical education, because of sport participation	___	___
2. Coaches as faculty members		
a. Coaches have an adequate opportunity to exercise the same rights and privileges as other faculty members in determining school and curricular matters	___	___
b. Coaches attend, and they are scheduled so that they may attend, faculty meetings	___	___
c. Coaches are not expected to assume more duties of a general nature than are other faculty members	___	___
d. Teaching tenure and other faculty privileges are available to coaches	___	___
e. Assignments for extra duties are made for coaches on the same basis as for other teachers	___	___
3. Participants encouraged to perform adequately in academic areas		
a. Athletes are held accountable scholastically at the same level as other students	___	___
b. Practices are of such length and intensity that they do not deter students' academic pursuits	___	___
c. Game trips do not cause the students to miss an excessive number of classes	___	___
d. Counseling services emphasize the importance of academic performance on career education	___	___
e. Athletes are required to attend classes on days of contests	___	___
4. Meeting philosophy of school board		
a. New coaches are made aware of the board policies and informed that they will be expected to follow them in spirit as well as to the letter	___	___
b. All coaches are regularly informed by the principal and athletic and activities director that they must conduct their programs within the framework of board policy	___	___
c. A procedure is available for the athletic and activities director and coaches to make recommendations regarding policy change	___	___
d. Noncoaching faculty members are made aware of board policy regarding sport so that they may discuss it from a base of fact	___	___
e. The philosophy of the board is written and made available to all personnel	___	___
5. Awards		
a. Only those awards authorized by local conferences, state high school athletic associations, and NCAA or similar organizations are awarded.	___	___
b. Diligence is exercised to ensure that outside groups do not cause violations of the award regulations	___	___
c. Care is taken to ensure that athletes are not granted privileges not available to the general student body	___	___

Continued

Evaluation of a High School Sport Program—Cont'd

	Yes	No
6. Projected program outcomes		
a. It is emphasized that participation in sport is a privilege	_____	_____
b. Development of critical thinking, as well as sport performance, is planned into the program	_____	_____
c. Development of self-direction and individual motivation are integral parts of the sporting experience	_____	_____
d. The athletes are allowed to develop at their own cognitive, psychomotor, and affective readiness level	_____	_____
e. Appropriate and accepted social values are used as standards of behavior both on and off the playing area	_____	_____
7. Guarding against student exploitation		
a. The student is not used in sport performance to provide an activity that has as its main purpose entertainment of the community	_____	_____
b. The student's academic program is in no way altered to allow continued eligibility with less than normal effort and academic progress	_____	_____
c. The students are not given a false impression of their ability through the device of suggesting the possibility of a college scholarship or professional career	_____	_____
d. The athletes are not given a false image of the value of their athletic prowess to the material and cultural success within the school and community	_____	_____

Source: Adapted from the National Council of Secondary School Athletic Directors.

---

ing to leagues and conferences rather than playing independently. Leagues and conferences often promote established procedures, rules, and regulations that are more likely to benefit the participant than if a team were organized independently.

Usually sports sponsored by educational institutions take special pains to provide for the health and safety of the participants. They frequently provide insurance options, physicians and athletic trainers, access to transportation, appropriate facilities and equipment, and other provisions that help guarantee safer participation.

Sometimes highly competitive sport programs in other organizations do not have the same concern for the safety and well-being of the players, especially as the participant gets older (e.g., senior leagues); as a result, players sometimes participate more at their own risk than do players in institutionalized school sport.

It would be helpful if all sport organizations would examine and apply many of the procedures and standards set forth in this chapter for educational institutions.

Management Guidelines for Sport for People with Varying Disabilities

Persons with disabilities can receive the same benefits as well as harm from a program of competitive sport as does their nondisabled peer group. The following reasons for including adapted or unified sport activities in the school sport programs are listed by Auxter, Pyfer, and Huettig (1993).

Many students assigned to an adapted physical education class are unable to correct an existing condition and also are unable to participate in regular physical education. A program of adapted sport would be ideal for such students because it

Eunice Kennedy Shriver, founder of Special Olympics International.

body under a variety of circumstances and assist in the physical conduct of daily living.

A certain amount of emotional release also takes place in sport activities, and this release is just as important to the student-athlete with a disability as it is for the nondisabled student-athlete.

The Joseph P. Kennedy Jr. Foundation probably has focused more attention on sport for persons with disabilities than any other single organization. The most visible activity promoted by the Kennedy Foundation is the Special Olympics, which was organized in 1968. It was designed to provide mentally retarded youths, 8 years of age and over, with opportunities to participate in a variety of sports and games on local, state, regional, national, and international levels.

The basic objectives of the Special Olympics follow:

- Encourage development of comprehensive physical education and recreation programs for the mentally retarded in schools, day-care centers, and residential facilities in every community.
- Prepare the retarded for sport competition—particularly where no opportunities and programs now exist.
- Supplement existing activities and programs in schools, communities, day-care centers, and residential facilities.
- Provide training for volunteer coaches to enable them to work with youngsters in physical fitness, recreation, and sports activities (Stein and Klappholz 1977).

would provide them additional opportunities to participate in various forms of physical activity.

Students in the adapted/developmental sport program need activities that have carryover value. They may continue exercise and fitness programs in the future, but they also need training in sports and games that will be useful in later life.

Adapted sports and games should help the person with disabilities learn to handle his or her

Since the enactment of the Amateur Sports Act of 1978, P.L. 95-606, the Committee on Sport for the Disabled (COSD) was established by the U.S. Olympic Committee, and other groups and associations have taken up the challenge to provide sport opportunities for athletes with disabilities (see Appendix E). In 1995 the Minnesota State High School League became the first state league to offer high school tournaments for

Title IX has provided increased opportunity for girls and women to participate in sport.

student-athletes with disabilities. Clearly we have a challenge within this crucial domain.

TITLE IX AND THE CHANGING ROLE OF GIRLS' AND WOMEN'S SPORT COMPETITION

Proponents of equality in girls' and women's sport and Title IX have opened the window of opportunity for participation in women's sport in recent years. Women have become accepted as athletes with full rights to experience the competitive urges so long restricted by our gender-dominated society.

Procedures and practices concerning interscholastic and intercollegiate sport competition for females vary from school to school, state to state, and university to university. Some schools

and colleges have wide-ranging programs of interscholastic and intercollegiate sports, whereas others still have few opportunities to compete at the varsity level. Most states have not set up specific requirements for girls' sport, but many believe that their established regulations apply to both girls and boys. Some states have athletic associations for girls that are similar to those for boys, and a few universities still maintain independent men's and women's athletic departments (e.g., University of Iowa, University of Minnesota, University of Tennessee, University of Texas at Austin, University of Arkansas, and Brigham Young University).

The National Association for Girls and Women in Sport (NAGWS) of AAHPERD (1977) believes that opportunities should be provided for all girls and women who want to participate in competitive sport. Adequate and equitable funds, facilities, and staff should be provided for these programs.

Title IX*

Although the 92nd Congress passed the Education Amendments Act on June 23, 1972, Section 901(a) (Title IX as it is commonly referred to) was not signed into law until 1975. The law mandated that all schools receiving federal assistance treat their admitted students without discrimination on the basis of gender. The "treatment" of students was considered inclusive of areas such as housing, course offerings such as physical education (presented in chapter 3), financial aid, insurance benefits, employment assistance, and sport participation. Although Title IX applied to all types of institutional programs, the most dramatically affected programs have been those associated with sport. This attention was not without reason. Research indicates that budget dollars directed toward women's intercollegiate athletics were approximately 2 percent compared to men's revenue share, even though 15 percent of the participants at this level were female. Legal suits concerning basketball, baseball, golf, tennis, and track and field were levied in states ranging

*Parts of this section have been taken directly from government documents relating to Title IX, particularly the following documents:

U.S. Department of Health, Education, and Welfare, Office of Civil Rights. 1995. *Final Title IX regulation implementing Education Amendments of 1972—prohibiting sex discrimination in education.* Washington, D.C.: U.S. Government Printing Office. July.

U.S. Department of Health, Education, and Welfare, Office for Civil Rights. 1975. *Memorandum to chief state school officers, superintendents of local educational agencies and college and university presidents; subject: elimination of sex discrimination in athletic programs.* Washington, D.C.: U.S. Government Printing Office. September.

Title IX of the Education Amendments of 1972, 1979. A policy interpretation: Title IX and intercollegiate athletics. *Federal Register* 44 (11 December): 227.

from New York to California (Eitzen and Sage 1993).

Since the passage of Title IX, girls' and women's sports programs have grown rapidly, and today, girls' and women's interscholastic and intercollegiate sport teams are in full evidence throughout the nation, providing athletes with challenges and championships on an equal basis with their male counterparts. Sport once again has contributed to breaking down discriminatory social barriers (e.g., gender, race, ethnicity, age), but although great strides have been taken, it is clear that we have a long way to go to total equality in sport opportunity and delivery (Vargyas 1994).

Provisions of Title IX Affecting Sport Programs

Chapter 3 contained some background information about Title IX of the Education Amendments Act of 1972 and how its interpretation has influenced physical education programs. The following section offers some of the provisions of Title IX specifically affecting sport programs.

- Separate teams for boys and girls, or a coeducational team, must be provided in schools and colleges. For example, if there is only one team in a particular sport, such as swimming, then students of both sexes must be permitted to try out for this team.

- Equal opportunities must be provided for both sexes in the educational institution in terms of competitive training facilities, equipment and supplies, facilities for practice and games, medical and training services, coaching and academic tutoring, travel allowances, housing and dining facilities, compensation of coaches, and publicity. Equal aggregate expenditures are not required; however, equal opportunity for men and women is mandated. In situations in which men are given the opportunity for athletic scholarships, women must be given the same opportunity. Contact and collision sports such as football, basketball, boxing, wrestling, rugby, and ice hockey may be offered either separately or on a unitary basis.

- The emphasis of Title IX is to provide equal opportunity for both sexes. In determining whether equal opportunity is provided, it is important to know whether the interests and abilities of students of both sexes have been met and whether such items as adequate facilities and equipment are equally available.

- Title IX guidelines provide that expenditures on men's and women's sport be proportional to the number of men and women participating. This standard of substantially equal per capita expenditures must be met unless the institution can demonstrate that the differences are based on nondiscriminatory factors, such as the costs of a particular sport (e.g., the equipment required in football) or the scope of the competition (national rather than regional or local). This proportional standard applies to athletic scholarships, recruitment, and other readily measurable financial benefits such as equipment, supplies, travel, and publicity.

- According to the Department of Health and Human Services, the policy is designed to eliminate, over a reasonable period of time, the discriminatory effects, particularly at the college level, of the historic emphasis on men's sport and to facilitate the continued growth of women's sport. It requires colleges and universities to take specific steps to provide additional competitive sport opportunities for women—opportunities that will fully accommodate the increasing interest of women participating in sport.

Procedures for Assuring Compliance With Title IX

To make sure the provisions of Title IX have been complied with by an educational institution, certain procedures should be followed. Each educational institution usually has some member of the faculty or staff coordinate a self-evaluation and ensure compliance. Some universities have employed a full-time compliance officer.

The steps that have been followed in some sport programs involve first developing a statement of philosophy that provides a guide for equality of opportunity for both sexes. Then student interest is determined about the activities in which students desire to participate. In addition, all written materials concerned with items such as mission statements, curriculum, employment, job descriptions, and organizational structures are reviewed to see that needed changes are made to ensure that equal and fair inclusion is described. Also, such factors as game and practice scheduling times for all teams, provision for supplies and equipment, travel expenses, number of coaches assigned to teams, and salaries of coaches are examined to see if any discrepancies exist between the sexes. The membership requirements for clubs and other student organizations associated with sport are also reviewed. The amount of publicity and information services provided for physical education and sport programs are checked. Eligibility requirements for scholarships and financial aid, medical and accident policies, award systems, and employment procedures are examined. Teaching loads, coaching assignments, coaches' gender, and facility (e.g. training, medical, housing, dining) assignments are also included in the appraisal.

According to AAHPERD (1977), many questions can be asked to determine if equality exists for men's and women's programs. For example, the question about *employment conditions* might be "Are men and women compensated the same for essentially the same work for both teaching and coaching?" For *physical education classes* the question might be "Are physical education requirements for graduation the same for boys and girls, men and women?" For *recreational sport opportunities,* "Are recreational sport programs provided for both sexes?" For *competitive sport,* "Does the total budget reflect comparable support to both the men's and women's programs?" Many other questions for determining if equality exists are listed in AAHPERD's publications.

However, the most effective method for ensuring compliance has been the Department of Health and Human Services' three-prong test for institutional compliance and its continuous policy interpretations. To be in compliance, athletic programs must demonstrate one of the following:

1) that intercollegiate participation opportunities for its students of each sex are substantially proportionate to its male and female undergraduate enrollments, or

2) a history and continuing practice of program expansion responsive to developing interests and abilities of members of the underrepresented gender, or

3) that the interests and abilities of the "underrepresented sex" are "fully and effectively" accommodated by the existing program.

Compliance is established by satisfying any one of these three tests (Kramer 1993).

The Office of Civil Rights is not only an enforcement agency, it can receive and initiate violation complaints. If found in violation, the institution has ninety days to voluntarily respond with a compliance agreement contract including a time frame for compliance attainment. Only when the institution fails to meet this agreement is it found in noncompliance; at that time, federal funds could be withheld or legal action seeking damages could be initiated.

A project of the Women's Equity Action League Educational and Legal Defense Fund has offered the following pros and cons of bringing a legal suit.

Some Pros of Filing a Complaint

It is possible to win! You may convince others to take legal action for other complaints. You may change discriminatory practices at your school or college. Many girls and women may benefit from your action. Your action may result in the Title IX compliance plan at your school becoming the subject of scrutiny. Schools that have been cited for complaints are more likely to come closer to compliance. You can seek and potentially win or settle for legal fees and damages.

Some Cons of Filing a Complaint

You can lose! You may lose your position or scholarship and be labeled a troublemaker. You may become frustrated in dealing with the many organizations' legal concerns involved. The procedure sometimes takes years to resolve.

Organizations that may be of help in case it is found that inequality exists are the Department of Health and Human Services; Office for Civil Rights; Equal Employment Opportunity Commission; Office of Federal Contract Compliance; and the U.S. Department of Labor–Wage and Hour Division of the Employment Standards Administration.

Title IX sport complaints have been filed against numerous institutions. The complaints are usually filed with the regional Office of Civil Rights and have been referred to the national headquarters in Washington, D.C.

Coeducational Sport and Title IX

Coeducational sport should be provided for students in schools and institutions of higher education because of the benefits that can accrue from such participation. In instances in which highly skilled females would not otherwise have the opportunity to participate in a particular sport, they must be allowed to participate on male teams. However, coeducational sport, in most cases, should be limited to the recreational sport level.

The primary reason for not advocating coeducational sport participation on interscholastic and intercollegiate levels in many sports is the physical difference between males and females. The ratio of strength to weight is greater in males than in females. Females thus would be at a decided disadvantage in those sports requiring speed, power, strength, and impact. As a consequence, teams would be male dominated.

The Impact of Title IX on Girls and Women in Sport

During the year before the birth of Title IX, 3,366,000 boys and 294,000 girls competed in interscholastic sport in the United States. After seven years, that figure increased to over 4 million boys and 1,645,000 girls, and today, the National Federation of State High School Associations reports that 2,367,936 of the 6,019,889 participants in interscholastic sports are girls. Girls' participation in interscholastic sport increased 460 percent during the interim. Furthermore, the participation of girls increased from 7 percent of the total number of students involved to 29 percent. Girls participate in more than twenty-nine high school sports. The three most popular sports, in terms of schools sponsoring teams and number of participants, are basketball, track and field, and volleyball. Approximately 500 colleges offer sport scholarships to women athletes. The Association for Intercollegiate Athletics for Women (AIAW), now defunct, had more than 1,000 member schools a decade ago and was the largest collegiate athletic association in the United States. Since that time, however, the NCAA has taken over control of women's sport in most colleges and universities and for more than 15 years has provided opportunities for young women to participate in myriad championship events.

Although sport programs for men and women are still not equal in terms of funding, budgets for boys' sport activities at the interscholastic level were on the average larger than the budgets for girls' sport activities.

Sport programs for male and female student-athletes on all levels are far more equal, as well as more numerous, in the 1990s than ever before. It is unfortunate that financial constraints are now also equally affecting men's and women's programs, resulting in some loss of both men's and women's sports, especially at the collegiate level.

Legislation such as Title IX has had a positive impact. One negative impact of Title IX is that the number of female coaches in girls' and women's sport programs has decreased dramatically, from about 90 percent in the early 1970s to around 50 percent in the mid-1980s (Acosta and Carpenter 1985; Acosta and Carpenter 1992).

Title IX, the Courts, and Prospects for the Future

Since the passage of Title IX, the courts have played a crucial role in effecting change toward equality. The courts have caused some changes in Title IX. The 1984 U.S. Supreme Court decision in *Grove City College v. Bell* changed the interpretation of Title IX as formerly held. The court ruled that only the student aid office at Grove City College was covered by laws barring sex bias, because the only federal money that the institution received came through student Pell Grants. In the case of private institutions that received direct federal aid, the U.S. Commission on Civil Rights stated that only the program or activity that actually received the aid need abide by Title IX regulations. In other words, the federal law barring sex discrimination in education, according to the Grove City ruling, did not apply to schools and colleges as a whole, but only to those parts or subunits of an institution that directly received federal aid. The court ruling meant, for example, that if the sport programs do not receive federal aid directly, they are not covered by Title IX. This ruling raised a storm of protest from the Office of Civil Rights and other organizations supporting the original concept of Title IX—if an institution received federal aid, then all programs within that organization are covered by Title IX regulations. On March 2, 1988, the U.S. Senate voted 75 to 14 to approve Senate Bill 557, the Civil Rights Restoration Act, which served to counteract the 1984 Grove City College decision and return the enforcement of Title IX to an institutional rather than specific subunit basis.

Each institution and each educational program will face continued challenges in complying with Title IX. This challenge is true particularly in light of the budget crises that many schools and colleges face at present. For example, it will be difficult for many institutions to increase, or even maintain, items such as support services, budgets, and facilities for an expanded sport program for girls without curtailing some other parts of the educational program at the same time. More realistically, it will become even more difficult to bear the increased costs of our present sport

The strength of women's athletics has greatly improved since Title IX was passed.

programming that now provide females and males with comparable sport programs. If proportioned equally, however, reductions in programs of compliance would further serve to reduce the opportunities for girls and women to participate. Class action suits at Brown University, Indiana University of Pennsylvania, and Colorado State University—because each institution attempted athletic department cost cutting by eliminating, respectively, women's gymnastics and volleyball, gymnastics and field hockey, and softball—attest to the ongoing battle to keep or reinstate programs that were discontinued. Each suit led to reinstatement.

Many changes have taken place to comply with the spirit of Title IX. Sports such as soccer, rowing, rifle/pistol shooting, skiing, and water polo have been rapidly expanding at the college level, where women make up approximately 37 percent of all athletes (a 22 percent increase since 1992). These changes and others, while not completely leveling the playing field, are positive

steps in breaking down the myth that women are physically or psychosocially inferior to men either in or out of the arena of competitive sport. Title IX has cleared the way for behavioral change to take place concerning women's participation not only in the domain of competitive sport but also in all of society.

SELECTED SPORTING ASSOCIATIONS

An individual school or college, by itself, finds it difficult to develop standards and control sport in a sound educational manner. However, uniting with similar schools and colleges makes such a formidable task possible. This coordinating has been done on local, state, and national levels in the interest of better sport for high schools and colleges. Establishing rules, policies, and procedures well in advance of playing seasons provides educators and coaches the necessary guidelines and control for conducting sound competitive sport programs. It aids them in resisting pressures of alumni, students, parents, spectators, community, media, and others who do not always have the best interests of the student-athlete and the program in mind.

Various types of sport associations exist. The ones most prevalent in high schools and colleges are student athletic associations, local conferences or leagues, state high school associations or leagues, the National Federation of State High School Associations, the National Association for Intercollegiate Athletes, the National Collegiate Athletic Association, and their respective conferences that exist throughout the nation.

The student athletic association or board is an organization within a school designed to actively promote and participate in the conduct of the school sport program. It is usually open to all students who elect to pay fees, which further help support the competitive sport program. Such associations are found in many high schools and colleges throughout the country. These associations assist in the mobilization of ticket sales, program and event promotion, and overall school enthusiasm. Once initiated, they add another educational component and dimension to the management structure of a well-managed sport program.

Various associations or boards, conferences, or leagues also bind together to facilitate sport competition and scheduling and to reduce travel. Usually several high schools within a particular geographical area will become members of a conference in order to construct schedules, assign officials, handle disputes, and maintain general guidance over the sport programs of the member schools.

The state high school athletic association or league that now exists in almost every state is yet another major influence in high school sport. The state association is usually open to all professionally accredited high schools within the state. It operates under a constitution, employs an administrative core of officers to conduct business, and usually possesses a board of directors. The number of members on the board varies widely but the board usually has a representative from each district or region. Fees or dues are usually as-

sessed by the association on a per school basis or sometimes according to the size of the school or number of sports offered. Some states have no fees because the necessary revenue is derived from the gate receipts, sponsorships, and/or television revenue from tournament competition. State associations are interested in sound programs of sport competition within the confines of the state. They concern themselves with the usual problems that have to do with sport, such as eligibility of players, certification of coaches and officials, conduct of coaches, handling of protests and disputes, and the organization and conduct of state tournaments. These state associations are interested in promoting sound high school sport practices, equalizing athletic competition, protecting participants, and guarding the health and welfare of players. In some states, such as Minnesota, the association operates drug awareness programs throughout the state. State associations have been a positive influence and have won the respect of school administrators, coaches, and educators.

National Association for Girls and Women in Sport

The National Association for Girls and Women in Sport (NAGWS) is one of the six associations of AAHPERD and is concerned with the governance of sports for girls and women.

The specific functions of the NAGWS are

- to formulate and publicize guiding principles and standards for the administrator, leader, official, and player
- to publish and interpret rules governing sports for girls and women
- to provide the means for training, evaluating, and rating officials
- to disseminate information on the conduct of girls' and women's sports
- to stimulate, evaluate, and disseminate research in the field of girls' and women's sports
- to cooperate with allied groups interested in girls' and women's sports in order to formulate policies and rules that affect the conduct of women's sports

- to provide opportunities for the development of leadership among girls and women for the conduct of their sport programs

The National Council of Secondary School Athletic Directors

AAHPERD's National Association for Sport and Physical Education (NASPE) established the National Council of Secondary School Athletic Directors. The increased emphasis on sport and the important position of athletic and activities directors in the nation's secondary schools warranted a council by which increased services could be rendered to enhance the services offered to the nation's youth. The membership in the National Council is open to members of AAHPERD who have primary responsibility in directing, administering, or coordinating interscholastic sport programs.

The purposes of the Council are:

- to improve the educational aspects of interscholastic sport and their articulation in the total educational program
- to foster high standards of professional proficiency and ethics
- to improve understanding of sport throughout the nation
- to establish closer working relationships with related professional groups
- to promote greater unity, goodwill, and fellowship among all members
- to provide for an exchange of ideas
- to assist and cooperate with existing state athletic directors' organizations
- to make available to members special resource materials through publications, conferences, and consultant services

The National Federation of State High School Athletic Associations

High school competition for boys began in Michigan in the late 1890s and, subsequently, a Michigan state athletic association was developed. By the turn of the century, Illinois and Indiana had followed Michigan's lead and inaugurated their respective state athletic associations. In New York, Luther Gulick established the New York City Public School Athletic League in 1903, which was followed in 1905 by the founding of a girls' branch under the direction of Elizabeth Burchenal.

The National Federation of State High School Athletic Associations was established in 1920 with five states participating. At present nearly all states are members. The National Federation is particularly concerned with the control of interstate sport competitions. Its constitution states this purpose:

> The object of this Federation shall be to protect and supervise the interstate athletic interests of the high schools belonging to the state associations, to assist in those activities of state associations, which can best be operated on a nationwide scale, to sponsor meetings, publications and activities which will permit each state association to profit by the experience of all other member associations, and to coordinate the work so that waste effort and unnecessary duplication will be avoided.

The National Federation has been responsible for many improvements in sport on a national basis, such as writing rule books for sixteen different boys' and girls' high school sports and working toward uniformity of standards.

The National Collegiate Athletic Association

The National Collegiate Athletic Association (NCAA) was formed in 1906. The alarming number of football injuries and the fact that there was no institutional control of the game led to a conference in New York City on December 12, 1905, attended by representatives from thirteen universities and colleges. Preliminary plans were made for a national agency to assist in the formulation of sound requirements for intercollegiate athletics, particularly football, and the name Intercollegiate Athletic Association (IAA) was suggested. At a meeting on March 31, 1906, a constitution and bylaws were adopted and issued. On December 29, 1910, the name of the IAA was

The NCAA conducts 79 championships in 21 sports.

changed to NCAA. The purposes of the NCAA are as follows:

- to uphold the principle of institutional control of, and responsibility for, all intercollegiate athletics in conformity with the association's constitution and bylaws
- to serve as an overall national discussion, legislative, and administrative body for the universities and colleges of the United States in matters of intercollegiate athletics
- to recommend policies for the guidance of member institutions in the conduct of their intercollegiate athletic programs
- to legislate upon any subject of general concern to the membership in the administration of intercollegiate athletics
- to study all phases of competitive athletics and establish standards therefor, to the end that colleges and universities throughout the United

States may maintain their athletic activities on a high plane

- to encourage the adoption by its constituent members of eligibility rules in compliance with satisfactory standards of scholarship, amateur standing, and fair play
- to establish and supervise regional and national collegiate athletic contests under the auspices of the association and establish rules of eligibility therefor
- to stimulate and improve programs to promote and develop educational leadership, physical fitness, sports participation as a recreational pursuit, and athletic excellence through competitive recreational and intercollegiate sport programs
- to formulate, copyright, and publish rules of play for collegiate sports
- to preserve collegiate athletic records
- to cooperate with other amateur athletic organizations in the promotion and conduct of national and international athletic contests
- to otherwise assist member institutions as requested in the furtherance of their intercollegiate athletic programs

Membership in the NCAA numbers more than 995 colleges and universities and 108 conferences categorized in three divisions. The NCAA requires that an institution be accredited and compete in a minimum of seven intercollegiate sports each year, with at least one sport sponsored in each of the three recognized sport seasons.

The services provided by the NCAA are as extensive as its stated purposes for existence. These services include publication of official guides in various sports, provision of a film and video library, establishment of an eligibility code for athletes and provisions for the enforcement of this code, provisions for national meets and tournaments with appropriate eligibility rules for competition, provision of financial and other assistance to groups interested in the promotion and encouragement of intercollegiate and recreational sport, and provision of administrative services for

U.S. universities and colleges concerning matters of international competition and student-athletes. The NCAA, which will be moving its headquarters from Kansas City to Indianapolis, offers 79 women's and men's championships in 21 sports (crew will soon be added) at the Division I, II, and III levels. In 1995, 107,605 young women and 176,607 young men participated under the NCAA umbrella, with more than 24,000 student-athletes participating in championship events.

The National Association of Intercollegiate Athletics

Another sport association on the college and university level is the National Association of Intercollegiate Athletics (NAIA), which has a membership of more than 365 institutions, mostly among the smaller colleges. This organization was instituted in 1940 as a basketball tournament association and by 1952 emerged as a total sport association. Its primary function is to provide national championship opportunities for young men and women competing below the "big-time" NCAA Division I level.

The National Junior College Athletic Association

The National Junior College Athletic Association (NJCAA) is an organization of junior colleges that has sponsored sport programs since its inception in 1937 in California. It now has regional offices with an elected regional director for each. Regional business matters are conducted within the framework of the constitution and bylaws of the parent organization. The regional directors, who are governed by an executive committee, hold an annual legislative assembly to determine the policies, programs, and procedures for the organization. The assembly's location rotates between NJCAA headquarters in Colorado Springs, Colorado (odd years), and regional sites (even years). The *Juco Review* is the official publication of the organization. Standing and special committees are appointed each year to cover special items and problems that develop. The role of the NJCAA closely follows that outlined by the NCAA.

National championships are conducted in sports such as basketball, cross country, wrestling, baseball, track and field, golf, and tennis. National invitation events are also conducted in activities such as soccer and swimming.

The NJCAA, with more than 300 institutional members, is affiliated with the National Federation of State High School Associations and the National Association of Intercollegiate Athletics. It is also affiliated with the U.S. Collegiate Sports Council, U.S. Olympic Committee and its respective federations, and AAHPERD.

Some of the services offered by the NJCAA to its members include recognition of organizations and athletes, recognition in official records, publications, film and video library, and participation in events sponsored by the association.

Amateur Athletic Union of the United States

Founded in 1888, the Amateur Athletic Union (AAU) of the United States is probably the oldest as well as the largest single organization designed to regulate and promote the conduct of amateur sport. Certainly it is one of the most influential organizations governing amateur sport in the world.

The AAU is a federation of sport and athletic clubs, national and district associations, educational institutions, and amateur athletic organizations.

Many persons associate the AAU only with track and field. However, the organization is involved with many more sports and activities, including basketball, baton twirling, bobsledding, boxing, diving, gymnastics, handball, judo, karate, luge, power lifting, swimming, synchronized swimming, volleyball, water polo, weight lifting, and wrestling. In addition to governing this multiplicity of sports and activities, the AAU is vitally concerned with ensuring that the amateur status of athletes is maintained at all times when participating in the amateur sport arena. To this end, the leaders of the AAU have developed and promulgated a precise set of guidelines describing amateurism.

Some of the other activities of the AAU include registering athletes to identify and control the amateur status of participants in sport events, sponsoring national championships, raising funds for the U.S. athletes for international competition and the Olympic Games, conducting tryouts for the selection of Olympic competitors, and sponsoring Junior Olympic competition. The AAU has established a number of committees (e.g., age group diving, track and field, youth activities, swimming) to help with the monumental task of performing the myriad duties associated with governing such a large number of sports and activities. An executive director housed in Indianapolis, Indiana, directs and coordinates all activities of the AAU.

Other Organizations

Higher education also has many leagues, conferences, and associations formed by a limited number of schools for sport competition. Examples are the Ivy League, Big Ten, Big East, Big Twelve, Pac 10, SEC, Southland, and Atlantic Coast Conferences. These associations regulate sport competition among their members and settle problems that may arise in connection with such competition.

Other groups related to sport and the sporting process include, but are not limited to, AAHPERD; the National Association of Collegiate Directors of Athletics (NACDA); and the U.S. Olympic Committee (USOC).

SUMMARY

The standards for competitive sport in schools, colleges, and other organizations have been clearly identified. There should be no doubt in any individual's mind about the types of interscholastic and intercollegiate programs that are educationally sound and operate in the best interests of student-athletes who participate in them. It is the responsibility of managers and others concerned with such programs to implement the various standards that have been established. The issue is not one of de-emphasis, but of re-emphasis along educational lines. Sound leadership will make the interscholastic and intercolle-

giate programs forces for quality education that have no equal.

Competitive sport is a part of the total Physical Activity and Sport Continuum. The objectives stated earlier in this text for physical education also apply to interscholastic and intercollegiate sport. Managers should evaluate their programs in terms of the extent to which the listed objectives are being achieved.

Sport has value if it is conducted in a sound educational manner. The management in charge of competitive sport is largely responsible to see that it is conducted in accordance with the standards that have been set. In so doing, managers may be confronted with problems that periodically occur in these programs because of sport's high public visibility and the economics involved. However, prudent managers know the goals to be achieved and the standards to be observed. Therefore, their responsibility is to see that the total competitive sport program is conducted accordingly.

SELF-ASSESSMENT ACTIVITIES

These activities will assist students in determining if material and competencies presented in this chapter have been mastered.

1. You are at a school budget hearing when a taxpayer attacks the varsity sport program as costing too much money for the values derived. As a member of the athletic staff, you are asked to react to the taxpayer's statement. What values can you cite to support the need for a varsity sport program?

2. Write profiles of what you consider to be the ideal director of athletics, coach, and athletic trainer.

3. Divide the class into teams that discuss the pros and cons of competitive sports at each educational level.

4. As a director of athletics and activities at a high school, what administrative policy would you recommend regarding the following: Gate receipts, tournaments and championships, eligibility, scholarships, recruiting, proselytizing, and scouting?

5. Develop a set of standards that could be used to evaluate a sport program at the junior high school level.

6. Identify the sporting association that governs your institution and the role it plays in the conduct of sport on your campus.

7. Prepare a report that provides pertinent facts about your school's competitive sport program and its compliance with Title IX.

REFERENCES

1. AAHPERD (American Alliance for Health, Physical Education, Recreation, and Dance) 1977. Equality in sports for women. Reston, Va.: AAHPERD.
2. Acosta, R. V., and L. J. Carpenter. 1985. Women in athletics—a status report. *Journal of Physical Education, Recreation, and Dance* 56(6):30–37.
3. Acosta, R. V., and L. J. Carpenter. 1992. *Women in intercollegiate sport: A longitudinal Study: Fifteen year update 1977–1992.* (Available from author, Brooklyn College, Brooklyn, NY 11210.)
4. AIAW (Association of Intercollegiate Athletic for Women) 1979. Code of ethics for coaches. *AIAW handbook.* Washington, D.C.: AAHPERD.
5. Arnheim, D. D.; and W. E. Prentice. 1997. *Principles of athletic training.* 9th ed. WCB/McGraw-Hill.
6. Auxter, D., J. Pyfer, and C. Huettig. 1993. *Principles and methods of adapted physical education and recreation.* 7th ed. St. Louis: Mosby–Year Book.
7. Coakley, J. J. 1994. *Sport in society: Issues and controversies.* 5th ed. St. Louis: 1994. Mosby–Year Book.
8. Eitzen, D. S., and G. H. Sage. 1997. *Sociology of North American sport.* Dubuque, Iowa: Brown & Benchmark.
9. Kramer, B. 1993. Title IX in intercollegiate athletics: Litigation risks facing colleges and universities. Washington, D.C.: Association of Governing Boards of Universities and Colleges. Public Policy Series No. 93-2. November.
10. Lopiano, D. 1986. The certified coach: Central figure. *Journal of Physical Education, Recreation and Dance* 51(9):32–33.
11. NASPE 1995. *National Standards for Athletic Coaches.* Dubuque, Iowa: Kendall/Hunt.
12. Sage, G. H. 1989. Becoming a high school coach: From playing sports to coaching. *Research Quarterly for Exercise and Sport* 60:81–90.
13. Stein, J. U. and L. A. Klappholz. 1977. *Special Olympics instructional manual.* Washington, D.C.: AAHPERD and The Kennedy Foundation.
14. Vargyas, E. J. 1994. *Breaking down barriers: A legal guide to Title IX.* Washington, D.C.: National Women's Law Center.

SUGGESTED READINGS

Andre, J., and D. N. James. 1991. *Rethinking college athletics.* Philadelphia: Temple University Press.

Coakley, J. 1994. *Sport in society: Issues and controversies.* 5th ed. St. Louis: Mosby–Year Book.
Provides a critical analysis of many of the salient sociological issues, concerns, and controversies in the sporting domain. Race, violence, social mobility, and politics as well as competitive sport are explored.

Cratty, B. J. 1989. *Psychology in contemporary sport.* Englewood Cliffs, N.J.: Prentice Hall.
Provides guidelines for coaches and athletes regarding various aspects of the psychology of sports, including psychological assessment, leadership, motivation, activation, aggression, and group dynamics. Also discusses characteristics such as coaching behavior, behavior modification, imagery, and team cohesion.

Frey, J., ed. 1982. *The governance of intercollegiate sports.* West Point, N.Y.: Leisure Press.
Examines the history of sport governance, sport cartels, alumni, law, and the "greening" of American athletes.

Graham, S., J. F. Wedman, and B. Gsarvin-Kester. 1994. Manager coaching skills: What makes a good coach? *Performance Improvement Quarterly* 7(2):81–94.

Houlihan, B. 1994. *Sport and international politics.* New York: Harvester Wheatsheaf.

Koehler, M. D. 1996. *Advising student athletes through the recruitment process.* Englewood Cliffs, N.J.: Prentice Hall.

Lumpkin, A., S. K. Stoll, and J. M. Beller. 1994. *Sports ethics: Applications for fair play.* St. Louis: Mosby–Year Book.

Orlick, T. 1980. *In pursuit of excellence.* Champaign, Ill.: Human Kinetics.
Explores the limits of human performance including commitment, self-control, goal setting, concentration, imagery, and dealing with coaching problems.

Paterno, J., 1985. Crystal balling with America's sports leaders. *Athletic Business,* January.
Nationally known sport leader predicts the future for college sports, women's sport programs, youth sport,

and the Olympic Games. Discusses academic standards, recruiting, economic problems, and Title IX.

Perry, R. H. 1987. Intercollegiate athletics in turmoil: So what else is new? *Journal of Sports Management* 1:82–86, January.

Traces the recurring problems of intercollegiate sport and discusses sports' external power brokers. Offers a prescription for future conduct of competitive sport.

Thoma, J. E., and L. Chalip. 1996. *Sport governance in the global community.* Morgantown, W. Va.: Fitness Information Technology.

Wuest, D. A., and C. A. Bucher. 1996. *Foundations of physical education and sport.* St. Louis: Mosby–Year Book.

Presents an overview of the various academic components of physical education; discusses sports-related careers, issues, and challenges facing the profession.

Management of Physical Education and Sport Programs in the Public and Private Sector

part

6 Physical Education and Sport Programs in the Public and Private Sector

Physical Education and Sport Programs in the Public and Private Sector

---

Instructional Objectives and Competencies To Be Achieved

After reading this chapter the student should be able to

- Identify physical education and sport careers and opportunities across the Physical Activity and Sport Continuum.

- Identify and describe the role of physical education and sport in public and private sector settings.

- Understand some of the management and program responsibilities involved in various employment settings.

- Illustrate organizational structures related to public and private sector physical education and sport programs.

- Identify current and future trends in public and private sector physical education and sport programs.

- Determine qualifications and preparation needed to successfully fulfill management responsibilities in the corporate and commercial health and fitness industry.

This text is devoted in great measure to the management processes, organizational structure, and functioning of physical education and sport programs housed within educational institutions at the elementary, secondary, and college levels. However, in recent years many potentially promising careers and employment opportunities have developed in settings other than schools and colleges (table 6-1). Corporations, businesses, athletic clubs, sports associations, therapeutic and rehabilitation centers, health clubs and spas, senior citizen centers, Ys, Jewish Community Centers (JCCs), and community centers have opened new windows of employment opportunity for physical educators.

This chapter is designed to provide the reader with information about representative public and private organizations at which physical educators may seek employment (even ownership) as instructors, personal trainers, consultants, and managers.

The chapter is divided into four sections. The first section presents corporate or workplace health and fitness career opportunities. Companies featured include Xerox Corporation, IBM, PepsiCo Inc., General Mills Inc., and Tenneco Inc. The second section provides a glimpse into

Table 6-1. Physical education and sport career opportunities

Teaching Opportunities

School Setting	Nonschool Setting
Elementary school	Community
Junior high school	recreation/sport
High school	programs
Junior/community	Corporate recreation
college	programs
College and university	Commercial sport clubs
Basic instructional	Youth-serving agencies
programs	Preschools
Professional	Health clubs
preparation programs	Military personnel
Adapted physical	programs
education	Resort sport programs
Overseas school	Geriatric programs
programs	Correctional institution
Military school	programs
programs	Sport tourism
International school	State high school
programs	leagues

Coaching Opportunities

Interscholastic programs	Commercial sport clubs
Intercollegiate programs	Community sport
Commercial sport	programs
camps	Military sport programs
International sport	AAU and club sport
camps	programs

Fitness and Health-Related Opportunities

Cardiac rehabilitation	Space fitness programs
Sports medicine	Corporate fitness
Movement therapy	programs
Health clubs	Sports nutrition
Community fitness	Athletic training
programs	Weight control spas
Personal fitness trainer	Military personnel
	programs

Sport Management Opportunities

Athletic administration	Sport organization
Aquatic administration	administration
Sport facility manage-	Health club
ment	management
Commercial sport club	Sport information
management	Sport retailing
Community recreation/	Corporate recreation
sport management	and wellness
Recreational sport/	Resort sport
campus recreation	management
U.S. Olympic Commit-	Bowl organizations
tee organizations	Sport conference
Sports governing bodies	commissioner
	Sport professional
	associations

Sport Media Opportunities

Sports information	Sport broadcasting and
Sport journalism	production
Sport photography	Sport art
Writing sport-oriented	Sport product advisor
books	
Sport publishing	

Sport-Related Opportunities

Player personnel and	Sport officiating
community relations	Game/event
Sport law	entertainment
Professional athlete	Sport statistician
Entrepreneur	Sport consulting
Research	Compliance director
Academic counseling	Golf club and turf
Sport agent	management
	Sport/educational
	psychologist

Source: Wuest and Bucher 1991.

the commercial fitness industry; Bally Total Fitness, Clark Hatch Fitness Centers, and the Radisson Hotel and Conference Center are presented. The third section explores various representative community-based programs, including a Y, a Jewish Community Center, a recreation and parks department, a local community recreation department, and an example of a state high school league program. The final section presents the professional qualifications necessary to meet the responsibilities in public and private sector physical education and sport programs.

CORPORATE OR WORKPLACE HEALTH, FITNESS, AND WELLNESS PROGRAMS

In the last decade, many large and small corporations and businesses have begun to offer employee health, fitness, and wellness programs. These companies have found that improved fitness among their ranks leads to improved health, decreased employee medical problems and absenteeism, and higher levels of employee job satisfaction. Corporations and businesses can also attract, recruit, and maintain top-notch employees by providing quality programs for both the employees and their families. Indeed, a survey by the U.S. Department of Health and Human Services (1987) reported that more than half of the U.S. companies with 750 or more employees, and almost 70 percent of the companies with 50 or more employees, offer some form of corporate or workplace health and fitness program. These in-house health, fitness, and wellness (e.g., nutrition, smoking cessation, stress management) programs save an estimated seven dollars for each one dollar invested, which is why an estimated seven billion dollars annually is spent in health and fitness-related corporate environs (Eitzen and Sage 1994). Since 1974 the American Association for Fitness Directors in Business and Industry (AAFDBI) has served both professional and potential students in the art of corporate fitness. The mission of the AAFDBI is to provide professional support and assistance in the development and maintenance of quality health, fitness, and wellness programs as well as to promote standards (e.g., American Council on Exercise

[ACE], American College of Sports Medicine [ACSM], National Strength and Conditioning Association [NSCA]) and professionalism. The AAFDBI disseminates information through its *Action* newsletter and its research publication *Footprints* and is housed at 60 Revere Dr., Suite 500, Northbrooke, IL 60062-1577.

The following pages present representative corporate or workplace programs that go well beyond the scope of the traditional employee fitness programs. The information about these creative programs has been gathered from the professional literature, from publications prepared by the corporations or companies, and directly from personnel of the respective organizations.

Xerox Corporation

Source of Information
Connie Kristen, Manager
Fitness and Recreation Services

General Information

In 1974, Xerox Corporation opened a centralized educational facility named the Xerox International Center for Training and Management Development in Leesburg, Virginia. The center is now known as Xerox Document University. In this environment, employees learn the latest techniques of selling and servicing information systems and products, and they develop themselves to meet the management challenges of the future. A crucial component of Xerox Document University's center for training and development is its Fitness and Recreation Service program.

Fitness and Recreation Services (FRS) establishes and manages program activities that contribute to effective use of employee leisure time and improve employee health and morale. It is also open through membership to the immediate community in order to build bridges between the corporate and public sectors.

Program Goals/Objectives

Since the opening of FRS in 1974, its primary objectives have been to (1) provide optimal physical and mental fitness for its employees through

Employees jog at Xerox Document University's Fitness and Recreation Center, Leesburg, Va.

organized and open fitness and recreation programs, (2) promote the constructive use of leisure time, and (3) provide an outlet for stress and tension.

Program Description

The Xerox Corporation offers numerous programs, which are designed to promote the effective use of leisure time as well as to enhance employee and community wellness and lifestyle. The program offers an individualized approach to fitness and wellness assessment and programming to employees, whether retired or active, and their families. Frequent fitness themes such as the Race to Atlanta—in which employees are awarded prizes for workout hours logged—are incorporated into the center's programming. Other activities, ranging from intramural basketball, tennis, volleyball, and wallyball to outward-bound pursuits, are offered to its management teams. The FSR also serves its corporate seminar user groups with ice breakers as well as stretch breaks ranging from aerobics to stress management.

Operation hours are 6 A.M. to 10 P.M. Monday through Thursday; 6 A.M. to 7 P.M. Friday; and 10 A.M. to 8 P.M. Saturday and Sunday.

Gymnasium #1 provides areas for volleyball and aerobic workouts, weight training and exercise equipment, one squash and two racquetball courts, a fitness assessment area, and a physical activity room.

Gymnasium #2 houses facilities for basketball, volleyball, badminton, and jogging as well as individual exercise equipment in various exercise stations.

Outdoor facilities include four tennis courts, two volleyball and paddle tennis courts, swimming pool, picnic area, jogging and bicycling trail, and an 18-station exercise trail.

Additional programs organized by the FRS include nutritional assessment and counseling, body composition profiles, golf league, tennis and volleyball clubs, fishing tournaments, and myriad special events focusing on family and community.

Personnel

Manager of fitness and recreation services
Fitness and recreation specialist
Fitness attendant
College interns

Contact Address

Xerox Document University
International Center for Training and Management Development
P.O. Box 2000
Leesburg VA 22075

International Business Machines (IBM)

Source of Information

Karen Orenstein, Program Manager
Fitness and Wellness Programs

General Information

IBM United States has a tradition of concern for the health of its employees, retirees, and their families, and offers a variety of wellness programs designed to encourage health, fitness, and work performance. Management believes that healthy employees/retirees are more productive

IBM is also active in sponsoring and promoting physical education and sport.

and enjoy a state of well-being that contributes to the quality of life and work in the home and company. IBM is also aware that enhanced health and fitness will slow the escalating cost of health-related corporate expense.

IBM United States has a workforce of approximately 300,000 employees, with more than 750,000 individuals (i.e., employees, retirees) spread over 200 locations eligible to participate in its fitness and wellness programs. Because of these numbers, operations are centralized and programming guidelines are relayed to on-site general managers for their location-specific implementation. Outside specialists are often utilized to manage the local IBM programs and provide a high level of expertise and service. The same program format is, for the most part, offered to all employees/retirees at all IBM locations.

Program Goals/Objectives

IBM's health promotion programs for employees and retirees grew out of a convergence of several factors—a concern for better health, the spiraling costs of medical benefits, a more fitness-oriented

population, and research indicating that personal care can be as important as medical science in improving health and wellness and extending the life span.

The objectives of IBM's health promotion programs are to improve/maintain the participants' health, reduce risks of developing disease, improve employee productivity and morale, reduce absenteeism, and slow the escalation of health-care expenditures.

Program Description

The IBM comprehensive program includes a voluntary health assessment (VHA). Since the VHA was initiated in 1968, more than 350,000 employees have taken advantage of this corporate benefit. The VHA provides a health profile based on age, gender, lifestyle, and family background.

The core of the IBM program, however, resides in its A Life Planning Account program (ALPA). This is a coordinated program offered at all IBM sites that enables employees and retirees to take a variety of classes (e.g., sexuality, parenting, humor, health, CPR and first aid) as well as participate in fitness and health-related activities ranging from solid soft-impact aerobic exercise to water exercise. The programs are conducted by specialists at the IBM locations as well as by local fitness, health and racquet clubs, Ys, and other community-based educational fitness program locations.

IBM also maintains recreation and fitness facilities at more than 30 locations across the country. These facilities vary, but many include sports fields, outdoor tennis and basketball courts, swimming pools, and exercise rooms. Flagship facilities (i.e., golf course) exist in Armonk, Poughkeepsie, Endicott, and Sands Point, New York, as well as in Boulder, Colorado, and San Jose, California.

Program Specifics

For the most part, IBM focuses on the ALPA program, which is offered at all of IBM's manufacturing, laboratory, and sales office sites. The ALPA consists of a series of comprehensive health-related classes (often conducted on location). These classes include exercise, weight management, smoking cessation, nutrition, first aid and CPR, parenting, and legal issues in caring for the elderly, just to mention a few. The classes are conducted in the morning, during noon hour, and in the evening to encourage as many employees as possible to attend.

Other ALPA components include physical activities ranging from aerobic exercise to water safety. Most of these activities are conducted off-site. Usually participants pay their own way to ALPA-coordinated offerings and IBM provides a tuition assistance reimbursement program, which pays up to the cost of the program (e.g., $175 for smoking-cessation class, $65 for water safety). Specific program completion reimbursement fees may also be used toward the cost of a membership to, for instance, a community-based YMCA or health and fitness club.

In 1987, IBM established a videotape library at most sites, focusing on topics ranging from fitness and stress management to AIDS and substance abuse. The tapes are available to employees and other community-based organizations at no cost.

Yearly health fairs are conducted at IBM locations nationwide, at which health-related assessments such as blood pressure, cholesterol, and body fat composition are developed into a health profile for each participant. IBM's Health Benefits staff also provides counseling twenty-four hours a day for all eligible IBM employees.

Personnel

Because of the decentralized nature of IBM's ALPA program, the personnel requirements may include an ALPA site coordinator (more than 200 nationally); however, for the most part, outside specialists are contracted to conduct both the on-site and off-site activities.

Contact Address

IBM HR-USA
Town of Mt. Pleasant, Rte. 9
Sleepy Hollow, NY 10591

Pepsi-Cola

Source of Information

Anne Tuite, Program Manager
Employee Wellness Services

General Information

Pepsi-Cola, a large soft drink producer, is under the larger PepsiCo umbrella, which also operates several restaurant/food divisions, including Frito-Lay, Pizza Hut, Taco Bell, and KFC. PepsiCo and all its divisions are committed to corporate fitness and wellness programs.

Program Goals/Objectives

The mission of the Pepsi-Cola Employee Wellness Services Program (EWSP) is to meet the cultural objectives of the company by focusing on family issues, employee involvement, and lifestyles conducive to better work and personal performance. "We are passionately dedicated to enriching the lives of all employees. Staff expertise and employee input direct the improvement of existing programs as well as creation of new programs designed to enhance the body, mind & spirit, helping all of us thrive in a dynamic business environment."

Goals include (1) the improvement of the social and physical profile of the company by increasing employee involvement over the previous year; (2) the increasing of the percentage of employees in the health, fitness, wellness, and recreation programs; (3) the promotion, internally and externally, of the Pepsi-Cola EWSP; and (4) the identification of the needs of employees in health, fitness, wellness, and recreation.

Program Description

Pepsi-Cola and the other divisions offer programs made up of the following four components:

1. General fitness: exercise testing and prescription, personal training
2. Recreation: intramurals, special events including ski and hiking trips
3. Health promotion: lunchtime lectures, programs and workshops (e.g., diet, nutrition, smoking cessation)

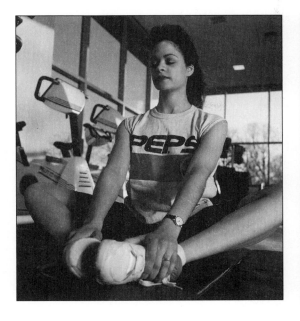

EMPLOYEE
WELLNESS
SERVICES

ENRICHING THE
BODY, MIND & SPIRIT

Trained professionals guide Pepsi-Cola Company's Employee Wellness Services Program.

4. Rehabilitation: injury prevention and care, massage therapy

Program Specifics

Of 1,700 employees at Pepsi-Cola corporate headquarters, 50 percent participate in the fitness, outdoor education, environment, and health promotion programs. An annual budget of $400,000 is appropriated for the Pepsi-Cola programs. Monthly special events (e.g., Family Month, Heart Month, Nutrition Month), tournaments, corporate leagues, and fitness and health incentives are all creatively packaged and promoted through their monthly *WellSource* newsletter and are aimed at total company involvement. The 15,200-square-feet center is available for use twenty-four hours per day and is supervised Monday to Friday 6:30 A.M. to 7:30 P.M.

Pepsi's wellness program focuses on the total person, combining the physical (e.g., fitness, nutrition), social (e.g., self and interpersonal skills and team-building activities), emotional (e.g., stress and crisis management, yoga), intellectual (e.g., personal fitness and health skills), and spiritual (e.g., volunteerism and mentoring programs). Pepsi-Cola also supports a wide range of charities, such as the Red Cross, and community programs, such as running and walking events and cycling tours.

Personnel

Program manager
Three fitness and recreation coordinators
One wellness coordinator
One administrative assistant

Contact Address

Pepsi-Cola World Beverage Headquarters
Health, Wellness and Fitness Program
1 Pepsi Way
Somers NY 10589-2201

General Mills, Inc.

Source of Information
Andrew Wood, Director
TriHealthalon Program

General Information

General Mills is a Midwest-based firm that consists of four divisions: Big G Cereal, Betty Crocker, Yoplait/Columbo, and Gold Medal.

Workplace health promotion began in earnest in the early 1980s under the title Framework—A Healthy Lifestyle Program. In 1984, the expanded TriHealthalon program began under the auspices of the Health and Human Services Department (figure 6-1). General Mills' Employee Service unit also promotes leisure-time recreation and sport clubs. The corporation is furthermore a strong supporter of the Olympic Games, Special Olympics, and other worthy community-based programs.

Program Goals/Objectives

The TriHealthalon is a program developed to improve the health of General Mills employees in the areas designated by the World Health Organization. These include the focal aspects of health—physical, mental, and social well-being.

- Physical well-being signifies exercising, eating well, controlling body weight, and being aware of the risk factors associated with cardiovascular heart disease and cancer.
- Mental well-being includes release of stress in one's life and involvement in activities that are recreational, relaxing, and entertaining.
- Social well-being focuses on improving interpersonal relations, controlling chemical usage, and being aware of personal safety.

Program Description

Every employee who completes the Personal Medical History and Lifestyle Appraisal forms is enrolled in the TriHealthalon program. Each participant receives a computer-analyzed health recommendation plan.

Health goals are determined, and three categories of participation are outlined in terms of physical, mental, and social well-being goals:

1. physical: fitness, nutrition and weight control, and cancer prevention

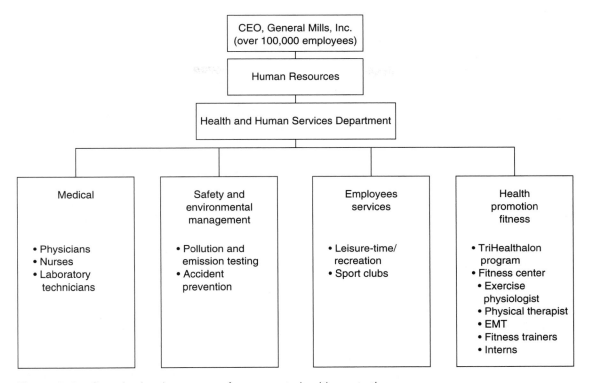

Figure 6-1. Organizational structure of a corporate health promotion program.

2. mental: stress management, recreation, relaxation, and entertainment
3. social: interpersonal relations, chemical usage, and safety

Program Specifics

The Fitness Center consists of 5,400 square feet of space and provides services from 6 A.M. to 8 P.M. Monday through Friday and 8 A.M. to 12 noon on Saturday. Completion of an orientation and a fitness/medical questionnaire is required before participation.

Health classes and seminars are routinely scheduled to provide participants with information about physical, mental, and psychosocial well-being. In addition, the program is promoted through the dissemination of materials and fliers. Furthermore, individualized physical fitness programs are prescribed to address specific employee needs, and fitness evaluations and follow-ups are ongoing.

The Fitness Center has weight training stations, stationary bicycles, treadmills, and rowing machines as well as other exercise apparatus. Available fitness classes range from beginning to advanced level in activities such as stretching, aerobic dance, conditioning, stepping, and progressive relaxation.

Personnel

Director
Exercise physiologist/physical therapist/ emergency medical technician
Physical fitness trainer
Physician
Nurses
Laboratory technicians
University interns

Contact Address

General Mills TriHealthalon Program
Health and Human Services, 3C
Number One General Mills Blvd.
Minneapolis MN 55426

Tenneco Energy

Source of Information
Melissa Simerly, Manager
Health and Fitness Program

General Information

Tenneco's health and fitness program evolved as a result of the chief executive officer's personal positive experience with exercise. The program was implemented in 1982 at corporate headquarters in Houston, Texas, in order to preserve Tenneco's most important asset—its more than 2,500 innovative and highly skilled employees. Since the program's inception, many of Tenneco's divisional headquarters have set up similar programs. Tenneco was the first oil company to provide "heart-healthy" cooking on oil rigs. The company was also the first to implement a Pipeline-to-Health promotion program in 125 field locations along their natural gas pipeline, which extends from Midland, Texas, to Emerson, Manitoba, Canada.

Program Goals/Objectives

The Tenneco program focuses on providing employees with the opportunity to learn about and maintain good health and fitness. Each year a joint planning meeting is conducted within the medical department to determine the program goals and objectives. The departmental mission statement is "a unified effort to expand our services into community and family." Step-Up-To-Health became the program name, and employee committees were reorganized around the themes of (1) Eating Right, (2) Smoke-Free, (3) Recreation, and (4) Fitness.

Program Description

The components of the Step-Up-To-Health program (health promotion, safety, medical, and employee assistance programs) are contained in the Tenneco Energy Medical Department. A holistic

Employees playing volleyball; Tenneco Energy's Health and Fitness Center, Houston, Texas.

health promotion program offers employees group and individual activities, screenings and assessments, and classes concerning a variety of topics. The safety program addresses safety issues at work and in the home and provides opportunities for aquatic, driving, first aid, and CPR certifications. Central to the department's success is the primary care medical clinic, which is organized under a preventive model. Employees who have medical problems, concerns, or questions come to the clinic and are seen by a nurse practitioner or physician. The 1,100 to 1,500 employees who are attended to each month not only get answers concerning their medical problems, but are also networked to other facets of the Step-Up-To-Health program. The employee assistance program provides psychological counseling, organizes various employee support groups, and designs classes in a wide range of personal growth topics including health and fitness.

Program Specifics

The health and fitness center occupies 25,000 square feet of the Tenneco Employee Center. It is equipped with weight-training equipment, bicycle ergometers, stretching areas, rowing machines, and stair climbing equipment. The most impressive exercise area is the 1/5-mile indoor track that encircles the entire building. A computer-based information system stores individual exercise data and provides employees with immediate feedback on caloric energy expenditure during their daily workouts. Tenneco's system is also equipped with a health topic dictionary that provides a quick source of information about common health questions and topics. The fitness center prides itself on delivering convenient and quality services to enhance the health, fitness, and education of each employee. Besides individually prescribed programs, also popular are classes in aerobics, yoga, and self-defense; tournaments in racquetball, wallyball, and basketball; and training for sport-specific events ranging from skiing to marathoning. Educational programs ranging from Muscle of the Week to six- to eight-week fitness incentive activities keep Tenneco's employees happy, active, and healthy.

Tenneco Energy's Health and Fitness Center.

Personnel

Medical director
Fitness manager
Fitness coordinator
Two fitness specialists
Clerical staff member
Six contract exercise teachers

Contact Address

Health and Fitness Center
Tenneco Energy
P.O. Box 2511
Houston TX 77252

COMMERCIAL HEALTH, FITNESS, AND WELLNESS INDUSTRY

The commercial (for profit) health and fitness industry has grown significantly in the last decade. Membership campaigns have attracted millions of men and women to health clubs and fitness centers (an estimated 12.9 million members), which seem to have become a permanent part of our society.

The commercial health and fitness industry focuses on adult fitness and sport pursuits, although most clubs are open to all age-groups. The commercial health and fitness industry is profit motivated ($8.25 billion), which differentiates it from many corporate and community-based physical education and sport programs.

Facilities at a typical center might include exercise and aerobic dance rooms, resistive-type exercise or strength training equipment like Cybex, Universal, or Nautilus machines as well as free and selectorized weights, treadmills, rowing machines, recumbent bicycles, stair climbing equipment, cross-country ski exercisers, swimming pools, whirlpools, saunas, steam rooms, massage rooms, cold plunges, oil baths, tanning rooms, and locker and shower areas, not to mention courts for volleyball, basketball, tennis, racquetball, and squash.

Programs in commercial enterprises also include such items as fitness assessment and prescription, weight training, yoga, aerobics of various types and intensity levels, stress management, day care, and sport competitions, both in-house and against other clubs. Personnel often include instructors (physical educators), business executives, and sales, marketing, and promotions specialists. The following descriptions are representative examples of the commercial health and fitness industry.

Bally Total Fitness

Source of Information

Keith Spennewyn, Training Director
Jarrett Hickman, Program Director

General Information

Bally Total Fitness was a branch of Bally's Manufacturing and Entertainment, which also oversaw equipment manufacturing, casinos, and the Health and Tennis Corporation of America. Bally Total Fitness was recently spun off into its own corporate enterprise and, according to *Business Industry* magazine, with its 350 fitness centers is one of the largest commercial fitness corporations in the world.

An exercise class is vital to a well-rounded fitness program.

Swimming remains a constant for both public and private sector fitness and exercise programs.

Program Goals/Objectives

Bally Total Fitness designs a personalized physical fitness program based on the member's needs (e.g., cardiovascular or muscular strength and endurance). The company is first on *Club Industry's* (1996) revenue list at $661 million and has as its mission to maintain their position as the leading provider of fitness services by offering a good product at a fair price, by attracting and retaining committed members, and by employing quality staff who are focused on meeting their customer's needs. Consonant with their mission, Bally's fitness centers adhere to a holistic approach to exercise in order to meet each individual's specific exercise needs.

Program Description

Each Bally Total Fitness center provides a wide array of programs, which include exercise and fitness, injury management, and a variety of counseling and assessment services. Exercise and aerobic classes include low-impact, intermediate, and advanced levels as well as muscle conditioning (e.g., 30-Minute Workout, Program Advance-ment) and aqua-aerobics. Exercise, fitness, and aerobic classes are provided for all ages from children to senior citizens.

In the area of injury management, Extended Care is a holistic program available to members. The program is designed according to the individual's physical limitations and his or her physician's recommended prescription for exercise. Counseling is also an integral part of the program and is available for basic nutrition and in conjunction with body composition assessment. Other assessment services that are tailored to meet individual needs are also offered (e.g., posture, cholesterol, blood pressure). As an added service to the Bally Total Fitness clientele, personalized trainers can be contracted for one-to-one instruction.

Program Specifics

Each Bally Total Fitness is well equipped with computerized resistance machines, exercise cycles, step ergometers, and rowing machines as well as an indoor jogging track and swimming pool. Some facilities also maintain racquetball, volleyball, and/or basketball courts.

Bally Total Fitness is open twenty-four hours a day, except holidays. Membership fees vary according to the local economy and state laws and regulations, with the average fee being $15 to $25 per month. Women make up approximately 55 percent of the total member population, and men make up about 45 percent. Each fitness center serves approximately 750 to 1,500 members daily and has on-site child care.

Personnel

Instructional staff are professionally trained and regularly updated with the most current principles and methods of fitness training. Standard black and teal sport uniforms identify Bally Total Fitness staff. Each center has a general manager in charge of sales and service, an operations manager for service and scheduling, five to seven personal fitness trainers, twenty to thirty aerobics and fitness instructors, receptionists, and day-care and maintenance staff.

Contact Address

Bally Total Fitness
4900 Excelsior Boulevard
St. Louis Park MN 55416

Clark Hatch Fitness Centers

Source of Information

Clark G. Hatch, Founder/President
William A. Monsen, Senior Vice President, Operations
John L. Sheppard, Senior Vice President, Development

General Information

An international chain of fitness centers with more than 25,000 members worldwide in fourteen countries, the Clark Hatch organization began in Tokyo, Japan, in 1965. There are now fifty-five locations, which are either wholly owned, co-owned, or managed by Mr. Hatch from his flagship center in the Hawaii Building, Honolulu, Hawaii. Clark Hatch has been the pioneer for physical fitness and health in the Pacific Rim, and his impact has set the pace and established the standard of quality, excellence, and professionalism for today's health and physical fitness manager.

Programs Goals/Objectives

Clark Hatch Fitness Centers offer in-house developmental and managerial fitness services to hotels

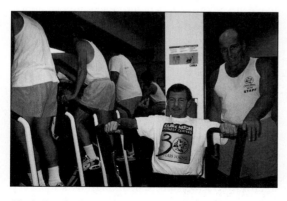

Clark Hatch Fitness Centers support a wide range of quality fitness activities.

and corporations throughout the world. The Clark Hatch program has carved out a special niche in the fitness industry, with more than forty of the centers being located in prominent world-class hotels, which serve not only the hotel clientele, but also its immediate multicultural community user.

Mr. Hatch's philosophy mirrors his personal fitness, vigor, and enthusiasm for the industry, and this, in turn, is reflected in the managers and staff he employs, trains, and continually updates through yearly, if not more frequent, managerial and instructor seminars. Clark Hatch Fitness Centers, although profit driven, are grounded in the underlying philosophy of promoting health and fitness throughout the world.

Program Description

Following an initial fitness assessment, which includes health history, injuries, nutrition, stress level, body measurements, and physical fitness appraisal, all members are scheduled for one-to-one exercise sessions. During these individualized sessions, a five-phase program of warm-up, aerobic exercise, flexibility, strength/conditioning, and cooldown is introduced. This individualized program provides a sound base from which all members progressively build more personalized programs under the direction of a well-trained staff.

Clark Hatch programs provide incentives such as educational seminars, newsletters, ongoing assessments, and program readjustments to inspire adherence as well as attainment of fitness goals. Personalized service, high-quality facilities, and sound managerial skill are evident throughout the Clark Hatch network.

Program Specifics

All centers are equipped with the most modern exercise equipment, an aerobics area, and one or more additional facilities (e.g., swimming pool, sauna, steam room, whirlpool, massage, and tennis, squash, or racquetball courts). Furthermore, the centers also sponsor outside events such as fun runs, hiking, outrigger canoeing, softball, and soccer. As an added amenity, members and hotel guests are provided with complimentary use of gym clothing, footwear, and towels.

Hours of operation vary from center to center (generally 6 A.M. to 10 P.M.). Members pay an initiation fee (e.g., Honolulu individual membership is $150) and monthly dues ($45 to $56), which vary markedly from country to country and center to center. Special husband/wife, student, off-peak hours, and corporate memberships are also available. Memberships offer unlimited usage and are fully reciprocal at Clark Hatch Fitness Centers throughout the world.

Table 6-2 presents a general representative breakdown of expenses for a Clark Hatch Fitness Center, which of course varies with country and location.

Table 6-2. Sample budget of a representative commercial fitness center

Clark Hatch Fitness Center Budget Sample

General & Administration Expenses	% of Gross Revenue
Payroll	34.0
Employee benefits	1.9
Rent	21.9
Repair/maintenance	3.2
Office expenses	1.7
Fitness center expenses	2.8
Advertisement/promotion/marketing	5.0
Entertainment/transportation/ seminars	0.7
General excise tax	4.0
License fee	0.2
Insurance	1.0
Professional fees/outside services	1.3
Temporary instructors	0.2
Parking/miscellaneous	0.2
Depreciation	3.8
	84.7
PROFIT MARGIN (varies by country and site)	15.3

Personnel

The worldwide Clark Hatch Fitness Center network is illustrated in Figure 6-2. Each location typically has a fitness center manager, senior fitness instructor(s), aerobic dance instructors, and support personnel ranging from on-site recreational staff to locker-room attendants, and from sales and marketing to maintenance. The personnel, regardless of level or location, are people-oriented and follow standardized corporation policies and procedures.

Contact Address

Clark Hatch Fitness Centers
Hawaii Building
745 Fort Street
Honolulu HI 96813

Radisson Hotel and Conference Center

Source of Information

Mike Serr, General Manager
Barry McLaughlin, Manager

General Information

The Radisson Hotel and Conference Center and its Fitness Center opened August 1, 1991. The fitness center caters to guests of the 243-room hotel and to its conferees who attend intensive meetings and conferences as well as to a limited membership who work or reside in the local community (figure 6-3).

Program Goals/Objectives

The objective of the Radisson Fitness Center is to provide exercise facilities and fitness programs for the guests of the Radisson Hotel and Conference Center and for club members from the surrounding community. The center seeks to promote fitness and adherence to an exercise prescription program as well as to provide physical activities during stretch breaks for those attending corporate seminars at the conference center. The key is availability, accessibility, and personalized cooperative programming planned in coordination with the various corporate seminar directors.

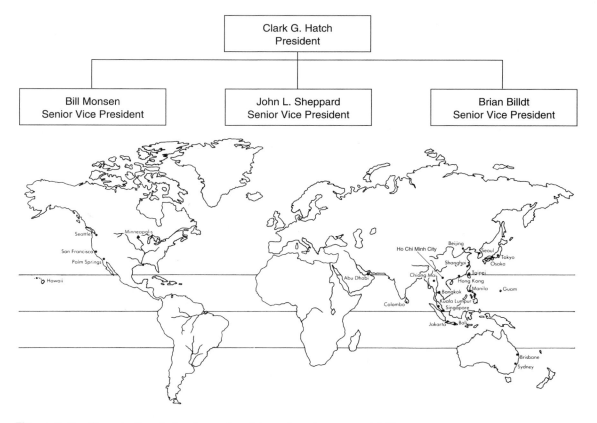

Figure 6-2. Organizational structure of an international commercial fitness center.

Program Description

The fitness center at the Radisson Hotel and Conference Center focuses on an exercise prescription program that is offered to all members. The program consists of a nine-phase fitness regimen designed to meet individual needs and to assist members in exercise adherence.

In order to meet the varied needs of the community clientele, the organization offers a wide range of membership options, including individual, joint, off-peak, alternate-day, nonprime-time, family, short-term, and corporate memberships. The Fitness Center is not as membership driven as most commercial fitness centers are, because its services and facilities are intimately tied into corporate sales packages. Service and long-range planning are keys to its success.

Program Specifics

The Radisson Fitness Center is housed in a three-story building separated from the hotel by a twenty-foot atrium entrance. The 20,000-square-foot complex includes a weight room that features selectorial, free weight, and Keiser, Cybex, and Trotter equipment, a 1,200 square-foot-aerobics room, and an exercise room equipped with step machines, rowing machines, treadmills, stationary bicycles, and cross-country skiing machines. The facility also has a swimming pool, sauna, and whirlpool as well as four racquetball courts, a

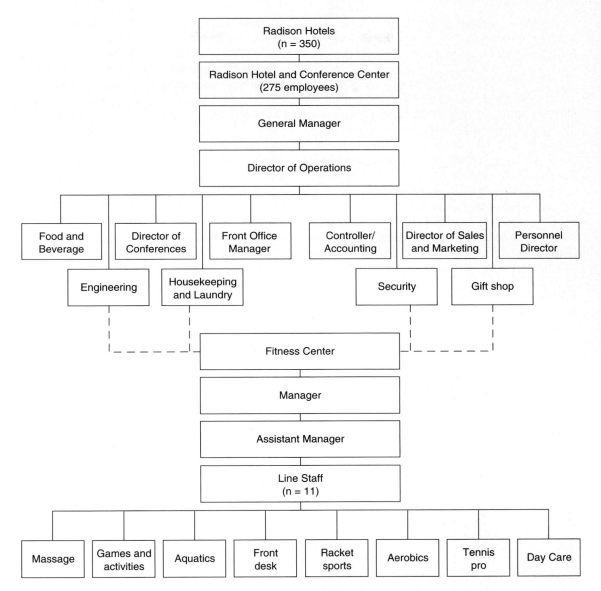

Figure 6-3. Organizational structure of a hotel-related fitness center.

basketball court, four outdoor lighted tennis courts, a sand volleyball court, and numerous jogging and biking trails in the immediate area. The center operates a basketball, volleyball, and racquetball league, a summer youth camp, and rents bicycles to hotel guests. Additional amenities include a suntan bed, a massage area, and a juice bar.

A schedule of aerobic dance and yoga classes provides instruction at twenty-one different times each week (usually mornings and evenings).

Hours of operation are 6 A.M. to 11 P.M. Monday through Friday, 7 A.M. to 11 P.M. on Saturdays, and 8 A.M. to 9 P.M. on Sundays.

Personnel

The fitness center is staffed by four full-time employees, which include a manager, an assistant manager, a front desk attendant, a fitness center attendant, and six part-time (twelve to twenty hours per week) employees. Responsibilities for all personnel involve front desk duties (e.g., communications/making reservations, accessibility, and some sales), directing fitness programs, stocking the locker room and juice bar, and general maintenance and cleaning. Education, certification (NSCA, AFAA), experience, appearance, and communication are requisite to employment.

Contact Address

Radisson Fitness Center
Radisson Hotel and Conference Center
3131 Campus Drive
Plymouth MN 55441

COMMUNITY-BASED PHYSICAL EDUCATION AND SPORT PROGRAMS

In addition to corporate fitness and commercial health, fitness, and wellness centers, there are other settings in which physical educators are finding employment and assuming management

Climbing has taken a foothold in many school and community-based physical education and sport programs.

responsibilities. Many of these opportunities exist in community-based programs such as YMCAs and YWCAs, Jewish Community Centers, and community education and senior centers. Other community-based delivery systems include organizations such as recreation and park departments, Boys' and Girls' Clubs, and local sport clubs. Some representative community-based physical education and sport organizations as well as a state high school league association are described here.

Young Men's Christian Association

Minnetonka, Minnesota
Source of Information
Russ Horsch, Executive Director
Sue Ericson, Associate Director

General Information

The Young Men's Christian Association (YMCA) was founded by George Williams in 1844 in London, England. Initially the YMCA offered programs designed to teach adults and children (with an emphasis on young males) the values of health and Christianity. This concept was transnationalized to Montreal, Boston, and New York in the 1850s and spread throughout the urban centers of the United States in the 1870s when a commitment to add physical education to its educational agenda and curriculum was adopted. YMCA programs were the cradle from which sprang the inventions of basketball (1891) and volleyball (1895). The YMCA continues to play an active role in the building of strong communities through innovative programs of health, wellness, fitness and sport.

Program Goals/Objectives

The YMCA is a worldwide fellowship united by a common loyalty with the purpose of developing strong kids, strong families, and strong communities and promoting values to building a better world. The goals for members include the following:

- Strengthen family life
- Improve physical, mental, and spiritual well-being of all persons

Ys have long been an integral part of many communities; Ridgedale Y, Minnetonka, Minn.

- Provide life-enhancing opportunities for disadvantaged persons
- Advance international understanding, justice, and peace
- Develop leadership skills among the community

Program Description

The YMCA program promotes a spirit-mind-body approach to the health and fitness of its members. The YMCA is supported not only by its membership, but also by donations from individuals who value the ideals of the organization, including honesty, caring, respect, and responsibility. Today's YMCAs are open to all users regardless of race, gender, or religion. They remain an active contributor to local communities from Minneapolis to Nairobi and from Kingston to Hong Kong. Their U.S. membership approaches the 7 million mark.

Program Specifics

Hours of operation at the Ridgedale YMCA are 5:30 A.M. to 10 P.M. Monday through Friday and 7 A.M. to 10 P.M. on Saturday and Sunday.

Movement exploration in the children's gym.

The facilities consist of a swimming pool, an indoor running track, four racquetball courts, and a gymnasium that can be partitioned to form two activity areas for basketball and/or volleyball. In addition, they have a free-weight room as well as rooms for weight-lifting equipment, exercise, and aerobic dance. The facilities include a children's gym and a conference and counseling area. State-of-the-art equipment in the exercise room includes eight stationary exercise bicycles, eight stair climbing machines, four rowing machines, and a full complement of gymnastic apparatus. Added attractions of the Ridgedale YMCA are a sauna and large whirlpool as well as a teen room, nursery, kitchen, and classroom facilities. The Y also has outdoor basketball and volleyball courts as well as day-camp facilities.

Programming includes exercise, fitness, and wellness instruction, classes in aerobic dance and weight management, and basketball and volleyball leagues. The YMCA also offers a children's sport program, teen nights, and a popular summer camp program. Most contemporary community-based YMCAs rival many of the best private fitness clubs for facilities and programming.

Personnel

The YMCA management structure consists of a director, associate director, and staff for the service and information desk. There are program directors and instructional staff for aquatics, adult fitness, gymnastics, children's programs, camps, and special events as well as for family and community relations.

Contact Address

Ridgedale YMCA
12301 Ridgedale Dr.
Minnetonka MN 55305
or
Your local YMCA/YWCA

Jewish Community Center

Schenectady, New York
Source of Information
Mitch Silver, Program Director

General Information

The Schenectady Jewish Community Center (JCC) is a committed community-oriented organization that provides exercise, sport and recreational facilities, and associated programming for a wide range of local clientele.

Program Goals/Objectives

The objective of the JCC is to provide health and fitness, sport, and recreational opportunities for children and adults in an atmosphere of fair play, cooperation, and family. These physical education objectives are couched within the overall JCC goals of enhancing the mind, body, and spirit as well as the cultural dimension of the Jewish faith.

Children's aquatic programs are important to community safety.

The family and cultural preservation are important parts of the JCC. The JCC, however, is secular in nature, with 40 percent to 50 percent of its users being non-Jewish.

Program Description

The JCC offers a wide range of programming to meet the physical education and recreational needs of its 1,200 members, which include boys and girls, adults, senior citizens, and especially families. Programming includes instruction in aquatics, aerobics, and tennis and sport leagues for soccer, basketball, softball, and volleyball. Programs for seniors (e.g., water walking), preschool movement offerings, and a popular after-school recreation program are also cornerstones of the JCC.

Program Specifics

The Schenectady JCC offers indoor facilities comprising a swimming pool, gymnasium, health

Golf lessons for children at a community course.

club with steam room and sauna, fitness room, television room, and kitchen area. Outdoor facilities consist of a $1.5 million family park complex, which includes a 300,000-gallon swimming pool, a spray pool, tennis courts, sand volleyball courts, playing fields, amphitheater, and picnic area. This beautiful area is rented for a nominal fee to many school, community, and family groups who take advantage of the modern facilities.

The focus of the department is the after-school recreation program as well as the adult recreation program. A number of activities are available on an adults-only basis. In addition, many aerobic activities are offered, including Lite Touch (low-impact aerobics), Bodyworks (intensive aerobics), and Aerobic Dance (high-impact and dance). Aquatics, ranging from Red Cross preschool programs and lifeguarding to YMCA certifications, are also very popular as are the

myriad games and physical activities offered in the after-school program.

The operational hours are 6:30 A.M. to 9:45 P.M. Monday through Friday, 9 A.M. to 5 P.M. Sundays, and 3 P.M. to 8 P.M. on Saturday (Shabbat). Saturday is devoted to family and recreation day, and no competitive activities or games are permitted.

Personnel

The health and physical education department of the Schenectady JCC comprises a director, who manages all recreation and fitness programming as well as oversees the maintenance of the facilities; an aquatics director, who directs the indoor pool activities, including a staff of twenty lifeguards; and the certified aerobics instructors, who provide instruction and leadership for the aerobic programs. The staff is small, well-qualified, and committed to the aims and objectives of the JCC.

Contact Address

Schenectady Jewish Community Center
2565 Balltown Road
Niskayuna NY 12309

Recreation and Parks Department

Brooklyn Park, Minnesota
Source of Information
Jay Lotthammer, Program Supervisor

General Information

The Brooklyn Park Recreation and Parks Department was started in 1965 by its current director, Dennis C. Palm. From its inception, the department has steadily grown to be one of the finest and most diverse departments in the nation and enjoys the distinction of being the first recreation program in the country to twice (1970 and 1981) receive the National Gold Medal Award for excellence in the field of park and recreation management.

Department Goals/Objectives

The basic objective of the Brooklyn Park Recreation and Parks Department is to provide facilities and a program of wholesome leisure-time activities to as many community residents as possible. Further goals of the organization are that the activities offered can assist both adults and children in gaining satisfaction, joy, and new friendships and that the activities provide an opportunity to improve skills while participating in meaningful leisure-time activities.

Program Description

The Brooklyn Park Recreation and Parks Department not only is well known for its comprehen-

sive and quality sport programs across all ages, but also offers more than 500 diverse recreational programs for its users. Age-group activities include instruction and recreational activities in art, music, drama, dance, safety, health, fitness, sport, and wellness, which form the focus of their well-rounded program. The department is committed to enhancing the social, cultural, and aesthetic environment of its diverse community and serves as a focal point for many community activities.

Program Specifics

In addition to designing and conducting the aforementioned 500 programs, the city of Brooklyn Park oversees a park system that contains 1,600 acres of community park land, including twenty-two neighborhood parks. The system also includes three nature areas, a communitywide trail system, ten school/park sites, three major sports complexes, five separate community public meeting facilities, and the Community Activity Center/ Armory, which is one of the finest centers of its kind in the nation. The park system also operates the restored Brooklyn Park Historical Farm, which showcases an 1890s farmstead, and two municipal golf courses (Brookland Executive Nine and Edinburgh U.S.A., which has been selected as one of the nation's top 50 public championship golf courses) and sponsors a Children's Art Festival with more than 5,000 participants.

The Community Activity Center is home to the department's management staff and houses a gymnasium, ice arena, community room, and racquetball, volleyball, and wallyball courts as well as conference rooms and classrooms. These areas are shared with groups ranging from the Lions to the National Guard. The facility also provides a nursery and day-care facility and programs for persons with varying disabilities.

The center opens daily at 6 A.M. and ice time is typically programmed to 1 A.M. Summer park hours extend daily from 8 A.M. to 10 P.M. There are user fees for golf, tennis, racquetball, the ice

Figure skating at Brooklyn Park Community Center.

arena, and the nursery, with other modest fees ($5 to $25) associated with each specific program. The center in this regard is user friendly!

Personnel

The department employs a director, three assistants, two program supervisors, and six program coordinators (youth, seniors, special populations, special events, aquatics, teens, and preschool), as well as 200 to 300 instructors and support staff necessary for providing first-class facilities and programming to all members of the community. The department also likes to provide summer jobs for qualified young men and women (high school/college). As implied by the depth, scope, and popularity of the programs, recreation and parks departments like Brooklyn Park offer many employment opportunities for qualified physical educators and recreation specialists.

Contact Address

Brooklyn Park Recreation and Parks Department
5600 85th Avenue North
Brooklyn Park MN 55443

Hopkins-Minnetonka Recreation Services

Source of Information
Ron Schwartz, Recreation Program Manager

General Information

Since 1967, the neighboring cities of Hopkins and Minnetonka as well as their respective school districts have combined in a joint powers agreement concerning the responsibility of management of a community recreation department. The program, in fact, serves seventeen communities that are housed in the three school districts. Operating costs for the recreation program are apportioned to the two cities' general fund tax base on the basis of the average user attendance. Although the program's administrative offices are housed in the Minnetonka City Hall, its facilities are primarily those of the two school districts as well as of the cities.

Program Goals/Objectives

The mission statement of this innovative organization is "to develop, promote, and provide quality diversified recreational programs, activities and facilities that will enhance the leisure-time needs and interests of the Hopkins-Minnetonka community." To accomplish this shared mission, the Hopkins-Minnetonka Recreation Services have established the following goals:

- to provide quality customer services
- to hire and maintain a staff that is professional in their abilities and responsive to the needs of the public
- to be fiscally responsible
- to strengthen the organization's identity in the community

Program Description

The comprehensive recreation program includes league play activity ranging from T-ball to high school and senior league competition in basketball, volleyball, broomball, ice hockey, softball, football, soccer, and baseball. Year-round aquatic programs, low-impact aerobics, slimnastics, morning stretch, senior tennis league ladder, indoor soccer, and figure skating as well as a nature environmental studies camp, sports clinics, and sport schools are other features of this multidimensional community-based program. Recreation Services also offers special programs ranging from Fabulous 4s (for parents and four-year-olds) to Over 55 and Fit and from New Horizons (integration of persons with disabilities) to monthly senior trips and recreational outings.

General activities include pool splash time, summer playground activities for preschool children, day camp, municipal swimming beach, ice skating rinks with warming houses, open gymnasiums, and an adaptive recreational program. Other services provided by the department are day centers, clubs, outings for senior citizens, group picnics, and Breakfast With Santa.

Program Specifics

Recreation Department activities are available to all residents of Hopkins, Minnetonka, and the surrounding school districts as well as any individuals who are employed full-time in either of these cities.

Programming for the department is developed and conducted by a joint recreation staff. Sport programs are low pressure in nature; they emphasize skill learning and development rather than highly competitive play.

An important focus for the Hopkins-Minnetonka Recreation Department is providing ample opportunity for senior citizens to engage in meaningful and enjoyable leisure-time activities. The department offers an active seniors schedule that includes hiking, square dancing, ballroom dancing, swimming, softball, tennis, and tai-ji-quan as well as ceramics and parlor games. In addition, senior trips, outings, and tours are organized and promoted via the *Senior Script* newsletter.

The department's programs run year-round, and except during summer, they operate after school and on weekends. The fees involved typically sustain each of the programs and provide a 30 percent profit margin for administrative cost and overhead.

Personnel

The Hopkins-Minnetonka Recreation Services is headed by the recreation director, who is supported by an assistant, a recreation supervisor, clerical and support staff, and more than 350 part-time instructors and supervisors who are responsible for the conduct of the various phases of the department's programs.

Contact Address

Hopkins-Minnetonka Recreation Services
14600 Minnetonka Boulevard
Minnetonka MN 55345

The Minnesota State High School League

Source of Information
David Stead, Executive Director
Dorothy McIntyre, Associate Director
Skip Peltier, Associate Director
Lisa Lissamore, Associate Director

General Information

The Minnesota State High School League (MSHSL) is a voluntary, nonprofit association of public and private schools with a history of service to Minnesota youth since 1916. The MSHSL has long been recognized as a national leader in student chemical health awareness and education (TARGET Minnesota), for its leadership in gender equity, and for developing activities and state championships for students with disabilities.

Program Goals/Objectives

The MSHSL mission is to provide educational opportunities through interscholastic athletics and fine arts programs for students and leadership and support for its more than 450 member schools. To achieve the mission, the MSHSL adheres to the following governing values:

- equity, fairness, and justice

Community-building programs focus on peer mentoring, youth, and leadership skills.

- activities that support the academic mission of schools
- fair play and honorable competition
- activities that support healthy lifestyles
- treating people with dignity and respect

Research indicates that students in league activities tend to have higher grade point averages, better attendance records, lower dropout rates, and fewer discipline problems than the general student population does.

Program Description

The MSHSL administers thirty-four athletic and fine arts state tournaments for its member schools. They have fourteen tournaments for girls, thirteen for boys, and since 1995, three (floor hockey, softball, and soccer) for students with disabilities. The MSHSL serves more than 200,000 students and involves more than 3,000 individuals in their committees and advisory boards.

Program Specifics

The MSHSL comprises more than 450 member high schools and is structured (see figure 6-4) in the form of an elected representative assembly and a twenty-member board of directors. The representative assembly is the rule- and policy-making body and develops bylaws that govern league activities. Member schools, activity associations, school board associations, and regional committees elect or appoint the members of the representative assembly. The league is financed primarily through state tournament gate receipts, broadcast rights fees, and corporate contributions. The league provides catastrophic insurance for league-sponsored programs and provides tournament liability insurance, rule books, a newsletter, training for contest officials and judges, and educational programs for coaches.

Contact Address

Minnesota State High School League
2100 Freeway Blvd.
Brooklyn Center MN 55430

PROFESSIONAL QUALIFICATIONS AND RESPONSIBILITIES OF PUBLIC AND PRIVATE SECTOR PHYSICAL EDUCATION AND SPORT PERSONNEL

The qualifications required in the various public and private sector physical education and sport professions are similar in nature but expanded in scope and intensity from that of the teacher, coach, or athletic director. Certainly a degree in physical education/kinesiology, recreation, sport management, exercise fitness (with basic business, marketing or counseling background), or some allied degree and certification (e.g., American College of Sports Medicine, Institute for Aerobic Research, National Strength and Conditioning Association, Aerobics Fitness Association, American Council on Exercise, etc.) is required. An internship in a public or private sector setting is also mandatory as is actual work experience in a similar setting.

Other qualifications that come in handy are the ability to repair and maintain equipment; create and design a wide range of exercise, fitness, health, and wellness programs (including nutrition, stress, and weight management); sell, promote, and market memberships; and develop or adopt a personality and communication style conducive to the specific workplace setting. The public and private sector job market is people-oriented, service and labor intensive, and demands a great deal from the employee.

The responsibilities of personnel involved with corporate and workplace organizations, commercial health and fitness industries, and community-based physical education and sport programs cover the total spectrum of work endeavor.

Sol (1981) identifies some responsibilities of health and fitness industry specialists as follows:

- Direct the exercise, fitness, and wellness program, which may be oriented to prevention and/or rehabilitation
- Train and supervise staff
- Develop and manage the program budget
- Design, manage, and maintain the exercise facility

MINNESOTA STATE HIGH SCHOOL LEAGUE
ORGANIZATION CHART

MEMBERSHIP

32 - AA Subregions
32 - A Subregions
 2 - Music A-AA
 2 - Speech A-AA
 2 - Athletic Directors Association
 2 - Coaches Association - Girls Sports
 2 - Coaches Association - Boys Sports
 8 - A School Board Representatives
 8 - AA School Board Representatives

LEGISLATION

REPRESENTATIVE ASSEMBLY *
The 90-member legislative
body of the MSHSL

* Enacts and amends activity rules
as submitted by:
1. Any five (5) member schools
2. A region committee
3. A coaches association
4. The Board of Directors

ADMINISTRATION

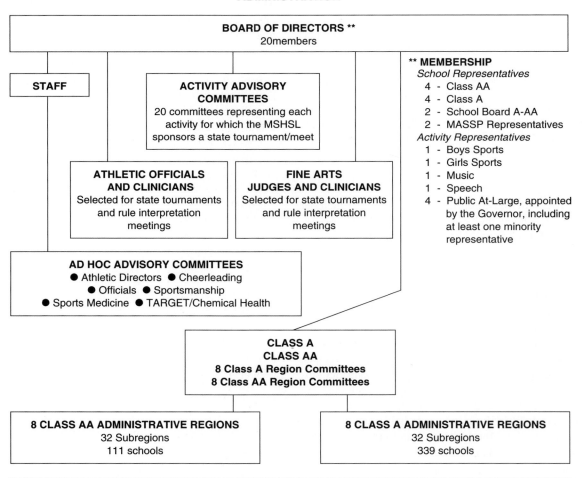

BOARD OF DIRECTORS **
20members

STAFF

ACTIVITY ADVISORY COMMITTEES
20 committees representing each
activity for which the MSHSL
sponsors a state tournament/meet

ATHLETIC OFFICIALS AND CLINICIANS
Selected for state tournaments
and rule interpretation
meetings

FINE ARTS JUDGES AND CLINICIANS
Selected for state tournaments
and rule interpretation
meetings

AD HOC ADVISORY COMMITTEES
● Athletic Directors ● Cheerleading
● Officials ● Sportsmanship
● Sports Medicine ● TARGET/Chemical Health

**** MEMBERSHIP**
School Representatives
4 - Class AA
4 - Class A
2 - School Board A-AA
2 - MASSP Representatives
Activity Representatives
1 - Boys Sports
1 - Girls Sports
1 - Music
1 - Speech
4 - Public At-Large, appointed
    by the Governor, including
    at least one minority
    representative

**CLASS A
CLASS AA
8 Class A Region Committees
8 Class AA Region Committees**

8 CLASS AA ADMINISTRATIVE REGIONS
32 Subregions
111 schools

8 CLASS A ADMINISTRATIVE REGIONS
32 Subregions
339 schools

450 MEMBER SCHOOLS
2 Official School Representatives from each member school to Region Meetings
Eligible: one school board member; one administrator or full-time faculty member

Figure 6-4. Minnesota State High School League organizational chart.

- Market the program and facility
- Evaluate, in conjunction with a physician, each participant's medical and physical activity history, as well as perform graded exercise and pulmonary function tests and various other fitness assessment procedures
- Develop individual exercise prescriptions and packages for participants
- Evaluate and/or counsel participants, on request, about nutrition, smoking, substance abuse, weight control, and stress reduction
- Accumulate program data for statistical analysis and research
- Maintain professional affiliations

This list of responsibilities, however, must be supplemented with the following tasks, which often fall in the domain of the corporate, commercial, and community-based program manager:

- Instruct a wide variety of skills (e.g., aerobic dance, racquetball, jogging, weight and circuit training)
- Participate with members in a wide variety of physical activity
- Counsel participants on skill, fitness, wellness, and technique development
- Serve as individual or personal trainers (IEP and computer analysis)
- Clean, maintain, and repair equipment (especially in an international setting where parts are unavailable)
- Inventory, select, purchase, and care for equipment
- Be an accountant and money collector (maintain daily, weekly, and monthly statements)
- Supervise groundskeeping, maintenance, and cleaning crews
- Supervise lifeguards
- Write newsletters, construct media guides, and design corporate health, fitness, and wellness handbooks
- Sell and sustain memberships (conduct tours of facilities)

- Budget, schedule, teach, promote, advertise, supervise, and evaluate programs and personnel
- Schedule members for interclub and intraclub activities and competitions (e.g., Boston Marathon, cycling tour of France, fun runs)
- Become a stress reducer for each member

These are just some of the responsibilities and duties required of personnel employed in a public or private sector physical education and sport environment. This profession offers a tremendous educational, physical, and psychosocial challenge (Ferreira 1988), one that requires commitment, endless vigor, and personal excellence.

SUMMARY

Physical education and sport programs are not limited to schools, colleges, universities, and other educational institutions. Many other programs and settings exist in the larger community, including the international domain. Corporate enterprises, health and fitness clubs, and other commercial fitness industry creations, as well as various community-based organizations ranging from Ys, community centers, and recreation- and park-related services to local and state associations now play, and will continue to play, a vital role in the delivery of health and fitness to the nation. These settings represent new, exciting, and challenging opportunities for well-trained and skilled physical educators seeking employment as instructors, consultants, managers, and potential owners.

SELF-ASSESSMENT ACTIVITIES

These activities will assist students in determining if material and competencies presented in this chapter have been mastered.

1. Conduct a survey of your county and state to determine various public and private sector physical education and sport programs providing employment opportunities.
2. Prepare a set of guidelines you would follow if asked to manage a commercial fitness club.
3. What physical education objectives might be accomplished in public and private sector physical education and sport programs?

4. Construct a job description for a manager of a corporate fitness and wellness center.

5. Conduct an interview with a public sector health and fitness manager and construct a top ten list of key employee responsibilities.

6. Design a plan to present to hotel chain management to convince them to include a fitness center component in their management scheme.

7. Describe how a community-based health and fitness center may cooperate with existing school district programs.

REFERENCES

1. Eitzen, D.S. and G.H. Sage. 1994. *Sociology of North American sports.* Dubuque, Iowa: William C. Brown Communications.
2. Ferreira, R.R. 1988. Effect of work shift and club size on employees. *Journal of Sport Management* 2:1–13.
3. Industry outlook. 1996. *Club Industry,* June, 1–22.
4. Sol, N. 1981. Graduate preparation for exercise program professionals. *Journal of Physical Education, Recreation, and Dance* 52(7): 76–77.
5. U.S. Department of Health and Human Services. 1987. National survey of worksite health promotion activities. Washington, D.C.: Office of Disease Prevention and Health Promotion, Summer.
6. Wuest, D.S. and C.A. Bucher. 1996. *Foundations of physical education and sport.* 12th ed. St. Louis: Mosby–Year Book.

SUGGESTED READINGS

Club Industry.
Monthly publication for the health and fitness industry. Published by Cardinal Business Media Inc., 1300 Virginia Drive, Suite 400, Ft. Washington, PA 19034.

Cordes, K.A., and H.M. Ibrahim. 1996. *Applications in recreation and leisure: For today and the future.* St. Louis: Mosby–Year Book.
Designed for students who are considering a career in recreation, physical education, and related professions. The appendices lists various organizations that may be of interest to physical educators.

Flatten, K. 1989. Fitness evaluation and programming for older adults. *Journal of Physical Education, Recreation, and Dance* 60(3): 63–78.
Discusses fitness evaluation, programming, and sport opportunities for the aging population and suggests the development of professional standards for their conduct.

Forouzesh, M.R., and L.E. Ratzker. 1984–85. Health promotion and wellness programs: Insight into the Fortune 500. *Health Education* 15(6):18–22.
Describes the nature and the extent of health promotion and wellness programs in Fortune 500 companies.

Kraus, R.G., and J.E. Curtis. 1990. *Creative management in recreation, parks, and leisure services.* St. Louis: Mosby–Year Book.
Describes recreation, parks, and leisure service programs for various special-interest groups, with a focus on physical education and sport. Outlines commercial and private recreation enterprises.

Lumpkin, A. 1994. *Physical education and sport: A contemporary introduction.* 3rd ed. St. Louis: Mosby–Year Book.
Provides lists of certifications and journals for newly entering professionals to the field of physical education and sport.

McNeal, R.B. 1995. Extracurricular activities and high school dropouts. *Sociology of Education* 68 (January): 62–81.

Pestolesi, R.A., and C. Baker. 1990. *Introduction to physical education: A contemporary careers approach.* Glenview, Ill.: Scott, Foresman.
Provides physical educators with an orientation to many diverse career pathways.

Thibault, L., T. Stack, and B. Hinings. 1994. Strategic planning for nonprofit sports organizations: Empirical verification of a framework. *Journal of Sport Management* 8:218–233.

Yiannakis, A. 1989. Some contributions of sport sociology to the marketing of sport and leisure organizations. *Journal of Sport Management* 3:103–115.
Discusses preparation and qualifications needed to be employed as a sport manager. Critical concerns of sport marketing, including product marketing features, target markets, positioning strategies, and other strategic planning phases are thoroughly addressed.

part IV

Management Functions

chapter 7

Human Resource Management and Supervision

Instructional Objectives and Competencies To Be Achieved

After reading this chapter the student should be able to

- Understand the need for personnel policies.
- State the basic principles underlying effective personnel or human resource management.
- Summarize the qualifications needed by physical educators and coaches who work in schools, in institutions of higher education, or in the private sector.
- Trace the process for recruitment, selection, hiring, orientation, preservice, and in-service training and for professional development of new staff members.
- Discuss the subject of supervision, including the qualities needed by supervisory personnel, the role of

group dynamics in the supervisory process, and the basic principles that should guide effective supervisory working relationships with staff members.
- State the various steps of procedural due process to which all personnel are entitled.
- Describe various methods of evaluating physical educators, coaches, and other personnel in physical education and sport programs.

This text has been concerned thus far with a discussion of management theory, organization, and structure and of the management of various kinds of physical education and sport programs. Part IV contains a discussion of the main functions and duties that managers must perform within these programs. The first of these is human resource management and supervision.

Originally, personnel management was mainly about selecting, placing, orienting, evalu-

ating, and retaining people who were staff members of an organization. Contemporary personnel management that is now referred to as human resource management, however, has taken on a more mature connotation. Management no longer regards personnel as overhead or cost factors to be manipulated for greater gain and glory but instead views personnel, or human resources, as assets worthy of investment (e.g., reward, compensation) in order that the social capital of the organization can accumulate. Elements of social organization such as trust, norms, values, standards, and networks that improve the efficiency and effectiveness of an organization by facilitating coordinated and meaningful actions are its social capital. Personnel are more likely to cooperate for mutual benefit in this horizontally managed environment and to seek collective solutions to problems as well as to perform at a high level. Recruitment, selection, hiring, training, motivating, and other considerations become the responsibility not only of management, but of all staff members. As a result, human resource management depends on various individuals and groups understanding and accepting each other and working closely together to ultimately achieve the organization's goals.

The nature of human resource management and supervision is changing because many institutions are adopting school-based management and responsibility-centered management concepts that provide for more decentralized decision making as well as responsibility. Managers and supervisors are consulting more closely with faculty and staff members before making final decisions on hiring, staffing, curriculum, scheduling, evaluations, and working conditions. Managers are also being required to negotiate with unions and nonunion workers in collective bargaining sessions. Management and supervisory positions are no longer considered isolated levels at which all decision making takes place. School-based and responsibility-centered management ensures that various faculty, staff, students and others who care about quality education have a voice in departmental or institutional policy making.

For all these reasons, human resources management and supervision are perhaps the most challenging responsibilities for an effective leader. Leaders who do not have the confidence and cooperation of their human resource assets will have great difficulty implementing any decision, policy, or program.

PERSONNEL POLICIES

With the help of staff members, management should see that a detailed handbook of personnel policies is developed. These policies should be sound, up to date, and consistent with contemporary human resource management theory. Selected areas that might be covered by a personnel policies manual include teachers' rights, terms of employment, assignments, promotions, due process, grievance procedure, harassment policy, separations, evaluations, hours of service and length of school year, compensation, schedules, fringe benefits, insurance, child care, absences, leaves, travel, in-service training, and conduct on the job.

In some cases, personnel policies are not developed by the management, but rather by a bargaining contract or exclusive representative (e.g., union, association, or federation). In such cases, the bargaining contract will probably affect the flexibility with which the manager and management may operate. It is crucial that management understand such exclusive representatives and that the guidelines prescribed are contained in full in the personnel policies handbook or manual (Hale, Hoelscher, and Kowal 1987).

PRINCIPLES OF HUMAN RESOURCE AND SUPERVISORY MANAGEMENT

Productive human resource management and supervision do not just happen. They occur as a result of adhering to a prescribed set of basic principles.

Cooperative effort between administrators, coaches, support staff, and athletes produces positive outcomes. Courtesy of: Special Olympics International. Photo by: David Otenstian

Cooperation and Trust

To achieve cooperation, build trust, and ensure that their service will be most productive and effective, the talents and unique abilities of individuals must be utilized, reinforced, and rewarded. Maintaining cooperation and trust among the staff will largely depend on staff satisfaction in the work environment and fulfillment of the organization's obligations and goals. The function of management and supervision is to see that these essentials as well as a wholesome work environment are provided and sustained.

The Individual as a Member of an Organization

Management and supervision should seek to imbue the organization with the idea that every individual is an asset and has a personal investment in the enterprise. The organization's undertakings can be successful only if all persons contribute by working to their fullest potential; then success brings satisfaction to all. Submergence of self to this end is necessary for achievement of the organization's goals. In this regard, Ouchi's Theory Z and Total Quality Management concepts discussed in chapter 1 are typically employed by high quality managers.

Final Authority

The existing authority of management belongs to the position and not to the person. Power and authority do not reside in one human being, but in the best thinking, judgment, and imagination that the organization can summon. This is the value of the school-based management approach. Individuals possess only the authority that goes with their position. In turn, this authority is respected and appreciated by other members whose work is closely allied to achieving the objectives for which the organization exists. Final authority rests in those who, because of their positions, are responsible for ultimate decisions.

Department heads, various committees, task forces, and staff consultants issue reports interpreting the facts. Their judgments, conclusions, and recommendations contribute to the formulation of final decisions, which are the responsibility of the manager (e.g., teacher, coach, athletic and activities director, principal). If these interpretations, judgments, conclusions, and recommendations are not accepted, the organization is not only weakened but may fail. Furthermore, individuals cannot be induced to contribute their full efforts to an organization that has little respect for their thinking. Authority permeates any organization and should be a shared concept.

Staff Morale

Management should continually strive to create conditions that facilitate good staff morale. The degree to which high staff morale exists will be in direct proportion to the degree to which such conditions are satisfied (Hunter 1989).

Leadership

The quality of management will, to a great degree, determine staff morale. From the top down, all leaders should be carefully selected. Other things being equal, individuals who contribute and produce more will possess better morale. These individuals usually have more respect for managers who are leaders in the true sense of the word. Leaders are managers who are a stride ahead in leading the way. Managers who possess a lucid, long-term vision for the future will empower employees, embrace diversity, and create and build trust and confidence. Leaders build social capital through sound human resource management.

Physical and Social Environment

A contributing physical and social environment is essential to good staff morale. The organization must provide for the physical health, wellness, and safety of the employee or student-athlete. It must also make provisions for mental and emotional health, including proper supervision and counseling, opportunity for advancement through professional and staff or student development, emergency plans, and avenues for intellectual enhancement (e.g., paid tuition, sabbatical leaves, paid staff development).

The social environment is also an important consideration. Individuals with whom a person interacts and the activities in which those individuals engage can strengthen or diminish a person's drive for excellence. Therefore it is important for a person to associate with those individuals who can serve as facilitators and motivators, important not only to accomplish the goals of the organization but also to build positive social relationships that are conducive to individual development and continued satisfaction.

Advancement

Each individual likes to believe that he or she is progressing in the world. Each member of an organization must be aware of what is essential for retention, progress, reward, and promotion. Opportunities should be provided for learning new skills and knowledge and for gaining new experiences. Encouragement, incentives, and resources should be provided to those individuals who wish to improve and are willing to devote extra time and effort to this end.

Recognition of Meritorious Service

Everyone possesses the need to be recognized. People who make outstanding contributions to the organization should be so honored. Investing in this positive reinforcement dimension is important to the future of the organization as well as to individual self-enhancement, self-esteem, and self-worth.

Individual Differences

Important principles of human resource management are recognizing individual differences, promoting diversity, and identifying different types of work. Individuals differ in many ways— abilities, skills, and training as well as physical, mental, and social qualities. Various types of work require different skills, abilities, personalities, preparation, and training. These differences should be recognized by the manager, who must make sure that the right person is in the right position at the right time. An individual who is a square peg in a round hole does not contribute to his or her own or the organization's welfare.

Recognition of accomplishment is valued at all levels. ALL American Katrein DeDecker, University of Minnesota.

The status granted any one person should be in line with the talents and capacities of that individual and with the importance of the function he or she performs. To be placed in a position that should be held by a person with lesser qualifications or vice versa is unjust and sometimes emotionally devastating and destabilizing. Many disruptive features can develop if individual abilities are not recognized or if proper incentives are not provided in accordance with training, qualification, and affirmative action.

Differentiated Staffing

Management must recognize staff members' interests, talents, training, and general suitability for each position or task that is delegated. Teachers and coaches should be assigned activities that are allied to their particular skills and abilities. Schools are also employing persons such as paraprofessionals, activity specialists, interns, teacher's aides, clerks, custodians, and equipment and facility managers to perform specialized tasks. All staff members must be carefully and selectively integrated into the whole so that each may develop to his or her fullest potential and add to the organization's efficiency and effectiveness.

PERSONNEL RECRUITMENT AND SELECTION

Personnel recruitment and selection are important functions of management. These functions include consideration of the special qualifications for teaching and coaching, the general qualifications of physical educators, and the unique qualifications of people working in other private and public sector physical education and sport settings. Orientation, pretraining, in-service training, and professional development are also responsibilities that go with staff recruitment, selection, and retention on what is hoped to be a long-term basis.

SPECIAL QUALIFICATIONS FOR TEACHING AND COACHING

The qualifications and the qualities of a good teacher and coach are synonymous. Many experts consider the following qualities to be desirable ones.

- thorough knowledge of the subject matter
- expertise in making an enthusiastic presentation of the fundamentals involved
- ability to take a personal interest in each student
- good preparation and organization skills
- respect from the students
- ability to stimulate and motivate the students to think and act
- ability to make the subject matter/sport come to life
- originality and creativity in his or her methods
- good communication skills
- neat, well-groomed appearance
- good sense of humor
- consistent, firm, fair, and honest approach in dealing with students
- understanding and kindness
- exemplary conduct and adherence to school policy and procedure

- emotional stability, self-control, and sensitivity in all situations

Beginning teachers, instructors, and coaches need considerable encouragement and support to hone their skills. Management should be aware of these needs and should work to ensure that those needs are met. A survey of fifty instructors indicated the following problems of new practitioners in the profession:

- difficulties with the administration or the person directly above
- difficulties arising from a lack of facilities
- large classes, making it difficult to instruct effectively
- instructional and other assignments in addition to the primary responsibility of teaching physical education and coaching
- discipline problems with students
- conflicting messages between what was learned during training and what is encountered in the workplace where traditional systems with established patterns and expectations of experienced teachers, coaches, and administrators seem dominant
- difficulty keeping records, reports, lesson plans, and other paperwork up to date
- problems encountered in obtaining books, materials, and supplies
- problems encountered in obtaining cooperative attitude from other teachers, instructors, and coaches
- lack of departmental meetings to discuss common problems
- inability to find time for personal recreation

MENTORING

Many organizations are using mentoring not only to improve productivity but also to develop managerial talents and potential successors. Mentoring is not a new concept, nor is it new to physical education, sport, or the sporting process. Greek literature notes that Mentor was hired by Odysseus to tutor/mentor his son before departing on his odyssey. In Japan, sumos have for centuries served as mentors (senpai) to develop future successors. Today, student teachers, and student coaches serve under cooperating teachers, and coaches, graduate assistants under head coaches, teaching assistants and research assistants serve under advisors, and even the U.S. Olympic Committee has an educational mentoring program. Mentoring usually takes place when a senior member advises and supports a junior member in order for that person to succeed and/or climb the professional ladder. All managers are encouraged to employ the various forms of mentoring—informal life, informal career, program, project, organizational, and external (community)—in the appropriate situation so that personnel may develop to their furthest potential.

QUALIFICATIONS FOR PHYSICAL EDUCATORS

One of the most important considerations in human resource management is recruiting, selecting, and hiring the most qualified personnel. The members of an organization determine whether it will succeed or fail. Therefore, management must recognize the following qualifications needed to meaningfully deliver physical education and sport.

The teacher/coach should be a graduate of an accredited institution that prepares professionals for a career in physical education and sport. Knowledge of the college or university that the potential employee has attended may play a part in the selection process.

Because physical education and sport is grounded in the sciences of anatomy, exercise physiology, biomechanics, sport sociology, and psychology, and sport management, physical educators and coaches should be well versed in these disciplines as well as in research methods tool, and strategies that will permit the teacher or coach to survey and apply appropriate research findings to the sport-specific situation.

The general education of physical educators and coaches is under continuous scrutiny and, at times, criticism. Knowledge of world affairs, mastery of the arts, and possession of other educational attributes are imperative. Because the position also requires frequent appearances in public, appearance and communication skills are deemed essential.

Physical education and coaching are strenuous and therefore demand that members of the profession be in good physical and mental condition in order to carry out their duties efficiently and effectively. Physical educators and coaches are supposed to help build healthy bodies and minds and are often expected by students, community, and management to be role models. Therefore, physical educators and coaches should be in good physical condition themselves.

Values, ethics, and morals are often developed through participation in games and other

Good coaches should have expertise in and be able to enthusiastically present the fundamentals of complex skills.

physical education activities. It is essential that professional physical educators and coaches stress ethics, discipline, fair play, and sound values. Their leadership should develop a recognition of the importance of high moral and ethical behavior and should significantly contribute to the development and enhancement of sound human relation and interpersonal skills.

Physical educators and coaches should have a sincere interest in and enjoy teaching, participating in activities, and helping others realize the thrill of participation and of becoming physically fit and physically educated. Unless the individual has a firm belief in the value of physical activity and a desire to help extend the benefits of such an endeavor to others, he or she will not be an asset to the profession.

The physical educator and coach should also possess an acceptable standard of motor ability and skill level. To coach and teach various games and activities to others and to fully realize the

Nadia Comenici conducts a coaches' clinic at the University of Minnesota to help present methods for stimulating and motivating students.

discipline, stress, and anxiety as well as the intricate finesse and strategies that accompany such activities, it is most helpful to possess the skills and ability to participate.

UNIQUE QUALIFICATIONS FOR PHYSICAL EDUCATION PROFESSIONALS IN OTHER SETTINGS

The professional who seeks employment in settings other than schools and institutions of higher education needs to possess those qualifications listed for physical educators and, in addition, the special training and qualifications needed for work in the activity-specific institution, agency, or area in which he or she seeks employment. For example, a physical educator who seeks employment in the corporate fitness and wellness setting should have as much experience as possible in exercise physiology, nutrition, and fitness assessment, because many of the duties will involve determining the health and fitness status of employees and planning and supervising programs to develop and maintain optimal physical fitness and wellness levels. It would also be helpful to be familiar with the various types of exercise equipment that are used in these programs. If the physical educator plans to seek a position in a community-based recreation program, he or she should have a wide variety of skills in activities that will interest adults and seniors. Furthermore, he or she will need to be familiar with program planning and structuring, scheduling, facility maintenance, public relations, marketing, and promotion.

To be successful in such settings as health and fitness clubs, ski areas, golf and tennis centers, senior centers, and youth-serving agencies, the physical educator should know the characteristics and needs of the population or user groups being served. For example, the professional working with the elderly must understand senior citizens—their lifestyles, interests, needs, fears, concerns, and physical fitness status—and the activities and programs that will contribute to their total well-being.

In a health and fitness club setting, the educator must be able to sell, promote, and market the program, to keep books, to design individualized fitness and wellness programs, and to supervise the implementation of those programs. The bottom line is that in order to gain meaningful employment, today's professional must be well educated, physically educated, highly skilled, and multitalented.

GUIDELINES FOR STAFF RECRUITMENT

Here are several guidelines for the recruitment of qualified personnel.

A job description that includes the various duties or job specifications and qualifications that the position requires should be prepared. This description is often preceded by a thorough and systematic job analysis. The job description should provide such details as the position title, a list of specific duties involved, salary and benefits, and educational and experience requirements (qualifications) as well as starting and closing dates. In addition, it is standard practice to declare that the employing organization or agency is an equal opportunity employer (in accordance with the Equal Opportunity Employment Act of 1972), to invite the application of qualified women, minorities, and people with disabilities, and to state that the organization complies with federal and state laws prohibiting discrimination in employment.

Notices of the position vacancy should be distributed within the organization, to professional programs and placement offices in colleges and universities, and to respected leaders and colleagues in the field; the vacancy should also be advertised in professional publications such as *JOPERD,* the *NCAA News,* and the *Chronicle of Higher Education* as well as in local and regional newspapers.

Candidates for the position should be asked to submit their resumes, college transcripts, and confidential references (or persons who can be contacted by the employing organization). A file should be prepared on each candidate that includes records of references and other pertinent information. Candidates should be duly notified when their files are complete or if more information might be needed to fulfill completion requirements. Completed files should be forwarded to members of the search committee or human resource department who are assigned the task of selecting the most promising candidates to bring in to interview.

GUIDELINES FOR SELECTION

Many organizations have a search or personnel committee as well as an affirmative action officer that recruits and interviews candidates for vacancies and makes recommendations to the management. Guidelines for the selection of personnel follow.

The search, personnel, or other committee or individual should review the files of all candidates, select three to five viable candidates for the position, and invite each of them for a personal interview. Persons within the organization who apply for the position should be evaluated by the same criteria as the outside candidates.

The personal interview offers an opportunity to meet the candidate firsthand and to discuss the position with him or her. During a personal interview, it is important to assess the candidate's personality, character, education, experience, demeanor under stress, and other specific qualifications. Questions asked might revolve around his or her interest in the position, qualifications, understanding of the employing organization, involvement in various professional activities, and background experience and education. The candidate's philosophy, leadership, and value judgments are also tested. Some organizations require that the candidate make a presentation before faculty, staff, and students. Many organizations find it useful to develop applicant qualification forms and interview assessment forms, not only to assist in quantifying applicants' qualifications and strengths but also to serve as a guide to the personnel or search committee on what the organization believes is crucial to the interview and selection process.

Based on the personal interview and a further examination of credentials, a recommendation should be made to management that includes either one or several applicants, giving management the prerogative to select the most qualified person for the position.

Another consideration that should be discussed is contracts. Contractual items such as salary and benefits, educational step level, length of employment, duties, tenure considerations, vacation time and sick days, and other job details should be made very clear to the prospective employee. These additional considerations could be the deciding factor that prompts an outstanding person to accept a position. Such benefits as health insurance, retirement, sick leave, annual leave, staff development, and travel allowances are an important consideration in the minds of many prospective employees. Managers should make sure applicants clearly understand all aspects of the position for which a candidate is being hired. Offers and acceptance of employment can be made orally at first, but should be followed up immediately with a written contract.

Staff orientation and in-service training are important for efficient functioning of any program.

Those candidates who were not hired should promptly receive a letter thanking them for their interest in the organization.

ORIENTATION OF NEW STAFF

The new staff member needs considerable orientation and help in adjusting to a new position. On hiring a new staff member, management should provide guidance and assistance concerning housing, transportation, educational system, hospitals, church, and other items necessary to getting settled into the community. A preorientation that familiarizes the person with the organization and management personnel should also be conducted before the opening of school in order to discuss, reinforce, and clarify the new staff member's duties and responsibilities. The new member should know the person to whom he or she is responsible and should know the lines of communication within the organization and any protocol including due process and grievance procedures that must be observed. The new person will have many questions; these should be expected and answered quickly and frankly. Quality preservice and orientation programs should result in a happier and more productive member of the organization. A mentoring program is also recommended.

IN-SERVICE TRAINING AND STAFF DEVELOPMENT

Because of the rapid changes occurring within the profession, staff members should attend regular in-service and staff development training programs. New methods of management, programming, teaching, assessment, and evaluation have implications for all professionals.

Some suggestions for in-service training and staff development include

- conducting workshops for staff members in which new trends and developments are examined
- holding faculty retreats or arranging programs that will enhance faculty and staff development by inviting consultants and professional colleagues who are specialists in facilities, curriculum development, methods, activity skills,

and computer techniques to meet with staff members and share new concepts and developments

- developing a professional library with the latest books, journals and periodicals, films, and videos and making them readily accessible to staff members
- devoting some staff meetings to discussions of new developments or issues like teacher burnout, sexual harassment, or substance abuse
- encouraging and subsidizing staff members' attendance at professional meetings and conferences
- using staff members with special talents to upgrade the knowledge and competence levels of other staff members (e.g., stress management, relaxation, creative thinking, cooperative learning, diversity training, and team building)
- providing presemester or summer orientation sessions for staff members
- conducting research and experimentation within the organization's own program and linking in-house information and research systems with local university information systems via fiber optics
- arranging for the local college or university to come to the school and conduct cohort group graduate classes and workshops or setting up an interactive TV link for distance learning opportunities
- providing training seminars in such activities as problem solving, teacher assistant teaming, social and emotional health issues, and mainstream collaborative modeling to enhance teacher performance
- encouraging sabbaticals, staff educational leave, and travel for professional enhancement

In-service training and staff development are vital to building a cooperative team of teachers and coaches. Such activities build esprit de corps and promote communication, enthusiasm, creativity, and sharing. Often these investments in personnel, or in the organization's assets, pay huge dividends in success and in high-quality programs. Professional enhancement opportunities should play a significant role in all management structures.

SUPERVISION

Supervision is the managerial function concerned with overseeing, assisting, and assessing the empowerment of the situation within each personnel function. The supervisor should act to improve the ability of teachers, coaches, or other personnel to complete their assigned duties. Supervisors must recognize each individual staff member and the contribution he or she makes to the organization, see that staff members are assigned to tasks in line with their abilities, be willing to delegate responsibility, establish high yet attainable standards, provide a complete analysis of each position in the organization, establish accountability for staff members, and help each member feel a sense of accomplishment.

Supervision will be effective if sound leadership is provided within the organization.

Qualities of the Supervisor Who Is a Leader

People years ago believed that leaders were born and not made, and that some people by virtue of beliefs or qualities lead and others follow. These statements are not valid. Instead, people today believe that personal characteristics, experience, and the ability to work independently determine leadership qualities.

Research indicates a relationship between personality factors and leadership. Group leaders are found to outperform other staff members in such areas as acceptance of responsibility, participation, scholarship, and socioeconomic status.

Research further reveals that the closer an individual conforms to the accepted norms of the group, the better liked he or she will be; the style of the leader is determined more by the expectations of the membership or group and the requirements of the situation than by the personal traits of the leader. The leader will be followed more faithfully the more he or she makes it possible for the members to achieve their personal goals along with the group goals, and in a small group,

Supervision is an applied art that must be learned and practiced.

authoritarian leadership is less effective than democratic leadership in holding the group together and getting its work done.

Hersey and Blanchard's (1993) Situational Leadership Theory suggests that to be an outstanding leader, the individual will change behavior with each situation. The theory is based on factors such as the interaction between the one who aspires to be a leader and the followers, the group's socioemotional support, two-way communication with the group, maturity level of followers, and education and experience of individuals or groups who are being led.

The physical educator or coach who desires to obtain and excel in a leadership and supervisory position in an organization should study the literature on management and supervision. This research will expose potential leaders to a variety of situations that may contribute to a greater understanding of the issues and concerns pertaining to leadership (Case 1984).

The physical educator and coach should also recognize that various personal qualities are essential for providing supervisory leadership. These personal qualities include a sense of humor, empathy, sensitivity, feeling of adequacy, ability to instill confidence and respect, enthusiasm, originality, sincerity, and resourcefulness. Supervision requires the ability to assist staff members in envisaging their own strengths and weaknesses, provide assistance in helping them solve problems, resolve personnel conflicts, improve morale, objectively judge and assess personal performance, and make recommendations for promotions, retention, and other rewards. To accomplish these tasks, the supervisor must be able to promote staff development, create effective channels of communication, establish staff accountability, set goals, provide effective motivation and adequate rewards, and supply a proper dosage of positive reinforcement.

GROUP DYNAMICS

Group dynamics are important in supervision. Group dynamics are about understanding the nature and role of groups in modern living. In this text, group dynamics are considered in light of the supervisory role in physical education and sport programs. Research has revolved around the structure of groups, how groups operate, the relationships of members within a group and between groups, the factors that affect group attitudes and productivity, and what types of leadership are most effective in varying group relationships.

Physical educators and coaches can benefit from the study of group dynamics because they work with various groups of people in their programs and because they are interested in getting groups to enter and participate in their activities and support their programs. Teamwork and cooperative effort are essential when working with organizations, agencies, and other groups. Managers and supervisors must be able to work comfortably both inside and outside the organizational framework and should be familiar with the various methodologies employed to examine group behavior.

Strategies for group dynamics are taught in winter survival course training.

Shaw (1971) has noted the following approaches to the study of groups:

- *Formal models research:* theoretical models of the structure and behavior of groups are developed
- *Field theory:* the behavior of groups and individuals within a group results from many interrelated and interdependent phenomena
- *Sociometric research:* the choices of the group on an interpersonal basis among members play a major role
- *Systems approach:* the group is viewed as a structure of interlocking elements, and group inputs and outputs are analyzed
- *Psychoanalytic approach:* the factors that groups and individuals use for motivation and defensive actions form the basis for investigation
- *Empirical approach:* groups are observed, observational behaviors are recorded, and statistical procedures are employed to develop basic concepts and guidelines regarding group decisions

Research has shown that supervisors must understand certain factors about groups in order to work effectively with them. These factors include an understanding of the group's mission in working with other groups, the power the group has over its own members, whether the group's activities are informal or highly structured, and the satisfaction derived by members of the group as a result of such group association. Other factors include the similarities of members of the group, the relationship of members with each other, the degree to which members actively participate in group activities, the case of access to group membership, significance of the group to its members, overall stability of the group, and the structure of the group as it affects the status of each of its members.

Shaw also suggests the following reasons why groups are effective:

- Group performance provides increased motivation over individual performance.
- Groups usually produce better solutions to problems than do people working alone.
- Groups are able to learn faster than individuals can by themselves.
- More new and different ideas are generated by both individuals and groups when there is an absence of critical evaluation.

An understanding of group dynamics can enhance the physical educator's and/or coach's role in the supervisory process. The study of group dynamics is an evolving area that has great potential for increasing the productivity and interpersonal relationships of any organization.

THE WORKING RELATIONSHIP BETWEEN SUPERVISORS AND STAFF

Effective working relationships between supervisors and staff members will be discussed in four sections: (1) responsibilities of supervisors, (2) responsibilities of staff members, (3) common points of conflict, and (4) a checklist for effective working relationships.

Responsibilities of Supervisors

Supervisors Should Possess a Sound Understanding of Human Nature to Work Effectively with People

Physical educators and coaches should not look on supervising as impersonal but should always keep in mind human dimensions and potentialities and give human problems high priority.

Supervisors Should Understand Their Own Behavior

Supervisors should see conflicts where they exist and not fabricate them where they do not exist. Supervisors should present an accurate account of group expectations although they may not be in agreement with those expectations. They should recognize the differences and rationale between their own views and those of others.

Supervisors Should Exercise Wisely the Authority Vested in Their Positions

Authority goes with the position, not with the person. Supervisors should recognize that the position exists to further the goals of the organization and that it should never be used for personal gain.

Supervisors Should Establish Effective Means of Communication among Members of the Organization

Opportunities should be readily available to discuss professional and personal (if appropriate) problems, new ideas, and ways to improve the effective functioning of the organization.

Supervisors Should Provide Maximal Opportunity for Personal Self-fulfillment

Each person has a basic psychological need to be recognized, to have self-respect, to be fairly rewarded, and to belong. Within the organizational structure, supervisors should strive to make this possible for every group member.

Supervisors Should Provide Leadership

Supervising requires leadership qualities that bring out maximal individual effort in the context of the total coordinated effort of the group.

Supervisors Should Provide Clear-cut Procedures

Sound procedures are essential to the effective and efficient functioning of an organization. Pro-

Supervisors provide clear-cut procedures that are essential to effective and efficient functioning.

cedures should be carefully developed; thoroughly discussed with those concerned; written and articulated in clear, concise language; implemented; and evaluated.

Supervisors Should Plan Meaningful Meetings

Staff meetings should be carefully planned and effectively conducted. Meetings should not be called on impulse or dominated by the supervisor. Agendas should be set and followed, and procedures agreed on at such meetings should be carried out.

Supervisors Should Recommend Promotions on the Basis of Merit, Without Politics or Favoritism

Recommendations for promotions, retention, tenure, and change of status or grade, when requested, should be attained through careful evaluation of each person's qualifications in relation to objective criteria. Each member of the staff (teaching or coaching) should be observed three to four times per year, with follow-up meetings and written evaluations submitted to management.

Supervisors Should Protect and Enhance the Mental and Physical Health of Staff Members

The supervisor should attempt to eliminate petty annoyances and worries that can weigh heavily on staff members. This concern in turn will increase the satisfaction each person derives from the organization, promote friendly relationships, develop esprit de corps, improve respect for the status of staff members, and establish a climate of understanding that promotes goodwill as well as personal and organizational development.

Responsibilities of Staff Members

Physical Educators and Coaches Should Support the Total Program

Each staff member must fulfill his or her responsibility to the program. This responsibility means serving on committees, attending meetings, contributing ideas, and giving support to worthy projects, initiatives, and developments regardless of the phase of the program to which he or she belongs. Staff members should view their own fields of specialization in proper perspective within the conceptual or total educational endeavor.

Physical Educators and Coaches Should Take an Interest in Supervision

By actively participating in policy formation and decision making, by role playing the problems and pressures faced by the supervisor, and by contributing ideas that will help cut down on red tape and thus streamline the process, physical educators and coaches can have significant impact.

Physical Educators and Coaches Should Carry Out Their Individual Responsibilities Efficiently

If each individual job is performed effectively, if proper procedure, attention to detail, and follow-up is maintained, the organization as a whole will function more efficiently.

Physical Educators and Coaches Should Be Prompt in Completing Administrative Responsibilities

Purchase requisitions, attendance, excuse and accident reports, lesson plans, curriculum, grade reports and many other administrative tasks have to be completed on schedule.

Physical Educators and Coaches Should Be Loyal

Each staff member must be loyal to the organization. Disagreement about supervision and differences of opinion can exist, but loyalty to the management and the organization is essential and must be maintained.

Common Points of Conflict between Supervisors and Staff Members

Areas in which poor working relationships occur include the following:

- the failure of supervisors to recognize physical education and sport as a vital part of the program
- the existence of authoritarian and undemocratic supervision
- the failure to clarify goals, tasks, and responsibilities for the organization and for each member of the organization
- the failure of supervisors to provide dynamic leadership
- the failure of supervisors to provide clearly defined procedures
- the failure of supervisors to build trust and respect with staff
- the practice of supervisors encroaching on classes and schedules without good reason or adequate previous announcement
- the assignment of unreasonable workloads
- the failure of staff members to read correspondence (bulletins, notices, E-mail) that contain important announcements
- the failure of supervisors to assume conscientiously the duties and responsibilities associated with supervision
- the existence of unsatisfactory working conditions
- the lack of adequate materials, supplies, and equipment

Physical Educators and Coaches Should Observe Proper Protocol

Staff members should discuss problems with immediate supervisors before going to higher authority. Lines of authority and chains of command should be recognized and followed.

Physical Educators and Coaches Should Be Professional

Professional and ethical behavior is essential in relationships with colleagues, supervisors, managers, administrators, parents, students, or the general public. Confidences should not be betrayed, and professional and personal problems should be settled within the appropriate management infrastructure.

PERSONNEL PROBLEMS REQUIRING SPECIAL ATTENTION

Selected personnel problems that need special attention are teacher burnout, stress management, unionism, affirmative action, use of certified and noncertified personnel, and grievance and due process.

Teacher Burnout

Teacher burnout has been described as a physical, emotional, and attitudinal exhaustion. Depression, fatigue, lack of concentration, anger, loss of sleep, and decreased productiveness are just some of the symptoms that seem to be prevalent in today's professions. Large classes, lack of administrative support, repetitiveness, lack of facilities, violence, shrinking employment opportunities, austere budgets, ill-conceived curricular movements, public criticism, lack of community support, heavier teaching loads or workloads, overemphasis on accountability, discipline problems, and inadequate salaries are a few of the conditions contributing to teacher burnout.

Some teachers and coaches are tired of their work and the many problems and pressures they face. As a result, the students are being short-changed by teachers and coaches who are complacent, dissatisfied, restless, and suffering emotionally and sometimes physically.

What can be done to cope with burnout? How can teachers and coaches who are suffering from it be helped? What procedures will result in self-renewal and revival for overburdened teachers and stressed-out coaches? More important, how can teacher and coach burnout be prevented?

Many suggestions have been made for eliminating and avoiding burnout. They are listed here so that beginning teachers and coaches as well as those currently on the job will be familiar with ways to avoid it or, if already afflicted, can find a cure for it.

A review of the literature suggests the following activities as antidotes to teacher and coach burnout: participate in visitations and exchange programs, participate in structured learning experiences, become involved in professional organizations, reassess teaching technologies, reevaluate curricular offerings, reassess reading habits, contribute to professional publications, develop a quest for new knowledge, join a staff fitness and wellness program, get involved in local service functions, and explore additional development opportunities.

Other potential solutions include the following: use holidays and vacations for personal and professional revitalization, change the way material is taught, transfer to another school, transfer to another position within the educational system, find a job outside education, or participate in professional development education. Horton (1984) points out that burnout must be attacked on several fronts because no single cause or solution exists. Therefore a teacher or coach experiencing burnout must recognize the problem and then develop a meaningful plan of correction. These plans can range from exercise to prayer and from study leaves to hobbies. Many educational and corporate environments now provide wellness counseling and self-help groups to alleviate this serious and growing problem.

Stress Management

Stress can be harmful or beneficial, depending on the nature of the stimulus or stressor, as the causal agent is called. Harmful stress affects the ability of the body to maintain stable conditions within itself. Beneficial stress can result in euphoria and greater personal achievements. Negative stress should be reduced to avoid developing physical or emotional health problems. In many cases, physical activity provides an excellent means of intervention and of stress reduction.

Some symptoms of stress that may represent danger signs are irritability, boredom, eating disorders, headaches, pain in the back, loss of appetite, nightmares, depression, emotional tension, and heart palpitations. The late Hans Selye, endocrinologist, philosopher, scientist, and pioneer in modern stress theory, defined stress as the "nonspecific response of the body to any demand placed upon it" (1976). He indicated that the body's response to stress follows a three-stage pattern:

Alarm state—the body mobilizes its resources to fight the hostile stressor.

Resistance state—the body adjusts to stress by using its maximal ability to withstand the stressor.

Exhaustion state—the body becomes devitalized and loses its ability to resist stress, leading to serious illness and even death. Many mental and physical reasons have been set forth proclaiming the benefits of physical activity and sport in stress reduction. Through physical activity, individuals can improve mind-body harmony and thus reduce harmful stress, thereby contributing to their own health, wellness, and fitness.

Exactly how physical activity reduces stress is not completely understood. It has been gener-

Teachers attend in-service training on stress management.

ally established that the mind can influence the body and the body can influence the mind. Research suggests that physical activity can result in a positive psychological response. One theory is that exercise burns up stress hormones. The human body reacts to stress by a response known as fight or flight. As a result, a number of hormonal and physiological changes take place as stress by-products are created.

If one responds to the stressor by engaging in physical activity, the stress by-products are depleted. Selye suggested that the person who exercises regularly is able to resist stressors better and that stressful situations do not represent as much harm to the physically active person as to the sedentary individual.

A second explanation is that activity helps to remove distress by releasing the tension that can accumulate when one is under stress. Activities such as jogging, bicycling, and brisk walking produce an increased target heart rate and respiration rate and result in significant stress reduction for tense persons. Physical activity also appears to provide a mental diversion from problems and concerns that cause stress (Krotee and Hatfield 1979). A stress-regulated and controlled lifestyle should provide a balance between work, exercise, rest, and structured relaxation training.

Many experts report that endurance exercise promotes the secretion of hormones called endorphins that produce the jogger's high. Endorphins are reported to be 200 times more powerful than morphine and serve as nature's way of rendering negative psychological feelings inert and of producing a natural feeling of well-being. Other experts point out that regular and vigorous exercise helps reduce stress by contributing to a lower heart rate, lower blood pressure, improved condition of blood vessels, fewer circulatory disorders, and improved body composition (Prentice 1994).

The negative image that some people have about their own body, whether the image is caused by obesity, weak muscular development, poor posture, or low fitness level, can also be a stressor. Exercise can not only improve body and

Selye's General Guidelines for Stress Reduction

Try not to be a perfectionist—instead, perform and work within your capabilities.

Spend your time in ways other than trying to befriend those persons who don't want to experience your love and friendship.

Enjoy the simple things in life.

Strive and fight only for those things that are really worthwhile.

Accent the positive and the pleasant side of life.

On experiencing a defeat or setback, maintain your self-confidence by remembering past accomplishments and successes.

Don't delay tackling the unpleasant tasks that must be done; instead, get at them immediately.

Evaluate people's progress on the basis of their performance.

Recognize that leaders, to be leaders, must have the respect of their followers.

Adopt the motto that you will live in a way that will earn your neighbor's love.

Try to live your life in such a way that your existence may be useful to someone.

Clarify your values.

Take constructive action to eliminate a source of stress.

Other Suggestions

Maintain good physical and mental health.

Accept what you cannot change.

Serve other people and some worthy cause.

Share worries with someone you can trust.

Pay attention to your body.

Balance work and recreation.

Improve your qualifications for the realistic goals you aspire to.

Avoid reliance on things such as drugs and alcohol.

Don't be narcissistic.

Manage your time effectively.

Laugh at yourself.

Get enough rest and sleep.

Don't be too hard on yourself.

Improve your self-esteem.

Exercise can contribute to stress reduction as well as maintain or improve fitness levels.

fitness level development, but it can also assist in enhancement of a person's self-image, self-concept, or body image.

Stress can also be managed by utilizing various kinds of interventions such as progressive relaxation techniques, biofeedback, cognitive restructuring, self-talk, and meditation. The box containing Selye's General Guidelines for Stress Reduction is provided here so that teachers and coaches can take full advantage of the suggested interventions to develop successful personalized stress management and coping programs.

Exclusive Representation, Unionism

Exclusive representation (e.g., federation of teachers, labor unions, professional organizations) is widespread, and management, teachers, coaches, and other staff members should understand the nature of such an association and be able to work effectively within their exclusive representative framework, including personnel and contractual agreements.

The emphasis in physical education and sport over the years has been for teachers and coaches to become involved in their professional organizations. But since the Public Employment Labor Relations Act of 1971 (PELRA), very little has been introduced to orient the manager, teacher, or coach to exclusive representation.

Managers, especially, need to understand teacher bargaining units, binding arbitration, and civil agreements to be able to work effectively with all personnel. If involved with exclusive representation negotiations, managers should look on negotiations as an opportunity to improve relationships rather than to harm such relationships. It is a time to adjust to negotiations and make the best of the working relationship, advance the organization, and improve its democratic atmosphere. The manager should insist on being a part of the negotiation process, protect the right to be the professional leader of the organization, and strive to promote mutual trust, understanding, respect, and cooperation. Other strategies contained in the Harvard Negotiation Project (Fisher and Brown 1988) and related literature should also be a part of the shared decision making in the negotiation process. Managers should know and be conversant as to their responsibilities in professional negotiations, and these responsibilities should be included within their job descriptions. If managers perform within the responsibilities as stated, they should receive solid backing from those whom they represent.

Teachers and coaches should understand that pursuant to PELRA, nothing contained in any exclusive representation agreement should be construed to limit, impair, or affect their right to express a view or opinion, to grieve, or to complain, as long as their duties are conducted faithfully.

Affirmative Action

Managers need to understand and conform to affirmative action guidelines. Among other things, these guidelines, first outlined in Title VII, Civil Rights Act of 1964, indicate that no discrimination can exist on the basis of gender, race, age, religion, color, ethnic background, handicap, or creed. All individuals must be afforded equal opportunities to achieve their destinies. In hiring personnel, attention must be given to adequate and appropriate publicity of vacancies (e.g., time, appropriate journals, newspapers), to equal consideration of all applications, and to selection based on each individual's qualifications. No discrimination can exist against members of minority groups in employment, retention, salary, or promotion. Also, organizations should strive to achieve representative diversity as well as to promote equal opportunity for professional growth and economic security.

Many organizations employ individuals whose responsibilities include promoting and overseeing the process of equal opportunity and affirmative action within their department, school, or division. Managers should continually consult with these individuals to see that affirmative action compliance is being met. If no such individual exists in an organization, the manager should be thoroughly familiar with and committed to affirmative action guidelines and goals.

Use of Noncertified and Temporary Personnel

A recent trend has been to use noncertified and temporary personnel in physical education and sport to teach and coach activities when permanent certified personnel are not available or when workloads have become too heavy for the full-time faculty. The profession has suggested the following guidelines:

- Activities and sports in which students and other consumers are interested in participating need to be conducted by regular full-time faculty members.

- In hiring new faculty, attention should be given to applicants who have the qualifications to teach and coach. If no certified faculty member is available to teach or coach an activity, certified part-time personnel should be hired. If no certified person is available, then noncertified temporary personnel may be considered.

- Noncertified personnel should have expertise in the activity to be taught or coached, and proper supervision should be provided for the noncertified person.

- The noncertified and/or temporary person should be replaced with regular full-time faculty when they become available.

There is considerable discussion in sport programs as to whether coaches should be certified. Kelley and Brightwell (1984) and Seefeldt

Use of certified human resources, including teachers, coaches, and sports administrators, is vital to attain positive outcomes.

(1992) have explored this question and, among other recommendations, believe that coaches need to be qualified and certified because tasks such as progressive training and conditioning programs as well as issues such as risk, safety, and legal liability can lead to serious problems if coaches are not well trained and well qualified.

Grievance and Due Process

In most educational organizations, a prescribed procedure is set forth to be followed by a staff member or other person who has a grievance. Grievance implies that the person believes he or she has been wronged or that a hardship, harm, or harassment has been realized and that he or she has a just cause for protest and complaint.

The established procedure usually includes discussing the grievance with persons in the chain of command and trying to solve and correct the problem at the grassroots level. If the problem cannot be solved at the lowest level, it moves on to a higher level or is submitted to a grievance committee. This committee discusses the facts in the case and attempts to arrive at a solution that is right and, if possible, satisfactory to all concerned.

Management should always be alert to situations in which grievances may occur and should try to solve personal and other problems before they reach the grievance stage. At the same time, some problems are impossible to solve, and therefore an established grievance procedure is essential.

Due process refers to an established procedure requiring certain prescribed steps that are designed to safeguard the legal rights of the individual under the Fourteenth Amendment. For example, when a person is accused of some wrongdoing and could be fired or suspended from the job or denied the right to participate in sport, that person is protected legally by having the right to pursue a judicial procedure that enables both sides to present their facts before a final decision is made. In general, procedural due process includes the individual's right (1) to be informed of all charges and complaints, (2) to a hearing, (3) to secure counsel, (4) to have adequate time to prepare and respond to the charge or complaint, (5) to present his or her side of the issue, (6) to call witnesses and to cross-examine opposing witnesses and parties, and (7) to a fair trial.

EVALUATION

Managers and supervisors need to establish methods to accurately assess staff effectiveness; to make sound decisions for retention, salary adjustments, promotion, and tenure; and to help staff members improve and grow. Management should encourage a program of evaluation. To evaluate is to determine the value or worth of someone (e.g., personnel) or something (e.g., program, facility). Evaluation should be viewed as a positive and ongoing cooperative venture based on the organization's objectives. It is usually accomplished by observations, reports of peers and students, and self-evaluations. Staff members need assistance and support to improve their effectiveness, and evaluation is one means to systematically achieve this goal. Records should be maintained to determine and chart progress. The checklist on p. 231 will help you formulate some questions to keep in mind when evaluating members of your program.

Here are some guidelines for evaluating staff members.

Appraisal should involve staff members themselves. Evaluation is a cooperative venture, and staff members should be included in developing the criteria for evaluation because they need to understand the process. There also is a place for self-evaluation.

Evaluation should be centered on performance. The job to be accomplished should be the focus, with extraneous factors considered as secondary.

Evaluation should be about helping staff members grow on the job. The purpose of evaluation is to help individuals evaluate themselves and develop or maintain strengths and reduce weaknesses.

Evaluation should look to the future. Evaluation should be concerned with developing an improved physical education and sport program and a better organization.

Evaluation of staff members should be well organized. A step-by-step approach with clearly outlined evaluation criteria should be provided for both teacher and coach.

Sturtevant (1984) suggests that the use of management techniques can be very helpful in assessing programs. Problems such as depressed economic conditions, changing enrollments, cost effectiveness, and increased travel and competition can be analyzed more objectively by using management techniques to improve productivity, increase efficiency, and reduce costs. When such techniques are employed and departmental and programmatic assessment has taken place and has been examined, then informed decision making can take place.

Methods of Evaluation

Some methods of evaluating instructors follow:

Observation of Teachers/Coaches

Teachers and coaches should be notified in advance that the observation will take place, and a conference should follow the observation, with the performance outcomes being discussed and evaluated. A written report should follow.

Student Progress

With the student progress method, standardized tests are used to determine what progress the student has made as a result of exposure to the teacher or coach.

Ratings

Ratings vary and may consist of an overall estimate of a teacher's or coach's effectiveness or consist of separate evaluations of specific teacher/coach behaviors and traits. Self-ratings may also be used. Ratings may be conducted by peers, by students, players, or by management personnel and may include judgments based on observation of student or team progress. To be effective, rating scales must be based on criteria that maintain objectivity, reliability, sensitivity, validity, and utility.

At colleges and universities, the evaluation of teacher performance is sometimes more difficult than at other schools because of the unwillingness of the faculty to permit managers or others to observe them. Various methods have been devised to rate faculty members, including statements from department heads and ratings by peers, students, supervisors, and other management personnel. The athletic director usually rates the coaches' performance.

What constitutes effective evaluation as it relates to a teacher/coach in a particular school or college? Research reveals, for example, only a slight correlation between intelligence and the rated success of an instructor. Therefore, within reasonable limits, the degree of intelligence a teacher possesses seems to have little value as a criterion. The relationship of knowledge of subject matter to effectiveness appears to depend on the particular teaching situation. A teacher's demonstration of good scholarship (e.g., publication record) appears to have little relationship to good teaching. Some evidence indicates that teachers who have demonstrated high levels of professional knowledge on national teachers' examinations are more effective teachers. The relationship of experience to teacher/coaching effectiveness

Checklist for Effective Working Relationships among Managers, Supervisors, Physical Educators, and Athletic and Activities Directors

	Yes	No
1. Job descriptions of all positions are formulated, written, and disseminated to each individual involved.	___	___
2. Policies are cooperatively formulated.	___	___
3. Staff members are encouraged to participate in the determination of policies. Management uses faculty committees to develop policies.	___	___
4. Policies cover priorities in the use of physical education and sport facilities.	___	___
5. Policies have been developed and are in writing for the major areas of the enterprise as well as specifically for physical education and sport.	___	___
6. Departmental policies and procedures are up to date and complete.	___	___
7. Board establishes and approves policies and programs.	___	___
8. Physical educators and coaches know the policies of their organization and work within this framework.	___	___
9. Open channels of communication are maintained between manager, supervisor, and staff.	___	___
10. Preservice, in-service, and staff development education is provided.	___	___
11. Staff members are encouraged to participate in the activities of professional organizations.	___	___
12. Supervisors act in an advisory, and not a managerial, capacity.	___	___
13. The teaching load of all instructors is equitable in that such factors as the following are considered: work hours per week and number of clientele per week.	___	___
14. Physical education and sport programs are open to all and conducted according to sound educational principles.	___	___
15. Policies that cover the organization and management of sport are in writing and disseminated.	___	___
16. Coaches are certified in physical education, teacher education, or coaching.	___	___
17. The group process is effectively used in staff and committee meetings.	___	___
18. There is a strong belief in and a willingness to have democratic management.	___	___
19. Staff meetings are well organized.	___	___
20. New staff members are oriented with respect to responsibilities, policies, and other items essential to their effective functioning in the organization.	___	___
21. Departmental budgets and other reports are submitted on time and in proper form.	___	___
22. Staff members attend meetings regularly.	___	___
23. Staff members participate in curriculum studies.	___	___
24. Class interruptions are kept to an absolute minimum.	___	___
25. Proper management channels are followed.	___	___
26. Relationships with colleagues are based on mutual integrity, understanding, and respect.	___	___
27. Management is interested in the human problems within the organization.	___	___
28. Maximal opportunity is provided for personal self-fulfillment consistent with organization requirements.	___	___
29. Department heads are selected on the basis of qualifications rather than seniority.	___	___
30. Staff members are enthusiastic about their work.	___	___
31. All personnel are provided opportunities to contribute to the improved functioning of the organization.	___	___

Checklist for Effective Working Relationships among Managers, Supervisors, Physical Educators, and Athletic Directors—cont'd

	Yes	No
32. The board's executive officer executes policy.	___	___
33. Faculty and staff assignments are educationally sound.	___	___
34. Management works continually to improve the working conditions of personnel.	___	___
35. Responsibilities are equitably distributed.	___	___
36. Management provides recreational and social outlets for the staff.	___	___
37. Management recognizes and rewards quality work.	___	___
38. Physical educators and coaches seek to improve themselves professionally.	___	___
39. Physical educators and coaches view with proper perspective their special roles and that of the profession in the total educational enterprise.	___	___
40. Physical educators and coaches organize and plan their programs to best meet the needs and interests of the participants.	___	___
41. Physical educators and coaches continually evaluate themselves and the professional job they are doing in the organization.	___	___
42. Budgetary allocations are equitably made among departments.	___	___
43. Management is sensitive to the specific abilities and interests of staff.	___	___
44. Physical educators and coaches take an active role in planning.	___	___
45. Physical education and sport objectives are consistent with general education objectives.	___	___
46. Management recognizes and gives respect and prestige to each area of specialization in the organization.	___	___
47. Physical educators and coaches are consulted when new facilities are planned in their areas of specialization.	___	___
48. Funds are available for professional library materials, professional travel, and quality in-service and staff development programs.	___	___
49. Physical educators and coaches carefully consider constructive criticism when provided by the management.	___	___
50. Management is skilled, informed, and up to date in organization and administration.	___	___

---

also seems to have questionable value. Experience during the first five years of teaching seems to enhance teacher effectiveness but after five years, effectiveness levels off. Little or no relationship has been found between teaching effectiveness and cultural background, socioeconomic status, gender, or marital status. More systematic research, however, must be accomplished in this domain to establish what constitutes sound teaching and coaching effectiveness.

Accountability

Accountability may be defined as a means of holding the teacher or coach (and other staff members) responsible for what the students or other individuals learn or achieve.

How can accountability be assessed? The first obstacle that must be overcome to have valid accountability is the acceptance by teachers and coaches of certain objectives that must be met. This acceptance can usually be accomplished by developing performance objectives. Once objectives have been developed, the student, coach, and instructor know what is expected of them. Accountability can be based on how well the students satisfy the stated performance objectives. Some people have suggested that student performance should be a basis for merit pay increases for teachers and coaches. This method of outcome-based education has its pros and cons.

Student Evaluations

The student is the one most exposed to the teacher or coach and his or her method. Therefore the student should have some input concerning the evaluation process. Some factors that students believe are related to teacher or coach effectiveness include knowledge of subject, fairness, interest in students, patience, leadership that is amicable but firm, enthusiasm, and skill in activities.

Many teachers are using student opinion questionnaires for teacher evaluation. The student is asked to respond to multiple choice or Likert scale questions that indicate items such as (1) interest level in activity, (2) skills learned, (3) time spent outside of class on activity, (4) knowledge gained, and (5) rating of instructor concerning course objectives, understandability of instructions, organization of presentation, enthusiasm, knowledge, skill, and accessibility to students. Space is often left for students to express in paragraph form any recommended changes in curriculum, teaching style, or method.

Self-Evaluation

An area of evaluation that is sometimes overlooked is self-evaluation, which is often the key to self-improvement. Physical educators and coaches should ask themselves some of the following questions: Have I been innovative? Do I alter my teaching to meet the different ability levels? Are my classes planned well in advance to ensure adequate teaching space, equipment, and facility use? Do I involve all my students and athletes? Do I stress cognitive, psychosocial, and behavioral objectives? Do I change my activities and practices from year to year and try new concepts such as contact grading, performance objectives, and self-directed and cooperative learning? Do I continually evaluate my programs? Do I try to improve myself by continuing my education?

Questions such as these can help the teacher and coach begin the process of self-evaluation.

Self-evaluation is not easy, but it can be a valuable assessment tool and may help improve performance.

Independent Evaluators

In recent years, the trend has been moving toward using independent evaluators because they may be more objective in assessing a teacher's or coach's abilities or a program's effectiveness. Independent evaluators should be thoroughly trained and familiar with the subject they are evaluating and should have a teaching, coaching, and administrative background. Often evaluators are drawn from consultant groups, professional organizations, or colleges and universities. The evaluators should have no previous links with present organizational personnel or the institution being evaluated.

Evaluating the Prospective Teacher and Coach

The competence of the prospective teacher and coach is an important facet of the total educational evaluation system. Traditionally the undergraduate education major was evaluated in terms of grade point average, completion of required course work including student teaching experience, and a minimum grade level in major subjects. Such evaluation techniques obviously are not sufficient to produce quality teachers. New assessment criteria must be established to include such factors as (1) comprehensive testing to ascertain mastery of both general and specific knowledge as well as teacher education objectives; (2) performance testing based on teaching task analysis; and (3) an internship to develop teaching and coaching skills.

The prospective teacher and coach should be field oriented, with much of his or her undergraduate training spent in school-related or community-based tasks. During undergraduate years, the individual should have experience in grading papers, keeping records, tutoring, and teaching and coaching. The teacher or coach who has graduated from such an experiential-based program and has satisfied the assessment criteria will be a better teacher or coach and will also have an easier and more enjoyable adjustment to the first few years of teaching. Some teacher preparation departments are extending their programs an additional year in the form of postbaccalaureate programs to provide such extensive in-school training and preparation.

Performance-Based Teacher Education

One trend today, as has been pointed out earlier in this text, is toward performance- or outcome-based teacher education. Under this plan, the prospective teacher or coach is evaluated not in terms of courses taken but in terms of certain competencies (skills, knowledge, abilities) that have been determined essential to satisfactory teaching or coaching. The prospective teacher is evaluated by scientific assessment techniques that are performance based. A major consideration is whether the individual possesses or can develop the skills requisite to changing student athlete behavior as well as performance through his or her teaching and coaching.

Evaluation of Physical Educators in Other Settings

Much of what has been said about the evaluation of teachers of physical education and coaches is also true about the evaluation of physical education professionals who work in capacities other than in school environs. They are also held accountable for the effective performance of assigned duties. This accountability is determined, for the most part, by on-the-job observation, by opinions elicited from persons who have been served by the instructors, and by their productivity. Productivity in a commercial establishment such as a health and fitness club, unfortunately, is judged by how many customers are attracted and maintained and what the bottom-line profit and loss statement says. This judgment is similar to looking at the win-loss ratio for the coach, which, although it may seem unfair, still appears to be the nature of the business.

The main concern of all physical educators and coaches, wherever they are employed, is to do the best job possible and let the evaluation take care of itself. In other words, one should be enthusiastic, develop as much expertise as possible about the position and responsibilities one has, and provide the best experience possible to all persons being served. One should also strive to develop good human relations and rapport with everyone. If these suggestions are followed, the physical educator and coach should not have to worry about the evaluation process. The satisfaction of doing the best job possible will lead to productivity, and advancement will result.

SUMMARY

One of the most important functions that management has to perform is that of human resource management. Management is responsible for such actions as establishing policies under which the staff will operate, seeing that staff morale is high, recruiting qualified members for the organization according to federal and state equal opportunity guidelines, providing adequate supervision, employing group dynamics and cooperative approaches in the achievement of organizational goals, and providing creative ways to prevent such problems as undue stress and teacher and coach burnout. Furthermore, managers must be able to work harmoniously with exclusive representatives and the various publics in general. Last, staff members need to be evaluated periodically in an objective and fair manner so that performance can be improved and deserving staff members are appropriately rewarded.

SELF-ASSESSMENT ACTIVITIES

These activities will assist students in determining if material and competencies presented in this chapter have been mastered.

1. Define what is meant by human resource management and supervision and describe the guiding principles for a physical education supervisor.

2. If you were hiring a physical educator for a health and fitness club or corporate setting, what qualifications would you look for?

3. Prepare a step-by-step procedure for the recruitment, selection, orientation, in-service, and professional development training of a new member of a physical education staff.

4. You are scheduled to be interviewed by a superintendent of schools who is looking for a person to supervise the work of coaches employed within the school system. Discuss the evaluation technique that you would employ to evaluate those coaches within your program. Present to your class what you told the superintendent. Then have the class decide whether you were hired for the position.

5. Develop a performance-based outcome rating scale you would use to evaluate the work of a physical educator at a senior high school.

6. Prepare a job description for a junior high or middle school girls' volleyball coach.

7. A teacher named in a misconduct complaint by a student should be entitled to what due process steps?

REFERENCES

1. Case, R. W. 1984. Leadership in sport—The situational leadership theory. *Journal of Physical Education, Recreation and Dance* 55 (January): 15.
2. Fisher, R., and S. Brown. 1988. *Getting together—Building relationships as we negotiate.* Boston: Houghton Mifflin.
3. Hale, R. L., D. R. Hoelscher, and R. E. Kowal. 1987. *Quest for quality.* Minneapolis: Tennant Company.
4. Hershey, P., and K. Blanchard. 1993. *Management of organizational behavior.* Englewood Cliffs, N.J.: Prentice Hall.
5. Horton, L. 1984. What to do about teacher burnout? *Journal of Physical Education, Recreation and Dance* 55 (March): 69.
6. Hunt, D. M. 1994. *Mentoring.* Hattiesburg, Miss.: Hunt Associates International.
7. Hunter, M. 1989. *Mastering coaching and supervision.* El Segundo, Calif.: Tip Publications.
8. Kelley, J. E., and S. Brightwell. 1984. Should interscholastic coaches be certified? *Journal of Physical Education, Recreation and Dance* 55 (March): 49.
9. Krotee, M. L., and F. C. Hatfield. 1979. *The theory and practice of physical activity.* Dubuque, Iowa: Kendall/Hunt.
10. Prentice, W. E. 1997. 5th ed. *Fitness for college and life.* St. Louis: Mosby–Year Book.
11. Seefeldt, V. 1992. Coaching certification: An essential step in reviving a faltering profession. *Journal of Physical Education, Recreation, and Dance,* May/June, 29–30.
12. Selye, H. 1976. *The stress of life.* New York: McGraw-Hill.
13. Shaw, M. 1971. Group dynamics: the psychology of small group behavior. New York: WCB/McGraw-Hill.
14. Sturtevant, M. 1984. Use management techniques to assess programs. *Journal of Physical Education, Recreation and Dance* 55 (May/June): 48.

SUGGESTED READINGS

Iacocca, L. 1984. *Iacocca—An autobiography.* New York: Bantam.
Tells the story of one of today's most successful managers in industry. As chief executive officer of the Chrysler Corporation, he transformed a dying company into a great success. Relates how he works with his staff to achieve results.

Kelly, B. C., and D. L. Gill. 1993. An examination of personal/situational variables, stress appraisal, and burnout in collegiate teacher-coaches. *Research Quarterly for Exercise and Sport,* March, 94–101.

Kraus, R. G., and J. E. Curtis. 1990. *Creative management in recreation, parks, and leisure services.* St. Louis: Mosby–Year Book.
Outlines the scope and process of personnel management, including information about such items as job descriptions, competency-based approaches to hiring personnel, professional preparation, employment standards, supervisory practices, training approaches, and working with unions.

Lehr, C. 1984. Meeting staff development needs of teachers. *Journal of Physical Education, Recreation and Dance* 55 (August): 73.
Presents what mature professional teachers want in the way of staff development. At the forefront are such factors as interaction with peers, self-awakening, and how to improve teaching and communication skills.

Marburger, C. L. 1988. One school at a time, school-based management, a process for change. Columbia, Md.: The National Committee for Citizens in Education.
Provides parents, students, school boards, and administrators with specific information about the concept of school-based management. Describes this new approach to decentralized organization in which decisions are made by those who know and care about quality education.

Morrison, A. M. 1992. *Diversity management and affirmative action.* San Francisco: Jossey-Bass Publishers.

Ouchi, W. G. 1981. *Theory Z: How American business can meet the Japanese challenge.* Reading, Mass.: Addison-Wesley.
Discusses the Theory Z management style in which employees are key to increased productivity and organizations foster close interchange between work and social life in order to build trust.

Peters, T. 1987. *Thriving on chaos.* New York: Alfred Knopf.
Introduces the revolution of personnel recruiting and covers topics such as reducing structure and the reorganization of the manager's role. Presents a model for empowering personnel and measuring what is important to the organization.

Rogers, E. J. 1982. *Getting hired.* Englewood Cliffs, N.J.: Prentice Hall.
Written by vice president and director of personnel for a large corporation. Illustrates the importance of such things as résumés, interviews, planning, and how to get off to a good start in a new position.

Weese, W. J. 1994. A leadership discussion with Dr. Bernard Bass. *Journal of Sport Management 8:* 179–89.
Discusses current issues and trends and provides a salient biography concerning leadership.

Zaleznik, A. 1989. *The managerial mystique: Restoring leadership in business.* New York: Harper and Row.
Describes the relationship of positive leadership to successful management, which can be applied to any organization or profession.

chapter 8

Program Development

Instructional Objectives and Competencies To Be Achieved

After reading this chapter the student should be able to

- Explain why program development is an important part of the management process and what programs of physical education and sport should accomplish.
- Identify the factors that influence program development.
- Outline a step-by-step process for program development, including the personnel or groups who will be involved.

- Describe a systems- and competency-based approach to program development.
- Discuss significant elements of program development.
- Develop a procedure for evaluating a program.

Chapter 7 focused on human resource management, one of the most important functions that directors, chairs, and other individuals involved with managerial aspects in physical education and sport have to assume. Chapter 8 presents another important function of management—to provide the leadership and support needed to design, develop, and deliver a program that will achieve the objectives of physical education and sport. A program can refer to a single event, such as an elementary school track and field day, a 5K fun run or a weekend coaching workshop, or it could be a planned sequence of curricular activities in team-building games. The key point is that the program depends on the "programmer," who provides expert intervention and services to facilitate the total development of the consumer.

The term *program development* as used in this text refers to the total learning experiences provided to consumers to achieve the objectives of physical education and sport. Program development is about the component parts of physical education and sport programs as well as the resources (e.g., human, physical, financial, informational/technological, and technical) involved in implementing or delivering these learning experiences. Physical education and sport management is involved with programs in schools and colleges as well as various public and private sector organizations. Contemporary program management demands a team approach with management, school or institution, and community as well as all people who share a need and concern about the delivery of quality physical education and sport programs. Today the trend is to provide carefully planned, value-based programs rooted in the following considerations: (1) the needs and abilities of the participant, consumer or user, (2) the needs of community and society, (3) the practical usefulness of various knowledge and skills, and (4) the social psychology of learning.

WHAT PROGRAM GOALS SHOULD PHYSICAL EDUCATION AND SPORT MANAGEMENT SUPPORT?

The main goals that physical education and sport programs should strive to accomplish pertain to four areas. The physical education and sport program should (1) develop health-related and motor performance-related fitness, (2) develop skill in a wide range of physical activities, (3) develop an understanding and appreciation of physical activity and sport, and (4) provide a meaningful psychosocial experience. This last goal may be accomplished by designing challenging physical activity opportunities (e.g., physical education, recreational sport, varsity sport) and having people (e.g., teachers, coaches, instructors, leaders) intervene in the social interaction. Such intervention should create and manipulate learning environments in a fashion that provides quality experiences for everyone participating in the physical education and sporting process.

Develop Health-Related and Motor Performance–Related Fitness

The physical education and sport program should develop such physical characteristics as adequate cardiovascular and respiratory endurance and function, proper body composition, strength, flexibility, body awareness, muscular power and endurance, coordination, speed, reaction time, balance, agility, and proper posture.

Develop Skill in Activities

The physical education and sport program should also develop skill in activities such as basic movement patterns and fundamentals (e.g., running, jumping, throwing, skipping) as well as in individual, team, and lifetime sports. Gymnastics,

Programs must balance student-athlete activities with academic pursuits.

aquatics, low organizational and cooperative games, and rhythmic activities (such as dance) that incorporate such factors as space, time, and flow should be integral components of the program. Management should also provide support for activities that will assist in any way the development of the various components of health-related and motor performance–related physical fitness (e.g., exercise, jogging, strength training, orienteering, outdoor pursuit). Mastery of the basic motor skills in both the physical education and sport program should be a primary target.

Develop an Understanding of Physical Activity

The program should also foster an understanding and appreciation of, among other things, the contribution of physical activity to physical health

Health-Related Physical Fitness Components

Item A: Distance Run
Fitness component: Cardiorespiratory fitness
Purpose: To measure the maximal function and endurance of the cardiorespiratory system
Item description:

Procedures and norms are provided for two optional distance run tests: the mile run for time and the 9-minute run for distance. The decision as to which of the two tests to administer should be based on facilities, equipment, time limitations, and personal preference of the teacher. For students 13 years of age and older, the 1.5 mile run for time or the 12-minute run for distance may be utilized as the distance run items.

Item B: Sum of Skinfolds (Triceps and Subscapular)
Fitness component: Body composition
Purpose: To assess the level of body fatness
Item description:

In a number of regions of the body, the subcutaneous adipose tissue may be lifted with the thumb and forefinger to form a skinfold. The skinfold consists of a double layer of subcutaneous fat and skin whose thickness may be measured with a skinfold caliper. The skinfold sites (triceps and subscapular) have been chosen for this test because they are easily measured and are highly correlated with total body fat.
Equipment: Harpenden or Lange skinfold calipers.

Item C: Sit-ups
Fitness component: Muscular strength/endurance
Purpose: To evaluate muscular strength and endurance of the abdominal muscles
Item description:

Students lie on their backs with knees flexed, feet on the floor with heels between 12 and 18 inches from the buttocks. The arms are crossed on the chest with hands on the opposite shoulder. Feet are held by a partner to keep them in touch with the testing surface. Upon the signal "go", students, by tightening their abdominal muscles, curl to the sitting position. Arm contact with the chest must be maintained. The sit-up is completed when elbows touch the thighs. Students return to down position until the midback makes contact with the testing surface. Repetitions are counted for a 60 second time period.

Item D: Sit and Reach
Fitness component: Flexibility
Purpose: To measure the flexibility of the lower back and posterior thigh
Item description:

The students remove their shoes and assume the sitting position with knees fully extended and feet against the sit and reach apparatus shoulder width apart. The arms are extended forward with the hands placed one on top of the other. The students reach directly forward, palms down, along the measuring scale. In this position, each student slowly stretches forward four times and holds the position of maximum reach on the fourth count for 1 second. The base of the apparatus, where the soles of the feet are placed, is at the 0″ or 23 cm level.

(reduction of risk factors, weight control, nutrition), biomechanical principles (role of gravity, levers, acceleration, force), human factors (the ability to integrate human movement with machines) and the contribution of physical health to mental health (relief of nervous tension and stress, building of self-esteem). Also, physical education and sport managers should help students and other individuals assess their own fitness level and personal developmental needs and assist them in setting goals that lead to a healthful lifestyle. The Health-Related Physical Fitness Components box contains examples of popular physical fitness test components employed by AAHPERD (Physical Best) and PCPFS (The President's Challenge).

Students learn the importance of stretching.

Provide a Meaningful Psychosocial Experience

Physical education and sport programs should provide for such psychosocial goals as the human desire for affiliation, mastery and success in play activities, cooperative effort, followership, recognition of ability, self-reliance, respect for leadership, self-discipline, concern for others, and increased cultural understanding. Managers (e.g., teachers, coaches, instructors) not only should build the program to provide meaningful psychosocial experiences through physical activity, but must themselves be proactive role models in the formation of their psychosocial capital (i.e., trust, norms, network, etc.).

IMPORTANCE OF PROGRAM DEVELOPMENT AND THE ROLE OF MANAGEMENT

Sergiovanni (1984) indicates that management should pay attention to three basic program development concerns. The first is what ought to be taught (the ideal program), the second is what is being taught (the real program), and the third is what can be taught (the practical program).

Program development should determine what must be learned and achieved and then should provide the means for seeing that these goals are accomplished. Because no two people are exactly alike, a wide range of physical activity and sport experiences that meet the needs of all individuals is requisite.

Management plays an important part in program design and planning. The goal of management is to provide quality teaching and coaching, an optimal learning environment, and healthful and safe experiences and activities to achieve the established program objectives. Because problems constantly arise and unmet needs continue to exist or remain unrecognized, continuous and adaptable planning and assessment is always a management priority. The manager, who may be the programmer, provides the leadership required to accomplish this dynamic task.

Program construction requires the selection, guidance, and evaluation of needs, experiences, and activities to achieve both long-term and more immediate short-term goals. Program construction provides for a periodic evaluation of the entire program to make changes whenever necessary. Consideration is given to factors such as participants, the community, the organization, existing facilities, personnel, time allotments, national trends, and state and federal laws and regulations. Program construction sets up a conceptual framework for a progressive plan that serves as a guide to physical education and sport personnel so that they are better able to achieve educational and organizational goals.

Although program development is in many cases a staff and faculty responsibility, management plays a very important role in bringing about program reform. Management assesses the organization's needs, assigns tasks, and sees that the mechanism is set in motion to develop and effectively deliver a quality program that meets not only the organization's objectives but those of the consumer (e.g., student-athlete) and the immediate community.

PROGRAM DEVELOPMENT PLAYERS

Program planning is a role and responsibility that involves the entire organization as well as crucial outside sources and resources. The considerations of managers, staff members, professional agencies, organizations and groups, participants, parents and community leaders, and other significant individuals are crucial to sound and effective program development.

Managers

Managers are key personnel in program planning. They serve as the catalytic force that sets curriculum and program studies into motion; as the leadership that encourages and stimulates interest in providing optimal learning experiences; as the barrier clearers who provide the time, place, and resources to accomplish the task; and as the implementers who help carry out appropriate recommendations of such plans.

McNeil (1981) points to the roles of principals and superintendents of schools in program development. The principal's role is to serve as a management link between the central office, parents, and staff when it comes to program development. Superintendents of schools influence program development by discussing curriculum and programs with boards of education, by seeing that state and federal government mandates are implemented, and by providing for preservice and in-service training and professional staff development of teachers and coaches.

Other management obligations are to place together a team of program developers who can work cooperatively and effectively, provide this team with direction (e.g., organizational philosophy and goals), and supply the team with the necessary motivation as well as human, financial, physical, technical, and informational/technological resources to accomplish the task of designing a quality program.

Staff

Staff members lie at the grassroots level of program development. The staff member can contribute his or her experiences and knowledge and can provide data to support recommendations of desired programmatic construction or change. Teachers' and coaches' comments, based on their immediate understanding of students' needs and interests, can make a valuable contribution. Committees are an effective way to use staff members. They can be established to study specific instructional or programmatic areas; identify deficiencies, weaknesses, and inequities; and recommend immediate needs of participants. Teachers and coaches can also serve to recommend solutions as well as implement changes. Staff input and perceived ownership are necessary before a program is designed and implemented and during its evaluative stage.

Professional Groups, Agencies, and Organizations

Most states have many groups, agencies, and organizations who can assist in physical education and sport planning. These include the state departments of public instruction, education, and/or health; colleges and universities; corporate groups; private voluntary organizations (PVOs); state high school associations or leagues; the NCAA; and state AAHPERD affiliates. All these organizations as well as various community-based service groups can provide meaningful input. These groups may provide program assistance, courses of study, volunteer teaching aids, mentors, materials, consulting services, advice, and even physical resources (e.g., space, facilities) that will prove to be invaluable in the planning and conduct of any program.

The Participant

The participants (ranging from student-athletes to older citizens) should play a part in program

Children and their student-teacher plan the next activity.

development. Their thinking in regard to what constitutes desirable or satisfying activities or instructional strategy for program content, intensity, duration, frequency, time, and delivery modality, for example, is vital. Participants today are more actively involved in expressing their program desires as well as their concerns and hesitations. They want to be heard, identified, included, and play a meaningful role in planning the various activities and experiences that a quality program should provide.

Parents, Significant Others, and Community Leaders

Dialogue with parents and other interested citizens can sometimes help communicate to the public what physical education and sport programs within the school or institution are trying to achieve. Parents and other community-minded people can make significant contributions by supplying input in terms of desired outcomes and other programmatic recommendations. In many instances, citizens support these programs with extra funding (e.g., equipment) as well as other resources that significantly add to program conduct and quality. Parents, students, and the community also actively express their desires, expectations, and views concerning program content and conduct. Ensuring the full participation and satisfaction of these people is vital to managing any program in an effective and efficient manner. The establishment of a parent and community liaison to serve alongside the program developer and the programmer is a useful strategy to meet this end.

Other Significant Individuals

Program development should employ the services of all interested individuals. Professionals such as physicians, nurses, lawyers, architects, bankers, construction workers, engineers, recreation leaders, and business leaders (e.g., finance and marketing executives) and virtually all citizens who reside in the community can make worthwhile contributions by examining offerings and providing input for various programmatic initiatives. It is management's charge to ensure the full participa-

Parents, teachers, and coaches play an active role in program development.

tion of all valuable human capital that may significantly contribute to building a quality program.

FACTORS THAT INFLUENCE PROGRAM DEVELOPMENT

Factors that directly and indirectly influence program development in physical education and sport include (1) the community; (2) federal and state legislation; (3) research; (4) professional organizations; (5) attitudes of managers, faculty, students, and consumers; (6) facilities and equipment; (7) class schedules; (8) class size; (9) physical education and coaching staff; (10) climate and geographical considerations; and (11) social forces ranging from culture to religion.

The Community

The community has considerable influence on physical education and sport program development. In public schools and other institutions in particular, the community provides the funds for the program; therefore there are vital implications for program development. The community wants to be, and should be, involved.

In the Darien, Connecticut, public schools, a task force on physical education curriculum was appointed by the board of education. The task force consisted of thirteen members who were active in the community. This group established the programmatic objectives they wished to accomplish and the strategy they would use to achieve their goals. The strategy provided for a survey of six hundred students in the school system, the district's coaches and staff members, one thousand Darien residents selected from tax rolls, and forty organizations with a direct or indirect interest in sport and recreation. Furthermore, the task force established evaluation criteria for program assessment.

This community involvement project resulted in rewriting K–12 curriculum guides, setting up student advisory boards and student recreational sport councils, creating a physical education inventory system, creating faculty manager positions in the secondary school, instituting a full-day in-service workshop for physical education teachers and coaches, holding regular meetings with community agencies, and developing a coaches' handbook (President's Council 1991).

Communities are becoming more aware of their role and responsibility in the planning and program development process, and good management practice allows for full and active participation. The manager in turn must be aware of the physical characteristics (boundaries, housing, parks) of the community's, who lives there, and economic base, political systems, and culture.

Federal Legislation

Although the governmental authority primarily responsible for education is the local authority and the state, the federal government is active in shaping educational programs. The Department of Health and Human Services is responsible for recommending many legislative changes in various fields, including education.

Title IX had a profound effect on physical education and sport programs by prohibiting sex discrimination in educational programs. As a result, many school districts have had to revise their curriculum to meet the mandate. Many more sports teams have also been brought into the educational fold, providing for marked increases in female participation at all levels.

P.L. 94-142, now IDEA and the Americans with Disabilities Act, and its continual upgrading has also had an effect on school programs in physical education and sport by requiring schools to provide educational services for persons with disabilities from birth through age 21. The upgrading of facilities and personnel has been a direct result of these mandates. Equal opportunity laws and affirmative action continue to play a role in the conduct and staffing of any program.

Sensitivity to issues of diversity has also brought about initiatives such as the Multicultural Education Project of the National Association for Sport and Physical Education (NASPE). Multicultural physical education shall

- include examination of prejudice based on race, ethnicity, language, religion, gender, and exceptionality
- be directed toward elimination of stereotypes and biases and toward achievement of full commitment to cultural pluralism
- be designed for students of both minority and dominant cultures
- promote equity and the maintenance of diverse cultural identities

To further clarify the definition, the following components were established:

- appreciation of (and pride in) a person's own unique cultural heritage, as reflected in history, philosophy and values, customs and traditions, and contemporary concerns
- appreciation of (and respect for) persons of different ethnic groups and their varying cultural perspectives
- appreciation of (and respect for) persons of both sexes and their differing cultural perspectives
- appreciation of (and respect for) persons of all racial groups and their varying cultural perspectives
- appreciation of (and respect for) persons of other religious affiliations and their varying cultural perspectives
- recognition of differences in goals of individuals within a culturally diverse population
- recognition of common goals and concerns of all persons within a culturally diverse population as a basis for positive personal interaction within and across cultural groups

Peer teacher promotes participation in a game of tug-of-war.

All programs, including those of physical education and sport, must lead the way to provide for inclusion and fair and equitable opportunity for all.

State Legislation

The state is the governmental authority primarily responsible for education. Local boards of education are responsible to the state for operating schools as well as recreation and park boards in their respective local school districts. They must adhere to the rules and regulations established by state departments of education. Most schools are also members of their state high school leagues, which in turn set regulations for participation in many extracurricular activities including sport.

State departments of education set policies about credits to be earned for graduation and courses (e.g., physical education, health) to be included in the curriculum and set requirements about physical education, including the number of hours and days per week as well as the opportunity for participation by persons with disabilities.

In most cases, the regulations adopted by state departments of education set minimum stan-dards. In an ideal situation, local school management sets the standards. Management must continue to play a proactive role in lobbying for daily physical education initiatives and sport programs at both the state and local governmental levels.

Research

Although some school districts rely on research to assist them in developing and revising their physical education and sport programs, too many schools fail to recognize the value of the latest research about health, physical education, and sport.

Important research studies that affect curriculum offerings in physical education are being conducted by researchers in a variety of disciplines. An example of the results of research that have influenced physical education programs is studies relating to the fitness of American children and youths. Results have indicated that a majority of American children and youths are lacking in many fitness components, and curricula have been revised accordingly to focus on the upgrading of physical fitness levels.

Relevant research in the social, psychological, and movement sciences as they relate to human movement and learning should guide physical education program planning. Researchers are investigating topics ranging from cooperative learning to effective movement patterns, from mainstreaming to exercise and fitness program adherence; their research has implications for program development at all levels of education. The closing of the decade of the 1990s provides researchers with an opportunity and challenge to meaningfully contribute to the classroom, field, pool, and gymnasium and build a path to the year 2000. This research dimension for the most part must be enhanced and advanced through cooperative program ventures, and the gap between research and practical application must be bridged. Needs analysis and market forecasts as well as evaluative assessment research should play a significant research role in the design, delivery, and upgrade of all physical education and sport programs.

Professional Organizations

National, state, and local professional organizations are constantly engaged in activities that influence physical education and sport programs. Through such activities as workshops, conferences, clinics, research, and publications, these organizations provide needed informational resources crucial to program development. Resources such as AAHPERD's *Physical Best* (1988), Jump Rope for Heart and Hoop Kits, and NASPE's *Basic Stuff Series I and II* (AAHPERD 1987) as well as its guidelines for elementary, middle, and secondary school physical education; and National Standards for Physical Education (1995) and Athletic Coaches (1995) the President's Council on Physical Fitness and Sports President's Challenge Physical Fitness Program (1996); the surgeon general's *Promoting Health/Preventing Disease: Year 2000 Objectives for the Nation* (1989) and *Healthy People 2000: National Health Promotion and Disease Prevention Objectives;* the U.S. Olympic Committee's K–9 enrichment units and their *Olympic Spirit: Building Resiliency in Youth* project materials, for example, can serve to guide, shape, and supplement program development.

AAHPERD also sponsors many national, regional, and state conferences of vital importance to physical education and sport professionals. Research studies; workshops; demonstrations of new activities, equipment, methods, and materials; and a general exchange of ideas are presented at these conferences. Also, on request, AAHPERD will suggest knowledgeable consultants to work with school and college personnel in program development, evaluation, and revision. The National Education Association, American College of Sport Medicine, and various sporting and coaching organizations ranging from sports federations such as the U.S. Soccer Federation and U.S.A. Triathlon to Special Olympics International also provide meaningful program and personnel support services.

State and local professional organizations also provide valuable program development resources and information. Physical educators and coaches should join and support these associations to keep abreast of the latest trends, issues, concerns, and activities. This participation is not only good public relations but also a way to keep the program in step with societal demands.

Arnold Schwarzenegger, former chair of the President's Council on Physical Fitness and Sports, addresses AAHPERD members.

Attitudes of Managers, Faculty, Students, and Participants

In education, the scope and content of physical education and sport programs are influenced by school managers, teachers, and coaches. If physical education and sport programs are viewed as an integral part of the school program, attempts will be made to provide the necessary support, financial and otherwise, for quality program development and delivery. If, on the other hand, they are viewed as extraneous, attempts may be made to diminish and downsize sound programs. The attitudes of teachers and students toward physical education and sport can also affect the kind of program offered.

Management has the responsibility for interpreting and setting the tone for the program to students, faculty, school boards, and the community. A written statement of philosophy and policies should be provided and included in the curriculum guide as well as in other school materials (e.g., orientation handbook, policy manual).

Students' and participants' attitudes should not be overlooked by program planners. The way students and student-athletes feel about their programs will influence their participation in, and support for, the program. A well-designed needs-and-opinions questionnaire is one way of determining attitudes toward physical education and sport programs. This questionnaire will enable the programmer to target program development and outline a strategic blueprint for operation and assessment.

Facilities and Equipment

The provision of adequate physical resources (e.g., facilities, equipment, maintenance, and upkeep) can help in influencing attitudes and facilitating programmatic success. Attractive indoor and outdoor facilities entice participation and adherence and thus help in shaping a quality program. The extent and nature of the facilities depend on such factors as the number of students, financial support, and the geographical location (e.g., urban, rural) of the program. Chapter 9 provides in-depth treatment of facility management.

Class Schedules and Sports Offered

The number of classes of physical education provided each week and the length of these classes affect the program. The minimum time for all subjects is set by state departments of education. However, local school managers can increase the amount of time spent on physical education just as they can for other subjects. Scheduling strategy such as block scheduling can also provide the programmer with creative opportunity.

The sports opportunities offered to males, females, and special populations also depend on attitudes, financial resources, and the interests of the community, school, and participants. It is the manager's role to marshal these human resources, to implement to full advantage the laws of the land (e.g., Title IX, IDEA), and to provide quality, equitable opportunities and programs for all.

Class and Team Size

The type of activity being taught and the number of teachers will determine the class size. Under normal circumstances, the number of children in a physical education class should not exceed thirty-five. Size of classes in adapted/developmental physical education should be determined by the specific needs of the students. In school districts in which physical education is accepted as an integral part of the school curriculum, class size is kept at a level that promotes optimal learning. The school management, and sometimes the local exclusive representative, can do much to see that class size is reasonable for achieving learning goals.

Team size should allow for inclusion of all participants who want the sporting experience within the limitations of quality staff and facility specifications. Title IX stresses equal opportunity for both physical education and sport programs.

Physical Education and Coaching Staff

The number of and qualifications of physical education and coaching staff members influence the program. Are teachers and coaches qualified and certified? Is there a supervisor of physical education and/or athletic and activities director to coordinate physical education and sport in the school district? These important questions need to be considered because sound physical education and sport programs depend on the quality of the teaching and coaching staffs. The faculty of every school should include personnel who have expertise and interest in physical education and sport.

Physical education specialists responsible for delivering the subject matter should have completed a sequence of courses relating to their specialty. Too often physical education is taught by individuals with limited physical education experiences. Coaches often are assigned because of willingness rather than qualification. Management should require that only qualified and certified personnel be employed in carrying out programmatic plans.

Climate and Geographical Considerations

The content of the program in physical education and sport is also influenced by environmental conditions including weather and geographical location. Program designers should take advantage of the environmental aspects of school locations. For example, many outdoor activities (e.g., rock climbing, sailing) can be scheduled in areas where the weather and terrain are favorable. Schools in areas with an abundance of water might offer various aquatic activities, whereas those located in northern environs might include skating, alpine and nordic skiing instruction, and winter camping. Management's role is to turn climatic and environmental barriers into challenges and to transform creative ideas into satisfying program offerings.

Social Forces and Pressure Groups

Social forces such as the civil and equal rights movements, culture, religion, booster clubs, mass communication, student activism, and sports promotion have implications for program development. Times, customs, and habits change; rules

Winter activities are more popular in some regions of the country that favor these programs.

vary; and the role of schools and institutions and their responsibilities to society are also altered over time.

Influential groups ranging from the National Rifle Association to labor unions, ROTC to PTOs, and alumni boards to booster clubs should be monitored in order to gain their positive support and potential contributions in program development and implementation.

SELECTED APPROACHES TO MANAGING PROGRAM EXPERIENCES

Many approaches and models have been designed for the development and organization of program and curriculum experiences. For example, Jewett, Bain, and Ennis (1995) describe what they believe are models for contemporary program development, models that are designed to provide a basis for decisions about the selection, structuring, and sequencing of educational experiences. These models are listed under the titles of developmental education, humanistic physical education, fitness, movement education, kinesiological studies, play education, and personal meaning.

Three approaches that have been employed to organize program experiences are the systems, conceptual, and competency-based approaches.

Systems Approach

In recent years, physical educators have tried to develop a more systematic means of determining what activities to include in a program. In some cases, formulas have been created; in other instances, step-by-step procedures have been developed to match activities to goals. Such methods of program development are encouraging because they represent an attempt to make program development a more scientific procedure.

A systems approach for developing a physical education program may be helpful to the physical educator because it provides a scientific, logical, and systematic method for program preparation that meets the needs of the participants. This systems approach to program development is composed of seven basic steps:

1. Identify the developmental objectives to be achieved in physical education (e.g., physical fitness and development, motor skill development, cognitive development, and social-emotional-affective development) or sport.

2. Divide each of the developmental objectives listed in the first step into subobjectives. Identifying the subobjectives brings into sharper focus what must be accomplished and makes the achievement of the developmental objective more manageable. The following are examples of some subobjectives of each of the development objectives:

Physical fitness and development objective

Subobjectives: health-related fitness components

Cardiovascular and cardiorespiratory endurance (e.g., 1-mile run/walk)

Muscular strength and endurance (e.g., pull-ups and sit-ups)

Flexibility

Relaxation

Subobjectives: motor performance–related components

Agility

Balance

Coordination

Posture

Reaction time

Speed and power

Motor skill development objective

Subobjectives

Locomotor (e.g., running, skipping, leaping) and nonlocomotor (e.g., stretching, pulling, pushing) skills

Movement fundamentals (e.g., throwing, catching, striking)

General motor ability and efficiency

Specific motor ability in game and sport skills (e.g., Hyde archery test, McDonald soccer test)

Cognitive development objective

Subobjectives

Understanding the principles of movement (e.g., gravity, force, time, acceleration, flow)

Knowledge of rules and strategies of games and sports (e.g., Scott badminton knowledge test, River Crossing cooperation game)

Knowledge of contribution of physical activity to health-related fitness

Awareness of contribution of physical activity to academic achievement

Problem-solving ability

Social-emotional-affective development objective

Subobjectives

Fair play

Values clarification

Cooperation in group work

Positive attitude toward physical education and sport

Development of self-concept

Respect for other students and teammates

3. Identify participant characteristics or norms in terms of each subobjective identified in step 2. A cardiorespiratory endurance characteristic, for example, of junior high or middle school students under the physical fitness and development objective is that they may tire easily during a 1-mile run/walk activity because of their rapid, uneven growth, whereas in grades 10 to 12, students possess a more mature physiological capacity and therefore are better equipped to engage in this type of vigorous activity.

The characteristics or norms of participants at each educational level must be determined in terms of each of the subobjectives identified in step 2. It is now possible to determine the relationship between the goals and specific participant growth and development characteristics.

4. Determine participant needs in relation to the characteristics outlined in step 3. For each

Children use an objectives chart for a balance beam activity.

subobjective, the needs of the participant must be identified. For example, a cardiorespiratory endurance characteristic of students in grades 7 to 9 indicates that they tire easily. Therefore a need exists for physical education and sport programming experiences that overcome fatiguing factors associated with time, distance, frequency, duration, intensity, and game pressures. Students also need guidance concerning nutrition habits, rest, and sleep.

5. Identify developmentally appropriate activities. For example, the activities scheduled for students in grades 7 to 9 that meet their needs should include large-muscle activities such as soccer, field hockey, lacrosse, or floor hockey. Use of modified rules, including shortened periods of play, smaller playing areas, frequent timeouts, and unlimited substitutions are recommended. Health-related fitness activities such as jogging, cycling, circuit training, strength training, and walking should also be prudently utilized.

6. List specific performance objectives for the participants in relation to their objectives, characteristics, norms, and needs and the activities appropriate to their age, fitness level, and ability. For each of the subobjectives, specific performance objectives should be listed. For example, a performance objective for the cardiorespiratory endurance subobjective for 7th to 9th grade students could be an exercise that measures cardiorespiratory endurance (e.g., the 600-yard run/walk) that the student is able to perform without undue fatigue and to promptly achieve heart rate recovery. A performance objective for 10th to 12th grade students might be having the student engage in a 1-mile run/walk and be able to perform without undue fatigue and with a quick recovery time as measured by pulse rate. Of course, all performance objectives should consider the characteristics and needs of the specific students involved. Performance objectives provide specific levels or standards of accomplishment that indicate whether progression toward the desired goals occurs.

7. Identify the teaching methods, instructional strategies, and procedures that will most effectively achieve the desired goals. These instructional strategies provide for variety and should incorporate sound learning theories (e.g., activity theory, cooperative learning). They reinforce concepts related to accomplishing the objectives (e.g., follow-through contributes to accuracy, a concept in motor skill development).

Methods that can be employed to develop the subobjective of cardiorespiratory endurance for 7th to 9th graders include viewing a laboratory experiment comparing conditioned and nonconditioned adults. Participants may also be educated and motivated by studying an explanation of the role and worth of cardiorespiratory endurance in physical fitness development and a presentation of research that outlines the comparative physical fitness level of their U.S. age-group, (such as the fitness levels found in the FITNESSGRAM) in figure 8-1, or with others throughout the world. Participation in activities that develop this type of endurance, together with an explanation of performance objectives and guidance in practice and self-evaluation, will assist the learner and facilitate efforts toward successful achievement of the objectives.

The seven-step systems approach to program development provides a logical, scientific, step-by-step method for determining the activities that will achieve the objectives, meet the characteristics and needs of participants, and provide the performance or outcome-based objectives to assess whether students are progressing or have met each objective. A systems approach may advance a meaningful physical education program aimed at helping participants become truly physically educated and making physical education a viable, well-planned offering that achieves specific educational and developmental goals.

Conceptual Approach

During the past two decades, many disciplines have instituted major program reforms that emphasize the conceptual approach to program and curriculum development. Curriculum models based on the conceptual approach have been designed for mathematics, science, biology, social studies, and health education.

In addition to studying national curriculum models, physical education program planners and other educators interested in the conceptual approach should also become acquainted with the theoretical aspects of concept development.

A definition of *concept* is needed to better understand the conceptual approach to program development. Woodruff (1964) defines a concept as "some amount of meaning more or less organized in an individual's mind as a result of sensory perception of external objects or events and the cognitive interpretation of the perceived data."

According to Woodruff, several kinds of concepts can be identified, including concepts that might be a mental construct, an abstraction, a symbolic response, or some other connotation. Although a concept might be a high-level abstraction, many concepts can be presented as concrete, easy-to-understand ideas. For example, a concept in health-related physical fitness could be related to the cardiac response to exercise: the heart rate increases during exercise. This concept can be illustrated by having students take their resting pulse rate, engage in one of AAHPERD's *Physical Best* (1988) or health-related physical fitness components (see box on page 239), and then take their pulse rate again to note the increase as a result of exercise. Concepts have been tested and found useful for students at the upper elementary school level.

The following example of the conceptual approach is based on movement activities. It is broken down into the key concept, the concept, and subconcepts. Some conceptual statements are then provided:

- *Key concept:* Individual development can be enhanced through movement activities.
- *Concept:* The development of locomotor skills is necessary for effective and efficient movement. These skills are also necessary for later development of competency in specialized games, sports, and other recreational and leisure activities.

Joe Jogger
Fitnessgram Jr. High School
FITNESSGRAM Test District

Instructor: Mr. James
Grade: 06   **Period:** 09   **Age:** 12

Test Date	Height	Weight
MO - YR	FT - IN	LBS
03.96	5.00	101
03.97	5.03	112

AEROBIC CAPACITY

HEALTHY FITNESS ZONE

One Mile Walk/Run

Needs Improvement	Good	Better
* * * * * * * * * * * *	* * * * * * * * * * * * * * * *	
* * * * * * * * * * * *	* * * * * * * * * * * * * * * *	

10 : 30   08 : 00

VO_{2max} Indicates ability to use oxygen. Expressed as ml of oxygen per kg body weight per minute. Healthy Fitness Zone = 35 + for girls & 42 + for boys.

Current	*Past*
min : sec	
8:56	9:12
ml/kg/min	
47	47

MUSCLE STRENGTH, ENDURANCE & FLEXIBILITY

HEALTHY FITNESS ZONE

Curl–up (Abdominal)

Needs Improvement	Good	Better
* * * * * * * *		
* * * * * * * *		

18   36

# performed	
12	10

Push–up (Upper body)

Needs Improvement	Good	Better
* * * * * * * * * * * *	* *	* * *
* * * * * * * * * * * *	* *	* * *

10   20

# performed	
27	20

Trunk Lift (Trunk Extension)

Needs Improvement	Good	Better
* * * * * * * * * * * *	* * * * * * * * * *	
* * * * * * * * * * * *	* * * * * * * * * *	

9   12

Inches	
10	10

The test of flexibility is optional. If given, it is scored pass or fail and is performed on the right and left.
Test given: Back Saver Sit–and–Reach

Right	P
Left	P

BODY COMPOSITION

HEALTHY FITNESS ZONE

Percent Body Fat

Needs Improvement	Good	Better
* * * * *		
* * * * *		

25.0   10.0

% Fat	
39.9	48.7

You can improve your abdominal strength with curl–ups 2 to 4 times a week. Remember your knees are bent and no one holds your feet.

Your upper body strength was very good. Try to maintain your fitness by doing strengthening activities at least 2 or 3 times each week.

To improve your body composition, Joe, extend the length of vigorous activity each day and follow a balanced nutritional program, eating more fruits and vegetables and fewer fats and sugars. Improving body composition may also help improve your other fitness scores.

Your aerobic capacity is in the Healthy Fitness Zone. Maintain your fitness by doing 20 - 30 minutes of vigorous activity at least 3 or 4 times each week.

Figure 8-1. The FITNESSGRAM provides profiles for an individual's level of fitness to help assess and improve exercise habits.

- *Subconcept:* Sprints and distance running are two specialized forms of one locomotor movement—running.

Examples of Conceptual Statements in Physical Education and Sport

Proper techniques and skill in starting are necessary for mastery of sprint running. The ability to understand and carry out the concept of pacing (the idea of running at a gradually increased speed to have enough energy left to sprint the last part of the race) is necessary for distance running. Leg strength is important in sprint running. Proper leg strength, endurance, and cardiovascular-respiratory endurance are important concepts in distance running. A knowledge of the cognitive aspects

Starting skills are crucial to sprint running.

related to both sprint and distance running and a positive attitude about running are necessary to the development of these running skills.

Basic Stuff Series I and II

The National Association of Sport and Physical Education (NASPE) of AAHPERD has created *Basic Stuff Series I and II* (1987). The purpose behind this project has been to identify the basic knowledge that applies to physical education programs and organize it in a manner that can be utilized by physical educators. It is applicable to elementary, middle, and secondary school children and youth at a time when the foundations are being laid down for adult years. It presents—in clear, concise language—basic concepts in the areas of exercise physiology, kinesiology, motor learning, psychosocial aspects of physical education, humanities (art, history, and philosophy), and motor development. A booklet has been prepared covering the basic concepts in each of the six areas; it is designed for preservice and inservice teachers. *Series I* represents the body of knowledge that supports the worth and interconnectedness of physical education.

The chapters in each pamphlet in the series share a similar organizational format relating to questions asked by students, such as (1) What do you have (e.g., self-concept, health, weight control) to help me? (2) How do I get it? (3) Why does it happen this way? Concepts are presented and then the student is shown how they can best be grasped, understood, and realized or controlled. It also explains why the concepts are valid and work.

Series II, which has been designed for teachers in the field, provides learning experience booklets with examples of instructional activities for early childhood (ages 3 to 8), childhood (ages 9 to 12), and adolescence (ages 13 to 18). The scientific knowledge in the six areas in *Series I* is related directly to physical education and sport and enables physical educators and coaches to have at their disposal the basic information and learning activities that will make it possible to educate the students. General concepts such as how to learn a new skill, how to better one's performance, and the beneficial effects of exercise are identified. The booklets also include ways to present the concepts in activity programs so that students may realize the importance of these concepts. This realization is accomplished by relating the concepts to the motives most children and young people possess. These motives are health (they want to feel good), appearance (they want to look good), achievement (they want to achieve), social (they want to develop aesthetic and affective qualities), and coping with the environment (they want to survive). Furthermore, the *Basic Stuff Series* makes it possible for teachers and coaches to tell and show students what concepts are important in physical education and sport as well as how and why they are important.

Basic Stuff Series I and II have been cooperatively developed by teachers and researchers who are experts in their particular disciplines.

Competency-Based Approach

Competency-based learning has evolved because of a public and professional concern for accountability. Students are taught by means of defined performance objectives based on cognitive, psychomotor, and affective tasks. Students are not in competition with each other, but with themselves and various norms. The teacher becomes a facilitator to learning rather than a taskmaster, and each student proceeds at his or her own rate. In addition, resource materials are made available to students to help further challenge their behavioral and cognitive skills.

How competency-based instruction or learning actually takes place can be better understood by reviewing the competency-based instruction at the high school level in Illinois. The performance objectives are developed and written by a team of physical educators and based on general physical fitness, motor skill, cognitive, and social-emotional-affective goals. A competency-based learning unit for 10th-grade gymnastics, for example, is divided into a 10-day introductory unit and a 3-week advanced unit. A lecture and demonstration of the 40 selected gymnastic stunts are presented to the students followed by an introductory unit in instruction, safety, and practice. The grading system for the introductory unit is based on performance mastery of the number of stunts as determined by the instructor:

$$16 \text{ to } 28 \text{ stunts} = A$$
$$10 \text{ to } 15 \text{ stunts} = B$$
$$6 \text{ to } 9 \text{ stunts} = C$$
$$3 \text{ to } 5 \text{ stunts} = D$$
$$0 \text{ to } 2 \text{ stunts} = F$$

The advanced unit might require a 3-week instruction demonstration period for the students continuing from the introductory unit. In this example, a student who satisfactorily completes 29 to 40 stunts might receive an A, 16 to 28 stunts, a B, 10 to 15 stunts, a C, and so on.

The Cripton Project (West Haven, Connecticut), entitled "Continuous Progress, K–12," provides another example of the competency-based approach. The project requires that student levels of achievement be divided into 10 blocks consisting of a total of 44 competency packages. Each student is regularly assessed, and a profile card that tracks each student's progress throughout his or her school experience is recorded, moved to computer, and kept on file.

Guidelines

Regardless of which program approach is used to organize students into learners, programmers must take into consideration the following factors when constructing the steps and stages of program development.

1. Motivation: What choices do students have about what is being taught and how it is being presented?

2. Activity: How do students get involved? Are equal and fair opportunities provided for all students?

3. Interaction: How will students discuss concepts? Can students try their ideas and receive feedback about their thinking or inquiry?

4. Integration: How do students connect what they are learning with their previous experience, and how do these concepts fit with other core courses?

Only when careful and thorough program development steps are outlined; only when students, learners, and team members are given a chance to become actively involved with the creation, design, implementation, operation, assessment, and revision of their program; and only when students' demonstrated performance is evaluated using clearly defined, concept- and context-specific criteria; only then will we truly optimize learning and personal growth and development. Figure 8-2 (page 257) provides an example of a program development model and the major steps involved.

STEPS IN PROGRAM DEVELOPMENT

Many dimensions should be studied when constructing a quality program. The systems approach presented in figure 8-1 illustrates some of the crucial ingredients of program development. Although ideally, perfect physical education and sport programs are implemented right from the start, the reality is that quality programs are developed over time by trial and enhancement within a systematic program development plan. The major steps involved in program development include (1) determining the organizational and climate objectives, (2) analyzing the objectives in terms of the program, (3) analyzing the objectives in terms of activities, (4) providing program guides and teaching aids, and (5) evaluating the program.

Determining the Organizational and Climate Objectives

Determining the objectives involves studying such factors as the philosophy and nature of the organization and society to be served; developmental program trends; the learning process; and the needs of the participant or target population; so that objectives may be clearly formulated.

If the main objective of physical education and sport is to produce a physically educated person, this should be the focus of the program objectives. For example, a physically educated person (NASPE 1995) is one who:

- demonstrates competency in many movement forms and proficiency in a few movement forms
- applies movement concepts and principles to the learning and development of motor skills
- exhibits a physically active lifestyle
- achieves and maintains a health-enhancing level of physical fitness
- demonstrates responsible personal and social behavior in physical activity settings

- demonstrates understanding and respect for differences among people in physical activity settings
- understands that physical activity provides opportunities for enjoyment, challenge, self-expression, and social interaction

Analyzing the Objectives in Terms of the Program

Having determined the organizational objectives and philosophy and knowing the characteristics of the participant as well as the various constraints associated with the task, those developing a program can now target, outline, and define broad categories of experiences and activities and assign relative emphases to the various phases of the design and program developmental process. The specialized fields of physical education and sport should be viewed as part of the total educational program and process. As a consequence, their specific objectives should relate to the overall objectives of the organization.

Analyzing the Objectives in Terms of Activities

The next step is to focus attention on the activities needed to achieve the set objectives and program goals. For example, the cognitive, affective, and psychomotor needs of the participants necessitate providing a wide range of physical activities as well as emphasizing the growth and development characteristics of participants throughout the life

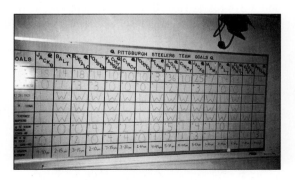

Goals are important to all physical education and sport programs.

span. In addition, enabling participants to become self-educative throughout their lives provides a tremendous challenge to program developers.

Providing Program Guides and Teaching Aids

Curriculum and program guides and teaching aids such as books, equipment, and visual aids offer opportunities to use educationally sound materials to achieve objectives during this program implementation phase. Computer software programs, videos, and behavior modification counseling are other means to support program operation. Well-qualified staff are vital to operationalize the program plan.

Evaluating the Program

Evaluation represents the culmination of the program development process—what actually takes place in the classroom, gymnasium, arena, fitness center, or natatorium. The learning that takes place, physical fitness level achieved, materials and human resources employed, and the outcomes accomplished determine the success or failure or worth of the program to both the organization and the community.

Evaluation is a dynamic process that helps determine the progress being made in meeting program objectives. It can identify strengths, weaknesses, and omissions and show where needed resources or emphases might be shifted in order to improve the program. It also helps the participants determine their own progress (e.g., competence, individuality, socialization, integration) within the program and is useful to the manager for interpreting and reporting program outcomes to both the organization and the public (see the box titled Management Principles to Consider in Program Development).

Management Principles to Consider in Program Development

Although program development varies from organization to organization, the following general principles are applicable to all situations:

Learning experiences and activities should be selected and developed to achieve desired outcomes.

The value of program development is determined by improved instruction and results.

Program development is a continuous and dynamic effort rather than one accomplished at periodic intervals.

The leadership in program development rests primarily with managers, supervisors, and programmers.

The management should consult (wherever possible and practical) teachers, coaches, laypeople, students, participants, state consultants, and other persons who can contribute to the development of the best program possible. The work should not, however, place an unreasonable demand on any person's time and effort.

Program development depends on a thorough knowledge of the needs and characteristics, developmental levels, capacities, and maturity levels of participants as well as an understanding of their environments and lifestyles.

Program development should permit staff members to explore sound principles of learning when selecting and developing experiences.

Physical education should be viewed in its broadest scope and include all activity based programs provided by the school, including recreational and varsity sports.

Physical education and sport should be integrated with other areas in the organization.

Physical education and sport activities should be selected using valid criteria including needs assessment.

Working relationships should be sought with recreational sport and athletic departments as well as with community-based and private-sector programs.

The relationship between program planning and evaluation should be recognized and understood by all individuals involved in the program. All programmatic learning experiences should be evaluated. Evaluation is primarily concerned with: (1) meeting participant needs, (2) meeting the objectives of the program, and (3) considering the requirements of parents, community, staff members, and organization members.

Goodlad (1964) indicates that program evaluation usually employs the following four means to determine the worth of a new program: (1) observing individuals who have been exposed to the new program and the progress they have made, (2) systematic questioning of people involved in the program, (3) testing participants periodically to determine their progress, and (4) comparative testing of participants under both the new and old programs to determine the progress of each.

Evaluation may be a yearly procedure, handled by members of a department, or it may be an examination of the entire organization by a visiting team of external specialists. The process of evaluation itself involves rating or judging the program according to selected criteria and standards. Some standardized forms have been developed to evaluate various phases of physical education programs (e.g., by NASPE/NCATE).

In situations in which standardized tests or norms are not available to judge programs or parts of programs, criteria based on authoritative research and textbook sources or the judgment of experts in the field must be established.

The following are sample questions, which may be answered *poor, fair, good,* or *excellent;* or may be scored on a scale of 1 to 10; or may be scored on a Likert scale wherein the respondent reacts to a five-point scale indicating *strongly agree, agree, uncertain, disagree,* or *strongly disagree.* Program areas are listed with sample questions about various factors that managers must take into full consideration. The Suggested Outline of a School Physical Education Program Evaluation Checklist box also provides a checklist of issues to help assess program curricula.

Cooperative games play an important role in program design.

Basic Instructional Physical Education Program

- Does the program devote equitable time to team, individual, and lifetime sports as well as to rhythms, aquatics, dance, cooperative games, and gymnastic activities?
- Are the available equipment and facilities adequate to allow for maximal as well as safe participation?
- Are reasonable budgetary allotments made for the program?
- Are accurate evaluation procedures conducted and records kept?
- Are minimal participation requirements met by all students?
- Are participants meeting proper physical education requirements in regard to participation?
- Are proper safety measures implemented in all activities?
- Are opportunities for developing student leadership being provided in the program?

Adapted/Developmental Program

- Do adequate screening and evaluation procedures exist for its participants?
- Are proper supervision and instruction afforded each individual participant?

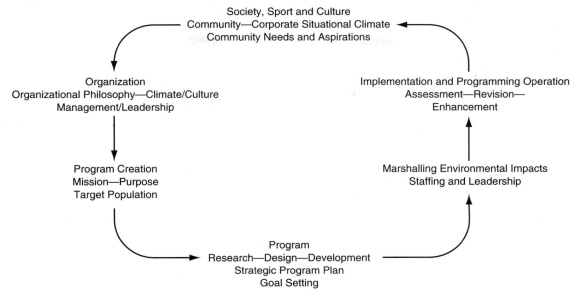

Figure 8-2. Krotee Program Development System (KPDS).

- Are adequate facilities, equipment, time, and space made available to the program?
- Is school and parental approval obtained for each individual's regimen of activity?
- Do participants engage in regular class activity as well as any recommended developmental classes?
- Are careful records and progress charts (e.g., IEP objectives) kept for each student?
- Is the financial allotment to the program reasonable?
- Does student achievement reflect the value of the program?

Recreational Sport Programs

- Are intramural, extramural, fitness, open, and club sports offered to all students, including the disabled?
- Are enough activities (e.g., level, coed, outdoor pursuit) offered to the student population?

- Has the percentage of participation in these programs increased during the past three years?
- Is prudent supervision available to all participants?
- Is adequate financial assistance given to this phase of the program?
- Are accurate records maintained about the participants and their awards, protests, and conduct violations?
- Does the reward or point system emphasize the joys of participation rather than focus on the value of the reward?
- Is the equipment utilized for the program safe and adequate for the number of participants?
- Is equipment properly maintained and stored to gain the most use from it?
- Are competitive experiences wholesome and worthwhile for all participants?
- Is the level of organization appropriate to the activity?

Suggested Outline of a School Physical Education Program Evaluation Checklist

The following evaluation checklist for physical education programs suggests methods of assessing curriculum development in this area.

	Yes	No
1. Does the physical education curriculum meet the established objectives?	_____	_____
2. Does the physical education curriculum provide for the keeping of records to chart student progress?	_____	_____
3. Is evaluation used to help each student find out where he or she is in relation to the program objectives?	_____	_____
4. Are objective, as well as subjective, measures used to determine the progress of students in attaining program objectives?	_____	_____
5. Are the students required to have medical examinations in order to participate?	_____	_____
6. Does the physical education curriculum provide for the administration of physical fitness tests to evaluate the fitness level of each student?	_____	_____
7. Does the physical education program provide for the testing of motor skills and use specific ability tests?	_____	_____
8. Does the physical education curriculum provide for cognitive testing of students?	_____	_____
9. Does the physical education curriculum provide for the testing of the social adjustment of each student?	_____	_____
10. Are the attitudes and interests of the students evaluated?	_____	_____
11. If scientific methods of testing are not feasible, does the physical education curriculum provide for teacher-made tests?	_____	_____
12. Does the physical education program use test results in planning and revising activity or program units?	_____	_____
13. Does the physical education curriculum provide for mobility of students based on evaluation results?	_____	_____
14. Does the physical education curriculum provide for student evaluation as well as teacher evaluation?	_____	_____
15. Does the physical education program provide for the recognition of curriculum problems and then try to bring about change?	_____	_____
16. Once change is needed in the curriculum, is it easy to bring about that change?	_____	_____
17. Is the physical education staff receptive to change?	_____	_____
18. Is there a provision for ongoing evaluation of programs in reference to satisfying objectives according to an established schedule?	_____	_____
19. Does the physical education curriculum provide for the needs of students with varying disabilities?	_____	_____

Interscholastic and Intercollegiate Sport Programs

- Is adequate financial support provided by the school for this program?
- Is there equitable financial support for all sports in the program?
- Are equal numbers of interscholastic sports available to boys and girls alike?
- Does the program meet established Title IX mandates?
- Are adequate health and safety standards being met in respect to number of practices and games, fitness level of participants, level of competition and certified equipment?
- Is competition provided by schools of a similar size?
- Is the program justifiable as an important facet of the educational process?
- Are academic standards for participants maintained?

Management should provide opportunities for gifted students to reach the highest level of skill development; USA National Junior Team. Courtesy of USA Basketball.

- Are good public relations with the community furthered through this program?
- Are sport offerings healthful and safe for all participants?
- Are medical personnel available at practices and games?

Staff and Faculty

- Is the teaching and coaching staff well qualified and capable of carrying out the program?
- Is the program run efficiently, with little loss of teaching time or space, and is maximal use made of facilities?
- Are professional or exclusive representative standards maintained regarding class size and teacher/coach assignment?
- Does the departmental organization function on a democratic basis, with members sharing in the decision-making process?
- Do members of the staff possess a professional outlook and attitudes?
- Do staff members attend professional meetings and keep up with the latest developments in the profession?
- Do staff members apply current research findings to various programmatic activities?

These are just a few sample questions that may be used in evaluating program management and conduct. A sample evaluation checklist for a school physical education program is also offered (see box on page 258). The key to successful evaluation of this type lies in the follow-up steps for program improvement.

Regardless of which evaluation method, style, or technique is used for physical education and sport programs, evaluation is an important and vital part of program development. Evaluation helps the programmer improve and service programs; analyzes the value of various component parts of programs (e.g., jump rope unit, booster club); should boost staff, student, or participant morale; and may even result in discovering new needs that should be addressed. Evaluation should be realistic, functional, systematic and continuous in order to fulfill its major purpose of providing meaningful and quality programs that benefit all involved.

MANAGEMENT AND PROGRAM CHANGE

Because evaluation is a continuous process, it effects future program development, establishes accountability to determine if program development goals are being met, and serves to change (e.g., reform, revise, cut, and enhance) existing programs. Many factors have an impact on programs, and the physical educator, coach, athletic and activities director, and program manager must make informed and prudent decisions about program change. Here are five questions that managers might ask themselves in evaluating changes:

1. *What are the functions of the organization?* How does the suggested change conform to the philosophy, culture, climate, and purpose of the organization?

2. *Am I sufficiently well informed to make an intelligent decision?* Managers need to be knowledgeable about the learning process; health-related fitness patterns; human growth and development; current program needs, issues, and mandates; and the needs and interests of the local community.

3. *How does the change relate to staff, facility, budget, future program development, and other important managerial considerations?*

The change must be practical to implement and make the best use of human and physical resources.

4. *What do the experts say?* What is the thinking, opinion, and position of professionals and organizations who have conducted research, thoroughly studied the problem, and piloted like programs? Expert testimony may be helpful in making sound program decisions.

5. *Who is the evaluation for, and who will take action based on the results?* Change is not accomplished in a vacuum and both personal and political motives for change must be studied.

Considerations in Program Change

Program revision cannot occur without considering the following:

1. *Participants.* The number of participants, their needs and interests, and other characteristics such as sociocultural background or gender need to be considered before initiating any program change.

2. *Staff members.* Staff members play a key role in program revision. Important considerations include, for example, the attitude of the faculty toward change, present workloads, comprehension of goals of the school, attitudes toward after-school sport programs, competencies in curriculum revision, and past training and experience. Change in curriculum might mean new members being added to the faculty or a different type of competency being represented on the staff.

3. *Physical facility.* The adequacy of the physical plant and facility for present and future programs must be considered. Information should be available on capabilities and limitations of the present physical plant (e.g., pool, arena, and field space). New demands may be placed on facilities through program revision that brings about changes in class size, scheduling, and alternative site planning.

4. *Budget.* The budget is another important consideration. What will the new sport program

cost? What are the sources of support? Before staff members expend time and effort to study program change, they need reasonable assurance that proposed changes are economically feasible. In systems using a planning-programming-budgeting-evaluation-system, or PPBES, budgets are formulated based on the objectives of the program; PPBES also provides for evaluation techniques that may require further program change or modification if goals are not being met.

5. *Program.* Because any new program proposal is likely to reflect current practices to some degree, it seems logical that the present program needs careful scrutiny to determine what has happened over the years, the degree to which staff members have brought about change, and the general direction in which the institution is moving.

6. *Legality.* New program additions or subtractions must conform to the laws of the land (e.g., Title IX, ADA). Programs and their resources must be equally apportioned.

7. *Management.* Staff members must take a hard look at the managerial leadership. The philosophy of management and its views toward change should be carefully weighed. Managers will need to approve budgetary and resource allocations as well as required expenditures in order to affect the proposed program initiative or change.

Research in Program Changes in Physical Education and Sport

Advancing the frontiers of knowledge in physical education and sport is urgently needed. Too many unsupported claims about the value of physical education and sport have been set forth. Its worth needs to be determined through valid research findings: basic research that will advance knowledge and perhaps more critically applied research that will determine the best ways to design and effectively implement this knowledge so individuals can come closer to realizing their full potential.

Many questions are still unanswered, such as: What is the most effective way to develop physical fitness? What activities are most effective for developing muscular strength and power? How many times per week is physical education needed to enhance self-concept? What activities can the employee on the job perform to enhance his or her physical fitness level? What are the fundamental patterns of human movement? What activities are best conducted cooperatively? What is the relationship of personality development to motor performance? What is the relationship of academic achievement to physical fitness level? What is the therapeutic value of physical activity? What types of feedback are most effective to promote exercise and sport adherence? How does family structure contribute to participation pattern and performance? What instructional strategies are most effective in mainstreaming? What about physical education and sport in other societies and cultures?

Research opportunity abounds in the classroom, arena, and gymnasium. There is no question that more systematic research is crucial to the development of the profession and that many program development improvements will result from such concerted research effort.

SUMMARY

Management has the responsibility to see that quality physical education and sport programs are developed, systematically reviewed, evaluated, and changed or modified when necessary to better meet the needs of the participant. This responsibility includes deciding what goals should be created and supported, enlisting the help of key individuals and groups in the construction of the program, taking into account the factors and groups who influence and are influenced by the program, following the proper procedures and selecting the best approach in program development, and being aware of the current trends and issues in the field for which the program is being targeted. In other words, management is responsible for providing effective leadership as well as the structural and support resources and motivation to fully, effectively, and efficiently carry out the program development process.

SELF-ASSESSMENT ACTIVITIES

These activities will assist students in determining if material and competencies presented in this chapter have been mastered:

1. Explain to the class what is meant by program development, the role of management in this process, and the ways in which program change occurs.

2. If you were an athletic and activities director of a junior high or middle school, what factors would influence the various activities included in your program?

3. You have been assigned to chair a committee to develop a physical education program for your school. Whom would you select to serve on a curriculum committee?

4. List and discuss several principles you would observe in developing a middle school curriculum.

5. Using the systems approach, trace the program development process for a high school.

6. You have been hired as a consultant to evaluate a physical education program in a developing nation. Describe the process you will follow in conducting this task.

7. Discuss various restrictions that may influence the shape and conduct of the physical education program at your institution.

REFERENCES

1. AAHPERD (American Alliance for Health, Physical Education, Recreation and Dance). 1987. *Basic stuff series, I and II.* Reston, Va.: AAHPERD.
2. AAHPERD (American Alliance for Health, Physical Education, Recreation and Dance). 1988. *Physical best.* Reston, Va.: AAHPERD.
3. Goodlad, J.L. 1964. *School curriculum reform in the United States.* New York: The Fund for Advancement of Education.
4. Jewett, A.E., L.L. Bain, and C. Ennis. 1995. *The curriculum process in physical education.* Dubuque, Iowa: Wm. C. Brown.
5. McNeil, J.D. 1981. *Curriculum: A comprehensive introduction.* Boston: Little, Brown.
6. NASPE (National Association for Sport and Physical Education). 1995. *Moving into the future: National standards for physical*

education—A guide to content and assessment. St. Louis: Mosby–Year Book.

7. NASPE (National Association for Sport and Physical Education). 1995. *National standards for athletic coaches.* Reston, VA: NASPE.

8. President's Council on Physical Fitness and Sports. 1996. President's Challenge Physical Fitness Program: *Test manual.* Bloomington, IN: Poplars Research Center.

9. Sergiovanni, T.J. 1984. *Effective department leadership.* Newton, Mass.: Allyn and Bacon.

10. U.S. Department of Health and Human Services. 1989. *Promoting health/preventing disease: Year 2000 objectives for the nation* (draft for public view and comment). Washington, D.C.: U.S. Government Printing Office.

11. U.S. Department of Health and Human Services. 1994. *Healthy people 2000: National health promotion and disease prevention objectives* (1994 update). Washington, D.C.: U.S. Department of Health and Human Services.

12. Woodruff, A.D. 1964. The use of concepts in teaching and learning. *Journal of Teacher Education* 20 (March): 84.

SUGGESTED READINGS

AAHPERD (American Alliance for Health, Physical Education, Recreation and Dance). 1988. Special focus: Playing fair. *Strategies* 1(3):5–21, 27–29.
Part of a series of articles dealing with coaching conduct and ethics. Provides a glimpse into coaching strategy and methodology.

Csikszentmihalyi, M. 1991. *Flow: The psychology of optimal experience.* New York: Harper Perennial.

Gensemer, R.E. 1985. *Physical education: Perspectives, inquiry, applications.* Philadelphia: Saunders.
Discusses perspectives of the philosophies and principles of physical education. Presents information about how the knowledge base of physical education and sport relates to career potentials. Tells what physical education is, what it examines, and how it is employed.

Lacy, A.C., and D.N. Hastad. 1989. Measurement and evaluation. *Strategies* 2(3):21–25.
Presents techniques to assess student progress in meeting program goals, including an easy-to-read chart that highlights the learning domains.

NASPE (National Association for Sport and Physical Education). 1995. *Moving into the future: National standards for physical education—A guide to content and assessment.* St. Louis: Mosby–Year Book.

Newell, S., and J. Swan. 1995. The diffusion of innovations in sport organizations: An evaluative framework. *Journal of Sport Management* 9:317–37.

Powell, K.E., G.M. Christenson, and M.W. Kreuter. 1984. Objectives for the nation: Assessing the role physical education must play. *Journal of Physical Education, Recreation, and Dance* 55(6):18–20.
Emphasizes three important aspects of the reports *Healthy People* and *Objectives for the Nation.* Discusses realistic goals for the profession as well as the need to garner the support of the American people. Challenges physical educators to promote lifelong health-related physical activity for all segments of the population.

Rink, J.E. 1993. *Teaching physical education for learning.* St. Louis: Mosby–Year Book.
Has implications for the implementation of the curriculum in physical education through the improvement of the efficiency of instruction, quality of teaching, and other factors that should be considered in seeing that students reap the greatest benefits from planned programs. Presents comprehensive coverage of sequential learning experiences.

Rossman, J.R. 1995. *Recreation programming: Designing leisure experiences.* Champaign, Ill.: Sagamore Publishing.

Sanborn, M.A. and B. Hartman. 1982. *Issues in physical education.* Philadelphia: Lea and Febiger.
Helpful for management personnel who need to make curricular decisions involving types of programs to be supported. Provides examples of the issues and resultant problems that can occur in program management.

Wilmore, J. 1982. Objectives for the nation: Physical fitness and exercise. *Journal of Physical Education, Recreation and Dance* 53(3):41–43.
Presents key points from the physical fitness and exercise section of the report *Objectives for the Nation.* Describes necessary preventive, promotive, legislative, and economic measures relative to the objectives. Delineates the specific objectives for the 1990s as well as the challenge for physical educators to work together within professional organizations and make a personal commitment to be role models of a healthy, active lifestyle.

Wuest, D.A., and B. Lombardo. 1994. Curriculum and instruction: The secondary school physical education experience. St. Louis: Mosby–Year Book.
Provides help in the development of a curriculum in physical education for the secondary school level. Includes such topics as objectives, curriculum planning, research, program organization, the curriculum guide, evaluation, and management guidelines for programs.

Facility Management

- -

Instructional Objectives and Competencies To Be Achieved

After reading this chapter the student should be able to

■ Prepare a list of principles that could be used by the management in planning, constructing, and utilizing facilities for physical education and sport programs.

■ List the procedures involved in working with an architect.

■ Describe the indoor facilities (type, size, location) needed for physical education and sport programs, and prepare guidelines for managers to follow in planning such facilities.

■ Describe the outdoor facilities (type, size, location) needed for physical education and sport programs, and prepare guidelines for managers to follow when planning such facilities.

■ Compute the number of teaching stations needed, given the total number of participants, size of classes, and periods per week.

■ Discuss contemporary features and developments in the construction of physical education and sport facilities.

■ Show how to provide facilities that will be conducive to a healthful and safe environment for conducting physical education and sport programs.

- —

Traditionally, at the K–12 school level and public sector venue (e.g., YMCA/YWCA, local sport clubs, etc.), facility management is usually a responsibility of those persons who are in charge of physical education and sport programs. The facilities for which they are responsible include outdoor facilities—such as playgrounds, courts, and fields—and indoor facilities—such as locker and shower rooms, natatoriums, racket sport courts, weight and exercise rooms, arenas, and gymnasiums. Facility management includes not only the effective scheduling and maintenance of such facilities but also, at times, planning new structures to keep pace with the demand for participation in physical education and sport programs. Contemporary sport facilities management at the university and community level, however, has taken on a whole new meaning. Facility management at many large universities, for example, has become a full-time profession. Facility management groups ranging from Spector to Ogden have matured into profitable multi-million-dollar businesses that professionally manage large sports complexes like the Hubert H. Humphrey

Metrodome or Three Rivers Stadium. In addition to their operation's traditional responsibilities, facilities managers are now involved in the Total Facility Management Package (see box below), which includes conceiving, planning, administering, marketing, financing, and learning the legal ramifications of facility management.

Additional developments have implications for facility management. The cost of materials and labor is rising as a result of inflation, making it very difficult for new capital building projects to go forward. High interest rates make it difficult to get bond issues passed for facility construction. Facilities must be accessible for persons with disabilities (per ADA) and must be brought up to code concerning myriad environmental standards. Energy conservation and sustained maintenance and repair costs must also be taken into consideration.

Because little or no money is available in some situations or because capital expenditure for building is so high alternative methods are being used to see that physical education and sport programs have the facilities necessary to conduct quality programs. Methods such as renovating and converting existing structures and instituting multiple use of present facilities are emerging. When funds are limited, fiscal responsibility involves following construction plans that are most economical not only in cost but in construction time and the use of energy.

Joint ventures and partnering between school, community and public and private sector interest groups (e.g., Ys, health and fitness clubs) are the wave of the future. Even though the partnering groups may not share the same goals, each entity desires quality facilities for its consumer or user groups. So from Boise, Idaho, to Springfield, Massachusetts, to Wayzata, Minnesota, Ys are sharing with communities and private health and fitness clubs are sharing with school districts to form common ground facilities projects. On a larger scale, enterprises such as Disney and corporations such as Toro and Cybex have also

---

Total Facility Management Package (TFMP)

Planning
  Feasibility strategies
  Market analysis
  Financial planning
  Site selection
  Team building

Administration
  Facilities programming
  Systems analysis
  Evaluation
  Personnel negotiating
  Networking

Operations
  Personnel hiring and training
  Concessions
  Security
  Event management
  Maintenance
  Parking/tailgating

Marketing
  Promotion
  Event procurements
  Public and media relations
  Televison and cable rights
  Sponsorship

Finance
  Accounting
  Budget analyses
  Ticketing and rentals
  Capital planning
  Inventory and purchasing

Legal
  Contract negotiations
  Sponsorship procurement
  Insurance
  Labor
  Employee relations

Source: Krotee 1997.

combined resources, for example, at Disney's 200-acre Wide World of Sports complex.

Physical plants require careful planning and consultation with specialists in architectural planning. Managers, physical educators, coaches, program specialists, consultants, and other personnel should participate in planning new facilities. Other participants, depending on the type of facility, should include the school board, institutional policy board, building and grounds, maintenance, director of public safety, and numerous building task force groups. The facility manager must be knowledgeable not only about the facility's specific structure, but also its functions and maintenance. Trends and innovative structural concepts should be thoroughly examined to provide a healthful, safe, and efficient physical plant.

The physical plant is a major consideration in most physical education and sport programs. New

The Hubert H. Humphrey Metrodome is shared by the community, Minnesota State High School League, and the University of Minnesota as well as the area's other intercollegiate and professional sport teams.

architectural ideas are constantly being introduced and new concepts developed that have a more economical, accessible, and functional management scheme. Some building concepts include *convertibility,* in which interiors are rearranged by employing movable walls, curtains, and partitions, such a concept facilitates using the gymnasium, cafeteria, and amphitheater as multipurpose activity stations that can accommodate small or large groups. This concept provides instruction and independent study spaces for a number of varied activities and is becoming a trend as plant space and fiscal restraint become crucial to the survival of programs.

Some resources that are aimed exclusively at facilities for physical education and sport are listed at the end of the chapter and should be consulted by those who desire a more thorough treatment of this subject.

PLANNING THE FACILITY

At the outset, two principles relating to facility management should be uppermost in the minds of physical educators: (1) facilities are built as a result of program needs, and (2) cooperative planning is essential to design and construct quality facilities. Program objectives; user group needs; activities; teaching methods, strategies, and materials; management philosophy; policies; equipment; and supplies all represent program considerations regarding facilities. The educational and recreational needs of both the school and community; the thinking of the managers, physical educators, and coaches; the advice of architects and engineers; and input from other groups mentioned earlier are other considerations if facilities are to be planned wisely.

Management guidelines and principles for facility planning that apply to all educational levels and organizations include the following:

- Facilities should be planned primarily for the participants and user groups.
- All planning should be based on goals that recognize that the total physical and nonphysical environments must be safe, secure, attractive, comfortable, clean, practical, and adapted to the needs of the individual.

- Facilities must be economical to operate and maintain.
- The planning should include a consideration of the total physical education and sport facilities of the community. The programs and facilities of these common areas are closely allied, and planning should be coordinated and cooperative, based on the needs of the total community.
- Facility planning must take into consideration protection for the community (e.g., sound, lighting). The facility must be accessible to user groups, yet isolated enough so that the activity is not a distraction to other programs.
- Facilities should be geared to health, safety, and legal codes and standards, which are important in protecting the health, welfare, and safety of user groups.
- Facilities should be planned so that they are easily accessible and secure for all individuals, including those with disabilities.
- Facility planning must be long-term in nature to include both adaptability and expandability to meet the needs of a changing society.
- Facilities play a part in a healthful environment. The extent to which organizations provide ample play area space, sanitary considerations, and proper ventilation, heating, and cleanliness will to some extent determine how effectively health and wellness are promoted.

Managers must make plans for facilities long before an architect is consulted. Technical information can be obtained in the form of standards and guides from various sources, such as state departments of health and education, sports organizations and federations, professional journals and literature (e.g., *Athletic Business, Facility Manager, Club Industry, Special Events, Aquatics*), as well as from appropriate groups such as the American Association of School Administrators, AAHPERD, NASPE, NCAA and the American Institute of Architects.

Standards may be used as guides and as a starting point; however, it is important to keep in mind that standards cannot always be implemented entirely as envisaged. They usually have to be modified in light of community needs, environmental conditions, and scarce inputs, including fiscal constraints.

Building safety and sanitation codes managed by the local and state departments of public health and the technical advice and consultation services available through these sources should be identified and implemented by managers during the planning phase as well as the construction phase of the facilities. Information about quality building materials, safety specifications, minimal standards of sanitation, sound and light, and other details may be procured from these sources.

Physical education and sport personnel should play important roles in planning, administering, operating, marketing, and promoting new and renovated facilities. The specialized knowledge and experience that such individuals have is important. Provisions should be made so that their expert opinion will be used to promote healthful, safe, optimal learning environments.

Facilities should be planned only after feasibility, market, and needs forecasting is performed. Too often, facilities are constructed, outdated, and outgrown within a very short time. Building units should be large enough to accommodate peak-load participation for various activities at all user group levels. The peak-load estimates should be made with future growth of both the user group and the activity in mind.

Planning should provide adequate allotment of space to each activity and program area. Space allotment should fit into an overall plan of program priorities (e.g., weight training, dance, open fitness, spectator sports). Office space and service and storage units, although important, should not be planned and developed in a spacious and luxurious manner that goes beyond efficiency and necessity.

Geographical, ecological, and climatic conditions should be considered when planning facilities. By doing this, the full potential for conducting activities outdoors as well as indoors can be realized.

*From construction to operation;
University of Minnesota Track and
Field Complex.*

Architects do not always pay as much attention as they should to the educational and health features when planning buildings and facilities. Therefore it is important that they be briefed on certain requirements that physical educators believe are essential so that the health, safety, and welfare of children, youth, and adults may be better served. Such a procedure is usually welcomed by the architect and facility planning committee and will aid them in rendering a greater service to the community.

Facilities should include all the safety features essential in physical education and sport programs. Health and sports medicine services

Role of Management in Facility Planning and Development

Kraus and Curtis (1990) have indicated the role of management in the planning and development of a facility, presented here in the following adapted form:

- Management should familiarize itself with background information pertinent to the facility plan and should be actively involved in all planning sessions.

- Management should meet and discuss the facility project with all people (e.g., user groups, community) who have a stake in the project. Management should be familiar with the views of such people and consider their suggestions carefully.

- Management should insist on being involved in selecting the architect or engineer who is going to do the plan. Management should press strongly for selecting competent and qualified people to do the job rather than the lowest bidder or the firm with political connections.

- Management should be at all planning conferences to present the department's point of view on facility design.

- Management should visit the site regularly after construction begins. All problems should be noted, recorded, and reported to the appropriate facility planning team.

- Management should insist that all details and standards incorporated in the project be carried out exactly as specified. Management should not approve any facility or authorize payment unless this has been done.

and office locations near the gymnasium, pool, arena, and other play areas, proper surfacing of activity areas, adequate space, temperature and humidity control, and proper lighting are a few of these considerations (see the Role of Management in Facility Planning and Development box).

The construction of school physical education and sport facilities often tends to set a pattern

and elicit a positive reaction that will influence community, civic leaders, parents, and others. This in turn promotes a healthful and safe environment for the entire community to take pride in.

HEALTH CONSIDERATIONS IN FACILITY PLANNING

The participant must be provided a safe, healthful, pleasant, and emotionally secure environment in which to participate. This environment also includes the outdoors, where everything possible should be done to protect and enhance land, water, air, and other delicate ecosystems. The total learning and working environment should be healthful and pleasant for all faculty members, staff members, and employees as well as all user groups.

Another set of principles basic to facility planning concerns the optimal promotion of a healthful environment for not only the participants but also the community. Included in this set of principles is the provision for facilities that consider the physiological needs of the participant, including proper temperature and humidity control, lighting, water supply, and acoustic (noise) level. A second principle is to provide safe facilities. The facilities should be planned so that the possibility of mechanical accidents, the danger of fire, and the hazards involved in traffic, and crowd safety and control would be eliminated or kept to a minimum. A third principle is to protect against disease. This means attention to items such as proper sewage disposal, sanitation procedures and policies, and quality water supply. A fourth principle is the need to provide a healthful psychosocial environment. This has implications for space, location of activities, color schemes, and elimination of distractions through such means as soundproof construction materials.

The general health features of the physical environment include site, building, lighting, heating and ventilation, plant sanitation, and acoustics.

A safe and healthful environment is necessary for positive academic performance.

Site

There are many aspects to consider in selecting a suitable site. These considerations will differ, depending on the community. Whether it is a rural or an urban community will have a bearing on the location of the site. In an urban community, it is desirable to have a school situated near transportation facilities but at the same time located away from industrial concerns, railroads, noise, heavy traffic, toxic fumes, and smoke. A rural facility site might bring more attention to readily accessible initiatives including cable and fiber optics, transportation, and parking as well as access to medical and fire services. Real estate, zoning, toxification, environment, security, and legal constraints also are crucial site variables. Consideration should also be given to demographic trends, population movements, and future development of the area in which the buildings and space for activity are planned. Adequate space for play and recreation should be provided. The play area should consist of a minimum of 100 square feet for each young child and 125 square feet for each high school student. Some school standards recommend 5 acres of land for elementary schools, 10 to 12 acres for junior high or middle schools, and 20 acres for senior high schools.

Attention also should be given to the aesthetic features of a site because of their effect on the physical and emotional well-being of participants and staff members as well as the community. The surroundings should be well landscaped, attractive, and free from disturbing noises or odors.

Building

The trend in schools and community-based building projects is toward one-story construction, with stress on planning from a functional rather than an ornamental point of view. The building should be constructed for *use* and, when possible, be multipurpose in design. The materials selected should make the building attractive and safe. Every precaution should be taken to protect against accidents, fire, slippery floors, and other dangers and risks. The walls should be painted with light colors and treated with acoustic materials. Doors should open outward. Space for clothing should be provided. Provisions for persons with disabilities and for older citizen community user groups, including ramps, walkways, split entrance accessibility, toilet facilities, and others discussed in chapter 3, should be major considerations when building or renovating an existing facility.

Lighting

Proper lighting is important to protect and conserve vision, prevent fatigue, and improve morale. In the past it had been recommended that natural light should come into the room from the left and that indirect artificial light should be provided as needed. There is a trend now toward allowing natural light from more than one direction. Artificial light (e.g., halide/vapor, fluorescent, incandescent), moreover, should come from many sources rather than one to prevent too much concentration of light in one place. Lighting intensity should be in accordance with recommended standards. Switches and other power sources for artificial light should be located in secure parts of the facility and of course should be recessed and enclosed for protection (Frier 1988).

In gymnasiums and swimming pools, light intensity should range from 50 to 100 foot-candles, depending on the activity being conducted. Glare

Proper lighting is a feature at Reily Recreation Center at Tulane University in New Orleans.

is an undesirable hazard that should be eliminated, especially in diving wells to ensure the safety of the participant or along sight lines for lifeguards and spectators. Overhead or other multistage lights should be properly installed, recessed, and adjusted for best results. Some new facilities are employing occupancy sensors to control their lighting systems. Strong contrasts of color such as light walls and dark floors should also be avoided if possible.

Heating and Ventilation

Efficiency in the classroom, gymnasium, exercise center, arena, special activities rooms, and other places is determined to some extent by thermal comfort, which is mainly determined by heating and ventilation.

The purposes of heating and ventilation are to remove excess heat and humidity, unpleasant odors, and in some cases, gases, vapors, fumes, and dust from the room; to prevent rapid temperature fluctuations; to diffuse the heat within a

room; and to supply heat to counteract loss from the human body through radiation and otherwise.

Heating standards vary according to the activities engaged in, the participant's clothing, and the geographic location of the facility.

For ventilation, the range of recommendations is from 8 to 21 cubic feet of fresh air per minute per occupant. Adequate ventilating and condensing systems are especially needed in dressing, shower, and locker rooms; toilets; gymnasiums; and swimming pools; in fact, all rooms require adequate ventilation. The recommended humidity level ranges from 40 percent to 60 percent. The type and amount of ventilation including air conditioning will vary with the specific needs of the particular activity area.

Plant Sanitation

Plant sanitation should not be overlooked. Sanitation facilities should be well planned and maintained. The water supply should be safe and adequate. If any question exists, the health department should be consulted. One authority suggests that at least 20 gallons of water per individual per day is needed for all purposes.

Drinking fountains of various heights should be recessed in corridor walls and should consist of material that is easily cleaned. A stream of water should flow from the fountain so that it is not necessary for the mouth of the drinker to get too near the water outlet or drain bowl.

Water closets, urinals, lavatories, and washroom equipment such as soap dispensers, toilet paper holders, waste containers, mirrors, bookshelves, and hand and hair drying facilities should be provided as needed, also keeping the person with disabilities in mind.

Waste disposal should be adequate. There should be provision for cleanup, removal, and recycling of paper and other materials that make the grounds and buildings a health and safety hazard as well as unsightly. Proper sewage disposal and prompt garbage, trash, and recycling services should also be provided. Weekly plant and facility sanitation audits are strongly encouraged.

Acoustics

Noise distracts, causes nervous strain, and detracts from many of the activities' benefits. Therefore noise should be eliminated as effectively as possible. This elimination can be achieved by acoustical treatment of such important places as corridors, gymnasiums, arenas, and swimming pools.

Acoustical materials include glazes, plasters, fibers, boards, acoustic tiles, and various fabrics. Floor covering that reduces noise should be used in corridors, and acoustical material should be used in walls and ceilings. Gymnasiums, arenas, swimming pools, and racket courts need special treatment to control the various noises associated with enthusiastic play and participation. Of course, sound and public address systems, when appropriate, must also be taken into full consideration.

DETERMINING NUMBER OF TEACHING STATIONS NEEDED

The teaching station concept should be considered when scheduling physical education and sport classes. A teaching station is the space or setting in which one teacher or staff member can conduct physical activities for one group of students. The number and size of teaching stations available together with the number of teachers on the staff, the size of the group, the number of times the group meets, the number of periods in the school or college day, and the program of activities are important items to consider when planning.

According to the participants in the National Facilities Conference, the following formulas should be used to determine the number of teaching stations necessary for effective teaching and learning (Flynn 1993).

Elementary Schools

The formula for computing the number of teaching stations needed for physical education in the elementary schools is:

$$\text{Minimum number of teaching stations} = \frac{\begin{array}{c}\text{Number of} \\ \text{classes or units} \\ \text{of students}\end{array} \times \begin{array}{c}\text{Number of Physical} \\ \text{Education periods} \\ \text{per week per class}\end{array}}{\text{Total periods in school week}}$$

For example, for an elementary school of six grades, with three classes at each level (approximately 450 to 540 students), ten 30-minute physical education periods per day, and physical education conducted on a daily basis, the teaching station needs are calculated as follows:

$$\text{Minimum number of teaching stations} = \frac{18 \text{ units} \times 5 \text{ periods/week}}{50 \text{ total periods in school week}} = \frac{90}{50} = 1.8$$

A rowing tank facility at Trinity College; Hartford, Conn.

Secondary Schools and Colleges

The formula for computing the number of teaching stations needed for physical education in secondary schools and colleges is as follows:

$$\text{Minimum number of teaching stations} =$$

$$\frac{\text{Number of students} \times \begin{array}{l}\text{Number of periods}\\\text{class meets each week}\end{array}}{\begin{array}{l}\text{Average number of}\\\text{students/instructor}\end{array} \times \begin{array}{l}\text{Total number of class}\\\text{periods in school week}\end{array}}$$

For example, if a school system projects its enrollment as 700 students and plans six class periods a day with an average class size of 30 students and physical education is required daily, the formula is as follows:

$$\text{Minimum number of teaching stations} =$$

$$\frac{700 \text{ students}}{30 \text{ per class}} \times \frac{5 \text{ classes/week}}{30 \text{ periods/week}} = \frac{3500}{900} = 3.9$$

THE TEAM APPROACH TO FACILITY PLANNING

Facility planning requires a team approach that includes many crucial players (Cohen 1996). The planning team may include the architect, engineer, business manager, physical plant and maintenance staff, physical education and sport managers, coaches, and consultants in facility safety, law, the environment, and health. In order to receive optimal results in obtaining a quality facility, certain facility planning procedural processes should be followed.

First, form a planning team (needs assessment team) that will identify needs, perform a feasibility study, and prepare a project proposal. Included on this team may be the project coordinator for the organization for whom the facility is being planned, the architect, a representative from the physical education and sport area, a community government representative, and a budget director or business manager. Team members should understand the role each plays in the facility planning process.

Second, secure consultants during the early stages of the project because team members may not have expertise in all aspects of facility design, multipurpose programming, or sustained maintenance and finance. Consultants can help close the gap between architectural theory and physical education and sport practice, not to mention fiscal shortcomings and legal responsibility.

Third, stress faculty, staff, student, and community involvement. Each of these representative team members should provide important input about their specific area of facility interest. These key players can also be used to form a public relations team to articulate or "sell" the facility to the community. For example, a physical education or adapted/developmental teacher, specialist in biomechanics, exercise scientist, aquatics director, park board member, dance instructor, or tennis, rowing, or swimming coach could provide meaningful information about his or her projected facility or laboratory space and needs.

Fourth, visit and gather materials and informational resources from other facilities and experts to obtain ideas and advice that may contribute to improving on your facility plan. Appendix F provides a thorough checklist for facility planners.

Finally, the plan, after approval by higher management, evolves into a request for proposals (RFP). The RFP issuance is a call for bids that outlines the overall facility picture and its fiscal outlook and requirements. Bids are received, presentations made, RFPs received, contracts negotiated, and, with luck, ground is broken.

The planning team should also be alert when making facility recommendations about long-term maintenance and operational costs. When construction is under way, not only the architect and consultants but also the physical education and sport specialists as well as other key members of the planning team should systematically monitor the work. By doing this, many potential errors may be avoided or corrected.

WORKING WITH THE ARCHITECT

The architect is the specialist in facility planning and leads the design team in the planning and construction of new physical education and sport facilities. The architect, through his or her train-

The architect and physical educators cooperatively planned for facilities at the Bob Carpenter Sports/Convocation Center at the University of Delaware, Newark.

Facilities must be accessible and must be planned with specific user groups in mind; Sports Pavilion, University of Minnesota, Minneapolis.

ing and experience, is a specialist who is competent to give advisory service in most aspects of facility management.

Ferreri (1985), a chief operations officer for a group of architects in Illinois, points out that a strong, positive relationship between the architect, the school, and the community is crucial for effective planning. Lines of communication within the school, between the school and the architect, and within the architect's office must be based on mutual understanding and teamwork. Communication about program and space needs and requirements must be continuous. These are the hallmarks of the satisfied and successful facility planner.

Physical educators and coaches should carefully think through their own ideas and plans for their special facilities and needs and submit them in writing to the planning team during the early stages of planning. The architect and physical education and sports specialists should have several team meetings in which they exchange views and consider architectural potentials, possibilities, and alternatives.

Many architects are limited in their knowledge about physical education and sport programs

and therefore welcome the advice of specialists. The architect might be furnished with such information as the names of institutions or communities where excellent facilities exist; kinds of activities that will constitute the program; space and rules requirements for various age-appropriate activities; storage and equipment areas needed; temperature requirements; relation of dressing, showering, and toilet facilities to the program; teaching stations needed; specific construction materials for activities; and lighting, acoustical, security, and accessibility requirements. The physical educator, athletic and activities director, and coach may not have all this information readily available, including some of the latest trends and standards recommended for his or her specific field or sport. However, such information can be obtained through the literature from professional organizations and federations as well as from other schools and organizations where excellent facilities have been developed, financed, constructed, and marketed.

The Donald Krotee Partnership, a professional planning and architectural firm, together with Comprehensive Planning Services, a Newport Beach, California, planning firm, has developed a procedural facility planning outline that lists some essential considerations for physical educators and sports administrators and managers when planning with architects and facility planning firms. Some of the main points follow.

Educational Specifications

Adequate educational specifications provide the basis for sound planning by the architect:

1. General description of the program, such as the number of teaching stations necessary to service the physical education program for a total student body of approximately (n = ?) boys and (n = ?) girls. The general description should also include school or institutional philosophy, primary user group (e.g., age and developmental level), size of team, number of spectators to accommodate, other user group specifications, and projected popularity of physical activities to be delivered.

2. Basic criteria that pertain to the gymnasium or facility being planned, including the number of teaching periods per day; capacities, number, size, and types of courts and lockers; and total multipurpose prioritized uses projected for the facility:

   a) Availability and accessibility to the community (e.g., foot, bicycle, wheelchair)

   b) Proximity to parks and community centers

   c) Parking, transportation, traffic patterns, and accessibility (e.g., persons with disabilities, medical emergency units, fire department)

   d) Popularity and type of activities for primary and other appropriate user groups (construct a prioritized list)

   e) Size and nature of groups and activities that will be accommodated after school hours

   f) Whether locker rooms and facilities will be made available for public use.

3. Specific description of various aspects of the physical education and sport program that affect the architects:

   a) Class size, scheduling, and number of instructors—present and future projection

   b) Preferred method of handling students or spectators—for example, flow of traffic in classrooms, gyms, pools, office areas, locker rooms, and shower rooms—and distance to outside play areas

   c) Storage requirements (e.g., size and space by square footage) and preferred method of handling permanent equipment and supplies

   d) Primary user groups and other extracurricular use of facilities (It helps the architect if the educational specifications detail a typical week's use of the proposed facility, which would include a typical daily program, after-school use, and potential community integration)

   e) Sport- or activity-specific requests such as synthetic tracks or fields, halide/incandescent underwater lights, spectator glass walls, acoustics, energy conservation power water pump system, skylights, wood surface floors, modular basaltic granite climbing wall system, and so on.

   f) Rules, regulations, laws (IDEA, Title IX, ADA, etc.), and safety codes concerning various user groups and physical activities should be reaffirmed. All user groups must be involved in the facility planning process.

Meeting with the Architect

At this point, it is advisable to meet with the architect to discuss specifications to ensure complete understanding and to allow the architect to point out certain restrictions or limitations that may be anticipated even before the first preliminary plan is made. There is no use creating elaborate plans if the only space available is one that is directly over an earthquake fault line!

Design

The following factors might be considered in the design of the facility and discussed with the architect.

1. *Budget.* An adequate budget should be allocated for the participants and the community to be proud of the completed project.

2. *Function.* Physical education and sport facilities should be long lasting (at least 50 years), durable, multipurpose, easily maintained, functional, safe, secure, and user friendly.

3. *Acoustics.* Use the service of acoustical consultants. Take their sound advice!

4. *Public address system.* How is it to be used—for instruction, sporting events, general communication?

5. *Aesthetics.* The design and color scheme should be compatible with surrounding environs, including existing structures, school colors, and the immediate community.

6. *Fenestration (window treatment).* Consider light control, potential window and skylight breakage, vision panel, natural light; windows in gymnasium areas and all high-traffic areas should have safety glass and be well protected and marked.

7. *Heating, ventilation, and air conditioning.* The area should be zoned for flexibility of use. This means greater ventilation when a larger number of spectators or users are present or a reduction for single class groups or in isolated areas such as locker and storage rooms. Special attention must be given to proper ventilation of uniform drying rooms, gymnasium storage areas, and locker, sauna, and shower areas. Ventilation, air exchange, heating, and air conditioning equipment should have a low noise level and maximal efficiency rating.

8. *Supplementary equipment in the gymnasium.* Such equipment should be held to a minimum. Supplementary equipment, such as fire boxes, drinking fountains, phone and electrical power sources should be recessed but accessible for all user groups.

9. *Compactness and integration.* Keep volume compact—large, barnlike spaces are unpleasant and are costly to heat and maintain. Integrate and divide the facility as far as budget permits.

10. *Mechanical or electrical features.* Special attention should be given to location of panel boards, chalk and bulletin boards, video monitors, fire alarms, folding doors, and drop nets. All must be easy to use and safe.

Further Critique with the Architect

The architect begins to develop plans from an understanding of the initial requirements he or she has considered in relation to the design factors listed. Aesthetics (how it looks), project budget, technology, and function will significantly determine the shape of your facility plans.

When the basic plan is set (e.g., square footage, cost estimate), the architect will usually call in consulting engineers to discuss the structural and mechanical systems before approval of the plan. These systems will have been outlined by the architect, but usually are not discussed with planning teams other than in generalities before the plan is in approximate final form.

More meetings are then conducted regarding approval of preliminary plans and proposed structural and mechanical systems, including the use of materials after the incorporation in the preliminary plans.

If supplementary financing by government or private sector agencies is involved, the plans or set of drawings will have been submitted to those agencies with a project outline or specifications as soon as the plan has been sufficiently developed. If the agency approves the application as submitted by the architect, the final preliminary working drawings are started.

Final Processing

It is advisable to settle all matters that can be settled during preliminary planning to save time and expense. If this method is employed, greater clarity is ensured and less changing or misunderstanding results (see the box titled Common Errors Made by Managers in Facility Planning and Development). On completion of the preliminary facility plan and agreement of the planning committee, the plans are then submitted to higher

Common Errors Made by Managers in Facility Planning and Development

Some common mistakes made by managers and athletic directors in facility planning and development include the following:

- Failure to adequately project enrollments and program needs into the future (facilities are difficult to expand or change, so this is a significant error).
- Failure to provide for multiple use of facilities.
- Failure to provide for adequate accessibility for students in physical education and recreational sport and also for myriad community user groups.
- Failure to observe basic health factors regarding lighting, safety, and ventilation.
- Failure to provide adequate space for the conduct of a comprehensive program of physical education and sport activities.
- Failure to provide appropriate accommodations for spectators and persons with disabilities.
- Failure to soundproof areas of the building in which noise will interfere with educational functions.
- Failure to meet with the architect to present views on program needs early in the planning process.
- Failure to provide adequate staff offices.
- Failure to provide adequate storage space.
- Failure to provide adequate space for privacy for medical services.
- Failure to provide entrances large enough to transport equipment.
- Failure to observe desirable current professional standards.
- Failure to provide for adequate study of cost in terms of durability, time, money, and effective instruction.

- Failure to properly locate teaching stations with service facilities.
- Failure to provide adequate locker and dressing space.
- Failure to plan dressing and shower area so as to reduce foot traffic to a minimum and establish clean, dry aisles for bare feet.
- Failure to provide a nonskid surface on dressing, shower, and toweling room floors.
- Inadequate provision for drinking fountains.
- Failure to provide acoustical treatment where needed.
- Failure to provide and properly locate toilet facilities to serve *all* participants and spectators.
- Failure to provide doorways, hallways, or ramps so that equipment may be moved easily.
- Failure to design equipment rooms for convenient and quick check-in and check-out.
- Failure to provide mirrors and shelving for boys' and girls' dressing facilities.
- Failure to plan locker and dressing rooms with correct traffic pattern to swimming pools.
- Failure to construct shower, toilet, and dressing rooms with sufficient floor slope and properly located drains.
- Failure to place showerheads low enough and in such a position that the spray is kept within the shower room.
- Failure to provide shelves in the toilet room.
- Failure to comply with ADA regulations.
- Failure to provide proper safety signage.

---

management (e.g., school board, board of regents) for approval, and competitive bids are sent out as described previously in the section titled The Team Approach to Facility Planning. A coopera-tive and coordinated effort including systematic walk-throughs and meetings between the planning team (representing the user), architect, and con-tractor remains in place until the facility is on-line. Even after opening, many consultations will be needed to ensure facility integrity.

INDOOR FACILITIES

Several special areas and facilities are needed by physical education and sport programs. These typically include such areas as management and staff offices; locker, shower and drying rooms; gymnasiums; special activity areas; and indoor swimming pools.

Management and Staff Offices

It is important, as far as practical and possible, for physical educators, coaches, and athletic and activities directors to have a section of a building set aside for management and staff offices. At minimum, the area should be a large central office with an outer office that can serve as a waiting room and reception area. The central office provides a place where secretarial and clerical work is performed; computer systems are housed; and records, files, and office supplies are secured. The waiting room may also serve as a reception point where people can wait for staff members.

Separate offices for the staff members should be provided, if possible. Separate offices provide a place where conferences can be conducted in private and without interruption. This is an important consideration for counseling, meeting with parents, and discussing other school-related business. If separate offices are not practical, a desk and office divider should be provided for each staff member. There should, however, be a private room available for conferences.

Other facilities that make the administrative and staff setup more efficient and enjoyable are staff locker and dressing rooms, a staff lounge, departmental library, conference room, and private toilet and lavatory facilities.

Locker, Shower, and Drying Rooms

Physical education and sport activities require facilities for storage of clothes and uniforms as well as for showering and drying. These facilities are essential to good health and to a well-organized program.

Locker rooms should present a healthful environment.

Locker and shower rooms should be readily accessible to all users and close to activity areas. Locker rooms should not be congested places that people want to get out of as soon as possible. Instead, they should provide ample room for storage and dressing lockers, stationary benches, mirrors, recessed lighting fixtures, scales, sauna, hair dryers, and drinking fountains.

A minimum of 20 square feet per individual at peak load, exclusive of the locker space, is generally required to provide proper locker room space.

Storage lockers should also be provided for each individual. An additional number of lockers equal to 10 percent of those needed should be installed for expanded enrollments or membership. Lockers are typically permanently assigned and can be used to hold essential clothing and other necessary supplies. They can be smaller than the dressing lockers; some recommended sizes are 7½ by 12 by 24 inches, 6 by 12 by 36 inches, and 7½ by 12 by 18 inches. Basket lockers are not favored by many experts because of hygiene problems, because an attendant is required, and because of the logistics involved in carting the baskets from place to place.

Dressing lockers are used by participants only when actually engaging in activity. They are large, usually 12 by 12 by 54 inches or 12 by 12 by 48 inches in elementary schools, and 12 by 12 by 72 inches or 12 by 15 by 60 for junior high, middle, and secondary schools and colleges as well as for community recreation programs.

Locker rooms should provide dressing and storage lockers for all participants. Adequate space should be provided so that dressing is not done in cramped quarters. Lockers should also have proper ventilation, be periodically inspected, and be kept clean at all times.

Shower rooms that have both group and cubicle showers should be provided. Some facility planners recommend that the number of showerheads be equal to 30 percent to 40 percent of the enrollment at peak load. Another recommendation suggests a 1:4 shower to person ratio at peak load; University National Standards insist on 10 showerheads for the first 30 users with an additional 1:40 ratio thereafter. Showers should be 4 feet apart or dispersed in a circular group pattern, and a graded change of water temperature is recommended. Shower rooms should also be equipped with liquid soap dispensers, good ventilation and heating, nonslip floors, and recessed plumbing. The ceiling should be constructed to prevent condensation. The shower area should be washed daily to prevent athlete's foot and other contaminations. A towel and laundry service should be initiated if it does not already exist.

A drying room adjacent to the shower room is essential. This should be equipped with proper drainage, good ventilation, towel bar, drinking fountain, mirrors, and appropriate hair drying equipment accessible to all user groups.

Gymnasiums

The type and number of gymnasiums that should be part of a school or physical plant depend on the number of individuals who will be participating and the variety of activities that will be conducted.

Dividing curtains and partitions create additional teaching stations.

Athletic Business (Tips 1984) lists some suggestions to consider when constructing or renovating a gymnasium. One of the major suggestions is to save money on the square footage, not on dollars per square foot. The wrong time to save money, the article points out, is when considering building materials. Careful planning makes it possible to buy the best materials and finishes. It is important to visit other facilities and talk to management to find out the advantages and disadvantages of materials that have been used and tested over time.

School gymnasiums are best located in a separate wing of the building to isolate the potential noise and to provide a convenient location for community-based groups that will be anxious to use such facilities.

Many gymnasiums have folding doors or curtains that divide them into halves, thirds, or fourths and allow activities to be conducted simultaneously. This has proved satisfactory where separate gymnasiums or teaching stations could not be provided.

General construction features for gymnasiums include smooth, acoustically treated walls,

A typical divided elementary school teaching station.
(Birchview Elementary School, Wayzata, MN.)

hardwood floors (maple—laid lengthwise—is preferred), recessed lights, recessed radiators, adequately screened or safety windows, and storage space for the apparatus and other equipment.

In elementary schools that need only one teaching station, a minimum floor space of 36 by 52 feet is suggested. Where two teaching stations are desired, floor space of 54 by 90 feet, which may be divided by a folding partition, is recommended. The general rule of 100 square feet per student and 4,000 square feet per gymnasium should be strived for in the facility planning process. The ceiling should be at least 22 feet high.

In junior, middle, and senior high schools where only one teaching station is desired, a minimum floor space of 48 by 66 feet is necessary. An area 66 by 96 feet exclusive of bleachers will provide two teaching stations of minimal size. The ceiling should be at least 24 feet high. If seating capacity is desired, additional space will be needed. If more than two teaching stations are desired, the gymnasium area may be extended to provide an additional station, or activity rooms may be added. Of course, the addition of a swimming pool also provides another functional teaching station.

Other considerations for gymnasiums might include provisions for basketball backboards, mountings for floor plates for various apparatus and standards that will be used, places for hanging and storing mats, outlets for various instruc-

tional aids (e.g., video, computer analysis, interactive videodisk), proper line markings for activities, bulletin boards, a false wall for rock climbing, and other essentials necessary for a well-rounded program.

Safe and properly constructed and maintained equipment should be a part of all physical education facilities. Adequate space should be provided for all the activity phases of the program, whether they are in the gymnasium, swimming pool, adapted room, dance area, or auxiliary areas. Mats should be used as a protective measure on walls, floors, and other areas in which participants may be at risk. Drinking fountains and cuspidors should be recessed, and doors should open away from the playing floor. Proper flooring should be used; tile-cement floors are sometimes undesirable where activity takes place. Accessibility and appropriate space should be provided for people with disabilities so that all facilities (indoor, outdoor, locker room, etc.) are fully accessible. Equipment storage space is a commodity often overlooked during facility planning. Proposed ventilation, storage racks and bins, and a workplace area for making minor equipment repair is also desirable.

Clothing and equipment used in physical education activities should meet health and safety standards. Appropriate, clean, and safe clothing, including nonscuff sport footwear, should be required.

Guidelines for Gymnasium Planning

The following guidelines are valid for management, architects, board members, consultants, and other persons involved in gymnasium planning. Many of these guidelines are overlooked by those responsible for gymnasium construction.

The Roof   If the roof is not properly designed before construction, costly changes in equipment installation may occur later. Ceiling support beams that may be part of the construction could also be employed by the physical educator to make maximal use of the facility. The design of the roof should allow for support beams strong enough to absorb the stress placed on them in various activities. Support beams should be placed to allow maximal flexibility for the placement of equipment such as scoreboards and gymnastic apparatus. Ceilings should reflect light and be acoustically treated. The distance from the floor to the exposed beams should be at least 22 to 24 feet for the main gymnasium and minimally 12 to 15 feet for specialty areas such as dance, wrestling, and weight training.

The Floor   The floor is a vital part of the gymnasium and should be constructed from hardwood, not tile. Although more expensive, hardwood is safer, more resilient, does not become slick, and is better for sports performance. Plates for floor apparatus such as the high bar or volleyball standards should be designed with safety and flexibility in mind. Floor markings should be placed after the prime coat of seal has been applied and before the application of the finishing coat. Synthetic surface may also be a consideration; however, for heavy use, wood is recommended.

The Walls   It is a good idea to provide a smooth, acoustically glazed, nonabrasive, nonmarkable wall for participants to practice their throwing, catching, and racket skills. A line could be taped along the wall to indicate the height of the tennis or badminton net. The wall can also be used for climbing or other assorted targets and goals. Walls behind baskets should be recessed and padded. Electrical outlets should be provided throughout the gymnasium so that audiovisual instructional strategies can be used at each teaching station. Computers, timing devices, scoreboards, public address systems, and outlets for the media should be kept in mind.

Lighting   Proper illumination that meets approved standards, with selective controls to vary intensity depending on activity, is a necessity. Fifty foot-candles is recommended for teaching stations and spectator consideration. Many gymnasiums are employing halide, fluorescent, or reo-stat quartz lighting used in combination with natural lighting. Durable lighting with recessed

and protected fixtures is essential. This helps prevent bulb or tube breakage from ball activities.

Acoustics   Noise control should be a primary consideration in any gymnasium construction. Acoustic treatment of ceilings and walls can help reduce or eliminate noise and provide for optimal learning.

Special Activity Areas

Although gymnasiums take up considerable space, there should still be additional areas for activities essential to physical education and sport programs.

Wherever possible, additional activity areas and teaching stations should be provided for remedial or adapted activities, apparatus, tennis (1 court/400 school population), racquetball/wallyball, handball, squash, weight training, combatives, dance, rhythms, fencing, and exhibitions and shows. The activities to be provided will depend on the interests of the user groups and type of activities involved in the program. The recommended size for such teaching stations is 30 by 50 by 24 feet, or 40 by 60 by 24 feet. A 75 by 90 foot auxiliary gymnasium is ideal. Many facilities are utilizing lower ceilings, ranging from 12 to 18 feet depending on their multipurpose usage requirements. The adapted/developmental activities room, if the school is fortunate enough

Special activity teaching stations should be well designed.

to have one, should be equipped with items such as horizontal ladders, mirrors, mats, climbing ropes, stall bars and benches, fixed and free weights, dumbbells, and other equipment and assessment materials suited to individual or small group instruction.

Regulation classrooms and other multipurpose space can be converted into additional teaching stations. This solution may be feasible in situations in which the actual construction of such costly facilities may not be practical.

Auxiliary Rooms

The main auxiliary rooms are equipment, supply, checkout, custodial, and laundry rooms.

Equipment and supply rooms should be easily accessible from the gymnasium and other activity areas. Balls, nets, standards, and other equipment and supplies needed for the program are stored, inventoried, and maintained in these rooms. Towels and uniforms can also be distributed from this area, as can first aid materials when necessary. The size of these rooms varies according to the number of participants, the number of activities offered, and the size of the program as well as the size of the physical plant.

Checkout rooms should be provided seasonally. They house the equipment and supplies used in various seasonal activities. They may be less centrally located and more proximate to fields, courts, arenas, or rinks.

Custodial rooms provide a place for storing some equipment and supplies used to maintain these specialized facilities. They too should be appropriately maintained and provide a comfortable environmental setting.

Laundry rooms should be large enough to accommodate the washing and drying of such essential items as towels, uniforms, and swimsuits. They should be well ventilated and possess the shelf space necessary for a well-organized and neat appearance.

Indoor Swimming Pools

Major design decisions must be made if an organization decides to construct a pool. These decisions

The University of Minnesota Aquatics Center in operation.

include items such as the nature of the program to be conducted, philosophy of management as well as user groups, type of overflow system, dimensions, shape and depth of pool, type of finish, type of filters and water treatment system, construction material, amount of deck area, dry and wet teaching stations, types of air handling and climate control systems, illumination and sound systems, and number of spectators to be accommodated.

Some mistakes that should be avoided in the construction of a pool include the following: locker rooms that open onto the deep rather than the shallow end of the pool; pool base that is finished with slippery material such as glazed tile; insufficient depth of water for diving; improper placement of ladders and guard rails; placement of starting blocks in the shallow end of the pool; water recirculation at an insufficient rate to accommodate peak participation loads; inadequate storage space; failure to use acoustic material on ceiling and walls; insufficient illumination; slippery tile on decks; and an inadequate overflow system at the ends of the pool.

Some trends and innovations in pool design and operation include the Rim-Flow Overflow

System, inflatable roof structure, the skydome design, pool tent cover, floating swimming pool complex including movable bulkheads, prefabrication of pool tanks, automation of pool recirculating and filter systems, regenerative cycle filter system, heat recovery and chiller preheating systems, adjustable height diving platform, variable bottom depths, pool lifts, fluorescent and incandescent underwater lights, portable underwater sound systems, automatic cleaning systems, computerized and interactive chemical control, in deck wiring systems for automatic timing, and wave-making machines. Play areas and sundecks are also growing in popularity.

Swimming pools have two main objectives: to provide instructional and competitive programs and to provide recreation.

The swimming pool should be located on or above the ground level, have a southern exposure, be isolated from other units in the building, and be easily accessible from the central dressing and locker rooms. Materials that have been found most adaptive to swimming pools are smooth, glazed, light-colored tile or brick.

The standard indoor pool is 75 feet 1 inch long. The width should be a multiple of 7 or 9 feet, with a minimum of 35 feet. Depths vary from 2 feet 6 inches at the shallow end to 4 feet 6 inches at the outer limits of the shallow area. The shallow or instructional area should make up about two thirds of the pool and be separated by pool lane dividers from the deeper areas, which taper to 9 to 12 feet in depth. An added important factor is a movable bulkhead that can be used to divide a large pool into various instructional or practice areas. Most colleges and many communities are moving toward 50-meter pools.

Water depth under the 1- or 3-meter board should be 12 feet or more and under any platform, 18 feet or more.

The deck space around the pool should be constructed of a nonslip, nonglazed material and must provide ample space for land drills, demonstrations, and potential spectators. The area above the water should be unobstructed. The ceiling should be at least 25 feet above the water and 20 feet above the diving board height if this is part of the complex. The walls and the ceiling of the pool area should be acoustically treated.

The swimming pool should be constructed to receive as much natural light as possible, with the windows located on the sides rather than on the ends. Artificial lighting should be recessed in the ceiling. Good lighting is essential, especially near the diving board, where glare should be eliminated. Underwater lighting is attractive but not essential.

There should be an efficient system for adequately heating and circulating the water. When possible, solar and self-heating systems should be adopted to save energy and reduce pool overhead costs. The temperature of the water should range from 78° to 82° F.

An office adjacent to the pool, with open vision to the pool, in which communication and first aid supplies can be stored is advisable. Such an office should be equipped with windows that overlook the entire length of the pool. Also, lavatory and toilet facilities should be available and, of course, the pool must be fully accessible.

The swimming pool is a costly operation. Therefore it is essential that it be planned with the help of the best advice obtainable. Specialists who are well acquainted with such facilities, including maintenance, cost control, and marketing, and who conduct aquatic activities should be brought into planning meetings with the architect, a representative from the public health department, and experts in essentials such as lighting, heating, acoustics, construction, and law. Figure 9-1 illustrates the planning of a large university aquatics program.

Health Considerations for Swimming Pools

Swimming pools need special attention whether indoors or outdoors. First, the pool should be properly constructed to provide for adequate filtration, circulation, and chemical treatment. The computer can assist in uniform regulation and conduct of these tasks. Next to water treatment, air handling is crucial to maintain a

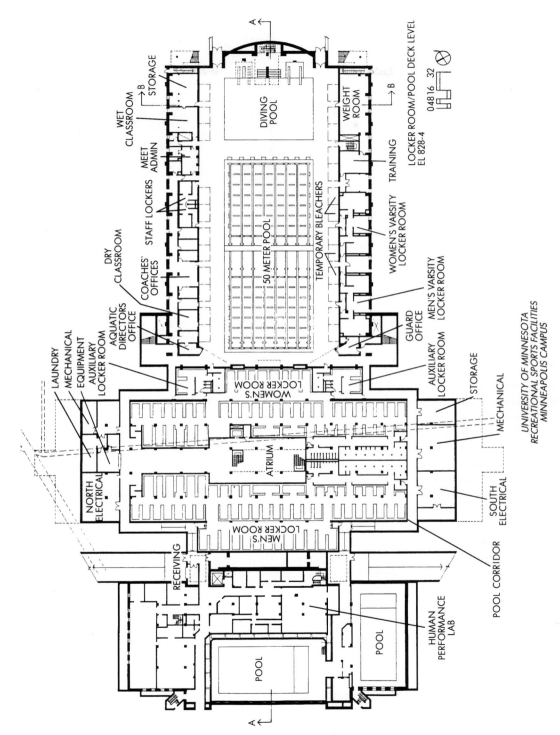

Figure 9-1. The planning of the University of Minnesota Aquatics Center.

proper educational and competitive environment. A daily log should be kept on information such as water temperature, water saturation index, facility humidity, hydrogen ion concentration, residual chlorine, and other important factors. Regulations and rules for pool use as well as safety and emergency procedures should be established and appropriately posted; all user groups should be acquainted with them.

Athletic Training and Sports Medicine Facilities

Athletic training, sports medicine, and health services are an important part of the program and require adequate facilities. These facets of physical education and sport are addressed in chapter 12.

OUTDOOR FACILITIES

The outdoor facilities discussed in this section are play areas, game areas, outdoor swimming pools, outdoor pursuit, facilities for persons with disabilities, and other special activity areas.

Play Areas

Many factors must be considered when planning outdoor facilities for schools and colleges. Before a site is selected, it is important to appraise the location, topography, soil drainage, water supply and table, acreage, shape, and natural features. The outdoor facilities should be as near the gymnasium and locker rooms as possible, yet far enough from the classrooms so that noise and activity will not be a distraction. Other factors that apply also to indoor facility planning, such as accessibility, integration with physical plant (e.g., gymnasium, school classrooms), adaptability, and expandability, should play a salient role in the facility planning process.

The play areas should serve the needs and interests of the students for the entire school year and at the same time provide a setting for activities during vacation periods. The needs and interests of the community must also be considered, especially in communities in which physical plants and facilities such as schools and recreation centers are shared. Because the community uses

Outdoor facilities are necessary for quality physical education programs.

the areas after the school day is over, a joint planning and management team with community input is strongly recommended.

The size of the area should be determined on the basis of the number and type of activities offered in the program and the number of individuals who will be using the facilities at peak load. Possibilities for expansion should also be kept in mind. Playing fields and playgrounds should have good turf and be clear of rocks, holes, and uneven surfaces. A dirty, dusty surface, for example, can aggravate conditions such as emphysema, chronic bronchitis, and allergies. Safety precautions should also be provided through regular inspection of facilities and replacement of worn equipment. Playfields and playgrounds should be fenced in, particularly where there is heavy traffic adjoining these facilities. Rubber, asphalt, synthetic materials, and other substances that require little maintenance and help to free an area from cinders, gravel, stones, and dust are being used on many outdoor surfaces. In some sections of the country, limited shelters are also being utilized to provide protection from the cold, rain, wind, and sun. All outdoor areas should have accessible sanitary drinking fountains and toilet facilities as needed.

Elementary School

The activities program in the K–6 learning environment suggests what facilities should be available. Children in the primary grades engage in large muscle activity involving adaptations of climbing, jumping, skipping, kicking, throwing, leaping, and catching. Children in the intermediate and upper elementary grades perform these fundamental skill activities and others in low organization games and various cooperative and team activities.

The playground area for an elementary school should be located near the building and should be easily accessible from the classrooms. Children in kindergarten should have a section of the playground for their exclusive use. This section should be at least 5,000 square feet and separated from the rest of the playground. It should consist of a surfaced area, a grass area, a play area, and a place for sand and digging. The sand area should be enclosed to prevent it from being scattered or shared by local pets. It is also wise to have a shaded area where storytelling and similar quiet activities may be conducted.

The surfaced area may serve as a year-round multipurpose activities center for both school and community. It can house basketball, tennis, and handball courts, games of minimal organization, and other creative activities. This area should be paved with material that provides resilience, safety, and durability. Rapid and efficient drainage is also essential. Lines may be painted on the area for various games.

The grass area provides space for varied and modified field and team games such as speedball, soccer, field hockey, softball, and fieldball. The play area should provide for essential equipment such as climbing bars in the form of a jungle gym, horizontal bars, swings, slides, seesaws, climbing and sliding structures, and built-in seats and tables also might be placed in this area. The area should have ample space for the safety of the participants. The shaded area may provide space for activities such as marbles, hopscotch, ring toss, and storytelling. Schools should allow additional space adjacent to this area for possible future expansion.

Other community-based recreation areas that have important implications for K–6 students include any landscaped, parklike areas. These provide a place for quiet activities such as dramatics and informal gatherings, fitness trails, hiking, jogging, walking, and a place for children to have gardening and picnic opportunities.

Junior High and Middle School

The junior high or middle school play and recreation area, planned and developed for the children who attend the school and also for the adults in the community, should be located on a site that consists of 10 to 25 acres. Local conditions will determine the amount of land available.

Many of the facilities addressed in the elementary school section may be incorporated in the junior high school. In many cases, however, the various play areas should be increased in size. The necessary facilities should provide for those activities that will be part of the basic physical education, recreational sport, and school sport programs. Oftentimes the community shares or may even possess co-ownership of this space, so ample field, court, arena, and gymnasium space with lighting is required for evening use.

A landscaped, parklike area should also be provided for various recreational activities for the students and the community. Activities such as walking, picnicking, in-line skating, bicycling, playing broomball, bocce, nordic skiing, sailing, and fly casting might be considered appropriate.

Senior High School

The senior high school physical education program is characterized by individual and lifetime sports as well as by team game activities. This emphasis, together with the popularity of recreational and interscholastic sport and the fact that facilities are typically needed for recreational use by the community, requires an even larger area than those for the two previous educational levels. Estimates range from 10 to 40 acres for such a physical plant.

Most of the environmental concepts and areas that have been listed in discussing the elementary and junior high schools should be included at the senior high level. Considerably more space for physical education class instruction and the various field games is necessary to provide full-sized official fields for softball, field hockey, soccer, speedball, lacrosse, basketball, tennis, football, and baseball, because recreational sport and the interscholastic programs as well as the community education and recreation programs usually share these facilities. Facility management and community and sometimes private sector partnering is therefore a crucial issue to the conduct of an effective and efficient program.

Football, soccer, and track can be provided for in an area of approximately 4 acres, with the football/soccer field placed within an enlarged track oval. Baseball and softball need an area of about 700 square feet to allow safe participation. With so many user teams practicing, however, game space should be protected from daily wear and tear, so additional field space with lighting capacity is strongly recommended. The more field space and creative configurations that can be adapted for small-sided games, the better.

Game Areas

The recommended dimensions for game areas for school physical education and sport programs as outlined by the profession are illustrated in table 9-1. One acre will accommodate four tennis courts, four handball courts, three badminton courts, and two volleyball courts.

Table 9-1. Recommended dimensions for game areas

	Elementary	Upper Grades	High School (Adults)	Side and End Safety Space
Basketball	40'×60'	42'× 74'	50'× 84'	6'; 8'
Volleyball	69'×50'	25'× 50'	30'× 60'	6'; 6'
Badminton			20'× 44'	6'; 8'
Paddle tennis			20'× 44'	6'; 8'
Platform tennis			30'× 60'	
Deck tennis			18'× 40'	
Tennis		36'× 78'	36'× 78'	12'; 21'
Ice hockey			85'×200'	
Field hockey			180'×300'	8'; 8'
Horseshoes		10'× 40'	10'× 50'	
Shuffleboard			10'× 52'	6'; 2'
Lacrosse			180'×330'	3'; 9'
Lawn bowling			14'×110'	
Tetherball	10' circle	12' circle	12' circle	
Croquet	38'×60'	38'× 60'	38'× 60'	
Bocce			18'× 62'	
Handball/Racquetball	18'×26'	18'× 26'	20'× 40'	
Baseball			350'×350'	
Archery		50'×150'	50'×300'	15'; 50'
Softball (12" ball)	150'×150'	200'×200'	250'×250'	
Football—with 400-yard track— 220-yard straightaway			300'×600'	
Touch football		120'×300'	160'×360'	
6-person football			120'×300'	
Soccer	40'×60'	165'×360'	225'×360'	8'; 8'
Squash			18.5'× 32'	
Water polo			66'×100'	
Wrestling/combatives			24'× 24'	5'; 5'

Source: Krotee 1997.

The game area should allow for basic instructional physical education classes and also provide fields for softball, field hockey, soccer, speedball, lacrosse, and court areas that include badminton, basketball, softball, team handball, volleyball, shuffleboard, and other activities. There should be appropriate space for track and field. A 400-meter oval, or at least a straightaway of 120 meters that is 6 to 8 meters wide, is mandatory. Most interscholastic sport complexes include a football/soccer field, a track, and baseball and softball diamonds as well as ample practice and scrimmage fields.

Winter activities should not be forgotten. With such activities gaining in popularity, provisions should be made for ice skating, nordic or cross-country skiing, broomball, ice hockey, and other winter activities.

One state recommends that the outdoor facilities for the basic needs of a physical education and recreation program for K–12 should consist of a minimum of 12 acres. This area should be divided into an elementary area of 3 acres; courts area of 1 acre; high school recreational sport area of 5 acres, and an interscholastic sport area of 3 acres.

A concept in game areas is the multipurpose sports court. This small, self-contained, lighted, fenced-in court provides for a variety of activities in a small area. The average sports court is 12 by 24 by 10.5 feet and may be completely enclosed (including ceiling). The floor is frequently a raised, weather-resistant, heated playing surface that allows for quick drainage and year-round play. When needed, pads or other roll-out playing surfaces can be laid over the surface. The court can then be used for basketball, volleyball, paddle/platform tennis, pickle-ball, handball, and other activities. This type of court is excellent for high-density urban school areas, corporate recreation programs, planned communities, and apartment complexes.

Outdoor Swimming Pools

The outdoor swimming pool is a popular and important facility in almost all communities. To a great degree, climatic conditions determine the advisability of such a facility.

Outdoor pools are built in various shapes, including oval, circular, T AND L-shaped, and rectangular. Rectangular pools are most popular because of easier construction, practicality of conducting competitive swimming events, and accommodation of various slides and standard equipment.

The size of pools varies, depending on the number of persons they are to serve. One recommendation has been made that 12 square feet of water space per swimmer be allotted for swimming purposes or, if the deck is taken into

Multisport winter facilities are popular in both schools and communities; evening broomball in Minneapolis, Minn.

Outdoor aquatic facilities must be secure at all times; Texas A&M University.

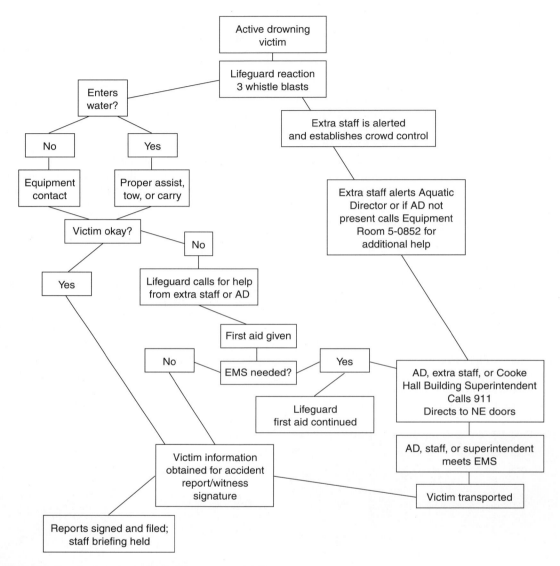

Figure 9-2. Active drowning emergency guidelines.

consideration, 20 square feet of space for swimming and walking area per swimmer.

The decks for outdoor pools should be larger than those for indoor pools. This larger space will accommodate more people and also provide space for lounging and sunbathing.

Shower facilities should be provided to ensure that every swimmer is clean before entering the water. A basket system for storing clothes has been found useful, but when the pool is located adjacent to a school, it is sometimes practical to use the school's locker and shower facilities. However, it is strongly advised that wherever possible, separate shower, locker, and toilet facilities be provided, and that safety and accessibility for all participants is ensured.

Because swimming is popular at night as well as in the daytime, lights should be provided

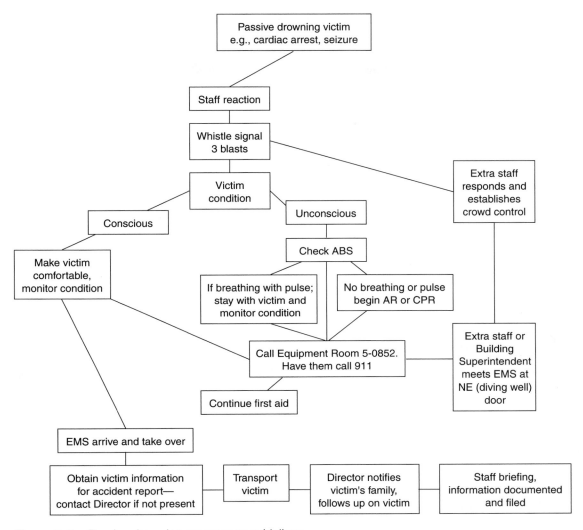

Figure 9-3. Passive drowning emergency guidelines.

so that the community may participate in this healthful and enjoyable activity.

Diving boards generally are constructed of fiberglass or plastic, and the standard heights of 1 and 3 meters are typically found in most outdoor aquatic facilities. The board or any diving takeoff area should have a nonskid surface, be securely fastened to the ground or foundation, and conform to state safety standards and recommendations for water depth as previously discussed in the section on indoor swimming pools.

The rules and regulations concerning the facility, including diving, should be clearly posted near the appropriate areas. Clear markings, firm dividers of shallow and deep water, and a certified and well-trained guard staff are also a must for all aquatic facilities. Management should provide clear emergency guidelines (Figures 9-2, 9-3, and 9-4) concerning active and passive drowning victims as well as facility emergency. These sample emergency guidelines should serve as models to develop emergency policies and procedures (for

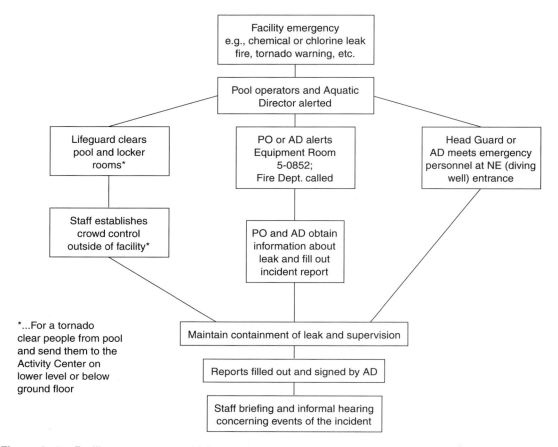

Figure 9-4. Facility emergency guidelines.

all facilities and programs) that are crucial to sound facility management.

Outdoor Pursuit

Because outdoor pursuits (hiking, rock climbing, skiing, small craft, camping, etc.) are becoming increasingly popular in both school and community recreational programs, they should receive full consideration for inclusion in a quality physical education or any activity program. Outdoor areas, including camping areas, should be located within easy reach of the school and community. They should be in locations desirable from the standpoints of scenic beauty, safety, accessibility, clear and unobstructed water, and natural resources pertinent to the program offered. Activities usually offered include hiking, rock climbing, orienteering, swimming, campcraft, boating and small craft, eco-study, fishing, and appropriate winter activities (e.g., alpine and cross-country skiing, snowshoeing). The natural terrain and other resources can contribute much toward such a program.

There should be housing, eating, sanitation, waterfront, and other facilities essential to outdoor pursuit. These facilities do not have to be elaborate, but they should provide adequate protection against the elements or in case of emergency. Facilities should also meet acceptable standards of health and sanitation. In general, camp structures should be adapted to the climatic and environmental conditions of the particular area in which the facility is located. It is wise to consult public health authorities, departments of natural resources, state and local park boards, or other appropriate professionals when selecting a campsite. Sometimes existing facilities can be shared (e.g., Ys, Scouts) or converted to camp use. Outdoor pursuit acreage could also be purchased outright by the school system or community, or acquired under a long-term lease agreement by coordinating with other local user groups or school districts.

FACILITIES FOR PEOPLE WITH DISABILITIES

Since the passage of P.L. 94-142, and more recently ADA, more consideration has been given to the facility needs of people with disabilities. Physical education and sport facilities in particular are concerned with the students' programs of specialized developmental exercises, perceptual-motor ability activities, health and fitness, modified sports, stress management, rest, and relaxation. Facilities for individuals with disabilities usually vary from school to school and according to the disabling conditions of those served.

Contemporary physical education and sport has the person with disabilities returning to the least restrictive environment (LRE) and to the gymnasium and activity whenever appropriate and possible. Special case teams design appropriate user IEPs, and some special equipment may be necessary; however, mainstreaming or inclusion back into the gymnasium as well as the classroom is the trend. This trend requires accessibility, sound planning, and a committed team effort by faculty and staff.

For those schools and communities that provide people with disabilities separate developmental space, a minimum area of 40 by 60 feet is recommended. Creative and committed teachers, however, can construct challenging curriculum utilizing much of the standard equipment and physical resources (e.g., aquatic facilities) already available.

Some schools also make use of nearby community or private facilities, and this trend will grow as more specialized resources and specific physical activity are legislated and supported by the community. With scarce financial inputs it is envisaged that the school and community will have to work even more closely together in order to meet the needs of this special user group.

OTHER SPECIAL ACTIVITY AREAS

Other special activity areas needing attention include those involving dance, gymnastics, weight training, wrestling, martial arts, racquetball, and squash. Research and assessment facilities, especially at colleges and universities, should also be provided not only for direct use by the students, staff, and faculty, but also to enable researchers to contribute to the body of knowledge of the profession.

Because dance has always been, and continues to be, a very popular activity, special facilities should be provided. It is recommended that a minimum of 100 square feet of space per student be provided. Full-length mirrors, a sound and video system, and practice bars on one wall at heights of 34 and 42 inches are required for

Renovated gymnastics room; University of Minnesota, Minneapolis.

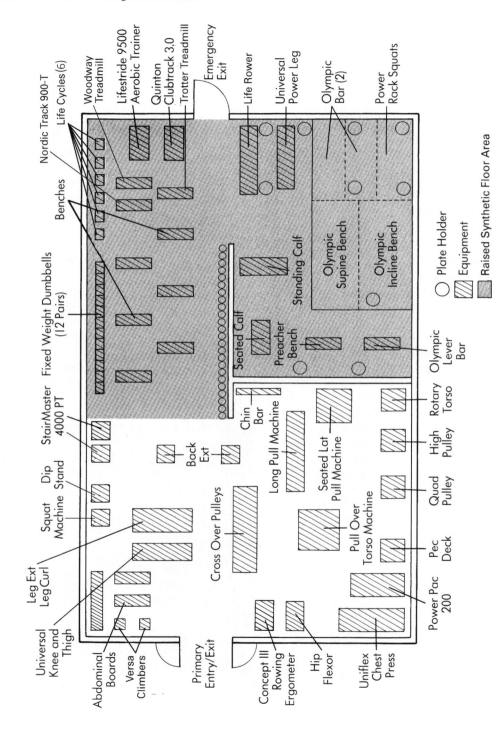

Figure 9-5. Weight training facility and design.

program enhancement. The floor is an important consideration, and it should consist of sealed and buffed hard northern maple. Proper acoustics, and other appropriate and wide-ranging dance-specific equipment and supplies should also be available.

Gymnastics is another special activity area, and recommended space allotment is 120 by 90 feet of floor space, with a minimum ceiling height of 23 feet.

Weight training and open fitness are very popular activities for both girls and boys. A minimum of 2,500 square feet should be provided with both fixed and free weights available. A weight room facility design is presented in Figure 9-5 (Hatfield and Krotee 1984).

A wrestling and martial arts area of a minimum 50 by 100 feet will provide enough space for two 42 by 42 foot mats. Judo, karate, and self-defense, among other combatives, have become popular activities for all age levels and should be housed in an appropriate space that is well ventilated and cleaned daily to prevent the spread of various communicable germs (e.g., impetigo, herpes simplex).

Racquetball and handball courts are common, particularly in colleges, universities, and club settings. Each four-wall court is 40 feet long and 20 feet wide, with a ceiling height of 20 feet. Multipurpose squash courts (18.5 by 32 feet) can also be housed within this area.

Such activities as indoor tennis, fencing, archery, golf, skating, skiing, and rock climbing also deserve full consideration when designing facilities. Technology ranging from synthetic floors to computerized golf has enabled many of these activities to be delivered indoors at any time of year.

An integral part of many facility designs, especially at the college and university level, are research and teaching laboratories or teaching stations. Space for exercise science (e.g., biomechanics, exercise physiology), psychosocial training (e.g., behavior, performance, and skill enhancement), and human factors, and resource centers as well as for sport medicine (training and first aid rooms) should be provided for all students, staff, and faculty. These integrated facilities must also be accessible, well-maintained, functional, and in budgetary alignment with the mission of the department, college, or community in which they are housed.

CONSTRUCTION TRENDS IN PHYSICAL EDUCATION AND SPORT FACILITIES

There are many new trends in facilities, supplies, and materials for physical education and sport programs (Turner 1987), including new paving and surface materials, roll-out floor systems, new types of equipment and personal storage units (lockers), air-supported structures, improved landscapes, new ceiling and lighting systems, new shapes for swimming pools, partial shelters, and synthetic grass and walls, just to name a few. Combination indoor-outdoor pools, including water slides, physical fitness equipment for outdoor use, all-weather tennis courts and games areas, and various kinds of climbing walls are other new developments that have had an impact on physical education and sport facility management as well as on program development.

In gymnasium construction, some of the new features include using modern engineering techniques and materials, which has resulted in welded steel and laminated wood modular frames; arched and gabled roofs; domes that provide areas completely free from internal supports; exterior surfaces of aluminum, steel, fiberglass, and plastics; hydraulic floors; different window patterns and styles; myriad floor surfaces including nonslip material; prefabricated wall surfaces; and better lighting systems with improved quality and quantity and reduced glare. Facilities are moving from using regular glass to using either a plastic and fiberglass panel or an overhead skydome. Lightweight fiberglass, sandwich panels, or fabricated sheets of translucent fiberglass laminated over an aluminum framework are proving popular. These require no painting; maintenance, labor, and material cost is lower; shades, curtains, or blinds are not needed to eliminate glare; and the breakage problem is reduced or eliminated.

The University of Idaho has a portable football field. The tartan turf is 200 feet by 370 feet and can be rolled up and stored on a 210-foot-long steel drum.

Locker rooms with built-in locks with combination changers, quiet tone control, and even coin-operated lockers have made their way into sport facilities where ID cards are now being scanned for admittance. Ceramic nonslip tile is used extensively because of its durability and low-cost maintenance. Wall-hung toilet compartments feature permit easier maintenance and sanitation with no chance for rust to start from the floor. Odor control is being effectively handled by new dispensers and dehumidification systems. New thin-profile heating, ventilating, and air-conditioning fan coil units are now being used to provide improved ventilation, heating, and lighting. More walls and floors are being constructed of easily cleansed materials, which aids in improving sanitation.

New developments in indoor swimming pools include computers that have direct control over all filters, chlorinators, chemical pumps, and lever controllers; much larger deck space areas constructed of nonslip ceramic tile; greater use of diatomaceous earth rather than sand filters to filter out small particles of matter including some bacteria; underwater lighting and sound; water level deck pools (the overflow gutters are placed in the deck surrounding the pool instead of in the pool's side walls, and provision is made for grating designed so that the water that overflows is drained to a trench under the deck without the possibility of debris returning to the pool); air-supported roofs that can serve as removable tops in a combination indoor-outdoor pool; and movable bulkheads.

New developments for outdoor swimming pools involve new shapes, including oval, wedge, kidney, figure-8, cloverleaf, and bean, as well as modern accessories, including wave-making machines, gas heaters, automatic water levelers, and retractable roofs and sides. More supplemental recreational facilities (such as shuffleboard courts, volleyball, and horseshoes) and more deck equipment (including guard rails, slides, pool lifts, and pool covers) are being included around larger pools.

New concepts have been put to good use in the facility planning of the following schools:

Oak Grove High School, San Jose, California. This school has a movable interior partitioning system with adjustable lighting, acoustics, and air conditioning that can accommodate different types of activities on short notice.

Wayzata High School, Wayzata, Minnesota. The Wayzata School District, the City of Plymouth, and Lifetime Fitness, a private health club, have joined in a public-public-private venture to construct a $5 million, 110,000-square-foot fitness center in addition to a new ice arena and aquatic complex. This fitness center is part of a larger $40 million new high school complex.

Andrews Senior High School, Andrews, Texas. Here the open court has a windowless exterior and faces inward to a concourse and a domed rotunda. Along the concourse are a swimming pool and gymnasium, and under the rotunda is an assembly area.

Holland High School, Holland, Michigan. This school constructed its plant on the multicampus plan, with four small schools sharing physical education and sports facilities.

Shattuck–St. Mary's School, Faribault, Minnesota. This school has recently expanded its ice arena to include new locker rooms. Eight tennis courts and a new synthetic track were also part of the expansion project.

Brooklyn Polytech, New York City. A bubble was erected on top of the physics building to house a gymnasium.

University of Texas at El Paso. This university covered its outdoor swimming pool with prefabricated material to have an all-weather, year-round facility.

LaVerne College, California. A "super tent," involving a cable-supported fabric roof structure made of fiberglass and Teflon, houses theater, gymnasium, cafeteria, bookstore, and health clinic.

Cuyahoga Falls, Ohio. Here a roof was installed over the swimming pool to provide residents with year-round swimming. In the summer, the roof is removed.

Thomas Jefferson Junior High School, Arlington, Virginia. This school has implemented the shared facilities concept by housing together performing arts, recreation, and physical education.

Texas A&M University, College Station, Texas. This university has recently completed a 286,000-square-foot student recreation center as well as an 87,000-square-foot outdoor activity area. The $36 million facility project includes two gymnasiums, five dance rooms, a lap track, fourteen racquet courts, three swimming pools, and a 3,500-square-foot climbing wall.

Lewis and Clark Elementary School, St. Louis, Missouri. A physical education partial shelter has been erected, with the sides of the open structure protected by banks of shrubbery.

Boston College, Chestnut Hill, Massachusetts. A roof design of hyperbolic paraboloids is used. This efficient structure spans a large area— 42,000 square feet of floor space.

University of Minnesota, Minneapolis. A 16,000-pound (2,000 pounds in water) movable bulkhead is used to divide its aquatic facilities into various recreational and competitive configurations. Its filter and chemical systems are fully computerized, controlling chemical analyses and water treatment.

Limited Shelters for Physical Education

The shelter or limited shelter provides protection from extremes of climate, uses the desirable elements of the natural environment, and creates an interesting background for physical education and sport activities.

The actual design of the shelter is determined by climate, number of participants, types of activity programs, and user groups. Methods of controlling air movement may be developed by using natural elements (trees and plantings), architectural elements (wall, roofs, and screens), and

Facilities such as the Super Tent at LaVerne College, Calif., and the Metrodome in Minneapolis, Minn., provide year-round playing opportunity.

mechanical devices (fan, moving walls, and dividers). Solar radiation may be controlled with natural shading and moving walls. These shelters cost about half as much as the traditional gymnasium.

Air-Supported Structures

An air-supported structure consists of a large plastic bubble that is inflated and supported by continuous air pressure. It is the least expensive building that can be erected, costing from one-fifth to one-half of what a solid structure may cost. These facilities have housed military equipment and have served as theaters, factories, swimming pools, tennis courts, indoor tracks, golf ranges, and gymnasiums.

The outside construction is usually made of vinyl-coated or Dacron polyester, which is lightweight, strong, and flexible. The fabric is flame-retardant, waterproof, tear-resistant, mildew-resistant, and sunlight-resistant. Installation is simple and may be completed in a few hours by a minimal crew. The installation process includes placement of the vinyl envelope and inflation. The bubble is supported by a blower that provides a constant flow of air pressure. The bubble may be easily dismantled by stopping the blower, opening the door, unhitching the attachments, and folding the bubble compactly.

Minigyms and Fitness Corners

Minigyms can be operated in the halls and alcoves of the school building. They may consist of climbing, pulling, and hanging apparatus that the students use between classes and at study hours, lunch, and recess. The concept is to distribute the gymnasium throughout the school. Some other suggestions include mats, chinning bars, incline benches and boards, walls to throw balls against, and carpeted corridors for stunts and tumbling.

Classrooms can also be turned into minigyms with creative fitness corners. Stationary bicycles, rowing machines and even desks can serve to promote quality physical activity.

Court Games and Other Facilities

Rubber-cushioned tennis courts are being used in many facilities. They consist of tough, durable material about 4 inches thick that has the individual advantages of clay, turf, and composition courts combined into one surface. Portable rollout surfaces are also being used by some school and community park systems for court games ranging from basketball to tennis and from badminton to pickle-ball.

Other New Developments

New developments in physical education and sport facilities are numerous. Sculptured play apparatus has been produced by a number of firms. It is designed to be more conducive to imaginative movements and creativity than is conventional equipment. Hard-surfaced, rubberized, all-weather running tracks; radiant heating of decks on swimming pools and outdoor elevated courts; heated wet rooms for teaching aquatics classes; floating roofs that eliminate non-load-bearing walls; interior climate control; better indoor and outdoor lighting; new cooling systems for ice rinks; padding for use under apparatus and on walls; outdoor skating rinks; translucent plastic materials for swimming pool canopies and other uses; and electrically operated machinery to move equipment, partitions, and bleachers are just a few of the many facility enhancements that have been, and continue to be, upgraded.

Other contemporary facility developments for physical education and sport include synthetic ice and snow, snowless ski hills, climbing walls, turntable skating, convertible roofs, mobile locker rooms, illuminated game lines, folding racquet courts, movable pool floors and lifts, computerized pool treatment, and myriad other factors that may influence the management and planning of a physical education and sport program. Security control systems, computerized energy conservation systems, and total facility communication systems, not to mention the new lines of fitness equipment, make facility management a challenge.

With the contemporary trend toward scarce inputs (e.g., lack of money and land), facility planning and creative and cooperative management of new and existing facilities are more crucial than ever.

FACILITY MAINTENANCE

Planning for the construction or remodeling of facilities is an important management function. An equally important responsibility of facility management is maintenance. With proper maintenance, a facility will last longer, provide a healthier environment, be less costly, and provide a more satisfying experience for user groups. Planning and constructing facilities in physical education and sport are team efforts. If proper plans, construction, and materials are selected, then maintenance should be made easier. Nothing is more embarrassing than a new facility that is a maintenance nightmare because of poor management decisions in the design and planning phases of the construction process. Given an adequate facility, it is up to the physical education, recreational sports, and athletic departments and all user groups as well as the custodial staffs to work together in taking pride in their facility and putting forth a special effort to see that it is maintained in as near perfect condition as possible.

SHARED FACILITIES

Schools and colleges continually receive requests to open their facilities to various community and other user groups. It is therefore imperative that management establish guidelines ensuring that appropriate precautions are taken (e.g., legal and fiscal) and that such facilities are used properly when approval is granted.

First, management should see that a written policy is established and approved by proper authorities regarding community and outside group use of facilities (who can use facilities, at what times, under what conditions). Second, procedures regarding outside use should be established. This usually includes such procedures as making a proper application, obtaining the liability insurance coverage necessary, setting the fee structure and type of payment, and making stipulations regarding maintenance and security. Third, management controls should be established to see that policies and procedures are carried out as specified in the user contract.

Schools Using Community Resources

Such facilities as parks, bowling alleys, golf courses, swimming pools, ski areas, Ys, fitness centers, and skating arenas can extend and en-

The tennis complex at Northwest Athletic Club promotes the shared facilities concept; Bloomington, Minn.

hance the school physical education program as well as related sports activities. Most community facilities can be used during off-hours or nonpeak hours, and the charge is frequently nominal. Sometimes barter and partnering agreements can be arranged. Those procedures described in community use of school facilities apply in reverse.

With bond issues and fiscal inputs becoming difficult to obtain, it is imperative that management and the community (public and private sector) work together to build model programs that might be impossible to accomplish alone. This cooperation is a challenge to management and all those intimately involved in long-range strategic facility planning.

SUMMARY

Facility management is an important managerial responsibility. It requires planning based on physical education and sport program philosophy and particular needs, taking health, safety, and environmental conditions into consideration. Working with an architect and planning team and being aware of the latest developments, issues, concerns, and laws in facility construction are also crucial parts of facility management. A basic knowledge of the requirements of both indoor and outdoor facilities is also important so that the needs of all participants, including those with disabilities, may be met. Facility management also includes establishing sound emergency procedures and policies. Management should be concerned with the renovation, multiple use, maintenance, and cleanliness of the facilities because these factors are crucial to effective and efficient programming. Furthermore, most physical education and sport facilities are used by people other than just the students and members of one institution or organization. It is common practice for community residents and other community-based organizations (e.g., youth groups, seniors) to use such facilities. Therefore consideration should be given to the development of policies, procedures, and priorities for such usage. Creative and cooperative facility management is requisite in this time of scarce financial inputs.

SELF-ASSESSMENT ACTIVITIES

These activities will assist students in determining if material and competencies presented in this chapter have been mastered.

1. List the basic considerations that should be followed by management in planning physical education and sport facilities.

2. As director of a physical education program, what steps would you follow in working with an architect in the construction of a gymnasium?

3. Prepare a sketch of what you consider to be an ideal indoor weight training facility.

4. Develop a list of standards for outdoor areas in physical education and sport, including a play

From Camden Yards Ball Park, Baltimore, Md., to the Londondome Arena and Exhibition Center, London, England; from Pro Player Stadium in Miami, Fla., to the Hong Kong National Stadium, Hong Kong, PRC, high-quality stadiums make an international statement about sport management prowess.

area and swimming pool, for a junior high or middle school.

5. You are a director of physical education in an elementary school with 500 students. Your school has five class periods a day with an average class size of 30 students, and physical education is required daily. What is the minimum number of teaching stations you will need?

6. Divide the class into teams and visit neighboring schools, interviewing students and staff about a facility needs assessment. Present your findings to the class.

7. Prepare a checklist for a physical education and sport facility that will ensure that it is safe, healthful, and accessible for all participants.

REFERENCES

1. Cohen, A. 1996. Togetherness. *Athletic Business,* October, 31–38.
2. Ferreri, J.P. 1985. Successful strategies for facility planning. *Athletic Business,* January, 64–67.
3. Flynn, R.B., 1993. *Planning facilities for athletics, physical education and recreation.* Reston, Va.: AAHPERD.
4. Frier, J.P. 1988. Keeping users out of the dark. *Journal of Physical Education, Recreation, and Dance* 12 (May):38–43.
5. Hatfield, F.C., and M.L. Krotee. 1984. *Personalized weight training for fitness and athletics.* Dubuque, Iowa: Kendall/Hunt.
6. Kraus, R.G., and J.E. Curtis. 1990. *Creative management of recreation, parks, and leisure services.* 5th ed. St. Louis: Mosby–Year Book.
7. Tips on gymnasium construction. 1984. *Athletic Business,* July, 20.
8. Turner, E. 1987. Facility design, trends and innovations. *Journal of Physical Education, Recreation, and Dance* 58 (January):34–35.

SUGGESTED READINGS

Clayton, R., and D.B. Thomas. 1989. *Professional aquatic management.* Champaign, Ill.: Human Kinetics.

Discusses a wide range of aquatic trends in facility management. Also includes a thorough overview of rules, procedures, and policies necessary for effective management.

Cohen, A. 1996. Togetherness. *Athletic Business,* October, 31–38.

Crompton, J.L. 1995. Economic impact analysis of sports facilities and events: Eleven sources of misapplication. *Journal of Sport Management* 9:14–35.

Dougherty, N.J. and D. Bonanno. 1985. *Management principles in sport and leisure services.* Minneapolis, Minn.: Burgess Publishing.

Discusses steps in the process of facility development, including the role of the manager, the planning process, operational considerations, and policies requisite to effective management.

Dunn, J.M., 1997. *Special physical education.* Dubuque, Iowa: Brown & Benchmark.

Discusses, suggests, and provides guidelines for adapted physical education facilities. Outlines how facilities can be modified and planned to meet the needs of persons with disabilities.

Farmer, P.H., J.D. Mulrooney, and R. Amman. 1996. *Sport facility planning and management.* Morgantown, W.Va.: Fitness Information Technology.

Flynn, R.B. 1983. Planning facilities. *Journal of Physical Education and Recreation.* 54 (June):19–38.

A gym by any other name is a multipurpose area. 1985. *Athletic Business,* March, 46.

Describes how modern technology and proper design principles make it possible to have a gymnasium that is multipurpose in construction as well as in usage.

McGuire, M. 1984. Skylit cluster design: Efficient space combined with aesthetic form. *Athletic Business,* July, 32.

Describes the multipurpose 130,000-square-foot physical education facility at the College of Du Page.

Olson, J.R. 1997. *Facility and equipment management for sports directors.* Champaign, Ill.: Human Kinetics.

Fiscal Management

Instructional Objectives and Competencies To Be Achieved

After reading this chapter the student should be able to

- Support the need for sound fiscal management in physical education and sport programs.
- Explain the budgeting process and formulate a physical education and sport budget.
- Apply a planning-programming-budgeting-evaluation system (PPBES) in the management of a physical education and sport program.

- Understand the role of school and college business managers or administrators in fiscal management.
- Outline principles necessary for managers to follow to ensure financial accountability in a physical education and sport program.
- Discuss zero-base budgeting as applied to a physical education and sport program.

---

crucial function of management involves securing the funds necessary to provide sound physical education and sport programs. Adequate funding must be procured, programs and budgets planned and implemented, and accountability for funds established. This chapter deals with this managerial function.

Fiscal management has become an increasingly important responsibility for management in light of current financial problems, issues, and constraints. In recent years, financial problems caused by inadequate financial forecasting and monitoring, insufficient levy referendum coverage, and rising operational costs have made it much more difficult to fund physical education

and sport programs even though sport is a multi-billion-dollar enterprise. Other compounding reasons for fiscal difficulty include the high price of supplies, equipment, insurance, security, and travel and transportation; the need to finance an increasing number of girls and women who are participating in physical activity and sport; crowd control costs at sporting events as a result of violence; expensive product liability and lawyer contingency funds; and an inflationary spiral that is resulting in rising costs for labor, teachers, coaches, athletic trainers, officials, and other associated personnel.

An analysis of the responses of directors of physical education and athletics in New York (more than 1,000 questionnaires) regarding the effect of budget cuts and austerity budget control on their programs disclosed the difficulties that managers of physical education and sport programs are having today. The survey revealed the following:

- Of the directors, 67 percent indicated that they had to cut supplies, transportation, specific sports, and levels of sports to balance the budget.
- Athletic programs conducted with private funds during cutbacks were markedly increasing.
- Volunteer coaches were used by 40 percent of the directors in part of their programs.
- Fund-raising activities such as booster club memberships, participation fees, sales, student work projects, and promotional activities such as lotteries and raffles were instituted to support programs.
- Regarding support for sport programs, the teachers' association (exclusive representation) was found to be the least supportive and the students the most supportive. The school management and community were also highly supportive.

Efficient fiscal management is an essential management function that ensures proper budgeting and financial accountability. Therefore managers must thoroughly understand the philosophy of the organization as well as the fiscal needs, objectives, and priorities of all the departments under their supervision. Budgeting deals with departmental requests as well as fiscal control. The fiscal management of an institution, department, or program deals with goal setting, design of a budget that is targeted to achieve these goals, the process of budget review and approval, and the actual management of the program. Fiscal management is a critical and challenging responsibility (American Management Association 1986).

IMPORTANCE AND FUNCTION OF FISCAL MANAGEMENT

The services that a program provides, whether personnel, facilities, or purchase of equipment, usually involve the gathering and disbursement of funds. This money must be secured from appropriate sources, be expended for proper purposes, and be accounted for item by item. The budget (from the French *bougette,* meaning bag or wallet), the master financial plan for the organization, is constructed with these purposes in mind.

Policies for raising and spending money must be set within organizational limits. Persons responsible should know the procedures for handling such funds with integrity, the basic purposes for which the program exists, as well as the laws, codes, and regulations concerning fiscal management. Only when funds are implemented wisely and in the best interests of all concerned can the outlay of monies be justified.

Place of Fiscal Management in Physical Education and Sport Programs

In schools, colleges, or other organizations, physical education and sport require a major outlay of funds. As much as 25 percent of many school and college physical resources (assets) are devoted to these programs. Human resources, health services, insurance, facilities, supplies and equipment, and transportation are only a few of the line items that quickly amount to significant sums of

Girls' and women's physical education and sport programs are expanding, as evidenced by the initiation of women's soccer into the Big Ten Conference.

The cost of equipment, programs, and personnel is increasing.

the public and private sector physical activity setting. In this regard fiscal management is similar to strategic planning; it is a team effort (see the box titled Purposes of Fiscal Management).

Formulating and preparing the budget are cooperative enterprises. They are based on information, reports, and forecasts that have been forwarded by staff members from various departments and subdivisions of the organization. These reports must contain accurate information on programs, projects, obligations that exist, funds that have been spent, and monies that have been received from various sources (e.g., interest-bearing benefits, endorsements, signage, user fees). Managers must have a conceptual or overall picture of the enterprise at their fingertips. They

money. Probably as many as 500,000 physical educators and coaches are collectively paid millions of dollars in annual salaries, and more than 60 million students participate in school physical education and sport programs. Gymnasiums, stadiums, arenas, aquatic complexes, athletic training and weight and exercise areas, playgrounds, and other school and college facilities are being constructed and stocked with state-of-the-art equipment at huge costs to the taxpayers as well as to students at institutions of higher learning.

What is true of fiscal management in schools and colleges is also true in community-based, corporate, and other public and private sector settings in which physical education and sport programs have become a multi-billion-dollar enterprise.

Responsibility

The responsibility for fiscal management, although falling largely on the shoulders of management (e.g., department chairs, athletic and activities directors, coaches), involves every member of the staff. In schools and colleges, students should also play an active part in fiscal management as should the member/consumer in

Purposes of Fiscal Management

Some of the principal purposes of financial management in physical education and sport programs are the following:

To prevent misuse and waste of funds that have been allocated to these special areas.

To help coordinate and relate the objectives of physical education and sport programs with the money appropriated for achieving such outcomes.

To ensure that monies allocated to physical education and sport will be based on research, study and a careful analysis of the pertinent conditions that influence such a process.

To involve the entire staff in formulating policies and procedures and in preparing budgetary items that will help ensure that the appropriate program directions are taken.

To use funds to develop the best physical education and sport programs possible.

To exercise control over the process of fiscal management to guarantee that the entire financial process has integrity and purpose.

To make the greatest use of human and physical resources, supplies, equipment, and other forms of assets and capital involved in accomplishing organizational objectives.

must be cognizant of the work being done throughout the organization, functions that should be carried out, needs and resources of every facet of the organization, and other items (e.g., capital improvements, maintenance, equipment) that must be considered in preparing the budget. The advent of the computer and its myriad software packages make budgeting a far less labor-intensive task as well as a far more accurate management venture.

BUDGETING

Budgeting is the formulation of a financial plan in terms of work to be accomplished and services to be performed. All expenditures should be closely related to the objectives the organization is trying to achieve. In this control aspect, management plays an important part.

Budgets should be planned and prepared with thought and vision to the future. They are an important part of management's three-year, five-year, or seven-year plan and the program of accomplishment outlined for a fiscal period. Projects of any size should be integrated progressively over many years. Thus the outlay of monies to realize such aims requires long-term, strategic planning. Downsizing or budget reduction as well as adding assets (e.g., a new women's sport to achieve gender equity) should also follow a similar planning path.

According to the strict interpretation of the word, a budget is merely a record of receipts or income and expenditures. As used here, however, it reflects the long-term planning of the organization, pointing up user needs and projected costs and then ensuring that a realistic program is planned and effectively implemented that will fit into the proposed financial plan. Budgets, forecasts, revenues, and expenses for a period of one year, known as the fiscal year, are the most common in school and college physical education and sport programs.

Types of Budgets

There are short-term and long-term budgets. The short-term budget is usually the annual budget.

The long-term budget represents long-term fiscal planning, possibly for a five- or ten-year period. Most physical education and sport managers will be concerned with short-term or annual budgets, whereby they plan their financial needs for a period covering the school year.

Budgets are also categorized into (1) object classification (e.g., supplies and equipment, travel, salaries), (2) functions (e.g., indoor, outdoor, aquatics), (3) organizational unit (e.g., football, swimming, lifetime sports), and (4) classification by fund (e.g., 0100-state, municipal bond, user fee).

Budgets are also classified into (1) operational, (2) equipment and supply, (3) human resource, and (4) capital outlay. Usually the first two types are directly managed by the chair or director of the respective physical education or sport program. Capital outlay management and human resource management, however, usually reside at a higher level (e.g., principal, executive director of finance, vice president) with top-down input usually applied.

Regardless of the type of budget, the budgeting process is a critical part of the management function and demands continuous attention to detail (see the box titled Purposes of Budgets).

Responsibility for Budgets

The responsibility for the preparation of the budget may vary from one locality or institution to another. In most school systems, the superintendent of schools is responsible. In colleges, budgeting may be the responsibility of the president, vice president, dean, or athletic director. In other organizations, the department chair or head coach plays a key role. It is often possible for school managers, department heads, teachers, professors, coaches, and members of the organization to participate in preparing the budget by submitting various requests for item expenditures. In other situations, a comprehensive budget may first be prepared and then submitted to the appropriate subdivisions or departments for consideration and input.

In some large school systems, the superintendent of schools frequently delegates much of the budget responsibility to an executive director of

Purposes of Budgets

They express the plan and program for physical education and sport. They determine things such as (a) size of classes, (b) supplies, equipment, and facilities, (c) methods used, (d) results and educational values sought, and (e) personnel available.

They reflect the philosophy and policies of the professions of physical education and sport. They provide an overview of these specialized areas.

They determine what phases of the program are to be emphasized and help analyze all aspects of physical education and sport programs.

They interpret the need and the funds necessary for physical education and sport.

In a school program, they help determine, together with the budgets of other subdivisions, the tax levy for the school district.

They make it possible to manage the physical education and sport programs economically by improving accounting procedures.

They make it possible, on approval by the proper authority, to authorize expenditures for physical education and sport programs.

finance, business manager, or assistant or associate superintendent. The final official school authority concerned with school budgets is the board of education and, in colleges, the board of regents or trustees. In some organizations other than schools, it is the controller who possesses authority to approve, reject, or amend budgets. Beyond the board of education rests the authority of the people, who in most communities, also have the right to approve, reject, or significantly influence budget proposals.

In colleges, the budget may be handled in the dean's office, or the director or chairperson of the physical education department may have the responsibility. In most cases, the director of athletics is responsible for the intercollegiate or interscholastic sport budget. Within school departments of physical education and sport, the

chairperson, supervisor, or director is the person responsible for the budget. However, he or she will usually consult with members of the department to consider their input, opinions, and projections. This type of bottom-up management is most effective in schools and community-based physical education and sport programs.

Criteria for a Sound Budget

A budget for physical education and sport should meet the following criteria:

- The budget clearly presents the financial needs of the entire program in relation to the objectives sought.
- Key persons in the organization have been consulted.
- The budget provides a realistic estimate of income to balance the expenditures anticipated.
- The budget reflects equitable allocations to boys' and girls' physical education and sport programs.
- The possibility of emergencies is recognized through flexibility in the financial plan.
- The budget was prepared well in advance of the fiscal year to leave ample time for analysis, thought, criticism, and review.
- Budget requests are realistic, not padded.
- The budget meets the essential requirements of students, faculty, staff members, community, and management.

Technology developments add to new budget items.

Budget Preparation, Planning, and Process

The budget process is continuous. Business management resources indicate seven basic steps to this process (Roe 1961):

Planning. Management uses the input power of staff and community in creative and cooperative planning as well as in identifying user needs. Past budgets and plans also play a significant role and serve as a solid reference point.

Coordinating. Management coordinates and integrates staff and community suggestions and recommendations into a unified whole that realizes the goals of the organization.

Interpreting. To have support for the budget, proper interpretation of plans and actions must be effectively communicated both within and outside the organization. Communication and consensus building are a continual part of the budgetary process.

Presenting. Management presents the budget in a simplified version so that it can be readily understood. Pictures, diagrams, graphics, and other visual materials make such a presentation more interesting and informative.

Approving. Adoption of the budget is but the formal approval of many projects that have been studied and considered throughout the year. In fact, this year's budget is usually based on last year's budget decisions with special attention to targeted areas. Management is continually planning, researching, and studying various budgetary items.

Administering. The budget, when approved, serves as management's guide throughout the year as to how monies will be allocated and spent and what activities will be conducted and supported.

Appraising. Appraisal is a continuous process indicating how the budget is functioning. Methods used include daily observation, cost accounting records and reports, surveys, audits, checklists, and staff studies.

There are four general procedures, or stages, in budget planning that physical education and sport personnel might consider. First is actual preparation of the budget by the chairperson of the department with his or her staff, listing the various estimated revenue, expenditures, and any other information that needs to be included, ranging from additional revenue streams such as grants to loss of state or local funding. Second, the budget is presented to the principal, superintendent, dean, board of education, or other person or group that represents the proper authority and has the responsibility and legal authorization for reviewing it. Third, after formal approval of the budget, it is used as a guide for the execution of the financial management plan of the department or organization. Fourth, periodic critical evaluation of the budget takes place to determine its effectiveness in meeting organizational needs, with notations being made for the next year's budget.

The preparation of the budget, representing the first step, is a long-term endeavor that cannot be accomplished in one or two days. The budget can be prepared only after a careful review of last year's program effectiveness and extensive appraisal. Oftentimes, economic forecasts, projections, and fiscal targets will be passed down from the administration. However, the actual completion of the budget usually is accomplished in the early spring after a detailed inventory of program needs has been taken. The director of physical education or athletics and activities, after close consultation with staff members, coaches, athletic trainers, the principal, dean, superintendent of schools, or other responsible management, should formulate the budget.

Involvement of Staff Members

Involving staff members (teachers, coaches, athletic trainers) in the budget-making process is very important. Klappholz (1989) provides some suggestions that permit dynamic involvement:

- Teachers and coaches should maintain inventory records that indicate supplies and equipment on hand.

- Teachers, coaches, and athletic and activity directors should keep accurate records of all expenditures for each activity, sport, or piece of equipment.
- Teaching staff and coaches should determine the items that were not a part of this year's budget, but that should be included in the budget for the coming year (e.g., new equipment, repairs, subscriptions to professional journals).
- Accurate records and receipts should be kept by staff members regarding funds allocated and spent each year. Then it should be determined whether funds were spent for purposes that were initially listed.
- When all pertinent information has been collected and analyzed, management should meet with all staff members and go over budget requests.
- Management should prepare total physical education or sport budgets, including all valid requests. The budget should not be padded, but provision should be made for emergencies.

Management and staff members must do their homework by having the latest price lists for supplies and equipment; the number of students or other user groups projected for the program; the cost of such items as officials, travel, phone, recruiting, meals, lodging, insurance, security, and medical supervision; the amount of money needed for teaching aids, film, video, equipment repair, and other teaching and coaching support and staff development needs, such as attending professional meetings, clinics, and seminars.

Many records and reports are essential to budget preparation and should be part of a central database. The inventory of equipment and supplies on hand will be useful, and copies of inventories, contracts, and budgets from previous years will provide good references and projection points. Comparison of budgetary items with those of organizations of similar size may also be of help. Accounting records are also a valuable source through which to review income and expenditure flow.

All records, reports, inventories, past budgets, and budget requests should be part of management's database. Lexington, Massachusetts, public schools provide such a fiscal system that enables each teacher and coach to project and assess their budgetary status and requirements.

The budget is based on forecasts that can be overtaken by reality; therefore, some flexibility for readjustment is necessary. It is difficult to accurately and specifically list each detail in the way it will be needed and executed; however, budgets should also be reasonably rigid (see the boxes titled A School Budget and Budgetary Allocations for Regular Instructional Programs).

The budget should represent a schedule that can be justified. This means that each budgetary item must satisfy the needs and interests of everyone concerned. Furthermore, each item that constitutes an expenditure should be reflected in budget specifications. A typical high school varsity sport budget and a sample intercollegiate recreational sport budget, accompanied by the monthly budget balance and year-to-date ledger balance with transactions for supplies, equipment, and other expenses, may be found in appendix G. Sample budgets for a community-based youth sport organization and YMCA are also included in this appendix.

Budget Organization

Budgets can be organized in many ways. One pattern that can prove useful for the physical education and sport manager is a four-phased program. First, a brief introductory message enables management to present the financial proposals in terms a person outside the educational domain might readily understand. This might include the philosophy, goals, and mission of the total organization.

The second phase presents an overall graphic view of the budget, with expenditures and anticipated

A School Budget

Proposed Budget Classification by Major Function

	Salaries, Fees, and Benefits	Equipment and Supplies	Services and Other Expenses	Totals
Board of Education and District Administration				
Board/district administration	$ 183,400	$ 11,400	$ 45,900	$ 240,700
District insurance			74,600	74,600
Claims, property tax, administrative costs			78,300	78,300
Category total				$ 393,600
Instruction				
Building administration	302,600	19,700	8,600	330,900
Salaries and materials	3,178,300	169,000	439,700	3,787,000
Guidance and health	264,200	2,900	14,600	281,700
Student activities	57,300	22,900	6,700	86,900
Category total				$4,486,500
Support Services				
Transportation	287,600	106,500	36,300	430,400
Operation and maintenance	362,000	42,900	378,400	783,300
School lunch program			5,000	5,000
Category total				$1,218,700
Employee Benefits	1,293,400			$1,293,400
Total operating expenses	$5,928,800	$375,300	$1,088,100	$7,392,200
Debt Service			765,600	765,600
TOTAL BUDGET				$8,157,800

revenues arranged clearly and systematically so that any person can compare the two.

Phase three includes a more detailed estimate of receipts and expenditures, enabling a principal, superintendent of schools, board of education, or other interested individuals or group to understand the specific budget item expenditure and projected income.

A fourth phase includes supporting documentation to provide additional evidence for the requests outlined in the budget. A budget often has a better chance of approval if it is accompanied by sufficient documentation to support

some items. For example, extra compensation for coaches may be supported by presenting salary schedules for coaches in cohort school systems.

Another form of budget organization consists of the following three parts: (1) an introductory statement of the objectives, policies, and programs of the physical education or sport department; (2) a resume of the objectives, policies, and programs interpreted in terms of proposed expenditures; and (3) a financial plan for meeting the needs during the fiscal period.

Not all budgets are broken down into these three or four divisions. For example, some larger

Budgetary Allocations for Regular Instructional Programs

The programs listed below describe the funding for regular classroom instruction. The costs of general classroom teachers in grades 1 through 5 are divided among the language arts, mathematics, and environment programs, according to the estimated percentage of instructional time each subject receives in the classroom curriculum.

Program costs in grades 6 through 12 are based on the division of staff members by academic specialization.

The unclassified group contains those general supply and equipment items that support the entire program and cannot be allocated by program.

	Salaries	Benefits	Equipment	Supplies	Services	Total
Art	$ 136,761	$ 38,434	$ 522	$ 10,401	$ 677	$ 186,795
Business education	66,465	18,681	2,150	1,638	1,350	90,284
Driver education	4,410	1,239	550	10,850	—	17,049
Environment	151,747	42,650	—	1,999	300	196,696
Health education	2,290	627	—	400	420	3,737
Home economics	39,609	11,313	—	3,341	447	54,528
Industrial arts	70,837	19,910	471	5,335	675	97,228
Kindergarten	47,203	13,267	—	1,255	—	61,725
Language arts	613,255	172,365	—	14,375	2,900	802,895
Foreign languages	158,078	44,430	—	5,361	1,715	209,584
Mathematics	452,918	127,291	710	7,489	560	588,968
Music	141,035	39,635	516	2,439	850	184,485
Physical education	233,176	65,552	2,147	6,069	2,590	309,534
Reading (special)	83,162	23,372	—	915	400	107,849
Science	333,804	87,083	3,124	11,140	1,850	437,001
Speech	10,751	3,018	—	261	—	14,030
Social studies	283,827	79,774	—	4,509	3,500	371,610
Unclassified	146,898	41,286	1,737	22,009	9,080	221,010
TOTAL	$2,976,226	$829,745	$11,927	$109,786	$27,314	$3,954,998

programs may organize their total budget into minibudgets, or cost centers that can usually be found on their organizational chart. This is a form of responsibility-based management. The same sound budget preparation and planning are still followed; however, each specific area (e.g., football, women's basketball, open fitness, aerobic dance) is broken out for scrutiny. Whatever their form, however, all budgets do present an itemized account of receipts and expenditures.

In a physical education or sport budget, common inclusions are items concerning instruction, such as extra compensation for coaches; matters of capital outlay, such as a new swimming pool or weight room; replacement of expendable equipment, such as basketballs and baseball helmets; and provision for maintenance and repair, such as refurbishing football uniforms or resurfacing the playground. Many of these items cannot be estimated without making a careful inventory and analysis of the condition of the facilities and equipment on hand. This analysis can be accomplished yearly (e.g., facility and inventory audit) and maintained in the computer database. This status can then be updated each year with adjustable or modified projections.

The capital outlay for a weight room is significant for many sport programs.

FUND-RAISING FOR PHYSICAL EDUCATION AND SPORT PROGRAMS

The sources of income for most school and college physical education and sport programs include the general school fund (e.g., local taxes, millage, state appropriations, bonds) or college fund, gate receipts, concessions, and general organization and activity fees. However, these sources usually do not provide sufficient monies to run quality programs.

The budget crunch in many school districts and institutions of higher education has caused physical education and sport directors to find additional ways of raising revenues for their programs. In Massachusetts, for example, school districts as well as physical education and athletic departments are getting business organizations to provide matching funds for specific programs by conducting fund-raising campaigns among alumni, by soliciting local citizens to make tax-free donations and gift provisions in their wills, and by selling two-for-one passes to the public for sport contests (What happens 1981).

Other sources of additional revenue streams are special foundation, governmental, or individual grants or gifts; sale of television and radio rights; concessions at sport contests and physical education events; and special fund-raising events such as games involving faculty vs. the media or a local professional team.

Many physical educators at the college level also look to replenish and supplement their funds with grants and external funding. Local and federal sources (e.g., Department of Education, National Institute on Aging) are approached with well-written proposals, as are various private foundations, corporations, and PVOs (e.g., Bush Foundation, Kellogg Foundation, Partners of the Americas, Pacific Cultural Foundation). Such proposals outline the proposed project, goals, projected budget, and outcomes of the project itself. These competitive funding channels are difficult to tap; however, all avenues to support worthwhile programs should be explored.

The principles of fund-raising are simple and easy to apply. A successful campaign is the combination of a good cause, careful planning, fact finding, and skillful communication. Good public relations are essential. Secondary schools and community-based programs have a product with which many people like to be associated: sport. Physical education is not quite as attractive to many potential sponsors; however, if presented in the right fashion with students as a point of focus, it also can be a recipient of fund-raising rewards. Indeed, many parent groups recognize the value of quality physical education and often provide additional funds to purchase equipment and support other programmatic and instructional needs.

To be effective, a program of fund-raising should have excellent organization, clearly articulated objectives, effective management, and a sound organizational philosophy.

Some illustrations of successful fund-raising are associated with booster clubs. The question of using booster clubs may be controversial because sometimes such clubs want to influence the operation of the physical education and sport programs. With proper guidelines and procedures, however, opportunity for this to occur is minimal.

Christian Brothers High School in Sacramento, California, has the La Salle Club, which raises money for the physical education and sport programs by means such as the Old Timer Baseball Night, a golf tournament, and a fireworks booth for the 4th of July. Davis Senior High School in Davis, California, has an annual Lift-A-Thon for their football program to raise money. Notre Dame High School in Sherman Oaks, California, uses their booster club membership as a major contributor to their sport fund. The Dell Rapids, South Dakota, school system sells advertising on their scoreboards to help finance their programs. Wayzata High School in Wayzata, Minnesota, has booster clubs for almost all their girls' and boys' sports. Pig roasts, potlucks, and the selling of T-shirts, sweatshirts, and other items raise ample sums of money that are used to employ assistant coaches and provide needed equipment or transport.

Some high schools across the country use professional organizations to do their fundraising. For example, the Revere Company has helped many schools to raise funds. Parke Techniques is a company that works through the schools selling everything from bookends to paperweights. Another company is the American Cap Company, which prints painter's caps. Win

Fund-raising to increase revenue is crucial to many physical education and sport programs; a booth at the Minnesota State Fair.

Popular Fund-Raising Activities

A-thons:	Jog-a-thon, swim-a-thon, bike-a-thon
Specialty sales:	Pizza, candy, cookie, holiday items, wrapping paper
Concessions:	Programs, food items, bake sales
Raffles:	Donated items from local merchants
Clothing sales:	Sweatshirts, T-shirts
Car washes	Preferred seating
Specialty meals:	"Roasts," dinners, breakfasts
Novelty sports competitions:	Basketball, volleyball, tug-of-war, faculty vs. ___ !
Summer sports camps and clinics	
Booster club:	Donations, sponsored activities
Souvenirs:	School items, key chains
Celebrity tournaments:	Local media vs. _____ !
Equipment sales	Used equipment "exchanges"
Sponsorship:	Local businesses supply uniforms

Craft Incorporated makes pom-pons, buttons, balloons, megaphones, cushions, and many other items. Most programs, however, usually rely on talented parents and a supportive community who are willing to get the job done in this ever-crucial process of budget supplementation. See the Popular Fund-Raising Activities box for ideas about raising additional revenues to help support physical education and sport programs.

PAY-TO-PLAY POLICY

Many high school sport and activity programs are requiring students who wish to participate to pay fees (Parkhouse and Dennison 1984). This plan is being initiated because school sport programs have outgrown their projected budgets. The National Council of Secondary School Athletic Directors indicates that the average high school athletic budget has been reduced by at least 25 percent and some even by 75 percent. This reduction seems to be the trend as the year 2000 approaches. Cuts in funding combined with increased costs are prompting schools to defray expenses through student participation fees ranging typically from $25 to $75 depending on the sport or activity. Some schools have been forced to drop various sport programs as well as to reduce teaching, coaching, and supervisory staff.

Although some states, such as Iowa and Michigan, have ruled against the pay-to-play practice, California courts have upheld user fees. A citizens' group called "The Coalition Opposing Student Fees" lost a suit against the Santa Barbara School Board. The ruling stated that fees were permissible because sport takes place outside the regular school day, students volunteer for the activity, fees are used only to pay the cost of running such a program, and fees do not violate the equal opportunity clauses of federal and state constitutions; that is, financially disadvantaged students are exempt from fees.

A school instituting a pay-to-play policy should make sure that the fee charged is reason-

Many sport programs have instituted a pay-to-play policy.

able, that disadvantaged students (those who are financially unable to pay) are exempt, and that fees are used solely to cover program operation costs on an equal and fair basis (e.g., both boys and girls and their teams have equal opportunities).

TRADITIONAL SOURCES OF INCOME
General School or College Fund

In elementary and secondary schools, the physical education and sport program usually is financed through the general fund (e.g., local taxes and state appropriation). At most colleges and universities, the general fund of the institution also represents a major source of income, especially for physical education and recreational sport programs. Today, most universities at the Division I and II levels (athletic scholarship providers) are being asked to be self-supporting. Division III and most junior colleges, however, still rely on general funds to conduct their programs. The

Stands such as those at the Metrodome in Minneapolis must be filled to meet budget projections.

issue of self-support for big-time sport will dominate the beginning of the twenty-first century.

Gate Receipts

In some schools, gate receipts play an important part in financing at least part of the physical education and sport program. Although gate receipts are usually less important at lower educational levels, some colleges and universities finance a large share of their sports programs, including recreational sports and physical education programs, through gate receipts. One example is at the University of Nebraska at Lincoln, where an assessment charge for each home football ticket will raise a projected $9.9 million toward the payment of their new campus recreation center used primarily for physical education and recreational sports. At a few high schools throughout the country, gate receipts have been abolished because of the belief that if sports represent an important part of the education program, they should be paid for in the same way that science and mathematics programs are financed. Table 10-1 shows a general organization financial statement of expenses and receipts.

Table 10-1. General Organization Athletic Account—Financial Report (Sept–Dec)

Program	Expenses	
Football		
Officials (four home games)	$ 480.00	
Equipment and supplies	2364.02	
Transportation	175.00	
Supervision (police, ticket sellers and takers)	952.00	
Reconditioning and cleaning equipment	1313.20	
Medical supplies	125.40	
Scouting	60.00	
Film/video	31.36	
Guarantees	520.00	
Football dinner	231.00	
Miscellaneous (printing tickets, meeting)	172.00	
TOTAL		$6423.98
Cross country		
State and county entry fees	$ 10.00	
Transportation	64.00	
TOTAL		$ 74.00
Basketball		
Supervision (three games)	$ 36.00	
Custodian (three games)	26.00	
Security (one game)	12.00	
TOTAL		$ 74.00
Cheerleaders		
Transportation	52.20	
Sixteen new uniforms	320.00	
Cleaning uniforms	96.00	
TOTAL		$ 468.20
Total expenses		7040.18
	Receipts	
Football games		
Newburgh	$ 1311.70	
Norwalk	1819.60	
Yonkers	1129.50	
Bridgeport	1100.00	
Guarantee (New Haven)	120.00	
Total receipts		$5480.80

General Organization and Activity Fees

Some high schools either require or make available to students separate general organization or activity fees and tickets or some other inducement that enables them to attend sporting, dramatic, and musical events. In colleges and universities, a similar plan is sometimes employed as a part of a student activity fee, thus providing students with reduced rates to the various extracurricular activities offered by the institution. Student referendums are another means to raise capital to construct new physical education and sport (both intercollegiate and recreational) facilities (e.g., University of Southern Mississippi, University of Texas at Austin, Texas A&M University, Kansas State University).

ESTIMATING RECEIPTS/CREDITS

Some steps for projecting receipts in the general school budget that also have application to physical education and sport budgeting include gathering and analyzing all pertinent data, estimating all income based on a comprehensive view of income sources and revenue streams, organizing and classifying receipts in appropriate categories (e.g., gate receipts, parking, concessions), estimating revenue from all gathered data, comparing estimates with previous years, and computing a final draft of credits as well as debits.

EXPENDITURES

In physical education and sport budgets, typical examples of expenditures are items of capital outlay, such as constructing or remodeling a swimming pool or weight room; expendable equipment, such as badminton shuttlecocks and soccer balls; and a maintenance and repair provision, such as towel and laundry service and the refurbishing of equipment and uniforms. See appendix G for a sample list of potential line-item expenditures to support various interscholastic sport programs.

Some expenditures are easy to estimate, but others are more difficult, requiring accurate inventories, past records, and careful analysis of the condition of inventoried equipment. Some items

and services, such as equipment cleaning and repair, will need to be figured by averaging costs over a period of years. Awards, new equipment needs, transportation, guarantees to visiting teams, insurance, security, and medical services for emergencies are other expenditures that must be projected.

Here are some sound procedures to follow in estimating expenditures: determine objectives and goals of the program; analyze expenditures in terms of program objectives; prepare a budgetary calendar that states what accomplishments are expected and by what date; estimate expenditures by also considering past, present, and future needs; compare estimates with expenditures from previous years; and thoroughly evaluate estimates before preparing a final budget draft.

Cost-Cutting Procedures

In light of current economic problems, some managers are cutting costs. They are, for example,

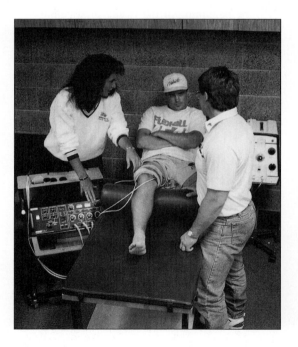

Medical personnel and equipment costs must be part of physical education and sport programs.

doing away with low participation or low revenue producing sports, reducing referees' pay, eliminating insurance, permitting fewer contests, reducing the number of coaches, using volunteer coaches, discontinuing the purchase of personally used equipment (e.g., bats, hockey sticks), lowering coaches' salaries, eliminating sports where rental facilities are used, and scheduling teams (e.g., girls' and boys' soccer) on the same day and combining transportation and coaches for these teams. Management must be more creative to keep programs intact as well as to provide more opportunities for all.

BUDGET PRESENTATION AND ADOPTION

After being prepared, school physical education and sport budgets are usually submitted to the superintendent through the principal's office. The principal is the person in charge of his or her particular building; therefore subdivision budgets should be presented to him or her for approval. Good management means, furthermore, that the budgetary items have been reviewed with the principal during their preparation so that approval is usually routine.

In colleges and universities, the proper budgeting channels should be followed. This might mean clearance through a dean or other management officer. Each person who is responsible for budget preparation and presentation should be familiar with the proper working channels.

For successful presentation and adoption, the budget should be prepared in final form only after careful consideration and consultation with appropriate budget committees so that little change will be needed. Requests for funds should be justifiable, and ample preliminary discussion of the budget with persons and groups most directly concerned (the fee payers) should be held so that needless fiscal conflict will be avoided and a unified proposal can be presented.

BUDGET MANAGEMENT

After the presentation and approval of the budget, the next step is to see that it is managed properly.

The budget should be followed closely with periodic checks (audits) on expenditures to see that they fall within the budget appropriations provided. The budget should be a guide to economical and efficient management.

Budget time frames such as Program Evaluation Review Techniques (PERT) and Critical Path Method (CPM) are often applied in budget management to assist in time expectation management. To employ these management techniques, the project must (1) have a clear objective and end point, (2) be divided into a series of stages or phases, (3) have projected due dates accompanying each assigned task, and (4) have a kick-off or starting date.

Numerous systems are employed in management of budgets. Line-item budgets (see appendix G) are most common and usually separate, via number codes, specific items such as salaries, uniforms, and insurance. Incremental budgeting is another common budgeting system that takes each line item and increases, decreases, or maintains its current status with each new budget plan. Other systematic forms of budgeting, such as zero-base budgeting and planning-programming-budgeting-evaluation, are explained next.

ZERO-BASE BUDGETING

Zero-base budgeting (Dirmith and Jablonsky 1979) is a procedure and system based on a justification for all expenditures of an organization at the time the budget is formulated. It allows management to, in effect, start over and not be influenced by previous budgets. Zero-base budgeting was developed and introduced by the Texas Instruments Company in 1969.

The traditional method of developing a budget is to use the previous year's budget as a base and then require a justification for any increase that is requested for the ensuing year. For example, if $500 had been allocated for recreational sports the previous year and the recreational sports director asked for $600 this year, then only the $100 incremental increase would have to be justified.

Zero-base budgeting, on the other hand, requires a justification of all expenditures that are requested. In the example just given, the entire $600 would have to be justified. In other words, each element, subdivision, or cost center of an organization that is allocated funds starts from zero, and all funds requested must be justified in light of their contribution to the achievement of the objectives of the organization.

Zero-base budgeting requires each subdivision or program of an organization to justify its request for funds. It requires planning for how these subdivisions can contribute to the achievement of the organization's goals and brings decision making into the procedure. Zero-base budgeting could mean that some elements of an organization have outgrown their usefulness and will no longer receive any funds whatsoever. It could also mean that new programs would be more likely to receive funds if they can be shown to be in line with, and capable of contributing to, organizational goals.

The steps to follow in zero-base budgeting include identifying the goals of the organization, gathering data about the program to be supported, planning a program to meet goals, identifying alternative ways to achieve goals in light of budgetary constraints, performing a cost analysis of the alternatives, and then arriving at a decision about what functions or alternatives should receive funding.

Zero-base budgeting could be especially valuable to organizations so steeped in tradition that they are not capitalizing on current trends and developments; they may need to implement new and creative ideas, programs, and projects. This system of budgeting can also make it possible to see that funds are used in the most effective way to achieve organizational goals.

PPBES: PLANNING-PROGRAMMING-BUDGETING-EVALUATION SYSTEM

PPBES came about as a solution to problems of fiscal accountability and optimal use of scarce inputs or limited resources.

A History of PPBES

PPBS, as it was originally known, started in 1949 when the Hoover Commission report on the organization of the executive branch recommended that the government adopt a budget based on function, activities, and objectives. In 1954, the Rand Corporation developed a performance budget for use in military spending. PPBS (Planning-Programming-Budgeting System) was the title given to this system. The DuPont Corporation and the Ford Motor Company were among the first to implement PPBS. In the early 1960s, Robert McNamara introduced the system to the Defense Department. The results of the system were so impressive that President Johnson ordered all federal departments and agencies to adopt PPBS by August 1965. PPBS became PPBES when the function of evaluation was added. At present, many schools, colleges, and other organizations are using this system, and many more are researching the feasibility of employing it.

Definition of PPBES

PPBES (figure 10-1) may be defined as a long-range plan to accomplish an organization's objectives by using continual feedback and updating of information to allow for greater efficiency in the decision-making process (Apostolou and Crumbley 1988). The four elements of PPBES are as follows:

1. *Planning*—establishing objectives
2. *Programming*—combining activities and events to produce distinguishable results
3. *Budgeting*—allocating resources; the financial plan for meeting program needs and objectives
4. *Evaluation*—determining how adequately the budget fits the program and the program meets the objectives; and evaluating the relationship of accomplishments to cost.

To implement PPBES, the objectives of the organization must be clearly defined. All activities that contribute to the same objective, regardless of placement in the organization, are clustered or grouped together. A financial plan designed to

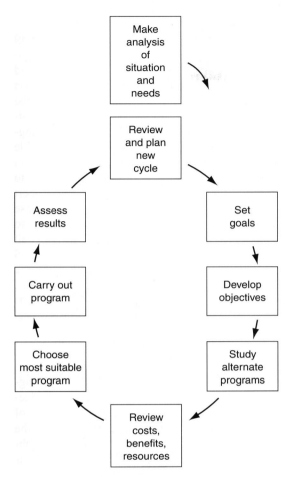

Figure 10-1. The PPBES cycle.

reach these objectives is formulated for a particular time period (PERT or CPM techniques may be utilized). An analysis document assesses long-range needs and evaluates the adequacy, effectiveness, costs, benefits, barriers, and difficulties inherent in the proposed program. Under PPBES, funds must be used with definitive goals in mind. Accountability for expenditures is stressed. In using PPBES, each activity and educational program is considered, not only by itself, but also with respect to other educational programs that make up the whole system. In this way, the needs of the entire school system or organization are considered.

Following are the steps necessary to apply PPBES:

1. *Goals and objectives.* Goals and objectives should be stated in terms of behavior and performance outcome. The results of the program should also be determined in relation to knowledge, skills, and attitudes.

2. *Statement of needs and problems.* Needs and problems of the particular organization and user group must be adequately defined.

3. *Determination of expected satisfaction of needs.* Numbers of persons and skills needed must also be determined.

4. *Constraints and feasibility.* Both these items must be evaluated to determine whether the system can overcome certain limitations (personnel, materials, facilities). The system may need modification in terms of needs or objectives to overcome existing limitations and barriers.

5. *Alternative programs.* These programs outline the different ways the organization can reach its goals. Alternative programs should be evaluated in terms of needs, goals, and constraints of the system.

6. *Resource requirements.* The resource needs of each alternative must be computed. One way to accomplish this might be to derive the faculty teaching cost per student credit hour and then add department overhead costs such as advising, counseling, management, equipment, and clerical support.

7. *Estimate of benefits.* The benefits of the program must be determined in relationship to student accomplishment at present and in the future.

8. *Development of an operating plan.* From the data collected, all alternatives should be weighed against fixed criteria such as cost of implementation and risk involved, estimated benefits, and future budget allocations.

9. *Pilot implementation of best alternative.* A pilot program should be conducted at a level

at which it could be modified or changed without involved or costly effort.

10. *Evaluation.* The data from the pilot program should be used to determine whether it is meeting the objectives of the organization. The program should be modified accordingly.

11. *Feedback and further modification.* Once PPBES is in process, it should be continually reevaluated and modified to ensure that the goals and objectives agreed on are being met.

12. *Situational analysis.* This is both a beginning and end process determined by the present state of the situation. This is a crucial and meaningful assessment of needs.

Advantages and Disadvantages of PPBES

Before implementing PPBES in an institution, management must be thoroughly familiar with the advantages and disadvantages of such a system. Each situation differs, and careful situational analysis before and after implementation is essential. Here are some of the advantages of PPBES:

1. The system assists in formulating goals, objectives, and identifying skills.

2. Curriculum and programs can be designed to meet the objectives formulated.

3. Staff members can be provided with prior planning experience and resource materials.

4. Alternative plans can be more systematically analyzed.

5. Costs, accomplishments, and risks may be systematically compared.

6. Staff members are more involved in decision making; and morale, motivation, and productivity may be increased.

7. Instructional and operational costs may be easily identified.

8. Innovation, integration, and coordination can be promoted in programs as well as within the entire organization.

9. New, creative ideas and programs that have been scrutinized and tested are continually applied to the system.

10. Public awareness, understanding, and communication are increased.

Here are some disadvantages of PPBES:

1. Staff time is limited, and staff members with sufficient technical skills in these areas may also be limited.

2. Implementation may lead to conflict and resistance from community members and sometimes from within the organization.

3. Cost-benefit analysis is difficult to quantify; some benefits from education are not easily measurable.

4. Communication among staff members may be limited as a result of centralization of system planning.

5. PPBES is a method of indicating the best use of funds; however, in doing so, funds are also expended, and limited budgets may not be able to justify implementation of such a system.

6. The vocabulary is vague to those who are not directly involved in using such a system.

7. PPBES may be mistakenly seen as a substitute for management rather than as a tool of management.

8. Alternatives with great potential are passed up because of their high risk or chance of failure according to PPBES criteria.

9. Some persons may feel that they are answerable to the "system" for their program; however, the system should be an aid, not a deterrent.

Using PPBES

Surveys indicate that more than 1,000 schools in the United States employ PPBES with their budgets. Michigan and California are two examples.

The Michigan program. Michigan has adopted PPBES in its publicly funded institutions of higher education. Although the system costs more money, it enables managers to have greater information for decision making and provides taxpayers a better indication of where their money is being spent.

The California program. Under the direction of the Advisory Commission on School District

Budgeting and Accounting, fifteen school districts piloted PPBES. The school districts simplified plans so that they were readily understandable to voters in the hope that the public's understanding would help the passage of school bond issues. When explained in terms of objectives and expected outcomes and accomplishments, budgets and programs were supported and approved.

It is obvious from the California and Michigan examples that PPBES is a system that can help organizations use available funds wisely, identify problem areas, and improve program weaknesses. In addition, the public is not only given input into the process, but also is offered clear and understandable data to assist in adopting and supporting sound fiscal budgeting.

How Can PPBES Be Applied to Physical Education and Sport Programs?

Physical education and sport have much to gain by implementing PPBES. If this system is used, physical education and sport programs and budget requests cannot be arbitrarily dropped or refused because of inadequate funding. Each segment of the program must be given equal emphasis according to objectives and benefits derived from meeting these objectives.

Pre-PPBES physical education and sport budgets were considered in terms of bats and balls rather than total program and user needs, objectives, and benefits. PPBES provides management with a situation assessment, a detailed list of goals and objectives, an analysis of problems and barriers, alternatives, solutions, and recommendations. The most important attribute of PPBES is the way it relates program costs and risks to expected outcomes and accomplishments.

COST ANALYSIS

Cost analysis of resources used in a program is a derivative of cost accounting. Cost analysis is needed to help the manager evaluate present operations and project future planning and budgets. Cost analysis is limited to the types of accounting systems being used as well as to designating the unit to be compared. It is particularly applicable to schools and colleges. For example, some schools operate on K–12, others, on K–6 or K–8 or some other educational pattern. Naturally, a great difference in expenditures per student would occur depending on the various patterns of organization.

Various units are employed in cost analysis in a school's general education fund. The number of students in attendance, the census, average daily attendance, and average daily membership or students enrolled in the school are some of those numbers used. Each of the various units has advantages and disadvantages.

As a raw measure of educational costs, the average daily membership is better than the average daily attendance. Teachers' salaries must be paid whether students are in 90 percent or 100 percent attendance, and desks and schoolbooks must be available whether students are in attendance or not. With respect to raw per capita units, the average daily membership is also a better unit to measure the educational costs than is the average daily attendance unit. Tradition, however, has favored the average daily attendance unit over average daily membership.

Cost analysis as it relates to equipment and supplies for physical education and sport may be simply handled by allowing a certain number of dollars per student or per participant, depending

Maintenance, equipment, and personnel must be considered when designing any budget.

on whether one is concerned with a school or another organizational program.

Some experts in fiscal management believe a per capita expenditure allocation for physical education and sport represents a good foundation program. However, they recommend in addition (1) an extra percentage allocation for program enrichment, (2) an extra percentage allocation for variation in enrollment, and (3) a reference to a commodity index (current prices of equipment and supplies) that may indicate need for changes in the per capita expenditure because of current increase or decrease in the value of the items being purchased.

The following example can be used as a guideline to determine the amount of money needed for physical education and sport programs. The director of physical education or athletic and activities director submits and substantiates the needs for the coming school year: increased expenditures—a sound estimate of projected increases of student program participation based on increased enrollments, student interest, program changes, and the anticipated cost of equipment and supplies to be used; inventory—equipment and supplies on hand and the condition of these items; and the previous year's budget—amounts allocated in the previous year or years. These items represent the basis on which most allocations of funds to physical education and sport programs are determined.

Directors of physical education and sport programs who were surveyed believed that the increases in per capita allocations that they were granted were the result of such factors as an increase in the number of participants, a careful evaluation of the number of participants and of the time those participants spent using the equipment and supplies, the cost per hour, and an excellent working rapport with the board of education.

THE EXECUTIVE DIRECTOR OF FINANCE OR BUSINESS MANAGER: FISCAL MANAGEMENT IN SCHOOLS AND COLLEGES

Schools and colleges today are in the business of education. The size of the physical plant and the large expenditures require the talents of a quali-

fied executive director of finance, or business manager. The school or college business manager is an integral part of the entire management team and ideally should possess experience in both business administration and education. Most business managers have earned a master's or a doctor's degree, usually in business administration. Some are certified public accountants, and others have taken courses from management institutes. Many college and university business managers are recruited from outside the academic world. The manager is primarily responsible for the efficient and economic management of business matters concerning the educational institution and often its physical education and sport programs.

Physical education and athletic and activity directors must understand and appreciate the vital role of the business manager. Many management functions of physical educators or public and private physical activity managers, including fiscal management, fall within the responsibility of the business manager. The business manager is a specialist in this area, and educators, coaches, and instructors should work closely with this individual in reference to business-related matters. It is up to teachers and coaches to supply the

Business managers, teachers and coaches must be experienced in fiscal management.

business manager with an accurate and up-to-date database (debits, receipts, equipment costs, membership trends, etc.).

The school, college, or private sector business manager is responsible for budget preparation and fiscal accounting, investment of endowment and other gift monies, planning and construction of buildings, data processing, management of research and other contracts, business aspects of student loans, and intercollegiate activities.

Regardless of who performs the role of business manager or what title he or she assumes, the functions outlined and the working relationship with physical education and sport personnel are similar to or have implications for physical educators in colleges and for other public and private sector organizations.

Function

The business manager's function is strictly limited by the size of the educational triangle—programs, receipts/credits, expenditures/debits (figure 10-2). The greater the perimeter of the triangle, the larger the sphere of operations. This applies to all departments within the system. Likewise, in times of inflation, the expenditures and receipts may increase, but the program side may remain stable. Hence it is obvious that the business manager must project both expenditures

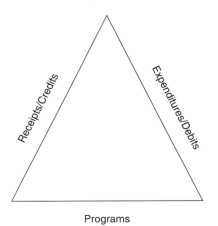

Programs

Figure 10-2. The business manager's isosceles triangle.

and receipts if a physical education or sport program is going to be maintained or expand.

The business office represents a means to an end, and it can be evaluated in terms of how well it contributes to the realization of the objectives of education.

Objectives

In serving schools and colleges, the business manager constantly has the goal of helping them obtain the greatest educational service possible from each tax, student fee, or other dollar spent. He or she should take a democratic approach to decisions affecting others, be they user groups, parents, alumni, coaches, or management. The decisions reached will then be for the best and will include assurances that the educational benefits are worth the cost and risks.

The business manager or finance director is part of the management team—along with principals, superintendents, board members, presidents, directors, and chairs—who may be expected to look into the years ahead and present long-term ideas regarding the future plans of the school or college as well as its programs.

Responsibilities

The business manager's responsibilities are varied. He or she must be familiar with employee health insurance and benefit programs as well as with state and federal allocations for education. In the smaller school districts, the business responsibilities may be incorporated into the duties of the chief school administrator. As districts enlarge, they need to hire a person to oversee all the noninstructional areas of the district so that the chief school administrator is free to devote more time to the educational programs of the district. No two districts are alike in handling business responsibilities.

The following are some of the business manager's duties as listed by Frederick W. Hill, past president of the Association of School Business Officials:

Budget and financial planning. This is an area in which the business manager has to be sensitive to the needs of staff members to carry out a program. A business manager also must have a sixth sense to understand how much the community can expend on the program. This experience can be related to the isosceles triangle in figure 10-2. A direct relationship must exist among all the components that make up the three sides of the triangle.

Purchasing and supply management. The business manager must use the best purchasing techniques to obtain maximal value for every dollar spent. After purchases are made and goods received, he or she is responsible for warehousing, storage, inventory control, and distribution. Equipment offered at the lowest bid price is not always the most economical to purchase.

Plans. The business manager works with administrators, teachers, coaches, architects, attorneys, and citizens of the community in developing plans for expansion, renovation, and construction of new facilities.

Human resources. The business manager's duties vary in relation to the size of the district. In a large district, he or she may be in charge of the nonteaching personnel, and in a small district, he or she may be in charge of all personnel. In this capacity, the manager has to maintain records and pay schedules, initiate payroll and retirement reports, and keep other human resource management records.

Staff development. The business manager is always interested in upgrading the people under his or her jurisdiction by providing workshops and in-service courses covering the latest developments in the field of fiscal management and services.

Community relations. Without community support the school would not operate. Some managers tend to forget this truism when they become too far removed from the community. There is always a need to interpret and effectively communicate the financial responsibility and accountability of the institution and program to the public.

Transportation. It has often been said that boards of education find themselves spending too much time on the three Bs—buses, buildings, and

Transportation costs add significant expenses to any budget.

bonds. When this occurs, it is time to look into hiring a business manager. Transportation is vital but is also one of the most complex and costly line items to control.

Food services. The business manager is responsible for the efficient and effective management of food services.

Accounting and reporting. The business manager establishes and supervises the financial records and accounting procedures.

Debt service. The business manager is involved with various capital developments and financial planning through short-term and long-term programs. The financial rating of a school district is judged in part on the way its debt service is handled.

Insurance. The business manager must be familiar with a large schedule of insurance provisions ranging from fire and liability to health and injury. He or she must maintain records for proof in case of loss.

Legal matters. The business manager has to be familiar with education and school law, and he or she must know when to consult with attorneys, who are typically retained by most school districts, colleges, corporations, and other public and private sector organizations.

Money raising. The business manager is frequently called on to lead or organize fund-raising drives for schools, colleges, and universities.

Grants and financial aid. The business manager must be aware of money available for programs through private, state, and federal agencies. Grants and financial aid and other monies available for scholarships from private and public sources should also fall into his or her domain.

Systems analysis. The business manager must constantly question and challenge existing systems to see if they can be improved so that managerial tasks can be performed more efficiently and effectively.

In many public schools, the collectibles and accountables are transferred via computer to the business manager's centralized database. Thus the role of the teacher and coach is to feed specialized information (e.g., equipment types and prices) to the central office. The business manager, via computer, can then check out the item, comparison shop, project and audit the existing equipment budget, evaluate alternative purchase offers, and produce vendor requisitions and purchase orders as well as update the existing equipment inventory and provide documentation back to the physical education chair or athletic and activities director.

Similar procedures for budgeting exist that ensure increased accuracy and standardized budget request forms, provide appropriate copies to affected management, and continually track and audit the existing budget area or cost center.

FINANCIAL ACCOUNTABILITY

The large amount of money involved in physical education and sport programs makes strict accountability mandatory. This accountability includes the maintenance of accurate records and receipts, proper distribution of materials, and adequate appraisal and evaluation of procedures. Financial accounting should provide a record of budget, income, and expenditures for all departmental transactions. With help from the computer, the process should also provide permanent records of all financial transactions, which can help form a pattern of expenditures as related to the approved budget. Documenting compliance with mandates and requests imposed either by law

or by administrative action, evaluating and accounting to ensure that funds are dealt with honestly, and managing properly with respect to control, analysis of costs, and reporting all fall within the domain of the business manager (see the box titled Reasons for Financial Accounting).

Management Policies for Financial Accounting

Management has the final responsibility for accountability for all monies, equipment, and supplies (see the box titled The Role of the Manager in Budgeting). Departments should establish and enforce policies covering loss, damage, theft,

---

Reasons for Financial Accounting

To provide a method of authorizing expenditures for items that have been included and approved in the budget. This means proper accounting records are being used.

To provide authorized procedures for making purchases of equipment, supplies, and other materials and to let contracts for various services.

To provide authorized procedures for paying the proper amounts (a) for purchases of equipment, supplies, and other materials, which have been checked upon receipt; (b) for actual labor; and (c) for other services rendered.

To provide a record of each payment made, including the date, to whom, for what purpose, and other pertinent material.

To provide authorized procedures for handling various receipts and sources of income.

To provide detailed information essential for properly auditing accounts, such as confirmation that money has been spent for specified items.

To provide informational resources for the preparation of future budgets.

To provide a tangible base for developing future policies relating to financial planning.

To serve as control for various cost centers.

The Role of the Manager in Budgeting

A. Preliminary considerations in preparing the budget
  1. Program additions or deletions
  2. Staff changes
  3. Inventory of equipment on hand
B. Budget preparation: additional considerations
  1. Athletic gate receipts and expenditures—athletic booster fund, other marketing revenue
  2. Board of education budget—allocations for physical education, including athletics and activities and recreational sport
  3. Coaches' requests and requests of teachers and department heads
  4. Comparison of requests with inventories
  5. Itemizing and coding requests
  6. Budget conferences with administration
  7. Justification of requests
C. Athletic and activities association funds: considerations
  1. Estimated income
    a. Gate receipts
    b. Student activities tickets
    c. Tournament receipts
    d. Concessions
  2. Estimated expenditures
    a. Awards
    b. Tournament fees
    c. Films and videos
    d. Miscellaneous
    e. Surplus
D. General budget: considerations
  1. Breakdown
    a. By sport or activity (cost center)
    b. By gender and per student
    c. Transportation
    d. Salaries
    e. Insurance and benefits
    f. Reconditioning of equipment
    g. Supervision
    h. General and miscellaneous
    i. Equipment
    j. Officials
    k. Security

  2. Codes (selected)
    a. Advertising
    b. Travel
    c. Conference fees
    d. Printing
    e. Office supplies
    f. Equipment
    g. Facility rental
    h. Postage, copying
E. Postbudget procedures
  1. Selection of equipment and supplies
  2. Preparation of list of deals to bid
  3. Request for price quotations
  4. Requisitions
  5. Care of equipment
  6. Notification to teachers and coaches of amounts approved
F. Ordering procedures
  1. Study the quality of various products
  2. Accept no substitutes for items ordered
  3. Submit request for price quotations
  4. Select low quotes or justify higher quotes
  5. Submit purchase orders
  6. Check and count all shipments
  7. Record items received on inventory cards or computer
  8. Provide for equipment and supply accountability and audits
G. Relationships with management
  1. Consultation—program plans with building principal and/or superintendent
  2. Make budget recommendations to administration
  3. Advise business manager of procedures followed
  4. Discuss items approved and deleted with business manager
  5. Advise teachers and coaches of amounts available and adjust requests
H. Suggestions for prospective directors of physical education and sport and activity programs
  1. Develop a philosophy and approach to budgeting

The Role of the Manager in Budgeting–cont'd

2. Consult with staff for their suggestions
3. Select quality merchandise
4. Provide proper care and maintenance of equipment and supplies
5. Provide for all programs on an equitable basis
6. Budget adequately but not elaborately
7. Provide a sound, well-rounded program of physical education and sport
8. Emphasize equality for girls and boys
9. Provide for balanced, basic instruction and adapted, recreational, and interscholastic sports programs
10. Conduct a year-round public relations program
11. Try to overcome these possible shortcomings:
    a. Board of education not oriented to needs of physical education and sport
    b. Program not achieving established goals
    c. Staff not adequately informed and involved in management process

misappropriation, or destruction of appropriate departmental resources. A system of accurate record keeping should be established and uniformly applied throughout the organization. The person to whom equipment and supplies are issued can be held accountable for these materials, and accurate inventories can be maintained. Once again the computer is user friendly for these types of systems.

Accounting for Receipts and Expenditures

A centralized accounting system, with all funds being deposited with the business manager, treasurer, or other responsible person, is advantageous. Purchase orders and other forms are usually then countersigned or certified by the proper official, thus better guaranteeing integrity in the use of funds. A system of bookkeeping wherein books and databases are housed in the central office by the business manager helps ensure better control of finances and allows all subdivisions, departments, or cost centers in a system to be uniformly controlled. The central accounting system fund accounts, in which the physical education and sports funds are located, should be audited annually by qualified persons. An annual financial report should be developed and publi-

From budgeting to data storage, computerization helps all dimensions of physical education and sport programs maintain accountability.

cized to indicate receipts, expenditures, and other pertinent data associated with the enterprise.

All receipts and expenditures should be properly recorded in the ledger or computer, providing important information like the fund into which the transaction has been deposited or from which it was debited. The money received from sources

Checklist for Budgeting and Financial Accounting

	Yes	No
1. Has a complete inventory been taken and itemized on proper forms as a guide in estimating equipment needs?	____	____
2. Does the equipment inventory include a detailed account of the number of items on hand, size and quantity, type, condition, date of certification, etc.?	____	____
3. Is the inventory complete, current, and up to date?	____	____
4. Are budgetary estimates as accurate and realistic as possible without padding?	____	____
5. Are provisions made in the budget for increases expected in enrollments, increased student participation, and changes in the cost of equipment, supplies, transportation, and insurance?	____	____
6. Has the business manager been consulted on the cost of new equipment?	____	____
7. Has the director of physical education or athletics and activities consulted with the staff on various budget items?	____	____
8. Has the director of physical education or athletics consulted with the school business manager in respect to the total budget for the department?	____	____
9. Are new equipment and supply needs for physical education and sport determined and budgeted at least 1 year in advance?	____	____
10. Was the budget prepared according to the standards recommended by the chief school administrator?	____	____
11. Are databases and information for previous years available as a means of comparison?	____	____
12. Is there a summary of receipts and expenditures listed so that the total budget can be quickly seen?	____	____
13. If receipts from sport or other funds are to be added to the budget, is this shown?	____	____
14. Are there alternate program plans with budgetary changes in the event the budget is not approved?	____	____
15. Has a statement of objectives of the program been included that reflects the overall educational philosophy of the total school and community?	____	____
16. Has the budget been prepared so that the major aspects may be viewed readily by those persons desiring a quick review and also in more detail for those persons desiring a further delineation of the budgetary items?	____	____
17. Is the period of time for which the budget has been prepared clearly indicated?	____	____
18. Is the physical education and sport budget based on an educational plan developed to attain the goals and purposes agreed on by management and staff within the framework of the total school's philosophy?	____	____
19. Is the physical education and sport plan a comprehensive one reflecting a healthful environment, physical education class, adapted, recreational sports, and interscholastic program?	____	____
20. Does the plan include a statement of the objectives of the physical education and sport programs, and are these reflected in the budget?	____	____

such as sport participation fees and organization dues should be recorded with sufficient credit cross-references and detailed information. Supporting vouchers should also be maintained and readily accessible for inspection. Tickets to sports and other events should be numbered consecutively and checked to get an accurate record of ticket sales. Students should not be permitted to handle funds except under the supervision of the management staff or faculty.

Checklist for Budgeting and Financial Accounting—cont'd

	Yes	No
21. Are both long-range and short-range plans for achieving the purposes of the program provided?	___	___
22. Have provisions been made in the budget for emergencies?	___	___
23. Are accurate records kept on such activities involving expenditures of money as transportation, insurance, officials, laundry and dry cleaning, awards, guarantees, repairs, new equipment, medical expenses, and publicity?	___	___
24. Are accurate records kept on the receipt of monies from such sources as gate receipts, sponsorships, and advertising revenue?	___	___
25. Once the budget has been approved, is there a specific plan provided for authorizing expenditures?	___	___
26. Are specific forms used for recording purchase transactions?	___	___
27. Are purchases on all major items based on competitive bidding?	___	___
28. Are requisitions used in obtaining supplies and equipment?	___	___
29. Are requisitions numbered and do they include such information as the name of the person originating the requisition, when the item to be purchased will be needed, where to ship the item, the description and/or code number, quantity, unit price, and amount?	___	___
30. With the exception of petty cash accounts, is a central purchasing system in effect?	___	___
31. Is the policy of quantity and cooperative purchasing followed whenever possible?	___	___
32. If quantity purchasing is used, are advanced thought and planning given to storage and maintenance facilities and procedures?	___	___
33. Are performance tests and inspections made on items purchased? Are state, regional, or national testing bureaus or laboratories utilized where feasible?	___	___
34. Are receipts of equipment and supplies checked carefully?	___	___
35. Is an audit made of all expenditures?	___	___
36. Are specific procedures in effect to safeguard money, property, and employees?	___	___
37. Is there an audit or check to determine that established standards, policies, and procedures have been followed?	___	___
38. Are procedures in operation to check condition and use of equipment and supplies?	___	___
39. Is a financial report made periodically?	___	___
40. Are there proper procedures for the care and maintenance and inventory of all equipment and supplies?	___	___
41. Are accurate records kept on all equipment and supplies, including condition, site, and age?	___	___
42. Have established procedures been developed and are they followed in regard to the issuance, use, and return of equipment?	___	___
43. Have provisions been made for making regular notations of future needs?	___	___

Purchase orders on regular authorized forms issued by the organization should be used so that accurate and standardized records may be kept. To place an order verbally without a written follow-up is a questionable policy. Preparing written purchase orders on regular forms and according to sound accountability procedure better ensures legality of contract together with prompt delivery and payment (see the Checklist for Budgeting and Financial Accounting box).

SUMMARY

The management of physical education and sport programs must be concerned with proper fiscal management. The lack of money from traditional sources such as the general fund of a school district or institution of higher education is prompting many organizations to look to government, foundations, the corporate sector, and other sources for help in meeting their fiscal needs and budgetary requirements. Other organizations are engaging in special fund-raising projects ranging from raffles to T-shirt sales and from "a-thons" to lotteries in order to secure the financial help they need to conduct quality programs. Management of funds also requires a knowledge of how to prepare and implement budgets; how to determine proper costs of supplies and equipment; how to apply systems such as zero-base budgeting, PPBES, and PERT; and how to provide for fiscal accountability within the organization. Computerization should also come into play to ensure greater accuracy and control of new revenue streams as well as to streamline fiscal operations.

SELF-ASSESSMENT ACTIVITIES

These activities will assist students in determining if material and competencies presented in this chapter have been mastered.

1. What are the reasons for fiscal management in physical education and sport programs?

2. Outline the procedure you would follow in preparing a zero-base budget if you were the chair of a department of recreational sports for a citywide program.

3. Develop a detailed PPBES plan for a department of athletics and activity at the junior high school level.

4. As a business manager in a school system, what aspects of fiscal management would involve you and the management of a physical education and sport program?

5. Identify the steps involved in the preparation of a budget that will be presented to the community at next month's school board meeting.

6. Design and defend a pay-to-play policy for an interscholastic varsity sport program.

REFERENCES

1. American Management Association. 1986. *Financial management.* New York: American Management Association.

2. Apostolou, N. G., and D. L. Crumbley. 1988. *Handbook of government accounting and finance.* New York: John Wiley and Sons.

3. Dirmith, M. W., and S. F. Jablonsky. 1979. Zero-base budgeting as a management technique and political strategy. *Academy of Management Review* 4(4):555–565, Oct.

4. Klappholz, L. A. 1980. Involving the staff in the budget-making process. *Physical Education Newsletter,* November.

5. Parkhouse, B. L., and M. Dennison. 1984. Pay for play: Solution or stopgap? *Athletic Business,* April, 12.

6. Roe, W. H. 1961. *School business management.* New York: McGraw-Hill.

7. What happens when the money runs out? 1981. *Athletic Purchasing and Facilities,* July, 44.

SUGGESTED READINGS

Austin, D. A. 1984. Economic impact on physical education. *Journal of Physical Education, Recreation and Dance* 55(May/June):35.
Discusses how sources of funds that affect physical education and sport programs have been cut back. Lists strategies for a lifetime game plan, the principle of which stresses that the way to sustain physical education is to provide excellent instructional programs. Explains that the value of being taught to actively engage in physical exercise should be continually stressed because the public is willing to supply funds to accomplish the objectives that result from such programs.

DeSchriver, T. D., and D. K. Stotlar. 1996. An economic analysis of cartel behavior within the NCAA. *Journal of Sport Management* 10:388–400.

DuBrin, A. J., R. D. Ireland, and J. C. Williams. 1989. *Management and organization.* Cincinnati, Ohio: South-Western Publishing.
Presents control methods and techniques relative to budgeting and finance. Discusses various network analysis techniques such as PERT and cost-profit schemes.

Graham, P. J. 1994. *Sport business: Operational and theoretical aspects.* Dubuque, Iowa: Brown & Benchmark.

Discusses financial management, including such aspects as operating versus capital budgets, types of budgets, preparing and presenting the budget, and sources of funding. Explores marketing tools and sponsorship.

Howard, D. R., and J. L. Crompton. 1995. *Financial sport.* Morgantown, W. Va.: Fitness Information Technology.
Discusses various financial resource avenues for public and private sector funding.

Lewandowski, D. M. 1984. Shoestrings and shoeboxes. *Journal of Physical Education, Recreation and Dance* 55(August):34.
Provides suggestions for how a school without sufficient cash can, through ingenuity, effort, and time, come up with solutions for insufficient space and equipment. It also provides suggestions in chart form for homemade equipment, how items can be constructed, and in what activities they can be used.

Needler, B. E., Jr., H. R. Anderson, and J. C. Caldwell. 1988. *Financial and managerial accounting.* Boston: Houghton Mifflin.

Sattler, T. P., and J. E. Mullens. 1993. How to budget simply, effectively. *Fitness Management,* February, 25.
Presents procedures and policies in accounting as well as in budget guidelines and format.

Steir, W. F. 1994. *Successful sport fund-raising.* Dubuque, Iowa: Brown & Benchmark.
Accentuates the need to raise funds for physical education and sport programs in schools and colleges. Suggests that such outside sources need to be tapped if these programs are to survive. Provides suggestions for procuring external funds.

Purchase and Care of Supplies and Equipment

Instructional Objectives and Competencies To Be Achieved

After reading this chapter the student should be able to

- Explain why sound supply and equipment management is important and explain the basis on which supplies and equipment should be selected for physical education and sport programs.

- Discuss the various procedures and principles that should be followed in purchasing supplies and equipment.

- List guidelines for the selection of an equipment manager and for the management of the equipment room.

- Establish a system for checking, issuing, and maintaining supplies and equipment.

- Justify the need for various types of audiovisual supplies and equipment for physical education and sport programs.

Chapter 10, fiscal management, showed that a large portion of the physical education and sport budget is allocated for the purchase of supplies and equipment. Management is responsible for seeing that the supplies and equipment that are purchased will meet program needs, be of good quality, be safe, measure up to code, and be acquired via a procedural pattern that reflects efficient and effective practices.

Physical education and sport programs use supplies and equipment that cost thousands of dollars. *Supplies* are those materials that are ex-

pendable and have to be replaced at frequent intervals, such as shuttlecocks, tennis balls, and adhesive tape. *Equipment* refers to those items that are not considered expendable, but are used for a period of years, such as parallel bars, volleyball standards, basketballs, soccer goals, canoes, and videotape recorders.

Because so much money is spent on supplies and equipment and because such materials are vital to the health and safety of participants, to good playing conditions, and to values derived from the programs, it is important that the man-

Proper care of supplies and equipment is crucial to all physical activity and sport programs.

agement aspects related to supplies and equipment are well planned and carefully developed. In addition, the purchase of supplies and equipment should be related to achieving program objectives designated by PPBES. Physical educators, coaches, and equipment room personnel should express their needs for supplies and equipment in terms of these programmatic goals.

Many different sources for purchasing equipment exist, many grades and qualities of materials are available, and many methods of storing and maintaining such merchandise are prevalent. Some of these sources, grades, and methods are good whereas others are extremely questionable. To obtain the best value for the investment of scarce financial inputs, basic principles of selecting, purchasing, and maintaining equipment need to be understood and applied. The checklist at the end of this chapter provides some guidelines that should be followed in the purchase and care of supplies and equipment.

DETERMINING SUPPLY AND EQUIPMENT NEEDS

Supply and equipment needs vary according to a wide range of factors, including the level of the program, age of the user group, activities being

offered, and, of course, finance. Other factors are the facilities and physical plant, athletic training rooms (see chapter 12), playing space available, and number of activities or sports being offered. Some organizations have only limited physical education and sport programs and facilities. Under such conditions, the supplies and equipment needed differ from those required in settings in which more spacious and sophisticated accommodations exist. Other factors to consider are the nature of the clientele (age, gender, and number), the length of playing seasons, the environment, and health and safety provisions. Those responsible for purchasing supplies and equipment should carefully study their own particular situations and estimate and project their needs objectively and realistically.

In the physical education instructional domain, all types of balls, apparatus, nets, standards, implements (e.g., gloves, bats, racquets), and racks will be needed for the conduct of individual and team sports as well as for aquatics, dance, and other physical activities. These same types of supplies and equipment may also be used in the recreational sport program and sometimes by community education. Many times, in fact, the

Specialized equipment being assembled for basketball.

Rolling equipment carts make it easy to transport, store, and account for costly equipment. University of California at Irvine.

same human and physical (facility, supplies, equipment) resources are utilized.

Physical education supply and equipment needs, and the manner by which they are determined, vary from organization to organization. For example, an elementary school may be given an equipment budget based on the number of students enrolled. Then, within the parameters of the budget, teachers request at the end of each year the equipment and supplies they will need the following year. Another procedure that might be followed in a high school, in which various units of different activities constitute the program, would be to have an inventory of supplies at the conclusion of each teaching unit. A third procedure followed in some cities and school districts is, in the interest of economy, ordering all supplies and equipment through a central office computer system for all schools within the city or district. In such cases, items are frequently kept in a warehouse, or central location from which they can be obtained as needed.

In sport programs, inventories are usually taken and purchase requests instituted at the end of each respective sport season. In this process, the sport-specific coach, equipment manager, and athletic and activities director usually cooperate to ensure that the necessary supplies and equipment are available for the beginning of the next season.

GUIDELINES FOR SELECTING SUPPLIES AND EQUIPMENT

Selection should be based on local needs. Supplies and equipment should be specified and selected because they are needed in a particular situation and by a particular user group. Items should be selected that represent materials needed to carry out the program as outlined and that represent essentials to fulfilling program as well as organizational objectives.

Selection should be based on quality. In the long run, the item of good quality is the least expensive and the safest. Bargain goods too often consist of inferior materials that wear out much

Weight training equipment is costly, yet if maintained properly, it can last for many years.

earlier and perhaps do not supply the protection needed for safe participation. Only the best grade of football equipment should be purchased. A study conducted on football deaths that occurred during a twenty-five-year period revealed that many of these deaths resulted from the use of inferior helmets and other substandard equipment. What is true of football is also true of other activities.

Selection should consider whether the product is both budget and maintenance friendly. When planning for everything from uniforms to artificial surfaces, management must consider not only the initial capital outlay for an item (e.g., shoulder pads, ice hockey breezers, pool lane dividers, golf mats), but also the maintenance, shelf life, and upkeep. If possible, managers should avoid buying the "label" of, for example, training equipment (Cybex, Nautilus, Sports Medicine Industries, OEI, Med X, Keiser, Polaris, Trotter, etc.) (Buyers guide 1991), because alter-

nate equipment may be found at significant savings without compromising quality.

Equipment that has readily replaceable parts that are "recommended by the manufacturer" for liability purposes should be the only type of equipment purchased and maintained.

Selection should be made by professional personnel. The persons selecting the supplies and equipment needed in physical education and sport programs should be knowledgeable and competent. Performing this responsibility efficiently means examining many types and brands of products; conducting comparative experiments to determine economy, durability, and safety; listing and weighing the advantages and disadvantages of different items; and knowing how each item is going to be used. The person selecting supplies and equipment should be interested in this responsibility, have the time to do the job, be a member of the Athletic Equipment Managers Association, and be able to perform the function efficiently.

Some organizations have purchasing agents who are specially trained in these matters whereas others use athletic equipment managers. In small organizations, the department chair, director, coach, physical education teacher or team leader, or equipment committee frequently performs this responsibility. One other point is important: Regardless of who the responsible person may be, the staff member who uses these supplies and equipment in his or her particular facet of the total program should have direct input concerning the specific items being considered for selection.

Selecting should be continuous. A product that ranks as the best available this year may not necessarily be the best next year. Manufacturers are constantly conducting research to develop and produce a safer and improved product. There is keen competition in the marketplace; management, therefore, cannot be complacent, thinking that because a certain product has served well in the past, it remains the best buy for the future. The search for the best product available must be a continuous process. With the help of the computer and expert equipment manager, these trends can be tracked.

Selection should consider service and replacement needs. Supplies and equipment may be difficult to obtain in volume. On receipt of merchandise, sizes of uniforms may be wrong, and colors may be mixed up. Additional materials may be needed on short notice (JIT, or just-in-time ordering). Therefore, one should select items that will be available in volume, if needed, and deal with business firms that will service and replace materials with manufacturer's approved parts and take care of emergencies without delay or controversy. Local merchants should be strongly considered in the purchasing process.

Selection should consider whether old equipment can be reconditioned successfully or whether new equipment should be purchased. Management should make this decision based on factors such as safety, cost, and suitability for effective use in activities in which the item is required. In some cases, repairing old equipment may be costly; therefore, buying new equipment

may be more beneficial. If the safety of participants is in question, the decision definitely should be in favor of new safety or protective equipment versus new jerseys or uniforms.

Selection should consider those persons with disabilities. Members of various special population user groups may need special types of equipment to participate in some of the activities that are a part of the physical education and sport program. Equipment may be needed for such aspects of the program as perceptual-motor activities or correction of postural deviations. For the most part, however, regular equipment can and should be adopted for those with disabilities, because the trend is to have students with disabilities integrated or "included" (inclusion) into as many regular classes as possible. This notion holds true with sport participation as well.

Dunn (1997) discusses equipment and supplies for special populations. Information about topics such as ordering and maintenance of equipment, safety, supervision required, and storage space is provided as well as a list of equipment suppliers.

Selection should consider acceptable standards for athletic equipment (Protective equipment 1985). The stamp of approval of the National Operating Committee on Standards for Athletic Equipment (NOCSAE) should be on football, lacrosse, baseball, and softball helmets. This seal will ensure that the helmet has been properly constructed and certified. NOCSAE researches sports equipment and encourages acceptable standards in manufacturing. They also distribute information about sport standards and safety to various organizations and individuals in the interests of safety, utility, and legal considerations. Furthermore, they provide an opportunity for individuals and organizations to study the problems regarding various aspects of sports equipment and how those problems can be solved.

Selection should consider trends in sports equipment and uniforms (Hart 1989). The emerging trends in sports equipment and uniforms also should be taken into consideration. Some significant changes include ventilated mesh cloth, wa-

Safety equipment such as helmets must be regularly inspected to meet acceptable standards.

Equipment and uniform selection should be up to date; University of Colorado, Boulder.

terproof and breathable Gore-Tex and similar materials, screen-printed lettering, and one-piece wrestling uniforms, not to mention the myriad fabrics (e.g., nylon filament, stretch nylon, spandex cotton, acrylic, polypropylene, and polyester). Additional accessories to basketball uniforms

(e.g., T-shirts might be worn under the uniform shirt and spandex tights under the pants) are also popular.

Developments in equipment are improving both safety and sport performance. Modifications in equipment ranging from ice hockey skate blades to composite tennis racquets and from eye protection to high-tech ski bindings have made continuous updating requisite to providing the most current, safe and effective equipment for the physical activity and sport consumer.

GUIDELINES FOR PURCHASING SUPPLIES AND EQUIPMENT

Purchases should meet the organization's requirements and have management approval. Each organization has its own policy providing for the purchase of supplies and equipment. It is essential that the prescribed pattern be followed and that proper management approval be obtained. Requisition forms that contain descriptions of items, amounts, and costs (figure 11-1), purchase orders that place the buying procedure on a written or contract basis (figure 11-2), and voucher forms that show date of receipt and the condition of materials received all should be used as prescribed by regulations. The physical education and sport manager and staff should all be familiar with and adhere to the purchasing policies of the organization and should be sure that their policies include standards such as those of NOCSAE and the U.S. Consumer Product Safety Commission.

Purchasing should be done in advance of need (Equipment innovations 1985). The majority of supplies and equipment for physical education and sport programs should be ordered in bulk and well in advance of the time the materials will be used. Late orders, rushed through at the last moment, may mean mistakes or substitutions on the part of the manufacturer. When purchase orders are placed early, manufacturers have more time to carry out their responsibilities efficiently and often better prices are available. Also, goods that do not meet specifications can be returned and replaced. Items needed in the fall should be ordered not later than the preceding spring, and

REQUISITION FORM
BLOOMINGTON SCHOOL DISTRICT 271

REQUISITION NO. 158236

ALL REQUISITIONS MUST BE TYPEWRITTEN

Name & Address of Vendor

SHIP TO: _____

Today's Date

Source of Price:
Estimate ☐   Catalog ☐   Contract ☐
Verbal Quote ☐   Written Quote ☐   (Attach copies of all quotes received)
Requisitions in excess of $1,000.00 require competitive written quotes.

Required Delivery Date

(Vendor Information Below This Line)

Quantity	Unit of measure	Catalog Number	Give complete information as to color, size, dimensions, copyright date, edition, etc. — state if book, film, magazine, etc.	Unit Price	Total Price Each
1.					
2.					
3.					
4.					
5.					
6.					
7.					
8.					
9.					
10.					

> ### PURCHASE REQUISITION
>
> Purchase requisitions are generally initiated by a school or department to cover requirements which are needed during the school year that are to be purchased from a supplier. Requisitions should be made in duplicate:
>
> 1. Original sent to business office for processing
> 2. Duplicate retained by initiating school or department

TOTAL

ADDITIONAL INFORMATION — (INFORMATION SHOWN BELOW THIS LINE WILL NOT GO TO VENDOR)
COMMENTS:

DIST.	SCHOOL & DEPT.	REQUESTED BY	DATE	PURCHASE ORDER	T	VEVDOR
271 4			39 44	45 50	51	52

G/E	FD	ORG	PRG	FIN	OBJ	CRS	C R	PURCHASE ORDER AMOUNT	P O C	B L T	C R	AMOUNT	T P 1	T P 2	INVOICE NUMBER	P T L
	9 10	11 13	14 16	17 19	20 22	23 25	26	27 37	36	26	27	37	38	58		68
						000										
						000										
						000										
						000										
						000										
						000										

Principal _____

District Administrator _____

PURCHASE ORDER
45   50

DATE OF ORDER
39   44

Figure 11-1. Requisition form.

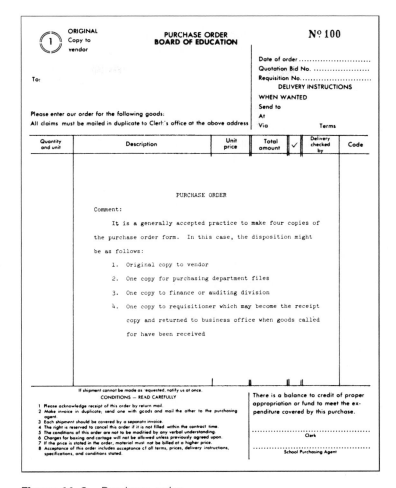

Figure 11-2. Purchase order.

items desired for spring use should be ordered not later than the preceding fall (see box titled Selected Management Goals Relating to the Purchase of Supplies and Equipment). Just after the postseason inventory is a recommended time to order new equipment. This early bird ordering as well as preday or early day plans may serve not only to save money but also establish a positive vendor relationship, which usually results in better service.

Supplies and equipment should be standardized. Ease of ordering is accomplished and larger quantities of materials can be purchased at a

saving when standardized supplies and equipment are used. Standardization means that certain colors, styles, and types of material are ordered consistently. This procedure can be followed after careful research to determine which are the best, most reliable, and most serviceable products for the money. However, standardization of supplies and equipment should never mean termination of further study and research to find the best materials to meet program objectives.

Specifications should be clearly set forth. The trademark or brand name, item serial number, catalog number, type of material, and other important specifications should be clearly stated when purchasing supplies, equipment, and other materials to avoid any misunderstanding of what is being ordered. This procedure ensures that quality merchandise will be received when it is ordered. It also makes it possible to objectively compare bids of competing business firms. For example, if a particular brand of baseball, basketball, or football is desired, the trademark, item serial number, and catalog number should be clearly stated on the bid form, along with a written notice that no substitutes will be accepted.

Cost should be kept as low as possible without loss of quality. Quality of materials is a major consideration. However, among various manufacturers and business concerns, prices vary for products of equal quality. Because supplies and equipment are usually purchased in considerable volume, a few cents per unit could represent a saving of many hundreds of dollars to departments and taxpayers. Therefore, if quality can be maintained, materials should be purchased at the lowest cost figure.

Purchases should be made from reputable business firms. In some cases, higher management authorities decide the firm from which supplies and equipment are to be purchased. In the event of such a procedure, this principle is academic. However, when physical education and sport personnel are determining the business firm from which purchases will be made, they are wise to deal with established, reputable businesses that are known to have reasonable prices, reliable materials, ample manufacturer-approved inventory for replacement, and good service. In the long run, purchasing from reputable companies is the best way to conduct business.

Direct purchasing is an expedient way of conducting business. Direct purchasing takes place when the school board, institution, or club enables the buyer (e.g., physical education teacher, coach) to purchase from whoever the buyer believes is the best supplier. Most schools or organizations have a direct purchasing policy limiting the buy to $100 to $500. The advantages of direct purchasing are that it is usually fast, local, and promotes good vendor relationships. The downside is that money may be directly handled and that favoritism and a higher price may result.

Central purchasing can result in greater economy. Some school districts and other organizations purchase supplies and equipment for several schools, school districts, or other groups. In this way, the purchasers can buy larger amounts at a reduced price per unit. In some cases, large school districts even go so far as to standardize their uniforms' colors, thus enabling them to purchase uniforms at lower prices. These systems also usually computerize their purchase orders,

---

Selected Management Goals Relating to the Purchase of Supplies and Equipment

- Try to standardize supplies and equipment as much as possible.
- Supervise the entire process of selection, specification, purchase, storage, and maintenance.
- Maintain an inventory (date purchased, date received, number, condition) of materials on hand (via computer database).
- Prepare specifications for items to be purchased.
- Secure bids for large purchases and those required by law.
- Decide on or recommend from where materials and supplies are to be purchased.
- Test products to see that specifications are satisfactorily met.
- Upon receipt, check supplies and equipment to determine if all that were ordered have been delivered and are in top condition. Inventory and date supplies and equipment.
- Expedite the delivery of purchases so that materials are available as needed.
- Seek new products that meet the needs of the program.
- Try to order NOCSAE and other approved equipment where appropriate.

contracts, and other records, not to mention their entire budgetary and purchasing process. Databases for maintaining inventory and equipment lists are also made immediately available. The physical educator and coach are called on for their valuable input.

Local firms should be considered. Management's main concern must be to obtain good value for money expended. If local firms can offer equal values, render equal or better service for the same money, and are reliable, then preference should be given to local dealers. In some cases, it is advantageous to use local dealers because they are more readily accessible and can provide quicker and better service than firms located farther away. Buying locally also makes for good public relations.

Bids should be obtained. A sound management procedure that helps eliminate any accusation of favoritism and helps obtain the best price available is competitive bidding. This procedure requires that special forms be distributed to the many dealers who handle the supplies and equipment desired (figure 11-3). These forms should

NOTICE TO BIDDERS

(For use in advertising)

The board of education of ___(legal name)___ School District

No. ____ of the Town(s) of _____ popularly known

as _____ , (in accordance with Section 103 of

Article 5-A of the General Municipal Law) hereby invites the submission of sealed bids on _____ for use in the

schools of the district. Bids will be received until _____ on the
(hour)

_____ day of _____ , 19 ____ , at _____
(date)   (month)   (place of bid

_____, at which time and place all bids will be publicly opened.
opening)

Specifications and bid form may be obtained at the same office. The

board of education reserves the right to reject all bids. Any bid

submitted will be binding for _____ days subsequent to the date of

bid opening.

Board of Education

_____ School District No. ____

of the Town(s) of _____

County(ies) of _____

_____
(Address)

By _____
(Purchasing Agent)

_____
(Date)

Note: The hour should indicate whether it is Eastern Standard or
Eastern Daylight Saving Time.

Figure 11-3. Sample notice to bidders form.

clearly state the specifics regarding the description (e.g., kind, make, model serial number), amount, and quality of articles desired. After bids have been obtained, the choice of vendor can be made. Low bids sometimes do not have to be accepted; however, a decision not to honor one must be justified. Such justification could be that a company's reputation is in question, the service rendered is poor, delivery cannot be made on time, or that the company is situated at such a great distance that communication and service are hampered.

Horine (1995) discusses the question of whether the competitive bidding process is desirable. He points out that this process sometimes increases costs, slows down the purchasing process, discourages bids from local dealers, and encourages dealers to cut corners in order to submit lower bids. Oftentimes the result leads to an inferior product being delivered.

Advantages of the bidding system are that it may stimulate honest competition, resulting in lower prices; it may promote on-time delivery; it can provide for better and more reliable service; it spreads the purchasing among more vendors; it eliminates favoritism; and it may reduce the risk of poor quality merchandise.

Gifts or favors should not be accepted from dealers. Some dealers and their representatives (reps) are happy to present management or staff members with a set of golf clubs, a nice training outfit, tennis racquet, or other gifts if, by so doing, they believe it is possible to acquire an account. In most cases, accepting such gifts or favors is poor policy. Accepting such a gift may place a person under obligation to an individual or firm and can result only in difficulties and harm to the program. A manager or staff member should never profit personally from any materials purchased for use in the programs. Therefore, such gifts or favors should be scrutinized carefully in light of professional ethics. Many vendors, of course, do leave sample items with the department to be tried and researched for further consideration.

Computers connected to centralized data banks help determine equipment needs as well as inventory.

At the high school level, sponsorships are now coming into play. This casts a gray area about the acceptance of free or discounted equipment and supplies. At the university level, however, large companies often have contracts with the administration or the coach to supply equipment. In this case, with approval of higher authority, gratis and reduced cost equipment may be received.

A complete inventory analysis is essential before purchasing. Before purchases are made, the amount of supplies and equipment on hand and the condition, including when these items were purchased, should be known. This knowledge prevents overbuying and having large stockpiles of materials that may be outdated or unsafe when they become needed. Inventories in some cases are taken periodically, whereas in other cases, computerization ensures that a perpetual inventory is maintained. In some organizations, inventories are taken at specified times, such as at the end of a sport season or semester or on an annual basis. In other organizations, the inventory is kept up to date on a continuing basis. Computerized inventories for departments, school districts, and other organizations are now in use in many places (Williams and Chiasson 1983). (See the box titled Steps in Purchasing Supplies and Equipment.)

Steps in Purchasing Supplies and Equipment

Need	Staff identifies need for equipment in program.
Consultation	Staff consults with management and grassroots personnel supporting need for equipment.
Initiation	A request is made for equipment to fulfill, augment, supplement, or improve the program.
Review of request	The proper management personnel approve or disapprove request after careful consideration of need. Sometimes the request is modified!
Review of budget allocation	A budget code number is assigned after availability of funds in that category has been determined.
Preparation of specifications	Specifications are prepared in detail, giving exact quality requirements, and made available to prospective contractors or vendors.
Receipt of bids	Contractors or vendors submit price quotations.
Comparisons	Careful evaluation is made to determine exact fulfillment of quality requirements.
Recommendations	The business manager prepares specific recommendations for approval.
Purchase order to supplier	After approval, a purchase order that fulfills the requirements at a competitive price is made.
Follow-up	Purchasing agent makes a follow-up inquiry if equipment is not received when due.
Receipt of goods	Warehouse receives goods, checks them against specifications, and returns purchase order with approval.
Payment	Purchasing agent and board of education approve purchase for payment, and accounting office pays.
Accountability	Goods are sent to the department that is held accountable for equipment.
User receives	Staff picks up equipment at designated place and inspects via safety audit before payment.
Inventory	Equipment staff inventories, labels, and stores equipment.

Maintaining an organized inventory is crucial to sound purchasing practices.

GUIDELINES FOR THE EQUIPMENT ROOM AND THE EQUIPMENT MANAGER

The equipment manager's position is very important. The money spent on uniforms, supplies, and equipment amounts to a large part of an organization's budget. Therefore, the person in charge of the equipment and supply room, whether a student or a paid employee, should be selected with care. A qualified person will be able to help make equipment and supplies last longer through proper maintenance, storage, cleaning, and care. Accountability for equipment will be better ensured because a system of good record keeping will be established and less equipment will be lost

```
┌─────────────────────────────────────────────────────────────────────┐
│                                                                       │
│                          EQUIPMENT ISSUE                              │
│                                                                       │
│                   Date .......................................        │
│                                                                       │
│   I .......................................................... have   │
│                                                                       │
│   accepted school property ........................................   │
│                                                                       │
│   ..................................( write in article and its number)│
│                                                                       │
│   and agree to return it clean and in good condition or pay for said  │
│   equipment.                                                          │
│                                                                       │
│                     Signed ......................................     │
│   Student I.D. #.................                                     │
│   Home Phone #........................ Home Address ................  │
│                                                                       │
└─────────────────────────────────────────────────────────────────────┘
```

Figure 11-4. Form for checking out physical education and sports equipment.

(figures 11-4 and 11-5). Also, a qualified manager will be able to make sound recommendations regarding the purchasing of athletic supplies and equipment. In light of such important responsibilities, the equipment manager selected should have qualifications that include technical equipment skills, organizational ability, computer skills, an interest in keeping equipment in excellent condition, an understanding of the care and maintenance of sports equipment and supplies, a willingness to learn, the ability to get along with people, trustworthiness, patience, the ability to supervise other people effectively, and communication skills. The equipment manager should also possess thorough understanding of the philosophy, goals, and objectives of the program and how this position fits in the total process.

The equipment and supply room is an important facility in physical education and sport programs. It is important to have sufficient space with proper ventilation to take care of the various purposes for which such a room exists (e.g., laundry, drying, storage). Space should be sufficient to store, label, and identify the equipment and supplies needed in the program. Adequate bins, shelves, and racks for equipment are needed. Space should be sufficient to permit movement

for handling the routine functions of issuing equipment and supplies. People working in the room should be able to move with ease throughout the facility. Space should be provided for drying equipment, such as football or soccer uniforms that have become wet when practices or games are held in the rain. The equipment and supply room should be well organized, secure, and a model of efficiency and sound organization.

GUIDELINES FOR CHECKING, STORING, ISSUING, AND MAINTAINING SUPPLIES AND EQUIPMENT

All supplies and equipment should be carefully inspected upon receipt. Supplies and equipment that have been ordered should not be paid for until they have been thoroughly inspected and inventoried as to amount, type, quality, size, and other specifications listed on the purchase order. Any discrepancies that are noted should be corrected before payment is made. This inspection is an important responsibility and should be followed carefully. It represents sound and prudent business practice in an area requiring business aptitude.

EQUIPMENT CHECKOUT RECORD

Player_____ Home Room_____

Address_____ Phone_____

Class_____ Height_____ Weight_____ Age_____

Parents Waiver_____ Examination_____ Insurance_____

- -

Football   Cross Country   Basketball   Swimming   Wrestling

Baseball   Track   Tennis   Golf   Softball

- -

	Out	In	Game Equipment	Out	In
Blocking pads			White jersey		
Shoulder pads			Maroon jersey		
Hip pads			White pants		
Thigh pads			Maroon pants		
Knee pads			Warm-up pants		
Helmet			Warm-up jacket		
Shoes			Stockings		
Practice pants					
Practice jersey					

I hereby certify that I have received the above-listed athletic equipment and will return same not later than the day following the last game of the season for the sport checked.

Signature_____

Figure 11-5. Equipment checkout record.

Supplies and equipment requiring organization identification should be labeled. Equipment and supplies are often moved from location to location and sometimes are part of an integrated or multiuser (e.g., physical education, recreational sports, community education) locker room system. It is a good practice to stencil or stamp inventory with the organization's logo in order to identify it. This identification system also helps to trace and locate missing articles, discourage misappropriation of such items, and determine what is and what is not departmental property.

Procedures should be established for issuing and checking in supplies and equipment. Considerable loss of material can result if poor accounting procedures are followed. Procedures should be established so that items are issued as prescribed, proper forms are completed, records are maintained, and all materials can be traced and located. Articles should be listed on the records according to various specifications of amount, size, or color, together with the name of the person or user group to whom the item is issued. The individual's record should be classified according to name, street address, telephone, locker number, social security number, student ID, or other information important for identification. In all cases, the person or persons to whom the supplies and equipment are issued should be held accountable.

In instances of multiple user groups, sound issuing procedures will enable management to track the amount of user time for each piece of equipment, which will not only justify the need for future purchasing considerations but also identify the user group budget that might be held accountable.

Equipment should be in constant repair. Equipment should always be maintained in a serviceable condition. This is sound preventive maintenance. Maintenance procedures for equipment should be routinized so that repairs are provided as needed. All used equipment should be checked and then repaired, replaced, or serviced as needed. Repair can be justified, however, only when the cost for such is within reason and when manufacturer's approved parts can be obtained. Supplies should also be replaced when they have been depleted.

Equipment and supplies should be stored properly. Equipment and supplies should be handled efficiently so that space can be properly organized for storing. A procedure should be established for identification and location, and proper safeguards should be taken to protect against fire and theft. Convenient bins, racks, shelves, hangers, and other accessories should be available. Temperature, humidity, lighting, and ventilation are also important considerations. Items going into the storeroom should be properly checked for quality and quantity before acceptance is confirmed. Cleanliness should also be requisite; many schools place the participant in charge of not only uniform cleaning but minor repairs as well. An inventory should be readily available for all items on hand in the storeroom. Computerization is strongly recommended for this function. Every precaution should be taken to provide for the adequate care of all materials so that investments are properly maintained and protected.

Garments should be cleaned and cared for properly. According to the Rawlings Sporting Goods Company, garment care has four catego-

Procedures for issuing and cleaning equipment should be developed to ensure a quality environment.

Equipment and uniforms must be properly cared for and stored.

Suggestions for Cleaning Sports Equipment

- The person responsible for cleaning should be informed about the need for special handling of the garments.

- Dry cleaning usually will remove dirt and stains but normally will not remove perspiration. Therefore, garments that can be cleaned by soap and water rather than by dry cleaning should be purchased.

- Garments of different colors should not be laundered together.

- Strong chemicals or alkalies should not be used because they will fade colors and may damage the material.

- Chlorine bleach should not be used.

- Water levels in washing equipment should be kept high if lower mechanical action is desired, but kept low if uniforms are badly soiled, to increase mechanical action. Do not overload washing equipment.

- When using a commercial steam press, it is recommended that garments should be stretched back to original size.

- Uniforms and other garments should be dry before being stored.

- Water temperatures above 120° F may fade colors and cause shrinkage.

- Specialized all-automatic athletic laundry facilities that are owned by the organization are recommended as a means of protecting garments against shrinkage, color fading, snags, and bleeding.

ries: (1) New garments should be kept in original packing boxes and stored in a cool, dry area with low humidity. (2) During the season, garments should be cared for immediately after a game. Before being sent to the cleaner, they should be inspected for tears or other defects and repaired immediately. (3) For away contests, garments should be packed for the trip and then hung up as soon as possible on arrival as well as on return. If an extended trip is being made, or if the trip home will not take place until the following day, the garments should be hung up for drying after each game. (4) Upon completion of the season, final cleaning, repair, and storage of the garments are crucial. If followed, proper cleaning and storing procedures will extend the life of the garments, help maintain attractiveness, and save time and money (see boxes on pages 346–347).

AUDIOVISUAL SUPPLIES AND EQUIPMENT

Audiovisual aids and materials have become an important part of physical education and sport programs.

A survey of 100 schools, colleges, and other sport-related organizations revealed that more than one-half used some form of audiovisual assistance in their programs. All the persons surveyed believed that audiovisual media are valuable supplements to instruction for acquiring motor skills and for encouraging and motivating people to be physically fit. The survey also revealed that videotaping and computer simulation are on the increase as instructional tools and that wall charts, slides, videocassettes, and instructional television were often utilized.

The most recent trends in the video realm, however, are computer simulation and the interactive videodisk. Computer simulation (e.g., golf and bowling) is beginning to earn its place in the classroom and gymnasium, while the interactive videodisk, which facilitates self-paced practice and learning, will most certainly have a tremendous impact on physical education and sport programs as the year 2000 approaches.

Reasons for Increased Use of Audiovisual Materials in Physical Education and Sport Programs

They enable the viewer to better understand concepts concerning the performance of a skill, event, game, and other experiences. Use of video, laser discs, graphics, or other materials provides a clearer idea of the subject being taught, whether it is how a heart functions or how to groove a golf swing.

Athletic Equipment Buyers' Almanac

MONTH	TYPE OF SPORTS EQUIPMENT			
	FOOTBALL	BASEBALL	BASKETBALL	TRACK
JANUARY	ORDER NEW EQUIPMENT	ORDER NEW EQUIPMENT	PRACTICE FREE THROWS	ORDER NEW EQUIPMENT
FEBRUARY	ORDER NEW EQUIPMENT	TIME IS RUNNING OUT		TIME IS RUNNING OUT
MARCH	ORDER NEW EQUIPMENT	DELIVERY	TAKE INVENTORY	
APRIL	TIME IS RUNNING OUT	MARK AND SAFETY CHECK EQUIPMENT	ORDER NEW EQUIPMENT	
MAY	PRINCIPAL'S RETREAT		ORDER NEW EQUIPMENT	ATTEND TAC MEETING
JUNE	ATTEND SCHOOL BOARD PICNIC	TAKE INVENTORY	ORDER NEW EQUIPMENT	TAKE INVENTORY
JULY	DELIVERY		ORDER NEW EQUIPMENT	
AUGUST	MARK AND SAFETY CHECK EQUIPMENT	ATTEND COUNTRY FAIR	TIME IS RUNNING OUT	
SEPTEMBER		SECURE METRODOME	DELIVERY	DELIVERY
OCTOBER		ORDER NEW EQUIPMENT	MARK AND SAFETY CHECK EQUIPMENT	MARK AND SAFETY CHECK EQUIPMENT
NOVEMBER	TAKE INVENTORY	ORDER NEW EQUIPMENT	FINAL FOUR MEETING	ORDER NEW EQUIPMENT
DECEMBER	ORDER NEW EQUIPMENT	ORDER NEW EQUIPMENT		ORDER NEW EQUIPMENT

■ ORDER NEW EQUIPMENT   ▥ TIME IS RUNNING OUT   ▭ YOU MAY BE TOO LATE

Management's Code of Ethics for Personnel Involved in Purchasing

1. To consider first the interests of the organization and the enhancement of the program.
2. To be receptive to advice and suggestions of colleagues, both in the department and in management, and others insofar as advice is compatible with legal and moral requirements.
3. To endeavor to obtain the most value for every dollar spent.
4. To strive to develop expertise and knowledge of supplies and equipment that ensure recommendations for purchases of best value and user impact.
5. To insist on honesty in the sales representation of every product submitted for consideration for purchase.
6. To give all responsible bidders equal consideration in determining whether their product meets specifications and the educational needs of the program.
7. To discourage and to decline gifts that in any way might influence a purchase.
8. To provide a courteous reception for all persons who may call on legitimate business regarding supplies and equipment.
9. To counsel and help others involved in purchasing.
10. To cooperate with governmental or other organizations or persons and help in developing sound business methods in the procurement of supplies and equipment.

They help provide variety to teaching. When audiovisual aids are used in addition to other teaching techniques, structures, and strategies, motivation is enhanced and the attention span is prolonged. The subject matter comes alive and is more exciting and meaningful.

They increase motivation on the part of the viewer. To see a game played, a skill performed, or an experiment conducted in clear, understandable virtual reality or graphic representation helps motivate a person to engage in a game, perform a skill more effectively, or want to know more about the relationship of physical activity to health. This motivation is particularly true in video replay or computer simulation, whereby a person sees how he or she performs a skill and then can compare the performance to a model program or movement pattern.

The recent innovation of the interactive videodisk carries the video concept one step further. Students not only view the video, but also are asked to respond to questions about strategies or skill execution. Correct responses allow the program to proceed whereas incorrect answers key the disk to repeat the learning sequence. This instructional strategy provides immediate feedback of results, is student-paced, and offers out-of-class learning options for students who need additional practice time.

They provide an extension of what can normally be taught in a classroom, gymnasium, or playground. Audiovisual aids enable the viewer to experience other countries and cultures as well as to view sporting events in other parts of the United States. All these experiences are important to the objectives of physical education and sport programs.

They provide a historical reference for physical education and sport. Outstanding and sometimes traumatic events (e.g., the 1972 Munich Olympics, Magic Johnson, Arthur Ashe, The Dream Team) in sports, physical education, and health that have occurred in past years can be brought to life before the viewer's eyes. In this way, the person obtains a better understanding of these events and the important role they play in our society as well as within the global village.

Guidelines for Selecting and Using Audiovisual Aids

Audiovisual materials should be carefully selected and screened before purchasing and use. Appropriateness for age and maturity level of students and others, accuracy of subject matter, technical qualities, inclusion of current information, cost, and other factors are important to ascertain before selecting audiovisual materials.

Instructional systems, including computers and audiovisual equipment, must be maintained and kept secure.

Management should see that the presentation of materials is carefully planned to provide continuity in the subject being taught. Instructors should select and use materials that amplify and illustrate some important part of the material being covered. Furthermore, audiovisual aids should be employed at a time that logically fits into the presentation of certain material and concepts.

Management should realize that slow-motion and stop-action projections are best when a pattern of coordination of movements in a skill or strategy is to be taught. When teaching a skill or strategy the physical educator or coach usually likes to analyze the various parts of the whole and also to stop and discuss aspects of the skill with the students.

Checklist of Selective Items to Consider in the Purchase and Care of Supplies and Equipment

	Yes	No
1. Selection of supplies and equipment is related to the achievement of the goals of physical education and sport programs.	____	____
2. Supplies and equipment are selected in accordance with the needs and capacities of the participants, including consideration for age, gender, skill, disability, and interest.	____	____
3. A manual or written policies have been prepared regarding the procedure for purchasing and care of all supplies and equipment.	____	____
4. Mechanics of purchasing such as the following are used: requisitions, specifications, bids and quotations, contracts and purchase orders, delivery data, receipt of merchandise, vendor invoices, and payment.	____	____
5. The relationship of functions such as the following to purchasing is considered: organizational goals, programming, budgeting and financing, auditing and accounting, property maintenance, legal regulations, ethics, and organizational philosophy.	____	____
6. Principles of purchasing such as the following are adhered to: quality, safety, quantity, storage, inventory, and salvage value.	____	____
7. A close working relationship exists between the department chairperson and school or college business manager or athletic and activities director.	____	____
8. Girls and boys provide and maintain their own equipment and supplies when appropriate.	____	____
9. Merchandise is purchased only from reputable manufacturers and distributors, and consideration is also given to replacement and the services provided.	____	____
10. The greatest value is achieved for each dollar expended.	____	____
11. Management possesses current knowledge and understanding of equipment and supplies.	____	____
12. Management is receptive to advice and suggestions from colleagues who know, use, and purchase supplies and equipment.	____	____

Checklist of Selective Items to Consider in the Purchase and Care of Supplies and Equipment—cont'd

	Yes	No
14. The director of physical education and athletics and activities consults with the business manager when supplies and equipment are needed and ordered.		
15. Regulations for competitive purchasing are followed.		
16. Supply and equipment purchases are standardized whenever possible to make replacement easier.		
17. Management is alert to improvements and advantages and disadvantages of various types of supplies and equipment.		
18. Brand, trademark, and catalog specifications are clearly defined in the purchase requisitions.		
19. Purchase orders are made on standardized school or institutional forms.		
20. Functional quality of merchandise and the safety it affords are major considerations.		
21. The inventory is used to plan for replacements and additions.		
22. Complete and accurate records are kept on all products purchased.		
23. New equipment and supply needs are determined well in advance.		
24. New materials and equipment are tested and evaluated before being purchased in quantity lots.		
25. New equipment complies with minimal safety requirements.		
26. Honesty is expected in all sales representation.		
27. State contracts are used when they are available.		
28. Management is prompt and courteous in receiving legitimate sales and business people.		
29. All competitors and vendors who sell merchandise are given fair and equal consideration.		
30. Gifts or favors offered by salespeople or manufacturers are refused.		
31. Materials received are checked with respect to quality and quantity and whether they meet specifications that have been indicated on school requisition forms.		
32. Prompt payment is ensured on contracts that have been accepted.		
33. All orders are checked carefully for damaged merchandise, shortages, and errors prior to officially signing for the shipment.		
34. Policies have been established for designating procedures to be followed when there is theft, loss, or destruction of merchandise.		
35. People who are issued supplies and equipment are held accountable for them.		
36. Inventories are taken periodically to account for all materials.		
37. A uniform plan is established for marking supplies and equipment.		
38. A written procedure has been established for borrowing and returning supplies and equipment.		
39. A procedure has been established for holding students accountable for school equipment that is not returned.		
40. Proper storage facilities have been provided for all purchases.		
41. Equipment is cleaned and repaired when necessary before replacements are ordered.		

Management should ensure that dependable, functional, and quality audiovisual equipment is purchased. Large capital outlays are required for audiovisual equipment and computers, whether used by equipment personnel or by staff and user groups. The new equipment should be compatible with that already used by the organization and should be secured and protected from the elements when not in use.

Management should carefully evaluate the audiovisual materials after they have been used. Whether materials are used a second time or purchased for the physical education and sport library should be determined on the basis of their value the first time they were implemented. Evaluation records should be maintained by the teacher, coach, media resource center, or other school or institutional personnel.

Management should see that equipment is properly maintained and repaired. Videotape players, computers, projectors, record and disc players, television and VCR equipment, and other materials need to be maintained in good operating condition and serviced on a regular basis. Using qualified operators ensures the longevity of equipment. An efficient and cost-effective audiovisual program and its accompanying staff development sessions are vital to every physical education and sport setting.

SUMMARY

Physical education and sport programs spend thousands of dollars on supplies and equipment in order to provide a meaningful and varied program of activities for their user groups. Because a large expenditure of funds is made for supplies and equipment, it is important that this management responsibility be carried out in a businesslike manner. Supply and equipment needs must be accurately determined, selection accomplished according to sound guidelines (e.g., user or organization needs and goals), and purchasing conducted within organizational requirements. Storage, security, maintenance, and repair of these items are also crucial to the effective and efficient operation of a well-managed physical education and sport program. The computer should be utilized in this vital management function.

SELF-ASSESSMENT ACTIVITIES

These activities will assist students in determining if material and competencies presented in this chapter have been mastered.

1. Why is supply and equipment management important, and what factors need to be considered regarding this management responsibility?

2. List and discuss five guidelines for equipment selection that should be followed before buying or tendering competitive bids.

3. Discuss the steps that should be considered in purchasing supplies and equipment.

4. Establish a job description for the position of equipment manager.

5. Prepare a management plan that you as chair of a physical education department would recommend for checking, issuing, and maintaining physical education supplies and equipment.

6. Prepare a volleyball lesson plan that includes the use of audiovisual aids and explain how and when audiovisuals could be used most effectively.

7. Design a model equipment room facility.

8. Construct a complete set of forms to assist a senior high school to purchase, maintain, and keep track of its athletic equipment.

    Construct models of the forms used by a senior high school to purchase, maintain, and keep track of the equipment softball team equipment.

REFERENCES

1. Buyers guide. 1991. *Athletic Business,* February.
2. Dunn, J. 1997. *Special physical education.* Dubuque, Iowa: Wm. C. Brown.
3. Equipment innovations: How they've changed the way we play. 1985. *Athletic Business,* January, 40.
4. Hart, K. 1989. Buying new uniforms. *College Athletic Management,* 1 (March) 8–10.
5. Horine, L. 1995. *Administration of physical education and sport programs.* Dubuque, IA: Brown & Benchmark.
6. Protective equipment: Getting the right fit makes the difference. 1985. *Athletic Business* March, 36.
7. Williams, H., and G. Chiasson. 1983. Computerized information retrieval: Options and issues for physical education and sport. *Journal of Physical Education, Recreation and Dance* 54:21–24.

SUGGESTED READINGS

Buyers guide. 1997. *Athletic Business,* February.
Provides a purchasing resource and reference base for physical education, sport, recreation, and fitness. Includes a facility specification guide, a manufacturers and suppliers directory, and a directory of associations to explore equipment purchase opportunities.

How to select and care for your wrestling, gym mats. 1982. *Athletic Purchasing and Facilities,* September, 60.
Shows how the materials and manufacturing methods that go into today's wrestling and gym mats have made tremendous gains. Also describes how the best mat will break down if not given proper care. Outlines several suggestions for keeping mats in good repair.

Jewel, D. 1992. *Public assembly facilities.* Malabar, Fla.: Krieger Publishing.
Presents various concepts and legal implications concerning care, safety, and maintenance of equipment.

Miller, G. 1991. A completion to purchasing. *College Athletic Management* 3(1):15–19.
Presents a procedure of setting goals and priorities, tracking performance, and power purchasing. Also explores various cost-cutting measures and multiple utilization of equipment.

Miller, L. K., L. W. Fielding, M. Gupta, and B. G. Pitts. 1995. Case study: Hillerich and Bradsby Co., Inc. *Journal of Sport Management* 9:249–62.

Presents views on just-in-time manufacturing, ordering, and purchasing concepts.

Raia, E. 1995. JIT in the '90s: Zeroing in on leadtimes. *Purchasing,* 12 September, 54–57.
Discusses the just-in-time concept revolution as well as *kanban* ordering.

Rosentsweig, J. 1984. Homemade strength equipment. *Journal of Physical Education, Recreation, and Dance* 55 (January):45.
Illustrates how homemade strength equipment can be inexpensively constructed. Provides a means whereby many organizations that cannot afford expensive strength training machines and devices can create and develop functional equipment on their own.

Stephenson, H., and D. Otterson. 1995. *Marketing mastery: Your seven step guide to success.* Grants Pass, Ore.: The Oasis Press/PSI Research.
Presents concepts on sales, purchasing, product images, distribution, and pricing.

Stauf, D. L. 1989. Anatomy of an efficient equipment purchasing system. *Athletic Business,* 13 (January):48–54.
Provides a guide to systematic purchasing procedures and policies.

Walker, M. L., and T. L. Seidler. 1993. *Sports equipment management.* Boston, Mass.: Jones and Bartlett.

Management and the Athletic Training Program

Instructional Objectives and Competencies To Be Achieved

After reading this chapter the student should be able to

- Understand and discuss the importance of a quality athletic training program and how it affects both the physical educator and the coach.

- Summarize the incidence of injuries among athletes.

- Understand the role of prevention and care of injuries in physical activity and sport programs.

- Discuss the qualifications, duties, and responsibilities of team physicians and certified athletic trainers.

- Discuss some risk management procedures that should be undertaken to emphasize safety in a school or other organized physical activity or sport program.

- Understand the functions and role of the certified athletic trainer.

- Identify the appropriate supplies that should be included in an athletic trainer's kit.

Throughout history, the profession of physical education and sport has had an intimate and complementary relationship with sports medicine and athletic training. Indeed, Michael Murphy, the famed University of Pennsylvania track coach and athletic trainer, authored the classic book *Athletic Training* in 1914; the American College of Sports Medicine (ACSM) was founded in New York in 1954 at the AAHPERD professional conference. This important relationship exists because the health and safety of students, student-athletes, and other user groups must be provided for by physical educators, coaches, directors of athletics and activities, and other members of the management team. The increasing number of participants in sports programs makes it particularly important to provide proper education, training, and conditioning; protective techniques; and other preventive measures to reduce the number of injuries that may occur in both physical education and sport programs. This chapter addresses the nature, scope, complementary relationship, and responsibilities of management in providing a quality athletic training program.

The number of athletes injured increases each year. One million sport injuries requiring hospital treatment occur each year; 50 percent of the 2.36 million girls and 3.6 million boys participating in interscholastic sport in 24,000 high schools will incur injury and one-sixth of these injuries will be time-loss classified (one to two lost days per year) (Stopka and Kaiser 1988). A survey by the Department of Health, Education, and Welfare (now known as the Department of Health and Human Services) reported that at least 111,000 serious sports-related injuries occur each year that cause students to miss three weeks of school or more; however, most injured athletes return to school within a few days of their injury (Whieldon and Cerny 1990).

Each year, more than 1 million boys participate in high school football, another 75,000 play at college, and still another estimated 300,000 participate in other community-based organizations (e.g., Pop Warner). An estimated 300,000 football injuries occur every year (39 percent of all varsity high school players). Injuries are caused by factors such as general trauma, illness, hazardous playing surfaces, and players returning to action before fully recovered from injuries (Arnheim and Prentice 1997).

Basketball has the second highest injury rate of all competitive sports. The National Athletic Trainers Association (NATA) projects that two

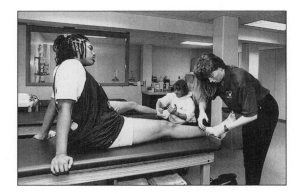

A student-athlete receives attention from a certified athletic trainer.

players on every high school team, regardless of gender, are likely to be injured. Injuries to the ankles and knees, stress fractures, and other serious contusions (hip, thigh, leg) are most prominent. In baseball and softball, most injuries occur to the hands, wrist, and arm (hit by the ball), and some injuries are caused by improper sliding techniques and spikes. With the tremendous growth of youth soccer, injuries in this sport have also increased. Lower extremity injuries (ankle and knee ligaments, fractures) are seen most often, while occasional heat exhaustion and dehydration also cause problems.

Chandy and Grana (1985) studied seven sports over a three-year period in 130 Oklahoma secondary schools. The study included 24,485 male athletes and 18,289 female athletes. The results revealed not only that female athletes had more injuries than did their male counterparts, but also that female athletes' injuries were more severe. Girls had injuries such as sprains and dislocations whereas boys sustained more strains and fractures. Knee injuries requiring surgery were more common among girls than boys. Of the sports studied, basketball had the highest injury rate.

Other research indicates that, with the exception of collision sports, in which males suffer more injuries, females seem to be more susceptible to injury. For example, female basketball player anterior cruciate ligament injury rates were three times higher than the rates of their male counterparts. The well-trained, conditioned female athlete is no more likely to sustain injury than is a male athlete (Rochman 1996). Therefore, to reduce the number of injuries, researchers recommend that a sound conditioning program be established to develop strength of the major muscle groups, particularly those muscle groups that protect the joints (Whieldon and Cerny 1990).

With the tremendous increase of individuals involved in physical education and sport (e.g., more than 6 million participants in interscholastic activities and more than 30 million children between ages 6 and 12 in out-of-school activities) and with subsequent reported and projected injury rates, the crucial need to provide quality sports medicine services at all levels of participation is evident. In 1990, The American Medical Association officially recognized athletic training as an allied health care profession.

Despite the well-documented need and crucial link between the professions of physical education and sport and athletic training, NATA reports that only 42 percent of the nation's 24,000 high schools provide certified athletic trainers for their programs (approximately 1:417 ATC (Athletic Trainer Certified): student-athlete ratio). The link and partnerships of the coach and athletic trainer are rapidly growing, because in 1988 only 10 percent of the nation's high schools provided such crucial services for its sports programs (Stopka and Kaiser 1988).

Although Division I and professional level sports are keeping pace with the needs of athletes (approximately 1:20–40 ATC: athlete), the picture in corporate and private sector physical education, sport, and fitness is, at best, dismal. NATA, however, projects that many certified athletic trainers will be filling this void as the year 2000 approaches (NATA 1988). The need and challenge are evident, and sound and prudent management practice mandates providing quality sports medicine services to all participants in physical activity and sport programs.

THE SPORTS MEDICINE MANAGEMENT TEAM

Although this chapter has strong implications for all persons who participate in physical education and recreational sport at all levels and ages, sports medicine services are especially important for student-athletes. It is therefore vital that the physical educator, coach, and athletic and activities director understand not only their role and responsibilities but also those of the athletic trainer in the overall scheme of their sport and physical activity settings. Not only does the growth of sport programs support this notion, but the legal community does as well. School systems and their coaches would be less likely to be held liable for injuries if a certified athletic trainer was

---

Sport Medicine Team Members

Physician team (general practitioner and orthopedic surgeon)
Athletic and activities director
Coach and physical education instructor
Certified athletic trainer
Sport psychologist/educator
School counselor/psychologist/social worker
Exercise scientist (physiology, biomechanics)
Dentist
Emergency medical technician
Nutritionist
Physical therapist
Chiropractor
School nurse
The athlete, family, and significant others

Source: Krotee 1997.

---

on staff. Even more crucial is the fact that contemporary management philosophy makes the individual student-athlete a high priority that mandates accessibility to quality sports medicine services. The complexities of student athletics (e.g., physical, psychological) and the rigor of training regimens, ranging from preseason to off-season, make it requisite that a team approach to total quality management of sports and sports medicine services be applied. This team approach includes all professionals who are concerned with enhancing the performance and health care of all participants engaged in physical activity and sport.

THE TEAM PHYSICIAN

A team physician must be selected with care. He or she must not neglect team responsibilities because of a growing practice or other commitments. The physician should remain objective and avoid being influenced by student-athletes, parents, and coaches. If a physician is needed and none is available, the local medical society, medical school, or HMO should be consulted for a recommendation of

The Team Physician's Duties

- Preparing and compiling medical histories of students, noting injuries and other health conditions.

- Examining athletes, reporting to coaches the results of such health status examinations, and making recommendations about whether the player can participate or under what conditions he or she can play.

- Supervising and advising athletic trainers and working with coaches, student-athletes, and parents in determining the best course of action to follow.

- Attending all games and also practices, if possible.

- Working cooperatively with the athletic trainer, coach, and the athletic and activities director in preparing emergency procedures.

- Examining, diagnosing, and treating all injuries and illnesses and making recommendations about the future play of the athlete. The player must receive the physician's approval to play.

- Providing time for students' queries regarding such matters as nutrition, conditioning, substance abuse, and injuries.

- Engaging in in-service self-education to keep abreast of the latest developments in prevention and care in sports medicine.

- Making recommendations to the athletic trainer and coaches regarding injury prevention, rehabilitation, and care.

- Verifying injuries when required for insurance, high school league, or NCAA purposes.

- Making recommendations about and helping to select and fit proper protective equipment.

- Working cooperatively with coaches, ATCs, and athletic and activities directors to promote and maintain a high level of health care for the student athlete.

The physician plays an important part in the sports medicine team.

Although it might be impossible to have a physician present for all sport contests, some suggestions for sport management in such cases might include the following:

- At contests or matches at which a physician cannot be present, have a telephone or beeper number where he or she can be contacted on short notice.

- Provide a certified athletic trainer.

- Refer the injured student-athlete to the family physician at parents' request. Have emergency contact number on file.

- Provide for emergency and ambulance service to the closest medical center emergency room.

- Prepare and keep on hand a complete athletic trainer's kit.

- Prepare and keep on file an accident report containing all essential injury-related information, including nature and extent of injury, date, time, place, and witnesses.

- Have medical prescriptions available for emergency treatment.

ATHLETIC TRAINERS

The importance of certified athletic trainers in sports injury prevention, education, treatment, and rehabilitation cannot be overlooked by management. It is unfortunate that in the secondary schools where athletic trainers are most needed,

one or perhaps several physicians who will jointly care for the team. A team dentist and physical therapist may also be identified in the same fashion. Some of the duties of the team physician are listed in the box titled The Team Physician's Duties.

they are poorly represented. Compounding this situation is the inadequate medical and injury prevention training of most coaches (i.e., 50 percent have not taken a first-aid course). Even if the coach has been well schooled in first aid and injury management, he or she simply does not have sufficient time to carry out both coaching duties and the responsibilities of an athletic trainer.

In 1980, 10.9 percent of public secondary schools had athletic trainers, but only 5 percent were certified by the NATA. Of the private secondary schools, 15.4 percent had trainers, but only 5 percent were NATA approved. On the college level, 16.1 percent of the two-year colleges had athletic trainers, but only 7 percent were NATA approved; 40 percent of the four-year colleges had athletic trainers, with 28 percent NATA approved. Those figures have improved because today NATA boasts more than 16,000 ATCs; however, many more are needed to bring the nation's junior and senior high school programs into the twenty-first century when it comes to providing quality health care for their student athletes. Only at major Division I colleges and universities and at the professional level do we seem to find acceptable athlete-to-ATC ratios (Booher and Thibodeau, 1994).

In the past the athletic trainer simply wrapped ankles and administered first aid to athletes. He or she usually had no special preparation for this role, but had learned through on-the-job training. Often such an individual had little scientific knowledge about the prevention and care of sports injuries.

Today, however, sports medicine and athletic training in particular has become a science as well as an art. The functions of the athletic trainer have become varied and complex, and the on-the-job-training philosophy, although crucial, is no longer all that is required. An explosion of scientific information about exercise, physiology, nutrition, biomechanics, sport psychology, and sociology as well as sophisticated rehabilitation and treatment equipment make it advantageous for the athletic trainer to have an undergraduate major in physical

A qualified NATA trainer looks after an injured student-athlete.

education, kinesiology, and/or sports medicine or athletic training with graduate work in physical therapy, athletic training, or sport management.

The qualifications for an athletic trainer (Arnheim and Prentice 1997) are both personal and professional. Personal qualifications include poise, good health, intelligence, maturity, emotional stability, compassion, cleanliness, ethics, fairness, and stamina. Professional qualifications include a knowledge of anatomy and applied physiology, psychology and sociology of sport, conditioning and training, nutrition, rehabilitation techniques, taping, methods for preventing injury, substance abuse, counseling, and protective equipment. Furthermore, the athletic trainer should have qualities that provide a harmonious and productive rapport with the team physician, coaches, sports managers, student-athletes, and the public in general. The athletic trainer must be able to practice good human relations as well as protect the student athletes' well-being. It is also strongly recommended that the NATA Code of Ethics be adopted (see appendix D).

NATA's basic minimum requirements for the professional preparation of athletic trainers are recommended by most experts in the field. These standards include graduating from an approved undergraduate or graduate program that meets specific criteria set forth by NATA or serving an

The Role of the Certified Athletic Trainer

- Prevention of athletic injury and illness
- Evaluation of athletic injury and illness including medical referral
- First aid and emergency care
- Rehabilitation and reconditioning under direction of a physician
- Organizational and administrative tasks (e.g., accident reports, injury records, etc.)
- Counseling and guidance
- Educational initiatives for coaches and student-athletes
- Help prepare training and conditioning programs
- Assist in selection and fitting of equipment
- Work cooperatively with coaching staff and medical team personnel

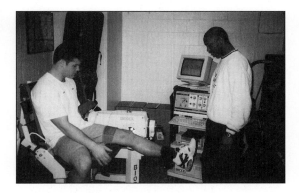

An athletic trainer assists in rehabilitation.

entails long hours, working closely with coaching staffs and other sports medicine personnel, and total commitment.

THE ATHLETIC TRAINING ROOM

Elaborate athletic training rooms and equipment are not always essential in sports programs. Indeed, most high schools do not have much in the way of a training room. A well-lighted and properly ventilated private room with an examining table, a desk, shelf space, phone, and a few chairs is the minimal requirement. However, a training room should be provided if possible, for it will serve both physical education and sport programs as a multipurpose place for first aid, physical examinations, bandaging and taping, rehabilitation, treating athletes, keeping records, and other functions concerned with the health of students, athletes, and staff members. The athletic training room should be near the dressing room, shower, and playing areas. A telephone, proper lighting, ice machine or refrigerator, whirlpool and, if possible, equipment for thermal and mechanical therapy, electrotherapy, and hydrotherapy should be provided.

internship that meets NATA specifications including coursework. NATA has voted to eliminate the internship option in the year 2004. Persons preparing for positions in athletic training must also be certified by NATA. To achieve this certification, they must have proper training and pass the NATA certification examination. Other important courses in preparing to be an athletic trainer (in addition to those previously mentioned) include kinesiology/biomechanics, first aid and safety, CPR, therapeutic modalities, psychology of sport injury, exercise physiology, health and disease, techniques of athletic training, psychosocial behavioral disorders (e.g., bulimia, anorexia nervosa), injury recognition and management, ethics, and communication.

Just as the traditional functions of the athletic trainer have changed, so has the opportunity for women to enter the profession. At present, 50 percent of the student athletic trainers involved in the athletic training educational process are women; NATA's female membership numbers 43 percent of its more than 16,000 members.

The athletic trainer's function is crucial and rewarding, but it is also very demanding and

If the sport program involves a great number of participants, special service sections or areas should be separated by low walls or partitions. For those institutions that desire more sophisticated facilities, separate sections would include those for taping, bandaging, and orthotics; thermal and mechanical therapy; electrotherapy; hydrotherapy; functional therapy (Swiss balls

A well-organized athletic training room is an important part of all physical education and sport programs.

and standard exercises). An assessment, reconditioning and rehabilitation area with equipment such as Cybex, Biodex, Kincom, treadmill and stair climbing machines, and stationary bicycles. Of course, there should be an area for storage so that adequate training supplies and well-stocked athletic training kits would always be readily available. The Checklist for Athletic Trainer's Kit box provides a list of requisite supplies for the athletic trainer's kit.

The athletic training room is crucial to any sport program. It is a meeting place, a safe haven for the student-athlete, and a place to share problems and gain counsel. The training room should be accessible, open, and staffed year-round and should be fully supported by management with the appropriate financial, physical, informational, technical, and human resources.

Checklist for Athletic Trainer's Kit*

		Activity								
Item	Amount	Football; Rugby; Lacrosse; Crew	Basketball; Volleyball; Soccer; Field Hockey	Wrestling	Baseball; Softball	Track; Cross-Country	Water Polo; Swimming; Diving	Gymnastics	Tennis; Squash; Golf	Ice Hockey
Accident reports		X	X	X	X	X	X	X	X	X
Adhesive bandages (1″ × 3″)	3 dozen	X	X	X	X	X	X	X	X	X
Adhesive tape										
½-inch (1.25 cm)	1 roll	X	X	X	X	X		X	X	X
1-inch (2.5 cm)	2 rolls	X	X	X	X	X	X	X	X	X
1½-inch (3.75 cm)	6 rolls	X	X	X	X	X	X	X	X	X
2-inch (5 cm)	1 roll	X	X	X	X	X	X	X	X	X

*Extra amounts of items such as tape and protective padding are carried in other bags.

Checklist for Athletic Trainer's Kit—cont'd

Item	Amount	Football; Rugby; Lacrosse; Crew	Basketball; Volleyball; Soccer; Field Hockey	Wrestling	Baseball; Softball	Track; Cross-Country	Water Polo; Swimming; Diving	Gymnastics	Tennis; Squash; Golf	Ice Hockey
Alcohol or iodine	4 ounces	X	X	X	X	X	X	X	X	X
Analgesic balm	½ pound	X	X	X	X	X	X	X	X	X
Ankle wraps	2	X	X		X	X			X	X
Antacid tablets or liquid	100	X	X	X	X	X	X	X	X	X
Antibacterial ointment	6 ounces	X	X	X	X	X	X		X	X
Antiglare salve	4 ounces	X			X					
Antiseptic powder	4 ounces	X	X	X	X		X	X	X	X
Antiseptic soap (liquid)	4 ounces	X	X	X	X	X	X	X	X	X
Aspirin, ibuprofen, acetaminophen tablets (with physician permission)	50	X	X	X	X	X	X	X	X	X
Butterfly bandages (sterile strip)										
Medium	3 dozen	X	X	X	X	X		X		X
Small	3 dozen	X	X	X	X	X		X		X
Contact case		X	X	X	X	X	X		X	X
Cotton balls (sterile)	1 ounce	X	X	X	X	X	X	X	X	X
Cotton-tipped applicators	2 dozen	X	X	X	X	X	X	X	X	X
CPR face shield	1	X	X	X	X	X	X	X	X	X
Elastic bandages										
3-inch (7.5 cm)	2 rolls	X	X	X	X	X		X	X	X
4-inch (10 cm)	2 rolls	X	X	X	X	X		X	X	X
6-inch (15 cm)	2 rolls	X	X	X	X	X	X	X	X	X
Elastic tape roll (3-inch)	2 rolls	X	X	X	X	X		X	X	X
Eyewash	2 ounces	X	X	X	X	X	X	X	X	X
Felt										
¼-inch (0.6 cm)	6 × 6 sheet	X	X	X	X	X		X	X	X
½-inch (1.25 cm)	6 × 6 sheet	X								
Flashlight or penlight		X	X	X	X	X	X	X	X	X
Flexible collodion	2 ounces	X	X	X	X	X		X		X

Checklist for Athletic Trainer's Kit—cont'd

Item	Amount	Football; Rugby; Lacrosse; Crew	Basketball; Volleyball; Soccer; Field Hockey	Wrestling	Baseball; Softball	Track; Cross-Country	Water Polo; Swimming; Diving	Gymnastics	Tennis; Squash; Golf	Ice Hockey
Foot antifungus powder	2 ounces	X	X	X	X	X	X	X	X	X
Gloves (latex)	2 pair	X	X	X	X	X	X	X	X	X
Glucose tablets	100	X	X	X	X	X	X	X	X	X
Heel cups/pads	2	X	X	X	X	X		X	X	X
Hydrogen peroxide	6 ounces	X	X	X	X	X	X	X	X	X
Insurance information		X	X	X	X	X	X	X	X	X
Instant cold pack	2	X	X	X	X	X	X	X	X	X
Liniment	2 ounces	X	X	X	X	X	X	X	X	X
Medicated ointment	2 ounces	X	X	X	X	X	X	X	X	X
Mirror (hand)	13	X	X	X	X	X	X			
Moleskin	6 × 6 sheet	X	X	X	X	X			X	X
Nonadhering sterile pad (3 × 3)	12	X	X	X	X	X			X	X
Oral thermometer	1	X	X	X	X	X			X	X
Paper and pencil		X	X	X	X	X	X	X	X	X
Peroxide	2 ounces	X	X	X	X	X	X	X	X	X
Plastic cups	1 dozen	X	X	X	X	X	X	X	X	X
Saline solution	6 ounces	X	X	X	X	X	X		X	X
Salt tablets	50	X	X	X	X	X			X	X
Scissors (tape, iris, cuticle)	1	X	X	X	X	X	X		X	X
Shoehorn	1	X	X	X	X	X			X	X
Skin lubricant	12 ounces	X	X	X	X	X			X	X
Sterile gauze pads (3 × 3)	6	X	X	X	X	X		X	X	X
Stethoscope	1	X	X	X	X	X	X	X	X	X
Sun lotion and block	12 ounces	X	X	X	X	X	X	X	X	
Tampon	2	X	X		X	X	X	X	X	
Tape adherent	6-ounce spray can	X	X	X	X	X		X	X	X

Checklist for Athletic Trainer's Kit—cont'd

Item	Amount	Football; Rugby; Lacrosse; Crew	Basketball; Volleyball; Soccer; Field Hockey	Wrestling	Baseball; Softball	Track; Cross-Country	Water Polo; Swimming; Diving	Gymnastics	Tennis; Squash; Golf	Ice Hockey
Tape remover	2 ounces	X	X	X	X	X	X	X	X	X
Tongue depressors	5	X	X	X	X	X	X	X	X	X
Triangular bandages	2	X	X	X	X	X	X	X	X	X
Tuff-skin	1 ounce	X	X		X	X			X	X
Tweezers	1	X	X	X	X	X		X	X	X
Underwrap or prewrap	2 rolls	X	X	X	X	X	X	X	X	X
Vinyl foam										
⅛-inch (0.3 cm)	6 × 6 sheet	X	X	X	X	X		X	X	X
¼-inch (0.6 cm)	6 × 6 sheet	X	X	X	X	X		X	X	
½-inch (1.25 cm)	6 × 6 sheet	X								
Waterproof tape (1-inch)	1 roll							X		X
Zinc oxide	6 ounces	X	X	X	X	X	X	X	X	X

MANAGEMENT'S RESPONSIBILITY IN ATHLETIC TRAINING

What is the management's responsibility in providing quality sports medicine services and preventing sports injuries? The first responsibility is to hire or subcontract, when possible, fully qualified and licensed physicians and coaches and certified athletic trainers who understand sports injuries and know how to prevent, treat, and rehabilitate them. These persons should be aware of the latest preventive measures necessary for sports safety. The American Medical Association's Committee on Medical Aspects of Sport and the National Federation of State High School Associations provide further elaboration on this topic, which may be found in the box titled Safeguarding the Health of the Athlete.

Other key elements of injury prevention are complete and thorough medical examinations, including blood and urine tests, for every athlete. Athletes who are immature physically, who have sustained previous injuries, or who are

Safeguarding the Health of the Athlete

A joint statement of the Committee on the Medical Aspects of the American Medical Association and the National Federation of State High School Associations.
A checklist to help evaluate five major factors in health supervision of sport.

Participation in sport is a privilege involving both responsibilities and rights. The athletes' responsibilities are to play fair, to train and to conduct themselves with credit to their sport and their school. In turn they have the right to optimal protection against injury as this may be ensured through good conditioning and technical instruction, proper regulations and conditions of play, and adequate health supervision.

Periodic evaluation of each of the factors will help ensure a safe and healthful experience for players. The checklist below contains the kinds of questions to be answered in such an appraisal.

PROPER CONDITIONING helps prevent injuries by strengthening the body and increasing resistance to fatigue.
1. Are prospective players given directions and activities for preseason conditioning?
2. Is there a minimum of 3 weeks of practice before the first game or contest?
3. Are precautions taken to prevent heat exhaustion and heat stroke?
4. Is each player required to warm up thoroughly before participation?
5. Are substitutions made without hesitation when players evidence disability?

CAREFUL COACHING leads to skillful performance, which lowers the incidence of injuries.
1. Is emphasis given to safety in teaching techniques and elements of play?
2. Are injuries analyzed to determine causes and to suggest preventive programs?
3. Are tactics discouraged that may increase the hazards and thus the incidence of injuries?
4. Are practice periods carefully planned and of reasonable duration?

GOOD OFFICIATING promotes enjoyment of the game and protection of players.
1. Are players, as well as coaches, thoroughly schooled in the rules of the game?
2. Are rules and regulations strictly enforced in practice periods as well as in games?
3. Are officials qualified both technically and emotionally for their responsibilities?
4. Do players and coaches respect the decisions of officials?

CORRECT EQUIPMENT AND FACILITIES serve a unique purpose in protection of players.
1. Is the best protective equipment provided for use in collision sports?
2. Is careful attention given to proper fit and adjustment of equipment?
3. Is equipment properly maintained and worn, with outmoded items discarded?
4. Are appropriate and safe areas for play provided and carefully maintained?

ADEQUATE MEDICAL CARE is a necessity in the prevention and control of injuries.
1. Is there a preseason health history and thorough medical examination?
2. Is a physician present at contests and readily available during practice sessions?
3. Does the physician make the decision as to whether an athlete should return to play following injury during games?
4. Is authority from a physician required before an athlete can return to practice after being out of play because of disabling injury?
5. Is the care given athletes by coach or athletic trainer limited to first aid and medically prescribed services?

inadequately conditioned are prone to sports injuries. Crash diets and dehydration (routinely practiced in wrestling and gymnastics) are injurious to an athlete's health and should be abolished. Train-

ing practices based on sound physiological principles are one of the best ways to avoid sports injuries. Of course, proper protective equipment must be used in appropriate sports. Facilities and

Water, rest, and sound training and conditioning procedures help prevent injury.

Athletic trainers assist in the design of sound training and conditioning programs.

equipment as well as educational curriculum (e.g., nutrition, substance abuse, behavior) must be developed with safety and health in mind, and sport safety and legal regulations must be reviewed. Research also must be conducted to improve and enhance all dimensions of the athletic training process.

Proper Conditioning of Athletes

Conditioning of athletes helps prevent sport injuries. This means preseason training as well as proper conditioning maintenance during the season. Certified athletic trainers, licensed educators, and coaches who know how to coach fundamentals and how to convey proper athletic training procedures are crucial to this process. Careful selection and fitting of equipment and protective strapping as well as counseling athletes about nutrition and rest also play an important part in the total conditioning package.

Conditioning exercises for athletics should be compatible with the athlete's capacity and fitness level and should include a warm-up, a progressive exercise routine both in-season and out-of-season, and special exercises to increase muscular strength and endurance, flexibility, and relaxation.

Protective Sports Equipment

Sports equipment that protects vulnerable parts of the athlete's body from injury is important, particularly in such collision sports as football, ice and field hockey, soccer, and lacrosse. For example, football helmets should be purchased in accordance with standards established by the National Operating Committee on Standards for Athletic Equipment (NOCSAE). The NOCSAE seal on a football, baseball, or softball helmet indicates that the manufacturer has complied with prescribed standards for protection of the head. Mouth guards and head or eye protection should be worn, when appropriate, in a number of sports (e.g., baseball, basketball, football, field hockey, ice hockey, squash, racquetball). Shoes and all other equipment should always be carefully selected to ensure proper fit, comfort, and maximal support and protection. Furthermore, proper equipment to protect the chest, ribs, elbows, knees, and shins is critical in certain sports (e.g., football, field hockey, lacrosse, volleyball, soccer).

Protective equipment must be tested for adequacy, must be maintained in good repair, and in essence be as good as new to prevent injury and avoid legal problems. The equipment, which, if possible, will be certified (e.g., Consumer Process Safety Commission, NOCSAE), should be selected with respect to the injury or potential trauma site (e.g., elbow pads in ice hockey), should fit properly, and should be continuously monitored and evaluated; educational information about its use should be effectively transmitted.

Taping, Bandaging, and Padding

Protective taping, bandaging, and padding can help prevent as well as provide care for injuries. Bandaging is needed at times to protect wounds from infection, to immobilize an injured area, to protect an injury, to support an injured part, to hold protective equipment in place, and to make arm slings and eye bandages. Padding and orthotic devices (e.g., usually made from malleable plastics such as polyethylene) are needed to cushion against injury, to restrict the athlete's range of joint motion, and to be used as foot pads. Orthotic devices can help in knee supports and shoulder braces. Taping, bandaging, and padding as well as shaping and fitting orthotic devices require special skill and knowledge.

Nutrition

Proper nutrition is important to the health of the athlete for physical fitness and stamina, for recuperation from fatigue, for energy, and for the repair and regeneration of damaged tissues. Athletes should include proper amounts of carbohydrates, fats, proteins, minerals, vitamins, and water in their diets. Substance abuse, eating disorders, stress, violence, and HIV are further examples of topics that should be presented in quality athletic training programs.

Ergogenic Aids

Ergogenic aids are supplements or agents that supposedly enhance sport performance. In other words, they are work-producing aids and are supposed to improve physical effort and performance outcome. They include drugs, food, physical stimulants such as caffeine and amphetamines, and even hypnosis. Some of these agents are questionable and unethical. The athletic trainer should be familiar with the ramifications of ergogenic aids as well as substance use and abuse.

Coaches, athletic trainers, and physical educators should endorse only ethically and morally sound training practices (Mangus and Ingersoll 1990). Under no circumstances should chemical substances, including over-the-counter (OTC) drugs (e.g., Doan's pills, acetaminophen, aspirin, diet pills), be administered to minor student-athletes for ingestion. Usually OTC first-aid preparations for skin wounds such as topical antibiotics are permitted, but the athletic trainer should refer to school policies.

Athletic trainers assist in measuring and fitting approved athletic equipment.

Protective equipment that fits well is crucial to all collision sports, including ice hockey.

Some athletic associations (e.g., NCAA, NF-SHSA) and sports medicine organizations have taken a strong stand against the use of agents or drugs that enhance performance through artificial means. Substances ranging from amphetamines (to reduce fatigue) to anabolic steroids (to gain weight and strength) and from dimethyl sulfoxide to crack cocaine and all illegal drugs have been placed on the banned substance list. The procedures and policies described in chapter 5 and appendix D fall well within the domain of those involved in athletic training.

SAFETY IN PHYSICAL EDUCATION AND SPORT

In light of the increased participation in physical education and sport, management must give attention to providing for the health and safety of persons engaging in these activities. Besides those maladies that might restrict active participation, injury to the participant is the paramount concern. Injuries are related not only to actual participation in these activities, but also to factors such as the equipment provided, conditions of athletic and playing fields, lighting, and myriad other factors associated with safe play.

Participatory growth in selected sports results in an increase in accidents and injuries. For example, during the 1980s there were an estimated 7.5 million racquetball players and more than 850 registered racquetball clubs. The increase in injuries to the eyes and the facial area was dramatic. Approximately 8,000 swimmers drown each year, and fatal or paralyzing football injuries, although not numerous, have increased. Injuries in basketball (640,755), bicycling (580,119), baseball (433,799), roller-skating (97,842), skateboarding (82,428), and now snowboarding, in-line skating, and women's ice hockey will all contribute to the estimated two million plus amateur athletes visiting U.S. emergency rooms each year. Given the large number of participants, especially the tremendous increase in girl's and women's sports and physical activities as well as accidents, the first risk management step should be to create an accident and injury policy that is prepared by each subunit involved in specific activities. Written policy has been a valuable tool not only in enforcing safety regulations but in lowering incidence of injury as well.

Another management recommendation is the appointment of an individual who will be responsible for the safety compliance program of the

The sports medicine team of the Pittsburgh Steelers consults daily on team injury status.

Helmets for bicycling, roller-skating, in-line skating, and skateboarding among other activities are commonplace and help prevent injury.

organization. In large organizations, such a position would pay for itself by reducing the accident rate and therefore the loss of production and other costs related to accidents and injuries. If a full-time professional cannot be employed, this responsibility should be assigned to a staff member (e.g., certified athletic trainer). This professional would have responsibilities such as developing policies and procedures, inspecting facilities and equipment, conducting safety research, developing educational materials, and reporting accidents to appropriate networks.

One such network organization that collects data on athletic injuries as related to consumer products is the National Electronic Injury Surveillance System (NEISS). Participating schools receive periodic reports about the number and types of injuries in various sports. The NCAA Injury Surveillance System (ISS) also provides its member institutions with injury data, as does the Big Ten Conference through its SIMS (Sports Injury Monitoring System) program. Another organization that is very much concerned with equipment standards and injury reduction in sports is the American Society for Testing and Materials (ASTM), an organization composed of manufacturers, consumers, and technical experts. One of the technical committees of this organization is NOCSAE. NOCSAE has a subcommittee concerned with helmets and face guards for sports such as football, baseball, softball, lacrosse, and ice hockey. ASTM also researches the number and types of injuries suffered by both male and female athletes. NATA sponsors a National High School Injury Registry (NHSIR). Developed in 1986, NHSIR also provides current and reliable data on injury trends in interscholastic sport. It provides a sport breakdown injury rate, both in practice and in game-related situations.

The development of a proper accident reporting system is another important management recommendation. According to the National Safety Council, a well-organized reporting system is essential to a safety program. The council points out that use of accident reports along with other systematic reporting helps prevent further accidents by getting at the causes of unsafe acts and unsafe conditions and by developing a program that results in the removal of such acts and conditions.

In schools, mandatory preparation of a school safety handbook is recommended. The handbook should contain specific guidelines for maintaining a safe physical activity and sporting environment, should identify individual responsibilities (e.g., student-athlete, parent, coach, athletic and activities director, certified athletic trainer), and should

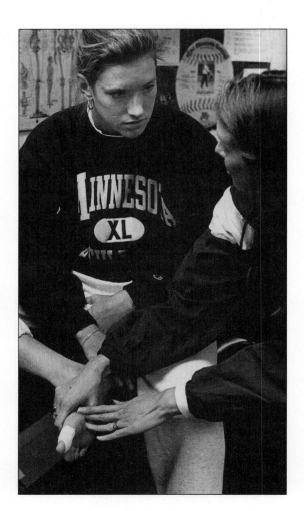

Certified athletic trainers do more than just treat injuries.

initiate and facilitate safety awareness and other creative risk management strategies.

A concluding management recommendation is the establishment of a safety committee. Safety committees have proved helpful in gaining organizational support for sound safety practices and awareness. The functions of such a committee are to develop procedures for implementing safety recommendations, to hold regular meetings for discussion of safety promotion, to conduct periodic inspections and safety audits, to investigate accidents, to recommend changes in equipment and the physical plant in order to eliminate hazards and reduce injury incidence, and to promote health and safety in all phases of the physical education and sport program.

SUMMARY

An important responsibility in physical education and sport management is to provide for the health and safety of participants. This responsibility requires establishing policies and procedures that will provide for proper sports medicine services, seeing that coaches have an understanding and skill in sound athletic training procedures, providing a full-time certified athletic trainer when possible, and ensuring that proper equipment and safe sport environs are provided.

The number of injuries that occur in sports programs today requires management to oversee the programs to make sure that sound sports medicine and athletic training policies, procedures, and practices exist so that such injuries are kept to a minimum and are treated effectively and efficiently. Risk management awareness and education are also crucial quality athletic training services and sound physical education and sport programs.

SELF-ASSESSMENT ACTIVITIES

These activities will assist students in determining if material and competencies presented in this chapter have been mastered.

1. Prepare an accident report that includes the nature and scope of the injuries that have just occurred at your junior high school volleyball match. Outline the procedures that were followed.

2. As a coach of a soccer team, what steps should you take in preventing injuries to your players? Describe the procedures you would follow if a player broke a leg in practice.

3. Discuss the role and relationship between one of the coaches at your university and the assigned certified athletic trainer.

4. Prepare a list of arguments to present to the board of education to justify the addition of a certified athletic trainer to the school staff.

5. List the desirable qualifications and functions of a certified athletic trainer.

6. Construct a risk management checklist for your university physical education department.

REFERENCES

1. Arnheim, D. D., and W. E. Prentice. 1997. *Modern principles of athletic training.* 9th ed. St. Louis: Mosby–Year Book.

2. Booher, J. M., and G. A. Thibodeau. 1994. *Athletic injury assessment.* 3d ed. St. Louis: Mosby–Year Book.

3. Chandy, T. A., and W. A. Grana. 1985. Secondary school athletic injury in boys and girls: A three-year comparison. *The Physician and Sports Medicine* 13(March): 106.

4. Mangus, B., and C. Ingersoll. 1990. Approaches to ethical decision making in athletic training. *Athletic Training Journal of the NATA* 25(4):340–43.

5. NATA (National Athletic Trainers Association). 1988. The future of athletic training. *NATA News* 1(1):5.

6. Rochman, S. 1996. Gender inequity. *Training and Conditioning* 6(5): 13–20.

7. Stopka, C., and D. Kaiser. 1988. Certified athletic trainers in our secondary schools: The need and the solution. *Athletic Training Journal of the NATA* 23(4):322–24.

8. Whieldon, T. J., and F. Cerny. 1990. Incidence and severity of high school athletic injuries. *Athletic Training Journal of the NATA* 25(4):344–50.

SUGGESTED READINGS

Avoiding aerobics injuries. 1985. *Athletic Business* 9 (March):10.
Discusses the fast-growing physical activity of aerobic dance and how overcrowded class conditions result in rising injury rates.

Buckley, W. L., R. Broxerman, and T. Lindey. 1996. Development for the athletic training profession: Where are we now? *Athletic Therapy Today* 1(1):23–26.

Clain, M. R., and E. B. Hershman. 1989. Overuse injuries in children and adolescents. *The Physician and Sports Medicine* 17(9):111–23.
Discusses the implications of overuse injury in young athletes in regard to growth plate damage, which can result in such problems as traction apophysitis and Little League elbow. Provides information about appropriate interventions that can prevent potential long-term complications.

Curtis, N. 1996. Job outlook for athletic trainers. *Athletic Therapy Today* 1(2):7–11.

Mathies, A. L., C. R. Denegar, and R. W. Arnhold. 1995. Changes in athletic training education as a result of changing from NATA-PEC to CAAHEP. *Journal of Athletic Training* 30 (June): 129–32.

Mueller, F. O., and C. S. Blyth. 1982. Fatalities and catastrophic injuries in football. *The Physician and Sports Medicine* 10 (October):135.
Compares football fatalities and injuries for the years 1976 through 1981 with earlier data, drawing implications for rule and equipment changes that have taken place since 1976.

Olson, J. R., and R. P. Bauer. 1984. Safety guidelines for gymnastic facilities. *Athletic Business* 8 (July):28.
Sets forth guidelines for a safe gymnastic program that includes maintaining constant supervision, conducting regular safety inspections, and making all repairs promptly.

Prentice, W. E. 1995. *Therapeutic modalities in sports medicine.* St. Louis: Mosby–Year Book.
Concerns the prevention, evaluation, management, and rehabilitation of athletic injuries.

Rankin, J. 1989. Athletic trainer education: New directions. *Journal of Physical Education, Recreation, and Dance* 60(6):68–71.
Presents a curriculum that provides prospective athletic trainers with a background in human performance as opposed to the traditional background in teaching.

Rankin, J. M., and C. Ingersoll. 1995. *Athletic training management: Concepts and applications.* St. Louis: Mosby–Year Book.
Provides a thorough overview of management concepts as they relate to the profession of athletic training.

Sports medicine groups of 1990. 1990. *The Physician and Sports Medicine* 18:131–42.
Provides a comprehensive listing of professional organizations and resource groups. References more than forty organizations and twenty-one groups including government agencies, sport federations, and statistic gathering groups.

Wilmore, J. H., and D. L. Costill. 1995. *Physiology of sport and exercise.* Champaign, Ill.: Human Kinetics.
Provides the sport practitioner, coach, athlete, certified athletic trainer, and team physician with a basic understanding of physiological principles underlying physical conditioning and performance in physical education and sport.

chapter 13

Legal Liability, Risk, and Insurance Management

Instructional Objectives and Competencies To Be Achieved

After reading this chapter the student should be able to

- Define each of the following terms: *legal liability, tort, negligence, in loco parentis, save harmless, assumption of risk, attractive nuisance, immunity, risk management,* and *insurance management.*

- Indicate the legal basis for physical education programs throughout the United States and the implications that this legal basis has for making physical education a requirement for all students.

- Discuss recent court interpretations regarding sport product liability, violence, and physical education activities held off campus.

- Describe what constitutes negligent behavior on the part of physical educators and coaches and what constitutes defense against negligence.

- Identify common areas of negligence in the conduct of physical education and sport programs, and explain what can be done to eliminate such negligence.

- Appreciate the relationship of Title IX to legal liability in the conduct of physical education and sport programs.

- Discuss precautions that physical educators can take to prevent accidents and provide for the safety of students and other individuals who participate in their programs.

- Recommend sound risk and insurance management plans for physical education and sport programs.

Among the most important management responsibilities of physical education and sport programs is conducting programs within limits provided by legislation and the law. Unlike other programs that relate to academic pursuits, physical education and sport programs take place in a variety of high-risk settings in which injuries

may occur. Therefore, every effort must be taken to provide preventive safety measures (i.e., risk assessment) that will keep such injuries to a minimum. These measures include hiring competent, qualified, and certified personnel to plan, conduct, and oversee programs and activities; purchasing approved and quality equipment;

Physical activity and sport injuries can lead to questions of legal liability.

The tremendous increase in participation in all physical education and sport endeavors across the Physical Activity and Sport Continuum (e.g., youth sport, increased women's participation, lifetime sport, health and fitness clubs and resorts, Sport for All) concomitant with our contemporary legal climate makes it requisite that all physical education and sport professionals be knowledgeable of not only injury incidence reduction but also the legal ramifications that are intimately interwoven with the profession (e.g., program, facilities, equipment, supervision, and safety policies).

That professional awareness must be increased is evidenced by the facts that physical educators are involved in more than 50 percent of the injuries sustained by students each year and that approximately 65 to 70 percent of all school jurisdiction accidents involving boys and 59 to 65 percent of those involving girls occur in physical education and sport-related programs. Furthermore, millions of boys and girls and adults will continue to participate in physical activity; an estimated 1 out of 30 to 35 students attending school will be injured; millions of people are involved in the public and private sector as well as in corporate- and community-based physical education and sport programs in which accidents and injuries will occur. These facts mandate that physical educators, athletic and activity directors, and coaches be more than just familiar with the topic of liability.

When an accident resulting in personal injury occurs, the question often arises about whether damages can be recovered. All employees run the risk of being sued by injured persons on the basis of alleged negligence that caused physical injury. Such injuries occur in playgrounds, sports fields (including the stands), parks, ski areas, golf courses, gymnasiums, arenas, fitness laboratories, and the myriad places where physical education and sport activities take place.

The legal rights of the individuals involved in such cases are worthy of study. Although the law varies from state to state and case to case, it is possible to discuss liability in a way that has implications for most settings in which physical

providing facilities and play areas that are safe and well maintained; and acquiring and recommending appropriate liability insurance to protect participants and personnel as well as the institution, organization, or program. Establishing procedures for skill progression, health status, and use of protective gear; educating the students to the risk of the activity; and selecting opponents to avoid dangerous mismatches are also factors to be fully considered. This chapter explores those aspects of legal liability, risk, and insurance management that are pertinent to the prudent management of physical education and sport programs.

According to *Black's Law Dictionary,* liability is the responsibility, the state of one who is bound in law and justice to do something which may be enforced by action (Black 1990). Other definitions describe liability as the condition of affairs that gives rise to an obligation to do a particular thing to be enforced by court action (Baley and Matthews 1984; Clement 1989; Kaiser 1986).

Most injuries in schools occur in physical education classes.

educators and coaches work.* First, it is important to understand the legal basis for physical education and sport and for those domains that fall under the Physical Activity and Sport Continuum that was presented in chapter 1.

LEGAL LIABILITY IN PHYSICAL EDUCATION AND SPORT

Physical education and sport legal liability cases show several trends over the last decade. Some experts have pointed to increased availability of legal services (e.g., more lawyers, contingency fees), a public more sophisticated about their legal rights, the modification of the doctrine of governmental immunity (e.g., state and local governments can now be sued), a public attitude that groups such as insurance companies and schools have endless sources of revenue, and the movement (approximately 39 states) toward the doctrine of comparative rather than contributory negligence, wherein prorated settlements evolve between litigious parties, as the main reasons for increased legal action. Other contributory litigious trends that directly affect physical education and sport management include litigation involv-

ing discrimination in respect to persons with disabilities, Title IX related cases, and increased legal negligence or foreseeability cases wherein participants were not properly warned that injury could result from their participation (Baley and Matthews 1984).

Some years ago the courts recognized the hazards involved in the play activities that are a part of the educational program. A boy sustained an injury while playing tag. The court recognized the possibility and risk of some injury in physical education programs and would not award damages. However, it pointed out that care must be taken by both the participant and the authorities in charge. It further implied that the benefits derived from participating in physical education activities such as tag offset the risk that occasional injury might occur.

The decision regarding the benefits derived from participating in physical education programs was handed down at a time when the attitude of the law was that no governmental agency (e.g., federal, state, local, public school, or college) could be held liable for the acts of its employees unless it so consented. Since that time, a changing attitude in the courts has been evident. The immunity derived from the old common-law rule that "the King or Sovereign could do no wrong" (*Russell v. Men of Devon,* 100 Eng. Rep 359 [1788]) and that a government agency cannot be sued without its consent is changing so that federal, state, and local governments may be sued (Kaiser 1986).

In 1959, the Illinois Supreme Court (*Molitor v. Kaneland Community Unit,* District No. 302, 163 NE 2d 89) overruled the immunity doctrine. The supreme courts of Wisconsin and Arizona and the Minnesota legislature followed suit; however, in 1963, the Minnesota legislature restored the rule but provided that school districts that had liability insurance were responsible for damages up to the amount of coverage. The principle of governmental immunity has also been put to the test in courts in Colorado, Iowa, Kansas, Montana, Oregon, Pennsylvania, and Utah. However, the courts in some of these states have been hesitant to depart from the precedent and insist

---

*If a legal issue does arise, seeking advice from the school, institutional, or association legal counsel or hiring a private attorney is recommended.

that the legislature of the state rather than the courts should waive the rule.

In some incidences, immunity has been upheld. In the case of *Cerrone v. Milton School District,* 479 A. 2d 675 (Pa. 1984), Cerrone received an injury while wrestling in high school. As a result of a suit against the Milton School District in Pennsylvania, the court ruled that the school district was immune from suit as provided by the Tort Claims Act (Appenzeller and Ross 1985). In another case, *Kain v. Rockridge Community Unit School District #300,* 453 NE 2d 118 (Ill. 1983), a football coach was granted immunity when Kraig Kain sued the Rockridge Community Unit School District for alleged negligent conduct by the coach, who let him play in a game without observing the required number of practices before participation (Appenzeller 1983b).

In most cases, governmental immunity has been modified, abrogated, or subjected to exceptions by either legislation or judicial decision. Schools and school districts may legally purchase liability insurance (many states expressly authorize school districts to carry liability insurance) to protect themselves when they become involved in lawsuits, although this insurance does not necessarily mean governmental immunity has been or will be waived. Of course, in the absence of insurance and save harmless laws (laws requiring that school districts assume the liability of the teacher whether negligence is proved or not), any judgment rendered against a school district must be met out of personal funds. School districts in Connecticut, Massachusetts, New Jersey, and New York have save harmless laws. Wyoming also permits school districts to indemnify or financially protect employees.

A strong belief exists among educators and many people in the legal profession that the doctrine of sovereign immunity should be abandoned. In some states, students injured as a result of negligence are ensured recompense for damages directly or indirectly, either because governmental immunity has been abrogated or because school districts are legally required to indemnify school employees against financial loss. In other states, if liability insurance has been secured, a possibility exists that students may recover damages incurred.

Although school districts have been granted governmental immunity in many states, teachers do not have such immunity. A 1938 decision of an Iowa court provides some of the thinking regarding teachers' responsibilities for their own actions (*Montanick v. McMillin,* 225 Iowa 442, 452–453, 458, 280 NW 608 [1938]):

> [The employee's liability] is not predicated upon any relationship growing out of his [her] employment, but is based upon the fundamental and underlying laws of torts, that he [she] who does injury to the person or property of another is civilly liable in damages for the injuries inflicted . . . The doctrine of *respondeat superior,* literally, "let the principle answer," is an extension of the fundamental principle of torts, and an added remedy to the injured party, under which a party injured by some act of misfeasance may hold both the servant and the master liable. The exemption of governmental bodies and their officers from liability under the doctrine of *respondeat superior* is a limitation of exception to the rule of *respondeat superior* and in no way affects the fundamental principle of torts that one who wrongfully inflicts injury upon another is liable to the injured person for damages. . . . An act of misfeasance is a positive wrong, and every em-

Signs with rules are important for activity areas.

ployee, whether employed by a private person or a municipal corporation, owes a duty not to injure another by a negligent act of commission.

Factors and Special Situations That Influence Legal Liability

Sports managers, teachers, and coaches have the responsibility and the duty to be aware of salient factors and special situations that can lead to litigation. Some potential litigious factors include: ignorance of the law, ignoring the law, failure to act, failure to warn, and time and expense (Lewis and Appenzeller 1985). Failing to provide accessibility for persons with disabilities to programs, ignoring Title IX mandates concerning equal opportunity, failure to check facilities and equipment on a regular basis, omitting warning and hazard signs or failing to issue warning statements during strenuous and potentially hazardous activities, and failure to properly repair and regularly inspect equipment are domains of litigation that have produced individual awards in excess of $1 million.

Most often, the physical educator, coach, or athletic and activities director is responsible for many of the ministerial or operational acts cited. This notion was upheld in the Michigan Court of Appeals in *Ross v. Consumer Power Company* (1984), in which it was contended that individual government employees are immune from liability only when they are

1. Acting during the course of their employment, and are acting, or reasonably believe that they are acting, within the scope of their authority
2. Acting in good faith
3. Performing discretionary-decisional, as opposed to ministerial-operational, acts

Hence, when a student in a beginning swimming class, as in *Webber v. Yio,* 383 NW 2d 230 (1985), dove into a pool and failed to surface, and efforts to revive him failed, the court held that the system of rescue was a discretionary act for which the instructor was immune from liability; however, the instructor's failure to warn participants about the danger and risks of the activity and the negligent supervision and resuscitation

procedures were ministerial acts for which the instructor may be held liable (Clement 1989).

The courts have also heard legal liability cases dealing in such areas as sport product liability, violence, travel, and off-campus physical education and sport activities.

Sport Product Liability

The sale of sporting goods is a multi-billion-dollar industry. As a result, the subject of sport product liability has arisen. The term *sport product liability,* according to Baley and Matthews (1984), refers to the liability of the manufacturer, processor, seller, lessor, or anyone furnishing a product to the person who uses the manufactured product and who sustains injury or damage as a result of using the product. Physical educators, coaches, and athletic and activities directors are being named as codefendants in approximately one-third of all sport product liability suits.

In the past, the buyer was responsible for inspecting the product before making the purchase. He or she assumed the risk of injury or damage to property. Today, however, the courts are placing more and more responsibility on the manufacturer to provide a reasonable standard of product to the market and to discover weaknesses and defects in the product. It is reasoned that the manufacturer or seller is in a better position than the consumer to become aware of, and to correct or eliminate, the defect. The manufacturer is required to exercise due care in designing, manufacturing, providing directions for specific use, and packaging labeling (e.g., warning labels if appropriate) of the product, including making available new replacement parts. The manufacturer guarantees the product to be safe for consumer use if the product is used in the specific way it was intended. Failure to do so is negligence in product liability. Therefore, when a high school student athlete was injured by a pitching machine whose manufacturer failed to include operating instructions, as in *Schmidt v. Dudley Sports Co.,* 279 NE 2d Indiana Court of Appeals, 2d Dist., 266 (1972), the jury found the company negligent.

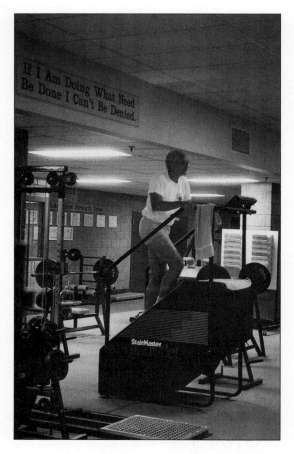

Careful selection of quality equipment keeps potential product liability suits to a minimum.

An estimated forty-two states have used the strict liability doctrine for some products (product liability litigation, Arnold 1978). Under this doctrine, the plaintiff must establish proof that the product contained a defect causing the injury or damage. In addition to this doctrine, a breach of the manufacturer's warranty in which the product or object fails to function according to its written specifications can also be just cause for awarding damages. A breached warranty does not require the injured party to prove negligence or recklessness.

The number of suits involving product liability has increased dramatically in the last few years. One reason is the possibility of large monetary settlements, especially in football cases in which an injury has occurred. Frequent targets of product liability litigation include the manufacturers of helmets, diving boards, flooring, and gymnastics and exercise equipment. These large awards result in skyrocketing insurance rates that are passed on to the institution, organization, user, or sport consumer.

Sporting goods manufacturers are now calling for a national product liability standard that would stabilize the rules under which they operate. However, legislators are having difficulty finding a solution acceptable to both consumers and business. At present the lack of certainty about how cases will be treated contributes to the high cost and the availability of product liability insurance (see the box titled Reducing the Risks Associated with Sport Product Liability).

Violence and Legal Liability

An increasing number of injuries that occur in sport contests are not accidental but intentional. These acts are referred to as intentional torts (e.g., assault, battery, reckless misconduct), and involve the harmful, unpermitted contact of one person by another. Awards for violence in sport, such as the case of the professional basketball player who was punched in the face and was awarded $3.3 million in damages, capture the headlines; however, reckless misconduct is also evident in cases ranging from *Nabozny v. Barnhill,* 31 Ill. App. 3d 212 (1975), in which a goalie was kicked in the head during a high school soccer match, to *Oswald v. Township High School District,* 84 Ill. App. 3d 723 (1980), in which a student sued another student for kicking him while participating in a physical education basketball class.

The coach or teacher is not necessarily free from liability in such cases of violence. Carpenter and Acosta (1980) cite two theoretical situations in which the coach may be held liable. The first situation is when a coach knows a player is likely to commit a violent act in a sport-specific situation, but still inserts the player into the lineup. In this case, the coach is not taking the necessary precautions to protect opponents from harm and

Reducing the Risks Associated with Sport Product Liability

- Become involved in collecting pertinent facts and information associated with illness and injury. This procedure can result in discouraging unwarranted claims.

- Purchase the best quality equipment available. Equipment should be carefully evaluated and tested. When equipment is purchased, records should be kept regarding such items as date of purchase, parts list, assembly directions, and operating instructions. Also, reconditioned and repaired items should be recorded.

- Purchase only from reputable dealers. Reputable dealers stand behind their products and provide replacements when called for.

- Use only reputable reconditioning equipment companies that have high standards. For example, the NOCSAE stamp of approval should apply to reconditioned football and lacrosse helmets.

- Follow manufacturer's instructions for fitting, adjusting, and repairing equipment, particularly protective equipment. Also, urge participants to wear protective equipment regularly.

- Be careful not to blame someone or something for the injury without just cause. Furthermore, it is best to confine such remarks to the accident report.

- Good teaching and supervising are important. Do not use any drills or techniques not approved by professional associations and respected leaders in the field.

- An emergency care plan should be prepared and ready to be implemented when needed.

- Insurance coverage for accident and general liability should be purchased or be available to all parties concerned, including students, athletes, staff members, and schools.

- When and if serious injuries occur, preserve items of evidence associated with the injury, such as pieces of equipment.

Adapted from Arnold DE: *Journal of Physical Education and Recreation 49;* 25, Nov/Dec 1978.

injury, and in the event injury occurs, the coach may be found negligent. The second situation is when a coach may instruct a player "to take Player X out of the game." In this case, the player who follows such an instruction is acting as an agent of the coach; as a result, a person who causes battery to be committed (in this situation, the coach) is just as negligent as the player who commits the act. In incidents such as these, which too frequently occur in the sporting process, coaches need to exercise common sense and sound ethical judgment to ensure that they and their team will conduct themselves in accordance with the proper standards, rules, and spirit of the game.

Off-Campus Activities and Legal Liability

Off-campus physical education and sport course offerings have become popular in many communities, schools, and colleges. In such cases, instruction in the activity may be provided by faculty members, or faculty members may provide only limited supervision, with the activity being instructed by a specialist not associated with the organization, school, or university. In fact, no faculty or staff member may even be present on a regular basis during the conduct of the off-site activity.

Although instruction may take place in off-campus settings by nonfaculty members, considerable responsibility and control still rests with the management and staff members of the organization sponsoring these activities. Arnold (1979) cites the case of a college that had a person not affiliated with the college teach a course at an off-campus equestrian center. The plaintiff was injured in a fall from a horse while receiving instruction. The plaintiff's attorney argued that the college was vicariously liable for the negligence of the riding academy. The court's ruling went in favor of the college, which did not have to pay damages on the grounds that a master-servant relationship did not exist between the plaintiff and the college. To show such a relationship, the plaintiff would have had to prove that,

Off-campus activities such as rock climbing and canoeing add increased risk to physical education programs.

among other things, the college could control the instruction taking place. Furthermore, the court ruled that the agency relationship did not result in the college authorizing the fall leading to the injury and that no complaints had been supplied regarding the instruction given.

When off-campus physical education activities are conducted (bowling, skiing, sailing, sport climbing, swimming), it is of primary concern whether due care is provided. The type of activity offered would indicate the amount of care that should be provided. For example, conducting a bowling class in a town bowling alley may not require as much care in most cases as an alpine skiing class. It is the responsibility of the organization and its management to exercise care and prudence in selecting the sites to be used for off-campus activities, providing quality personnel to see that proper instruction is being given, and ensuring that proper supervision is provided.

Required Physical Education

One legal implication for schools is that of requiring students to enroll in physical education classes. The schools should be flexible enough to provide alternatives for those cases in which activities such as dancing or swimming may be against a participant's sociocultural principles or religion.

Supervision

Legal experts estimate that almost 80 percent of all court cases concerning sports injuries deal with some dimension of supervision. Whether

Proper supervision is required for safe participation in physical activity and sport.

checking on the health status of the participant or managing a weight room or teaching a physical education class, supervision is vital. In Michigan, a high school principal and athletic director were sued for allegedly breaching their duty to a fifteen-year-old boy who was severely injured when weights fell on him (*Vargo v. Svitchan,* 301 NW 2d 1 [Mich. 1981]). The boy accused the administration of negligence for failing to supervise his coach, to provide for proper ventilation in the weight room, and to observe rule violations for illegal summer football practice. The boy further charged the school's athletic director with negligence for failing to supervise the sports program. The Michigan court noted that the athletic director had the responsibility of enforcing the rules and supervising activities because of his

specialized training in sports. It also reasoned that the athletic director had the authority to eliminate unsafe practices engaged in by the coaches under his direction.

Human Resources

Although covered in chapter 7, human resource issues deserve another mention. Too often management employs unqualified and incompetent personnel to support their programs. Sometimes management, especially in off-campus activities and in the fitness (e.g., aerobics instructors, personal trainers) and recreation areas, incorrectly classify employees by assigning them independent contractor status. The proper classification of employees has serious liability implications. Personnel reflect directly on management in all settings, and the courtroom is no exception. Management—whether at the school, college, or corporate level, whether it's hiring volunteer youth coaches or fitness club personnel—retains the responsibility and liability to provide competent, certified, properly classified, and well-trained human resources, that is, teachers, coaches, instructors, and supervisory personnel.

Equipment, Facilities, and Physical Plant

Those people responsible for the conduct of physical education and sport programs should set policies and procedures for the inspection of equipment, facilities (including floors and arena and field conditions), and other associated physical plant systems (e.g., pool filters, heating, ventilation). Safety audits and periodic inspections, maintenance, repair, and status reports should all be included on a database file. Names, areas, times, places, purchase and requisition orders, serial and catalog numbers, and manufacturers' warnings and operating guides should all be a matter of record.

It is hoped that these legal liability suggestions will serve to eliminate risks before they become injurious as well as potential legal entanglements.

Recommendations Regarding Helmets

- Only the best as well as certified and approved equipment should be purchased.
- *All* players should have the proper equipment.
- The coach should see that the helmet fits properly.
- The helmet should be inspected weekly.
- In event of injury, no one should remove the helmet during transportation to the hospital.
- The helmet should be removed safely.
- Both players and parents should be informed about risk involved in using the helmet as well as the risk of engaging in the activity.

Adapted from Appenzeller H, Ross CT: *Sports and the courts.* Charlottesville, VA, 1983, The Michie Company.

TORT

A *tort,* derived from the Latin *torquere* meaning to twist, is a legal wrong resulting in direct or indirect injury to another individual or to property or to one's reputation. A tortious act is a wrongful act, and damages can be collected through court action. Tort can be committed through *omission* or *commission.* An act of omission results when the accident occurs during failure to perform a legal duty, such as when a teacher fails to obey a fire alarm after he or she has been informed of the procedure to be followed. An act of commission results when the accident occurs while an unlawful act, such as assault, battery, reckless misconduct, or defamation, is being performed. (An example was previously provided in the violence and legal liability section.)

The National Education Association (1950) points out that

A tort may arise out of the following acts: (a) an act which without lawful justification or excuse is intended by a person to cause harm and does cause the harm complained of; (b) an act in itself contrary to law or an omission of specific legal duty, which causes harm not intended by the person so acting or omitting; (c) an act or omission causing harm which the person so acting or omitting did not intend to cause, but which might and should, with due diligence, have been foreseen and prevented.

The teacher, coach, or other sport manager (e.g., of an aquatic center, fitness club, ice arena, ski area) not only has a legal responsibility as described by law, but also has a responsibility to prevent injury. This responsibility means that in addition to complying with certain legal regulations such as proper facilities (e.g., lighting, pool depth), the teacher must comply with the principle that children should be taught without injury to them and that prudent care, such as a parent would give, must be exercised. The term *legal duty* does not mean only those duties imposed by law but also the duty owed to society to prevent injury to others. A duty imposed by law would be one such as complying with housing or traffic regulations. A duty that teachers and coaches owe to society, in general, consists of allowing children to learn in a risk-free environment.

It is important to understand the legal meaning of the word *accident* in relation to the topic under discussion. According to *Black's Law Dictionary* (Black 1990),

An accident is an unforeseen event occurring without the will or design of the person whose mere act causes it. In its proper use, the term excludes negligence. It is an event which occurs without fault, carelessness, or want of proper circumspection for the person affected, or which could not have been avoided by the use of that kind and degree of care necessary to the exigency and in the circumstance in which the person was placed.

Stehn v. Bernarr McFadden Foundation, Inc., 434 F. 2d 811 (6th Cir. Tenn. 1970) showed that omission of a legal duty was involved in an inexperienced volunteer wrestling coach's failure to teach a wrestling escape. An eighth-grade wrestler's spinal cord was severed during a match, and the pivotal legal question involved the qualifications of the volunteer coach. The paralyzed youth was awarded $385,000.

In another tort example, *Bourque v. Duplechin,* 331 So. 2d 40 (La., Ct. App. 1976),

Only qualified personnel should deal with injury.

during a recreational league softball game Duplechin slid into second base, breaking the jaw and seven teeth of second baseman Bourque. The umpire ejected Duplechin from the game. The court found for Bourque for intentional tort and against Duplechin's contestment of assumption of risk.

The courts are now taking a hard look at assumption of risk (many states have abolished or extensively modified it), and if a player violates the rules and if the act injures an individual, that player as well as the teacher, coach, official, and athletic and activities director who enforce the rules may be held liable.

NEGLIGENCE

Questions of liability and negligence occupy a prominent position in connection with the actions of those involved in physical education and sport programs. Negligence is the failure to exercise reasonable or ordinary care.

The law in America pertaining to negligence is based on common law, previous judicial rulings, or established legal procedure. This type of law differs from statutory law, which has been written into the statutes by lawmaking bodies.

Negligence implies that someone has not fulfilled his or her legal duty or has failed to do something that according to common sense reasoning should have been done. Negligence can be

avoided by acting reasonably and being prudent in various situations. One of the first things that must be determined in the event of an accident is whether negligence has occurred (Baley and Matthews 1984). Negligence is "the omission to do something which a reasonable (person), guided by those ordinary considerations which ordinarily regulate human affairs, would do, or the doing of something which a reasonable and prudent (person) would not do" (Black 1990).

The National Education Association's report (1950) contains a more detailed explanation:

> Negligence is any conduct which falls below the standard established by law for the protection of others against unreasonable risk of harm. In general, such conduct may be of two types: (a) an act which a reasonable person would have realized involved an unreasonable risk of injury to others, and (b) failure to do an act which is necessary for the protection or assistance of another and which one is under a duty to do.

The National Education Association's report (1950) includes the following additional comment:

> The law prohibits careless action; whatever is done must be done well and with reasonable caution. Failure to employ care not to harm others is a misfeasance.

Negligence may be claimed when the plaintiff has suffered injury either to self or to property, when the defendant has not performed his or her legal duty and has been negligent, and when the plaintiff has constitutional rights and is not guilty of contributory negligence. Negligence is sometimes defined in degrees such as negligence, gross negligence, and willful, wanton, and reckless misconduct. The teacher, coach, fitness specialist, or leader (even volunteer) of children in such cases is regarded as *in loco parentis,* that is, acting in the place of the parent in relation to the child, and this relationship is sufficient to create a legal duty (see the box titled An Employee May Be Negligent Because of the Following Reasons).

Negligence implies failure to act as a reasonably prudent and careful person; therefore, necessary precautions should be taken, danger should

An Employee May Be Negligent because of the Following Reasons:

- Appropriate care was not taken.

- Although due care was exercised, he or she acted in circumstances that created risks.

- His or her acts created an unreasonable risk of direct and immediate injury to others.

- He or she set in motion a force that was unreasonably hazardous to others.

- He or she created a situation in which third persons such as students or inanimate forces, such as gymnastic equipment, may reasonably have been expected to injure others.

- He or she allowed students to use dangerous devices although they were untrained to use them.

- He or she did not control a third person such as a special child, whom he or she knew to be likely to inflict intended injury on others.

- He or she did not give adequate warning.

- He or she did not look out for persons, such as students, who were in danger.

- He or she acted without sufficient skill and care.

- He or she did not make sufficient preparation to avoid an injury to students before beginning an activity in which such preparation is reasonably necessary.

- He or she failed to inspect and repair mechanical equipment or devices to be used by students.

- He or she prevented someone, such as another teacher, from assisting a student who was endangered, although the student's peril was not caused by his or her negligence.

Source: Adapted from Garber 1957.

be anticipated, and common sense should be exercised. For example, if a teacher permits a group of very young children to venture up a high slide alone and without supervision, he or she is not acting prudently.

Four factors of negligence must be proved before a lawsuit can be decided. First, there must be conformance to a standard of behavior that avoids subjecting a person to reasonable risk or injury. Second, a breach of duty must be shown. Third, the breach of legal duty must be the proximate cause of injury to the victim. The final factor that must be proved is that injury did occur. A student at Chatham Junior High School in Chatham, New Jersey, was severely injured in an accident while participating in physical education class (*Miller v. Cloidt and the Board of Education of the Borough of Chatham,* No. L-7241-62 (N.J. Sup. Ct. Law Div. Morris County; Oct. 31, 1964). The testimony revealed that the physical education teacher was not present when the accident occurred but was treating another child for a rope burn. However, the teacher had continually warned the class not to use the springboard at any time he was out of the room. (The injured student was trying to perform an exercise in which he would dive from a springboard over an obstacle and finish with a forward roll.) The prosecution argued that the warning had not been stressed sufficiently and that the teacher's absence from the gymnasium, leaving student aides in charge, was an act of negligence. The court ruled negligence and awarded the boy $1.2 million for injuries. His parents were awarded $35,140. On appeal, the award to the boy was reduced to $300,000, and the award to the parents remained fixed.

Considerable weight is given in the law to the foreseeability of danger. One authority points out that "if a danger is obvious and a reasonably prudent person could have foreseen it and could have avoided the resulting harm by care and caution, the person who did not foresee or failed to prevent a foreseeable injury is liable for a tort on account of negligence" (Baley and Matthews 1984). If a person fails to take the needed precautions and care, he or she is negligent. However, negligence must be established on the basis of facts in the case, not on mere conjecture.

Physical educators must realize that children will behave in certain ways, that juvenile acts will cause injuries unless properly supervised, and that hazards must be anticipated, reported, and eliminated. The question raised by most courts of law is: "Should the physical educator have had enough prudence to foresee the possible dangers or occurrence of an act?"

Two landmark court actions point to legal reasoning on negligence as interpreted in one state. In *Lane v. City of Buffalo* (1931), the board of education was found not liable. In this case, a child fell from a piece of apparatus in the schoolyard. It was found that the apparatus was in good condition and that proper supervision was present. In a similar court action, the defendant was found liable. The City of Buffalo owned a park supervised by the park department. While ice skating on the lake in the park, a boy playing crack-the-whip hit a twelve-year-old boy who was also skating. Workers and a guard had been assigned to supervise activity and had been instructed not to allow rough or dangerous games.

Although there are no absolute, factual standards for determining negligence, certain guides have been established that should be familiar to teachers, coaches, fitness instructors, and other people engaged in physical education and sport programs. Attorney Cymrot (Proceedings 1953), in discussing negligence at a conference in New York City, suggested the following:

1. The person must be acting within the scope of his or her employment and in the discharge of his or her duties in order to obtain the benefits of the statute.

2. There must be a breach of a recognized duty owed to the participant.

3. There must be a negligent breach of such duty.

4. The accident and resulting injuries must be the natural and foreseeable consequence of the person's negligence arising from a negligent breach of duty.

5. The person must be a participant in an activity under the control of the instructor, or, put in another way, the accident must have occurred under circumstances in which the instructor owes a duty of care to the participant.

The ability to foresee potential danger is crucial to physical educators and coaches.

6. A person's contributory negligence, however modified, will bar his or her recovery for damages.

7. The plaintiff must establish the negligence of the instructor and his or her own freedom from contributory negligence by a fair preponderance of evidence. The burden of proof on both issues is on the plaintiff.

8. Generally speaking, in a school situation, the board of education alone is responsible for accidents caused by the faulty maintenance of physical plant and associated equipment.

Some states have a save harmless law that provides for protection of their employees. For example, in New Jersey the law reads:

> Chapter 311. P.L. 1938 Boards assume liability of teachers. It shall be the duty of each board of education in any school district to save harmless and protect all teachers and members of supervisory and administrative staff from financial loss arising out of any claim, demand, suit or judgment by reason of alleged negligence or other act resulting in accidental bodily injury to any person within or without the school building provided such teacher or member of the supervisory or administrative staff at the time of the accident or injury was acting in the discharge of his duties within the scope of his employment and/or under the direction of said board of education; and said board of education may arrange for and maintain appropriate insurance with any company created by or under the laws of this state, or in any insurance company authorized by law to transact business in this state, or such board may elect to act as self-insurers to maintain the aforesaid protection.

Negligence Concerning Instruction

Many cases result from situations concerning improper instruction or educational malpractice in an activity. For example, if a child in physical education class is injured in a basketball game or diving from a diving board, his or her parents may try to show that instruction had been either inadequate or unreasonable. These cases are often found in favor of the student because of the inherent danger of the activity. Other students and their families have sued teachers because the teachers did not follow the class syllabus that many states require of their teachers. Such a syllabus outlines the course content and proper progression, and if injury occurs in an unlisted activity, then a basis for suit may be apparent. Teachers have also been held liable when joining in on class activity.

In *Dibortolo v. Metropolitan School District of Washington Township,* 440 NE 2d 506 (1982), a student injured her mouth performing a preliminary run as part of the jump-and-reach test. The jury found for the plaintiff due to erroneous instruction, because the student should have begun the test from a stationary position and because the teacher should have demonstrated the skill. In another case, a mainstreamed special education student who fell while vaulting in a regular physical education class sued. The Sanchezes (*Sanchez v. School District 9-R,* 902 P. 2d 450 [Colo. App. 1995]) sued because no aides or support services were in class to assist the physical education teacher.

Negligence Concerning Equipment and Facilities

Defective or otherwise hazardous equipment or inadequate facilities are often the cause of injuries that lead to court action. If a physical educator or coach has noted that the equipment is defective, he or she should put this observation in writing for personal future protection. A letter should be written to the principal and superintendent of schools or other responsible managerial personnel stating that danger exists and noting the areas and specifics of such danger. A copy should be maintained on file. In these cases, the courts tend to find for the student even if dangerous conditions had been noted. Conditions cannot only be recognized, but also must be corrected or removed. Therefore physical educators and coaches should see to it that defective equipment (e.g., frayed ropes, splintered bats, warped arrows, holes in field) is either repaired, or destroyed and discarded.

Litigation concerning slippery surfaces (*Paul v. Roman Catholic Church of Innocents,* 641 NYS. 2d 330 [New York App., 2 Dept. 1996]), cramped playing fields (*Ward v. Community Unit School District 220,* 614 NE 2d 102 [Ill. App. 1 Dist. 1993]), and unprotected gymnasium walls (*Hendricks By and Through Martens v. Weld,* 895 P. 2d 1120 [Colo. App. 1995]) have also surfaced, bringing to realization that facility and equipment

Expert teaching, careful supervision, and quality equipment make for fun as well as safe participation.

Cardinal Principles of Supervision

- Always be there!
- Be qualified (first aid, CPR)
- Be active and hands-on
- Know students' health status
- Monitor and enforce rules and regulations
- Monitor and scrutinize the environment
- Inform students of safety and emergency procedures
- Be vigilant
- Be prudent, careful, and prepared

Source: Krotee, 1997

checks and recorded audits are crucial to conducting a safe program.

Negligence in Sport Participation

Many injuries are related to participation in sport. Unequal competition is often the cause of sport accidents. Physical educators should consider gender, age, size, and skill of students in grouping players for an activity, especially an activity classified as collision or contact.

In *Benitez v. City of New York,* Bronx Supreme Court, Index No. 7407/85 (May 29, 1986), a nineteen-year-old was injured in a high school football game. The plaintiff, who injured his neck, received a 70 percent contributory award of $875,000 because A vs. B teams had been scheduled.

Negligence in Supervision

Failure to properly supervise physical activity is another frequently litigated situation. Supervision should be active, maintained over the entire area or group, and never ending. Supervision implies the duty to protect those who are being supervised from negligently injuring themselves by engaging in inappropriate and inherently dangerous activities. Supervision entails ensuring that rules and regulations governing the area are maintained as well as warning participants about their actions or the dangers of the activities in which they are engaged. Professionals should be aware of their responsibilities: Negligence can occur through failure to warn students about the risk and danger of activities, failure to provide competent spotters, failure to establish locker-room safety procedures, or failure to render immediate and adequate first aid (see the box titled Cardinal Principles of Supervision). The teacher, coach, or supervisor should never leave the class unattended; the school should have an established policy for emergency situations. The defendant in cases of negligence in supervision must have been able to prevent the injury that has occurred.

Defenses Against Negligence

Although an individual may be found negligent, the plaintiff, to collect damages, must show that the negligence resulted in or was closely connected with the injury. The legal question in such a case is whether the negligence was the *proximate* cause (legal cause) of the injury. Furthermore, even though it is determined that negligence is the proximate cause of the injury, a defendant may base his or her case on certain defenses (see the box titled Coaches' Guide to Avoid Charges of Negligence).

Coaches' Guide to Avoid Charges of Negligence

- Be familiar with the health status of students.
- Require medical clearance of students who have been seriously injured or ill.
- Render services only in those areas in which one is fully qualified and certified.
- Follow proper procedures in the case of injury or illness.
- See that medical personnel are available at all games and are on call for practice sessions.
- See that all activities are conducted in safe areas.
- Be careful not to diagnose or treat a student's injuries.
- See that protective equipment is properly fitted and worn by players who need such equipment.
- See that teaching and coaching methods and procedures provide for the safety of students.
- See that only qualified personnel are assigned responsibilities.
- See that proper instruction is given before students are permitted to engage in class or contests.
- See that a careful and accurate record is kept of injuries and illness and procedures followed.
- Act as a prudent, careful, and discerning teacher or coach whose students are the first consideration.

Proximate Cause

The negligence of the defendant may not have been the proximate cause of the plaintiff's injury. In most cases, the test for actual causation is whether the plaintiff has established that the harm would not have occurred but for the negligent conduct of the defendant. Thus, in *Markowitz v. Arizona Parks Board,* 705 P. 2d 937 (Ariz. 1985), in which the plaintiff dived into shallow water and sued for failure to post warning signs, the lack of signs was found not to be the proximate cause of injury so as to impose liability for the injury on the parks board. In another case, *Chudasama v. Metropolitan Government of Nashville,* 914 SW 2d 922 (Tenn. App. 1995), a seventh-grade female requested permission to use the locker-room bathroom, where she was assaulted by several female classmates. Even though the teacher could not be in the class and in the boys' and girls' locker rooms at the same time, the case was dismissed due to unforeseeable circumstances. Negligence requires some causal connection between the defendant's conduct and the plaintiff's injury.

Act of God

An act of God is a situation that exists because of certain conditions beyond the control of human beings. For example, a lightning storm, gust of wind, cloudburst, tornado, or other such factor may result in injury. However, this assumption applies only in cases in which injury would not have occurred had prudent action been taken. Emergency procedures and procedures in these cases should be outlined, published, distributed to parents, and followed.

Assumption of Risk

Assumption of risk is especially pertinent to games, sports, and other phases of the physical education and sport program. It is assumed that an individual takes a certain risk when engaging in various games and sports, especially in activities in which collision and contact are frequent, in which balls, implements, and apparatus are used, and in which open and obvious field conditions are played on voluntarily. Participation in such activity indicates that the person assumes a normal risk. Only the risk created by negligent conduct of the defendant can be litigated. The participant, however, must know, be forewarned and informed of, and fully appreciate the risk involved.

Assumption of risk is a defense to negligence and strict liability. Assumption of risk has several

Individuals assume risk when participating in collision sports such as soccer.

**THE ATLANTA COMMITTEE
FOR THE OLYMPIC GAMES
1996 OLYMPIC GAMES SPECTATOR RULES**

(1) SPECTATORS ASSUME ALL RISKS AND DANGER INCIDENTAL TO THE EVENT, whether occurring prior to, during or after the event, including, among other things, injuries caused by other Spectators. Spectators assume all risks of property loss. (2) This ticket is a personal . . .

Implied consent to assumption of risk as printed on the back of a ticket to the 1996 Atlanta Olympic Games.

dimensions, including express consent, implied consent, duty, and misconduct. Express consent is when the user, student, or player relieves the defendant of obligation, usually by signing a waiver form; implied consent is present when a ticket to a game is purchased (and is sometimes printed on the back of the ticket). Duty means that the plaintiff voluntarily entered into an agreement such as an employee contract knowing that risks were involved in the activity, and misconduct is when the plaintiff knows the risk but continues to play in an unsafe environment.

In *Scala v. City of New York,* 102 NYS. 2d 790, 1951, the plaintiff was injured when playing softball on a public playground but at the same time was aware of the risks caused by the curbing and concrete benches near the playing field. The courts decided that the plaintiff must be held to

have voluntarily and fully assumed the dangers and, having done so, must abide by the consequences.

In an action by Maltz (*Maltz v. Board of Education of New York City,* 114 NYS. 2d 856 [1952]) for injuries, the court held that a nineteen-year-old (who was injured when he collided with a doorjamb in a brick wall two feet from the backboard and basket in a public school basketball court and who had played on that same court several times before the accident) knew the basket and backboard were but two feet from the wall, had previously hit the wall or gone through the door without injury, was not a student at the school but a voluntary member of a team that engaged in basketball tournaments with other clubs, knew or should have known the danger, and thus assumed the risk of injury.

Rutter v. Northeastern Beaver County School District, 496 Pa. 590, 437 A. 2d 1198 (1981), in which a sixteen-year-old lost an eye during summer football practice, indicates that the decision to assume the risk must be free and voluntary and that the participant needs to clearly understand what dangers exist in order to be able to assume such a risk.

Contributory and Comparative Negligence

Another legal defense is contributory and comparative negligence. A person who does not act as a normal individual of similar age and nature thereby contributes to the injury. Typical examples are individuals who fail to obey the rules or to heed warnings or who do not follow the sequence of instructions provided by the teacher, coach, or leader. In such cases, negligence on the part of the defendant might be ruled out. Individuals are also subject to contributory negligence if they expose themselves unnecessarily to dangers. The main considerations that seem to turn the tide in such cases are the age of the individual, the nature of the activity, and the documentation, of the practices or "informed" conduct of activities by the defendant.

Contributory negligence, an all-or-nothing concept, has been modified to include the concept of comparative negligence; that is, the fault is prorated. In other words, the plaintiff and the defendant both share at times some of the fault for the injury or damage. In cases in which comparative negligence exists, damages are awarded on a prorated or percentage basis.

Appenzeller (1983b) reports that thirty-nine states have adopted the comparative negligence doctrine and that other states are trying to adopt this concept. Contributory negligence is usually a matter of defense, and the burden of proof is

placed on the defendant to convince the jury of the plaintiff's fault and of causal connection with the harm sustained. Minors may not be held to the same degree of care as is demanded of adults.

Contributory and comparative negligence have implications for a difference in the responsibility of elementary and high school teachers. The elementary school teacher, because the children are immature, has to assume greater responsibility for the safety of the child. That is, accidents in which an elementary school child is injured are not held in the same light from the standpoint of negligence as those involving high school students who are more mature. The courts might say that a high school student was mature enough to avoid doing the action that caused him or her to be injured, whereas if an elementary school child engaged in the same action, the courts could say that the child was too immature and that the teacher should have prevented or protected the child from doing the act that caused the injury.

Sudden Emergency

Sudden emergency is pertinent in cases in which the exigencies of the situation require immediate action on the part of a teacher or coach, and as a result, an accident occurs. For example, an instructor in a swimming pool is suddenly alerted to a child drowning in the water. The teacher's immediate objective is to save the child. He or she runs to help the drowning person and, in doing so, knocks down another student who is watching from the side of the pool. The student who is knocked down is injured. This would be a case of sudden emergency, and if legal action is taken, the defense may be based on this premise.

LAWSUITS

Lawsuits need only a complaint to exist. The NCAA Committee on Competitive Safeguards and Medical Aspects of Sports assumes that those who sponsor and govern sport programs have accepted the responsibility of attempting to keep the risk of injury to a minimum. Because lawsuits

Proper equipment and certified personnel reduce risk.

are apt to arise in cases of injury that occurred despite the efforts of teachers, coaches, athletic directors, and event managers, attempts should be made to ensure legal protection. The committee contends that the principal defense against an unwarranted complaint is documentation that adequate measures have been taken and programs have been established to minimize the risk inherent in sport. No checklist is ever complete, but the legal avoidance checklist that follows should serve as a review of safety considerations for those people responsible for the management of interscholastic and intercollegiate sport programs. The list can also certainly be extrapolated for use in all physical activity environments and settings.

LEGAL AVOIDANCE CHECKLIST

Preparticipation Medical Examination

Before a student or athlete is permitted to participate in physical education, organized sport, or physical activity, he or she should have a health status evaluation including a thorough medical examination by a well-trained physician. An annual update of a student's health history, with the use of referral exams when warranted, is sufficient. The NCAA Committee on Competitive Safeguards and Medical Aspects of Sports and the National Interscholastic Athletic Administrators Association (NIAAA) have developed health questionnaires and guidelines to assist in conducting preparticipation medical examinations as well as other sports medicine procedures.

Health Insurance

Each student-athlete should have, by parental or guardian coverage or institutional plan, access to customary hospitalization and medical benefits for defraying the cost of a significant injury or illness.

Preseason Preparation

Particular practices and controls should protect participants from premature exposure to the full rigors of the sport. Preseason conditioning recommendations from the coaching staff will help the candidates arrive at the first practice in good condition. Attention to heat stress, dehydration, and cautious competitive matching of candidates during the first weeks are additional considerations.

Acceptance of Risk

Informed consent or waiver of responsibility by student athletes, or their parents if the athlete is a minor, should be based on an informed awareness and acceptance of the risk of injury as a result of the student athlete's participation in the sport. Not only does the individual share responsibility in preventive measures, but he or she also should fully appreciate the nature and significance of the risk involved. The forms should be discussed with the student and parent during a team meeting, and both students and parents should sign the forms.

Planning and Supervision

Proper supervision of a sizable group of energetic and highly motivated student athletes can be attained only by appropriate planning. Such planning should ensure both general supervision and organized and professionally sequenced instruction. Instruction should provide individualized attention to the progressive refinement of skills and conditioning. First aid evaluation should also be included with the instruction. Planning for specific health and safety concerns should also take into consideration conditions encountered during travel for competitive purposes.

Equipment

As a result of the increase in product liability litigation, purchasers of equipment should be aware of impending, as well as current, safety standards recommended by authoritative groups and should purchase materials only from reputable dealers. In addition, attention should be directed to the proper repair and fitting of equipment.

In accordance with the preceding paragraph, one should know, for instance, that NOCSAE has established a voluntary football helmet standard that has been adopted by the NCAA, the National Association for Intercollegiate Athletics, the National Junior College Athletic Association, and the National Federation of State High School Associations. All new helmets purchased by high schools and colleges must bear the NOCSAE seal. According to NCAA football rules, if a helmet is in need of repair, it must be reconditioned according to the NOCSAE Football Helmet Standard recertification procedures.

Facilities

The adequacy and condition of the facilities, including fields used for all sports, should not be overlooked. The facilities should be examined and inspected regularly. Inspection should include warm-up areas, locker and shower rooms, and adjacent spectator areas as well as the actual competitive playing area.

Emergency Care

The NCAA guidelines state that attention to all possible preventive measures will help to eliminate sports injuries. At each practice session or game, the following should be available:

- The presence or immediate availability of a person qualified and delegated to render emergency care to an injured participant.
- Planned access to a physician by phone or nearby presence for prompt medical evaluation of the situation when warranted.
- Planned access to a medical facility—including a plan for communication and transportation between the sport or event site and medical facility—for prompt medical services when needed.
- A thorough understanding by all persons involved in the contest, class, event, or practice, including the management of visiting teams, of the personnel and procedures involved.

Records

Documentation is fundamental to management. Authoritative sports safety regulations, standards, and guidelines should be kept current and on file. Permission slips and waiver forms may not pre-

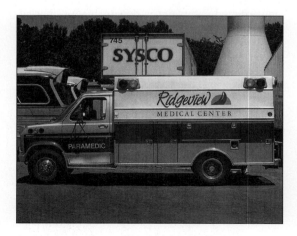

Paramedics and immediate medical transportation should be available at all sporting events.

vent lawsuits, but they help reflect organizational control and attention to injury control. These forms need to be kept up to date as does the student athletes' health status and eligibility (see the box titled Precautions to be Taken).

Daily and weekly lessons and practice plans (including handouts) documenting the method and effort to inform students of safety and risk issues as well as planned progressions of activity should be maintained by both teachers and coaches. Injury, accident, and incident reports must also be thorough and retained on record (see figure 13-1).

Precautions to Be Taken by the Physical Educator to Avoid Possible Legal Liability

- Be familiar with the health status of each person in the program.

- Inform students of the potential risk involved in the activity.

- Consider each individual's skill level when teaching new activities.

- Group participants together on equal competitive skill, fitness, and developmental levels.

- Perform proper progression leading up to all activities.

- Be sure equipment, uniforms, facilities, and environs are safe.

- Organize and carefully supervise the class. Never leave the class unattended—even in emergencies. If an emergency occurs, secure a replacement before leaving the room.

- Administer only first aid and CPR—never prescribe or diagnose.

- Use only qualified personnel to aid in classrooms.

- Keep accurate accident records.

- Provide adequate instruction, especially in potentially dangerous activities.

- Make sure any injured person receives medical attention.

NUISANCE

Action can be instituted for nuisance when the circumstances surrounding the act are dangerous to life or health, result in offense to the senses, are in violation of the laws of decency, or cause an obstruction to the reasonable use of property.

The National Education Association (1950) states the following about nuisance:

> There are some conditions which are naturally dangerous and the danger is a continuing one. An inherent danger of this sort is called by law a "nuisance"; the one responsible is liable for maintaining a nuisance. Liability may be predicated upon negligence in permitting the continuing danger to exist, but even without a showing of negligence the mere fact that a nuisance does exist is usually sufficient to justify a determination of liability. For example, a junk pile in the corner of the grounds of a country school was considered a nuisance for which the district was liable when a pupil stumbled over a piece of junk and fell while playing at recess (*Popow v. Central School District No. 1, Towns of Hillsdale et al.,* New York, 1938). Dangerous playground equipment available for use by students of all ages and degrees of skills has also been determined to be a nuisance (*Bush v. City of Norwalk,* Connecticut, 1937).
>
> On the other hand, allegations that the district has maintained a nuisance have been denied in some cases; for example, when a small child fell into a natural ditch near the schoolyard not guarded by a fence, the ditch was held not to be a nuisance for which the district would be liable (*Whitfeld v. East Baton Rouge Parish School Board,* Louisiana, 1949). The court said this ditch did not constitute a nuisance; nor did the principle of *res ipsa loquitur* apply. Under this principle the thing which causes the injury is under the management of the defendant and the accident is such that in the ordinary course of events, it would not have happened if the defendant had used proper care.

In addressing the Health Education Division of the New York City Schools, Cymrot (Proceedings 1953) had the following to say about an "attractive nuisance":

> Teachers need to be aware of decisions of the courts pertaining to "attractive nuisance," . . . an attractive

INCIDENT REPORT FORM

A. NAME ______________________ SEX ____ AGE ____ GRADE _____ SCHOOL __________

PARENT/GUARDIAN ________________ HOME ADDRESS ____________________ PHONE ________

DATE/TIME INCIDENT OCCURRED ___________________________

ADULT IN CHARGE ____________________________ ADULT PRESENT? YES _____ NO _____

WITNESS: NAME ______________________________ POSITION _____________ PHONE __________

B. NATURE OF INJURY/INCIDENT

1. Abrasion__________
2. Amputa.__________
3. Bite__________
4. Breath__________
5. Bruise__________
6. Burn__________
7. Dislocate__________
8. Elect.Schock_______
9. Foreign Body______
10. Fracture__________
11. Head Inj.__________
12. Lacera/Cuts_______
13. Poisoning_________
14. Puncture__________
15. Scratches_________
16. Sprain/Strain______
17. Other (Specify)____ __________________

C. PART OF THE BODY INVOLVED

1. Abdomen________
2. Ankle__________
3. Arm__________
4. Back/Neck_______
5. Chest/Rib________
6. Ear__________
7. Elbow__________
8. Eye__________
9. Face__________
10. Finger/Thumb_____
11. Foot/Toes________
12. Hand__________
13. Head__________
14. Hip__________
15. Knee__________
16. Leg__________
17. Mouth__________
18. Nose__________
19. Shoulder_________
20. Tooth__________
21. Wrist__________
22. Other (Spe)_______

D. LOCATION

1. Athletic Field______
2. Auditorium________
3. Cafeteria__________
4. Classroom_________
5. Corridor__________
6. Gymnasium________
7. Home Econ._______
8. Laboratories_______
9. Locker___________
10. Locker Rm_______
11. Pool___________
12. Restroom_________
13. Sch. Grds._______
14. Stairs__________
15. To/Fr Sch________
16. Field Trip________
17. Ice Arena________
18. Weight Room_____
19. Other (specify)____

E. ACTIVITY

1. Athletics/Phy. Ed.______ What?______________
2. Recess/playground______ What?______________
3. Equip. a. athletics/PE/recess/plg______________
   b. classroom______ c. other_________________
   What?_________________________________
4. Medication-related_________________________
5. Name of Unit____________________________

Figure 13-1. Incident report form.

DESCRIPTION OF INCIDENT

F.

1. Description of the incident:

2. Description of the injury:

3. First Aid treatment:

ACTION TAKEN AND FOLLOW-UP

G.

1. Returned to class_____ 2. Sent Home_____ Referred to Nurse_____

3. Sent to physician (name)_____

4. Sent to hospital (name)_____

5. Parent/other notified?_____ Time_____ By Whom?_____

6. School Insurance: Yes_____ No_____ Claim Form to Parent_____

7. Report to: Principal_____School Nurse_____ Adm Bldg._____
               Date   Date   Date

8. Follow-up Report_____

9. Person completing report:_____ Date/Time of report:_____
               (Name)   (Position)

Figure 13-1. (Continued)

contrivance which is maintained, alluring to children but inherently dangerous to them. This constitutes neglect. But it is not every contrivance or apparatus that a jury may treat as an "attractive nuisance." Before liability may be imposed, there must always be something in the evidence tending to show that the device was something of a new or uncommon nature with which children might be supposed to be unfamiliar or not know of its danger. Many courts have held, however, that for children above the age of 10 years the doctrine of "attractive nuisance" does not hold. Children are expected to exercise such prudence as those of their age may be expected to possess.

The following cases present representative court rulings concerning nuisance. In *Iacono v. Fitzpatrick* in Rhode Island in 1938, a seventeen-year-old boy, while playing touch football on a playground, received an injury that later resulted in his death. He was attempting to catch a pass and crashed into a piece of apparatus. The court held the apparatus was in evidence and the deceased knew of its presence. It further stated the city had not created or maintained a nuisance.

A seven-year-old child playing with his friends on a golf course had his eye put out when hit by a golf ball (*Lyshak v. Detroit,* 351 Mich. 230, 88 NW 2d 596 [1958]). The court found that signs and fences were inadequate in this example of attractive nuisance.

GOVERNMENTAL VERSUS PROPRIETARY FUNCTIONS

The government in a legal sense is engaged in two types of activity: governmental and proprietary.

The *governmental function* refers to particular activities of a sovereign nature. This theory dates back to the time when kings ruled under the divine right theory, were absolute in their power, and could do no wrong. As such, sovereigns were granted immunity and could not be sued without their consent for failing to exercise governmental powers or for negligence. Furthermore, a subordinate agency of the sovereign could not be sued. The state college or university, public high school, or municipality, according to this interpretation, acts as an agent of the state in a governmental capacity. The logic behind this reasoning is that the municipality is helping the state govern the people who live within its geographic limits.

Many activities are classified under the governmental function, such as education, police protection, and public health. The courts hold that public education is a governmental function and therefore is entitled to state's immunity from liability for its own negligence. As has previously been pointed out, however, the attitude of the courts has changed and for the most part the doctrine of immunity has been neutralized.

Proprietary function pertains to government functions similar to those of a business enterprise. Such functions are for the benefit of the constituents within the corporate limits of the governmental agency. An example of this would be the manufacture, distribution, and sale of some product to the public. Renting a school's gymnasium or ice skating rink to the private sector is a proprietary function. In proprietary functions, a governmental agency is held liable in the same manner that an individual or a private corporation would be held liable.

In *Watson v. School District of Bay City* (324 Mich. 1, 36 NW 2d 195), a decision was handed down by the supreme court of Michigan in February 1949. In this case, a fifteen-year-old girl attended a high school night football game. In going to her car, she was required to walk around a concrete wall. As she attempted to do this, she fell over the wall and onto a ramp. She suffered paralysis and died eight months later. The parking area was very poorly lighted. The supreme court held that staging a high school football game was a governmental function and refused to impose liability on the district.

From this discussion, it can be seen that education, recreation, and health are governmental functions. The distinction between governmental and proprietary functions precludes a recovery from the governmental agency if the function was governmental. However, if the high school had rented its stadium to another entity and the same action occurred, the outcome might have been different because a proprietary function would have been involved.

FEES

Many public recreation activities, facilities, and the like are offered free to the public. However, certain activities, because of the expenses involved, necessitate a fee to stay in operation. For example, golf courses and ice arenas are expensive, and charges are usually levied so that they may be maintained. This charge is sometimes also found at facilities such as camps, bathing beaches, and swimming pools.

The fees charged have a bearing on whether the activity is a governmental or a proprietary function. The courts in most states have upheld recreation as a governmental function because of its contribution to public health and welfare and also because its programs are free to the public at large. When fees are charged, however, the whole or conceptual picture takes on a different aspect.

The attitude of the courts has been that the amount of the fee and whether the activity was profitable are considerations in determining whether recreation and sport is a governmental or a proprietary function. Incidental fees used in the conduct of the enterprise do not usually change the nature of the enterprise. If the enterprise is run for profit, however, such as a health and fitness club, the function changes from governmental to proprietary.

LIABILITY OF THE MUNICIPALITY

It has been previously noted that a municipality as a governmental agency performs both governmental and proprietary functions.

When the municipality is performing a governmental function, it is acting in the interests of the state, it receives no profit or advantage, and it is not liable for negligence on the part of its employees or for failure to perform these functions. However, these factors would not hold if a specific tort claim statute imposed liability for negligence. When the municipality is performing a proprietary function—some function for profit or advantage of the agency or people it comprises—rather than the public in general, it is liable for negligence of the people carrying out the function. As previously pointed out, many states and municipalities have instituted specific statutes and permitted purchase of insurance recognizing the trend to permit injured citizens to recover damages from the managing agency for the torts of its employees.

LIABILITY OF THE SCHOOL DISTRICT

As a general rule, the school district is not held liable for acts of negligence on the part of its management or employees, provided a state statute does not exist to the contrary. The reasoning behind this is that the school district or school board in maintaining public schools acts as an agent of the state. It performs a purely public or governmental duty imposed on it by law for the benefit of the public and, in so doing, it receives no profit or advantage.

Some state laws, however, provide that school districts may be sued in cases of negligence in the performance of certain duties, such as providing for a safe environment and competent and qualified leadership. Furthermore, the school district's immunity in many cases does not cover acts that bring damage or injury through trespass of another's premises or where a nuisance exists on a school district's property, resulting in damage to other property. Just as protection of the state and municipality is on the wane, so too is that of the school district.

LIABILITY OF SCHOOL BOARD MEMBERS

In general, school board members are not personally liable for any duties in their corporate capaci-

ties as board members that they perform negligently. Furthermore, they cannot be held personally liable for acts of employees of the district or organization over which they have jurisdiction on the theory of *respondeat superior* (let the master pay for the servant). Board members act in a corporate capacity and do not act for themselves. For example, in the state of Oregon, the general rule about the personal liability of members of district school boards is stated in 56C.J., page 348, section 223, as follows:

> School officers, or members of the board of education, or directors, trustees, or the like, of a school or other local school organization are not personally liable for the negligence of persons rightfully employed by them in behalf of the district, and not under the direct personal supervision or control of such officer or member in doing the negligent act, since such employee is a servant of the district and not of the officer or board members, and the doctrine of *respondeat superior* accordingly has no application; and members of a district board are not personally liable for the negligence or other wrong of the board as such. A school officer or member of a district board is, however, personally liable for his own negligence or other tort, or that of an agent or employee of the district when acting directly under his supervision or by his direction.

However, a board member can be held liable for a ministerial act (an act or duty prescribed by law for a particular administrative office) even though he or she cannot be held for the exercise of discretion as a member of the board. If the board acts in bad faith and with unworthy motives, and if this can be shown, the board can also be held liable. Furthermore, acts of individual board members beyond their legal scope of duties are *ultra vires* (beyond their authority) acts, for which they may be held liable.

LIABILITY OF THE ADMINISTRATOR/ SUPERVISOR

The doctrine of *respondeat superior* does not apply to administrators and supervisors, and thus, in the absence of a statute imposing liability, such officials are not liable for the tortious conduct of their subordinates when liability is based solely on supervising responsibility (Kaiser 1986). The administrator/supervisor may, however, be liable if improper training or negligence in hiring is found.

LIABILITY OF TEACHERS, COACHES, AND LEADERS

The individual is responsible for negligence of his or her own acts. With the exception of specific types of immunity, the teacher, coach, or leader in programs of physical education and sport is responsible for what he or she does. The Supreme Court has reaffirmed this principle, and everyone should recognize its important implications. Immunity of a government agency such as a state, school district, or board does not release the teacher, coach, or leader from liability for his or her own acts.

In New York (*Keesee v. Board of Education of City of New York,* 5 NYS. 2d 300 [1962]), a junior high school girl was injured while playing line soccer. She was kicked by another player. The board of education syllabus listed line soccer as a game for boys and stated that "after sufficient skill has been acquired two or more forwards may be selected from each team." The syllabus called for ten to twenty players on each team and required a space of thirty to forty feet. The physical education teacher divided into two teams some forty to forty-five girls who did not possess any experience in soccer. An expert witness in such matters testified that to avoid accidents, no more than two people should be on the ball at any time and criticized the board syllabus for permitting the use of more than two forwards. The expert also testified that students should have experience in kicking, dribbling, and passing before being permitted to play line soccer. The evidence showed that the teacher permitted six to eight inexperienced girls to be on the ball at one time. The court held that possible injury was at least reasonably foreseeable under such conditions, and the teacher's negligence was the cause of the student being injured.

Teachers and leaders are expected to conduct their various activities carefully and prudently. If such conduct is not observed, they are exposing themselves to lawsuits for their own negligence. The National Education Association (1950) has the following to say about management:

> The fact that administrators (speaking mainly of principals and superintendents) are rarely made defendants in pupil-injury cases seems unjust to the teachers who are found negligent because of inadequate supervision, and unjust also to the school boards who are required to defend themselves in such suits. When the injury is caused by defective equipment, it is the building principal who should have actual or constructive notice of the defect; when the injury is caused by inadequate playground supervision, the inadequacy of the supervision frequently exists because of arrangements made by the building principal. For example, a teacher in charge of one playground was required to stay in the building to teach a make-up class; another teacher was required to supervise large grounds on which 150 pupils were playing; another teacher neglected the playground to answer the telephone. All of these inadequacies in playground supervision were morally chargeable to administrators; in none of these inadequacies in playground supervision did the court action direct a charge of responsibility to the administrator. Whether the administrator in such cases would have been held liable, if charged with negligence, is problematical. The issue has not been decided, since the administrator's legal responsibility for pupil injuries has never been discussed by the courts to an extent that would make possible the elucidation of general principle; the administrator's moral responsibilities must be conceded.

Many schools and agencies in states that have passed indemnification statutes allow the district or agency to pay tort damage judgments against their employees. This payment is not mandatory, however, and includes only those actions that are within the scope of the job. Actions outside the scope of their job that result in negligent behavior may find even the volunteer (who is classified as an employee) personally liable. All teachers, coaches, and leaders (even if volunteers) should check with their employers to determine the type and extent of liability coverage and plan accordingly for complete professional coverage.

ACCIDENT-PRONE SETTINGS

Because many accidents occur on the playground, during recess periods, in physical education classes, and at sport events, some sample test cases are offered here to serve notice that professionals involved in these settings must be aware.

Playground and Recess Games

The unorganized games played during recess and noon intermissions are more likely to result in injuries than the organized games played in physical education class. Playground injuries may be pure accidents, such as when a student ran against the flagpole while playing (*Hough v. Orleans Elementary School District of Humboldt County,* California, 1943) or when a student was hit by a ball (*Graff v. Board of Education of New York City,* New York, 1940). The courts have said in connection with this type of injury that every act of every student cannot be anticipated. However, the school district should make rules and regulations for students' conduct on playgrounds so as to minimize dangers. For example, it was held to be negligence to permit students to ride bicycles on the playground while other students were playing (*Buzzard v. East Lake School District of Lake County,* California, 1939).

Playgrounds should be supervised during unorganized play and such supervision should be adequate. One teacher cannot supervise a large playground with more than 100 students playing (*Charonnat v. San Francisco Unified School District,* California, 1943), and when the supervision is either lacking or inadequate, districts that are not immune are liable for negligence in not providing adequate supervision (*Forgnone v. Slavadore Union Elementary School District,* California, 1940). Students are known to engage in fights and may be expected to be injured in fights; it is the responsibility of the school authorities to attempt to prevent such injuries. The misconduct of other students could be an intervening cause to break the chain of causation if the supervision is adequate, but when the supervision is not adequate, misconduct of other students is not an intervening superseding cause of the injury.

Playground activities also need to be supervised.

If a student wanders from the group during playground games and is injured by a dangerous condition into which he or she places himself or herself, the teacher in charge of the playground may be liable for negligence in student supervision (*Miller v. Board of Education, Union Free School District,* New York, 1943), although the district would not be liable in a common-law state because of its immunity (*Whitfield v. East Baton Rouge Parish School Board,* Louisiana, 1949).

Supervision of unorganized play at recess or noon intermission should be by competent personnel. A school janitor is not qualified to supervise play (*Garber v. Central School District No. 1 of Town of Sharon,* New York, 1937).

When children of all ages share a playground, extra precautions should be taken to prevent accidents, because some children are more adept in using equipment than others and some playground equipment is dangerous to the unskilled.

Physical Education and Sport Events

Student injuries in this area occur when playground or gymnasium equipment is defective, when students attempt an exercise or sport for which they have not been sufficiently trained, when there is inadequate supervision of the exercise, when other students conduct themselves in a negligent manner, and even when the students are merely spectators at sports events.

It has been held that physical education teachers, coaches, or the school district in states where the district is subject to liability are responsible for injuries caused by defective equipment. For example, there was liability for the injury to a student who was injured in a tumbling race when the mat, not firmly fixed, shifted on the slippery floor (*Cambareri v. Board of Education of Albany,* New York, 1940).

Defects in equipment should be known to the physical education teacher or coach. There may be either actual knowledge or constructive notice of the defect. The term *actual knowledge* is understood; *constructive notice* means that the defect has existed for a sufficient time so that the instructor should have known of its existence, whether he or she did or not. Physical education teachers and coaches should make periodic examination of all equipment at frequent intervals and maintain appropriate records; otherwise, they may be charged with negligence in not having corrected equipment defects that have existed long enough that ignorance of the defect is a presumption of negligence.

Physical education teachers may also be liable for injuries that occur to students who attempt to do an exercise that is beyond their skill level. A running-jump somersault is one such instance (*Govel v. Board of Education of Albany,* New York, 1944), and a headstand exercise is another (*Gardner v. State of New York,* New York, 1939). These exercises were found to be inherently dangerous by the courts, and the evidence showed that previous instruction had been inadequate and the students had not been warned of the dangers. However, when the previous instruction and the supervision during the exercise are both adequate, there is no liability so long as it cannot be proved that the teacher is generally incompetent (*Fuller v N.Y.C. Board of Education,* 614, NYS. 2d [A.D. 2 Sept. 1994]). These cases suggest that teachers should not permit students to attempt exercises for which they have not been fully prepared through the use of warnings of the dangers and preliminary exercises to develop the required fundamental lead-up skills, confidence, and strength.

The physical education teacher is not liable if the injury occurred without his or her negligence. If caused by the negligence of another student, the teacher will likely be relieved of liability if the other student's misconduct was not foreseeable. Pure accidents occur in both physical education and sport; if there is no negligence, there is no liability (*Pomaro v. Community School District 21,* 662 NE 2d 438 [Ill. App. 1 Dist. 1995]).

Sports events to which nonparticipating students and even the public are invited raise other problems of liability for the district or the physical education teacher, coach, or sport manager in charge. If the locality is in a common-law state in which the district is immune, the charge of an admission fee does not nullify the district's immunity or make the activity a proprietary function as an exception to the immunity rule (*Watson v. School District of Bay City,* Michigan, 1949). If a spectator is accidentally hit by a ball, there is no liability; even when a student was injured by being hit by a bottle at a game, there was no liability because the misconduct of the other spectator was not foreseeable (*Weldy v. Oakland High School District of Alameda County,* California, 1937).

COMMON AREAS OF NEGLIGENCE

Common areas of negligence in physical education and sport activities include situations involving poor selection of activities, failure to take protective measures, hazardous conditions of buildings or grounds, faulty equipment, inadequate supervision, and poor selection of play area (Dougherty et al. 1994; Uberstien 1996). Cases involving each of these common areas of negligence are described here.

Poor Selection of Activities

The activity must be suitable and developmentally appropriate to the child or youth. In *Rook v. New York,* 4 NYS. 2d 116 (1930), the court ruled that tossing a child in a blanket constituted a dangerous activity.

Failure to Take Protective Measures

The element of foreseeability enters here, and proper protective measures must be taken to

Protective gear and proper instruction significantly reduce risk.

provide a safe place for children and youth to play. In *Roth v. New York,* 262 App. Div. 370, 29 NYS. 2d 442 (1942), inadequate provisions were made to prevent bathers from stepping into deep water. When a bather drowned, the court held that the state was liable.

Hazardous Conditions of Buildings or Grounds

Buildings and grounds must be safe. Construction of facilities and their continual repair must have as one objective the elimination of hazards. In *Novak et al. v. Borough of Ford City,* 141 Atl. 496 (Pa. 1928), unsafe conditions were caused by an electric wire over the play area. In *Coronel v. Chicago White Sox Ltd.,* 595 NE 2d 45 (Ill. App. 1 Dist. 1992), unsafe conditions were caused by failure to erect a protective screen, and in *Henig v. Hofstra University,* 553 NYS. 2d 479 (N.Y. App. Div. 1990), a field was not maintained during an intramural football game.

Faulty Equipment

All play and other equipment must be in good condition and properly maintained at all times. *Van Dyke v. Utica* (203 App. Div. 26, 196 NY Supp. 277 [1922]) concerned a slide that fell over on a child and killed him. The court ruled that the slide was defective.

Inadequate Supervision

Qualified supervisors must be in charge of all play activities. In *Niles v. San Rafael,* 116 Cal. Rptr. 733 (Ca. 1974), a city park was held responsible for failure to properly supervise a physical activity when a student was hit over the head with a bat during a softball game. The nature, location, training, and number of supervisors should also be of concern to prudent management.

Poor Selection of Play Area

The setting for games, sport, and physical activity should be selected with the safety of the participants in mind. In *Morse v. New York,* 262 App. Div. 324, 29 NYS. 2d 34 (1941), sledding and skiing were permitted on the same hill without adequate barriers to prevent participants in each activity from colliding with each other. The court held that the state was liable for negligence.

SUPERVISION

Children are entrusted by parents to physical education and sport programs, and parents expect that adequate supervision will be provided to minimize the possibility of accidents. Questions of liability regarding supervision pertain to two points: (1) the extent of the supervision (number of children and location) and (2) the quality of the supervision (certification and experience).

The first point, the extent of supervision, raises the question of whether adequate supervision was provided. This question is difficult to answer because it varies from situation to situation. However, the answers to these questions help determine adequate supervision: "Would additional supervision have eliminated the accident?" and "Is it reasonable to expect that additional supervision should have been provided?"

The second point, the quality of the supervision, addresses expectations that competent personnel should handle specialized programs in physical education and sport. If the supervisors of such activities do not possess proper training in such work, the question of negligence can be raised.

It is crucial to have preservice, in-service, and continual professional development for all employees to ensure that proper training is an ongoing feature of the management scheme.

WAIVERS, PERMISSION SLIPS, AND CONSENT FORMS

Waivers and consent forms are not synonymous. A waiver is an agreement whereby one party waives a particular right. A consent form or permission slip is an authorization, usually signed by the parent, permitting a child to take part in a particular activity.

A parent cannot waive the rights of a minor. Parents who sign waiver slips are merely waiving their right to sue for damages. Kaiser (1986) points out that although the courts have a penchant not to enforce liability waivers (*Wagenblast v. Odessa School District*, 758 P. 2d 968 [Wash. 1988]) such waivers are still helpful in risk management programs because they may discourage lawsuits and enhance legal defense of assumption of risk by increasing the participant's awareness of programmatic risk, rigors, and hazards.

Consent forms offer protection from the standpoint of showing that the child has the parent's permission to engage in an activity.

THE COURTS AND ELIGIBILITY RULES

When eligibility regulations have been challenged, courts have traditionally been reluctant to substitute their judgment for the judgments of school athletic associations (Appenzeller 1983a). In recent years, however, federal judges have been finding eligibility rules unconstitutional (*Regents of University of Minnesota v. NCAA*, 1976). Physical educators and sport managers have noted this change in court attitude and rulings, and many colleges have employed compliance officers, as well as legal counsel, to ensure due process concerning eligibility issues.

Due process refers to the rights guaranteed under the Fourteenth Amendment that entitle the accused (e.g., student, teacher, coach, athletic director) to (1) the name of the accuser and witnesses, (2) an oral or written report on the facts to which each testified, (3) an opportunity to present a defense, and (4) an opportunity to produce witnesses or testimony on his or her behalf. The right to due process is the right to be treated fairly; the right to a standardized procedural process; the right to be heard; if needed, the right to have counsel; and if found guilty, the right that the penalty imposed be proportional to the offense committed. Denial of participation in sport as a punishment can be as serious as school suspension and may be regarded as the denial of a student's legitimate entitlement to public education as found in the landmark due process case of *Goss v. Lopez*, 419 US 565 (1975) (Huggins and Vacca 1979).

Court decisions in which eligibility rules have been found to be segregationist have been consistently found unconstitutional. For example, a ruling in Alabama found that having racially based athletic associations was unconstitutional. The U.S. Circuit Court has also ordered the Louisiana High School Athletic Association to admit private black high schools.

Sample rulings about eligibility include a recent federal court order voiding the Indiana High School Athletic Association rule that prohibited married students from sport participation. Another significant decision involved the Iowa High School Athletic Association and the suspension of a student athlete because he was riding in a car that was transporting beer. The student was not drinking, and the event occurred in the summer when school was not in session. In addition, no state or federal law was broken. The eligibility law was found to be unreasonable, and the student was reinstated.

TITLE IX AND THE COURTS

As was presented in chapters 3 and 5, recent years have found the courts vigorously involved on numerous cases involving discrimination against women in sport. In fact, from the passage of Title IX in 1972 until 1988, the office of Civil Rights received 1,025 official complaints. In 1978 a federal judge in Dayton, Ohio, ruled that girls may not be barred from playing on boys' school sport teams, even in such collision sports as football and wrestling. In the decision, the judge pointed out there might be many reasons why girls would not want to play on boys' teams, such as "reasons of stature or weight, or reasons of temperament, motivation, or interest. This is a matter of choice. But a prohibition without exception based on sex is not." The judge also indicated that the ruling would have national implications.

A ruling by the State Division on Civil Rights of New Jersey requires Little League baseball teams to permit girls to play. New Jersey was the first state to have such a ruling. The order also requires that both boys and girls be notified of team tryouts and that children of both sexes be treated equally. An amendment to the Education Law of New York State provides that no one may be disqualified from school sports teams because of sex, except by certain regulations of the state commissioner of education.

In *Yellow Springs Exempted Village School District v. Ohio High School Athletic Association,* 647 F. 2d 651 (1981), it was found that the OHSAA rule preventing girls from playing on boys' teams was unconstitutional. The Indiana Supreme Court has also ruled that it is discriminatory for a high school to sponsor a boys' team and not a girls' team.

Title IX ensures that physical education and sport opportunities are open to everyone. Coeducational flag football is popular at many schools.

Three decisions, *Haffer v. Temple* (1981), *Poole v. South Plainfield Board of Education* (1981), and *Wright v. Columbia* (1981) seemed to continue to set the early course for Title IX intervention. Conflict, however, arose when other judgments, *Othen v. Ann Arbor* (1981), *Bennett v. West Texas* (1981), and *University of Richmond v. Bell* (1982) reflected differing opinions. The Supreme Court landmark decision in *Grove City v. Bell* (1984) overruled Haffer and further set back Title IX initiatives. Following the Grove City decision, 674 complaint investigations and 79 ongoing cases were dropped or severely limited (Shaw 1995). This situation continued until 1988, when the Civil Rights Restoration Act of 1987 (20 U.S.C. Sec. 1687) placed Title IX back on track. *Cohen v. Brown University,* 991 F. 2d 888 (1st Cir. 1993), in which the university chose to drop four sports (men's golf and water polo, and women's volleyball and gymnastics); *Favia v. Indiana University of Pennsylvania,* 812 F. Supp. 578 (W.D. Pa. 1993), in which similar configurations of men's and women's sports were also eliminated; and *Roberts v. Colorado State University,* 814 Supp. 1507 (D. Colo. 1993), in which women's softball was dropped, serve to keep alive the Title IX push for equality and a level playing field. In each case, the institution was found in violation of the Title IX compliance, and the women's sports teams that were targeted for elimination were restored.

Discriminatory action, however, is still taking place toward due process, opportunity, equal financial aid, and support. *Haffer v. Temple University of the Commonwealth System of Higher Education* (1987); *Lantz v. Ambach,* 620 F. Supp. 663 (D.C. N.Y. 1985); *Ridgeway v. Montana High School Association,* 633 F. Supp. 1546 (1986); *Clay v. Board of Trustees of Neosho County Community College,* 905 F. Supp. 1488 (D. Kan. 1995); *Gonyo v. Drake University,* 879 F. Supp. 1000 (S.D. Iowa 1995), and *Pederson v. Louisiana State University,* 912 F. Supp. 892 (M.D. La. 1996) serve as examples of actions that have been filed in the continuing process to come into compliance with the law of the land.

RISK MANAGEMENT

Risk management is the systematic process by which management protects not only the participants from personal injury but also the organization from financial loss through claims for damages. Risk management is an ongoing process of risk identification, analysis, and control as it relates to instruction, programming, supervision, and operations. Risk management is a team effort; however, each organization should appoint a risk manager whose duties are to develop policy and procedure and to ensure their implementation to avoid, limit, control, and reduce risk.

It is important to take every precaution possible to prevent accidents by providing for the safety of students and other individuals who participate in physical education and sport programs (see the box titled Safety Code for the Physical Education Teacher or Coach). If such sound risk management precautions are taken, the likelihood of injury is lessened, of a lawsuit is diminished, and of negligence is minimized. The following are recommended precautions to which the teacher, coach, or sport manager should adhere:

- Be properly trained, licensed, certified, and qualified to perform specialized work.
- Require medical examinations of all participants. Know current health status of the student.
- Be present at all organized activities (e.g., meetings, workshops, staff development, etc.) in the program.
- Organize classes properly according to class size, activity, physical fitness level, and other factors that have a bearing on safety and health of the individual.
- Have a planned, written program for proper disposition of participants who are injured or become sick or in case of other emergencies.
- Make regular inspections of items such as equipment, apparatus, ropes, or chains, testing them and taking other precautions to make sure they are safe. These items should also be checked for deterioration, looseness, fraying, and splinters.

Safety Code for the Physical Education Teacher or Coach

The following safety codes should be followed by the physical education teacher or coach:

Have a proper and current teaching certificate and coaching license.

Operate and teach at all times within the scope of employment as defined by the rules and regulations of the employing board of education and within the statutory limitations imposed by the state.

Provide the safeguards designed to minimize the dangers inherent in a particular activity.

Provide the required amount of supervision for each activity to ensure the maximal safety of all the students.

Inspect equipment and facilities regularly to determine whether they are safe for use.

Notify the proper authorities forthwith concerning the existence of any dangerous condition as it continues to exist.

Provide sufficient instruction in skill acquisition of any activity before exposing students to its hazards.

Be certain the activity is approved by the employing board of education and is age appropriate for the students involved.

Do not force a student to perform a physical feat the student obviously feels incapable of performing.

Act promptly and use discretion in giving first aid and CPR to an injured student, but nothing more.

Exercise due care in practicing his or her profession.

Act as a reasonably prudent person would under the given circumstances.

Anticipate the dangers that should be apparent to a trained, intelligent person (foreseeability).

- Avoid overcrowding at sport and other events, adhere to building specifications and codes and fire regulations, and provide adequate lighting and proper safety signs for all facilities.

- Use protective equipment, such as mats, helmets, and eye guards, wherever needed. Any hazards such as projections or obstacles in an area in which physical activity is taking place should be eliminated. Floors should not be slippery. Shower rooms should have surfaces conducive to secure footing.

- Require the wearing of gym shoes on gymnasium floors and safe and appropriate clothing for each activity.

- Adapt activities to the age and developmental, maturity level, and fitness level of the participants; provide proper and competent supervision; and use trained spotters in gymnastics and other similar high-risk activities.

- Utilize teaching methods, procedures, and progressions that are consistent with professional and institutional guidelines and standards.

- Instruct students and other participants in the correct use of apparatus and performance of physical activities, and duly warn them of the risk involved. Any misuse of equipment should be prohibited.

- Inspect the buildings and other facilities regularly for safety hazards such as loose tiles, broken fences, cracked glass, and uneven pavement. Defects should be recorded and reported immediately to responsible persons, and necessary precautions taken.

In planning play and other instructional activities, the following precautions should be taken:

Space should be sufficient for all games. Games using balls and other equipment that can cause damage should be conducted in areas containing minimal danger of injuring someone. Quiet games and activities requiring working at benches, such as arts and crafts, should be undertaken in places that are well protected.

In the event of an accident, the following or similar procedure should be followed:

1. The nearest teacher, coach, or sport manager should immediately proceed to the scene, no-

Special care should be provided for activities such as scuba diving.

tifying the person in charge and medical personnel, if available, by phone or messenger.

2. A preliminary first aid survey of the injured person will provide some idea of the nature and extent of the injury and the emergency of the situation. If necessary, the person in charge should call 911 for emergency medical services (EMS).

3. If the teacher or coach at the scene is well versed in first aid, assistance should be given, paying particular attention to the ABCs of first aid (airway, breathing, and circulation). A current first aid and CPR certificate and the undertaking of proper procedures will usually absolve the teacher of negligence.

Every teacher, coach, and sport manager should hold first aid and CPR certification. In any event, everything should be done to make the injured person comfortable until EMS or care by a physician can be secured.

4. After the injured person has been provided for, the person in charge should fill out the

The rapid growth of collision sports such as soccer have led to an increase in risk management issues.

appropriate accident report forms, take the statements of appropriate witnesses, and file the report for future reference. Reports of accidents should be prepared promptly and sent through appropriate managerial channels.

5. There should be a complete follow-up of the accident, an analysis of the situation, and an eradication or correction of any existing hazards or flaws in the school safety program.

The Standard Student Accident Report Committee of the National Safety Council listed the following reasons why detailed injury reports are important for school authorities:

1. They aid in protecting school districts and school personnel from associated publicity and from liability suits growing out of student injury cases.

2. They aid in evaluating the relative importance of the various safety areas and the time that each area merits in the total school safety effort.

3. They suggest modification in the structure, use, maintenance, and repair of buildings, grounds, and equipment.

4. They suggest curriculum adjustments to meet immediate student needs and safety requirements.

5. They provide significant data for individual student guidance.

6. They give substance to the school managers' appeal for community support of the school safety program.

7. They aid school management in guiding the school's safety activities for individuals and user groups.

INSURANCE MANAGEMENT

Insurance management is an element of risk management that seeks to divert or shift risk onto another party (the other elements include assignment and agreement indemnification).

Schools and other organizations employ three major types of insurance management to protect themselves against loss. The first is insurance for property. The second is insurance for liability protection when financial loss might arise from personal injury or property damage for which the school district or organization is liable. The third is insurance for crime protection against a financial loss that might be incurred as a result of theft or other illegal act. This section on insurance management addresses liability protection.

A definite trend can be seen in school districts toward having some form of school accident insurance not only to protect students against injury but to shield teachers, coaches, and staff against injury and liability as well. The same is true wherever physical education and sport pro-

Accident procedures and care should be well managed.

Some Common Features of Insurance Management Plans

Premiums are paid for by the school, by the parent, or jointly by the school and parent.

Schools obtain their money for payment of premiums from the board of education, general organization fund, or a pooling of funds from gate receipts of league games.

Schools place the responsibility on the parents to pay for any injuries incurred.

Blanket coverage is a very common policy for insurance companies to offer.

Insurance companies frequently offer insurance coverage for athletic injuries as part of a package plan that also includes an accident plan for all students.

Most schools have insurance plans for the protection of athletes.

Hospitalization, X-ray and MRI examinations, emergency transportation, medical fees, and dental fees are increasingly becoming part of the insurance coverage in schools.

grams are conducted. Along with this trend can be seen the impact on casualty and life insurance companies that offer insurance policies. The premium costs of accident policies vary from community to community and also in accordance with the age of the insured, type of plan offered, and sport to be covered. Interscholastic sport has been responsible for the development of many state athletic protection plans usually available through state high school leagues as well as the issuance of special policies by commercial insurance companies, ranging from basic athletic injury to lifetime catastrophic injury. Because accidents are the primary cause of death among students between the ages of five and eighteen, adequate and ample protection is requisite to a well-managed program of physical education and sport (see the box titled Some Common Features of Insurance Management Plans).

Common Features of School Insurance Management Plans

Some school boards have found it a good policy to pay the premium on insurance policies because full coverage of students provides peace of mind for both parents and teachers. Furthermore, many liability suits have been avoided in this manner.

Other school officials investigate the various insurance plans available and then recommend a particular plan, and the student athlete's parents or guardians deal directly with the company or through the school to guarantee coverage. Such parent-paid plans are frequently divided into two options: (1) they provide coverage for the student on a door-to-door basis (to and from school, while at school, and in school-sponsored activities) and (2) they provide 24-hour accident coverage with premiums usually four times higher than those of the school-only policy. The school-only policy rates are based on age, with rates for children in the elementary grades lower than for high school students. These policies usually run only for the school year.

Student accident insurance provides coverage for all accidents regardless of whether the insured is hospitalized or treated in a doctor's office. Some medical plans, such as Blue Cross and Blue Shield as well as various HMOs, may be limited in the payments they make. Student accident insurance policies, as a general rule, offer reasonable rates and are a good investment for all concerned. Parents should be encouraged, however, to examine their existing family policies before taking out such policies to avoid overlapping coverage.

A survey of nine school districts in Ohio disclosed the following practices for and problems with selecting an insurance policy for sport:

1. The chief school administrator was the person who usually selected the insurance company from whom the policy would be purchased.
2. Medical coverage on policies purchased ranged from $30 to $5,000 and dental coverage from zero to $500.
3. Companies did not follow through at all times in paying the amount for which the claim was made.
4. Most insurance companies writing sport policies have scheduled benefit plans.
5. Catastrophe clauses were absent from all policies.
6. Athletes' coverage ranged from 80 percent to 100 percent.
7. In most cases, part of each athlete's premium was paid for from a school athletic fund.
8. Football was covered by a separate policy.

As a result of this survey, the following recommendations were made:

1. Some person or group of persons, preferably a committee of experts, should be delegated to review insurance policies and, after developing a set of criteria, should purchase the best one possible.
2. Where feasible, cooperative plans with other schools on a county, district, association, state high school league, or other basis should be encouraged to secure less expensive group rates.
3. Criteria for selecting an insurance policy should, in addition to cost, relate to such important benefits as maximum medical coverage, excluded benefits, maximum hospital coverage, dental benefits, dismemberment, surgery, X-ray and MRI examinations, and physical and rehabilitation therapy.
4. The greatest possible coverage for cost involved should be an important basis for selecting a policy.
5. For football programs especially, a catastrophic clause should be investigated as possible additional coverage.
6. Deductible clause policies should not be purchased, if possible.
7. Dental injury benefits are an important consideration.
8. Determine what claims the insurance company will and will not pay.
9. The school should insist on 100 percent enrollment in the athletic insurance program.
10. Schools should have a central location for keeping insurance records, and an annual survey should be conducted to ascertain all the pertinent facts about the cost effectiveness and quality of coverage.

Procedure for Insurance Management

Every school should be covered by insurance. Five types of accident insurance may be obtained: (1) commercial insurance policies written on an individual basis, (2) student medical benefit plans written on a group basis by commercial insurers, (3) state high school athletic association benefit plans, (4) medical benefit plans operated by specific city or district school systems, and (5) self-insurance. Before adoption by any school, each type of insurance should be carefully explored and weighed so that the best coverage is obtained for the type and scope of program sponsored.

Sport and Insurance Coverage

Some schools and colleges do not provide a sport insurance program. If a student is injured in a sporting event, the family is then responsible for all medical expenditures. No provision is made for the school or college to reimburse the family for its expense. Of course, the school or college is always open to a lawsuit by the parents as well as by the student in an effort to reclaim expenses. A lawsuit is expensive for the school or college, because if the claim is settled in favor of the participant and parents, the school's or college's insurance premiums for the next few years are increased and because of the intangible effect to the school's or college's reputation and public image. In these cases, the high school is usually, through its membership in a state high school association, supplied with catastrophic insurance to supplement the individual's personal coverage.

An alternative is to provide an opportunity for students to purchase athletic insurance (many high schools provide this option) or, better yet, for the school or college to purchase a policy for student-athletes (most collegiate athletic departments provide insurance). Of course, the latter is the best method because all students are then covered, regardless of their economic status, and the students' liability policy is not subject to suit. Most parents are interested only in recovering monies actually spent, and they are satisfied accordingly. Usually a blanket policy purchased by the school or college can be obtained at a lower unit cost than a policy purchased by individuals. The athletic insurance program should be managed through the business office of the school district or of the athletic department or by a local or regional broker, relieving the school or college of going into the insurance business.

It is the responsibility of the director of physical education or athletics and activities to maintain and supply accurate lists of participating students to the business office before the beginning of the various sport seasons. It is also imperative that the coaches and athletic trainers be made aware of the types of insurance coverage plans so that when accidents happen, they can

The most inexpensive insurance policy is the employment of master teachers and coaches.

inform the athletes of the proper procedure to follow in seeking appropriate care as well as in filing reports and claims. Usually the business or athletic office will supply policies for every participant in a covered sport team or program.

Not only should the coach be knowledgeable about insurance coverage, but he or she should also show concern for accident victims as well as injured players. This concern is not only a form of good public relations, but it may also make the difference in the parents' minds about potential litigation. The coaches must also be instructed by management in the proper attitude to take when such mishaps occur. Legal counsel, if required, should be made available through the school, institution, or agency. If not, a private attorney should be retained (see the box titled The Prudent Manager).

School Sport Insurance

Sport protection funds usually have these characteristics: they are a nonprofit venture, they are not compulsory, a specific fee is charged for each person registered with the plan, and provision is made for recovery for specific injuries. Generally the money is not paid out of tax funds, but instead is paid either by participant fee or by the school or other agency.

The Prudent Manager

The following exercise should provide personal guidance for management as to the establishment of an appropriate degree of prudence commensurate with the professional as well as legal responsibility of the contemporary manager in physical education and sport.

	Degree of compliance			
The prudent manager:	**Always**	**Frequently**	**Rarely**	**Never**
1. Seeks to prohibit the situation that may lead to litigation through constant foresight and care inherent in the professional role he or she holds.	___	___	___	___
2. Assigns instructional and supervisory duties for an activity to only those people who are qualified for that particular activity.	___	___	___	___
3. Conducts regular inspections of all equipment used and insists on full repair of faulty items before use.	___	___	___	___
4. Establishes procedures and enforces rules for safe use of equipment and proper fitting of all uniforms and protective gear.	___	___	___	___
5. Has written plans with adequate review procedures to ensure that participants do not move too rapidly into areas of skill performance beyond their present skill level.	___	___	___	___
6. Selects opponents for each participant/team with care to avoid potentially dangerous mismatching.	___	___	___	___
7. Establishes and scrupulously enforces rules regarding reporting of illness or injury, to include compilation of written records and names and address of witnesses.	___	___	___	___
8. Does not treat injuries unless professionally prepared and certified to do so.	___	___	___	___
9. Regularly updates first aid, CPR, and emergency medical care credentials.	___	___	___	___
10. Does not permit participation in any activity without medical approval following serious illness or injury.	___	___	___	___
11. Readily recognizes the presence of any attractive nuisance, and initiates firm control measures.	___	___	___	___
12. Posts safety rules for use of facilities, and orients students and colleagues to danger areas in activities, facilities, and personal conduct.	___	___	___	___
13. Does not place the activity area in the control of unqualified personnel for *any* reason.	___	___	___	___
14. Relies on waiver forms, not as a negation of responsibility for injury, but only as a means of ensuring that parents/guardians recognize students' intent to participate.	___	___	___	___
15. Does not permit zeal for accomplishment or emotion of the moment to suppress rational behavior.	___	___	___	___

The Prudent Manager—cont'd

	Degree of compliance			
	Always	Frequently	Rarely	Never
16. Provides in letter and spirit nondiscriminatory programs for all students.	____	____	____	____
17. Cancels transportation plans if unable to be thoroughly convinced of the personal and prudent reliability of drivers, means of transportation, and adequacy of insurance coverage.	____	____	____	____
18. Does not conduct a class or practice or contest without a plan for medical assistance in the event of injury, regardless of the setting.	____	____	____	____
19. Holds professional liability insurance of significant dollar dimensions and pertinent applicability to professional pursuits involving physical activity.	____	____	____	____
20. Does not permit excessive concern about legal liability to prohibit the development of a challenging and accountable physical education/sport experience for each participant.	____	____	____	____

This material is reprinted with permission from the JOPERD (Journal of Physical Education, Recreation & Dance), January, 1979, p. 45. JOPERD is a publication of the American Alliance for Health, Physical Education, Recreation and Dance, 1990 Association Drive, Reston, VA 22091-1599.

In connection with such plans, an individual, after receiving benefits, could in most states still bring action against the coach or other leader whose negligence contributed to the injury.

States vary in whether they pay for liability and accident insurance out of public tax funds. Some states do not permit tax money to be used for liability or accident insurance to cover students in physical education and sport activities. On the other hand, the state legislature of Oregon permits school districts to carry liability insurance. This section is stated as follows in the revised code, O.R.S.:

332.180 Liability insurance; medical and hospital benefits insurance. Any district school board may enter into contracts of insurance for liability coverage of all activities engaged in by the district, for medical and hospital benefits for students engaging in athletic contests and for public liability and property damage covering motor vehicles operated by the district, and may pay the necessary premiums

thereon. Failure to procure such insurance shall in no case be construed as negligence or lack of diligence on the part of the district school board or the members thereof.

Some athletic insurance plans in use in the schools today are entirely inadequate. These plans indicate a certain amount of money as the maximum that can be collected. For example, a boy may lose the sight in one eye. According to the athletic protection fund, the loss of an eye will draw $1,500. This amount does not come close to paying for such a serious injury. In this case, as a hypothetical example, the parents sue the athletic protection fund and the teacher for $50,000. In some states, if the case is lost, the athletic fund will pay the $1,500 and the teacher will pay the other $48,500. It is evident that some of these insurance plans do not give complete and adequate coverage and protection to all concerned.

In many states, physical educators and coaches need additional protection against being sued for accidental injury to students and student athletes. Legislation is needed permitting school funds to be used as protection against student injuries. In this way, a school would be legally permitted, and could be required, to purchase liability insurance to cover all students, teachers, and coaches.

THE EXPANDED SCOPE OF LAW AND SPORT

The tremendous growth and development of physical activity and sport has been accompanied by the expanded role that law has played in ensuring a safe, smooth, and level playing field. This growth includes antitrust regulations, collective bargaining, eligibility, lease negotiations including concessions; parking; advertising; stadium boxes; players and sports team representation; media negotiations; sponsorship; taxes; worker compensation; and team licensing, just to mention a few. Although these topics seem out of the range of this text, today's professional involved in physical education and sport will nonetheless be called on to explore, extract, and extrapolate relevant knowledge from such topics. It is strongly recommended that further study (see Suggested Readings) into sport and law be undertaken by all professionals involved in physical education and sport.

SUMMARY

Legal liability, risk, and insurance management are important functions of management of physical education and sport programs. In managing such programs, the persons in charge should be familiar with the laws and legal basis for physical education and sport programs and the responsibilities associated with factors such as product liability, negligence in the conduct of activities, common areas of negligent behavior, safety precautions necessary to prevent accidents, and provisions to be implemented for sound risk and insurance management programs. Furthermore, management should be aware that citizens (e.g., parents and student athletes) are becoming increasingly aware of the meaning of laws that concern their programs and of their individual rights, including due process in such matters. As a result, the prospect of litigation has significantly increased. Management, therefore, should be prepared to do all it can to prevent not only injury but also possible litigation.

SELF-ASSESSMENT ACTIVITIES

These activities will assist students in determining if material and competencies presented in this chapter have been mastered.

1. Without consulting your text, construct a definition for each of the following terms: *legal liability, tort, negligence, in loco parentis, save harmless law, assumption of risk, attractive nuisance, immunity, insurance management,* and *risk management.*

2. Prepare a set of guidelines that teachers of physical activity in grades K–12 should follow to prevent negligence.

3. Discuss sport product liability and the methods you would take to ensure adequate protection for your ice hockey team.

4. Arrange a mock trial in your class. Have a jury, prosecutor, plaintiff, defendant, witnesses, and other features characteristic of a regular court trial. The case before the court is that the coach of a high school football team, in the final minutes of a game, used a player who had incurred a head injury in the first quarter. The player later suffered brain damage.

5. Conduct a risk management survey of the physical education and sport facilities at your college and identify any areas of concern that might exist. If any problem areas are found, recommend how they can be eliminated.

6. Prepare a step-by-step list of emergency safety procedures that should be followed by every physical education teacher at a junior high school to provide for the welfare of all students and student-athletes.

7. Take a field trip to a local community playground and chart the various safety concerns observed.

REFERENCES

1. Appenzeller, H. 1983a. *The right to participate.* Charlottesville, Va.: Michie Company.
2. Appenzeller, H. 1983b. Sports and the courts: Trends in tort liability. *Physical Education and Sports Law Quarterly.* Greensboro, N.C.: Guilford College Summer Law and Sports Conference, June.
3. Appenzeller, H., and C.T. Ross. 1985. Sports and the courts. 6(Spring):15.
4. Arnold, D.E. 1978. Sport product liability. *Journal of Physical Education and Recreation* 49(November/December):25.
5. Arnold, D.E. 1979. Legal aspects of off-campus physical education programs. *Journal of Physical Education and Recreation* 50(April):21.
6. Baley, J.A., and D.L. Matthews. 1984. *Law and liability in athletics, physical education, and recreation.* Boston: Allyn and Bacon.
7. Black, H.C. 1990. *Black's law dictionary.* 8th ed. St. Paul, Minn.: West Publishing.
8. Carpenter, L.J., and R.V. Acosta. 1980. Violence in sport—Is it part of the game or the intentional tort of battery? *Journal of Physical Education and Recreation* 51 (September):18.
9. Clement, A. 1989. *Law in sport and physical activity.* Carmel, Ind.: Benchmark Press.
10. Dougherty, N.J., D. Auxter, A.S. Goldberg, and G.S. Heinzman. 1994. *Sport, physical activity, and the law.* Champaign, Ill.: Human Kinetics.
11. Garber, L.O. 1957. *Law and the school business manager.* Danville, Ill.: Interstate Printers and Publishers.
12. Huggins, H.C., Jr., and R.S. Vacca. 1979. *Law and education: Contemporary issues and court decisions.* Charlottesville, Va.: Michie Company.
13. Kaiser, R.A. 1986. *Liability and law in recreation, parks, and sport.* Englewood Cliffs, N.J.: Prentice Hall.
14. Lewis, G., and H. Appenzeller. 1985. *Successful sport management.* Charlottesville, Va.: Michie Company.
15. National Education Association Research Division for the National Commission on Safety Education. 1950. *Who is liable for pupil injuries?* Washington, D.C.: National Education Association.
16. Proceedings of the City Wide Conference With Principals' Representatives and Men and Women Chairmen of Health Education. 1953. Brooklyn: City of New York Board of Education, Bureau of Health Education.
17. Shaw, P.L. 1995. Achieving Title IX gender equity in college athletics in an era of austerity. *Journal of Sport and Social Issues* 19(1): 6–27.
18. Uberstien, G.A., ed. 1996. *The law and professional and amateur sports.* Deerfield, Ill.: Clark Boardman Callaghen.

SUGGESTED READINGS

Berg, R. 1984. Catastrophic injury insurance: An end to costly litigation? *Athletic Business* 8(November):10.
  Discusses the Ruedlinger Plan, a plan endorsed by forty-eight state high school athletic associations that is designed to provide lifetime care for catastrophically injured athletes and protection from lawsuits for the schools.

Carpenter, L.J. 1995. *Legal concepts in spot: A primer.* Reston, Va.: AAHPERD.
  Addresses topics such as sexual harassment, corporal punishment, and product liability.

Drowatzky, J.N. 1993. *Legal issues in sport and physical education management.* Champaign, Ill.: Human Kinetics.
  An edited monograph discussing such topics as accountability, duty, negligence, and facility liability.

Hart, J.E., and R.J. Ritson. 1993. *Liability and safety in physical education and sport.* Reston, Va.: AAHPERD.
  Provides guidelines for teachers and coaches to assist in evaluating the adequacy of their program to avoid liability-producing circumstances.

Jordan, D. ed. 1996. Risk management. *Journal of Physical Education, Recreation and Dance 7* (67): 29–36.
  Presents risk management issues dealing with supervision of vertical adventures as well as of urban and wilderness areas.

Krotee, M.L., and E.S. Lincoln. 1981. Sport and law. *Choice* 18:1055–65.
  Delves into sport and law in regard to sports injuries, sex discrimination, education, contracts, and taxation. Describes the role of law in society and its effect on prudent management.

Mitchell, C.B. 1995. *Gender equity through physical education and sport.* Reston, Va.: AAHPERD.
  Presents rationale behind Title IX and offers strategies and materials to enhance Title IX efforts.

Ross, C.T. *Sports and the courts.* P.O. Box 2836, Winston-Salem, N.C.
  A physical education and sports law newsletter providing information about various legal issues, concerns, and cases.

Stotlar, D.K., and S.D. Butkie. 1983. Who's responsible when a spectator gets hurt? *Athletic Purchasing and Facilities* 7(April):22.
  Explains how the courts have ruled that spectators at sports events assume certain risks. Also explains

steps managers can take to reduce potential negligence on their part.

Uberstien, G.A., ed. 1996. *The law and professional and amateur sports.* Deerfield, Ill.: Clark Boardman Callaghen.

Gives a thorough overview of the multi-billion-dollar industry that is associated with sport, entertainment, and recreation that cover topics from antitrust law to violence and from collective bargaining to spectator rights.

van der Smissen, B. 1990–95. *Legal liability and risk management for public and private entities.* 3 vols. and supp. Cincinnati, Ohio: Anderson Publishing.

A three-volume exploration of physical education and sport and the law. Thoroughly treats legal liability and risk management for public and private sports-related organizations.

Wong, G.M. 1994. *Essentials of amateur sports law.* Westport, Conn.: Praeger.

Presents an overview of the court systems in the United States along with those entities that govern amateur sport. Contract law, tort law, drug testing, and sex discrimination cases are explored.

Wong, G.W., and M. Burke. 1993. Informed consent. *Athletic Business 17* (December):10.

Discusses the pros and cons of liability waivers and shows how they can discourage lawsuits and enhance legal defenses by increasing participant awareness.

Wong, G.M., and R.S. Ensor. 1985. Torts and tailgates. *Athletic Business 9*(May):46.

Pre- and postgame tailgating are popular among sport fans, but institutions can be held liable if reasonable precautions are not taken, particularly precautions related to alcohol.

chapter 14

Public Relations

Instructional Objectives and Competencies To Be Achieved

After reading this chapter the student should be able to

- Define the term *public relations* and its purpose and importance to physical education and sport programs.
- Understand the relationship of marketing to a public relations program.
- Recognize the constituents and needs of various publics in physical education and sport.
- Describe key principles that should guide a sound public relations program.
- Be familiar with various public relations media and how they can best be used to promote physical education and sport programs.

- Describe the four Ps as they relate to marketing strategy.
- Be familiar with the construction of a news release.
- Identify some professional organizations that can serve as resources for the conduct of public relations programs.
- Understand the importance of interpersonal and mass communications to the public relations and marketing agenda.

Abraham Lincoln once said, "Public sentiment is everything. With public sentiment, nothing can fail; without it, nothing can succeed." The management teams of physical education and sport programs need positive public recognition that the programs under their jurisdiction are meeting the needs of consumers. To accomplish this, the consumer and the public in general should be familiar with, understand, and support the services these programs render. Therefore, to have sound public relations, quality programs must exist, effective and continuous marketing must take place, communication channels with the various publics must be kept open, and media must be utilized in a manner that effectively presents the objectives of the organization to the public at large.

Public relations is an all-encompassing term. It is commonly defined as the planned effort to influence opinion through good character and socially responsible performance, based on mutually satisfactory two-way communications (Cutlip and Center 1978). Public relations indicates the positive relationship of the institution or organization and its total complement of human resources as well as its public constituencies (Williams 1985). *Public Relation News* further adds that it is the management function that evaluates public attitudes, identifies the policies and procedures of an individual or organization with the public interest, and plans and executes a program of action to earn public understanding, linkage, and acceptance. Two key ingredients of public relations are careful planning and proper conduct, which in turn will result in public understanding and confidence. Public relations includes attempts to modify and shape the attitudes and actions of the public through persuasion and to integrate the attitudes and actions of the public with those of the organization or people who are conducting the public relations as well as its marketing program. Public relations is the entire body of relationships that makes up our impressions of an individual, institution, organization, or idea.

These concepts of public relations help clarify its importance for any organization, institution, or group of individuals trying to develop an enterprise, profession, or business. Public relations considers important factors such as consumer or user interest, human relationships, public understanding, and goodwill. In business, public relations attempts to show the important place that specialized enterprises have in society and how they exist and operate in the public interest. In education, public relations is concerned with improving public opinion, proclaiming the needs of the school or college, and acquainting constituents with the value of programs and what is being done in the public interest. Public relations also should acquaint the community with problems and challenges that must be solved and overcome for education to render a greater service.

Purposes of school public relations include: (1) serving as a public information source about school activities; (2) promoting confidence in the schools or school-related organizations; (3) gathering support for school or organizational funding and programs; (4) stressing the value of education for all individuals; (5) improving communication among students, teachers, coaches, parents, and community members; (6) evaluating school and organization programs; and (7) correcting misunderstandings and misinformation about the aims and objectives of the school, its programs, and other organizations.

Physical education and sport need public relations because the public does not always understand the positive contributions that these programs make to all the people of a community. Many individuals believe that these programs are appendages to schools' academic programs and are sources of entertainment rather than education. Sound public relations and marketing programs both internally (e.g., faculty, staff, students, parents, alumni) and externally (e.g., community, business) are needed to correct these misunderstandings and ensure that an effective communication network is established based on research analysis, needs, and how these needs can be satisfied through the delivery of quality physical education and sport programs.

The goals of physical education and sport as presented in chapter 2 are educational and individual in nature and can be achieved through well-planned and effectively and efficiently managed programs as well as through the hiring of expert teachers, coaches and support personnel. These facts should be communicated to the public, both internal and external, through various media as well as through the pursuit of excellence in the programs.

The practice of public relations has been related to education since a publicity bureau was established at Harvard in 1900. Since that time, public relations has invaded all areas of human endeavor, including education, business, politics, religion, military, government, and labor as well as physical education and sport (e.g., AAHPERD's Physical Education Public Information Commission, or PEPI). A sound public relations program is not hit-or-miss. It is planned with considerable care, employing the steps outlined previously in the planning process. Great amounts of time and effort are necessary to produce meaningful results. Furthermore, it is not something in which only top management, executives, or administrative officers should be interested. For any organization to have a good program, all members must be conscious of public relations.

The extent to which interest in public relations has grown is indicated by the number of individuals specializing in it. A recent edition of the *Public Relations Directory and Yearbook* listed more than 5,000 directors of public relations with business firms, approximately 2,000 of whom are associated with trade and professional groups, and nearly 1,000 associated with social organizations. Some of these people are involved in physical education and sport programs. Indeed, almost every NCAA Division I institution designates a school official to manage its public relations efforts (e.g., sports information, public or external affairs or relations).

Public relations is steadily being recognized for the impact it may have in not only the business or corporate world, but also the realm of physical education and sport. All programs need public support and understanding to survive. A sound program of public relations helps not only to sustain our programs but also to make them grow and flourish. A lot of work has yet to be accomplished in public relations at both the grassroots and the national level, especially in regard to our physical education programs.

MARKETING PHYSICAL EDUCATION AND SPORT PROGRAMS

In the past, U.S. corporate structures manufactured goods and then made every effort to sell them. Today, management teams adhere to a strict policy of marketing analysis, or identifying the needs of the consumer, and then trying to satisfy these desires. Management is marketing oriented rather than production oriented. In other words, nothing should be manufactured or supplied unless there is a demand for it. This concept applies to physical education and sport as well as to the corporate arena.

Steps in Strategic Marketing Management

Analyze consumer or user group
  Consumer needs
  Consumer demographics, motivations, etc.
  Forecasting data collected and considered
Target consumer group population or segment
  Gather more detailed information, such as psychographics, social patterning and lifestyle, etc.
  Form or consult databases and other marketing information systems
  Identify barriers and limitations to promotion plans
  Cost, distribution, competitor groups, culture, technology, etc.
Select plan
  Consider all questions, issues, and concerns
  Evaluate alternative plans
  Initiate pilot study
Implement plan
  Including internal and external (print and electronic media) promotion
Review and evaluate plan
  Including process, outcome, and consumer satisfaction

Source: Krotee, 1997.

The term *marketing* includes areas such as analysis (including identifying recurring market patterns, frequencies, and tendencies), promotion (furthering the growth and development of something), and coordination. Marketing involves a strategic game plan for the various factors that relate to persuading the public to endorse, purchase, support, and utilize a product or service. In so doing, marketing tries to find out things such as what products and services customers want, who wants them, what the target population is (e.g., opinion research), and how best to present the product or service to the targeted public. In practical terms, marketing has several dimensions, sometimes called the marketing mix. These dimensions include consumer research to identify a target population, product planning, pricing, public relations, advertising or positioning, promotion, packaging, distribution, and servicing. Management is responsible for coordinating all the dimensions of the market process into an effective and satisfying program.

A marketing-oriented organization starts with the consumer and his or her needs and interests, which have been identified by sound marketing research. A determination is made between specialization and diversification—whether to stress one or several services or products.

In essence, marketing refers to the relationship of the producer to the consumer. In physical education and sport programs, marketing relates to the various services provided and programs implemented and to how well these services and programs meet the needs of the consumer (students, administration, alumni, faculty, community, and the population in general) as well as the nonconsumer. Marketing is the process by which the objectives of the physical education and sport programs can be best achieved. A marketing strategy or plan that will enable the organization to accomplish its objectives as efficiently and effectively as possible should be developed. This strategic marketing plan should be grounded in the organization's objectives, operated within its

All programs need public support and sponsorship.

financial resources or budget, and based on factors that can be controlled. These factors are often referred to as the four Ps of marketing (McCarthy 1960). The four Ps include the *product* (e.g., team); the *price* (e.g., admission); the *place* (e.g., indoor vs. outdoor stadium); and the *promotion* (e.g., public relations, advertising, publicity). Marketing therefore has a significant relationship with the conduct of an effective promotions and public relations effort.

THE MANY PUBLICS

For public relations and marketing programs to be successful, accurate facts must be gathered and articulated to the public in a meaningful fashion. To establish what facts are to be packaged and presented to the public, management needs to identify the consumers, user groups, or target population of the product or service. Marketing people call this market segmentation. Such factors

Successful marketing campaigns bring championship events, as well as revenue and recognition, to programs, schools, and communities; Target Center, Minneapolis, Minn.

as socioeconomic status, age, proximity, transportation, parking, and other product-service needs are used to identify the target population. These factors play a significant role in helping management select which population it wishes to target, segment, and direct its efforts toward (Graham 1994).

A public is a group of individuals drawn together by common interests who are in a specific geographic location or area or are characterized by some other common feature (e.g., age, interest, motivation). The United States, because of its diversity, is made up of hundreds of different publics—farmers, senior citizens, organized workers, students, professional and blue-collar workers, veterans, teens, and so on. The various publics may be national, regional, and local. They can be classified according to race, gender, ethnicity, age, religion, occupation, politics, disability, income, profession, economic level, or background (business, fraternal, or educational). Each organization or group with a special interest represents a public. All publics possess common elements to which public relations and marketing efforts must be sensitive. Each public (e.g., internal, external, immediate, associated) usually needs to belong, wants to have input, and desires to be included (psychosocial ownership) in order to maintain its interest and enhance its reputation. Public relations-minded and dependent organizations (e.g., education, physical education, sport) should always think in terms of the publics with which they wish to interact and serve in order to promote understanding as well as to determine how those publics can best be reached and satisfied.

To have a meaningful and purposeful public relations and marketing program, it is essential to visit and interact with the community; obtain accurate facts about these publics; and gain an understanding of their needs, interests, lifestyle practices, and likes and dislikes as well as other essential information. It is also important to consider what is good for most of the people in the community.

Public opinion, along with other factors, helps determine whether a profession (e.g., physical education and sport) is important, whether it meets an essential need, and whether it is making a meaningful contribution to society. Public opinion can influence the success or failure of a department, program, school, institution, business, bond issue, event, or, indeed, an entire profession. Public opinion is dynamic and results from the interaction of people, the media, and all those involved with the physical education and/or sporting process. Public opinion has great impact, and any group, institution, or organization that wants to survive, sustain, and succeed should learn as much about its process as possible.

To gather information on what the public thinks, why it thinks as it does, and how it reaches its conclusions, various techniques may be explored. Surveys, questionnaires, opinion polls, interviews, expert opinions, discussions, town meetings, observations, and other methods have proved valuable. Anyone interested in public relations and marketing should be acquainted with these various techniques.

Some forms of public opinion are shaped as a result of influences in early life, such as the effect of parents, peers, coaches, and school and community environment. Individuals' everyday lifestyles and culture and what they see, hear, and experience in other ways also contribute to the establishment of public opinions. Furthermore, the media, including newspapers, magazines, radio, television, and the Internet, play a significant role in influencing the formation and strength of people's opinions. One must not only be aware of these facts but also remember that one is dealing with many different publics (e.g., unaware nonconsumer, aware nonconsumer, competitor, sanctioner, support, media consumer, light user, dropout, etc.). Each public requires a special source of research, data gathering, and study in order to plan the most meaningful way to develop, organize, and manage an effective, efficient, and beneficial public relations and marketing campaign.

The Rolling Timberwolves display their skills.

Public relations promotes everyone involved in physical education and sport.

PLANNING THE PUBLIC RELATIONS PROGRAM

Public relations and marketing programs are more effective when they are planned by a team of interested and informed individuals and groups. Individuals and groups such as school boards, management personnel, teachers, students, administrators, coaches, and citizens' committees can provide valuable input and assistance in certain areas of the public relations program. These people, serving in an advisory capacity to physical education and sport professionals, can help immeasurably in planning a community public relations program by following these specific steps:

■ Establish a sound public relations policy.
■ Identify the services, programs, and products that will yield the greatest dividends.
■ Obtain facts about what consumers and nonconsumers do and do not know and believe about educational values and needs.
■ Decide what facts and ideas will best enable consumers and nonconsumers to understand the benefits obtained from quality programs.

■ Decide what program or personnel improvements will improve service or programs.
■ Make full use of effective planning techniques to generate mission statements, policies, goal setting, understanding, and appreciation.
■ Relate cost to opportunity for participants to learn, experience, maintain, and improve health and achieve fitness.
■ Decide who is going to perform specific communication tasks at particular times.

After the public relations plan is put into operation, it is important to assess and evaluate its results to see if its goals are being met and to improve the quality of the program.

PRINCIPLES OF PUBLIC RELATIONS

The role of management to provide sound public relations is vital to any institution or organization. Following are common principles to observe in developing a good public relations program:

■ Public relations should be considered internally before being developed externally. The support of all substructures and representatives within the organization, from top management to operational staff, should be obtained. A team effort is crucial! Furthermore, such items as mission and purpose of program, person or persons responsible, funding sources, media involvement, and self-controlled communication tools to carry on the program should be primary considerations before implementation.

- Managers involved in the public relations process must determine the organization's image from the public's point of view, relate this finding to the organization's public relations authority, and make suggestions on how this image can be positively enhanced before the public relations plan is set.

- A public relations program should be outlined and put in writing, and members of the organization should have meaningful input as well as the responsibility to become familiar with the program. The better its mission, goals, and objectives are known and understood, the better chance the program has of succeeding.

- The persons directly in charge of the public relations program must have thorough knowledge of the professional services being rendered, the attitudes of members of the profession and of the organization represented, and the nature and reaction of the consumers and of all the publics directly or indirectly related to the task at hand.

- After all relevant information has been gathered, a program that meets the needs of the organization and the public or community should be developed. The program should be based on market or opinion research and not on the whims of management.

- Adequate funds should be made available to do the job. Furthermore, all support services necessary to allow the public relations program to succeed should be mobilized to ensure the campaign a fair chance to meet its stated objectives.

- The formation of a public relations staff will be determined by the needs of the organization, the amount of money available, the attitude of the management, and the size, philosophy, and resources of the organization. If additional staff members are needed, specific job descriptions should be developed so that talented indi-

Public relations and marketing are coordinated and cooperative efforts.

viduals can be sought for the public relations team.

- Individuals who are assigned public relations work should, if deemed appropriate by the nature of the program, stay in the background instead of seeking the limelight.

- Public relations workers should keep abreast of the factors and influences that affect the program and develop and maintain a wide sphere of public contacts.

- As a public relations program is developed, the following items should be checked. Does the organization have a handbook, manual of guidelines, or newsletter to keep members informed as to both their role and place in the overall picture? Does the organization have a system for disseminating information to local electronic (i.e., radio, television, web site) and newsprint outlets? Has the organization created a booklet, flyer, or printed matter that tells its story? Do members of the organization participate in community activities? Has the organization made provisions for a speakers' bureau so that civic and service clubs, schools, and other organizations may obtain someone to speak on various topics? Does the organization hold open houses, clinics, or seminars for interested persons? Does the organization have a video or other visual or printed material that explains and interprets the work of the organization that can be shown and distributed to interested groups? Are interinstitutional or intrainstitutional E-mail and web pages utilized to their fullest capacity?

- A good public relations program will employ all available human, technical, and informational resources to disseminate crucial information to the public to ensure adequate dialogue between the consumer, potential consumer, and the organization.

PUBLIC RELATIONS, MARKETING, AND THE MEDIA

Many media (e.g., electronic and newsprint) can be employed in a public relations and marketing campaign. Some media have more significance than others in certain localities (e.g., your local

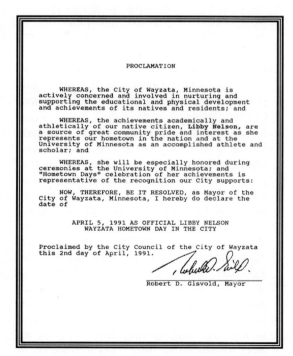

PROCLAMATION

WHEREAS, the City of Wayzata, Minnesota is actively concerned and involved in nurturing and supporting the educational and physical development and achievements of its natives and residents; and

WHEREAS, the achievements academically and athletically of our native citizen, **Libby Nelson**, are a source of great community pride and interest as she represents our hometown in the nation and at the University of Minnesota as an accomplished athlete and scholar; and

WHEREAS, she will be especially honored during ceremonies at the University of Minnesota; and "Hometown Days" celebration of her achievements is representative of the recognition our City supports:

NOW, THEREFORE, BE IT RESOLVED, as Mayor of the City of Wayzata, Minnesota, I hereby do declare the date of

APRIL 5, 1991 AS OFFICIAL LIBBY NELSON
WAYZATA HOMETOWN DAY IN THE CITY

Proclaimed by the City Council of the City of Wayzata this 2nd day of April, 1991.

Robert D. Gisvold, Mayor

Many communities are recognizing the contributions of student-athletes.

sports writer), and some are more readily accessible than others (e.g., local cable television). Physical educators, athletic and activity directors, and coaches should survey their communities to determine which media networks they have access to and which can be used most effectively and meaningfully to promote their programs and the institutions and communities they represent.

Program and Staff

The program and the staff represent perhaps the best opportunities for establishing an effective public relations program. Any school, college, department, or profession can build much goodwill by providing leadership, activities, and experiences (e.g., clinics, presentations, workshops, health fairs).

Some of the most effective community relations occurs on a person-to-person basis. This contact might be teacher to student, student to parent, teacher to citizen, or physical educator or coach to participant. Research about communication, persuasion, and voter patterns indicate that one-to-one communication is a very effective tool. Data from the fitness industry about the popularity of personal training also seems to support this notion. Sport managers must enter and experience the community if the profession is to be meaningful and sustained.

Print Media/News Releases

The newsprint medium is one of the most common and useful means for disseminating information. It reaches a large audience and can be helpful in presenting and interpreting physical education and sport to the public at large. Here are some questions that might be asked to determine what makes a good news story: Is the news of interest to the public? Are the facts correct? Is the style direct? Is it written in the third person in nontechnical terms, and is it well organized? Does it include news about individuals who are closely related to the local community, school, college, or other organization? Does the article have a goal, theme, or plan of action, and does it play a significant part in interpreting the program?

When a story or news release is going to be submitted to a newsprint medium, phone contact should take place prior to the preparation of the manuscript. In some cases, a news advisory is preferable to a story or news release.

The following guidelines (Cutlip and Center 1978) should be followed when formulating a news release to promote an event:

- Complete the news release; get the message across.
- Use AP (Associated Press) writing style.
- Be concise; one page should do it.
- Identify the market segment (target population) that should be addressed.
- Identify the primary players (e.g., media experts, local feature editors) to whom releases should be mailed, E-mailed, or faxed.
- Contact these key media people and explain the importance of the news release, to the program and community as well as to society.
- Avoid the majority fallacy by targeting the release to the appropriate following (e.g., heavy consumer, light consumer, nonconsumer).
- Mail the release in plenty of time (two to three weeks before the event). Events like National Physical Education and Sports Week (May 1–7), National Girls and Women in Sports Day (first Thursday in February), the Great American Workout, or National Employee Health and Fitness Day are just a few of the themes that may be utilized.
- Include any other relevant materials (e.g., program brochure, annual report, media guide, description, schedule).
- Follow up the mailed news release with a call to be sure it is "on-line" and to answer any questions.
- Send a note of thanks.

There are no guarantees when dealing with the newsprint media. Many times, a supposedly great story may be submitted and will never appear before the public. Some of the most common reasons for rejecting material include limited reader interest, poor writing, inaccuracies, and insufficient information. The discretion that the media exercises over the public relations domain can be discouraging. The best bet is to just be persistent; get to know the key media people and learn who can be relied on for the release of important information (e.g., stories, features, events). Mixing up strategies for releasing information may be helpful. Use word of mouth, press releases, personal letters, phone calls, and so on. Never give out incorrect information or information based solely on hearsay; memories are long in the media business and serious repercussions often result in subsequent negative publicity or, worse, neglect.

Thousands of popular magazines, professional journals, trade publications (e.g., *Sports Market Place*), and other periodicals provide another challenging outlet for building sound public relations. National newsprint media such as *Newsweek, Sport Magazine, Sports Illustrated,* and *Reader's Digest* are excellent for publicity purposes. So are journals such as *JOPERD, Health Education, NIRSA, National Aquatic Journal, Parks and Recreation, Journal of Sport and Social Issues, NATA News, Journal of Sport Management, Sport Marketing Quarterly, Strategies, International Journal of Comparative Physical Education and Sport,* and *National Strength and Conditioning Association Journal,* just to name a few. However, just like breaking into a major daily newspaper, getting manuscripts or notices in these journals is difficult because of their rigid requirements.

Many of the major media outlets like to cover the stories with their own staff writers. Many times, suggesting ideas to these sources is better than submitting a manuscript. The public relations person can attempt to interest the editors in some particular work being done and ask them to send a staff writer to cover the story. It might be possible to get a freelance writer interested in the organization, program, or event and have him or her develop a story. Someone on the department staff with writing skill can also be assigned to write a piece for newsletter or magazine consumption and then also submit the story to various periodicals for consideration.

In many cases, however, it is not necessary to get a story in a national magazine. Many local and community print outlets provide excellent exposure and are geared specifically to one community or a specific topic. Sound public relations must be built and nurtured, and working with the local paper, magazine, cable, radio, or television outlet will provide an extra personalized boost to the physical education or sport program.

The newsprint media can be used effectively by any school or other organization. To be most effective, however, the information must be related to the readership of that particular publication and must meet the needs of the target population. To this end, the focal point of public relations or marketing is still providing crucial information to the target audience at the most opportune time.

Pictures and Graphics

Pictures represent an effective medium for public relations. Two words should be kept in mind by the persons who take and select the pictures for publication: action and people. Pictures that reflect action are more interesting and appealing than stills. Furthermore, pictures with people in them are more effective than those without people. Usually a few people are better than many. Finally, such considerations as background, accuracy in details, clarity, taste, and educational significance should be taken into consideration. Some newspaper outlets require that photographs be taken by union or newspaper-employed photographers. Permission should always be secured and rules checked (e.g., NCAA, agents) to ensure that the photo and its use is within all legal and jurisdictional guidelines.

Educational matters such as budgets, statistical and demographic information about growth and diversity of school population, information about participation in various school or college activities, and many other items relating to schools and other organizations can be made more interesting, intelligible, and appealing if

Public relations and marketing campaigns can be very effective in sending messages to targeted populations.

presented through colorful and creative graphics. Pictures, flowcharts, and graphs should relate specifically, of course, to the age, gender, level of activity, and message that is being publicized. The computer software packages now available have increased and enhanced the visual effects employed by public relations and marketing personnel.

Communications

Knowledge and expertise in both mass and interpersonal communications is imperative if sport managers are to affect any public relations or marketing programs. Management, including teachers, coaches, and other personnel, needs to deal effectively with the reporters, columnists, and broadcasters who will encode and transmit messages concerning the program or event. Clear, concise, consistent, and accurate messages based on the objectives of both the organization and the program must be articulated. Public speaking can be another effective medium for achieving good public relations. Addresses to schools and civic and social groups in the community as well as at public affairs, gatherings, and professional meetings afford good opportunities for interpreting a profession to the public. However, it is important to do a commendable job, or the result can be marginal, rather than good, community relations.

Public interaction helps to promote a positive image for physical education and sport programs.

To make an effective speech, a person should observe many fundamentals, including mastery of the subject, sincere interest and enthusiasm, concern for putting thoughts rather than the speaker across to the public, directness, straightforwardness, preparation, brevity, and clear and distinct enunciation.

If the educational or sport organization is large enough and has several qualified speakers within it, a speakers' bureau may also be an asset. Various civic, school, college, church, and other leaders within a community can be informed of the services the organization has to offer. Then, when the requests come in, speakers can be assigned on the basis of qualifications and availability. The entire department or organization should set up facilities and make information and resources available for the preparation of such presentations. If desired by the members of the organization, in-service training, seminars, or courses could be developed in conjunction with the English Communications or marketing departments, to provide hints for public speaking. Public speaking is not easy, and young professionals and student-athletes should all be exposed to such positive experiences, although only after appropriate practice.

Student athletes in many high schools and colleges are being mobilized to speak at local K–12 schools on academics, reading, Just Say No campaigns, substance abuse, and other crucial topics. Communications and public speaking skills are requisite for all people involved in the physical education and sport professions.

Discussion and Advisory Groups

Discussion groups, forums, coffee klatches, and other similar meetings are frequently held in educational institutions and communities. At such gatherings, representatives from the community, including educators, industrialists, business people, physicians, lawyers, clergy, labor leaders, politicians, and others, discuss topics of general interest. These gatherings provide an excellent setting for sport managers to enlighten civic leaders, clarify issues, clear up misunderstandings, and discuss the pros and cons of their programs and projects. These meetings are a good way to get to know the market (Frigstad 1995). Physical educators, coaches, and public and private sector sport managers should play a larger role in such meetings than in the past. Much good could be done for all through this medium of public relations.

Someone once said, "There is no such thing as an original idea." Time allows ideas, methodologies, and concepts to be refined over and over again. Sport managers must not be afraid to listen to people who are in the community. One of the most effective ways to keep current on the pulse of community sentiment is to form an advisory group. The purpose of the group is simple—to stay in touch with community needs, feelings, opinions, and desires. Members of an advisory group will invariably be from all walks of life. The group may be started with friends in the business community or parents of children in the organization who have an interest in certain opportunities that the program can offer.

The group should meet as often as is reasonable to discuss and brainstorm about the possibilities that exist in the immediate community to promote your programs and attract participants. Surprising results can be achieved by information relayed through school or company newsletters, word of mouth, payroll envelope or mail box stuffers, and other ideas that have been generated at these informal meetings. In addition, allowing ownership in the program by including outside parties and making them feel that they are part of the program can only serve to expand the organization's programmatic and informational resource base for the future.

Radio and Television

Electronic media such as radio and television are powerful because of their universal appeal. These media are well worth the money spent for public relations. However, the possibilities of obtaining free time should be thoroughly explored. The idea of public service will influence some radio and television station managers to grant free time to an organization. This publicity may be in the nature of an item included in a newscast program, a spot public service announcement (PSA), or a public service program that might range from fifteen to thirty minutes.

Some radio and television stations reserve, and make available, spots for educational purposes. One example is the "Kids and Arnold" PSA developed by the President's Council on Physical Fitness and Sports, which has captured an estimated $2.8 million in comparative advertising value. These possibilities should be investigated. Many local communities, schools, and colleges have stations (e.g., cable, radio) of their own and these resources should be fully utilized.

Sometimes a person must take advantage of these media on short notice; therefore it is important for an organization to be prepared with written plans that can be put into operation immediately. The following include some short list items of preparation that might be kept on file:

- Know your message—health, Physical Best, Move to Improve, stop smoking, Jump Rope or Hoops for Heart, National Youth Sports Program (NYSP), fair play
- Know the program—style, format, audience participation, time
- Know the target audience—seniors, teens, upscale, nonconsumers, fans
- Tailor the message—construct and shape according to audience interest
- Tailor the presentation—to the show, time, audience
- Practice—rehearse, speak in lay terms, be brief and concise

Being prepared to contribute might make the difference between being accepted or rejected for a media opportunity. The organization must also be prepared to assume the work involved in rehearsing, gathering research and background materials, preparing scenery, arranging facility availability, or other factors essential in presenting such a program.

Television has provided positive attention to sport at all levels.

Radio and television offer some of the best means of reaching a large number of people at one time. What people see and hear has a great impact on them. Organizations concerned with physical education and sport should continually translate their message into material that can be used by the media. This, in turn, will assist in the building and maintaining of quality programs.

Films and Video

Film and video productions can present dramatic and informative stories ranging from an organization's public service to highlights of the training of its student athletes. Such a production constitutes an effective medium for presenting a story. A series of visual impressions will remain long in the minds of the viewers.

Because a vast majority of Americans enjoy films and videos, it is important to consider them in any public relations or marketing program. Film and video are not only a form of entertainment, but also an effective medium to use to inform, educate, and motivate. They stimulate attention, create interest, and provide a way of getting across information not inherent in printed material. They can be a powerful tool if effec-

tively incorporated into an organization's public relations campaigns.

Movies, videos, slide films, educational television, web pages, and other visual aids have also been used by a number of physical education and sports organizations not only to present their programs to the public but also to interest individuals in their message (e.g., health, fitness, wellness, school and community-building).

Posters, Exhibits, Brochures, Demonstrations, Miscellaneous Media

Posters, exhibits, and brochures are important in any public relations program concerned with physical education and sport. Well-illustrated, brief, and attractive brochures can visually and informatively depict activities, facilities, projects, opportunities, and services that a department or organization has to offer as part of its total program.

Drawings, paintings, charts, graphics, pictures, and other aids, when placed on posters and properly packaged and distributed, will illustrate activities, show progress and concern, and present information visually. These media will attract and interest the public.

Exhibits, when properly prepared, placed, and presented, such as in a store window or

Coaching clinics serve as effective community relations-builders.

gymnasium entryway, school foyer, or some other prominent spot, can do much to demonstrate work being done by the school or organization.

Demonstrations that entertain, inform, and present the total program of an organization or profession are a unique aspect of any community relations program. The main objectives for a physical education or sport demonstration are (1) to inform the public and provide an outlet for interest in physical education and sport programs by community members, (2) to provide an opportunity for members of an organization to work together toward a common goal, (3) to demonstrate the need, value, and benefit of physical education and sport to all participants, (4) to provide opportunities for the general public to see the physical education and sport program in action, (5) to contribute to the objectives of the organization, (6) to include all participants in the activities, (7) to reflect the needs of the consumer in the present and in the future, and (8) to contribute to the health and social and emotional well-being of participants and spectators.

Other miscellaneous media, such as correspondence in the forms of letters and messages to parents, student publications, and newsletters and reports, offer opportunities to develop good public relations and favorable understanding toward schools, colleges, and other organizations and the work they are doing and the linkages they have with the community. Every opportunity must be used to build and sustain positive public relations.

A student athlete gymnastics exhibition at Northrop Mall, University of Minnesota.

PUBLIC RELATIONS IN ACTION

Many publics play a vital role in the arena of physical education and sport. Each demands a personalized public relation agenda which must be a vibrant part of the profession's coordinated marketing strategy. Effective public relations and their accompanying marketing programs are a vibrant aspect of the profession of physical education and sport. AAHPERD, through various public relations efforts such as its Jump Rope and Hoops for Heart Programs, provides quality programs and resources (e.g., books, manuals, standards, videos, kits, and speakers) for public consumption. NASPE (National Association for Sport and Physical Education) over the years has contributed public relations initiatives ranging from its Physical Education Public Information (PEPI) project, Physical Best, PE-TV, and Move to Improve to the Hershey Youth Project and Skate in Schools Program. These activities all serve to bring to the public the values of active participation in physical education and sport programs.

Organizations such as the President's Council on Physical Fitness and Sport, the Institution for

---

President's Council on Physical Fitness and Sport Performance Checklist

Yes   No

☐ ☐ Physical fitness is not a part-time agenda. Does your school provide at least one period per day of instruction in vigorous physical activity?

☐ ☐ Play alone won't develop physical fitness. Is a part of each physical education period devoted to activities like running, calisthenics, agility drills, and strength training?

☐ ☐ Skill in sport is a valuable social and health asset. Does your school program offer instruction in lifetime sports like tennis, swimming, golf, skiing, and jogging?

☐ ☐ Most physical problems can be alleviated if discovered early enough. Does the school give a screening test to identify those students who are weak, inflexible, overweight, or lacking in coordination?

☐ ☐ All children can improve with help. Are there special physical education programs for students with varying disabilities?

☐ ☐ Testing is important to measure achievement. Are all students tested in physical fitness at least twice a year?

What to do to change the "No" answers to "Yes"
First: Make sure you know what your local school code says about physical education and what is specified in state laws or regulations.
Then:
1. Speak to the physical education teacher in your child's school. You will find him or her very cooperative and willing to answer your questions.
2. If the physical education teacher can't help, speak to the school principal.
3. If significant changes are needed in the school's priorities or scheduling, try to encourage your parent/teacher organization to support a regular physical education program with an adequate emphasis on physical fitness.
4. If the problem is one of policy in the entire school district, take up the issue with your local Board of Education.
5. If your school is doing all it can at this time, make certain your child gets at least one-half hour of vigorous physical activity every day before or after school.
For additional information or help in setting up a program of vigorous physical activity for your child, write:
THE PRESIDENT'S COUNCIL ON
PHYSICAL FITNESS & SPORTS
HHH Building, Room 738H
200 Independence Avenue, S.W.
Washington, DC 20201

International Sport, and some institutions of higher education among others have also played crucial roles in not only getting out the message, but also determining through research what the message should be and how the message should be delivered as it makes its way into the global community. Some examples of the profession's public relations initiatives follow. (The President's Council on Physical Fitness and Sport Performance Checklist provides a means for determining the effectiveness of a fitness program.)

Jump Rope and Hoops for Heart

One of the most successful public relations activities of AAHPERD is the Jump Rope for Heart (JRFH) program. The American Heart Association (AHA) and AAHPERD cooperate to sponsor rope-skipping exhibitions, Jump Rope for Heart, and Jump-Rope-a-Thons to raise funds. Student groups who have been involved in demonstrations have been very well received. This project has raised considerable money to benefit the AHA as well as to augment AAHPERD funds and remains

Jump rope provides a good cardiovascular workout and also serves as an AAHPERD public relations initiative.

a tremendous public relations vehicle that focuses on community involvement. JRFH has completed more than fifteen years of providing students with jump rope skills as well as knowledge, attitudes, and understanding about the positive effects that cardiovascular fitness can play in prevention of various forms of heart disease. AAHPERD has recently added a Hoops for Heart Program in an effort to reach out to an even greater share of their targeted public (youth). AAHPERD provides thorough media training supplements that are helpful to any educator who wishes to implement these or any other AAHPERD public relations programs.

Move to Improve

The recent Move to Improve initiative by NASPE focuses on why children need physical education. Because of the continuing fiscal problems facing our school systems, NASPE provides the professional pertinent information concerning the 1987 H. Con. Res. 97 and the first Surgeon General's Report on Physical Activity and Sport (published in July 1996) that encourages all K–12 schools to provide quality physical education and sport programs that promote healthy behaviors and individual well-being. NASPE provides the following recommendations about quality physical education:

- It should be taught daily.
- It should be taught by a certified physical education teacher.
- It provides logical progression, K–12.
- It allows for all children, including those with disabilities, to participate and succeed at their own level.
- It encourages students to use the skills and knowledge acquired in class.

NASPE also provides guideline and program appraisal checklists for K–12 physical education programs as well as a Sport and Physical Education Advocacy Kit (SPEAK) that includes models for presentations, news releases, public service announcements, contemporary fitness facts, and a twelve-minute video that will be a service to any professional in the field. Indeed, all K–12 teachers should be familiar with NASPE's initiatives, such as Physical Best, Skate in School, the Pro-Link Program, the Hershey Youth Project, and the PETT Project (gender equity).

Institute for International Sport

The Institute for International Sport (IIS) is housed at the University of Rhode Island and for more than a decade has brought to the public events such as the World Scholar-Athlete Games and National Sportsmanship Day ("Dare to Play Fair" programs). The IIS selects outstanding Sports Ethics Fellows (e.g., Bonnie Blair, Joan Benoit Samuelson, Joe Paterno), promotes research into fair play, and provides practical application through its coordinated outreach programs ranging from its International Senior Games to its international scholar-athlete competitions.

The Tucker Center for Research on Girls and Women in Sport

The vision and pioneering spirit of Dorothy McNeil Tucker led to the establishment of the Tucker Center for Research on Girls and Women in Sport at the University of Minnesota in 1993. Housed in the College of Education and Human Development's School of Kinesiology, the Tucker Center's mission is threefold: (1) to conduct, sponsor, and promote basic and applied research; (2) to support and enhance the education, training, and mentorship of graduate students; and (3) to engage in community outreach and public service by disseminating research findings and educational materials to targeted constituencies.

Since its inception, the Tucker Center has provided centralization, organization, scientific excellence, and national leadership on issues of great national and local significance. Through its direction and leadership, the center encourages researchers, policy makers, educators, parents, and practitioners to work together to better the lives of girls and women in ways that go far beyond the playing fields.

National Girls and Women in Sports Day in Minnesota.

National Girls and Women in Sports Day

The National Association for Girls and Women in Sports (NAGWS) began National Girls and Women in Sports Day in 1987 to honor former volleyball great Flo Hyman. With themes such as "Get in the Game" and with wide support from the Girl Scouts of America, the YWCA, the Women's Sport Foundation, and J. C. Penney, NAGWS encourages young girls and women to become active participants and believers not only in the potential of sport but in themselves. NAGWS, as well as the sponsors just listed, can provide numerous publications and resources for professionals (NAGWS 1988).

National Physical Fitness and Sports Month

National Physical Fitness and Sports Month was established in 1983 by the President's Council on Physical Fitness and Sports and is endorsed by the president of the United States and supported by AAHPERD.

The President's Council on Physical Fitness and Sports

The President's Council on Physical Fitness and Sports (PCPFS) was established by executive order in 1956 by President Eisenhower as part of a national campaign to help shape up America's younger generation. Some of the council's programs include the Youth Fitness Campaign, the Presidential Sports Award, the President's Challenge Physical Fitness and Health Awards, the President's Council Performance Checklist (see page 425), and National Physical Fitness and Sports Month.

May is usually designated as National Physical Fitness and Sports Month, and various public relations plans are utilized to motivate the public into action. Slogans such as "Shape up America" and "Spring Into Action" and public relations messages delivered by the president and governors as well as by celebrities such as Arnold Schwarzenegger, Florence Griffith Joyner, Ralph Boston, Pam Shriver, Tom McMillen, and Zina Garrison-Jackson are used to alert people of all ages that physical education, sport, and fitness remain a top priority and a national concern. As a result of this promotion, many communities, schools, and businesses across the country sponsor various physical education and sport activities and other health-related fitness events during the month of May. AAHPERD provides posters and its May: National Physical Fitness and Sports Month/Week Kit to serve as a further resource to help promote physical education and sports programs.

PUBLIC RELATIONS IN SCHOOL AND COMMUNITIES

Research conducted by the authors of this textbook in various school systems concerning the nature and scope of their public relations programs has revealed the following information about physical education and sport.

The policies that govern the programs indicated that the director of physical education and/or athletics and activities was usually directly responsible for public relations press releases. All printed material needed the approval of the director and/or the superintendent of schools before being

Poster used in public relations effort to promote National Physical Education and Sport Week and quality daily physical education.

released. The coaches of interscholastic sport were responsible for preparing all sport-specific releases regarding their programs. Each physical educator and coach was urged to recognize that his or her activities were an integral part of the professional and public relations programs of the school district.

Communications media employed included the physical education and sport program, newspaper, posters, films, videos, public speaking, school publications, newsletters, letters to parents, demonstrations and exhibits, personal contact, pictures, radio, television, window displays, brochures, sports days, and bulletin boards. The five media found to be the most effective in their professional and public relations programs were (1) the total physical education and sport program, (2) personal contact, (3) newspapers, (4) public speaking, and (5) demonstrations and

Public Relations and Fund Raising Promotional Ideas

Art auction	Cross-country skiing marathon	Reading marathon
Arts and crafts fair	Garage sale	Roller-skating marathon
Backgammon tournament	Golf tournament	Sailing regatta
Bake sale	Greeting card sales	Showing films and videos
Ballroom dancing	Guest speakers	Silent auction
Basketball marathon	"Guiness" risk activities	Skating marathon
Bicycle marathon	Hayrides	Soccer clinic
Bingo	Historical and/or house tour	Softball tournament
Book sale and fair	Holding a dance	Spaghetti or chili dinners
Bowling contest	Marathon—10K, 5K, walking	Sport camp
Candy, cookie, or fruit sales	Monopoly marathon	Swimming marathon
Canoe race	Night golf	T-shirt and sweatshirt sales
Car wash	Pageant (male or female)	Talent show
Carnivals	Pancake breakfast	Tennis tournament
Church supper	Picture taking	Used equipment swaps
Club exhibitions	Pizza sales	Weiner and pig roasts
Concert	Radio marathon	Wrapping paper sales
Coupon book sales	Raffles	

exhibits (see the box titled Public Relations and Fund Raising Promotional Ideas).

All the directors of physical education and sport indicated that sport received more publicity than the physical education program. When asked why they thought this was so, some typical comments were: "the public demands it," "because of public interest," and "the newspapers will only accept and print releases on athletics."

When the directors were asked what message they were trying to convey to the public, the following were typical answers: the value of the total physical education and sport programs, the importance of the programs to the student, recognition and achievement of all students in all areas of physical education and sport, efforts and energies being expended to give each person a worthwhile experience in physical education and sport, the role of the physical education and sport programs in enhancing the health and welfare of the participant, and the aims and objectives of the total physical education and sport programs.

In summary, the professional and public relations programs in the school districts surveyed

were conducted in light of the following principles:

- Each physical education and sport department recognized the importance of an active public relations program.
- Sound policies guided the program.
- Responsibility for public relations was shared by all members of the department, with central authority residing with the director.
- Many different communications media were used to interpret the program to the numerous publics.
- The total physical education and sport program was recognized as being the most effective medium of professional and community relations.
- Efforts were made to interpret accurate facts about physical education and sport to the public.
- Considerable planning was needed for the effective use of public relations media.

Communities have also assisted schools and other public and private sector organizations and associations in the promotion of physical

Partners of the Americas in cooperation with the University of Minnesota and Special Olympics International play host to a Uruguyan coach and gold medal winning athlete.

education and sport. Rotary Clubs, Lions Clubs, American Legion Posts, The American Red Cross, Junior Chamber of Commerce, Partners of the Americas, and Special Olympics International, among other service organizations, have a long tradition of assisting in the positive public relations of physical education and sport programs.

SUMMARY

Public relations and marketing are important responsibilities for all managers of physical education and sport programs. Public support for these programs is essential if the necessary funds, facilities, staff, and other support essentials are to be provided. Therefore, sound principles should guide the public relations and marketing programs in a way that will communicate the objectives of these programs to the various publics who are interested. Furthermore, all the faculty, staff, and members of the organization should be involved in both the public relations and marketing programs to ensure that the content and

delivery of such programs are of the highest standard.

SELF-ASSESSMENT ACTIVITIES

These activities will assist students in determining if material and competencies presented in this chapter have been mastered.

1. As a manager, you are conducting a staff meeting in your school. Explain to the staff why you believe that an in-service program in public relations would be valuable to staff members and managers alike.

2. What is meant by the term *marketing,* and what are its implications for promoting physical education and sport programs?

3. What is meant by the fact that physical education and sport organizations are dealing with not just one but many publics? Identify two different publics and how they differ; indicate what type of public relations program you would employ with each.

4. List the principles that should be observed in a public relations program. Apply five of these principles in communicating the importance of a strong physical education program in your school.

5. Prepare a two-minute news release to be published or broadcast to the public about some event or phase of a physical education or sport program. Present it to the class and have the class evaluate it.

6. Present a fund-raising plan that would serve to build public relations in your elementary physical education program.

7. Prepare a five-minute speech to present to a local civic organization about the role of sport in community building.

REFERENCES

1. Cutlip, S. M., and A. H. Center. 1978. *Effective public relations.* Englewood Cliffs, N.J.: Prentice Hall.
2. Frigstad, D. B. 1995. *Know your market.* Grants Pass, Ore.: Oasis Press.

3. Graham, P. J. 1994. *Sport business: Operational and theoretical aspects.* Dubuque, Iowa: Brown & Benchmark.

4. McCarthy, E.J. 1960. Basic marketing: A managerial approach. Homewood, Ill.: Richard D. Irwin.

5. NAGWS. 1988. *Get in the Game Community Action Kit.* Reston, Va.: AAHPERD.

6. Williams, J. 1985. Public relations. In *Successful sport management,* edited by G. Lewis and H. Appenzeller. Charlottesville, Va.: Michie Company.

SUGGESTED READINGS

AAHPERD, Jump Rope for Heart, Hoops for Heart, and Sport and Physical Advocacy publicity kits, 1900 Association Drive, Reston, VA 22091.

AAHPERD and NASPE provide excellent materials by way of publicity kits that assist in forming vigorous promotion for physical education and sport programs.

AAHPERD. 1985. *Shaping the body politic: Legislative training for the physical educator.* Reston, Va.: AAHPERD. A publication prepared by the American Alliance Public and Legislative Affairs Office. Offers some helpful advice for educators charged with developing a school public relations program.

Brooks, C. M. 1994. *Sports marketing: Competitive business strategies for sports.* Englewood Cliffs, N.J.: Prentice Hall. Presents an environmental or climate assessment approach to various marketing strategies. Examines topics ranging from priority seating to internal and external sport competitions in order to facilitate better strategic market planning processes.

Buturusis, D. 1984. Gaining and keeping support for physical education. *Journal of Physical Education, Recreation and Dance* 55 (August):44. Discusses various ways physical education can achieve public support. Stresses such requisites as direct communication with parents and other segments of public, staff involvement, assessing community needs, and prudent media utilization.

Cousens, L., and T. Slack. 1996. Using sport sponsorship to penetrate local markets: The case of the fast food industry. *Journal of Sport Management* 10: 169–87.

Frigstad, D. B. 1995. *Know your market.* Grants Pass, Ore.: Oasis Press.
Presents an overview of the market research process including forecasting, market analysis, and setting up a market information system.

Fullerton, S., and R. Dodge. 1995. An application of market segmentation in a sports marketing arena: We all can't be Greg Norman. *Sport Marketing Quarterly* 4(3): 43–47.

Helitzer, M. 1992. *The dream job: Sports publicity, promotion, and public relations.* Athens, Ohio: University Press.

Horine, L. 1995. *Administration of physical and education sport programs.* Dubuque, Iowa: Brown & Benchmark.

Jackson, J. J. 1981. *Sport administration.* Springfield, Ill.: Charles C. Thomas. Presents the theoretical base for various aspects of management, including public relations, then links it with specific situations in physical education, sport, and recreation.

Marken, G. A. 1987. Thirteen ways to make enemies of the press. *Public Relations Quarterly* 32 (winter):30–31. Discusses guidelines for management when dealing with the press. Provides information on how to work in cooperative spirit with the media.

Roloff, B. D. 1985. Public relations: Objectives for physical education. *Journal of Physical Education, Recreation and Dance* 56 (March):69.
Sets forth fifteen objectives for public relations that, when properly implemented, will achieve public understanding and support for physical education.

Stotlar, D. K. 1993. *Successful sport marketing.* Dubuque, Iowa: Brown & Benchmark.

Sutton, W. A., and R. Watlington. 1994. Communicating with women in the 1990s: The role of sport marketing. *Sport Marketing Quarterly* 3(2): 9–13.

Tenoschok, M., and S. Sanders. 1984. Planning an effective public relations program. *Journal of Physical Education, Recreation and Dance* 55 (January):48. Describes how concerned parents and administrators are more willing to offer support if they know how the physical education program helps their children, what concepts are developed, and why activities are offered. Suggests various techniques for accomplishing these goals.

Yiannakis, A. 1989. Some contributions of sport sociology to the marketing of sport and leisure organizations. *Journal of Sport Management* 3:103–15.
Presents a detailed analysis of critical concerns involving sport marketing, consultative assistance, target market identification, and product marketing. Also discusses the marketing mix of product, price, place, promotions, and people.

chapter 15

Office Management

Instructional Objectives and Competencies To Be Achieved

After reading this chapter the student should be able to

- Appreciate the importance of office management in a physical education and sport program.
- Understand and appreciate the role of the computer in accomplishing management tasks.
- Justify the need for office personnel in the management of a physical education and sport program.
- Identify and describe the role that "boundarylessness" can play in sound office management.

- Identify basic office management procedures that should be used in carrying out the tasks of a physical education and sport program.
- List the records and databases that should be maintained in a physical educator's or athletic and activities director's office.

Managers of physical education and sport programs know that efficient office management determines to a great extent the success of their programs. Therefore, along with integrated functions such as facility management, fiscal accountability, public relations, and marketing, office management is a crucial management component.

Office management has often been neglected by physical educators, coaches, directors of athletics and activities, and other sport managers. Efficient office management indicates a well-run department. The office is the place for first impressions, communication between student and teacher or athlete and coach, the focus of management duties and functions, and a point of contact

for the management and staff and, oftentimes, the public.

An effective and efficiently managed office provides a place in which teachers, coaches, and sports managers are assisted and relieved of myriad duties by well-trained office personnel. Office personnel also provide service to students and other user groups, which serves to engender sound public relations. Whether an organization is large or small, staffed with student workers or volunteers, the office should be properly maintained, including up-to-date office equipment, and follow a well-established plan of office procedures so that assigned office tasks can be professionally carried out.

OFFICE MANAGEMENT TASKS

Although many office management tasks have been moved to a centralized location (e.g., principal's or district business manager's office) and the computer has enabled office personnel to instantly retrieve relevant information (e.g., student medical status, budget, eligibility, equipment inventory, schedule), office personnel are still responsible for many important tasks including the following:

Communication

The office is the nerve center of the organization, where information is received and transmitted to staff members, user groups, and others by means such as face-to-face or video conferences, telephone, fax, correspondence, intercom, pager, and electronic mail systems. Communication systems and procedures ranging from personally recorded voice mail to call waiting should be in place to effectively and promptly service, record, transmit, and distribute messages. Proper procedure should be followed and professional courtesy always extended.

Offices serve as hubs for effective communication and management.

Correspondence

The office is the setting for preparing and filing letters and reports for managers and staff members and for handling and sorting their incoming and outgoing mail.

Supplies and Equipment

The office is the place for requesting, receiving, ordering, and disbursing supplies and equipment needed for conducting the organization's various activities. It should be a place that safeguards programmatic assets.

Processing Materials

The office is a central point for recording, duplicating, typing, and word processing data, information, and materials pertinent to the management of the program.

Record Keeping

The office is the place in which records containing information on staff, students, athletes, and other materials are housed or made available via computer database. Calendars, schedules, attendance, and medical status reports are usually priorities of well-run offices. The computer has made centralized housing and storing of student files more accessible and efficient than were traditional manual filing systems.

Personnel Concerns

The office serves as a central location for employment interviews, counseling, and small conferences.

Report Preparation

The office is a place for preparing and retrieving data and information and for finalizing reports for various faculty and staff members and other personnel to whom the management is required to report.

Budget Preparation and Implementation

The office is where budget information is prepared, payrolls are initiated and may be distributed, revenues and expenditures are recorded, and financial reports and summaries are compiled and stored or electronically filed and fed to a central database.

Community and Public Relations

The office is a key communications center for the conduct, planning, and management of community-based and professional projects that are closely related and important to the achievement of the goals and functions of the organization. Reception and receiving of visitors as well as other personnel is crucial to the program.

Emergencies

The office is a focal point for meeting day-to-day emergency situations that call for immediate action. Instant communication and location of personnel and students necessitate precise and up-to-date record keeping.

IMPORTANCE OF OFFICE MANAGEMENT

Colleagues, community leaders, business contacts, new staff members, potential employees, vendors, students, and other visitors frequently have their initial contacts with physical education and sport managers and departments in the central office (Schaffer 1988). Their reception, the courtesies they are promptly shown, the efficiency and attitude with which the office work is conducted, and other covert operational details leave lasting impressions. Friends, alumni, employees, and recruits are often made or lost at this strategic control point.

Communications Center

Office work, broadly defined, is the handling and management of information. The office is usually the place in which schedules are arranged and distributed; telephone calls made and received; fax and electronic mail transmitted; reports typed, word processed, duplicated, and file transferred; mail received, opened, and distributed; bulletins prepared and issued; conferences arranged and held; appointments made and confirmed; visitors received and greetings voiced and exchanged. The office represents the hub of activity around which revolves the effective and efficient functioning of the physical education and coaching personnel. Unless these functions are carried out with dispatch, accuracy, and courtesy, the entire management process begins to break down.

Focus of Management Duties

The chief management personnel (e.g., department chair, athletic amd activities director, office manager, etc.), secretarial assistants, and clerical help constitute the office staff. The filing system (e.g., computer), key records and files, and reports are usually housed in the office. When inventories need to be examined, budgets audited, letters pulled from files, or the program chair or director consulted on important matters, the office is frequently the point of contact. Management responsibilities are carried out in the office, making this space a focal point for the entire organization.

Handbook or Manual of Tasks

Every office should be well organized, and one way to assist office personnel is to develop a manual or handbook for office procedures. This manual will serve as a guide not only for accomplishing office tasks, assignments, and duties but also for all office conduct.

Point of Contact for Management and Staff Members

Staff members visit the office regularly. Mailboxes are located there, and telephone calls, faxes, messages, and electronic mail may be taken and transferred by the office. Conferences and appointments with students and visitors often bring staff members to the office. Constant communication and dialogue take place between the management and staff members in this setting. The atmosphere in the office can and should create high staff morale, efficiency, a friendly and

Offices can take on many shapes and forms, but they are always crucial to the management process.

secure climate, and a feeling of working toward common goals.

RELATIONSHIP OF MANAGEMENT TO OFFICE STAFF MEMBERS

The management should establish a good working relationship with office staff members. Secretaries and other office personnel should have a feeling of belonging and a recognition that they are an important part of the organization. This form of "boundarylessness" or co-location (that should be practiced throughout the organization) serves as a behavior definer, a way of getting people outside of their organizational boxes and offices, and working together faster. The work each one performs, and their ideas, are essential to the achievement of the organization's goals.

Most managers depend heavily on their office staff members to carry out day-to-day duties and routines efficiently and productively. Well-trained and highly motivated office personnel are a must to effectively accomplish this task. Furthermore, managers (e.g., teachers, athletic and activities directors, coaches) are frequently away from their desks on organization assignments, and in their absence, the office must function in the same manner as when the manager is present. These goals cannot be achieved unless an excellent working relationship exists between the management and office staff members.

In-Service Education of Office Staff Members

The management should encourage office staff members to engage in in-service education and training and be aware of the updating of any office procedures. Areas in which improvement might take place include word processing skills, computer programming, computer graphics, updating the filing system, simplifying record keeping, and human relations skills (e.g., assertiveness, multicultural, diversity, and self-development training).

Office staff should also be encouraged to continue their formal education and keep in good physical condition; it is hoped that management will see that these might be built into the office staff 's busy schedule.

Sexual Harassment

Sexual harassment is a problem that has been highlighted in recent years. Electronic and print media stories and court cases have described how sexual harassment in educational settings has resulted in dismissals as well as psychological trauma. Managers must recognize that such conduct cannot be tolerated. Departmental procedures should be established, and staff should be encouraged to attend workshops concerning this crucial issue.

OFFICE SPACE

The central office for the physical education and sport departments should be readily accessible. If physically possible, the office should be near health service and athletic training offices,

Reception areas with viewing windows are popular in health and fitness centers.

gymnasiums, arenas, exercise rooms, locker rooms, fields, pools, and other departmental facilities.

Most central offices for physical education and sport should consist of at least three divisions including (1) a general reception area, (2) clerical work stations, and (3) private offices. Other desirable features to be considered are a rest room, storage and duplicating room, and conference room for staff and other meetings and functions.

General Reception Area

The general reception area is used by visitors as a waiting room, reception room, or information center; for staff members to pick up their mail, conduct appointments, or acquire information; and for office services in general. The area should be attractive and well maintained, with comfortable chairs, current and attractive bulletin boards, and other items essential to carrying out necessary management routines. The area should create a warm, friendly, professional atmosphere. A counter, railing, or desk divider should separate the general reception area from the rest of the office facilities and

work stations. This division helps ensure greater privacy and security and more efficient conduct of office responsibilities.

Clerical Work Stations

The clerical work space should be separated from the general reception and waiting area. It should be equipped with computer, typewriters, files, tables, telephones, copying and fax machines, laser printer, and scanner. It is often desirable to have a private alcove or office for one or more of the secretaries, depending on the size of the department and office space. Office dividers are also effective in providing personalized work stations. Privacy is often needed for word processing, typing, preparing reports, or for the convenience of visitors and other personnel. Ample lighting and sufficient space for freedom of movement should ensure that duties can be carried out comfortably and with minimal confusion, traffic, and difficulty.

Private Offices

The chairperson or director of the department or program and possibly other staff members, depending on the school size and educational domain (college, university), should have private offices. The offices should be large enough (at least 120 square feet) so that the persons in managerial positions can concentrate on their work without interruptions, conduct private conferences and tutorials with students, interact with staff members or visitors, and in general carry out their duties as efficiently as possible. The offices should be well lighted, wired for cable, air conditioned, equipped appropriately, well maintained, and secure. Desks should be functional, and calendars, schedule pads for appointments and conferences, and other essential organizational materials should be provided. Filing and storage cabinets, bookshelves, resource material, and other office equipment (e.g., computer, laser printer, VCR, etc.) should be provided as needed.

Private staff offices are necessary for maximal efficiency.

OFFICE PERSONNEL

The number of office personnel depends on the size and mission of the program or department. The staff can consist of receptionist, secretaries, and word processors in a large department. However, most offices, especially at the school level, usually consist of one principal secretary. In some small schools, student workers, interns, and volunteers may be the only office personnel available. This is why the selection and qualities of office personnel (usually only a secretary) and the interpersonal relationships established are vital to any physical education and sport program.

Following are brief descriptions of the roles of various specialized office personnel, but as mentioned, these duties are usually collapsed into one or, if fortunate, two top-notch secretaries.

The position of *receptionist* will vary with the program. In some departments, a receptionist is a greeter who presents an attractive appearance and is polite, courteous, and helpful to visitors and callers. The receptionist should be knowledgeable about how to deal with routine departmental matters and where to direct inquiries that can be handled better elsewhere. Some departments also assign to this person certain word processing, typing, filing, and supply room responsibilities.

The *secretary* should be a solid contributor to the chairperson and to the department as a whole. To be most helpful, he or she will be a master typist and word processor, a stenographer, a public relations representative, an expert computer operator, and be efficient at photocopying, faxing, and time management. He or she will see that the office runs smoothly. The secretary should know where documents and materials are filed and be able to access them quickly, should assist management with minor details (e.g., appointments, calendar, copying), and should see that accurate records are maintained, databases established, and reports sent out on time. Without question, the secretary is crucial to a well-managed office.

The duties and functions of an outstanding secretary range from keeping managerial calendars to maintaining public relations, from taking minutes to control and security (e.g., keys, locks), and from completing endless forms to laboring over reports and manuscripts. The secretary is the backbone of most departments and should both command respect from and show respect for all personnel involved in the managerial process.

A *transcribing word processing operator* listens to dictated material on a playback mechanism, then word processes the material in accordance with the instructions provided. This technical skill usually carries over into the operation of the facsimile (fax) machine and other general office duties as well.

Office personnel should be selected very carefully. Experience, intelligence, character, personality, honesty, common sense, appearance, and ability should play important roles in the selection process. The secretary should be well educated, experienced or at least exposed to a secretarial course of study, and possess a solid background in word processing, computer applications, bookkeeping, and English as well as the requisite psychosocial qualities (e.g., discretion, loyalty, integrity). In small elementary schools, high schools, and colleges, the manager may have to rely partially or entirely on students (e.g., work study) to perform much of the clerical work.

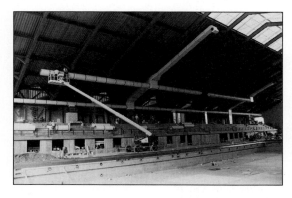

Office space should be considered when planning any new or remodeled facility.

In-service education should take place for these student workers to ensure that acceptable procedures are followed in the conduct of their work. Student help is a necessary part of most management teams and should provide a meaningful experience for the employee. This responsibility usually resides with the senior secretary, but sometimes the manager must embrace this important duty.

EQUIPMENT AND SUPPLIES

Whether an office is efficient and effective sometimes depends on the equipment and supplies available. The materials needed vary with the size of the organization. In smaller organizations, equipment such as computers and duplicating machines might be centrally located rather than in departmental offices. The following are some of the physical resources that should be considered when conducting a functional analysis of office requirements (FAOR):

Bookcases

Bulletin boards

Cabinets (lockable)

Calendars

Calculator

Camera

Cellular phone

CD-ROM

Chairs

Clips

Coat racks

Clock

Computer package and stand (laser printer, mouse, modem, appropriate software such as Internet browser, spreadsheet, database, word processor, graphics package, etc.)

Copying machine

Desk baskets and dividers

Desk lamps

Desk pads

Desks

Dictionaries

Facsimile machine

File cabinet (lockable)

First aid cabinet

Letter trays

Magazine racks

Modem

Paper cutter

Paperweight

Paste, glue, tape

Pencil sharpeners (manual and electric)

Pencils and pens

Phone directory

Pictures or posters

Reproducing machines

Rulers

Safe

Scale for postage

Scanner

Scissors

Scrapbooks

Stamps

Stapling machine, three ring punch

Stationery and paper

Tables

Telephone

Typewriters

Umbrella rack

Video and VCR

Wardrobe cabinets (lockable)

Wastebaskets

Although physical resources (e.g., equipment, supplies, and other materials) are vital for effective and efficient office functioning and/or communicating and for maintaining and storing records, recording appointments, and controlling supplies and equipment, the well-trained and committed human resource is still the most crucial commodity and is the key to successful office management.

COMPUTER APPLICATIONS IN OFFICE MANAGEMENT

In 1983, sales of personal computers reached approximately 3.5 million units. Today, 65 percent of all professional, managerial, and administrative jobs depend on computers, and expenditure relating to computer utilization has reached almost 13 percent of our gross national product. Indeed, over the last twenty years, the government has spent more than $300 billion to move its information technology systems into the twenty-first century.

The computer age is here, but it is accompanied by many problems and concerns (e.g., expenses, literacy apprehension, application viruses, and training). Computer systems can contribute substantially to cost reduction of office management through increased efficiency and productivity in the performance of routine clerical tasks. All twenty-one schools involved in the survey mentioned in chapter 14 indicated the presence of a computer for departmental use; however, more than half noted that the technology was not fully integrated into their physical education programs.

The Department of Parks and Recreation in Hartford, Connecticut, realized the potential of the computer in its project titled Leisure Match. The department developed a computer informa-

Computers play an important role in office management.

tion service for Hartford residents to familiarize them with the leisure opportunities the city was offering. The computer service enabled interested individuals to match leisure interests to leisure opportunities, helped people to better understand and enjoy new and different leisure experiences, and provided management with a computerized information system that not only resulted in a better program but also contributed to future planning and resource allocation (Jensen 1984).

Public and private sector physical fitness and wellness organizations have also significantly increased their efficiency as well as reduced their costs by adopting computer technology. Member attendance, activity preferences, attendance and front desk control, member billing, and market segmentation all contribute to satisfied customers and good public relations. Tenneco Energy maintains a computer system to help achieve the goals of its corporate health and fitness program. The computer has been particularly helpful in providing demographic, fitness, and medical assessment data on employees and in providing exercise and nutritional analyses, in which the employee keeps a daily record of activity workouts including caloric expenditure (see figure 15-1).

Technology is not only useful in parks and recreation programs and the corporate fitness setting, but it also plays a significant role in the operation of physical education and sport programs.

The Lexington, Massachusetts, public schools have used their computer system to link all physical education staff members to an electronic mail system. This link enables physical education teachers and their supervisors to communicate instantaneously within all school buildings through the use of desktop computers linked to the school system's mainframe computer. This system eliminates delays caused by use of interoffice mailing systems and provides for immediate communication to individuals or specified groups on the network.

The Lexington school system has also developed a computerized program for tracking students in grades 3 through 12 as they participate in AAHPERD's Physical Best. Teachers in each school, upon completion of the testing, enter the raw data from their desktop computer into a user-friendly, menu-driven mainframe program. This program converts entered data instantaneously to national normed percentiles, maintains a progressive student database, and provides an individualized fitness report card. The program also offers predesigned graphics packages to help with program evaluation, parent conferences, and public relations.

Another feature of the Lexington program allows each physical education teacher and coach, after being assigned a predetermined budget amount, to enter a computerized catalog of physical education and sport equipment and purchase requirements. These orders are sorted and compiled into a singular bid list and sent to a variety of vendors. When the bids are returned and analyzed, the computer writes the purchase orders automatically. The manager or supervisor can keep up to date on purchases and budget expenditures and their projected implications through specified procedures and continuous staff input concerning needs (e.g., equipment, travel, tournaments, etc.).

Computer Contributions to Management

A computer is a machine that can, among other things, program managerial functions in areas such as physical education and sport (Mohnsen 1991). It possesses a memory and will carry out a given set of instructions almost instantaneously. It can process data about physical education and sport programs (e.g., budget, test scores) by performing mathematical and logical operations. The computer can instantaneously transfer or move information and can store it as well.

The main advantages for management in using a computer include *speed;* it saves a considerable amount of time (e.g., the addition that one person could do in 100 days can be done in 5 seconds or less via computer). A second advantage is *accuracy;* the computer does not make errors if the correct input is applied. A third advantage is that it *imposes discipline;* a person

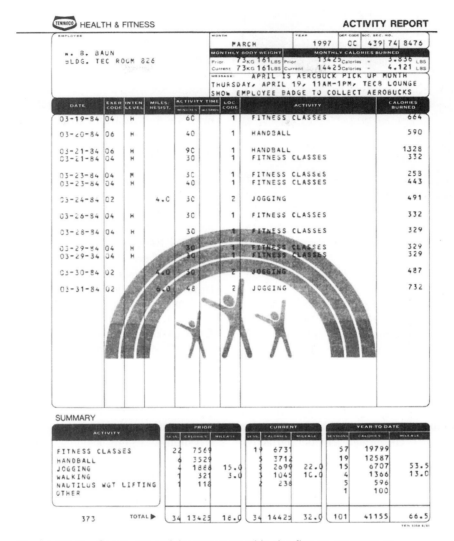

Figure 15-1.   Computer activity report used in the fitness program at Tenneco Energy in Houston, Texas.

must thoroughly understand a problem before programming the computer to arrive at the correct answer. A fourth advantage is *versatility;* the computer can score, add, subtract, multiply, divide, sort, compare, correct, simulate, draw, transfer, and store information as well as perform a variety of other potentially helpful operations (Porter and Miller 1985).

The computer processes most likely to be applied by management include word processing, database, spreadsheets, desktop publishing, and networking through the Internet, CD-ROM accessing, and the World Wide Web.

Word processing is the computer function most called upon by management. Letters, memos, and other correspondence; manuscripts;

From budget preparation to data analysis and from E-mail to accessing the World Wide Web, computers play an important role in physical education and sport.

reports; curriculum guides; playbooks; forms; and evaluations, among other items, are common word processing outcomes that can be stored and manipulated through mail merge, spell checking, and graphics applications.

Database has transformed worn phone books, old student records, mailing lists, and past scouting reports, along with other collectibles into functional bits of information for the business manager, teacher, coach, and athletic and activities director.

Spreadsheets assist the manager with inventory, purchasing, facility utilization and scheduling, budgeting, and other countables. Spreadsheets permit the manager to forecast, or see how the future will be affected by potential decisions such as budget reduction or attendance gain.

Desktop publishing allows the user to design newsletters and produce fliers and overhead transparencies as well as curriculum guides and playbooks with graphics. Scanners transfer data from texts, ledgers, and videos onto disks for editing and storage.

Networking through the Internet is a means to link the staff to a centralized data bank. Depending on the software, this communication may range from departmental electronic mail to

international computer conferencing and BINET, which connects about 1,500 organizations. Internet provides the user with not only E-mail but file transfer (FTP) and remote log-on which enable the user to log on to another computer to access information from a remote work station.

CD-ROM (Compact Disk-Read Only Memory) is a high storage capacity, optimal disk that can hold approximately 275,000 typewritten pages. CD-ROMs often contain large databases, ranging from government census information to dissertation abstracts. DATRIX, SPORT Discus, PsyLIT, and MedLine are examples of professional literature abstracts that teachers, coaches, and administrators can access.

The World Wide Web (WWW) is a universal network of servers that permits the user to connect to a wide range of resources—everything from Supreme Court decisions to university graduate programs' home pages.

Computer Utilization in Physical Education and Sport

Physical education and sport programs can make effective use of the computer. It can be programmed to aid in management decision making at all levels. The bottom line is recognizing that many management tasks—budgeting, class scheduling, record keeping, talent assessment, direct mail public relations—can be handled by the computer at a far more accurate and efficient pace than manually by the clerical staff.

The computer can be especially valuable in the areas of budget and finance, personnel, program and scheduling, and facilities. The computer can be helpful in such budget and finance tasks as handling payrolls, inventories, budget control and allocation (figure 15-2), cost analysis, purchasing, and general accounting. In the area of personnel, the computer can save much clerical work in tasks like student registration, grade reporting and recording, faculty assignments, and staff retention. The computer can assist in programming, designing curricula and instructional strategies, and in scheduling students (e.g., demand analysis) or other clientele for particular classes or activities.

INSTRUCTIONAL SUPPORT SERVICES
ACCOUNTING PERIOD 12

REPT FIN333 16

SORT KEYS: NBR-PRG-EXP

OBJ	DESCRIPTION		YTD-EXPENDED	A YTD-EXPENDED	B YTD-ENCUMBER	C BUDGET	C – (A + B) BUDGET–BALANCE	%EXP
200	DISTRICT CONTEST	TOTAL	0.00	1,315.82	0.00	3,500.00	2,184.18	37.6
220	ATHLETIC DIR OFFICE	TOTAL	18,579.35	72,336.13	0.00	264,540.00	192,203.87	27.3
221	FOOTBALL–BOYS	TOTAL	2,984.03	70,129.30	0.00	90,010.00	19,880.70	77.9
222	BASKETBALL–BOYS	TOTAL	5,131.51	6,139.85	0.00	42,980.00	36,840.15	14.3
223	HOCKEY–BOYS	TOTAL	6,626.46	7,371.31	0.00	49,360.00	41,988.69	14.9
224	BASEBALL–BOYS	TOTAL	0.00	994.00	0.00	34,880.00	33,886.00	2.8
226	SOCCER–BOYS	TOTAL	1,182.73	34,109.46	0.00	37,580.00	3,470.54	90.8
227	GYMNASTICS–BOYS	TOTAL	197.00	12,144.11	0.00	17,480.00	5,335.89	69.5
228	SWIMMING–BOYS	TOTAL	2,883.37	5,987.47	0.00	24,760.00	18,772.53	24.2
229	CC–SKIING–BOYS	TOTAL	797.64	797.64	0.00	5,640.00	4,842.36	14.1
230	WRESTLING–BOYS	TOTAL	2,568.20	3,560.79	0.00	27,960.00	24,399.21	12.7
231	TRACK–BOYS	TOTAL	265.26	1,283.61	0.00	26,570.00	25,286.39	4.8
232	CC–RUNNING–BOYS	TOTAL	5.82	4,219.30	0.00	5,360.00	1,140.70	78.7
233	GOLF–BOYS	TOTAL	373.43	389.48	0.00	9,980.00	9,590.52	3.9
234	TENNIS–BOYS	TOTAL	0.00	82.20	0.00	12,540.00	12,457.80	.7
235	SLALOM/SKIING–BOYS	TOTAL	520.55	520.55	0.00	6,320.00	5,799.45	8.2
240	VOLLEYBALL–GIRLS	TOTAL	803.90	24,915.16	0.00	34,780.00	9,864.84	71.6
241	BASKETBALL–GIRLS	TOTAL	6,303.42	9,886.92	0.00	41,380.00	31,493.08	23.9
242	GYMNASTICS–GIRLS	TOTAL	2,724.62	2,724.94	0.00	16,980.00	14,217.06	16.2
243	CC–SKIING–GIRLS	TOTAL	717.66	717.66	0.00	5,380.00	4,662.34	13.3

Figure 15-2. A school district sport budget control document.

It can record facts about students' interests, faculty availability, complex scheduling, and staff use (Minor 1989).

To be more specific, physical educators and sport managers are interested in having complete demographic records on faculty and staff: names, addresses, phone numbers, teaching background, health status, accomplishments, and teaching loads. The computer is a tremendous asset in having such records filed and immediately accessible. Registration of students and class scheduling can be better accomplished. The computer can accurately report which gymnasiums, swimming pools, tennis courts, weight rooms, basketball courts, baseball fields, and other facilities are in use at any particular time. The computer can be used to keep physical fitness assessment data, health status, and accident reports on every student or member of an organization.

Support staff no longer has to keep individual index cards on each person; the computer can generate a master file of physical fitness data for each person, compare the data to state and national norms, and print out a report card. The computer can keep attendance records, compare prices for equipment and supplies, and locate every book and periodical related to physical education and sport in your library (Mohnsen 1991). Additionally, some institutions, such as the Big Ten and the University of Chicago, have formed cooperative information management consortiums so that their library resources are electronically available to each other's members.

For facilities management, the computer can help in configuring the best use of building space, availability of facilities, equipment inventory, cost of building maintenance and energy, and projected future needs of buildings and other facilities. This information is crucial to long-range planning as well as to efficient and effective facility usage.

Uses for the computer in sport programs include scheduling games and practice facilities, gathering data on players in a school or organiza-tion, and identifying players' tendencies, weaknesses, and strengths. The computer can also keep individual statistics on every team member as well as on the opponents.

Other database uses of the computer in physical education and sport may include long-range scheduling, newsletter construction, travel arrangements and transportation schedules, news releases, fitness forms, grade or report cards, locker and lock assignments, media guides, injury reports, playbooks, ticket generation, eligibility lists, potential sponsors for fund-raising, trend analysis, scoreboard graphics, maintenance inventory, and a host of other applications that can reduce time and increase the efficiency and effectiveness of office and program operation (Andrus and Lane 1989).

Without question, office management and the profession of physical education and sport have been revolutionized by the computer. From desktop curricular guides to E-mail and E-journals, from computer-assisted instruction and simulation to MEEC's Sports XL Collection (e.g., Athletic Director, Club/League Organizer, Soccer), and from the Virtual Library Home Page on the World Wide Web to spell checking and Quick Cam, the computer and its endless supply of software programs has permeated contemporary society including the arena of physical education and sport.

The functions described here are only some of the applications of the computer to physical education and sport. The challenge, moving into the twenty-first century, is to become computer literate and conversant in order to function more effectively and to better contribute to society. Computer literacy is requisite for all students and should play an ongoing role in the professional development of all teachers, coaches, athletic and activities directors, and sport managers.

MANAGEMENT ROUTINE

The management routine (Tedesco and Mitchell 1987), or manner in which the day-to-day business of the organization, center, or department is carried out by the organization's office personnel, represents the basic reason why such a facility exists. Although technology has reduced labor intensity and time and has even omitted some office procedures, there are still offices and management in transition; therefore, the following aspects of management routine should continue to receive careful consideration and attention for maximal office efficiency and effectiveness.

Office Hours

The office should be open during regular hours. This usually means from 7:30 or 8:00 A.M. to 4:30 or 5:00 P.M. in most school and institutional settings. During this time, someone should always be present to answer the telephone, greet visitors, field questions, and carry out the regular functions of the office. Some exceptions to these hours may be made (e.g., flextime), but in all cases, office hours should be posted and publicized as widely as possible. Staff members should post regular office hours indicating when they will be accessible, and these hours should also be on file in the central office. Staff members should faithfully observe their office hours and keep office personnel informed of their whereabouts. Alternative times should be supplied to the central office if for some circumstance (e.g., attendance at national meeting, professional growth seminar), office hours cannot be observed; the result will be that requests for information and assistance can be properly handled and staff members can be reached if necessary.

Assignments

All assignments for office personnel should be in writing, with job descriptions and tasks clearly outlined and appropriately publicized. Office personnel may be required to turn on, check, and audit office machines; duplicate materials; prepare weekly bulletins; distribute and account for supplies; check, update, and prepare the calendar of events; recycle office mater-

Office professionalism and conduct are important for all personnel.

ials; contact students; deliver mail; and assist in general office cleanup. These duties, among others, should be clearly understood and carried out at the proper time. Specific responsibilities should be fixed, appropriate work priorities established, and a schedule of duties prepared to prevent any misunderstanding. Any misunderstandings should be quickly and amicably resolved because respect, pride, cooperative spirit, motivation, and efficiency of the organization must be maintained.

Correspondence

Correspondence represents a most effective public relations medium. Letters and messages can be written and transmitted in a cold, impersonal manner, or they can carry warmth, respect, and courtesy and help interpret what a program reflects and is trying to accomplish for student, staff, faculty, or other person or organization. Letters, memos, and messages should be prepared carefully, using proper grammar and a format that meets the highest standards of secretarial practice. If a staff member must prepare his or her own letters, these same standards should be met. All correspondence should convey the feeling that the department is anxious to assist, support, and serve wherever possible. Even with the advent of computer spell checking, all correspondence should be proofread and all addresses checked. Letters and memos should be distributed promptly, and follow-up memos should be sent in a timely fashion. Copies of all important correspondence should be stored for future reference. Creative office personnel should also improve and refine appropriate office forms, and keep a word processing file of standard correspondence to reduce turnaround time.

Files and Filing

For vertical filing, the office should contain metal filing cases that can be secured. The filing system employed depends on the number of personnel involved and the person doing the filing, but in any case, it should be simple and functional and should be used for storing only the most current information. Other records, data, and information should, when possible, be stored on computer disk or microfiche. Files usually consist of correspondence and informational material. For ease of retrieving material, some form of alphabetical filing should be applied, although numerical filing may at times be practical. The alphabetical files utilize a name or subject designator (e.g., "Brown, Charles A.," "Medical Examinations," or "Equipment") and a manila or hanging folder to hold all the material to be filed under that name or subject. Cross-references should be included to facilitate locating material. Guide cards can be used to show which divisions of the file pertain to each letter of the alphabet, thus facilitating the search for material.

Office files should be maintained accurately. The person responsible for the files should take care to see that any letter or other material borrowed from a file is returned to the proper folder and that the folder is returned to its correct location. Filing should also be kept up to date. A periodic review of the files should be made to cull material that is no longer pertinent to the department. Files that for any reason are removed from the file cabinet should be signed out and signed in

on return. If files are stored via computer, backup copies are a must.

Telephone, Facsimile Machine, and E-Mail

The use of the office telephone, fax machine, and E-mail is a major consideration for good departmental public relations. Here are a few simple rules that should be observed.

Promptness

The telephone and all communications should be prioritized and answered as promptly and courteously as possible. Answering promptly reflects efficient office practice and consideration for the person calling. Answering machines, voice mail, and phone rollover to the central office should be considered.

Professional Purposes

The telephone, fax, and electronic mail are installed in an office for professional purposes. Office personnel should not be permitted to talk for long periods of time about personal matters. The telephone and other forms of communication linkages, including copying machines, should be kept clear for business important to the achievement of organizational objectives.

Courtesy, Friendliness, and Helpfulness

The person answering the phone should be pleasant and courteous and should desire to be of assistance to the caller. This manner represents a professional responsibility that should be standard procedure at all times.

Messages

At times staff members who are being called will not be available. A memo pad should be kept at hand for recording day, time, name, and phone number of callers in such cases. A definite procedure should be established for relaying these messages (e.g., phone, E-mail, file transfer, fax, telex, packages, etc.) to the proper persons. Voice and electronic mail have become popular aids in this procedure; however, a central number should be made available at which the caller can speak to a real live person as opposed to a totally automated voice mail menu.

Appointments

Appointments should not be made unless it is believed they can be kept. Furthermore, all appointments should be kept as close to the time scheduled as possible. Many times, the person making an appointment has arranged his or her day with the understanding that the conference will be at a certain time. If this time is not adhered to, the schedule has to be altered, and complications frequently arise as a result. The secretary should keep an accurate list of appointments. If no secretary is available, the staff member should keep his or her own schedule of appointments and check it regularly to see that all appointments are honored.

Meetings

Meetings—including staff meetings, office personnel meetings, and orientation for new office team members—should be regular and requisite. Regular meetings reaffirm that a line of open communication exists and provide a time for building, monitoring, and assessing interpersonal relationships and evaluating how the management system is functioning. Meetings should begin on time, have an agenda that has been distributed at least a day before, and stay on task. Good meetings are crucial to smooth, efficient, and effective office management as well as to solid departmental functioning.

RECORDS AND REPORTS

At times, records and reports are not prepared and maintained accurately because the directions provided by management or staff members are not clear and definite. When complicated reports are to be prepared, oral instructions alone will usually not be sufficient. Instead, directions (e.g., format, style, computer compatibility, and a prototype or model) should be written, typed, and distributed. The preparation of a sample method and preferred style will save time and energy and will also help ensure better results.

Managers are often responsible for poorly kept records, inaccurate reports, and late submissions. Directions and deadlines should be made clear, and managers should receive announcements at regular intervals and reminders of when reports are due. A prompt check of report status will indicate whether the reports have been submitted, or are on-line. Any omissions, updates, or other inaccuracies in records and reports should be corrected immediately.

The survey of twenty-one school systems discussed in chapter 14 also determined the types of records that were kept in departmental files for physical education (figure 15-3). The results of this survey showed that some of the schools' departments were conscientious in record keeping and others were not.

The survey also revealed that in some schools, records concerning health status, fitness level, and attendance were kept in the physical education department, whereas in other schools, records were kept in the central office. The same was true of budgetary and inventory records. In some schools, department heads kept these records, and elsewhere, the business manager or principal kept them.

Most department heads and teachers admitted that they should put more time and effort into this phase of management. The result of the survey indicated that office management procedures are in a state of transition, with most departments having access to technology but few using it to maintain records. Contemporary management must lead the way to build effective, efficient functioning at this crucial management level (see the Checklist box for some guidelines for effective office management).

Figure 15-3. Physical education records used in twenty-one school systems.

X denotes records kept	Accident reports	Adapted program	Application for participation in interscholastic sports	Attendance	Cumulative class record	Equipment	Extracurricular activities	Financial	Game reports	Health	Interscholastic sports	Intramurals	Inventory	Medical form for interscholastic sports	Medical form for physical education	Parental permission sports participation	Physical fitness scores
School 1	x			x	x			x		x	x	x	x				x
School 2					x							x	x			x	x
School 3	x	x		x					x	x	x					x	x
School 4	x			x		x							x	x	x	x	x
School 5					x						x				x	x	x
School 6		x		x	x			x	x		x				x	x	x
School 7	x			x								x					x
School 8	x		x	x			x				x	x	x			x	x
School 9				x	x												
School 10	x			x							x				x	x	
School 11	x		x	x								x			x	x	x
School 12		x		x							x	x	x				
School 13	x			x		x					x	x	x			x	x
School 14		x		x		x	x					x	x				
School 15	x	x		x					x		x					x	x
School 16	x			x						x					x		
School 17			x	x	x	x		x		x						x	
School 18												x				x	x
School 19				x						x					x		x
School 20	x			x										x		x	x
School 21	x		x	x	x	x	x	x		x	x	x		x			x

Checklist of Some Important Considerations for Office Management

Space and Working Conditions — Yes / No

1. Does the reception area provide ample space for waiting visitors?
2. Is the clerical space separated from the reception room so that office work is not interrupted by the arrival of guests?
3. Are there private offices for the director of physical education and athletics and activities and as many staff members as possible?
4. Is there a health suite that provides an office and other essential facilities for medical personnel?
5. Is there adequate space and equipment for filing?
6. Are file drawers arranged so that papers can be inserted and removed easily and with space for future expansion?
7. Is the office arranged so that as many workers as possible get the best natural light, with glare from sunlight or reflected sunlight avoided?

Checklist of Some Important Considerations for Office Management—cont'd

	Yes	No
8. Has the office space been painted in accordance with the best color dynamics?		
9. Have provisions been made so that unnecessary noise is eliminated, distractions are kept to a minimum, and cleanliness and a smoke-free environment prevail?		
10. Are there good ventilation, appropriate artificial lighting, and satisfactory heating conditions?		
11. Is the value of the computer fully integrated?		

Personnel

	Yes	No
12. Is a receptionist available to greet guests and answer queries?		
13. Is there a recorded analysis of the duties of each secretarial position?		
14. Are channels available for ascertaining causes of dissatisfaction among office personnel?		
15. Do secretaries dress appropriately?		
16. Do secretaries maintain a desk that has an orderly appearance?		
17. Do secretaries concern themselves with the efficiency of the office?		
18. Are secretaries loyal to the department and staff members?		
19. Do staff members have regular office hours?		
20. Are appointments kept promptly?		
21. Is up-to-date and appropriate reading material furnished for waiting guests?		
22. Do office personnel continually pay attention to maintaining offices so that they are neat, with papers, books, and other materials arranged in an orderly manner?		
23. Are the secretaries knowledgeable about departmental activities so that they can answer intelligently queries about staff members and activities?		
24. Do secretaries assist guests promptly and courteously?		
25. Is work arranged neatly, free from errors, and presented appropriately?		
26. Is correspondence handled promptly?		
27. Is the filing system easily learned and is the filing done promptly so that the work does not pile up?		
28. Does the office routine use human resources efficiently, eliminating duplicate operations?		
29. Are the most effective and efficient office methods used?		

Procedures

	Yes	No
30. Is the clerical output satisfactory, with work starting promptly in the morning and after lunch, and breaks taken according to schedule?		
31. Has a streamlined procedure been developed so that telephones are answered promptly, guests are treated courteously, and personal argument and gossiping are minimized?		
32. Are essential records properly maintained and kept up to date?		
33. Have procedures for typing, word processing, and duplicating course outlines, committee reports, examinations, bulletins, fliers, letters, and announcements been developed to eliminate uncertainty or confusion on the part of staff members?		
34. Are regular office hours for staff posted and known so that office staff members can make appointments as needed?		
35. Are secretaries acquainted with such details as securing films and other visual aids, obtaining reference material, helping in registration, duplicating material, and obtaining additional forms and records?		
36. Is the office staffed continuously during working hours?		
37. Does the office have a personnel policy and an office manual or handbook?		

SUMMARY

Office management is an important consideration in the management of physical education and sport programs. Office management concerns such matters as communication, correspondence, materials processing, record keeping, meetings, in-service training, and public relations. The office is the nerve center of the operation; therefore, if the group, center, program, department, or other unit of the organization is to be efficiently run, much attention must be given to office management. Space, personnel, human relations, equipment, computers, management routine, records, evaluations, and reports must receive continual and careful attention.

SELF-ASSESSMENT ACTIVITIES

These activities will assist students in determining if material and competencies presented in this chapter have been mastered.

1. Why is sound office management essential to effective public relations?

2. What are some important reasons why "boundarylessness" office management is important to a department of intercollegiate athletics?

3. In what ways can the computer be used in physical education and sport programs?

4. As a manager of a large high school physical education program, describe the office personnel and equipment you would need and then justify your request.

5. Construct a class or departmental home page directory, including information about faculty, staff, and programs.

6. Prepare a set of sample records that you would want to maintain as part of a junior high or middle school physical education program.

7. Form a team and make an appointment with your department head or manager of a community-based physical activity or sport setting and conduct an office management audit via observation. Report your findings to the class.

REFERENCES

1. Andrus, S., and S.A. Lane. 1989. Computerizing the athletic department. *College Athletic Management* 1(March):30–34.

2. Jensen, M.A. 1984. Computer applications: An introduction. *Journal of Physical Education, Recreation, and Dance* 55(April):32.

3. Minor, R.O. 1989. Computer technology can manage curriculum, link learning to instruction. *NASSP Bulletin* 73(521):75–79.

4. Mohnsen, B. 1991. Using computers—Helping physical education administrators. *Journal of Physical Education, Recreation, and Dance* 62(January):40–43.

5. Porter, M.E., and V.E. Miller. 1985. How information gives you the competitive edge. *Harvard Business Review,* July/August, 149–60.

6. Schaffer, G. 1988. *Functional analysis of office requirements: A multiperspective approach.* New York: John Wiley and Sons.

7. Tedesco, E.H., and R.B. Mitchell. 1987. *Administrative office management systems.* New York: John Wiley and Sons.

SUGGESTED READINGS

Asbury, G. 1983. Bringing your operations into the computer age. *Athletic Purchasing and Facilities* 7(March):20.

Baun, W.B. and M. Baun. 1984. A corporate health and fitness program: Motivation and management by computers. *Journal of Physical Education, Recreation, and Dance* 55(April):42.
Describes how Tenneco Inc. uses computers in its corporate fitness program to achieve departmental goals and objectives.

Bay, R. 1993. The four C's for computer success. *School Business Affairs,* May, 10–18.

Bridges, F.J., and X. Roquemore. 1996. *Management for athletic/sport administration: Theory and practice.* Decatur, Ga.: Educational Services for Management.
Devoted to management procedures and functions with many implications for office management.

Henderson, R.I. 1994. *Compensation management: Rewarding performance.* Englewood Cliffs, N.J.: Prentice Hall.

Key, J. 1994. Reaching out with interest. *Journal of Physical Education, Recreation, and Dance* 65(February):21–24.

MECC/University of Minnesota. 1988. Improving the use of technology in schools: What are we learning?

Research Bulletin #1. Minneapolis, Minn.: Center for the Study of Educational Technology.
Covers the impact of technology on education. Focuses on computer-based programs, desktop procedures, and pursuing quality instructional software.

Djang, P.A. 1993. Selecting personal computers. *Journal of Research on Computer Education* 32 (spring):327–38.
Tells how to choose a computer that fits the needs of any particular organization or program.

Turner, J.A. 1985. A personal computer for every freshman: Even faculty skeptics are now enthusiasts. *Chronicle of Higher Education,* February.
Describes how some colleges and universities are providing students with computers and how those computers are being integrated throughout campus.

Physical Education and Sport with a Purpose

- International Charter of Physical Education and Sport (UNESCO)
- A Global Vision for School Physical Education and Sport and the Physically Educated Person (AAHPERD/CAHPERD)
- Year 2000 Objectives for the Nation: Physical Activity and Exercise (USDHHS)

INTERNATIONAL CHARTER OF PHYSICAL EDUCATION AND SPORT (UNESCO)

The General Conference of the United Nations Educational, Scientific and Cultural Organization, meeting in Paris at its twentieth session, this twenty-first day of November 1978,

Recalling that in the United Nations Charter the peoples proclaimed their faith in fundamental human rights and in the dignity and worth of the human person, and affirmed their determination to promote social progress and better standards of life,

Recalling that by the terms of the Universal Declaration of Human Rights, everyone is entitled to all the rights and freedoms set forth therein without discrimination of any kind as to race, color, sex, language, religion, political or other opinion, national or social origin, property, birth or other consideration,

Convinced that one of the essential conditions for the effective exercise of human rights is that everyone should be free to develop and preserve his or her physical, intellectual and moral powers, and that access to physical education and sport should consequently be assured and guaranteed for all human beings,

Convinced that to preserve and develop the physical, intellectual and moral powers of the human being improves the quality of life at the national and the international levels,

Believing that physical education and sport should make a more effective contribution to the inculcation of fundamental human values under-lying the full development of peoples,

Stressing accordingly that physical education and sport should seek to promote closer commun-ion between peoples and between individuals, together with disinterested emulation, solidarity and fraternity, mutual respect and understanding, and full respect for the integrity and dignity of human beings,

Considering that responsibilities and obliga-tions are incumbent upon the industrialized coun-tries and the developing countries alike for reduc-ing the disparity which continues to exist between them in respect of free and universal access to physical education and sport,

Considering that to integrate physical educa-tion and sport in the natural environment is to enrich them and to inspire respect of the earth's resources and a concern to conserve them and use them for the greater good of humanity as a whole,

Taking into account the diversity of the forms of training and education existing in the world, but noting that, notwithstanding the differences between national sports structures, it is clearly evident that physical education and sport are not confined to physical well-being and health but also contribute to the full and well-balanced development of the human being,

Taking into account, furthermore, the enor-mous efforts that have to be made before the right to physical education and sport can become a reality for all human beings,

Stressing the importance for peace and friendship among peoples of co-operation be-tween the international governmental and non-governmental organizations responsible for physi-cal education and sport,

Proclaims this International Charter for the purpose of placing the development of physical education and sport at the service of human progress, promoting their development, and urg-ing governments, competent non-governmental organizations, educators, families and individuals themselves to be guided thereby, to disseminate it and to put it into practice.

Article 1. The practice of physical education and sport is a fundamental right for all

1.1 Every human being has a fundamental right of access to physical education and sport, which are essential for the full development of his personality. The freedom to develop physical, intellectual and moral powers through physical education and sport must be guaranteed both within the educational system and in other aspects of social life.

1.2 Everyone must have full opportunities, in accordance with his national tradition of sport, for practicing physical education and sport, developing his physical fitness and attaining a level of achieve-ment in sport which corresponds to his gifts.

1.3 Special opportunities must be made avail-able for young people, including children of pre-school age, for the aged and for the handi-capped to develop their personalities to the full through physical education and sport programs suited to their requirements.

Article 2. Physical education and sport form an essential element of lifelong education in the overall education system

2.1 Physical education and sport, as an essen-tial dimension of education and culture, must develop the abilities, will-power and self-discipline of every human being as a fully inte-grated member of society. The continuity of physical activity and the practice of sports must be ensured throughout life by means of a global, lifelong and democratized education.

2.2 At the individual level, physical education and sport contribute to the maintenance and im-provement of health, provide a wholesome leisure-time occupation and enable man to over-come the drawbacks of modern living. At the community level, they enrich social relations and develop fair play, which is essential not only to sport itself but also to life in society.

2.3 Every overall education system must as-sign the requisite place and importance to physi-cal education and sport in order to establish a balance and strengthen links between physical activities and other components of education.

Article 3. Physical education and sport programs must meet individual and social needs

3.1 Physical education and sport programs must be designed to suit the requirements and personal characteristics of those practicing them, as well as the institutional, cultural, socio-economic and climatic conditions of each country. They must give priority to the requirements of disadvantaged groups in society.

3.2 In the process of education in general, physical education and sport programs must, by virtue of both their content and their timetables, help to create habits and behavior patterns conducive to full development of the human person.

3.3 Even when it has spectacular features, competitive sport must always aim, in accordance with the Olympic ideal, to serve the purpose of educational sport, of which it represents the crowning epitome. It must in no way be influenced by profit-seeking commercial interests.

Article 4. Teaching, coaching and administration of physical education and sport should be performed by qualified personnel

4.1 All personnel who assume professional responsibility for physical education and sport must have appropriate qualifications and training. They must be carefully selected in sufficient numbers and given preliminary as well as further training to ensure that they reach adequate levels of specialization.

4.2 Voluntary personnel, given appropriate training and supervision, can make an invaluable contribution to the comprehensive development of sport and encourage the participation of the population in the practice and organization of physical and sport activities.

4.3 Appropriate structures must be established for the training of personnel for physical education and sport. Personnel who have received such training must be given a status in keeping with the duties they perform.

Article 5. Adequate facilities and equipment are essential to physical education and sport

5.1 Adequate and sufficient facilities and equipment must be provided and installed to meet the needs of intensive and safe participation in both in-school and out-of-school programs concerning physical education and sport.

5.2 It is incumbent on governments, public authorities, schools and appropriate private agencies, at all levels, to join forces and plan together so as to provide and make optimum use of installations, facilities and equipment for physical education and sport.

5.3 It is essential that plans for rural and urban development include provision for long-term needs in the matter of installations, facilities and equipment for physical education and sport, taking into account the opportunities offered by the natural environment.

Article 6. Research and evaluation are indispensable components of the development of physical education and sport

6.1 Research and evaluation in physical education and sport should make for the progress of all forms of sport and help to bring about an improvement in the health and safety of participants as well as in training methods and organization and management procedures. The education system will thereby benefit from innovations calculated to develop better teaching methods and standards of performance.

6.2 Scientific research whose social implications in this sphere should not be overlooked, must be oriented in such a way that it does not allow of improper applications to physical education and sport.

Article 7. Protection of the ethical and moral values of physical education and sport must be a constant concern for all

7.1 Top-class sport and sport practiced by all must be protected against any abuse. The serious dangers with which phenomena such as violence, doping and commercial excesses threaten its moral values, image and prestige pervert its very nature and change its educative and health-promoting function. The public authorities, voluntary sports associations, specialized non-governmental organizations, the Olympic Movement, educators, parents, supporters' clubs, trainers, sports managers and the athletes themselves must combine their efforts in order to eliminate these evils. The media have a special role to play, in keeping with Article 8, in supporting and disseminating information about these efforts.

7.2 A prominent place must be assigned in curricula to educational activities based on the values of sport and the consequences of the interactions between sport, society and culture.

7.3 It is important that all sports authorities and sportsmen and women be conscious of the risks to athletes, and more especially to children, of precocious and inappropriate training and psychological pressures of every kind.

7.4 No effort must be spared to highlight the harmful effects of doping, which is both injurious to health and contrary to the sporting ethic, or to protect the physical and mental health of athletes, the virtues of fair play and competition, the integrity of the sporting community and the rights of people participating in it at any level whatsoever. It is crucial that the fight against doping should win the support of national and international authorities at various levels, and of parents, educators, the medical profession, the media, trainers, sports managers and athletes themselves, to ensure that they abide by the principles set out in the existing texts, and more particularly the International Olympic Charter against Doping in Sport. To that end, a harmonized and concerted policy must guide them in the preparation and application of anti-doping measures and of the educational action to be undertaken.

Article 8. Information and documentation help to promote physical education and sport

8.1 The collection, provision and dissemination of information and documentation on physical education and sport constitute a major necessity. In particular, there is a need to circulate information on the results of research and evaluation studies concerning programs, experiments and activities.

Article 9. The mass media should exert a positive influence on physical education and sport

9.1 Without prejudice to the right of freedom of information, it is essential that everyone involved in the mass media be fully conscious of his responsibilities having regard to the social importance, the humanistic purpose and the moral values embodied in physical education and sport.

9.2 Relations between those involved in the mass media and specialists in physical education and sport must be close and based on mutual confidence in order to exercise a positive influence on physical education and sport and to ensure objective and well-founded information. Training of personnel for the media may include elements relating to physical education and sport.

Article 10. National institutions play a major role in physical education and sport

10.1 It is essential that public authorities at all levels and specialized non-governmental bodies encourage those physical education and sport activities whose educational value is most evident. Their action shall consist in enforcing legislation and regulations, providing material assistance and adopting all other measures of encouragement, stimulation and control. The public authorities will also ensure that such fiscal measures are adopted as may encourage these activities.

10.2 It is incumbent on all institutions responsible for physical education and sport to promote a consistent, overall and decentralized plan of action in the framework of lifelong education so as to allow for continuity and co-ordination between compulsory physical activities and those practiced freely and spontaneously.

Article 11. International co-operation is a prerequisite for the universal and well-balanced promotion of physical education and sport

11.1 It is essential that States and those international and regional intergovernmental and non-governmental organizations in which interested countries are represented and which are responsible for physical education and sport give physical education and sport greater prominence in international bilateral and multilateral co-operation.

11.2 International co-operation must be prompted by wholly disinterested motives in order to promote and stimulate endogenous development in this field.

11.3 Through co-operation and the pursuit of mutual interests in the universal language of physical education and sport, all peoples will contribute to the preservation of lasting peace, mutual respect and friendship and will thus create a propitious climate for solving international problems. Close collaboration between all interested national and international governmental and non-governmental agencies, based on respect for the specific competence of each, will necessarily encourage the development of physical education and sport throughout the world.

A GLOBAL VISION FOR SCHOOL PHYSICAL EDUCATION AND SPORT AND THE PHYSICALLY EDUCATED PERSON (AAHPERD/CAHPERD)

Physical Education—Building on a Valuable Tradition

The need for children and youth to engage in regular physical activity [PA] as one of the prerequisites for achieving optimum health and quality of life has long been recognized. The UNESCO Charter of Physical Education and Sport established in 1978 was one of the first international statements espousing these beliefs.

While many children and youth, particularly those with concerned parents, learn physical skills and participate in community settings, only the schools can reach and influence all children. Physical education [PE] is vital to all aspects of normal growth and development of children and youth—not only physical but social and emotional growth as well. Enhanced learning, better concentration, improved self-control and self-confidence, as well as promotion of healthy, posi-

tive, and lifelong attitudes toward PA are well documented benefits of quality PE in schools. In addition, school PE establishes the foundation of skills for a lifetime of participation while at the same time building a natural immunizing effect against many sedentary lifestyle diseases.

Rationale for Global Vision

Despite widespread public acceptance of the need for PA, quality PE is not seen as a priority for many policymakers in most school systems. Where PE exists today it is under strong attack. It occupies a tenuous place in the school curriculum, and in some cases it is being replaced and moved out of the curriculum. Budget cutbacks, inadequate and aging facilities, the absence (and continued attrition) of PE specialists, insufficient allocations of time within the school timetable, as well as societal factors, such as impact of a technology-based economy, are contributing to its perilous status.

There is a misconception among the general public that existing school programs have the capacity to meet the PA requirements of our children and youth. However, the average school curriculum does not allot sufficient instructional time to PE for skill acquisition, health related fitness, and the attainment of a positive attitude and appreciation for PA.

The lack of opportunities for daily PE at school, coupled with the continuing decline in PA within the home setting is leading to the development of sedentary lifestyle patterns that will continue into adulthood and throughout life. Furthermore, efforts to recognize PA as a strategy to offset healthy behaviors have not been realized.

The need to promote active, healthy lifestyles among children and youth is great. Increasing numbers of children and youth are exposed to [a] wide variety of social ills and behaviors which put their health and lifestyles at risk. This is evidenced by growing reports of poor self image, inadequate nutrition, family problems, stress, higher drop-out rates, youth violence, early sexual activity, increases in smoking, declining activity levels, increasing obesity and increasing sedentary health risk factors, alcohol and drug abuse, within our young population.

The North American Regional Forum feels that we must reverse this negative trend if we are to significantly influence the personal well being of all children and youth as we journey into year 2000 and beyond. As a consequence of our beliefs in the importance of quality, daily school PE, the Canadian Association for Health, Physical Education, Recreation and Dance and the American Alliance for Health, Physical Education, Recreation and Dance have collectively developed the Global Vision for School Physical Education.

Statement of Beliefs

We believe that:

- All students in every grade have the right and the opportunity to experience sustained, vigorous physical activity [PA] and participate in quality, daily physical education [PE] programs;
- All aspects of a quality, PE program have a positive impact on the thinking, knowing, and doing (or the cognitive, affective, and physical) domains of the lives of children and youth and that physically educated children and youth will go on to lead active, healthy, and productive lives;
- All teachers responsible for teaching PE must be professionally prepared physical educators. Through their preparation and ongoing professional development, all teachers will have a sound knowledge of the contribution of movement to the total education of children and youth;
- Each school must have at least one professionally prepared PE specialist who can act as the leader resource teacher assisting all teachers in developing the total PE program;
- Quality, PE programs are equitable (gender, culture, race, ability, etc.) in all respects;
- Local school officials, school boards, and departments of education have a responsibility to provide appropriate support services to teachers in PE as well as adequate facilities, resource supplies, and equipment.

The Physically Educated Person

Physically educated persons have ACQUIRED skills enabling them to perform a variety of physical activities which can help them maintain health related fitness levels; they PARTICIPATE regularly in physical activity [PA] because it is enjoyable and exhilarating; they UNDERSTAND and VALUE PA and its contribution to a healthy lifestyle.

1. Acquired Skills

- Physically educated persons move efficiently using body and space awareness and are able to differentiate between personal and general space.
- They have competence in manipulative, transport and balance skills and can perform each of these skills along or with others; they have ability in a variety of activities; and they have the ability to process new skills.
- They are able to assess personal needs, design a realistic fitness program, and achieve and maintain a level of personal fitness.
- Physically educated persons have acquired culturally normative physical skills that provide a base for ongoing participation throughout life.

2. Participation

- Physically educated persons lead physically active lives and can select and integrate regular PA into their lifestyles through participation with others and/or alone.

3. Understand and Value

- Physically educated persons understand that PA provides lifelong opportunities for enjoyment, self-expression, and social interaction. They understand that there are many reasons to value and enjoy PA: to fulfill their human development potential, adapt and control their physical environment, relate and interact with others, and learn to live in and with the world around them.

- Physically educated persons accept and appreciate the differences and abilities of self and others. They understand risks, safety factors, and appropriate behaviors associated with PA. They value PA and its impact upon physical, emotional, social, and spiritual well being. They display positive personal and social responsibility.

Solutions Expected From Schools

As families and social institutions become transformed, many people increasingly look to schools for solutions. The educational institution is the agency with the potential to positively impact attitudes and behaviors of all children and youth as a captive audience, regardless of sex, age, ability, ethnicity, or socioeconomic status.

While there exists mounting concern for health and quality of life, many education policymakers fail to recognize the role of physical activity [PA] and its contribution. A narrow perception exists among some education leaders that the primary role of schools is to educate students only for academic achievement. There is a failure to recognize the important connection between PA, health, and vitality on the one hand and academic performance, productivity, and success in school on the other. With schools expected to teach students to lead productive lives, there should be community commitment to schools as health promoters through quality physical education.

Our Vision for Global School Physical Education—Learner-Centered and Comprehensive

- In our vision, physical education [PE] plays a valued and vital role in providing a quality, balanced education for all students in the world.
- The well being of the students and the quality of the skills, knowledge and values they will ultimately derive from PE is the driving force of PE principles and practices.

- PE is a planned program of instruction and complementary activities, such as intramurals, interscholastics, and leadership opportunities. The core instructional component of the program provides the opportunity to develop skills, fitness, knowledge, attitudes, and appreciation while intramural programs provide all students with the opportunity to utilize learned behaviors in a recreational setting. The interscholastic and leadership components represent the enrichment opportunities to those so inclined.
- Students are physically educated in a creative, safe, and caring atmosphere which recognizes the students' individual interests, needs as central factors in curriculum design, and program implementation.
- PE is conducted in various environments, including the outdoors, allowing personal growth in environmental citizenship and ethics.
- PE involves students in a variety of activities, including games, sports, gymnastics, dance, outdoor pursuits, fitness, and aquatics.
- PE programs utilize appropriate assessment techniques to enhance the learning of the students.
- PE is actively interfaced with other disciplines such as science, the arts, humanities, and mathematics.
- PE enables students to become responsible decisionmakers relative to their own physical well being.
- PE provides the necessary skills, knowledge, and attitudes to integrate physical activity into daily living during the school years and beyond.
- PE programs are designed and implemented by professionally prepared physical educators.
- PE contributes to the promotion of lifelong active and healthy lifestyles and the prevention of disease.
- PE is inclusive and equitable. It excludes no students on the basis of gender, race, ability, ethnicity, socioeconomic level, religion or language.

YEAR 2000 OBJECTIVES FOR THE NATION: PHYSICAL ACTIVITY AND EXERCISE (USDHHS)

Specific Objectives	Goal	Baseline (Year)
Health Status Objectives		
Reduce deaths due to coronary heart disease.	100/100,000 people	135/100,000 people
Reduce prevalence of overweight.	20% for people 20 years and older; 15% for youths 12–19 years	26% for people 20 years or older; 15% for youths 12–19 years (1976–1980)
Risk Reduction Objectives		
Increase number of people who engage regularly, preferably on a daily basis, in light to moderate physical activity for at least 30 minutes/day.	30% for people 6 years and older	22% for people 18 years or older who were active 5 or more times/week; 12% active 7 or more times /week (1985)
Increase number of people who engage in vigorous physical activity that promotes the development and maintenance of cardiorespiratory fitness 3 or more days/week for at least 20 minutes/session.	30% for people 18 years or older; 75% for children and youths 6–17 years	12% for people 18 years or older (1985); 66% for children and youths 10–17 years (1984)
Reduce number of people 6 years and older who engage in no leisure-time physical activity.	15%	24% for people 18 years or older (1985)
Increase number of people 6 years and older who regularly engage in physical activities that promote and maintain muscular strength, muscular endurance, and flexibility.	40%	
Increase number of people 12 years and older who are overweight and have adopted sound dietary practices combined with regular physical activity to attain an appropriate body weight.	50%	30% of women and 25% of men 18 years or older (1985)
Services and Protection Objectives		
Increase number of children and youths in grades 1–12 who participate in daily school physical education.	50%	36% (1984–1986)
Increase proportion of school physical education class time that students spend actively engaged in physical activities, preferably in lifetime physical activities.	50%	27% (1983)
Increase number of worksites offering employer-sponsored physical activity and fitness programs.	20%–80% depending on size of worksite	14%–54% depending on size of worksite (1985)
Increase availability and accessibility of community physical activity and fitness facilities.		
Hiking, biking and fitness trails (miles)	1/10,000 people	1/71,000 people
Swimming pools	1/25,000 people	1/53,000 people
Parks and recreation open space (acres)	4/1,000 people	1.8/1,000 people

From Public Health Service, US Department of Health and Human Services: *Promoting health/preventing disease: year 2000 objectives for the nation,* Washington DC, 1989, US Government Printing Office.

The Role of the Parent

- Notice of an Educational Assessment/Reassessment Plan for Parent's Permission
- Referral Review and Assessment Determination for Parent's Information
- Notice of Special Education Services Presented to Parents for Their Consent
- Parents' Rights Form
- Individual Education Program Plan

Educational Service Center I.S.D. 279 11200 93rd Avenue North Maple Grove, Minnesota 55369	**NOTICE OF AN EDUCATIONAL ASSESSMENT/REASSESSMENT PLAN**

Learner's Full Name: _____

ID: ☐☐☐☐–☐☐☐–☐☐–☐☐☐☐   Birthdate: ☐☐–☐☐–☐☐

Month / Day / Year: _____

School: _____ Grade: _____

Dear_____:

We are requesting your permission to assess your child's current educational functioning in order to determine your child's possible eligibility for special education services. The specific reasons and plans for assessment are on the next page.

☐ This notice is for an **Initial Assessment.** The district must receive your signed permission before we can begin.

☐ This notice is for a **Reassessment.** The school will begin the assessment unless you object in writing within 10 school days after receiving this request. If you sign and return this form right away, it will allow us to do the assessment without waiting.

The assessment will be conducted at _____
and is provided at no cost to you. The assessment procedures may include a review of school records, diagnostic teaching, observation of your child's activities, personal interviews, and consultation with you or others you recommend, along with individual testing as outlined. *(See next page)*

It is important to know your rights. Please read the enclosed **Parent Rights and Procedural Safeguards** brochure.

If you have questions, please contact me.

Sincerely,

Name	*Position*	*Telephone*

Address

PARENT RESPONSE

DIRECTIONS TO PARENT: Please **check** one of the options below, **sign** this form, and **return** the original of this page.

A. ☐ I give permission to the district to proceed as proposed.

B. ☐ I need further information. Please contact me to schedule a meeting to explain the reasons for the assessment.

C. ☐ I do not give permission for the district to proceed with the assessment as proposed. I understand that you will be contacting me to offer a conciliation conference where my concerns will be discussed. I also understand that I may choose not to participate in the conciliation conference and may proceed directly to a due process hearing.

X_____ _____ _____
Parent Signature (or Learner, if of legal age) *Daytime Telephone* *Month, Day, Year*

Educational Service Center I.S.D. 279 11200 93rd Avenue North Maple Grove, Minnesota 55369	**REFERRAL REVIEW AND ASSESSMENT DETERMINATION**

Learner's Full Name: _____

ID: ☐☐☐☐–☐☐☐☐–☐☐–☐☐☐☐ Birthdate: ☐☐–☐☐–☐☐

Month / Day / Year: _____

School: _____ Grade: _____

Person Referring: _____ Title: _____

A. Review of Referral

1. Briefly describe the reason for referral. *(You may attach district referral form.)*

2. Attach documentation of the two required interventions for learning and/or behavior problems, including their design and outcome. *(Interventions are not required for reassessment.)*

3. If the interventions have been waived, please check here ☐ and attach rationale.

4. Does the learner have limited proficiency in English? ☐ Yes ☐ No ☐ Previously received LEP services

B. Review of Learner's Performance

Review each of the following areas and determine if there is a need to assess.	Do we need to assess?
1. Intellectual Functioning	☐ Yes ☐ No
2. Academic Performance	☐ Yes ☐ No
3. Communicative Status	☐ Yes ☐ No
4. Motor Ability	☐ Yes ☐ No
5. Sensory Status	☐ Yes ☐ No
6. Health/Physical Status	☐ Yes ☐ No
7. Emotional and Social Development and Behavior Skills	☐ Yes ☐ No
8. Functional Skills	☐ Yes ☐ No
9. Vocational, Occupational Potential, and Transition	☐ Yes ☐ No

Comments:

C. Assessment Determination

As a result of our review, the team has decided that:

☐ 1. No special education assessment is necessary.

☐ 2. An Initial Assessment Plan is needed. (Complete Notice of an Educational Assessment/Reassessment Plan form.)

☐ 3. A Reassessment Plan is needed. (Complete Notice of an Educational Assessment/Reassessment Plan form.)

D. Persons Who Reviewed the Referral

_____   _____

_____   _____

_____   _____

Educational Service Center I.S.D. 279 11200 93rd Avenue North Maple Grove, Minnesota 55369	**NOTICE OF** **SPECIAL EDUCATION SERVICES**

Learner's Full Name: _____

ID: ☐☐☐☐–☐☐☐–☐☐–☐☐☐☐ Birthdate: ☐☐–☐☐–☐☐

Month / Day / Year: _____

School: _____ Grade: _____

Dear _____.

This notice is required whether or not you attended the Individual Education Program (IEP) Team meeting on _____(month/day/year).

The team recommends that:

1. ☐ your child begin to receive special education services. The school district will not proceed without your written consent. *(IEP attached)*

2. ☐ your child's special education placement or services be changed as noted in the IEP. The school district will proceed with this change unless you object in writing within 10 school days of receiving this notice. *(IEP attached)*

3. ☐ all current special education services be discontinued. The school district will proceed with this change unless you object in writing within 10 school days of receiving this notice. *(Supporting documentation attached)*

4. ☐ all special education services be discontinued. Your child is graduating from high school with a diploma. *(Supporting documentation attached)*

The reasons for the above recommendations, the basis upon which they are made, and all factors affecting this decision are in the attached documents.

Comments:

Please read the enclosed **PARENT RIGHTS AND PROCEDURAL SAFEGUARDS,** complete the "Parent Response" portion of this form, and return the original to me. Sincerely,

_____	_____	_____
Signature of IEP Manager	*Position*	*Telephone*

_____
Address

PARENT RESPONSE

DIRECTIONS TO PARENT: Please check one of the options below, sign this form, and return the original.

A. ☐ I give permission for the district to go ahead as proposed above.

B. ☐ I need further information. Please contact me to schedule a conference.

C. ☐ I do not give permission for the district to proceed with this recommendation for my child's special education services. I understand that you will be contacting me to offer a conciliation conference where my concerns will be discussed. I also understand that I may choose not to participate in the conciliation conference and may proceed directly to a due process hearing.

X

_____	_____	_____
Parent Signature (or Learner, if of legal age)	*Daytime Telephone*	*Month, Day, Year*

Date Received by District	**COPIES:**	Learner File Parent IEP Manager

ENCLOSED: **PARENT RIGHTS AND PROCEDURAL SAFEGUARDS**
IEP PLAN or SUPPORTING DOCUMENTATION

463

Educational Service Center
I.S.D. 279
11200 93rd Avenue North
Maple Grove, Minnesota 55369

Parent Rights

and

Procedural Safeguards

presented to protect
the rights of you and your child

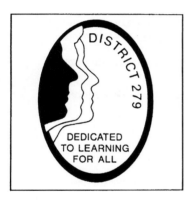

DISTRICT 279

DEDICATED
TO LEARNING
FOR ALL

Dear Parent:

This pamphlet is designed to explain your rights when planning for your child's education. As a partner in making educational decisions for your child, it is important that you read and understand your rights. The information in this pamphlet is taken from federal and state laws, rules, and regulations. Some of the items may not relate directly to you because they are intended to cover a number of actions.

You may contact "Parents Advocacy Coalition for Educational Rights," (PACER) for consultation.

PACER Center, Inc.	(612) 827-2966
4826 Chicago Avenue So.	(TTY & Voice)
Minneapolis, MN 55417-1055	(800) 537-2237

Also, the following are low-cost legal services:

Legal Advocacy for Persons	(612) 332-1441
with Developmental Disabilities	(800) 292-4150
or **Client Assistance Project**	TTY: ⇃
or **Mental Health Law Project**	(612) 332-4668
222 Grain Exchange Building	
323 Fourth Avenue South	
Minneapolis, MN 55415	

Legal Advocate for the Blind	(612) 339-1431
NorthStar East Center	
608 2nd Ave. So., Suite 380	
Minneapolis, MN 55402	

Other resources:

Minnesota Dept. of Education	(612) 297-2843
Office of Monitoring & Compliance	
Administrative Review & Complaint Specialist	
550 Cedar Street	
Capitol Square Building	
St. Paul, MN 55101	

We are committed to serving all children with handicapping conditions who live in the district. If you have questions or concerns, please call. Your interest and communication are appreciated.

Be Informed of Your Rights

1. You have the right to review and receive copies of all records or other written information regarding your child which are in the school's possession.

2. You have the right to participate as a team member in developing and determining your child's educational program, including special education services, and/or to provide information relative to his or her assessment and the development of the program plan. *A convenient time to meet will be set with you and you will be informed of the procedures for planning your child's program.*

3. You have a right to have an interpreter present if you do not speak or understand English well, are hearing impaired or use some other mode of communication. You may also invite an advocate.

4. You have the right, prior to the meeting and upon request, to receive interpretations of assessment or reassessment procedures, instruments and data or results, and of the program plan from a knowledgeable school employee. You also have the right for this meeting to be held in private. *The specific procedures and time for this meeting will be explained following your request.*

5. You have the right to have included, on the team that interprets the assessment data and/or develops the individual education program (IEP) plan, a person who is a member of the same minority or cultural background or who is knowledgeable concerning the racial, cultural, or handicapping differences of your child. *The specific procedures and time for this team meeting will be explained following your request.*

6. You have the right to obtain an independent assessment at your own expense. You also have the right to request information from the district about where an independent assessment may be obtained. You may obtain an independent assessment at public expense if you disagree with an assessment obtained by the district. However, a district

may initiate a due process hearing to show that its assessment is appropriate after the offer of at least one conciliation conference. If you refuse the offer of conciliation or if the matter is not resolved in conciliation, the district shall initiate a due process hearing to show that its assessment is appropriate. If the hearing officer's final decision is that the district's assessment is appropriate, you still have the right to an independent assessment, but not at public expense. *Whenever an independent evaluation is at public expense, the criteria under which the evaluation is obtained, including the location of the evaluation and the qualifications of the examiner, must be the same as the criteria which the district uses when it initiates an evaluation.*

7. You have the right to know that the district will not proceed with its proposed initial formal assessment or proposed initial placement without your prior written consent. "Initial" means the first time the district has proposed to assess your child or place your child in any special education program in this district. *If you do not respond to the initial assessment or placement, a conciliation conference will be offered by the school. If this is not the first assessment or first placement by the district, the district will proceed with the proposal within ten school days of your receipt of the notice unless you object in writing.*

8. You have the right to discuss placement and service options which are available for your child.

9. You have the right to know that your consent for assessment or placement is voluntary and that you may revoke it at any time. If you do revoke your consent, however, the district may not agree, in which case the due process procedures on the reverse side of this sheet would be followed.

If you disagree with the school proposal, see other side.

Note to Non-Custodial Parent:
Please contact your child's school for information regarding your rights.

Procedural Safeguards Available to Parent

If you disagree with what the school is proposing, please be informed that:

- You have the right to object to the district's proposed action (assessment or placement) in writing. If you object, you will be requested to attend a conciliation conference which will be held at a mutually agreeable time and place. If this is an initial assessment or placement and you do not respond to the notice, a conciliation conference will be offered to you by the district.

- You have a right to proceed directly to an impartial due process hearing and bypass the conciliation conference. Even if you do attend a conciliation conference, if you do not agree with action proposed by the school you always have a right to a due process hearing.

- You have the right to be represented by counsel or another person of your choosing at the conciliation conference or the impartial due process hearing.

- You have the right to be assured that, unless you and the district agree otherwise, your child will not be denied initial admssion to school and your child's educational program will not be changed as long as you object in writing to the proposed action.

- You have the right to be represented in preparation for, and at, the hearing by legal counsel or other representatives of your choice.

- You have the right, in accordance with laws relating to confidentiality, to examine and receive copies of your child's school records before the hearing, including tests, assessments, reports, or other information concerning the educational assessment or reassessment upon which the proposed action may be based.

- You have the right to call your own witnesses and to present evidence, including expert medical, psychological, and educational testimony and relevant records, tests, assessments, reports or other information.

- You have the right to request the attendance of any official or employee of the providing or resident school district or any other person who may have evidence relating to the proposed action and you have the right to be informed of the manner and time in which to do so.

- You have the right to present evidence and cross-examine any employee of the school district(s) or other persons who present evidence at the hearing.

- You have the right to have your child, who is the subject of the hearing, present at the hearing.

- You have the right to a closed hearing unless you want to request an open hearing.

- You have a right to obtain a record of the hearing, including the written findings of fact and decisions, whether or not you appeal.

- You have the right to be informed that, if a due process hearing is held and your position is upheld, you may be awarded attorney's fees and costs.

- You have the right to be informed of any free or low cost legal service.

- Each form you receive from the district proposing action will have a place for your response. The form will also identify the district employee to whom it should be returned and to whom questions may be directed.

ED-01878-02
cc: Learner File, Parent, IEP Manager

Educational Service Center
I.S.D. 279
11200 93rd Avenue North
Maple Grove, Minnesota 55369

**INDIVIDUAL
EDUCATION PROGRAM (IEP)
PLAN**

A. LEARNER INFORMATION

Learner Name (Last, First, M.I.)

Doe, Lisa

Birthdate
2/15/83

Current Address (Street, City, State, Zip)

**301 Maple Lane
Maple Grove, MN 55069**

Learner's Primary Language
English

Sex
M F **X**

Grade
4

ID# **5 5 4 4 - 2 3 3 - 1 2 - 3 7 8 9**

School of Enrollment
Crest View

School Telephone Number
(612) 555-4230

District No.
#279

Learner's Permanent Residence Address (If Different Than Above)

District No.

B. PARENT/GUARDIAN INFORMATION

Name(s) of Parent(s)
Glenn and Carol Doe

Home Telephone Number
(612) 555-4230

Other Telephone Number
( )

Address (If other than Learner's Permanent Residence Address)

District No.

Guardian(s)/Surrogate Parent(s) Name(s)

☐ Guardian(s)   ☐ Surrogate Parent(s)

Address (if other than Learner's Permanent Address)

Home Telephone No.
( )

Other Telephone No.
( )

District No.

C. IEP INFORMATION

Federal Child Count Information
3 Learning Disabilities

IEP Manager Name
Leslie Childs

Telephone Number
(612) 555-3629

Date IEP Written
1/3/96

IEP Type
☐ Initial **☒** Annual ☐ Interim

Date of Last Comprehensive Assessment
12/18/95

Periodic Review Date
Month **6** / Year **96**

D. IEP PLANNING MEETING

Date of Planning Meeting **1/5/96**	List Names of All Team Members	Indicate Attendance
Parent	Glenn Doe	☒ Yes ☐ No
Parent	Carol Doe	☒ Yes ☐ No
Administrator/Designee	Dan James	☒ Yes ☐ No
Special Education Teacher	Leslie Childs	☒ Yes ☐ No
Regular Education Teacher	Judy Black	☒ Yes ☐ No
Speech/Lang. Teacher	Renee Green	☒ Yes ☐ No
Adap. PE Teacher	Mary Brown	☒ Yes ☐ No
Occup. Therapist	Kris Smith	☒ Yes ☐ No
		☐ Yes ☐ No
		☐ Yes ☐ No
		☐ Yes ☐ No
		☐ Yes ☐ No

E.	
PRESENT LEVELS OF PERFORMANCE AND SPECIAL EDUCATION NEEDS	

Carefully consider and document data from all sources in the following areas: (Include information and observation provided by parent(s).)

1. Intellectual Functioning	* 9. Vocational, Occupational Potential, and Secondary Transition
2. Academic Performance	A. Jobs and Job Training
3. Communicative Status	B. Recreation and Leisure
4. Motor Ability	C. Home Living
5. Sensory Status	D. Community Participation
6. Health/Physical Status	E. Post-Secondary Training and Learning Opportunities
7. Emotional and Social Development and Behavior Skills	
8. Functional Skills	

* Area Number 9 must be summarized for all learners who have reached the 9th grade or age 14 and younger learners for whom the team determines it is applicable.

Present Levels of Performance	Special Education Needs
In years when an initial assessment or reassessment is conducted, attach the Assessment Team Summary Report for performance level information.	
1. Intellectual Functioning Lisa scored in the low average range on the WISC-R and Columbia Mental Maturity Scale. (12-6-94)	
2. Academic Performance Lisa's reading skills are approximately 2 years delayed; math skills are approximately 1 year delayed; spelling and written language approximately 2 years delayed. Other content area courses (i.e. science, health, and social studies) are modified for her. (12-18-94)	2. Academic Performance a. Lisa needs to improve her decoding and comprehension reading skills. b. Lisa needs to improve her math computation and problem solving skills. c. Lisa needs to improve her written language and spelling skills.
3. Communicative Status Lisa scored in the moderately low range for vocabulary and concept understanding and usage. Her expressive language has made great gains. Her articulation has made continued growth. (11-16-94)	3. Communicative Status a. Lisa needs to improve her articulation skills. b. Lisa needs to improve her vocabulary and concept usage and understanding.
4. Motor Ability Lisa has difficulty in the areas of balance, bilateral coordination, muscular strength, and endurance. (11-20-94)	4. Motor Ability a. Lisa needs to improve her physical fitness level in the areas of muscular strength and endurance. b. Lisa needs to improve gross motor areas of balance, motor planing, coordination, and mainstream curriculum skills.
5. Sensory Status Lisa's visual perception skills in the areas of form and space perception, sequencing, and visual memory are low. Her auditory memory is in the low average range. (12-3-94)	5. Sensory Status a. Lisa needs to improve visual perceptual skills in the areas of form and space perception, sequencing, and visual memory.
6. Health/Physical Status Lisa has been diagnosed as having Attention Deficit Hyperactivity Disorder without hyperactivity or impulsiveness and is not receiving medication. (11-12-94)	
7. Emotional and Social Development and Behavior Skills (11-6-94). Lisa is a well-adjusted child without social or emotional deficits.	

E.   PRESENT LEVELS OF PERFORMANCE AND SPECIAL EDUCATION NEEDS

Carefully consider and document data from all sources in the following areas: (Include information and observation provided by parent(s).)

1. Intellectual Functioning
2. Academic Performance
3. Communicative Status
4. Motor Ability
5. Sensory Status
6. Health/Physical Status
7. Emotional And Social Development and Behavior Skills
8. Functional Skills

* 9. Vocational, Occupational Potential, and Secondary Transition
  A. Jobs and Job Training
  B. Recreation and Leisure
  C. Home Living
  D. Community Participation
  E. Post-Secondary Training and Learning Opportunities

* Area Number 9 must be summarized for all learners who have reached the 9th grade or age 14 and younger learners for whom the team
  determines it is applicable.

Present Levels of Performance	Special Education Needs

In years when an initial assessment or reassessment is conducted, attach the Assessment Team Summary Report for performance level information.

8. Functional Skills
   Lisa's functional skills are age
   appropriate.   (11-19-94)

9. Vocational, Occupational Potential,
   and Secondary Transition

   This area will be addressed when Lisa
   turns 14 years old or when she enters
   the 9th grade.

Page 3 of IEP
Date _____ 1/3/96 _____   Learner's Name: _____ Lisa Doe _____

F.
ANNUAL GOALS, SHORT-TERM INSTRUCTIONAL OBJECTIVES

Use one **PAGE 3** for each goal. Thoroughly state the goal. List objectives for the goal, including attainment criteria for each objective.	GOAL # 7 OF 8 GOALS

GOAL:
Lisa will improve her physical fitness level in the areas of muscular strength and endurance.

Short-Term Instructional Objectives

1. Given activities to improve abdominal strength and endurance, Lisa will perform 30 correct curl-ups in 60 seconds.

2. Given activities to improve upper body strength and endurance, Lisa will perform 12 mature push-ups in 30 seconds.

3. Given activities to improve cardiovascular endurance, Lisa will run/walk 1 mile at the 15% level for her age-group norms.

G.
IEP PERIODIC REVIEW

Date Reviewed: 6-4-96   Progress made toward this goal and objectives:

The learner's IEP:

[X] Meets learner's current needs and will be continued without changes.

[ ] Does not meet learner's current needs and the modifications (not significant) **listed below** will be made without an IEP meeting unless you contact us.

[ ] Does not meet learner's current needs and the **significant changes listed below** require a revised IEP. We will be in contact soon to schedule a meeting.

NOTE TO PARENT(S): You are entitled to request a meeting to discuss the results of this review.

ED-01878-02

Learner's Name:_____ Lisa Doe

H.	ADAPTATION OF REGULAR AND SPECIAL EDUCATION

Describe changes in regular and special education that will be made to permit successful accommodation and education of this learner: e.g., grading, credits, staff, transportation, facilities, materials, equipment, technology, adaptive devices, curriculum, methods, and other services.

```
        Transportation - small bus
        Classroom - Self-Contained
        Curriculum methods/grading - modified
```

Describe use of regulated behavioral interventions. *Attach more information, if necessary.*

```
        Not applicable for Lisa at this time.
```

Describe any regular education secondary graduation standards modified for this learner.

```
This will be addressed when Lisa enters 9th grade.
```

I.	SPECIAL EDUCATION AND RELATED SERVICES

* SERVICE(S)	MIN./WEEK Indirect	MIN./WEEK Direct	STARTING DATE	SERVICE PROVIDER AND TELEPHONE	BUILDING NAME AND ROOM (If another school district, provide district name)
SCLD		900	1/5/96	Leslie Childs 555-3629	Crest View 9
Speech		90	1/5/96	Renee Green 555-3629	Crest View 15
OT		60	1/5/96	Kris Smith 555-3629	Crest View 12
APE		60	1/5/96	Mary Brown 555-3629	Crest View 8

* The duration of these services may not exceed 1 year from the date of this IEP. This IEP is in effect for:
- [X] a normal school year.
- [ ] an extended school year. Explain:
- [ ] less than a normal school year. Explain:

ED-01878-02

Learner's Name:_____ Lisa Doe _____

J.	**LEAST RESTRICTIVE ENVIRONMENT (LRE)**

Check all sites and settings in which special education and related services will be provided:

SITE
- [X] School building learner would attend if did not have handicapping condition(s)
- [ ] Alternative regular school within the district
- [ ] Alternative regular school outside of the district
- [ ] Alternative special school within the district
- [ ] Alternative special school outside of the district
- [ ] Home-based/Homebound
- [ ] Community-based site other than a school or home
- [ ] Residential school
- [ ] Hospital or treatment center
- [ ] Other _____

> **NOTE:**   **Please use this setting and site information to determine the federal child count placement category for all learners, birth through age 21, and enter in Part C. on front page of IEP Plan.**

SETTING
- [X] Regular education
- [X] Special education
- [ ] Integrated community
- [ ] Other _____

8 4 0	min./week
1 1 1 0	min./week
	min./week
	min./week

Explain why options selected above are the most appropriate and the least restrictive.

Due to Lisa's academic deficits, she requires structured, small group instruction so that she may experience academic gain.

Describe any other options considered, and provide reasons those options were rejected.

LENGTH OF DAY
- [ ] Check here if the learner's school day is shorter or longer than peers without handicapping conditions. *If checked, Commissioner of Education approval is required.*

K.	**DESCRIPTION OF ACTIVITIES WITH LEARNERS WITHOUT HANDICAPPING CONDITIONS**

For a learner who is served more than half-time in a special education setting, include any activities in which the learner will be participating with learners who do not have handicapping conditions (e.g., lunch, assembly periods, club activities, field trips, and other special events).

Lisa interacts with her mainstream peers in science, health, art, physical education, music, media, and social studies. She also participates in other special activities as they are appropriate.

NOTE:	**Attach Notice of Special Education Services form when needed.**

appendix C

Approaches to Crowd Control

- Approaches to Crowd Control: Summary (AAHPERD)
- Share the Spirit of Fair Play: Be a Good Sport (MSHSL)

APPROACHES TO CROWD CONTROL: SUMMARY

The Sixth National Conference of City and County Directors of AAHPERD spent considerable time on the subject of crowd control at sport contests. A summary of their discussions follows.

Approaches to Crowd Control: Summary

The nature and seriousness of the problems in crowd control have recently become more drastic and bizarre as they have occurred with increasing frequency. They take on the collective character of a deliberate attempt to either ignore or confront the system. This social problem may be impossible to eliminate completely, but an attempt must be made to cope with the immediate symptoms. Our only hope is for imaginative and coordinated efforts by the school and sport management, the majority of students, and community authorities to promote standards of conduct conducive to continuing spectator sports in comparative tranquility. The alternatives are to allow a disruptive element to completely negate the nature of school

sport, to play with no spectators, or to abandon the activity.

The following will present some causes of crowd control problems and some approaches to solutions.

Some Causes of Problems

- Lack of anticipation of, and preventive planning for, possible trouble
- Lack of proper facilities
- Poor communication resulting in lack of information
- Lack of involvement of one or more of the following: school administration, faculty, student body, parents, community, press, law enforcement, and security agencies
- Lack of respect for authority and property
- Attendance at games of youth under the influence of illegal substances
- Increased attitude of permissiveness
- School dropouts, recent graduates, and outsiders including gangs

Some Approaches to Solutions

Develop written policy statements, guidelines, and regulations for crowd control

1. Consult the following before writing policy statements or promulgating regulations: school administration, athletic and activities director, conference representatives, coaches, faculty members involved in the school sports program, school youth organizations, parents, community education department, local police departments, and community leaders

2. Properly and efficiently administer regulations and provide for good communications

3. Constantly evaluate regulations and guidelines for their relevance and effectiveness

4. Make guidelines and regulations so effective that the director of athletics who follows them is secure in knowing he or she has planned with the staff for any eventuality and has sufficient help to cope with any situation that may arise

Provide adequate facilities

1. Plan and design stadiums, fieldhouses, arenas, and gymnasiums for effective crowd control

2. Provide for adequate rest room facilities

3. Establish a no-smoking and drug-free school and promote these policies during contests

4. Provide for complete preparation of facilities including security before and after the game or event

Teach good fair play throughout the school and the community

1. Begin education in good sportspersonship in the earliest grades and continue it throughout the school life

2. Make frequent approving references to constructive and commendable behavior

3. Institute a fair play and sportspersonship award for both teams and fans at events and competitions

4. Arrange for program appearances by faculty members and students jointly to discuss the true values of sport competition including good sportspersonship

5. Make use of all news media through frequent and effective television, radio, and press presentations and interviews, commentaries, and frequent announcement of good sportspersonship slogans and awards

6. Distribute a printed Code of Conduct for Good Sportspersonship

7. Include the good sportspersonship slogan in all printed programs at sports events

8. Urge the use of sports events as an example in elementary school citizenship classes, stressing positive values of good conduct at school games and events, during the raising of the flag and singing of the national anthem; also emphasize courtesy toward visitors

9. Involve teachers in school athletic associations, provide them with passes to all sports events, and stress the positive values of their setting an example of good sportspersonship

Intensify communications before scheduled games

1. Arrange for an exchange of speakers at school assembly programs; the principals, coaches, or team captains could visit the opposing school

2. Discuss with appropriate personnel of the competing school the procedures for the game, including method and location of team entry and departure

3. Provide superintendent or principal, athletic director, and coach with a copy of the written policy statement, guidelines, and regulations

4. Meet all game officials and request them to stress good sportspersonship before, during, and after all contests

5. Meet with coaches and instruct them not to question officials during a contest; stress the importance of good sportspersonship and that their conduct sets the tone for spectator reaction to game incidents

6. Instruct students, parents, fans, coaches, and athletes about what to expect and what is expected of them

7. Schedule preventive planning conferences with local police to be assured of their full cooperation and effectiveness in spectator control

Inform the community

1. Request coaches and athletic directors to talk to service groups and other community groups
2. Invite community leaders and their families (nonschool people) to attend sports events on a regular basis
3. Post on all available notice boards around the community and in businesses, factories, and other public places, posters showing the Sportspersonship Code of Conduct
4. Release constructive information and positive statements to news media and request publication of brief guidelines on sports pages
5. Provide news media with pertinent information as to ways in which the community may directly and indirectly render assistance in the crowd control problem

Involve law enforcement personnel

1. Police and other security personnel should be strategically located so as to afford the best possible control
2. Law enforcement professionals should handle *all* enforcement and disciplining of spectators
3. Strength in force may be shown by appearance of several police officers, motorcycles, police cars, etc., at and near the site of the game
4. Police may be stationed in rest rooms
5. Civil Defense organizations could patrol parking areas
6. A faculty member from the visiting school may be used as a liaison with police and local faculty in identifying visiting students
7. Attendants, police, security, EMTs, county sheriffs, and deputies should be in uniform. Uniformed authority figures command greater respect

Use supervisory personnel other than police

1. Carefully select teacher supervisors who are attentive and alert to signs of possible trouble

2. Identify faculty members by armbands, T-shirts, or other means
3. Provide for communication by means of walkie-talkie or cellular phone
4. Assign some faculty members to sit behind the visiting fans; this reduces verbal harassment of visitors
5. Employ paid ticket takers and paid chaperones to mingle strategically among the crowd and to remain on duty throughout the game, including halftime
6. Issue free or complimentary passes to elementary and junior high physical education teachers and coaches to provide more adult supervision

Plan for ticket sales and concession stands

1. Arrange for advance sale of student tickets to avoid congestion at the gate
2. Sell tickets in advance only to students in their own schools, and avoid sale of tickets to outsiders and nonstudents
3. Provide for a thorough security check at the gate or entrance
4. Arrange for concession stands to be open before the game, during halftime, and after the game
5. Channel the flow of traffic to and from concession stands using ropes or other means; keep traffic moving and away from the playing area

Prepare spectators and contestants

1. Encourage as many students as possible to be in the uniforms of the athletic club, pep club, booster clubs, band, majorettes, cheerleaders
2. Provide transport for participants to and from the game site
3. Have participants dressed to play before leaving for a game or contest
4. Adhere to established seating capacity of stadiums, arenas, and gymnasiums
5. Try to arrange for a statewide athletic association regulation prohibiting all noisemakers including musical instruments except for the

school band or orchestra under professional supervision

6. Request the assistance of visiting teams and clubs

7. Educate cheerleaders, student leaders, band captains, pep squads, and faculty supervisors by means of a one-day safety and conduct seminar

8. Keep spectators buffered from the playing area as much as practical

9. Request that elementary school children be accompanied by an adult

Miscellaneous

1. Inform and involve school superintendents when problems arise in connection with sports events

2. Impose appropriate penalties on faculty, coaches, and students guilty of poor conduct

3. Publish the identity of offenders at games and notify parents if possible; any penalties inflicted should also be noted (Note: If the offense leads to juvenile court action, care should be taken not to contravene laws about publishing names of juvenile offenders)

4. Consistently enforce rules and regulations; this is a necessity

5. Work toward the assumption of responsibility for strong regulation and enforcement of team

behavior on the part of the state athletic leagues and associations

6. Attempt to work with the courts toward greater cooperation

7. Avoid overstressing the winning of games

8. After-game incidents away from the proximity of the stadium, arena, or gymnasium are out of the control of school officials, but they do cause bad public relations

Summary

Safety and crowd controls at school sport functions are imperative! Greater concentration on treating the causes of the problem is essential. Preliminary planning and groundwork is the key to good crowd control. Coordination and cooperation of school, community, and law enforcement agencies are keys to success.

Youths should be taught to know what to expect and what is expected of them. Consistent enforcement of rules and regulations is a necessity if youth are to respect authority. Adult behavior should be such that it may be advantageously and admirably emulated by youth whose actions may result in deserving praise instead of negative criticism and disapproval.

The school sport program is a constructive and valuable educational activity. It should be permitted to function in a favorable, healthful, positive, and friendly environment.

SHARE THE SPIRIT OF FAIR PLAY: BE A GOOD SPORT

Sharing the Spirit of Fair Play is an important part of any sports program. It teachers young people a valuable life skill that is applicable to far more than sports. That is why the Minnesota State High School League and its corporate partner, First Bank, are proud to sponsor a sportsmanship awards program for schools participating in our state tournaments. To earn an award, a school's spectators, coaches, cheerleaders, bands, and players must honor their parts of the Sportsmanship Code of Conduct.

Sportsmanship Code of Conduct

Spectators:

1. Take part in cheers with the cheerleaders and applaud good performances.
2. Work cooperatively with game officials and supervisors in keeping order.
3. Refrain from crowd booing, foot stomping or making negative comments about officials, coaches and/or participants.
4. Stay off the playing area at all times.
5. Show respect for public property and equipment.

Coaches:

1. Follow the rules of the contest at all times.
2. Accept the decisions of game officials.
3. Avoid offensive gestures or language.
4. Display modesty in victory and graciousness in defeat.

5. Avoid public criticism of game officials and/or participants.

Participants:

1. Show respect for opponents at all times.
2. Accept the decisions of game officials.
3. Avoid offensive gestures or language.
4. Display modesty in victory and graciousness in defeat.
5. Show respect for public property and equipment.

Cheerleaders:

1. Know the contest rules and cheer at proper times.
2. Lead positive cheers which support and uplift your team.
3. Encourage support for any injured participant.
4. Show respect for opposing cheerleaders.
5. Avoid offensive gestures or language.

Bands:

1. Choose appropriate music and time for performing.
2. Dress in school-approved uniforms.
3. Show respect at all times for officials, opponents and spectators.
4. Show respect at all times for public property and equipment.
5. Avoid offensive gestures or language.

appendix D

Drugs and Alcohol

- -

- Intercollegiate Drug and Alcohol Education, Testing, and Rehabilitation Program
- NCAA Division I Intercollegiate Consent to Participate Statement
- Junior High School Rules Concerning Mood-Altering Chemicals and Informed Consent
- National Athletic Trainers' Association Code of Ethics
- TARGET Minnesota (Courtesy of the Minnesota State High School League)
- High School Pledge of Honor

- -

U OF M INTERCOLLEGIATE ATHLETICS DRUG AND ALCOHOL EDUCATION, TESTING, AND REHABILITATION PROGRAM

Illicit drug use and alcohol abuse are major problems in America today, and they are present on all college and university campuses. Student-athletes are as prone to the ills of drug use and alcohol abuse as anybody else and the Departments of Men's and Women's Intercollegiate Athletics believe it is their responsibility to do everything possible to protect the health and welfare of the student-athletes and to eradicate the problem. Drug testing is appropriate to help ensure the safety of student-athletes while they participate in athletic contests. In addition, a program to prevent the use of performance-enhancing drugs promotes

fair competition in intercollegiate athletics. The NCAA has established a drug testing program for athletes and the University of Minnesota program serves the same purposes. It is reasonable for the University to require a student to submit to drug testing as a condition of the privilege of participating in intercollegiate athletics. Toward that end, the Men's and Women's Athletic Departments have formulated a comprehensive drug and alcohol program that focuses on Education, Testing, and Rehabilitation.

Purposes of the Intercollegiate Athletic Drug Program

1. To adhere to NCAA, Big Ten, and University of Minnesota rules and procedures regarding licit or illicit drug use by student-athletes.

477

2. To disseminate information and educate student-athletes about problems associated with drug and alcohol abuse.

3. To identify student-athletes who are using illicit drugs or abusing alcohol or other illicit drugs and provide avenues for remediation.

4. To assure all athletes, parents, and University officials that the University of Minnesota Men's and Women's Intercollegiate Athletic Departments are committed to providing a drug-free environment for the conduct of all athletic programs.

5. To protect the reputation fnd integrity of the University of Minnesota athletic programs.

Drug Education

At least once each academic quarter, a Chemical Dependency Consultant, physician, and/or Head Coach will meet with all departments to discuss drug and alcohol use and to review the University of Minnesota Intercollegiate Athletic Drug Program, including all policies and procedures. Behavioral responsibilities and disciplinary expectations will also be fully discussed at that time.

NOTE: All freshman student-athletes will meet as a group in the fall with a drug counselor and Head Coaches to discuss in detail the University of Minnesota Intercollegiate Athletic Drug and Alcohol Program. This meeting will be administered through the Center for Student-Athlete Development Program.

Additionally, a resource pool of educational materials, films, and speakers will be made available for use by the coaches and student-athletes at any time throughout the year.

Each fall, a copy of the drug and alcohol program will be provided for all newly entering student-athletes. Parents or guardians will be encouraged to contact the athletic department regarding any questions they might have.

Voluntary Participation

Any athlete who feels that he/she has a problem with alcohol or other drugs, and who has not had a previous positive test, may request assistance through the Trainer, Team Physician, Chemical Dependency Consultant, or other staff member. Such a request *shall not* be treated as a positive test, and the athlete shall be treated/counseled in a manner appropriate to his/her problem. Any positive test (or equivalent) occurring after such voluntary participation shall be treated as a first positive test.

Athletes' Responsibility

As a member of any University of Minnesota Athletic Department team participating in any events or activities authorized by the department, you are required to provide proof of compliance with the U of M Drug and Alcohol Education, Testing, and Rehabilitation Program. It is your responsibility to present a urine specimen free from banned substances or evidence of inappropriate use of alcohol or illicit medications. Any urine sample testing positive will be considered valid and that of an active user.

Selection of the athlete or team for testing will be determined by the Athletic Director of the University of Minnesota Men's/Women's Intercollegiate Athletic Department or their designate. In NCAA postseason competition and championships or bowl games, each athlete/team selected to represent the University of Minnesota will undergo testing. If an athlete's test is positive for a banned substance, the athlete will be disqualified and another athlete may replace him/her. The athlete's replacement must likewise be tested. If tests are conducted more than 30 days prior to the game, those athletes/teams are subject to re-testing closer to the time of the games. Athletes/teams with a previous positive test will also be tested.

Athletes participating in NCAA, WCHA, etc. are subject to further testing by those organizations. Tests will be conducted on the top three athletes/teams and three other athletes/teams at random. Both the University of Minnesota and the NCAA will honor State and Federal confidentiality laws.

Alcohol and Prescription (Licit) Medication

The University recognizes that alcohol and prescription medications are two of the most commonly used and abused drugs in our society. For this reason, any use of alcohol that results in harmful consequences (i.e., assault, theft, public intoxication, property destruction, underage drinking, and others) to the athlete or others shall be treated as a positive drug test and dealt with according to the conditions of this drug program. *Athletes are reminded that the legal age for consumption of alcohol in the State of Minnesota is 21.*

Drug Counseling Staff

The drug counseling staff shall consist of:

Team Physician
Chemical Dependency Consultant
Senior Associate Director or Designate
Head Coach
Head Athletic Trainer
Director of Student-Athlete Development Program

The Team Physician and the Chemical Dependency Consultant shall be the overall coordinators for the counseling staff. Physicians and counselors who are responsible for direct patient care shall be qualified in their respective fields in accordance with community standards and regulations. All members of the counseling staff are expected to have training in the field of alcohol and other drug use/abuse appropriate to their job description.

Screening for Illicit Drug Use

At unannounced dates throughout the academic year, student-athletes will be asked to give urine samples as part of the drug testing program. *Refusal to provide a urine specimen will be considered as a positive test.*

Each athlete should be expected to be tested at least once a year for selected drugs including, but not limited to:

alcohol	heroin
amphetamines	LSD
anabolic steroids	marijuana
barbiturates	PCP
cocaine	quaaludes
diuretics	

Use of any of the above drugs by a student-athlete at the University of Minnesota is prohibited, except as may be prescribed by a licensed physician to treat specific medical conditions. All athletes should declare all medications routinely taken, prescription or nonprescription, to their team trainer prior to the beginning of their season.

Testing Procedures

All urine samples for testing will be collected under direct observation to eliminate substitutions. Procedures will be designed to preserve the integrity, accuracy, and confidentiality of the testing process.

Containers and samples will remain under constant supervision of Athletic Training Staff members until they are delivered to the Hennepin County Medical Center (HCMC) Toxicology Laboratory or another appropriate facility for testing.

Upon completion of the testing, the Supervisor/Lab Manager of the HCMC Toxicology Lab will telephone the Head Athletic Trainer to report the results *regardless of whether or not all specimens were found to be negative, or if positive samples were found.* The Head Athletic Trainer will then notify the respective Head Coach of the laboratory's findings. If positive specimens are identified, the Head Athletic Trainer will also notify the Senior Associate Athletic Director, the Head Team General Physician, the Director of the Center for Student-Athlete Development, and the Chemical Abuse/ Dependency Counselor of any positive samples.

The Supervisor/Lab Manager of the HCMC Toxicology Lab will also submit a *written* report of *all* test results to the Head Team General Physician, who will review all measurements and data listed on the report. The Team Physician will identify samples below the minimum specific gravity threshold, or those whose measurements are suspect. These athletes will produce another sample as instructed until they have provided a sample approved by the Head Team Physician. It is the athlete's responsibility to report as instructed at the proper place and time until cleared by the medical staff. The athlete's coach will be notified of any delinquencies in this regard, and the coach will impose appropriate discipline. The Head Athletic Trainer will submit summary statistical reports to the Athletic Director upon his/her request.

Policy Regarding Positive Tests

All positive results will be re-tested from a reserve sample for verification. If the positive test is verified, the Head Coach, Athletic Trainer, or Team Physician will notify the athlete of the results and explain the procedure to be followed.

1. First Positive Test

The Sports Medicine Coordinator/Director of Student Services will arrange an appointment with the Team Physician or Drug Counselor for the purposes of evaluation, education, and if necessary, treatment or counseling. The evaluation will include a diagnosis using standard diagnostic instruments, history, and if necessary, physical examination. Information from other sources will be solicited for the purposes of the evaluation. These sources include, but are not limited to, coaches, academic advisors, trainers, dormitory personnel, other athletes, and members of the athletic department staff. Such information shall be used for the purposes of obtaining the clearest view possible of the athlete's clinical picture. Upon completion of the interview, a diagnosis will be formulated, which will characterize the athlete in one of five general categories with respect to alcohol/drug use. These categories include experimental use, social use, chemical abuse, chemical dependency, and an indeterminate category. In the case of the chemical abuse and dependency categories, diagnosis shall be made in accordance with the Diagnostic and Statistical Manual (current edition) or the criteria of the National Council on Alcoholism.

In some cases disposition may include simple education and limit-setting techniques. In the case of chemical dependency, structured treatment will be a prerequisite to the athlete's continued participation in athletics. When problems other than chemical use/abuse are uncovered, the physician/counselor may refer the athlete to other appropriate resources. The athlete will also be subject to periodic re-tests on any given date throughout the calendar school year of the first positive test. These tests will be done under the supervision of the drug counselor and/or team physician. Although a first positive test may warrant no specific sanctions, other than referral to a Drug/Alcohol Counselor for guidance, it does not preclude a coach from enforcing a team policy or team rule.

In addition to the evaluation process, the athlete will be required to participate in a conference call with his/her parents, guardian, or spouse, the Athletic Director (or designee), Head Coach, Physician, or Counselor.

Refusal or failure of the athlete to meaningfully participate in the evaluation/counseling process, as defined by the counselors, shall result in immediate suspension from the team until such time as the athlete shall cooperate with counseling and evaluation measures.

Prior to implementation of any suspension, or as soon thereafter as is practical, the athlete will have the opportunity to fully discuss the matter with the drug counseling staff and present evidence contesting the accuracy of the test or any mitigating circumstances the athlete believes are important.

2. Second Positive Test

A second positive test, by its very nature, indicates a more serious problem requiring more formal intervention. Upon confirmation of the second positive test the athlete will be suspended from all competition for a period equivalent to 10 percent of his/her regular season games. The suspension shall be served starting with the next scheduled game and will be in effect for both regular and playoff competition. If the infraction occurs at the end of the season or during the off-season, the suspension will be served in the next season. If the infraction occurs at the end of the regular season but before a playoff, it shall be served during the playoff.

In addition, the player will be reevaluated by the team physician or drug counselor and will be referred to appropriate treatment on or off campus. Athletes who receive treatment for chemical dependency will be required to attend weekly meetings of an appropriate self-help group such as Alcoholics Anonymous (AA) or Cocaine Anonymous (CA). In addition, the athlete will be responsible for carrying out the discharge plans of the treatment facility. Athletes will sign appropriate authorization forms to ensure that results of treatment, treatment plans, etc. are available to the Team Physician, Drug Counselor, and Athletic Director. Failure to comply with Athletic Department Drug Policy or treatment program recommendations will result in immediate suspension from all competition, practice, and training until compliance is achieved. A second positive test could result in the suspension of the athlete from related financial aid.

The athlete will also be subject to periodic re-tests on any given date throughout the calendar school year of the second positive test. These tests will be done under the supervision of the drug counselor and/or team physician.

Prior to implementation of the treatment/penalties, or as soon thereafter as is practical, the athlete will have the opportunity to fully discuss the matter with the drug counseling staff and present evidence contesting the accuracy of the test or any mitigating circumstances he/she believes are important.

In addition to the evaluation process, the athlete will be required to participate in a conference call with his/her parents, guardian, or spouse, the Athletic Director (or designee), Head Coach, Physician, or Counselor.

3. Third Positive Test

Upon confirmation of a third positive test, the athlete will be suspended from all competition, practice, and training for one year. In addition, athletic financial aid will be revoked for the same period. The athlete's parents, guardian, or spouse will be notified by the Athletic Director or designee concerning said suspension.

After appropriate treatment and aftercare (including regular attendance at AA, CA, etc.), and at the end of the suspension, the athlete shall be eligible to apply for reinstatement to the athletic program. Reinstatement will not be considered automatic. A panel including the Athletic Director (or designee), Team Physician, Drug Counselor, Head Trainer, Head Coach, and others deemed appropriate by the Athletic Director shall review and determine the outcome of the petition for reinstatement. Participation in and cooperation with treatment goals, maintenance of sobriety, academic performance, and social functioning shall be considered as requirements for reinstatement. During this conference, the athlete will have appropriate opportunity to present his/her case for reinstatement.

Prior to implementation of the suspension, or as soon thereafter as is practical, the athlete will have the opportunity to fully discuss the matter with the drug counseling staff and present evidence contesting the accuracy of the test or any mitigating circumstances he/she feels are important.

In addition to the evaluation process, the athlete will be required to participate in a conference call with his/her parents, guardian, or spouse, the Athletic Director (or designee), Head Coach, Physician, or Counselor.

Relapse

The University of Minnesota recognizes that chemical dependence (as opposed to chemical use or abuse) is a chronic disease requiring abstinence from all mood-altering chemicals (including alcohol) and is associated with the possibility of relapse. Any athlete having been diagnosed as having the disease of chemical dependency, and having cooperated with appropriate treatment, who sustains a relapse, may not be treated as having a third positive test if the athlete reacquires his/her sobriety, cooperates with relapse treatment recommendations, or if necessary, reenters treatment and aftercare. If a second relapse occurs, the athlete will be subject to the consequences of a third positive test.

Appeal Process

After an appeal or presentation of mitigating circumstances to the Drug Education Committee, any athlete who is found to test positive for a banned substance has the right to register an appeal to the Athletic Director. The Athletic Director will implement appropriate procedures to review the appeal. This procedure involves discussions with the athlete involved, the Drug Counseling Staff, the athlete's Head Coach and appropriate Assistant Coaches, and any other person the Athletic Director feels has relevant bearing on the appeal.

Reinstatement

Reinstatement of the athlete to athletic participation would be made possible only after the provision of proof of successful completion of appropriate Certified Drug Education and/or Rehabilitation Program (on or off campus), drug testing results, and approval by the counseling staff and athletic department.

Refusal of the student-athlete to meaningfully participate and cooperate in the evaluation and counseling program will result in *immediate suspension from the team, immediate revocation of aid, and ineligibility for athletic aid for the subsequent year.*

Reinstatement may involve a behavioral contract with the Athletic Director (or designee), Physician, Counselor, or Head Coach, outlining their expectations.

Violations of Criminal Law

Any athlete arrested and/or charged with violations of city, county, state, or federal criminal statutes related to alcohol or illegal drug use shall be immediately suspended from participation in athletics pending the outcome of an investigation of the charges against the individual. Conviction for any felony offense shall result in a one-year suspension from athletic participation. At the end of said period, the athlete may apply to the Athletic Director for reinstatement. Reinstatement shall be contingent on the satisfactory serving of any sentence applied by the court system, including completion of treatment for chemical dependency and cooperation with aftercare recommendations.

Conclusion

It is believed and hoped that the implementation of this University of Minnesota Intercollegiate Athletic Drug Education and Testing Program will serve to benefit all connected with intercollegiate athletics at the University of Minnesota.

NCAA DIVISION I, BIG TEN U OF M INTERCOLLEGIATE ATHLETICS CONSENT TO PARTICIPATE STATEMENT

Consent to Participate

I certify by my signature below that I have read and reviewed the University of Minnesota Intercollegiate Athletics Drug Program. I recognize and understand that I will be asked to provide urine for drug analysis. I consent to any such testing conducted as a part of the University of Minnesota Intercollegiate Athletics' Program and agree that I will not refuse to take any such test or otherwise dispute the University's right to perform such tests. Likewise, I hereby agree to abide by the treatment program and guidelines set forth in the University of Minnesota Intercollegiate Athletics' Drug Program for a *First Positive Test, a Second Positive Test, and a Third Positive Test.*

I understand that the University will abide by State and Federal Laws and the Data Privacy Act to maintain the confidentiality of all matters related to drug tests and other information to be performed pursuant to this policy.

I further agree to inform the Team Physician or Head Trainer of any and all medications I may take from time to time, either under prescription or self-administered. I recognize that this information is necessary to assist my Team Physician and Trainer in providing me with the best possible care, should such care be needed.

I also authorize the Team Physician to make a confidential release to the Athletic Director, Head Coach, and Head Trainer, and to contact my parents, legal guardian, or spouse with information relating to positive test results, in accordance with terms of the University of Minnesota Intercollegiate Athletics Drug Program.

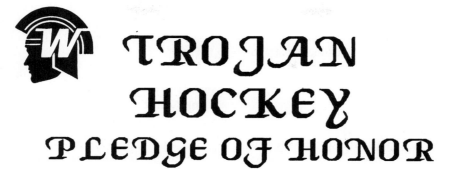

TROJAN HOCKEY
PLEDGE OF HONOR

I, _Rob Krotee_ , as a member of Wayzata High School's hockey team, recognize my responsibility to my teammates and coaches to follow the training rules set forth by the Minnesota State High School League and any other rules set by my coaches for the 1996-97 hockey season. By signing this contract, I pledge and promise not to use or possess alcoholic beverages, illegal drugs, or tobacco products during the 1996-97 hockey season.

If I am tempted to break training, I will gain the strength to abstain by remembering the trust my teammates and coaches have in me, my own self respect, and the pride I take in being a member of the Wayzata Trojan hockey team.

Robert L. Krotee   _11/23/97_
Player's Signature   Date

Derek Schwach
Rick Etzel   Team Captains
Chris Isaacson

I have read this contract signed by my son.

Leslie Krotee
Parent's Signature

I understand that the University of Minnesota's Counseling Center and other help is available to me should I have any difficulty with drugs, alcohol, or any other personal matter, or with any questions regarding the University of Minnesota Intercollegiate Athletics Drug Program.

To the extent set forth in this document and the University of Minnesota Intercollegiate Athletics' Drug Program, I waive any privileges I may have in connection therewith.

The Regents of the University of Minnesota, its officers, employees, and agents are hereby released from legal responsibility or liability and the release of such information and records as authorized by this form.

Print Full Name

Signature   Date

Signature of legal guardian if student-athlete is not 18 by September 1.

Signature   Date

OLSON JUNIOR HIGH SCHOOL ELIGIBILITY INFORMATION BULLETIN FOR INTERSCHOLASTIC ATHLETICS

Scholarship Rules

1. First semester 7th graders must have been promoted from the 6th grade.
2. Second semester 7th graders and 8th graders must be making satisfactory progress in completing course work toward promotion.

Mood-Altering Chemicals

1. Philosophy and Purpose

The Bloomington Schools recognize the use of mood-altering chemicals as a significant health problem for many adolescents, resulting in negative effects on behavior, learning, and the total development of each individual. The misuse and abuse of mood-altering chemicals for some adolescents affect extracurricular participation and development of related skills. Others are affected by misuse and abuse by family, team members, or other significant persons in their lives.

2. Rule

During the school year, regardless of the quantity, a student shall not (1) use a beverage containing alcohol, (2) use tobacco, or (3) use or consume, possess, buy, sell, or give away any other controlled substance (including steroids).

A. The rule applies to the entire school year and any portion of an activity season that occurs before the start of the school year or after the close of the school year.

B. It is not a violation for a student to be in possession of a controlled substance specifically prescribed for the student's own use by her/his doctor.

3. Penalties for Athletic Activities

A. First Violation
   Penalty: After confirmation of the first violation, the student shall lose eligibility for the next two (2) consecutive interscholastic contests or two (2) weeks of a season in which the student is a participant, whichever is greater. No exception is permitted for a student who becomes a participant in a treatment program.

B. Second Violation
   Penalty: After confirmation of the second violation, the student shall lose eligibility for the next six (6) consecutive interscholastic contests or two (2) weeks of a season in which the student is a participant, whichever is greater. No exception is permitted for a student who becomes a participant in a treatment program.

C. Third and Subsequent Violations
   Penalty: After confirmation of the third or subsequent violation, the student shall lose eligibility for the next twelve (12) consecutive

interscholastic contests in which the student is a participant. If after the third or subsequent violations, the student on his/her own volition becomes a participant in a chemical dependency program or treatment program, the student may be certified for reinstatement in MSHSL activities after a minimum period of six (6) weeks. Such certification must be issued by the director or a counselor of a chemical dependency treatment center.

D. Penalties shall be accumulative beginning with and throughout the student's participation on Junior High and Senior High athletic teams.

E. A student shall be disqualified from all interscholastic athletics for nine additional weeks beyond the student's original period of ineligibility when the student denies violation of the rule, is allowed to participate, and is subsequently found guilty of the violation.

- -

Statements to be Signed by Participant & Parent or Guardian

I have read, understand, and acknowledge receiving the Athletic Eligibility Information, which contains a summary of the eligibility rules for interscholastic athletics at Olson Junior High School.

Informed Consent for Athletes: By its nature, participation in interscholastic athletics includes risk of injury, which may range in severity. Although serious injuries are not common in supervised school athletic programs, it is impossible to eliminate the risk. Participants can and have the responsibility to help reduce the chance of injury. Players must obey all safety rules, report all physical problems to their coaches, follow a proper conditioning program, and inspect their own equipment daily.

_____

Student's Signature

_____

Grade in School

_____

Date

_____

Parent or Guardian's Signature

_____

Date

Tear off and return signed statement to your school prior to practice or participation.

NATIONAL ATHLETIC TRAINERS' ASSOCIATION CODE OF ETHICS

PRINCIPLE 1:
Members shall respect the rights, welfare and dignity of all individuals.

1.1 Members shall neither practice nor condone discrimination on the basis of race, creed, national origin, sex, age, handicap, disease entity, social status, financial status or religious affiliation.

1.2 Members shall be committed to providing competent care consistent with both the requirements and the limitations of their profession.

1.3 Members shall preserve the confidentiality of privileged information and shall not release such information to a third party not involved in the patient's care unless the person consents to such release or release is permitted or required by law.

PRINCIPLE 2:
Members shall comply with the laws and regulations governing the practice of athletic training.

2.1 Members shall comply with applicable local, state, and federal laws and institutional guidelines.

2.2 Members shall be familiar with and adhere to all National Athletic Trainers' Association guidelines and ethical standards.

2.3 Members are encouraged to report illegal or unethical practice pertaining to athletic training to the appropriate person or authority.

2.4 Members shall avoid substance abuse and, when necessary, seek rehabilitation for chemical dependency.

PRINCIPLE 3:
Members shall accept responsibility for the exercise of sound judgment.

3.1 Members shall not misrepresent in any manner, either directly or indirectly, their skills, training, professional credentials, identity or services.

3.2 Members shall provide only those services for which they are qualified via education and/or experience and by pertinent legal regulatory process.

3.3 Members shall provide services, make referrals, and seek compensation only for those services that are necessary.

PRINCIPLE 4:
Members shall maintain and promote high standards in the provision of services.

4.1 Members shall recognize the need for continuing education and participate in various types of educational activities that enhance their skills and knowledge.

4.2 Members who have the responsibility for employing and evaluating the performance of other staff members shall fulfill such responsibility in a fair, considerate, and equitable manner, on the basis of clearly enunciated criteria.

4.3 Members who have the responsibility for evaluating the performance of employees, supervisees, or students, are encouraged to share evaluations with them and allow them the opportunity to respond to those evaluations.

4.4 Members shall educate those whom they supervise in the practice of athletic training with regard to the Code of Ethics and encourage their adherence to it.

4.5 Whenever possible, members are encouraged to participate and support others in the conduct and communication of research and educational activities that may contribute knowledge for improved patient care, patient or student education, and the growth of athletic training as a profession.

4.6 When members are researchers or educators, they are responsible for maintaining and promoting ethical conduct in research and educational activities.

PRINCIPLE 5:
Members shall not engage in any form of conduct that constitutes a conflict of interest or that adversely reflects on the profession.

5.1 The private conduct of the member is a personal matter to the same degree as is any other person's except when such conduct compromises the fulfillment of professional responsibilities.

5.2 Members of the National Athletic Trainers' Association and others serving on the Association's committees or acting as consultants shall not use, directly or by implication, the Association's name or logo or their affiliation with the Association in the endorsement of products or services.

5.3 Members shall not place financial gain above the welfare of the patient being treated and shall not participate in any arrangement that exploits the patient.

5.4 Members may seek remuneration for their services that is commensurate with their services and in compliance with applicable law.

TARGET MINNESOTA
It's Cool to Be Chemically Free

While adults can only imagine it, teenagers know what it's like for high schoolers in today's pressure-packed society where drugs and alcohol can be easy to get and hard to resist.

TARGET Minnesota, a League service program, taps that teen knowledge of their times to lead the way into a new era. It puts student

leaders out front, showing their peers in League activities that it's "cool" to be chemically free.

TARGET is about responsibility. Students taking responsibility for themselves. Parents for their children. Schools for training student leaders and communicating with parents. Communities for supporting all three in their efforts to teach and foster healthy, chemically free lifestyles.

Students Lead the Way

TARGET Minnesota training teaches student leaders how to recognize chemical-use behavior, to listen, to express concern, to say:

"I care" and tell a friend or teammate why she/he is concerned;

"I see" and describe the actions that have caused concern;

"I feel" and talk about feelings of disappointment, anger, hurt, or fear;

"I want" and express her/his expectations for a behavior change;

"I will" and express how, as a student leader, she/he will support a student's efforts and commitment to change.

Parent Responsibility

Parents should attend the pre-season meeting(s) their schools offer, with their teenagers, to openly and clearly express how they feel about the use of alcohol, drugs, or tobacco. They should then follow through by verifying their teens' whereabouts. (Most drinking goes on at parties where there is no supervision.)

Communicating with other parents; getting to know their sons' and daughters' friends; praising their teen's efforts as well as their accomplishments; supporting coaches/advisors, their rules and principles, shows support for teen attempts to free their schools of chemical use.

Parents should know about the "691 reporting law" which states that any adolescent whom the police apprehend for possession of alcohol, drugs or paraphernalia will have the police report forwarded to the school. Parents should understand their liability for consequences that occur as a result of having served alcohol to minors in their homes.

Region Responsibility

Grassroots support of TARGET Minnesota comes from the Minnesota State High School League's 16 regions. Each has a TARGET TEAM which supports the program with information and annual training workshops/meetings held in schools, hotels, conference centers, or outdoor camps. Here, school personnel and students share their successes and lessons learned from their TARGET affiliated program.

Each school's Target coordinator gets information through TARGETalk, a special section in the League *Bulletin,* and from special mailings.

The League office stands ready to help with resources and information. TARGET banners, pins, T-shirts, and sweatshirts are available by calling the League office at 612/569-0491.

School Responsibility

TARGET Minnesota helps member schools to identify, train, support, and recognize chemically free students and to put the program to work for their students, in just six steps.

Step One: Select Student Leaders

Schools determine a selection process which defines student leaders, i.e., students who show the qualities of good leaders, who have demonstrated leadership, or whose peers have selected them as leaders.

Coaches, advisors, couselors, and teachers help by recommending students for the program.

Step Two: Provide Leadership Training

Training teaches potential leaders about the qualities of motivational, positive leaders and:

- how to learn from those leaders
- how to learn from their own personal mistakes
- how to recognize the needs of their group
- how to focus on issues important to their group
- how to intervene with peers who experience/ create problems for the group

Regularly held TARGET leadership support group meetings also provide an outlet for pressures and a place to mutually discuss and resolve problems.

Step Three: Present Role Modeling Opportunities

Student leaders can become role models for elementary and middle school students, carrying the message of:

- personal and team consequences of chemical use
- effects of chemical use on school performance
- how to refuse when pressured to use mind-altering chemicals
- the importance of telling someone when they are facing a problem(s)

Step Four: Recognize Commitment

Emblem/pins for TARGET student leaders to wear recognize the commitment they bring to the program. Articles that profile individual students in school and local newspapers give deserved recognition.

Other recognition can come through public service announcements promoting students' choices to be chemically free and through special awards to chemically free student leaders at awards ceremonies.

Opportunities for students in the TARGET program to speak to community organizations publicly rewards students' efforts and broadens their leadership experience.

Step Five: Support Student Leaders with Coach/Advisory Training

Student leaders can be most effective when working with adult coaches or advisors who know how to lend their support. Students learn from them how to recognize the signs and symptoms of chemical use as it affects an individual or team activity.

Coaches/advisors have to examine their own attitudes about the use of mood-altering chemicals; clarify their roles in establishing team/group standards about use; and develop their skills for "care-fronting" use by team/activity member.

They have to be ready for student expectations that they will be role models concerned with individuals, not just with winning. Students will look for them to have a "we can do this" attitude and to show respect for students.

Students will expect them, as coaches/advisors, to avoid showing favoritism; to be knowledgeable about their activities; to be good listeners; to give constructive criticism; to be able to have fun; to motivate team unity; and to relate to students.

Step Six: Bring Parents into the Circle

Schools can give parents a chance to speak out, to state their positions on chemical use, to communicate their feelings, and to show their support for the TARGET program. They do this by including TARGET in at least one pre-season parent-student meeting each year where schools introduce and discuss Minnesota State High School League athletic and fine arts activities.

Or schools may choose to schedule a separate meeting for TARGET and for each League activity to promote communication, cooperation, and mutual support among parents, coaches/advisors, and school administrators.

Meetings provide a setting for signing the League *Eligibility Information Brochure* indicating an understanding of and support for League and school rules. They are an opportunity to inform parents and the general public of the school's leadership program and the expectations and goals for the year.

Meetings also send a community-wide message about chemical usage among teens and about interscholastic activities available to students.

Putting TARGET to Work

Here is a step-by-step check list for schools to follow as they put the TARGET program to work for their students.

Identify TARGET program goals.

Develop a committee to define programs, i.e., identify the student selection process, membership requirements, consequences for rules violations, and other necessary elements for the program.

Develop clear, consistent and enforceable rules, and define the roles of school personnel.

Conduct a training session for athletic coaches, fine arts advisors, and other activity directors.

Establish support groups for student leaders and trained group facilitators.

Conduct leadership training for identified students.

Conduct a pre-season meeting to develop communication, cooperation and support between students, coaches/advisors, school administrators, and parents.

Develop strategies for providing regular communication to students, administrators, coaches/advisors, and parents.

Conduct chemically free activities for students with the involvement of parents in the school's community.

Develop an evaluation procedure to compare and monitor the TARGET program and its activities.

appendix E

Selected Associations for Athletes with Disabilities

American Athletic Association of the Deaf
3607 Washington BLVD., #4
Ogden, UT 84403-1737
(801) 393-8710

American Hearing Impaired Hockey Association
Irvin G. Tiahnybik
1143 West Lake Street
Chicago, IL 60607
(312) 226-5880

American Wheelchair Bowling Association
George Snyder
5809 NE 21st Ave.
Ft. Lauderdale, FL 33308
(954) 491-2886

Canadian Wheelchair Sports Association
1600 James Naismith Dr.
Gloucester, Ontario, Canada K1B 5N4
(613) 748-5685

Disabled Sport USA
Kirk Bauer, Executive Director
451 Hungerford Dr., Suite 100
Rockville, MD 20850
(301) 217-0960

Eastern Amputee Athletic Association
Jack Graff, President
2080 Ennabrock Road
North Bellmore, NY 11710
(516) 221-0610

Handicapped Scuba Association
1104 El Prado
San Clemente, CA 92672
(714) 498-6128

International Foundation for Wheelchair Tennis
Peter Burwash
2203 Timberlock Place, Suite 126
The Woodlands, TX 77738
(713) 363-4707

International Paralympic Committee
Dr. Robert Steadward
Rick Hansen Centre
W1-67 Van Vliet Centre
University of Alberta, Edmonton
Alberta, Canada T6G 2H9
(403) 492-3182

International Wheelchair Road Racers Club, Inc.
Joseph M. Dowling, President
30 Mayano Lane
Stamford, CT 06902
(203) 967-2231

National Beep Baseball Association
James Mastro
38-66 Way NE
Fridley, MN 55432
(612) 574-9317

National Foundation of Wheelchair Tennis
Brad Parks, Director
15441 Redhill Ave., Suite A
Tustin, CA 92680
(714) 259-1531

National Handicapped Sports and Recreation
Association
1145 19th St. NW, Suite 717
Washington, DC 20036
(301) 652-7505

National Wheelchair Basketball Association
Stan Lebanowich
110 Seaton Building
University of Kentucky
Lexington, KY 40506
(606) 257-1623

National Wheelchair Softball Association
Jon Speake, Commissioner
1616 Todd Court
Hastings, MN 55033
(612) 437-1792

North American Riding for the Handicapped
Association
12041 Tejon
Broomfield, CO 80028
(303) 452-1212

Ski for Light, Inc.
Mary Mosbey
1455 West Lake Street
Minneapolis, MN 55408
(612) 827-3232 or (612) 779-9151

Special Olympics International
Joseph P. Kennedy, Jr., Foundation
1325 G St., NW, Suite 500
Washington, DC 20005
(202) 628-3680

United States Association for Blind Athletes
Charlie Huebner, Executive Director
33 North Institute
Colorado Springs, CO 80903
(719) 630-0422

United States Cerebral Palsy Athletic Association
200 Harrison Ave.
Newport, RI 02840
(401) 848-2460

United States Organization for Disabled Athletes
143 California Ave.
Uniondale, NY 11553
(516) 485-3701

Wheelchair Sports, USA
3595 East Fountain Blvd., Suite L-100
Colorado Springs, CO 80910
(719) 574-1150

Your State's Special Olympics
Minnesota Special Olympics
400 South Fourth Street, Suite 915
Minneapolis, MN 55415-1423
1-800-783-7732

appendix F

Checklist for Facility Planners

	Yes	No

General

1. A clear-cut statement has been prepared concerning the nature and scope of the program and the special requirements for space, equipment, fixtures, lighting, safety, and facilities dictated by the activities to be conducted.

2. The facility has been planned to meet the total requirements of the program as well as the special needs of those who are to be served, including those with disabilities.

3. The plans and specifications have been checked by all governmental agencies (city, county, state, and federal) whose approval is required by law.

4. Plans for areas and facilities conform to local, state and federal regulations and to accepted standards and practices.

5. The areas and facilities planned make possible the programs that serve the interests and needs of all people.

6. Every available source of property or funds has been explored, evaluated, and utilized whenever appropriate.

7. All interested persons and organizations concerned with the facility have had an opportunity to share in its planning (professional educators, users, consultants, administrators, engineers, architects, environmental experts, program specialists, building managers, and builder—a team approach).

8. The facility and its appurtenances will fulfill the maximal demands of the program. The program has not been curtailed to fit the facility.

9. The facility has been functionally planned to meet the present and anticipated needs of specific programs, situations, and publics.

10. Future additions and phases are included in present plans to promote economy of construction.

Checklist for Facility Planners—cont'd

	Yes	No
11. Instructional stations and offices are isolated and insulated from sources of distracting noises.		
12. Storage areas for indoor and outdoor equipment are adequately sized. They are located adjacent to the gymnasiums.		
13. Shelves in storage rooms are secure and slanted toward the wall.		
14. All passageways are accessible: free of obstructions; fixtures are recessed.		
15. Facilities for health services, athletic training, health assessment and instruction, and the first aid and emergency-isolation rooms are suitably interrelated.		
16. Buildings, specific areas, and facilities are clearly identified and hazards noted.		
17. Locker rooms are arranged for accessibility and ease of supervision.		
18. Offices, teaching stations, and service facilities are properly interrelated.		
19. Special needs of persons with disabilities are met, including a ramp into the building at a major entrance and accessibility to all floors and areas.		
20. All "dead space" is used.		
21. The building is compatible in design and comparable in quality and accommodation to other organizational structures.		
22. Storage rooms are accessible to the play area and free of doorway center mullions or thresholds.		
23. Workrooms, conference rooms, and staff and administrative offices are interrelated.		
24. Shower and dressing facilities are provided for professional staff members and are conveniently located.		
25. Thought and attention have been given to making facilities and equipment as durable and vandalproof as possible.		
26. Low-cost maintenance features have been adequately considered.		
27. This facility is a part of a well-integrated master plan.		
28. All areas, courts, facilities, equipment, climate control, security, etc., conform rigidly to detailed standards and specifications.		
29. Shelves are recessed and mirrors are supplied in appropriate places in rest rooms and dressing rooms.		
30. Dressing space between locker rows is adjusted to the size and age of participants.		
31. Drinking fountains are conveniently placed in locker room and activity areas or immediately adjacent thereto.		
32. Special attention is given to provision for the locking of service windows and counters, supply bins, carts, shelves, and racks.		
33. Provision is made for the repair, maintenance, replacement, and off-season storage of equipment and uniforms.		
34. A well-defined program for laundering and cleaning of towels, uniforms, and equipment is included in the plan.		
35. Noncorrosive metal is used in dressing, drying, and shower areas except for enameled lockers.		
36. Antipanic hardware is used where required by fire regulations.		

Checklist for Facility Planners—cont'd

	Yes	No
37. Properly placed hose bibbs and drains are sufficient in size and quantity to permit flushing the entire area with a water hose.		
38. A water-resistant, coved base is used under the locker base and floor mat, and where floor and wall join.		
39. Whiteboards and/or tackboards with map tracks are located in appropriate places in dressing rooms, hallways, and classrooms.		
40. Bookshelves are provided in toilet areas.		
41. Space and equipment are planned in accordance with the types and number of participants.		
42. Basement rooms, being undesirable for dressing, drying, and showering, are not planned for those purposes.		
43. Spectator seating (permanent) in areas that are basically instructional is kept at a minimum. Portable rollaway bleachers are used primarily. Balcony seating is considered as a possibility.		
44. Well-lighted and effectively displayed trophy cases or walls of fame enhance the interest and appearance of the lobby.		
45. The space under the stairs is used for storage.		
46. Department heads' offices are located near the central administrative office, which includes a well-planned conference room.		
47. Workrooms are located near the central office and serve as a repository for department materials and records.		
48. The conference area includes a cloakroom, sink, and toilet.		
49. In addition to regular secretarial offices established in the central and department chairperson's offices, a special room to house a secretarial pool for staff members is provided.		
50. Staff dressing facilities are provided. These facilities may also serve game officials.		
51. The community and /or neighborhood has a planning "round table."		
52. All those (persons and agencies) who should be a party to planning and development are invited and actively engaged in the planning process.		
53. Space and area relationships are important. They have been carefully considered.		
54. Both long-range plans and immediate plans have been made.		
55. The physical comfort of the student and other participants, a major factor in securing maximal learning, has been considered in the plans.		
56. Plans for quiet areas have been made.		
57. In the planning, consideration has been given to the need for adequate recreation areas and facilities, both near and distant from the homes of people.		
58. Information and security cameras, monitors, and consoles have been strategically integrated into the plan.		
59. Every effort has been exercised to eliminate hazards.		
60. The installation of low-hanging door closers, light fixtures, signs, and other objects in traffic areas has been avoided.		
61. Warning signals, both visible and audible, are included in the plans.		
62. Ramps have a slope equal to or less than a 1-foot rise in 12 feet.		

Checklist for Facility Planners—cont'd

	Yes	No

63. Minimum landings for ramps are 5 feet × 5 feet, they extend at least 1 foot beyond the swinging arc of a door, have at least 6-foot clearance at the bottom, and have level platforms at 30-foot intervals on every turn.
64. Adequate locker and dressing spaces are provided.
65. The design of dressing, drying, shower, and sauna areas reduces foot traffic to a minimum and establishes clean, dry aisles for bare feet.
66. Teaching stations are properly related to service facilities.
67. Toilet facilities are adequate and equal in number. They are located to serve all user groups.
68. Mail services, outgoing and incoming, are included in the plans.
69. Hallways, ramps, doorways, and elevators are designed to permit equipment to be moved easily and quickly.
70. A keying design suited to management and instructional needs is planned.
71. Toilets used by large groups have circulating (in and out) entrances and exits.

Climate control

1. Provision is made throughout the building for climate control—heating, ventilating, humidity control, and air conditioning.
2. Special ventilation is provided for locker, dressing, shower, drying, toilet, and equipment storage rooms.
3. Heating, humidity, ventilation, and air conditioning plans permit both area and individual room control.
4. Research areas where small animals are kept and where chemicals are used have been provided with special ventilating equipment.
5. The heating and ventilating of the wrestling and combatives gymnasiums have been given special attention.
6. Thermostats are centrally controlled and secure.

Electrical

1. Shielded, vaporproof lights are used in moist areas.
2. Lights in strategic areas are key controlled.
3. Lighting intensity conforms to approved standards.
4. An adequate number of electrical outlets are strategically placed.
5 Gymnasium lights are controlled by dimmer or user capacity units.
6. Locker room lights are mounted above the space between lockers.
7. Natural light is controlled properly for purposes of visual aids and other avoidance of glare.
8. Electrical outlet plates are installed 3 feet above the floor unless special use dictates other locations.
9. Controls for light switches, phone, cable, computer, VCR, and projection equipment are suitably located and interrelated.
10. All lights are shielded. Special protection is provided in gymnasiums, arenas, court areas, and shower rooms.
11. Lights are placed to shine between rows of lockers.
12. Lights are easily accessible for replacement and maintenance.
13. Indirect lighting has been used or integrated whenever possible.

Checklist for Facility Planners—cont'd

	Yes	No

Walls

1. Movable and folding partitions are power-operated and controlled by controlled keyed switches.
2. Wall plates are located where needed and are firmly attached.
3. Hooks and rings for nets are placed (and recessed in walls) according to court locations and net heights.
4. Materials that clean easily and are impervious to moisture are used where moisture is prevalent.
5. Showerheads are placed at varying and appropriate heights—4 feet (elementary) to 7 feet (high school, university)—for each school level.
6. Protective matting is placed permanently on the walls in the wrestling room, at the ends of basketball courts, and in other areas in which such protection is needed.
7. An adequate number of drinking fountains is provided. They are properly placed (recessed in wall).
8. One wall (at least) of the dance studio has full-length mirrors.
9. All corners in locker rooms are rounded.
10. All walls and surfaces of gymnasiums and court sports (e.g., handball, racquetball, wallyball, squash) are flush.
11. The lower parts of walls are glazed for ease of maintenance.
12. Walls should be acoustically treated and pastel colored if feasible.

Ceilings

1. Overhead-supported apparatus is secured to beams engineered to withstand stress.
2. The ceiling height is adequate for the activities to be housed.
3. Acoustical materials impervious to moisture are used in moist areas.
4. Skylights, being impractical, are seldom used because of problems in waterproofing roofs and controlling sun rays (gyms).
5. All ceilings except those in storage areas are acoustically treated with sound-absorbent materials.
6. Most ceilings are painted off-white.

Floors

1. Floor plates are placed where needed and are flush-mounted.
2. Floor design and materials conform to recommended standards and specifications.
3. Lines and markings are painted on floors before sealing is completed (when synthetic tape is not used).
4. A coved base (around lockers and where wall and floor meet) or the same water-resistant material used on floors is found in all dressing and shower rooms.
5. Abrasive, nonskid, slip-resistant flooring that is impervious to moisture is provided on all areas where water is used—laundry, swimming pool, and shower, sauna, dressing, and drying rooms.
6. Floor drains are properly located, and the slope of the floor is adequate for rapid drainage.

Checklist for Facility Planners—cont'd

	Yes	No

Gymnasiums and special rooms

1. Gymnasiums are planned so as to provide safety zones (between courts, end lines, and walls and for best use of space.
2. One gymnasium wall is free of obstructions and is finished with a smooth, hard surface for ball-rebounding activities.
3. The elementary school gymnasium has one wall free of obstructions, a minimum ceiling height of 18 feet, a minimum of 4,000 square feet of teaching area, and a recessed area for housing appropriate equipment and teaching aids.
4. Secondary school gymnasiums have a minimum ceiling height of 22 feet; a scoreboard; electrical outlets placed to fit with bleacher installation; wall attachments for apparatus and nets; and a power-operated, sound-insulated, and movable partition with a small pass-through door at one end.
5. A small spectator alcove adjoins the wrestling and combatives room and contains a drinking fountain (recessed in the wall).
6. Cabinets, storage closets, supply windows, and service areas have locks.
7. Provisions have been made for the cleaning, storing, and issuing of physical education and sport equipment and uniforms.
8. Weight rooms have racks for all free weights and dumbbells.
9. Special equipment is provided for use by persons with disabilities.
10. Special provision has been made for audio and visual aids, including intercommunication systems, radio, television, and interactive videodisk linkage.
11. Team dressing rooms have provision for:
    a. Hosing down room
    b. Floors pitched to drain easily
    c. Hot- and cold-water hose bibbs
    d. Windows located above locker heights
    e. White chalk, tack, and bulletin boards, and movie and video projection
    f. Lockers for each team member
    g. Drying facility for uniforms
12. The indoor rifle range includes:
    a. Targets located 54 inches apart and 50 feet from the firing line
    b. 3 feet to 8 feet of space behind targets
    c. 12 feet of space behind firing line
    d. Ceilings 8 feet high
    e. Width adjusted to number of firing lines needed (1 line for each 3 students)
    f. A pulley device for target placement and return
    g. Storage and repair space
13. Dance facilities include:
    a. 100 square feet per student
    b. A minimum length of 60 linear feet for modern dance
    c. Full-height viewing mirrors on one wall (at least) of 30 feet; also a 20-foot mirror on an additional wall if possible

Checklist for Facility Planners—cont'd

	Yes	No

d. Acoustical drapery to cover mirrors when not used and for protection if other activities are permitted

e. Dispersed microphone jacks and appropriate wiring for speaker installation for music and instruction

f. Built-in cabinets for record, tape, computer simulation, and video players, microphones, and amplifiers, with space for equipment carts

g. Electrical outlets and microphone connections around perimeter of room

h. An exercise bar (34 inches to 42 inches above floor) on one wall

i. Drapes, surface colors, floors (maple preferred), and other room appointments to enhance the room's attractiveness

j. Location near dressing rooms and outside entrances

14. Athletic training rooms include:

   a. Rooms large enough to adequately administer proper treatment, assessment, and rehabilitative services

   b. Sanitary storage cabinets for medical supplies

   c. Installation of drains for whirlpool, tubs, etc.

   d. Installation of electrical outlets with proper capacities and voltage

   e. High stools for use of equipment such as whirlpool, ice tubs, etc.

   f. Sink, toilet, sauna, and shower

   g. Extra sink, freezer and refrigerator in the athletic trainer's room proper

   h. Adjoining dressing rooms

   i. Installation and use of hydrotherapy and diathermy equipment in separate areas.

   j. Space for the athletic trainer, the physician, and the various services of this function

   k. Rehabilitative exercise laboratories located conveniently and adapted to the needs of persons with disabilities

15. Coaches' room should provide:

   a. A sufficient number of dressing lockers for coaching staff and officials

   b. A security closet or cabinet for athletic equipment such as timing devices

   c. A sufficient number of showers and toilet facilities

   d. Drains and faucets for hosing down the rooms where this method of cleaning is desirable and possible

   e. Whiteboard, scheduling chart, and tackboard

   f. A movie screen, video monitor, VCR, cable connection, and projection table for coaches to review films and videos and view games

Persons with disabilities

Have you included those considerations that would make the facility fully accessible? These considerations include:

1. The knowledge that persons with disabilities will be participants in almost all activities, not merely spectators, if the facility is to conform to the Americans with Disabilities Act.

2. Ground-level entrance(s) or stair-free entrance(s) using inclined walks(s) or inclined ramp(s).

Checklist for Facility Planners—cont'd

	Yes	No

3. Uninterrupted walk surface; no abrupt changes in levels leading to the facility.
4. Approach walks and connecting walks no less than 4 feet wide.
5. Walks with gradient no greater than 5 percent.
6. A ramp, when used, with rise no greater than 1 foot in 12 feet.
7. Flat or level surface inside and outside of all exterior doors, extending 5 feet from the door in the direction that the door swings, and extending 1 foot to each side of the door.
8. Flush thresholds at all doors.
9. Appropriate door widths, heights, and mechanical features.
10. At least 6 feet between vestibule doors in series, i.e., inside and outside doors.
11. Access and proximity to parking areas.
12. No obstructions by curbs at crosswalks, parking areas, etc.
13. Proper precautions (handrails, etc.) at basement window areas, open stairways, porches, ledges, and platforms.
14. Handrails on all steps, ramps, and rest rooms.
15. Precautions against the placement of utility covers or barriers in primary or major sidewalks.
16. Corridors that are at least 60 inches wide and without abrupt pillars or protrusions.
17. Floors that are nonskid and have no abrupt changes or interruptions in level.
18. Proper design of steps and accompanying railings.
19. Access to rest rooms, water coolers, telephones, food-service areas, lounges, dressing rooms, play area, elevators, and auxiliary services and areas.
20. Elevators in multiple-story buildings.
21. Appropriate placement of controls to permit and prohibit use as desired.
22. Sound and braille signals for the blind, and visual signals for the deaf as counterparts to regular sound and sight signals.
23. Proper placement, concealment, or insulation of radiators, heat pipes, hot water pipes, drain pipes, etc.

Swimming pools

1. Has a clear-cut statement been prepared on the nature and scope of the design program and the special requirements for space, equipment, safety, and facilities dictated by the activities to be conducted?
2. Has the swimming pool been planned to meet the total requirements of the program to be conducted, as well as any special needs of the clientele to be served?
3. Have all plans and specifications been checked and approved by groups such as the local board of health?
4. Is the pool the proper depth to accommodate the various age-groups and types of activities it is intended to serve (e.g., wet classroom)?
5. Does the design of the pool incorporate the most current knowledge and best experience available regarding swimming pools?

Checklist for Facility Planners—cont'd

	Yes	No
6. If a local architect or engineer who is inexperienced in pool construction is employed, has an experienced pool consultant, architect, or engineer been called in to advise on design and equipment?		
7. Is there adequate deep water for diving (minimum of 12 feet for 1-meter boards and 3-meter boards, and 18 feet for 10-meter towers)?		
8. Have the requirements for competitive swimming been met (7-foot lanes; 12-inch black or brown lines on the bottom; pool 1 inch longer than official measurement; depth and distance markings)?		
9. Is there adequate deck space around the pool? Has more space been provided than that indicated by the minimum recommended deck-pool ratio?		
10. Does the aquatic director's or swimming instructor's office face the pool? And is there a window through which the instructor may view all the pool area? Is there a toilet-shower-dressing area next to the office for instructors?		
11. Are recessed steps or removable ladders located on the walls so as not to interfere with competitive swimming turns?		
12. Does a properly constructed overflow gutter extend around the pool perimeter?		
13. Where skimmers are used, have they been properly located so that they are not on walls where competitive swimming is to be conducted?		
14. Have separate storage spaces been allocated for maintenance and instructional equipment?		
15. Has the area for spectators been properly separated from the pool area?		
16. Have all diving standards and lifeguard stands been properly spaced and anchored?		
17. Does the pool layout provide the most efficient control of traffic from showers and locker rooms to the pool? Are toilet facilities provided for wet swimmers separate from the dry area?		
18. Is the recirculation pump located below the water level?		
19. Is there easy vertical access to the filter room for both people and material (stairway if required)?		
20 Has the proper pitch to drains been allowed in the pool, on the pool deck, in the overflow gutter, and on the floor of shower and dressing rooms?		
21. Has adequate space been allowed between diving boards and between the diving boards and side walls?		
22. Is there adequate provision for lifesaving equipment? Pool-cleaning equipment?		
23. Are inlets and outlets adequate in number and located so as to ensure effective circulation of water in the pool?		
24. Has consideration been given to underwater lights, observation windows, and speakers?		
25. Is there a coping around the edge of the pool?		
26. Has a pool heater been considered in northern climates in order to raise the temperature of the water?		
27. Have underwater lights in end racing walls been located deep enough and directly below surface lane anchors, and are they on a separate circuit?		

Checklist for Facility Planners—cont'd

	Yes	No

28. Has the plan been considered from the standpoint of persons with disabilities?

29. Is seating for swimmers provided on the deck?

30. Has the recirculation-filtration system been designed to meet the anticipated future bathing load?

31. Has the gas chlorinator (if used) been placed in a separate room accessible from and vented to the outside?

32. Has the gutter waste water been valved to return to the filters, and also for direct waste?

33. Can a computer be used to control chemical balance?

34. Are bottom drain covers secure?

35. Are proper warning signs placed where appropriate?

36. Are depth markers (4 or more inches in height) conspicuously placed both in and on pool deck?

37. Are starting blocks placed in the deep end or in at least 5 feet of water?

38. Are proper safety equipment and emergency procedures kept current and practiced?

Indoor pools

1. Is there proper mechanical ventilation?

2. Is there adequate acoustical treatment of walls and ceilings?

3. Is there adequate overhead clearance for diving (20 feet above low springboards and 3-meter boards, and 15 feet for 10-meter platforms)?

4. Is there adequate lighting (50 foot-candles minimum)?

5. Has reflection of light from the outside been minimized by proper location of windows or skylights (windows on side walls are not desirable)?

6. Are all wall bases coved to facilitate cleaning?

7. Is there provision for proper temperature control in the pool room for both water and air?

8. Can the humidity of the facility be controlled?

9. Is the wall and ceiling insulation adequate to prevent "sweating"?

10. Are all metal fittings of noncorrosive material?

11. Is there a tunnel around the outside of the pool, or a trench on the deck that permits ready access to pipes?

Outdoor pools

1. Is the site for the pool in the best possible location (away from railroad tracks, heavy industry, trees, and dusty open fields)?

2. Have sand and grass been kept the proper distance away from the pool to prevent them from being transmitted to the pool?

3. Has a fence been placed around the pool to ensure safety when not in use?

4. Has proper subsurface drainage been provided?

5. Is there adequate deck space for sunbathing?

6. Are the outdoor lights placed far enough from the pool to prevent insects from dropping into the pool?

7. Is the deck of nonslip material?

Checklist for Facility Planners—cont'd

	Yes	No
8. Is there an area set aside for eating, separate from the pool deck?	_____	_____
9. Is the bathhouse properly located with the entrance to the pool leading to the shallow end?	_____	_____
10. If the pool shell contains a concrete finish, has the length of the pool been increased by 3 inches over the official size in order to permit eventual tiling of the basin without making the pool too short?	_____	_____
11. Are there other recreational facilities nearby for the convenience and enjoyment of swimmers?	_____	_____
12. Do diving boards or platforms face north or east?	_____	_____
13. Are lifeguard stands provided and properly located?	_____	_____
14. Has adequate parking space been provided and properly located?	_____	_____
15. Is the pool oriented correctly in relation to the sun?	_____	_____
16. Have windscreens been provided in situations where heavy winds prevail?	_____	_____
17. Is there appropriate above ground and underwater lighting?	_____	_____
18. Are ladders recessed?	_____	_____
19. Does pool design allow an additional inch for electrical timing pads (more space is needed if movable bulkheads are part of the aquatic plan)?	_____	_____
20. Are telephone and emergency equipment and procedures readily available?	_____	_____

Adapted and updated from National Facilities Conference, Planning Areas and Facilities for Health, Physical Education, and Recreation, Washington, D.C., 1965, AAHPER.

Sample Budgets

- -

■ Typical Suburban School District Budget and Funding Sources
■ Typical High School Varsity Sport Budget
■ Intercollegiate Recreational Sport Budget
■ Community-Based Youth Sport Budget
■ YMCA Revenue and Expenditures

- -

TYPICAL SUBURBAN SCHOOL DISTRICT BUDGET AND FUNDING SOURCES*(1 HIGH SCHOOL AND 2 JUNIOR HIGH SCHOOLS)

Typical suburban school district budget and funding*
(1 High School and 2 Junior High Schools)

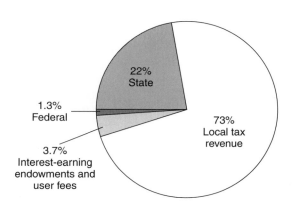

22%
State

1.3%
Federal

3.7%
Interest-earning
endowments and
user fees

73%
Local tax
revenue

Total budget: $45,000,000 - $75,000,000

Physical education and recreational sports:
$500,000 - $700,000

Varsity sports: $500,000 - $700,000
(Less than 2% of budget)

* Dependent on commercial and residential tax base of the school district

503

TYPICAL HIGH SCHOOL VARSITY SPORT BUDGET

**Expenditures
090685**

**Fund: General
Location: INSTRUCTIONAL SUPPORT SERVICES—003**

	Budget Code	Actual Expenditures	Budget	Proposed Budget
Interscholastic Athletics—221 Boys				
*Casual	132		$ 4,374.00	$ 4,920.00
*Extra assignment	152		-0-	-0-
*Athletics	155		158,196.00	177,880.00
General supplies	330		23,100.00	25,450.00
Postage and express	332		-0-	-0-
Printing and publishing	422		1,810.00	2,400.00
Rental equipment	432		1,050.00	1,300.00
Use of vehicles	447		31,260.00	33,000.00
Facility use	450		51,550.00	54,050.00
Telephone and fax	452		200.00	300.00
Repair equipment	462		-0-	3,700.00
Laundry	486		2,500.00	2,650.00
Official expense	492		16,270.00	16,270.00
*Other contract services	499		17,430.00	20,270.00
Travel and expense	902		800.00	800.00
Dues and memberships	905		-0-	-0-
TOTAL DEPARTMENT			$308,540.00	$342,990.00
Interscholastic Athletics—240 Girls				
*Casual	132		$ 3,070.00	$ 3,450.00
*Extra assignment	152		-0-	-0-
*Athletics	155		126,784.00	143,976.00
General supplies	330		14,550.00	16,700.00
Postage and express	332		-0-	-0-
Printing and publishing	422		270.00	500.00
Rental equipment	432		500.00	600.00
Use of vehicles	447		22,360.00	23,480.00
Facility use	450		38,850.00	40,850.00
Telephone and fax	452		100.00	150.00
Laundry	486		1,500.00	1,850.00
Official expense	492		12,510.00	12,510.00
*Other contract services	499		8,432.00	10,090.00
Travel and expense	902		800.00	800.00
Dues and memberships	905		-0-	-0-
Repair equipment	462		-0-	500.00
TOTAL DEPARTMENT			$230,596.00	$255,456.00

*Negotiated—increase pending

INTERCOLLEGIATE RECREATIONAL SPORT BUDGET MANAGEMENT SUMMARY INCOME/EXPENSES

Expenses	Current Fiscal Year				
Item Name	**Month**	**%**	**YTD**	**%**	**Budget**
Planning and operations	26,286.14	6	106,615.66	27	387,338.00
Intramurals	18,331.12	7	59,551.53	25	232,771.00
Fitness and open recreation	11,547.36	6	58,031.02	33	171,881.00
Sport clubs	8,707.33	5	101,777.11	69	147,237.00
Facilities	33,036.08	10	96,087.53	31	309,027.00
Instructional	15,747.30	8	63,121.88	34	183,652.00
Aquatics	27,434.09	10	73,438.59	28	259,386.00
Special events	6,871.91	14	13,743.95	29	46,438.00
SUBTOTAL	$147,961.33		$572,367.27		$1,737,730.00
Income	**Current Fiscal Year**				
Item Name	**Month**	**%**	**YTD**	**%**	**Budget**
Planning and operations	15,660.00	*	323.06	*	0.00
Intramurals	955.00	0	17,803.85	14	123,475.00
Fitness and open recreation	8,065.62	10	17,392.24	22	77,800.00
Sport clubs	2,227.00	26	2,244.00	26	8,500.00
Facilities	26,812.03	11	89,178.94	39	227,500.00
Instructional	10,253.44	11	31,780.83	35	89,500.00
Aquatics	950.00	2	15,332.00	36	42,500.00
Special events and student service fees	354,127.40	31	464,344.28	41	1,168,455.00
SUBTOTAL	$387,730.49		$638,399.20		$1,737,730.00

COMMUNITY-BASED YOUTH SPORT BUDGET

Wayzata Youth Hockey Association

Gross Receipts/Sales

Registrations (726)	$17,170.00	
Sponsors	5,750.00	
Blue Line Boosters	31,138.19	
Ice time	10,699.07	
Wayzata Tournament (2)	10,607.12	
General donations	250.00	$75,614.38

Expenses and Cost of Sales

League fees, referees, and ice time	$13,523.38	
Registration expense	1,269.50	
Equipment	14,462.21	
Rink and arena maintenance	5,260.58	
Outside tournaments and playoffs	3,265.00	
Wayzata tournament costs	3,892.68	
Insurance	694.00	
Interest on loan	347.59	
Loan payment	2,000.00	
Blue Line Boosters	20,525.41	
Concession commission to school district	1,732.18	
Travel team coaches' expense	1,487.30	
Miscellaneous administrative expense	517.35	68,977.18
Net results of Operations—Gain		$ 6,637.20
Beginning cash: Association Checking Account	$11,113.53	
Blue Line Boosters Accounts	1,804.39	
Savings Account (Capital Improvement)	7,072.34	$19,990.26
Plus Interest on Savings		478.56
		$20,468.82
Ending cash: Association Checking Account	$18,043.81	
Blue Line Boosters Accounts	1,511.31	
Savings Account (Capital Improvement)	7,550.90	27,106.02
Net cash increase		$ 6,637.20

NOTE: The savings account is held as collateral for the $3,000 loan at Anchor Bank.
The Association Account and Blue Line Account are held for capital improvements and season start-up costs.

YMCA Revenue and Expenditures

Revenue - $2,383,912

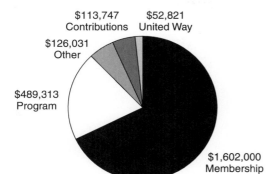

$113,747
Contributions

$52,821
United Way

$126,031
Other

$489,313
Program

$1,602,000
Membership

Expenditures - $2,383,809

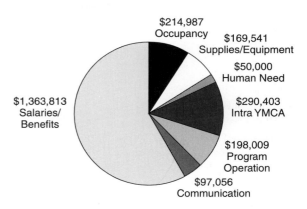

$214,987
Occupancy

$169,541
Supplies/Equipment

$50,000
Human Need

$290,403
Intra YMCA

$1,363,813
Salaries/
Benefits

$198,009
Program
Operation

$97,056
Communication

index